KANT'S THEORY OF TASTE

This book constitutes one of the most important contributions to recent Kant scholarship. In it, one of the preeminent interpreters of Kant, Henry E. Allison, offers a comprehensive, systematic, and philosophically astute account of all aspects of Kant's views on aesthetics.

Since the structure of the book maps closely on to the text of the *Critique of Aesthetic Judgment* (the first and most important part of the *Critique of Judgment*), it serves as a kind of commentary, with chapters serving as companion pieces to the different sections of Kant's work. This makes the book useful to both specialists and students tackling the *Critique of Judgment* for the first time and seeking an authoritative guide to the text.

The first part of the book analyzes Kant's conception of reflective judgment and its connections with both empirical knowledge and judgments of taste. The second and third parts treat two questions that Allison insists must be kept distinct: the normativity of pure judgments of taste, and the moral and systematic significance of taste. The fourth part considers two important topics often neglected in the study of Kant's aesthetics: his conceptions of fine art, and the sublime.

No one with a serious interest in Kant's aesthetics can afford to ignore this groundbreaking study.

Henry E. Allison is Professor of Philosophy at Boston University. His two most recent books, both published by Cambridge University Press, are *Kant's Theory of Freedom* (1990) and *Idealism and Freedom* (1996).

MODERN EUROPEAN PHILOSOPHY

General Editor

Robert B. Pippin, University of Chicago

Advisory Board

Gary Gutting, University of Notre Dame
Rolf-Peter Horstmann, Humboldt University, Berlin
Mark Sacks, University of Essex

Some Recent Titles:

Frederick A. Olafson: *What Is a Human Being?*
Stanley Rosen: *The Mask of Enlightenment: Nietzsche's Zarathustra*
Robert C. Scharff: *Comte after Positivism*
F. C. T. Moore: *Bergson: Thinking Backwards*
Charles Larmore: *The Morals of Modernity*
Robert B. Pippin: *Idealism as Modernism*
Daniel W. Conway: *Nietzsche's Dangerous Game*
John P. McCormick: *Carl Schmitt's Critique of Liberalism*
Frederick A. Olafson: *Heidegger and the Ground of Ethics*
Günter Zöller: *Fichte's Transcendental Philosophy*
Warren Breckman: *Marx, the Young Hegelians, and the Origins
of Radical Social Theory*
William Blattner: *Heidegger's Temporal Idealism*
Charles Griswold: *Adam Smith and the Virtues of the Enlightenment*
Gary Gutting: *Pragmatic Liberalism and the Critique of Modernity*
Allen Wood: *Kant's Ethical Thought*
Karl Ameriks: *Kant and the Fate of Autonomy*
Alfredo Ferrarin: *Hegel and Aristotle*
Cristina Lafont: *Heidegger, Language and World-Disclosure*
Nicholas Wolterstorff: *Thomas Reid and the Story of Epistemology*
Daniel Dahlstrom: *Heidegger's Concept of Truth*
Michelle Grier: *Kant's Doctrine of Transcendental Illusion*

KANT'S THEORY OF TASTE

A Reading of the *Critique of Aesthetic Judgment*

HENRY E. ALLISON

Boston University

CAMBRIDGE
UNIVERSITY PRESS

PUBLISHED BY THE PRESS SYNDICATE OF THE UNIVERSITY OF CAMBRIDGE
The Pitt Building, Trumpington Street, Cambridge, United Kingdom

CAMBRIDGE UNIVERSITY PRESS
The Edinburgh Building, Cambridge CB2 2RU, UK
40 West 20th Street, New York, NY 10011-4211, USA
10 Stamford Road, Oakleigh, VIC 3166, Australia
Ruiz de Alarcón 13, 28014 Madrid, Spain
Dock House, The Waterfront, Cape Town 8001, South Africa

http://www.cambridge.org

First published 2001

Printed in the United States of America

Typeface New Baskerville 10/12 pt.   *System* QuarkXPress™ 4.04 [AG]

A catalog record for this book is available from the British Library.

Library of Congress Cataloging in Publication data

Allison, Henry E.
Kant's theory of taste: a reading of the Critique of aesthetic judgment / Henry E. Allison.
p. cm – (Modern European Philosophy)
Includes bibliographical references and index.
ISBN 0-521-79154-5 – ISBN 0-521-79534-6 (pbk.)
1. Kant, Immanuel, 1724–1804. Kritik der èsthetischen Urteilskraft. 2.
Aesthetics – Early works to 1800. 3. Judgment (Aesthetics) – Early works to 1800. I.
Title. II. Series.
B2784 .A45 2000
111'.85–dc21   00-03426

ISBN 0 521 79154 5 hardback
ISBN 0 521 79534 6 paperback

To Renee

CONTENTS

ix

ACKNOWLEDGMENTS

As is almost always the case with works of this sort, which reflect the labor of many years, one is indebted to too many people to mention. Particular thanks are due, however, to Hannah Ginsborg for her careful reading of virtually the entire manuscript in its "semifinal" form. Although I am sure that she will still have much to criticize, I am convinced that it is a significantly better piece of work as a result of her comments than it would otherwise have been. I am likewise grateful to Béatrice Longuenesse for her valuable comments on the first chapter of the book, where I attempt to make use of some of her own very exciting work, as well as to two anonymous referees for Cambridge University Press, whose suggestions I have frequently followed.

I also owe a major debt to my many students in the seminars on the third *Critique* that I have given in the past ten years at UCSD, Boston University, and the University of Oslo. Since this, like my earlier books on Kant, is largely a product of my interchange with my students (and occasionally faculty) in the seminars, I am grateful to them for their comments, questions, criticisms, and, indeed, for their interest. And, once again, I must express my deep gratitude to my wife, Norma, for her continued support of my work despite the great disruption in both of our lives (but especially hers) caused by our move from the West to the East Coast.

Finally, I would like to thank the Hackett Publishing Company for their kind permission to quote extensively from their edition of Werner Pluhar's translation of Kant's *Critique of Judgment;* to Katrien Vander Straeten for her invaluable assistance in the preparation of the manuscript; and to Mary Troxell for the laborious task of preparing the index.

NOTE ON SOURCES AND KEY TO
ABBREVIATIONS AND TRANSLATIONS

Apart from the *Critique of Pure Reason,* all references to Kant are to the volume and page of *Kants gesammelte Schriften* (KGS), herausgegeben von der Deutschen (formerly Königlichen Preussischen) Akademie der Wissenschaften, 29 vols. (Berlin: Walter de Gruyter, 1902). References to the *Critique of Pure Reason* are to the standard A and B pagination of the first and second editions. Specific works cited are referred to by means of the abbreviations listed below. The translations used are also listed below and, except in the case of the *Critique of Pure Reason,* are referred to immediately following the reference to the volume and page of the German text. It should be noted, however, that I have frequently modified these translations, particularly in the case of citations from the *Critique of Judgment.* Where there is no reference to an English translation, either the translation is my own or the text is referred to but not cited.

A/B	*Kritik der reinen Vernunft* (KGS 3–4). *Critique of Pure Reason,* N. Kemp Smith, trans. New York: St. Martin's Press, 1965.
Anthro	*Anthropologie in pragmatischer Hinsicht* (KGS 7). *Anthropology from a Practical Point of View,* Mary J. Gregor, trans. The Hague: Nijhoff, 1974.
Anthro B	*Anthropologie Busolt* (KGS 25).
Anthro C	*Anthropologie Collins* (KGS 25).
Anthro F	*Anthropologie Friedlander* (KGS 25).
Anthro M	*Anthropologie Mrongovius* (KGS 25).
Anthro P	*Anthropologie Pillau* (KGS 25).
BDG	*Der einzig mögliche Beweisgrund zu einer Demonstration des Daseins Gottes* (KGS 2).
Beob	*Beobachtungen über das Gefühl des Schönen und Erhabenen* (KGS 2). *Observations on the Feeling of the Beautiful and Sub-*

lime, John T. Goldthwait, trans. Berkeley and Los Angeles: University of California Press, 1960.

BL   *Logik Blomberg* (KGS 24). *The Blomberg Logic, Lectures on Logic,* Michael Young, trans. (*The Cambridge Edition of the Works of Immanuel Kant.* Cambridge: Cambridge University Press, 1992), pp. 5–246.

Br   *Kants Briefwechsel* (KGS 10–13).

Diss   *De Mundi sensibilis atque intelligibilis forma et principiis* (KGS 2). *Concerning the Form and Principles of the Sensible and Intelligible World* (The Inaugural Dissertation), David Walford and Ralf Meerbote, trans. and eds. *The Cambridge Edition of the Works of Immanuel Kant; Theoretical Philosophy, 1755–1770.* Cambridge and New York: Cambridge University Press, 1992, pp. 377–416.

FI   *Erste Einleitung in die Kritik der Urteilskraft* (KGS 20). First Introduction to the *Critique of Judgment. Critique of Judgment,* Werner Pluhar, trans. Indianapolis: Hackett, 1987, pp. 385–441.

Fire   "Meditationem quarandum de igne succincta delineatio" (KGS 1).

Fort   *Welches sind die wirklichen Fortschritte, die die Metaphysik seit Leibnitzens und Wolf's Zeiten in Deutschland gemacht hat?* (KGS 20).

Gr   *Grundlegung zur Metaphysik der Sitten* (KGS 4). *Groundwork of the Metaphysics of Morals,* H. J. Paton, trans. New York: Harper & Row, 1964.

GTP   *Über den Gebrauch teleologischer Principien in der Philosophie* (KGS 8).

IAG   "Idee zu einer allgemeinen Geschichte in weltbürgerlicher Absicht" (KGS8).

JL   *Jäsche Logik* (KGS 9). *The Jäsche Logic, Lectures on Logic,* Michael Young, trans., pp. 521–640.

KpV   *Kritik der praktischen Vernunft* (KGS 5). *Critique of Practical Reason,* Lewis White Beck, trans. Indianapolis and New York: Bobbs-Merrill, 1956.

KU   *Kritik der Utreilskraft* (KGS 5). *Critique of Judgment,* Werner Pluhar, trans.

LB   *Lose Blatter zur Kritik der reinen Vernunft* (KGS 23).

LBu   *Logik Busolt* (KGS 24).

LD-W   *Logik Dohna-Wundlacken* (KGS 24). *The Dohna-Wundlacken Logic, Lectures on Logic,* Michael Young, trans., pp. 438–516.

LPh   *Logik Philippi* (KGS 24).

LPö   *Logik Pölitz* (KGS 24).

MAN   *Metaphysische Anfangsgründe der Naturwissenschaften* (KGS 4). *Metaphysical Foundations of Natural Science,* James Ellington, trans. Indianapolis, New York: Bobbs-Merrill, 1970.

MD   *Metaphysik Dohna* (KGS 28). *Lectures on Metaphysics,* Karl Ameriks and Steve Naragon, trans. and eds. *The Cambridge Edition of the Works of Immanuel Kant.* Cambridge: Cambridge University Press, 1997, pp. 357–94 (selections).

Mensch   *Menschenkunde (KGS 25).*

ML$_1$ *Metaphysik L$_1$* (KGS 28). *Lectures on Metaphysics,* Karl Ameriks and Steve Naragon, trans., pp. 3–106.

ML$_2$ *Metaphysik L$_2$* (KGS 28). *Lectures on Metaphysics,* Karl Ameriks and Steve Naragon, trans., pp. 299–356.

MM   *Metaphysik Mrongovius* (KGS 29). *Lectures on Metaphysics,* Karl Ameriks and Steve Naragon, trans., pp. 108–288.

MS   *Die Metaphysik der Sitten* (KGS 6). *The Metaphysics of Morals,* Mary Gregor trans. Cambridge: Cambridge University Press, 1991.

MS Vor   *Vorarbeiten zu die Metaphysik der Sitten* (KGS 23).

Ton   "Von einem neuerdings erhobenen vornehmen Ton in der Philosophie" (KGS 8).

MSV   *Metaphysik der Sitten Vigilantius* (KGS 27).

Mor M II   *Moral Mrongovious* II (KGS 29).

MV   *Metaphysik Vigilantius* (K3) (KGS 29). *Lectures on Metaphysics,* Karl Ameriks and Steve Naragon, trans., pp. 417–506.

NG   *Versuch den Begriff der negativen Grössen in die Weltweisheit einzuführen* (KGS 2). *Attempt to introduce the concept of negative magnitudes into philosophy, Theoretical Philosophy, 1755–1770,* David Walford and Ralf Meerbote, trans., pp. 203–41.

Pro   *Prolegomena zu einer jeden künftigen Metaphysik die als Wissenschaft wird auftreten können* (KGS 4). *Prolegomena to any Future Metaphysics,* Lewis White Beck, trans. Indianapolis: Bobbs-Merrill, 1950.

R   *Reflexionen* (KGS 15–19).

Re   *Die Religion innerhalb der Grenzen der blossen Vernunft* (KGS 6). *Religion within the Boundaries of Mere Reason,* Allen Wood, trans. *The Cambridge Edition of the Works of Immanuel Kant, Religion and Rational Theology,* Allen Wood and George

Di Giovani, eds. Cambridge: Cambridge University Press, 1996, pp. 57–215.

TP   *Über den Gemeinspruch: Das mag in der Theorie richtig sein, taugt aber nicht für die Praxis* (KGS 8).

UE   *Über eine Entdeckung nach der alle Kritik der reinen Vernunft durch eine ältere entbehrlich gemacht werden soll* (KGS 8).

WH   "Was heisst: Sich im Denken orientiren?" (KGS 8). "What Does it Mean to Orient Oneself in Thinking?" *Religion and Rational Theology*, Allen Wood trans., pp. 7–18.

WL   *Wiener Logik* (KGS 24) *The Vienna Logic, Lectures on Logic*, Michael Young trans., pp. 251–377.

INTRODUCTION

The eighteenth century, usually known as the "Age of Reason," has also been characterized as the "Century of Taste."[1] If this juxtaposition seems strange to us today, it is because we have lost sight of the ideal, normative element, which, as Gadamer points out, was essential to the concept of taste as it developed in the seventeenth and eighteenth Centuries.[2] Thus, whereas for us to say that a question or evaluation is a matter of taste is to imply that it is merely a private, subjective matter lacking any claim to normativity, this was not at all the case in the eighteenth century. On the contrary, as Gadamer also points out, taste was thought of as a special way of knowing, one for which rational grounds cannot be given, but which nonetheless involves an inherent universality.[3] In short, it was not a private but a social phenomenon, inseparably connected with a putative *sensus communis*.[4] Moreover, taste, so construed, was not limited to the realm of the aesthetic, but also encompassed morality, indeed, any domain in which a universal order or significance is thought to be grasped in an individual case.[5]

It is therefore in terms of this widely shared viewpoint that we must understand both Kant's lifelong concern with the question of taste and his definitive account of it given in the *Critique of Judgment*. For in this respect, as in so many others, he was very much a man of his time, even though, as we shall see, this did not prevent him from breaking with the orthodoxy of the day on a number of crucial points regarding taste.

Kant's earliest significant discussion of taste is contained in his *Observations on the Feeling of the Beautiful and the Sublime* (1764). This brief and stylistically elegant work stems from a period in which Kant still thought, in agreement with the British moral sense tradition, that morality was based on feeling, and in which he, like many of his contemporaries, insisted on an intimate linkage between moral feeling and the aesthetic feelings of the sublime and the beautiful. Thus, in discussing the principles underlying true virtue, Kant remarks that they are not speculative rules, but "the consciousness of a feeling that lies in every human breast

and extends itself much further than over the particular grounds of com-
passion and complaisance," a feeling which he identifies as that of "*the
beauty and the dignity of human nature*" (Beob 2: 217; 60). Moreover, this
work is not an aberration, since a continuous concern with questions of
taste or matters aesthetic can be traced through the surviving transcripts
of his lectures, particularly the recently published lectures on anthropology, as well as the associated *Reflexionen*.[6] And throughout these discussions Kant, like many of his contemporaries, emphasized the social nature of taste, its inherent claim to universality.[7]

What is particularly noteworthy, however, is that Kant's interest in the
nature of taste and its putative claim to universality survived the radical
change in his moral theory (and his whole philosophical orientation) an-
nounced in his Inaugural Dissertation (*On the Form and Principles of the Sensible and the Intelligible World*) of 1770. The essential feature of this important work, which is usually regarded as "semicritical" because it
contains the essential elements of the account of space and time as forms
of human sensibility found in the Transcendental Aesthetic of the *Critique
of Pure Reason*, is the sharp distinction between sensible and intellectual
cognition (with the latter including what Kant later distinguished as understanding and reason) and their respective spheres of application or
"worlds." Given his understanding of this distinction, Kant was naturally
led to link morality and its principles with pure intellect rather than feeling (sensibility), which meant that he could no longer maintain its close
connection with taste.[8] Correlatively, the latter was conceived more narrowly as relating merely to the aesthetic domain and, therefore, as lacking any direct connection with either morality or cognition.[9]

Nevertheless, this rationalism did not lead Kant (at least not immediately) to the marginalization or outright excision of the concept of taste
from his systematic philosophical program. In fact, taste figures prominently in the outline of his incipient project that Kant conveyed to Marcus Herz in two well-known letters from early in the so-called silent
decade.[10] In both letters, the fundamental concern is with metaphysics
or, more properly, the possibility thereof, and the projected work that is
intended as a prelude to metaphysics is given the title "The Limits of Sensibility and Reason." In the first of these letters, Kant tells Herz that this
projected work "is intended to contain the relation of the fundamental
concepts and laws destined for the sensible world, along with an outline
of what constitutes the nature of the doctrine of taste, metaphysics and
morals."[11] In the second letter, he goes into more detail concerning the
structure of the proposed work. He says that it is to consist of two parts,
a theoretical and a practical; and the latter, which alone concerns us here,
will supposedly consist of two sections: the first dealing with general principles of feeling, taste, and the sensible desires, and the second with the
first grounds of morality.[12] Consequently, it appears from these letters

that in spite of the sharp separation of taste from both morality and cognition, and its assignment to the domain of feeling, in the early seventies Kant continued to recognize the philosophical importance of taste.

By the time of the publication of the *Critique of Pure Reason,* however, taste, together with any concern with feeling, seems to have been removed entirely from the framework of Kant's emerging transcendental philosophy. Thus, in a footnote to the Transcendental Aesthetic, wherein he is concerned to reserve the term "aesthetic" for his account of sensibility and its *a priori* conditions, rather than for a theory of taste, Kant remarks:

> The Germans are the only ones who now employ the word 'aesthetics' to designate what others call the critique of taste. The ground for this is a failed hope, held by the excellent analyst Baumgarten, of bringing the critical estimation of the beautiful under principles of reason, and elevating its rules to a science. But this effort is futile. For the putative rules or criteria are merely empirical as far as their sources are concerned, and can therefore never serve as *a priori* rules according to which our judgment of taste must be directed, rather the latter constitutes the genuine touchstone of the correctness of the former. For this reason it is advisable again to desist from the use of this term and preserve it for that doctrine which is true science (whereby one would come closer to the language and the sense of the ancients, among whom the division of cognition into αἰσθητα; καὶ; ροητα was very well known. (A21)[13]

Nevertheless, in late December of 1787, after having completed both the revisions for the second edition of the *Critique of Pure Reason* and the composition of the *Critique of Practical Reason,* Kant writes to Reinhold that he has discovered a new *a priori* principle that governs the feeling of pleasure and displeasure. The latter, for Kant, is one of three faculties or capacities of the mind, the other two being the cognitive faculty and desire or will. These two faculties had already been assigned their *a priori* principles in the first and second *Critiques* respectively, the former stemming from understanding (the "lawgiver to nature") and the latter from reason (construed as practical reason). And for a time Kant thought that this was sufficient to complete the critical project, since, on the one hand, it enabled him to lay the foundations for the two parts of metaphysics (a metaphysic of nature and a metaphysic of morals) for which the *Critique of Pure Reason* was intended as the propaedeutic,[14] while, on the other, he continued to hold to the view expressed in the first edition of the *Critique* that any putative rules or principles governing taste could only be empirical.

However, as a result of his discovery that the feeling of pleasure and displeasure has its own *a priori* principle, irreducible to those of the other two mental faculties, Kant tells Reinhold that he now recognizes three parts of philosophy. In addition to theoretical and practical philosophy (the subjects of the first two *Critiques* and their corresponding metaphysics of nature and morals), there is also teleology, which is presumably grounded in this new principle and relates to the feeling of pleasure and pain. Moreover, he also tells Reinhold that he is now at work on a new manuscript dealing with this third part of philosophy, which is to be entitled "Critique of Taste," and which he hopes to have in print by Easter.[15]

As usual, Kant was overly optimistic regarding the time required for the completion of his project, since the promised work eventually appeared in April 1790, or some two years after the projected date. And, of course, it took the form of a critique of *judgment*, dealing with both aesthetic and teleological judgment, rather than a critique of *taste*, which is somehow supposedly itself concerned with teleology.[16] But in spite of this significant change in title, it is clear from the Preface to the *Critique of Judgment* that Kant's major concern is still with taste and the possibility of its having a distinct *a priori* principle. For in introducing the idea and putative subject matter of a critique of judgment, Kant states that it will deal with the following three questions:

> Does judgment, which in the order of our cognitive powers is a mediating link between understanding and reason, also have *a priori* principles of its own? Are these principles constitutive or merely regulative. . . . ? Does judgment give the rule *a priori* to the feeling of pleasure and displeasure, the mediating link between the cognitive faculty and the faculty of desire (just as understanding prescribes laws *a priori* to the cognitive faculty and reason to the faculty of desire)? (KU 5: 168; 5)

Although taste is not mentioned in this list of questions, it is unmistakably that to which they all point. For what Kant endeavors to demonstrate in the *Critique* itself is that, contrary to his earlier view expressed in the first *Critique* that judgment, as a merely subsumptive faculty, has no rules or principles of its own (A134–5/B173–4), judgment does in fact have a unique principle and that it is "constitutive," that is, normative, for the feeling of pleasure and displeasure. Moreover, as normative or "rule-giving" for this feeling, the principle of judgment is precisely a principle of taste, understood as a capacity to judge or discriminate by means of this feeling. Thus, it is judgment's legislation to feeling through judgments of taste concerning the beauty of objects of nature and art that makes a critique of judgment both possible and necessary. It makes such a critique possible because it is only if a cognitive faculty lays claim to some *a priori* principle that it becomes the appropriate subject matter for a critique in the Kantian sense, which is just an examination of the grounds and limits of such a claim. It makes it necessary because any such claim, even one regarding taste, requires an examination of its grounds and limits before it can be accepted.

What greatly complicates the story and led to the transformation of the initial relatively modest, apparently self-contained project of a critique of taste into a full-scale critique of judgment is the introduction of a distinction between determinative and reflective judgment. The former concerns judgment's subsumptive activity on which Kant focused in the first *Critique,* and he continued to hold that, *qua* determinative or subsumptive, that is, insofar as it merely applies previously established concepts or rules to given particulars, judgment neither has nor needs an *a priori* principle of its own. Thus, as it were by default, the *a priori* principle supposedly governing taste is assigned to judgment in its reflective capacity, which essentially involves a movement from particulars to universals.

It turns out, however, that the reflective capacity of judgment is concerned with far more than judgments of taste, or even aesthetic judgment broadly construed (to include judgments of sublimity as well as beauty). For Kant argues in both Introductions that reflective judgment is deeply involved in the empirical investigation of nature and that in such an investigation it is governed by its own *a priori* principle, namely the purposiveness of nature, which, though merely regulative, is nonetheless necessary. In fact, it is claimed to be necessary in a twofold sense, or, more precisely, there are two forms of purposiveness necessarily involved in the pursuit of empirical knowledge. One, which Kant terms "logical" or "formal purposiveness," is necessarily presupposed in the search for empirical concepts under which particulars given in experience can be classified, in the quest for empirical laws in terms of which these same particulars can be explained, as well as in the unification of these laws into theories. The other, termed "real" or "objective purposiveness," is required for the empirical investigation of certain products of nature, namely organisms, whose possibility and mode of behavior we can only make comprehensible to ourselves in terms of the idea of a purpose or end [*Zweck*]. The former mode of purposiveness is a central topic of both Introductions, whereas the latter is the concern of the *Critique of Teleological Judgment.*[17]

Kant also argues in the Introductions, however, that even though both of these modes of purposiveness belong to the subject matter of a critique of judgment, since they rest upon a reflective use of judgment, by themselves they do not warrant a separate critique or division of philosophy. On the contrary, he insists that an investigation of them, "could at most have formed an appendix, including a critical restriction on such judging, to the theoretical part of philosophy" (KU 5: 170; 7). Thus, again, it is only taste or the capacity for aesthetic judgment, through which judgment legislates to the feeling of pleasure and displeasure, that necessitates a separate critique. Or, as Kant puts it in the Second Introduction, "In a critique of judgment, the part that deals with aesthetic judgment belongs to it essentially" (KU 5: 193; 33).

Kant's clear privileging of taste from the standpoint of transcendental critique is perhaps the major reason for the title selected for the present work. It should also be noted, however, that, like the third *Critique* itself, this work is concerned with far more than Kant's theory of taste narrowly conceived. For the analysis of this theory that I attempt to provide is framed, on the one side, by an account of his underlying conception of reflective judgment and its principle of logical or formal purposiveness, which I try to show is central to Kantian epistemology, quite apart from its connection with taste; and, on the other side (in the last two chapters), by discussions of Kant's accounts of fine art and genius, that is, his analysis of artistic production or "creation aesthetic," and of the sublime. Neither of these latter two topics falls within the province of a theory of taste, though both certainly pertain to aesthetics as it is usually construed. Thus, I believe it fair to say that the present work deals with virtually all of the central topics of the *Critique of Aesthetic Judgment.*

It does not, however, discuss in systematic fashion the *Critique of Teleological Judgment,* which is the second part of the *Critique of Judgment.* Consequently, it does not deal explicitly with the thorny question of the unity of the *Critique of Judgment,* that is, whether the two parts of the work (and the discussion of logical purposiveness in the Introductions) are parts of a coherent whole, a single investigation into the various forms of reflective judgment, or constitute merely a set of distinct investigations externally linked by Kant's architectonic.[18]

Initially it had been my plan to deal with this broader issue. Operating on the principle, which I still take to be valid, that Kant's critical philosophy as a whole revolves around three great ideas, namely, the transcendental ideality of space and time, the freedom of the will, and the purposiveness of nature, and having already written books on the first two, I set out some years ago to complete my Kantian trilogy by producing a book on the third.[19] The idea was to show that the concept of purposiveness, which is the *a priori* principle of judgment in its logical, aesthetic, and teleological reflection, does, indeed, provide a unifying principle.

After having worked on this project for some time, however, I came to recognize two considerations which led me to revise my overly ambitious agenda and narrow my focus to the topics discussed in the *Critique of Aesthetic Judgment.* One was the great variety of the senses that Kant gave to the notion of purposiveness and the difficulties involved in reconciling them with one another.[20] Although I continue to believe that it is both possible and important to do so, the issues, particularly as they involve teleological judgment, are extremely complex, and an adequate treatment of them would have both increased the size of the present work beyond reasonable proportions and threatened its integrity.[21] The other, and perhaps more serious consideration, was my lack of sufficient expertise in biology, and the history and philosophy thereof, to do justice to Kant's account of teleological judgment. Thus, rather than contenting myself with a relatively superficial discussion of Kant's extremely interesting views on biology, which would not add anything of substance to the existing literature, I decided to leave that topic for those who are better equipped than I am to deal with it.[22] Nevertheless, the *Critique of Teleological Judgment* is not neglected completely.[23] In fact, since there is much in that portion of the third *Critique* (and in the brief discussions of teleological judgment in the two Introductions) that is directly relevant to the issues discussed in this work, I turn to it at several key points in my analyses, including the discussion of the production of fine art.

Apart from this Introduction, the book as a whole is composed of thirteen chapters and is divided into four parts. The first part, consisting of the first two chapters, is concerned with Kant's conception of reflective judgment as articulated in the two Introductions and its connection with his theory of taste. The first chapter, which could stand by itself as an independent essay, offers a fairly detailed analysis of reflection and reflective judgment, their role in the formation of empirical concepts, and their connection with the transcendental principle of the formal or logical purposiveness of nature. It also analyzes and defends Kant's deduction of this principle, which it treats as at once an answer to Hume's skepticism regarding the rational grounding of induction and as a third way or "critical path" between Locke's conventionalism and Leibniz's metaphysical essentialism. Building on this analysis and following the suggestion of Béatrice Longuenesse that what is distinctive in the third *Critique* is not the conception of reflective judgment as such, but the idea that there might be a "merely reflective judgement" (reflection without a corresponding determination),[24] the second chapter examines Kant's account of judgments of taste as aesthetic judgments of reflection in the First Introduction and the corresponding account of an aesthetic representation of purposiveness in the Second. Its major concern is thus to try to understand the connection between the reflective activity of judgment in judgments of taste and Kant's broader views about the epistemic role of reflection.

The analysis of Kant's theory of taste as it is contained in the body of the *Critique of Aesthetic Judgment* constitutes the heart of the book and is concerned with two questions, which, in opposition to many interpreters, I insist upon keeping sharply separate: the question of the normativity of judgments of taste (their supposed right to demand the agreement of others), and the question of the moral or systematic significance of taste.[25] These are the concerns of the second and third parts respectively.

The second part, consisting of Chapters 3 through 8, is organized around Kant's famous distinction between the *quid facti* and the *quid juris,* which to my knowledge has never before been applied to the third *Critique.* Its central claim is that the four moments of the Analytic of the

Beautiful, each of which is treated in a separate chapter, are concerned with the *quid facti,* which is understood to refer to the conditions under which a judgment of taste can be pure, while the Deduction of Pure Judgments of Taste (Chapter 8) addresses the *quid juris.* An important consequence of this mode of analysis, which I endeavor to defend, is that although Kant succeeds reasonably well in the Deduction in showing that a pure judgment of taste makes a rightful demand on the agreement of others (and thus possesses genuine normativity), it turns out to be impossible in a given case to determine whether a particular judgment of taste is pure.

The third part (Chapters 9 through 11) completes the analysis of taste and the experience of beauty by considering the question of their moral and systematic significance. Since this relates directly to Kant's famous reference to the necessity of a transition or *Übergang* from nature to freedom, I devote the initial chapter to this issue as it is discussed in the Second Introduction and earlier texts. On the basis of this analysis, I then discuss in the next two chapters two related, though distinct, ways in which taste and the experience of beauty contribute to such an *Übergang* (and therefore to morality): first, by making possible an intellectual interest in natural beauty, which, by providing "hints" and "traces" that nature is on our side (is amenable to our morally required projects), helps to support the moral endeavors of radically evil agents such as ourselves (Chapter 10); and second, by serving as a symbol of morality (Chapter 11). Since the latter claim is the culmination of the Dialectic of Aesthetic Judgment, I preface my treatment of it with a detailed analysis of the Antinomy of Taste and the doctrine of aesthetic ideas, which I argue is essential to understanding how the beautiful can symbolize morality.

Finally, as already noted, the fourth part of this book (Chapters 12 and 13) deals with two topics that are of considerable intrinsic interest but stand apart from the systematic structure of Kant's theory of taste: his conceptions of fine art and genius, and his account of the sublime. Appealing to Kant's term highlighted by Derrida, I refer to these topics as "parerga" to the theory of taste because of their "extra-systematic" status.[26]

The first of these topics is parergonal because Kant's theory of taste as such is concerned exclusively with the nature and normativity of aesthetic *judgment.* Thus, as Gadamer suggests, the concept of a "pure judgment of taste" may be viewed as a "methodological abstraction, only obliquely related to the difference between nature and art."[27] But in order to apply this account to artistic beauty, Kant is forced to deal with the ways in which it differs from natural beauty. And this leads him inevitably to a consideration of the creative process, the centerpiece of which is his conception of genius.

Since a full treatment of Kant's views on fine art and genius would amount to a book-length work in its own right, I focus my analysis on the conditions which, according to Kant, must be met by a product of art if it is to be deemed beautiful, namely, it must seem like nature, though we must be conscious of it as art. The tension between these two requirements, I suggest, generates much of the interest in Kant's philosophy of art and is the key to understanding his conception of genius. Within this framework I return to the theory of aesthetic ideas and attempt to show that the account of beauty (both natural and artistic) is not only compatible with the formalism of the Analytic but is its necessary complement. In addition, I attempt to relate the conception of fine art to the free-adherent beauty distinction of the Analytic and to explore the diverse ways in which Kant views "representation" in the domain of art.

The account of the sublime, as the second species of pure aesthetic judgment, completes the study and is the longest and perhaps most complex chapter in the book. Both the length and complexity of the discussion derive partly from the many strands of thought that collide in Kant's account of the sublime and partly from the relatively undeveloped nature of his analysis. The latter I take to be a symptom of his deep ambivalence toward this conception, and I believe that this ambivalence underlies the apparently last-minute nature of his decision to include a discussion of it in the *Critique of Judgment*.

In particular, I emphasize the tension between the sublime and the underlying concept of the purposiveness of nature. The central problem is that whereas the beautiful provides intimations (not amounting to anything like evidence) that nature is on our side in the sense previously stipulated, the sublime provides us with a sense of our allegedly "supersensible" nature and vocation and, therefore, of our independence of nature. The latter is certainly crucial for Kant's understanding of morality, reflecting what I term the "Stoic side" of his moral theory; but the sense of purposiveness that it involves can no longer be readily viewed as that of nature, except in an indirect and Pickwickian sense.

KANT'S CONCEPTION OF
REFLECTIVE JUDGMENT

REFLECTIVE JUDGMENT AND THE PURPOSIVENESS OF NATURE

As the title indicates, the *Critique of Judgment* is concerned with the faculty of judgment [*Urteilskraft*]. Following a long tradition, Kant assumes that judgment, together with understanding and reason, constitute the three "higher" cognitive faculties (sensibility being the "lower" faculty), and the question he poses at the beginning of both Introductions is whether a separate critique of this faculty is necessary or, indeed, possible. To anticipate a topic to be explored at length later in this study, the necessity for such a critique stems from the mediating function that judgment supposedly plays between the faculties of understanding and reason, which were the main concerns of the first and second *Critiques* respectively.

What is of immediate interest, however, is not so much the systematic function that judgment is supposed to play in the overall critical enterprise, but rather the condition under which it is alone capable of a critique in the first place. As already indicated in the Introduction, this condition is that it must be the source of some claims that rest on an *a priori* principle unique to judgment as a faculty (otherwise there would be nothing stemming specifically from judgment requiring a transcendental critique).

In the *Critique of Aesthetic Judgment* (the first part of the *Critique of Judgment*), Kant argues that judgments of beauty fit this description, since they lay claim to a certain kind of universality and necessity. But the initial problem with which Kant deals in the Introductions is the direct outgrowth of the first two *Critiques*, namely that judgment, in contrast to both the understanding, which is normative with respect to nature, and reason (here understood as practical reason), which is normative with respect to freedom),[1] does not appear to have its own sphere of normativity. And this, expressed in terms of the political metaphor that Kant uses in the Second Introduction, is because, unlike them, judgment has no "domain" [*Gebiet*] (KU 5: 174–5; 12–13).

Accordingly, Kant's primary concern in both Introductions is to show that, in spite of this lack of a domain, judgment does have its unique *a priori* principle (the purposiveness of nature), albeit one that is operative only in its reflective rather than its determinative capacity. This account is the subject matter of the present chapter, which is divided into four parts. The first provides a sketch of Kant's conception of judgment, beginning with the formulation in the first *Critique,* and of the distinction (and relationship) between its determinative and reflective functions that Kant only makes explicit in the third. The second analyzes in some detail the reflective function of judgment with respect to the formation of empirical concepts and, more generally, the logical use of the understanding. To this end, I make significant use of some of the analyses provided by Béatrice Longuenesse in her recent book.[2] The third section is devoted to an examination of Kant's claim in both Introductions that the principle of judgment has a transcendental status and of the considerations that lead him to assert the need for a new transcendental deduction of this principle. The fourth section then analyzes the actual deduction as it is contained in Section V of the Second Introduction. By connecting this deduction with what Kant terms the "heautonomy" of judgment, this analysis sets the stage for the discussions that Kant provides in the two Introductions of the relationship between reflective judgment and taste, which is the subject of the second and final chapter in the first part of this study.

I

If one approaches the question of whether the faculty of judgment has a distinct *a priori* principle from the standpoint of the first *Critique,* the situation does not look promising. For judgment is there defined in contrast to the understanding (the faculty of rules) as "the faculty of subsuming under rules; that is, of distinguishing whether something does or does not stand under a given rule (*casus datae legis*)" (A132/B171), and Kant emphasizes that general logic can provide no rules for judgment so conceived. This is because the stipulation of rules for the application of rules obviously leads to an infinite regress. Thus, at some level the very possibility of cognition (and practical deliberation as well) requires that one simply be able to see whether or not a datum or state of affairs instantiates a certain rule. The capacity for such nonmediated "seeing," or, as we shall later see, "feeling," apart from which rules could not be applied, is precisely what Kant understands by judgment, which he famously describes as a "peculiar talent which can be practiced only, and cannot be taught" (A133/B172).

To be sure, Kant limits this independence of governing rules to judgment as considered from the point of view of general logic. Indeed, his main concern in introducing the topic is to underscore the point that things look very different from the standpoint of transcendental logic.

For, as Kant puts it, "Transcendental philosophy has the peculiarity that besides the rule (or rather the universal condition of rules) given in the pure concept of understanding, it can also specify *a priori* the instance to which the rule is to be applied" (A136/B175).

These *a priori* specifiable instances are the schemata of the various pure concepts, which provide the conditions under which these concepts are applicable to the data of sensible experience. And Kant proceeds to delineate them in the Schematism chapter, which constitutes the first part of the "Transcendental Doctrine of Judgment" (A137/B170). From the point of view of the third *Critique*, however, the crucial point is that the rules for which judgment specifies the application conditions stem not from itself but from the understanding, and that no additional rules are introduced on the basis of which such specification is possible. Accordingly, it might seem that whether judgment be considered from the standpoint of general or of transcendental logic, there is no basis for assigning any distinctive rules or principles to this faculty and therefore no grounds for a separate critique.

Nevertheless, in both Introductions to the third *Critique* Kant attempts to carve out space for a distinct *a priori* principle of judgment by distinguishing between the reflective and determinative functions of this faculty. In the First Introduction he states:

> Judgment can be regarded either as mere[ly] an ability to *reflect*, in terms of a certain principle, on a given representation so as to [make] a concept possible, or as an ability to *determine* an underlying concpet by means of a given empirical representation. In the first case it is the *reflective*, in the second the *determinative faculty of judgment*. (FI 20: 211, 399–400)[3]

In the Second Introduction he writes:

> Judgment in general is the ability to think the particular as contained under the universal. If the universal (the rule, principle, law) is given, then judgment, which subsumes the particular under it, is *determinative* (even though [in its role] as transcendental judgment it states *a priori* the conditions that must be met for subsumption under that universal to be possible). But if only the particular is given and judgment has to find the universal for it, then this faculty is merely *reflective*. (KU 5: 179; 18–19).[4]

As presented here, reflection and determination are seen as contrasting operations of judgment (the movement from particular to universal, and from universal to particular), and it is quite clear that Kant draws no such contrast in the first *Critique*. Indeed, since his concern in the Transcendental Analytic is with the determination and justification of the *a priori* principles of possible experience, his focus is largely on the movement from the top down, that is, on the determinative operation of judgment. Admittedly, in the Appendix to the Transcendental Dialectic Kant does deal with the problem of moving from particulars to universals, and in the process appeals to the line of argument that he later develops in the Introductions to the third *Critique;* but this is all presented in terms of an account of the proper regulative use of the ideas of reason, which makes no reference to judgment and a distinct reflective function (A641/B670–A668/B696).[5]

Notwithstanding the lack of an explicit formulation of this distinction in the first *Critique,* however, it remains an open question whether the contrast that Kant draws in the Introductions to the third *Critique* really marks a major change in his conception of judgment. Recently, Béatrice Longuenesse has argued forcefully for the view that it does not. On her reading, what is unique to the third *Critique* is not the affirmation of a distinct reflective activity of judgment, but rather the idea that there are judgments (aesthetic and teleological) that are *merely* reflective. In other words, for Longuenesse, reflection and determination are complementary aspects of judgment from the very beginning of the "critical" period (if not before).[6] Moreover, she finds important confirmation of this view, which is primarily based on a close analysis of the functions of discursive thinking and the "concepts of comparison" to which Kant appeals in the Amphiboly chapter, in a passage from the First Introduction. The following is the passage with her translation and emphases:

> With respect to the universal concepts of nature, under which in general a concept of experience (without any particular empirical determination) is possible, reflection has in the concept of nature in general, i.e. in understanding, already its direction [*ihre Anweisung*] and *the power of judgment does not need a particular principle for its reflection, but schematizes it a priori* [*die Urteilskraft bedarf keines besonderen Prinzips der Reflection, sondern schematisiert dieselbe a priori*] and applies these schemata to each empirical synthesis, without which no judgment of experience would be possible. This power of judgment is here *in its reflection at the same time determinative,* and the transcendental schematism of the latter is at the same time a rule under which empirical intuitions are subsumed. (FI 20: 212; 401)[7]

Actually, though it is deeply suggestive, this text to which Longuenesse attaches such significance is less informative on the main point at issue than her account suggests. Kant is here obviously referring back to the schematism of the pure concepts and the passage makes three closely related points. The first is that, like all concepts, the categories as distinct concepts are themselves the product of a reflective activity. This is a centerpiece of Longuenesse's interpretation, since she insists that the categories operate at two levels: pre-reflectively as the logical functions of judgment guiding the sensible syntheses of the imagination, and post-reflectively as concepts under which objects are subsumed in objectively valid judgments of experience.[8]

Although a detailed consideration of the issue would take us well beyond the scope of this study, it must be noted that she is undoubtedly correct on this important point. As she appropriately reminds us, Kant makes clear in his response to Eberhard that, in spite of their *a priori* status, neither the categories nor the forms of sensibility are innate. They are rather "original acquisitions," and in the case of the categories, Longuenesse suggests that this acquisition results from a reflection on the product of the synthetic activity of the imagination under the direction of the logical functions of judgment (which are alone original).[9]

The second major point that Kant makes in the passage is closely related to this, namely that the reflection involved in the formation of the categories as clear concepts does not require a distinct principle, but is based on their very schematization. In other words, in providing *a priori* the instance corresponding to the rule thought in the pure concept, that is, the transcendental schema, judgment provides all that is necessary to arrive at a clear concept of this rule, that is, the categories as full-fledged, reflected concepts under which objects may be subsumed in judgments.

The third point, which is really just a clarification of the second, is that here judgment is both reflective and determinative ("in its reflection at the same time determinative"). With respect to Longuenesse's central thesis about judgment involving both reflection and determination, this is presumably the most important. Nevertheless, the text under consideration is less than decisive because it is explicitly limited to the *transcendental* function of judgment with respect to the schematization of the categories. Consequently, unless one assumes that what holds at the transcendental level *ipso facto* holds at the empirical as well, the question of whether ordinary empirical judgment (the subsumption of empirical intuition under a concept) necessarily involves both determination and reflection is really unaddressed.

Moreover, at first glance at least, the text of the Second Introduction appears far less supportive of Longuenesse's general thesis than the First. For rather than bringing reflection and determination together, at least in the case of the categories and their schematization, Kant now seems to separate sharply these activities. Thus, in connection with the schematization of pure concepts, he remarks that "Determinative judgment, under universal transcendental laws given by the understanding, is only subsumptive" (KU 5: 179; 19). And from this he concludes in accordance with the claim of the first *Critique* that such judgment requires no distinct principle. By contrast, reflective judgment, here understood in its empirical function, does require a distinct principle in order to proceed from the particular in nature to the universal (KU 5: 180; 19). Accordingly, the picture suggested by this text is of determinative and reflective judgment as two distinct faculties, united only by a common concern of connecting universals to particulars, which they attempt to do in two diametrically opposed ways: the former by subsuming particulars under given concepts (mainly pure concepts of the understanding or categories), which is made possible by providing schemata for these concepts, and the latter by ascending from empirical intuition to empirical concepts and principles, which requires the presupposition of the principle of the (logical) purposiveness of nature.

Given Kant's intent to introduce a distinct transcendental principle for judgment in its reflective capacity, this way of characterizing the distinct activities of judgment is perfectly understandable. Indeed, from this point of view the fact that reflection is required for the acquisition of the categories as full-fledged concepts is beside the point, since, as Kant points out in the First Introduction, this reflection does not require a distinct principle of judgment. And this is probably why Kant omitted any reference to this point in the more compact published Introduction.

Nevertheless, the picture that Kant provides there is somewhat misleading for the very reasons that Longuenesse suggests. For there Kant gives no indication of the fact that, in his view, *all* theoretical judgments, including ordinary empirical ones, contain what may be termed a "moment" of reflection as well as determination. Moreover, the recognition of this fact is crucial for the proper understanding of both Kant's "deduction" of a special transcendental principle of judgment in its empirical reflection and his account of pure judgments of taste as resting on "mere reflection." Accordingly, in the remainder of this section I shall try to indicate why this must hold true of all empirical judgment by showing that an account of judgment solely in terms of determination is inherently incomplete, requiring as its complement the activity that Kant terms "reflection." This should then set the stage for an analysis of the latter activity in Section II.

To begin with, we must attempt to get clear about what Kant means by "determination" with respect to judgment. This turns out to be a more complicated matter than it first appears, however, since there are three different subjects of such determination. In the previously cited passage from the First Introduction, Kant indicates that it is a *concept* that is determined, and that this determination occurs by providing it with a corresponding intuition. To determine concepts in this manner is, of course, essential for Kant, since he famously maintains that "Thoughts without content are empty" (A51/B75).

For an understanding of Kant's conception of judgment, however, the fundamental point is that all judgment (whether it be analytic or synthetic) is determinative insofar as it makes a claim about its purported object.[10] Thus, what is determined from this point of view is the *object* (or set thereof) referred to in the judgment, which Kant usually characterizes as "x" in order to indicate its indeterminacy prior to the judgmental act. In a judgment of the categorical form, this determination occurs through the subsumption of the intuition of this x under a subject-concept, which, in turn, makes possible further subsumption or subordination under additional concepts in the judgment.[11]

Finally, since through such subsumption the *intuition* is determined as the intuition of an object of a particular kind, it is likewise a subject of determination in a judgment. In other words, the determination of the object occurs in and through the conceptual determination of its intuition. And this is precisely what Kant had in mind in the introductory portion of the Transcendental Logic, when he characterized a judgment [*Urteil*, not *Urteilskraft*] as "the mediate knowledge of an object" (A68/B93).

Interestingly enough, Kant there uses one of his favorite examples of an analytic judgment, "all bodies are divisible," in order to illustrate this thesis. Although perhaps surprising, there is nothing improper in this, since the analysis of the structure of judgment pertains to general logic, where the distinction between analytic and synthetic judgments does not arise.[12] According to Kant's analysis, the broader concept "divisibility," which is presumably also applicable to abstract entities such as lines, planes, and numbers, is here applied to the concept of body (he should have said the *extension* of this concept), while this, in turn, is applied to "certain intuitions [or appearances] that present themselves to us" (A68–9/B93).[13] Thus, both the intuitions and the objects thereof (appearances) are "determined" by being brought under a hierarchy of subordinate concepts, and by this means, as Kant puts it, "much possible knowledge is collected into one" (A69/B94).

Later, in §19 of the B-Deduction, Kant returns to a consideration of this act of judgment in light of the conception of the "objective unity of apperception" developed in §17 and §18. His avowed concern is to correct the logicians who define a judgment simply as the "representation of a relation between two concepts." In addition to applying only to categorical judgments, Kant faults this account for failing to specify in what this relation consists. And in an endeavor to answer this question he writes:

> I find that a judgment is nothing but the manner in which different cognitions are brought to the objective unity of apperception. This is what is intended by the copula 'is'. It is employed to distinguish the objective unity of given representations from the subjective. (B141–2)

By characterizing the unity of representations attained in a judgment as "objective," Kant is not simply distinguishing it from a merely subjective unity based on association (though he is, of course, doing that); he is also indicating that objective validity is a definitional feature of judgment as such, rather than a property pertaining only to some judgments, namely, those that are true.[14] This is not to be understood, however, as suggesting that every unification of representations under a judgmental form is thereby "true," that is, conforms to its object. The point is rather that every cognitive judgment makes a claim about its purported object and therefore has a truth *value* (is either true or false).[15] Moreover, as I have already indicated, it is precisely because a judgment involves a reference to an object that it may be said to be *determinative* of its object. And this suggests that every judgment insofar as it is objectively valid is determinative.

Obviously, much more needs to be said in order to provide anything like an adequate account of Kant's conception of the act of judgment as contained in the first *Critique*. In particular, it is important to bring out the connection between this act and the table of logical functions, which is the focal point of much of Longuenesse's analysis, and which Kant himself attempts to do in §19 and §20 of the B-Deduction. Nevertheless, even without this, it should already be apparent that an account of judgment solely in terms of determination is radically incomplete. For in order to judge that the x's in question are divisible (and therefore "determined" by the concept), I must first recognize that they fall under the concept of body. Moreover, in order to do this, I must already possess this concept, through the analysis of which I can then infer divisibility as one of its marks.

In the preliminary analysis in the first *Critique*, Kant treats these concepts as already at hand and available for analysis and subsumption. Elsewhere, however, he makes it clear that the concepts under which objects are subsumed in judgment are themselves only attained through a complex act of (logical) reflection. This makes such reflection an essential ingredient in what Longuenesse, following Kant, terms the "capacity to judge" [*Vermögen zu urteilen*], which is identified with the "capacity to think" [*Vermögen zu denken*] (A81/B106).[16] And given this, it is incumbent upon us to provide an account of this act on which the entire architecture of the third *Critique* is ultimately based.

II

Kant's fullest account of the nature of reflection is in the First Introduction where he writes:

> To *reflect* (or consider [Überlegung]) is to hold given representations up to, and compare them with, either other representations or one's cognitive faculty, in reference to a concept that this [comparison] makes possible. The reflective faculty of judgment [*Urteilskraft*] is the one we also call the power of judging [*Beurteilungsvermögen*] *(facultas dijudicandi)*. (FI 20: 211; 400)

Kant here characterizes reflection in the broadest possible terms so as to include not only the logical reflection involved in the formation of concepts, but also transcendental reflection, which he presents in the first

Critique as the antidote to the amphibolous use of concepts of reflection by Leibniz, and, more importantly, the type of "mere reflection," which, as he will go on to argue, is involved in aesthetic judgments. Although these differ markedly from each other, they share the common feature of involving a comparison based on given representations. Indeed, this also applies to the extended sense of reflection that Kant attributes to animals in the next paragraph, even though they are (in his view) incapable of conceptual representation. As he there puts it, "even animals reflect, though only instinctively, that is, not in reference to acquiring a concept, but rather for determining an inclination" (FI 20: 211; 400). Unfortunately, Kant does not elaborate upon this brief reference to animal reflection, but his main point presumably is that animals may be said to "reflect" (in an extended sense) insofar as they compare intuitions or sensations, say of odors, in order to determine which is preferable. The essential difference is that rather than being based on some principle (as is the case with regard to rational beings), such animal "reflection" occurs instinctively.[17]

Our present concern, however, is solely with the kind of reflection that is requisite for the generation of empirical concepts. This is what Kant terms in the first *Critique* "logical" as opposed to "transcendental" reflection; and its systematic significance stems from the fact that, unlike the latter, it supposedly rests upon a principle unique to judgment.[18]

In order to understand the mechanics of this type of reflection, it is necessary to turn from the third *Critique* to the *Jäsche Logic*.[19] Underlying this account is the distinction between the matter (or content) and the form of a concept. Empirical and pure concepts differ with respect to the former and its origin, since for pure concepts the content is either given *a priori* or made, that is, constructed (as in the case of mathematical concepts), whereas for empirical concepts it is derived from experience. But notwithstanding this difference in *content*, all concepts (pure, mathematical, and empirical) share the same *form*, namely universality.[20] And it is the origin of this form, also termed the "logical origin," with which Kant is concerned in the *Jäsche Logic*.[21]

In the frequently discussed §6 of this text, Kant refers to the "logical acts" of comparison, reflection, and abstraction as the source of this universality and therefore of concepts with respect to their form. And after not very helpful characterizations of these operations he attempts to illustrate the whole process in a note:

> To make concepts out of representations one must thus be able *to compare, to reflect,* and *to abstract,* for these three logical operations of the understanding are the essential and universal conditions for generation of every concept whatsoever. I see, e.g., a spruce, a willow, and a linden. By first comparing these objects with one another I note that they are different from one another in regard to the trunk, the branches, the leaves, etc.; but next

I reflect on what they have in common among themselves, trunk, branches, and leaves themselves, and I abstract from the quantity, the figure, etc., of these; thus I acquire a concept of a tree (JL 9: 94–5; 592).

At first glance at least, this account of the formation of the concept of a tree seems highly problematic. For one thing, as Longuenesse has pointed out, the chronology that Kant describes is totally implausible. It cannot be the case that we first note the differences between the various trunks, branches, and leaves, then reflect that the objects being compared have in common the fact that they all have these features, and only then abstract from their differences. If this account is to make any sense, comparison, reflection, and abstraction must be seen as aspects of a single, unified activity, not as temporally successive operations.[22]

Even if this be granted, however, difficulties remain, since the process seems hopelessly circular. We supposedly arrive at the concept of a tree by reflecting on precisely those features of the perceived objects (trunk, branches, leaves, etc.) in virtue of which we recognize them to be trees, and by abstracting from those that are irrelevant. But how could one recognize and select these "tree-constituting" features unless one already had the concept of a tree, which is precisely what was supposed to have been explained? In short, it seems that on Kant's account one must already have the concept of a tree before one is able to acquire it.[23]

The nature of the difficulty concerning the Kantian theory of empirical concept formation can be clarified by comparing it to a similar problem in Hume. Since the latter held that every idea is a copy of a corresponding impression, he would not merely acknowledge but actually insist upon there being a perfectly acceptable sense in which the mind could be said to have a "concept" (idea) before having it, namely in the form of an impression with precisely the same content as the corresponding idea.

The problem for Hume, however, arises regarding the origin of what Kant terms the "form of universality." Since he was committed by the so-called copy thesis to hold that all ideas are particular, Hume naturally sided with Berkeley in denying the existence of abstract general ideas. But he went beyond Berkeley in offering an account of how ideas that are in themselves particular can become "general in their representation" by referring to (and calling to mind) any number of other resembling ideas. As Hume puts it in the *Treatise:*

> When we have found a resemblance among several objects, that often occur to us, we apply the same name to all of them, whatever differences we may observe in the degrees of their quantity and quality, and whatever other differences may appear among them. After we have acquired a custom of this kind, the hearing of that name revives the idea of one of these objects, and makes the imagination conceive it with all its particular cir-

cumstances and proportions. But as the same word is suppos'd to have been frequently applied to other individuals, that are different in many respects from that idea, which is immediately present to the mind; the word not being able to revive the idea of all these individuals, only touches the soul, if I may be allow'd so to speak, and revives that custom, which we have acquir'd by surveying them.[24]

The problems with this account begin at the very first step with the appeal to resemblance. Setting aside the fact that the identification of ideas with faint copies of impressions precludes the possibility of even recognizing resemblances (the mind can have resembling impressions but not an impression of their resemblance), it would seem that the capacity to recognize such resemblances and to abstract from the differences already presupposes a concept and therefore cannot be used to explain its origin.[25]

More interestingly, much the same may also be said for the role assigned to custom, which does so much of the work by calling to mind the relevant particulars. Consider, for example, Hume's account of its role in reasoning regarding triangles, which follows shortly upon the passage cited. Consistently with his principles, Hume suggests that the mention of the term "triangle" occasions the formation in the mind of the idea of a particular one, say an equilateral triangle with sides of three inches. At this point custom takes over, bringing forth images of various other particular (nonequilateral) triangles that have previously been associated with the term, and this supposedly prevents the mind from drawing false inferences regarding all triangles from the particular features of the one it is contemplating.[26] This is an ingenious attempt to account for mathematical reasoning on the basis of association, but it is clearly a failure. For how could the images of other triangles supposedly produced by the custom be recognized as counterexamples unless the mind could already grasp the properties essential to all triangles, that is, unless it had the concept of a triangle?

By rejecting Hume's conflation of concepts and images, Kant clearly avoided the problem in its Humean form. But it is not immediately apparent that he was able to avoid it altogether, that is, that he could provide a nonquestion begging account of the origin of empirical concepts as general representations. Indeed, it might even seem that the problem is exacerbated for Kant by his conception of experience. Since, in contrast to empiricists such as Hume, he identified experience with empirical knowledge rather than merely the reception of the raw material for such knowledge (impressions), Kant was committed to the view that experience presupposes the possession and use of concepts. And this naturally gives rise to the question of the genesis of those concepts that are required for the very experience through which empirical concepts are supposedly formed.

It is important to recognize that the problem in its specifically Kantian form cannot be avoided simply by claiming that the concepts presupposed by experience are the pure concepts of the understanding, which, as the description suggests, have a nonempirical origin in the very nature of the understanding. For one thing, we shall see later in this chapter that the categories and the principles based upon them are not of themselves sufficient to account for the possibility of acquiring empirical concepts (and laws); and, for another, that they cannot themselves be applied as concepts independently of empirical concepts.[27] How, for example, could one apply the concept of causality to a given occurrence unless it were already conceived as an event of a certain kind, for example, the freezing of water?

Although she does not pose the problem in this way, I believe that Longuenesse provides the basis for an answer, in fact, for the very answer to which Kant himself alludes in various texts without ever making fully explicit. The key lies in Kant's understanding of the "logical act" of comparison, which, as we have seen, is carried out "with respect to a concept that is thereby made possible" (FI 20: 211; 400).

In contrast to the kind of comparison (or reflection) practiced by animals, which is itself obviously akin to the association, which, for Hume, generates customs or habits, this may be described as "universalizing comparison."[28] In other words, it is a comparison that is directed from the beginning toward the detection of common features in the sensibly given, and it is so directed because it is governed by the implicit norm of universality, with the goal being to elevate these common features into the marks of concepts that may be subsequently applied in judgments. According to Longuenesse, this is because such comparison is in the service of the logical functions of judgment (or the "capacity to judge"), and occurs only under the guidance of the "concepts of comparison" delineated in the Amphiboly chapter (identity and difference, agreement and opposition, inner and outer, matter and form) (A63/B319–A268/B324).[29]

Leaving the latter aside for the present, however, our immediate concern is with the items to be compared in this "universalizing comparison," which Longuenesse identifies as various schemata. In support of this reading, she refers us to a *Reflexion* dated somewhere between 1776 and 1780, in which Kant remarks: "We compare only what is universal in the rule of our apprehension" (R2880 16: 557).[30] Since what is universal in a rule governing or ordering our apprehension of an object is equivalent to what the *Critique* characterizes as a schema, it follows that the comparison leading to the formation of concepts is a comparison of schemata rather than merely of impressions or images, as it is for Hume, and therefore of something that already has a certain universality.

If we reconsider Kant's account in the *Jäsche Logic* in this light, we can see that in comparing the trunks, branches, leaves, and so forth of the various trees for the sake of forming a general concept of a tree, what one is really comparing are the patterns or rules governing the apprehension of these items, that is, their schemata. And it is from a reflection on what is common to these patterns of apprehension or schemata, combined with an abstraction from their differences, that one arrives at the (reflected) concept of a tree.

This seems to provide at least a partial answer to the objection since it explains how one can reflect upon those very features that constitute the defining characteristics or marks of the not-yet-formed concept of a tree. It is clearly only a partial answer, however, since it immediately suggests at least two further questions: (1) How is it possible to have a schema before acquiring the concept which it purportedly schematizes? And (2) How does the schema of an empirical concept itself originate, since it obviously cannot be viewed as given *a priori?* Although we cannot here pursue Longuenesse's answers to these questions, particularly the second, in the detail they require and deserve, it will be helpful to outline her basic conclusions.

As Longuenesse points out in a note, the initial resistance to the idea that a schema might antedate its concept stems from the fact that when Kant introduced the topic of the schematism in the first *Critique,* his concern was with the conditions under which a concept that is supposedly already formed may relate to a sensible object. This requires a schema, which is its sensible expression or "presentation"; so without its corresponding schema a concept would have no application.[31] Indeed, we could go further and claim that one cannot really be said to possess a concept without also having its schema, which is just the rule for its application. For it is the schema that tells us what counts as falling under a given concept; and one clearly cannot have a concept with knowing the kind of thing (or property) that instantiates it.

Longuenesse also suggests, however, that if one considers the relation between concept and schema from the perspective of the Metaphysical and Transcendental Deductions, the priority is reversed.[32] For in the former, Kant clearly maintains that synthesis is the result of the imagination, that "blind but indispensable function of the soul," whereas the function of the understanding is to "bring this synthesis to concepts," by which we first obtain "cognition properly so-called" (A78/B103). Moreover, in the A-Deduction this is elaborated into the doctrine of the threefold synthesis, the last stage of which is termed "recognition in the concept." Correlatively, in the B-Deduction, where the role of the imagination is supposedly downplayed, Kant claims that the "*analytic* unity of apperception [which belongs to every concept as such] is possible only under the presupposition of a certain *synthetic* unity" (B133 and attached note).

These texts from both editions of the first *Critique* strongly suggest that Kant held that the conceptual recognition required for "cognition properly so-called" arises from a subsequent reflection upon (a bringing to *concepts* of) an order or structure initially imposed upon the sensible manifold by the "blind," that is, not consciously directed, synthesis of the imagination. Moreover, this, in turn, suggests that one might have and make use of a schema (rule of apprehension) prior to and independently of the discursive representation of this rule (as a set of marks) in a concept.

Returning to Kant's own example of the different types of tree, it seems clear that one could have a capacity to distinguish, say, a spruce from a willow on the basis of perceived structural features of their trunks, branches, and leaves, without also having the capacity to list the defining marks of the distinct species. Since the former capacity is prelinguistic (and therefore preconceptual) it does not amount to "cognition properly so-called." Nevertheless, it is also the source of the content, which when raised to the form of universality through the "logical operations" of the understanding, does yield such cognition.[33]

In order to illustrate the rule-governedness of the apprehension that precedes the formation of concepts in which these rules are expressed discursively, Longuenesse cites an example given by Kant of an apprehension that is *not* so rule-governed. As Kant describes the situation:

> If, for example, a savage sees a house from a distance, whose use he does not know, he admittedly has before him in his representation the very same object as someone else who knows it determinately as a dwelling established for human beings. But as to form, this cognition of one and the same object is different in the two cases. In the former it is *mere intuition*, in the latter it is simultaneously *intuition and concept* (JL 9: 33: 544–5).[34]

Even though Kant himself indicates that what the savage lacks is the *concept* of a house, I believe that Longuenesse is correct in emphasizing that he is also missing the *schema* (which is, after all, a necessary condition for possessing the concept). Thus, as she suggests, the savage, never before having seen anything like a house, receives the same sensible data as someone familiar with such objects, but he has no procedure at hand for processing it in a determinate way. As she puts it, "there is no rule guiding him to privilege certain marks and leave aside others, so that a concept of house might apply."[35] In other words, the savage lacks not only the concept of a house but also the precondition for acquiring it, namely its schema.

How, then, is a schema or rule of apprehension acquired in the first place? Unless this question can be answered, our initial worry about empirical concept formation has merely been replaced by a parallel one regarding schemata, rather than resolved.[36] Moreover, Longuenesse's answer, though perfectly consistent with her underlying analysis, nonetheless appears puzzling, at least initially. For according to her account, the "schemata arise from the very same acts of universalizing comparison of which they are the object."[37] In other words, acts of this type produce *both* the full-fledged reflected concepts by means of a comparison of schemata and the very schemata that are to be compared.

Clearly, the major puzzle suggested by this response concerns the initial or foundational schema-generating comparison. How is such a comparison to proceed, since *ex hypothesi* it does not yet have "what is universal in the rule of our apprehension," that is, a schema? And how can schemata both provide the terms of a universalizing comparison and be themselves products of such a comparison? The very idea appears to threaten us with either an infinite regress or a replay of the same circularity that plagued Kant's original account of concept formation.

If I understand her correctly, the gist of Longuenesse's answer is that this comparison does not begin with a blank slate. This is because the mind, in its universalizing comparison, is guided by the very same concepts of reflection that are operative in the comparison of schemata that leads to the formation of reflected concepts. Presumably, at this level, however, the comparison leads the mind to seek similarities and differences, which can first be codified as schemata governing apprehension and then reflected as concepts. And this is possible, according to Longuenesse, because this comparison is oriented from the beginning toward the acquisition of concepts applicable in judgments.

Thus, Kant's savage, never having seen a house, initially had no basis of comparison to order his apprehension. But after seeing many similar objects, which he presumably relates by association, he will begin to perceive relevant similarities and differences, which, in turn, leads (under the implicit guidance of the concepts of comparison) to the formation of a schema of a house as a rule governing apprehension, and possibly even the full-fledged concept.

I find this reading appealing and the doctrine it attributes to Kant both internally coherent and plausible, albeit seriously underdeveloped. In addition to providing at least the outlines of a much more nuanced and sophisticated account of concept formation and the conditions of its possibility than is possible on the basis of the sparse materials of classical empiricism, this reading avoids the circularity problem with which our reflections began. Contrary to what initially seemed to be the case, one does not need already to have a schema in order to acquire it in the first place. All that is required (from the side of the mind) is, in Longuenesse's terms, "the capacity to judge," which is initially exercised in a universalizing comparison of associated representations under the guidance of the concepts of reflection.

Both textual support for this reading and an indication of how the account of concept formation fits within the overall framework of Kant's theory of reflective judgment is provided by another *Reflexion* (also cited by Longuenesse) that stems from the same group as the one linking com-

parison to "what is universal in the rule of our apprehension." In this related *Reflexion*, Kant remarks with regard to a "*communicatio objectiva*," by
which he apparently means a collection of representations in a single
mark [*nota*] for which some kind of objectivity or applicability to a set of
objects is claimed, that "This general validity [*Gemeingültigkeit*] presupposes a comparison, not of perceptions, but of our apprehension, insofar
as it contains the presentation [*Darstellung*] of an as yet undetermined
concept, and is universal in itself [*an sich allgemein ist*]" (R2883 16: 558).[38]

Three points are to be noted regarding this brief but highly significant
text. First, Kant clearly does refer to a comparison of apprehensions,
which can only mean a comparison of the *contents* of various acts of apprehending (such as that of the apprehendings of the different kinds of
tree in the example from the *Jäsche Logic*). Second, these apprehendings
are compared with respect to their presentation (or exhibition) [*Darstellung*] of "an as yet undetermined concept." Since this presentation is
equivalent to the schema of the concept, and since the concept is not yet
determined, it follows that the comparison is between schemata of concepts that have not yet been formed. Indeed, as already indicated, this
comparison is precisely the basis on which the concepts are formed.
Third, and most important, the contents of these acts of apprehension
contain something "universal in itself." The latter may reasonably be
taken to refer to the schemata, since a schema must have a universal nature if it is to serve as the exhibition of a concept.[39] But it may also refer
to the apprehended content on the basis of which the schemata themselves are formed, insofar as this content is to provide the foundation for
a universalizing comparison.

The significance of the latter point stems from the fact that it indicates
both the need for and the nature of the principle to which judgment must
appeal in its logical reflection directed toward the acquisition of empirical concepts for use in judgment. Clearly, reflection, so construed, rests
on the assumption that there is something "universal in itself" encoded,
as it were, in our experience, which provides the basis for the formation
of both schemata and reflected concepts. For without this presupposition
the process of reflection would never get off the ground.

Longuenesse nicely brings out this fundamental, yet frequently neglected, aspect of Kant's position by means of a brief comparison with
Locke's view on universals. As she correctly notes, Kant seems close to
Locke in holding that the form of a concept as a discursive representation is always something made (rather than discovered), which is analogous to Locke's thesis that "[G]eneral and *universal* belong not to the real
existence of things; but are the inventions and creations of the understanding made for its own use."[40] She also points out, however, that Kant
refused to follow Locke in viewing the concepts formed by the mind as
arbitrary inventions, without any connection with the nature of things.

On the contrary, perhaps because he viewed concepts as "predicates of possible judgments" (A69/B94), and judgments as involving an inherent claim to objective validity, Kant assumed the right to maintain that the concepts formed through the logical operations of the understanding somehow reflect or correspond to the nature of things.

To leave it at this, however, would be to run the danger of simply collapsing Kant's position into that of Leibniz. For in Book III of his *New Essays on Human Understanding,* the latter attacks Locke's conventionalism as it is expressed in the contrast between real and merely nominal essences, and insists that the nominal essences or abstract ideas of sorts manufactured by the understanding have a basis in the nature of things or real essences. In Leibniz's own terms, which, as we shall see, are highly significant for understanding Kant's view, "every outer appearance is grounded in the inner constitution," and "whatever we truthfully distinguish or compare is also distinguished or made alike by nature."[41]

Clearly, Kant could not simply help himself to such an ontologically grounded realism. This is precluded not only by the transcendental theory of sensibility, which denies the human mind access to anything like Leibnizian real essences, but also by Hume's critique of the rational credentials of the belief in the uniformity of nature. In fact, these two worries about the conditions of reflection are strictly correlative. For, on the one hand, without the assumption of something like the Leibnizian principle, there is no basis, apart from a purely *ad hoc* hypothesis such as occasionalism, which clearly had no appeal for Kant, for assuming the uniformity of nature; while, on the other hand, without the presupposition of such uniformity, there are no grounds for assuming that the similarities and differences noted on the basis of experience correspond to intrinsic (and therefore permanent) similarities and differences in things. Thus, while it may very well be the case that experience has taught us up to now that all substances with the perceptual properties associated with the term "gold" also have the causal property of being soluble in *aqua regia,* this, of itself, provides us with neither an insight into the intrinsic nature of gold nor a guarantee regarding the future correlation of its properties. Moreover, for reasons to be considered shortly, such a guarantee is also not provided by the Transcendental Deduction in the first *Critique.*

Accordingly, it seems that the analysis of the nature and conditions of logical reflection leads to what is nothing less than a new transcendental problem. This problem concerns the "empirical as such," and it may be described in two alternative ways, which in the end come to much the same thing. According to one description, it is to find a third way between the Leibnizian realism of universals (real essence) and the Lockean conventionalism (nominal essence), just as in the first *Critique* Kant affirmed a third way between the former's "noogony" and the latter's sensualism (A271/B327). According to the other, it is to ground the inference from the observed to the unobserved (the focus of the Humean problematic) in a rational norm.[42] And, as I am about to argue, it is to this end that Kant introduces in both versions of the Introduction to the third *Critique* a distinct transcendental principle for judgment in its reflective capacity.

<h1 style="text-align:center">III</h1>

In both versions of the Introduction, Kant describes the required transcendental principle as that of the purposiveness of nature. In the first version, this purposiveness is characterized more specifically as "logical" (FI 20: 216–7; 404–5), and in the second as "formal" (KU 5: 180–1; 20); but in both cases it clearly signifies the contingent agreement of the order of nature with our cognitive needs and capacities. Moreover, in both versions Kant explicitly links this principle with familiar formulas or maxims, such as "nature takes the shortest way" (the principle of parsimony), "nature makes no leap in the diversity of its forms" (the principle of continuity), and "principles must not be multiplied beyond necessity" (KU 5: 182; 21–2; see also FI 20: 210; 399).[43] As these formulas suggest, the basic idea is that we look upon nature *as if* it had been designed with our cognitive interests in mind; though, of course, we have no basis for asserting that it was in fact so designed. In the formulation of the Second Introduction, which proved to be of great significance to the young Hegel, Kant describes the principle thusly:

> [S]ince universal natural laws have their ground in our understanding . . . the particular empirical laws must, as regards what the universal laws have left undetermined in them, be viewed in terms of such a unity as [they would have] if they too had been given by an understanding (even though not ours) so as to assist our cognitive faculties by making possible a system of experience in terms of particular natural laws. (KU 5: 180; 19)[44]

This formulation of the principle in terms of a system of empirical laws (or, as it is often referred to in the literature, of "systematicity")[45] is prevalent in both Introductions. It is not, however, the only way in which this principle and its function are characterized. For example, in the First Introduction it is presented as the principle that "for all natural things *concepts* can be found that are determined empirically," which is then glossed as "we can always presuppose nature's products to have a form that is possible in terms of universal laws which we can cognize" (FI 20: 211–12; 400). By contrast, in the Second Introduction Kant appears to argue that its main function is not simply to systematize empirical laws but to ground their very necessity, that is, their claim to nomological status (see KU 5: 183; 22). In fact, in various places in the Introductions, Kant suggests that the principle of the purposiveness of nature is necessary for the formation of empirical concepts, the classification of "natural forms" into genera and species, the unification of empirical laws into a system (theory construction), the formulation of empirical laws in the first place, and the attribution of necessity to such laws.[46]

Nevertheless, it is possible to find some coherence in this variety of formulations, if we simply keep in mind the essential function of reflective judgment, namely, to find universals for given particulars. First of all, this search for universals can take the form either of finding empirical concepts under which particulars can be subsumed for the sake of classification or of finding empirical laws in terms of which their behavior can be explained. Moreover, as Hannah Ginsborg has pointed out, these two types of universal are themselves closely connected, as are a taxonomic classification of "natural forms" in terms of genera of species and a systematic organization of empirical laws. For one thing, without assuming something like natural kinds, we could not even begin to look for empirical laws or hope to distinguish such laws from contingent regularities. For another, determinate empirical concepts presuppose known causal laws, since the inner properties in terms of which we conceptualize and classify things must include causal properties. Finally, the necessity and therefore the nomological character of relatively specific laws, such as that of the solubility of gold in *aqua regia,* are a function of their derivability from higher-level laws, such as those that hold at the molecular and atomic levels.[47]

Perhaps of greater immediate relevance, the same connections can also be spelled out in terms of Kant's conception of judgment. To begin with, we have seen that concepts for Kant serve as predicates of possible judgments, which means that the whole purpose of bringing intuitions under concepts is to make possible determinate judgments about their corresponding objects. The judgments in which Kant is interested are, however, of a particular type, namely "judgments of experience," that is, objectively valid, grounded claims about objects of possible experience, which are contrasted in the *Prolegomena* with mere "judgments of perception."[48]

Although Kant never says so explicitly, it seems clear from a consideration of his account of judgments of experience in the *Prolegomena* that in order to qualify as such, a judgment must either be itself a statement of empirical law or be derivable from such a law.[49] Accordingly, the search for empirical concepts that can serve as predicates in judgments of experience is inseparable from the search for empirical laws; and since, as suggested, the latter is inseparable from a hierarchical organization of such laws, it follows that the quest for the conditions of the possibility of empirical concepts and for the systematic organization of empirical laws are best seen as two poles of a quest for the conditions of the empirical knowledge of nature *qua* empirical, or equivalently, for judgments of experience.

When Kant first introduced the conception of a judgment of experience in the *Prolegomena* and distinguished it from a judgment of perception, it was to underscore the role of the categories with regard to the former. As we shall shortly see in some detail, however, the central claim in both Introductions to the third *Critique* is that the categories and the transcendental principles based upon them are not sufficient to account for the possibility of such judgments. An additional transcendental principle is required, and this is the role played by the principle of the purposiveness of nature. At least that is what I take to be the import of the "transcendental deduction" of this principle, which Kant provides in the Second Introduction.

Before we are in a position to analyze this deduction, however, further consideration of this principle and the multiple uses to which it is put is required. And here I shall focus on the more expansive account in the First Introduction. Of particular interest in this regard is Kant's insistence that, even though the principle of purposiveness is transcendental, it is "merely a principle for the *logical use of judgment*," and that its function is to allow us to "regard nature *a priori* as having in its diversity the quality of a *logical system* under empirical laws" (FI 20: 214; 402).

The "logical use of judgment" is to be distinguished from its transcendental use, which, according to the first *Critique*, is to provide the schemata that are the sensible conditions for the application of the categories. The former consists in the formation of empirical concepts and their organization into genera and species, which makes possible the subordination of these concepts in judgments and the connection of the judgments in syllogisms.[50] Insofar as our concepts are orderable in a single set of genera and species, they have the form of a logical system, and insofar as this order reflects the actual order of nature, the latter may be thought of as a "logical system under empirical laws."

Such a view of nature has, of course, merely the status of a regulative idea; but, as Kant points out, in light of it we can proceed to investigate nature either from the bottom up or from the top down. The former procedure begins with the classification of diverse particulars as members of a single species; then distinct species are unified on the basis of common properties into a genus, and different genera into higher genera, and so forth. Ideally, the process culminates in the unification of all these higher-order genera into a single highest genus. Conversely, the movement from the top down is one of increasing specification, wherein differentiations are continually introduced between items that were initially taken to be members of a single species.[51] Appealing to the language of teachers of law and Aristotelian logicians, Kant also suggests that in this procedure of specification, the genus is (logically considered) the matter and the species the form (FI 20: 214–15; 402–3).[52]

Kant's view of the significance of such an ideal scheme for empirical knowledge is best expressed in two footnotes in the First Introduction. The first of these notes is attached to the previously cited formulation of the principle as "for all natural things concepts can be found that are determined empirically" (FI 20: 211; 400). In the note Kant attempts to argue that, even though this principle may seem to be merely logical and tautologous, it is actually synthetic and transcendental because it expresses nothing less than "*the condition under which it is possible to apply logic to nature*" (FI 20: 211–12; 400) [my emphasis].

By "logic" Kant does not, of course, mean formal logic, but rather our discursive, conceptual abilities, what Longuenesse terms "the capacity to judge." The initial claim is that some such systematic structure (approaching the ideal of a logical system) is necessary for the successful exercise of this capacity because this exercise is based on comparison (the logical act), and comparison requires something to compare. In light of this Kant concludes that, as a condition of the possibility of its own logical activity, reflective judgment

> must assume that nature, with its boundless diversity, has hit upon a division of this diversity (into genera and species) that enables our judgment to find accordance among the natural forms it compares, and [so] enables it to arrive at empirical concepts, as well as at coherence among these by ascending to concepts that are more general [though] also empirical. In other words, judgment presupposes a system of nature even in terms of empirical laws, and it does so *a priori* and hence by means of a transcendental principle. (FI 20: 212n; 400)

Although at the end of the note Kant repeats the unexplained transition from empirical concepts to a system of empirical laws made in the text to which it is attached, the main focus is on the conditions of forming a set of empirical concepts that cohere with one another. Some degree of coherence is clearly necessary if the concepts obtained through comparison are to be connectable with one another in judgment, that is, if they are to function as concepts at all; and this is what is provided by their systematic ordering in terms of the relation of genera and species.

It would be a mistake, however, to regard such an ordering merely as a kind of supplemental requirement or desideratum, rather than as a necessary condition of the possibility of the concepts themselves. On the contrary, the necessity for a hierarchical ordering in terms of genera and species follows from the very nature of a concept. Consider once again the concept "gold," understood as a yellow metal, soluble in *aqua regia*, and so forth. It is composed (in part) of these distinct concepts, which constitute its intension, and it stands to each of them in the relation of species to genus (or logical form to matter). Thus, "gold" designates at once a species of yellow objects, of metal, of things soluble in *aqua regia*, and so forth. But at the same time the concept also functions as a genus under which different types of gold (or of things composed of gold) are to be distinguished as species. Moreover, this is not something unique to the concept of gold, but is a feature of every empirical concept. In short, every concept (except for that of the highest genus)[53] is itself both a species of the concepts contained in it and a genus for the concepts falling under it. And from this it follows that the very possibility of concepts as general representations presupposes a system of concepts subordinate to one another in terms of the relation of genera and species.

If this is correct, then it follows that such a system of hierarchically organized concepts is a necessary condition for the application of logic to nature, that is, for empirical judgment. It does not, however, follow that such a system is, as such, also sufficient to account for the kind of judgment in which Kant was really interested, namely, judgments of experience, which, as I have suggested, either themselves state or are derivable from empirical laws. Accordingly, it is worth exploring a second note in the First Introduction in which Kant seems to go further. In this frequently discussed text Kant writes:

> One may wonder whether Linnaeus could have hoped to design a system of nature if he had had to worry that a stone which he found, and which he called granite, might differ in its inner character from any other stone even if it looked the same, so that all he could ever hope to find would be single things – isolated, as it were, for the understanding – but never a class of them that could be brought under concepts of genus and species. (FI 20: 215–16n; 403)

Where this appears to go beyond the preceding note is in making explicit the requirement that a classificatory system reflect an underlying order of nature. Thus, whereas any number of such systems might be possible, the assumption is that there is one (and only one) that, as it were, "carves nature at its joints." And the goal or regulative idea of a systematizer such as Linnaeus is to provide the system that reflects this order (or at least comes as close as possible to doing so). Moreover, since the classification of phenomena has to be based on observed uniformities and differences, the operative assumption must once again be that outer similarities and differences correspond to inner or intrinsic ones. To use Kant's own example, objects with the observable features of granite must also be similar in their inner character; for otherwise there would be no basis for inferring from the fact that an object has granite-like features that it will behave similarly to other objects with these features.

In light of this, it is instructive to consider Kant's cryptic account of the "inferences" of reflective judgment in the *Jäsche Logic*. According to this account, which is crucial to an understanding of Kant's views on empirical knowledge, there are two species of such inference, that is, two ways of inferring (empirical) universals from particulars, namely induction and analogy. The former moves from the particular to the universal according to what Kant terms the "principle of universalization" [*Princip der Allgemeinmachung*]: *"What belongs to many things of a genus belongs to the remaining ones too."* The latter moves from a similarity between two things with respect to a particular property to a total similarity according to the corresponding "principle of *specification:* Things of one genus, which we know to agree in much, also agree in what remains, with which we are familiar in some things of this genus but which we do not perceive in others" (JL 9: 133; 626). Moreover, these principles are themselves specifications of the higher-order principle governing the inferences of reflective judgment as a whole, namely *"that the many will not agree in one without a common ground, but rather that which belongs to the many in this way will be necessary due to a common ground"* (JL 9: 132; 626).

Although Kant does not make the point, it seems clear that induction and analogy are the inference-forms through which judgments of experience are grounded. In Humean terms, they describe the thought processes through which we move from something observed (a present impression) to something unobserved. Or, in more contemporary language, they are the vehicles through which predicates are "projected," either from some instances of x to all x's (induction), or of a given x on the basis of other predicates already known to pertain to that x (analogy). It is also clear that the principle on which they are based, and which therefore licenses such inferences or "projection" of predicates, is itself an application of the principle of purposiveness. For to claim that "the many will not agree in one without a common ground" is just to claim that observable regularities are not merely incidental, but reflect an underlying ground or order of nature, or, simply put, that "the outer is an expression of the inner."

Finally, it follows from this that the stakes involved in a deduction of the principle of purposiveness are high indeed, amounting to nothing less than the vindication of induction. More specifically, the issue in its Kantian form is whether inductive procedures (construed in a broad sense to include reasoning by analogy as well as induction proper) can be given a rational justification within the framework of reflective judgment.[54] For only such a justification could be capable of providing an answer to Hume's skeptical doubts regarding the rational credentials of inferences from the observed to the unobserved, without falling back on some variant of the dogmatic metaphysical assumptions underlying Leibniz's response to Locke.

IV

The "official" deduction is contained in Section V of the Second Introduction, which is given the heading: "The Principle of the Formal Purposiveness of Nature Is a Transcendental Principle of Judgment" (KU 5: 181; 20). As a prelude to the actual deduction, Kant tries to show that this principle is genuinely transcendental and that it is required because the task that it performs is not already accomplished by the transcendental principles of the understanding established in the Transcendental Analytic of the first *Critique*.

In the First Introduction, where Kant likewise insisted on the transcendental nature of the principle, the alleged problem was that, because of its connection with empirical concept formation, it seemed to be merely logical and tautological, rather than synthetic and transcendental. As we have already seen, Kant there argues for its transcendental status by trying to show that it is the condition of the possibility of applying logic to nature. By contrast, in the Second Introduction this latter claim is dropped, together with any reference to a worry that it might be merely a tautologous, logical principle. Instead, Kant insists that the principle cannot be merely empirical or psychological, since it makes a normative claim about how we *ought to judge*, rather than simply describing how we do, in fact, judge (KU 5: 182; 22). In support of this, he appeals to the previously mentioned maxims of judgment, which serve as an *a priori* basis of the investigation of nature (KU 5: 182; 21).

Kant's major departure from his initial formulation, however, consists in the claim that the principle is transcendental rather than metaphysical. Kant had appealed to this distinction in the *Metaphysical Foundations of Natural Science* in order to contrast the complete generality and independence of any empirical assumptions of the transcendental principles of the first *Critique* with the principles of that work, which, though still *a priori*, presuppose the empirical concept of body as the movable in space.[55] Thus, whereas the transcendental principle of causality, which, in its perfect generality, is not limited merely to bodies, states that every alteration of substance must have a cause, the more restricted metaphysical version maintains that it must have an *external* cause (KU 5: 181; 21).

Since the principle of the logical purposiveness of nature is explicitly concerned with the empirical as such (concepts and laws), one might think that it should be viewed as metaphysical rather than transcendental by that criterion. Nevertheless, Kant denies this on the grounds that the concept of objects *qua* viewed as subject to this principle is "only the pure concept of objects of possible empirical cognition in general and contains nothing empirical" (KU 5: 181–2; 21). In other words, even though the objects to which this principle is applied are themselves empirical, this application does not rest upon any specifically empirical predicates, for example, the possession of mass or mobility in space.[56]

By showing that the principle is transcendental, Kant also shows that it requires some kind of deduction or justification. Even granting this, however, one might still argue that a separate deduction would be redundant on the grounds that the basic task was already accomplished in the first *Critique*. In order to deflect any such possible objection and to underscore the unique nature of formal purposiveness as a principle of *judgment,* Kant takes great pains to argue that the need for such a deduction is not obviated by the Transcendental Deduction of the first *Critique*.

The basic point is that the transcendental laws laid down in the Analytic of the first *Critique* do not themselves guarantee the existence of a cognizable order at the empirical level. Since these laws concern merely the "formal" conditions under which objects can be cognized together in a single spatiotemporal framework (the unity of experience), they are compatible with any number of different empirical orderings. Or, simply put, they underdetermine the particulars falling under them. Thus, even though these laws ensure the existence of *some* order in nature, it need not be one discernible in appearances by the human mind.[57] For example, the most discussed of these transcendental laws (the principle of causality) states that for any event-b, there must be some antecedent condition-a, such that given a, b necessarily follows. This licenses the search for causes, but it hardly ensures that it will be possible to find them, that is, to distinguish between a merely accidental succession a-b and one that is genuinely causal.[58] For, as far as this transcendental law is concerned, experience might present few (if any) *discernible* lawlike regularities capable of supporting induction. But if this were the case, then, *a fortiori,* we could neither discover empirical laws in terms of which particular phenomena can be predicted or explained nor connect these laws in overarching theories. As Kant puts it in a passage that constitutes part of the elaboration of the deduction:

> For it is quite conceivable that, regardless of all the uniformity of natural things in terms of the universal laws, without which the form of an empirical cognition in general would not occur at all, the specific differences in the empirical laws of nature, along with their effects, might still be so great that it would be impossible for our understanding to discover in nature an order it could grasp, i.e., impossible for it to divide nature's products into genera and species, so as to use the principles by which we explain and understand one product in order to explain and comprehend another as well, thereby making coherent experience out of material that to us is so full of confusion (though actually it is only infinitely diverse and beyond our ability to grasp). (KU 5: 185; 25[59]

This passage raises a specter that is both reminiscent of, and significantly different from, the more famous specter that Kant raises in connection with the Transcendental Deduction in the first *Critique*. In introducing the problematic of that deduction, Kant suggested that, for all that had been shown so far, "Appearances might very well be so constituted that the understanding should not find them to be in accordance with the conditions of its unity" (A90/B123). This may be termed "transcendental chaos" (disorder at the transcendental level). Clearly, one of the major concerns of that deduction is to exorcize this specter, which Kant attempts to do by showing that the possibility that appearances are not so constituted is ruled out on the grounds of its incompatibility with the conditions of the unity of apperception. For the goal of the Transcendental Deduction in both editions is to prove that everything given to the mind in accordance with its forms of sensibility, that is, all appearances, which includes everything that could possibly become an object of empirical consciousness, must be subject to the conditions of this unity, and therefore to the categories (which are just the rules governing this unity).

By contrast, the present specter may be termed that of "empirical chaos" (disorder at the empirical level), and it can be characterized as a scenario in which something like Hume's "uniformity principle" does not hold.[60] Or, in its specifically Kantian form, it is a scenario in which the uniformity that nature necessarily exhibits in virtue of its conformity to the transcendental laws imposed by the very nature of the understanding does not translate into an empirically accessible uniformity, understood as one which could support induction and analogy.

Since the operative assumption is that this possibility is left open by the Transcendental Deduction of the first *Critique*, even though the latter succeeded in its appointed task of establishing the necessary conformity to law of experience at the transcendental level, the specter obviously cannot be exorcized by appealing to the unity of apperception and the transcendental laws derived therefrom. Indeed, the problem arises precisely because the possibility of empirical chaos or lack of sufficient uniformity is not precluded by these laws, which ensure, for example, that nothing happens without a cause, but not that these causes are discoverable on the basis of empirical regularities. In both Introductions Kant expresses this point by noting that an empirically cognizable order of nature is contingent with respect to these transcendental conditions, which just means that it cannot be deduced as a consequence thereof.

As Kant suggests in the Dialectic of Teleological Judgment, this contingency may be seen as a consequence of an even more fundamental one that is endemic to our discursive understanding, namely, the contingency that the "particular, as such" [*als ein solches*] has with respect to the universal supplied by the understanding (KU 5: 404; 287). For since, as should be clear from Kant's account of the nature of judgment in the first *Critique*, our understanding proceeds from universals (concepts and laws) to the particulars that are to be subsumed under them, and since these particulars, as sensibly given, are not themselves products of the act of understanding, it follows that there is an unavoidable element of contingency in the fit between universal and particular. Moreover, if this is the case, then the same contingency must also apply to judgment in its reflective activity of seeking universals under which to subsume sensible particulars.

Nor, once again, can it be objected that the assertion of an ineliminable contingency of fit between universal and particular conflicts with the results of the Transcendental Deduction and threatens to resurrect the specter of transcendental chaos that has supposedly been exorcized by it. For the Transcendental Deduction was not concerned with the "particular as such," but merely with it *qua* spatiotemporal entity or event; and taken under that description it remains fully subject to the categories. But the question of empirical lawfulness does concern precisely the "particular as such." Consequently, such lawfulness is contingent with respect to the universal, and the specter of empirical chaos remains in place.

It follows from this that if this latter specter is to be dealt with, a distinct transcendental principle is required. And it likewise follows, given Kant's definition of purposiveness as the "lawfulness of the contingent as such" (FI 20: 217; 405), that it must take the form of a principle of purposiveness.[61] This principle cannot be used, however, to deny the very possibility of empirical chaos in anything like the manner in which the transcendental unity of apperception denies the possibility of the transcendental variety, that is, by somehow proving that nature, in its empirical diversity, necessarily conforms to our cognitive needs. Any such *objective* deduction, even one subject to the standard "critical" limitation to objects of possible experience or phenomena, is precluded by virtue of the ineliminable contingency of fit between the [empirically] universal and the particular.

Nevertheless, this does not rule out the possibility of a *subjective* deduction, which would leave the results of the Transcendental Analytic of the first *Critique* in place but go beyond them.[62] The goal of such a deduction would not be to remove the specter by showing it to be incompatible with the transcendental conditions of experience (since that is impossible), but merely to render it idle. Moreover, this is precisely what Kant's actual deduction attempts to accomplish by establishing the subjective necessity of presupposing the purposiveness of nature in the process of empirical inquiry. In other words, the claim is not that nature is purposive, that is, that we have some sort of *a priori* guarantee that it is ordered in a manner commensurate with our cognitive capacities and needs. Nor is it even that we must believe it to be purposive in this sense (which is basically Hume's position). The claim is rather that we are rationally constrained to approach nature *as if* it were so ordered. Or, in Kant's own terms, at the basis of all reflection on nature (the search for empirical laws) lies the *a priori* principle that "a cognizable order of nature in terms of these [empirical] laws is possible" (KU 5: 185; 24).

Since Kant's reasoning here is akin to that underlying the well-known claim in the *Groundwork* that we can act only under the idea of freedom, it may prove useful to examine the latter briefly.[63] There the "specter" is that in spite of the resolution of the Third Antinomy, which showed only that transcendental freedom is compatible with causality according to laws of nature, our apparent practical rationality and agency might be ultimately tropistic; that even though we take ourselves to be rational self-determiners, we are really moved by underlying causes, for example, instinct. In the language of the first *Critique,* it is the possibility that what we call freedom, "may . . . in relation to higher and more remote operating causes, be nature again" (A803/B831).

Kant's ultimate response to this problem, given in the *Critique of Practical Reason,* is that our consciousness of standing under the moral law (the "fact of reason") assures us of our freedom from the practical point of view.[64] Kant does not take this route in the *Groundwork,* however, arguing instead that freedom is a necessary presupposition of reason insofar as it regards itself as practical. Here the point is not that we must believe ourselves to be free in order to believe that we are agents rather than automata; it is rather that we must act *as if* we were free, which is just what it means to act under the idea of freedom. In other words, the idea of freedom has an essentially normative force. To act under this idea is to place oneself in the "space of [practical] reasons," and therefore to take oneself as subject to rational norms (of both a moral and prudential sort), rather than merely to causal conditions. Thus, even though it remains alive as a metaphysical possibility, from the practical point of view (that of agency) the specter that we might be merely automata is perfectly idle.

The suggestion, then, is that the presupposition of the logical or formal purposiveness of nature be understood in essentially the same way, that is, as having normative or prescriptive force. In investigating nature we *ought* to treat it as if it were purposive because this is just what is involved in "applying logic" to it. For reasons that should now be clear, there is simply no other procedure possible for judgment in its reflection on nature, at least not if the goal is to form empirical concepts that can be combined in something like judgments of experience. Appealing once again to a variation of that deeply suggestive but perhaps overused metaphor, one might say that the principle of purposiveness defines the "space of judgment," since it provides the framework in which alone rational reflection on nature is possible. Moreover, this serves to explain Kant's emphasis on the *a priori* nature of the principle. There is nothing optional about approaching nature in this way, just as there is nothing optional about presupposing freedom insofar as we take ourselves as rational agents. But, of course, this no more proves that nature really is purposive than the latter proves that we really are free.

Kant indicates the true nature and function of this principle when he claims that through it, "judgment prescribes, not to nature (which would be autonomy) but *to itself* [my emphasis] (which is heautonomy), a law for the specification of nature" (KU 5: 185–6; 25). Thus, even though the principle concerns nature as the *object* of investigation, its prescriptive force is directed back to judgment itself. In order to emphasize the purely reflexive, self-referential nature of this principle, Kant coins the term "heautonomy."[65] To claim that judgment is "heautonomous" in its reflection is just to say that it is both *source* and *referent* of its own normativity. In fact, this is what distinguishes judgment's *a priori* principle, from those of the understanding, which legislates transcendental laws to nature, and of (practical) reason, which prescribes the objectively necessary laws of a free will.

This conception of the heautonomy of judgment is also the key to understanding Kant's answer to Hume, insofar as it is contained in the third *Critique*. Admittedly, one might think that by appealing to a merely subjective necessity to presuppose logical or formal purposiveness, Kant is really conceding Hume's point regarding the uniformity principle rather than answering him. Or, even worse, that he is guilty of the very error of which he accused Hume's Scottish common sense critics, namely of taking for granted what Hume doubted and of demonstrating what he never thought of doubting (Pro 4: 258; 6–7).

This would, however, be a mistake. For as in the case of causality and the other *a priori* concepts and principles that are at stake in the first *Critique*, Kant saw clearly that the basic question between himself and Hume was one of normativity or right, not simply indispensability or pragmatic necessity, which Hume certainly did not deny in the case of the uniformity principle. Thus, whereas Hume accounts for our commitment to this principle on the basis of custom or habit, which explains why we necessarily believe past regularities to be guides to future ones, Kant grounds the principle of purposiveness (which, as we have seen, amounts to his alternative to Hume's uniformity principle) in the heautonomy of judgment. It is *right*, that is, rationally justified, to presuppose the principle of purposiveness because judgment legislates it to itself as a condition of the possibility of its self-appointed task: the application of logic to nature.[66] Moreover, lest this seem a peculiar type of deduction, we shall see later in this study that the principle of the heautonomy of judgment (of which the principle of the logical or formal purposiveness of nature is a consequence) likewise underlies the deduction of pure judgments of taste.

For the present, however, the point to note is that the heautonomy of judgment not only provides the basis for an answer to Hume, but also makes it possible for Kant to find the desired third way between Locke's conventionalism (nominal essences) and Leibniz's metaphysical essentialism (real essences). Thus, given this conception and the account of judgment that is inseparable from it, Kant can maintain with Locke, and against Leibniz, that the conceptual scheme with which we approach nature is manufactured by the human understanding (or, in Kant's case, judgment) for its own use, and therefore cannot be assigned any ontological significance (even with regard to phenomena). At the same time, however, he can also uphold with Leibniz, and against Locke, the right to presuppose that "every outer appearance is grounded in the inner constitution," and "whatever we truthfully distinguish or compare is also distinguished or made alike by nature." Presumably, the latter is also at least part of what Kant had in mind when, at the end of his polemical response to Eberhard (published in the same year as the *Critique of Judgment*), he suggests that "the *Critique of Pure Reason* might well be the true apology for Leibniz" (UE 8: 250).[67]

REFLECTION AND TASTE IN THE
INTRODUCTIONS

At first glance at least, the account of reflective judgment and its a *priori* principle, the purposiveness of nature, analyzed in the preceding chapter, does not seem to have much, if anything, to do with taste and aesthetic judgment. Nevertheless, Kant himself clearly intended it to serve as a prelude to his accounts of both aesthetic and teleological judgments, which together constitute the main business of the *Critique of Judgment*. Accordingly, it is essential to consider the connections that Kant attempts to draw in both Introductions between the faculty of reflective judgment and aesthetic judgment.

The present chapter is therefore devoted to this task and is divided into five parts. The first analyzes the conception of a merely reflective judgment, which Kant introduces in the First Introduction, and the distinction between teleological judgment and aesthetic judgment of reflection as two species thereof. Although anything approaching an adequate analysis of teleological judgment is beyond the scope of this study, we shall nevertheless find that a brief consideration of Kant's treatment of the topic in the First Introduction is useful in understanding how aesthetic judgment might involve reflection. The second and third parts jointly examine the account of aesthetic judgment of reflection given in the First Introduction. The fourth considers the more succinct treatment of this topic in the Second Introduction, where the reference to an aesthetic judgment of reflection is dropped and the focus is instead on the nature and possibility of an aesthetic representation of purposiveness. Although there is no substantive disagreement between these two accounts, the terminological differences point to a significant difference of emphasis, which justifies their separate treatment. Finally, the fifth section deals with a problem that is common to both Introductions and that provides a transition to the concerns of the second part of this study, namely Kant's apparent identification of the principle underlying judgments of taste with the principle of purposiveness presupposed in the investigation of nature and analyzed in Chapter 1.

I

As was argued in the last chapter, reflection and determination are best seen as complementary poles of a unified activity of judgment (the subsumption of particulars under universals), rather than as two only tangentially related activities pertaining to two distinct faculties. Accordingly, every ordinary empirical judgment involves moments of both reflection and determination: The former consists in finding the concept under which the given particulars are to be subsumed, and the latter in the determination of the particulars as being of such and such a type by subsuming them under the concept. What we now learn from the First Introduction is that this reciprocity is not complete. Although every determinative judgment involves reflection (as a condition of the very concepts under which particulars are subsumed), not every reflective judgment involves a corresponding determination. For it turns out that there is such a thing as a "merely reflective judgment" [*ein bloss reflectirendes Urteil*] (FI 20: 223; 412).[1]

According to Kant, there are two species of merely reflective judgment: aesthetic judgment of reflection (later to be subdivided into two classes: judgments of taste and judgments of the sublime) and teleological judgment. Our concern here is only with the former, or, more precisely, with the judgment of taste. But since teleological judgment is also classified as "merely reflective," albeit for very different reasons, and since these differences are important for an understanding of Kant's conception of the judgment of taste, I shall begin with a brief consideration of teleological judgment, with a focus on what makes it merely reflective.[2]

Teleological judgments are primarily about certain "products of nature," which Kant terms "natural purposes" or "natural forms," that is, organic beings. For reasons which cannot be examined here, Kant claims that in order to understand the inner possibility or intrinsic nature of such beings, it is necessary to regard them "as if they were products of a cause whose causality could be determined only by a *representation* of the object" (FI 20: 232; 421).[3] In other words, they must be considered as products of an intentional causality or design, rather than merely of a causality operating according to mechanistic laws. Such judgments are reflective, according to Kant, because they are based on a comparison of the object given in empirical intuition with reason's idea of a system (a whole that precedes and makes possible the connection of its parts) (FI 20: 221; 409).

For present purposes, however, the essential point is not that teleological judgments are reflective, but that they are *merely* reflective. Indeed, since they have the form of cognitive judgments about empirical objects, one might think that, like the judgments of experience discussed in Chapter 1, they must be determinative as well as reflective. Nevertheless,

Kant denies this on the grounds that they do not actually subsume their objects under the concept of a causality according to purposes (which *would* make them determinative), but merely express how, given the nature of our cognitive capacities, such objects must be reflected upon, if an empirical concept corresponding to their inner nature is to be possible. Otherwise expressed, they rest upon a methodological claim to the effect that these objects must be investigated *as if* they were products of such a causality, rather than a straightforwardly causal claim that they are, in fact, such products. Thus, as in the case of logical purposiveness, it is a matter of heautonomy, of judgment legislating to itself rather than to nature (FI 20: 234; 423); and this is what makes teleological judgment merely reflective.

However, if the problem regarding teleological judgment is to understand why it should be merely reflective (and not also determinative), the difficulty with aesthetic judgment is precisely the opposite. Since, as we shall see in more detail shortly, such a judgment for Kant is noncognitive, it is obviously nondeterminative, so that the operative question becomes how it can be reflective at all.[4] As a first step in dealing with this question, we must briefly revisit the initial account of reflection discussed in Chapter 1.

We saw there that, according to Kant, "To *reflect* or consider is to hold given representations up to, and compare them with, either other representations or one's cognitive faculty, in reference to a concept that this [comparison] makes possible" (FI 20: 211; 400). Although it was noted that this is intended as a generic characterization of reflection, when it was first considered it was with an eye toward understanding the logical reflection that, as we have seen, underlies all concept formation. Our present concern, however, is to determine whether this generic characterization also enables us to understand other forms of reflection, particularly the act of "mere reflection" [*blossen Reflexion*], which supposedly occurs in aesthetic judgments of reflection (FI 20: 220; 408).

To begin with, this account of reflection, taken together with Kant's other remarks on the topic, enables us to make the following generalizations regarding the nature of this activity: (a) the objects of reflection are always given representations; (b) the activity of reflection consists essentially in a comparison involving these representations; (c) this comparison is primarily directed toward the formation of concepts; and (d) there are two species of this activity: one in which representations are compared with others (in order to determine commonality and difference), and the other in which they are compared with one's cognitive faculty (transcendental reflection).[5] In addition to the logical reflection analyzed in Chapter 1 and the transcendental reflection discussed in the Amphiboly chapter in the first *Critique*, this clearly applies to teleological judgment. For as we have just seen, such judgments involve a comparison of the empirical intuition of certain kinds of objects (organic beings) with reason's idea of systematicity, for the purpose of forming an empirical concept of such objects that would be usable for classification and explanation.

By contrast, when considered in light of this list of features, aesthetic reflection appears to be something of an anomaly. Like all reflection, it consists essentially in a comparison involving a given representation, and like transcendental reflection, this comparison is with one's cognitive faculties rather than other representations. But it differs from the other forms of reflection in that, as aesthetic, it does not seem to be properly characterizable as involving reference to a "concept that this makes possible." On the contrary, what is produced through aesthetic reflection is not a concept at all but a *feeling*. Accordingly, the problem is to explain how such a thing as an aesthetic judgment of reflection is possible. Moreover, this is crucial, not merely because judgments of taste fall within this category, but also because it turns out that it is the connection with reflection (and therefore with the subjective conditions of cognition) that creates the conceptual space for the normativity of such judgments.

II

The First Introduction's account of the possibility of an aesthetic judgment of reflection is contained in the latter portion of Section VII and Section VIII and can be divided into two main parts. The first part (Section VII) focuses on the peculiar form of "mere reflection" involved therein, and the second (Section VIII) on its aesthetic nature. This, in turn, leads to an important discussion of the nature of feeling and the contrast between these judgments and mere aesthetic judgments of sense. The entire discussion is introduced by the following passage, in which Kant provides a cryptic summary of his views regarding the elements of a judgment that is *not* merely reflective, that is, which involves determination as well as reflection, and therefore issues in an empirical concept applicable to a sphere of objects, that is, a cognition:

> Every empirical concept requires three acts of the spontaneous cognitive power: (1) *apprehension* (*apprehensio*) of the manifold of intuition; (2) *comprehension* [*Zusammenfassung*] of this manifold, i.e. synthetic unity of the consciousness of this manifold, in the concept of an object (*apperceptio comprehensiva*); (3) *exhibition* [*Darstellung*] (*exhibitio*), in intuition, of the object corresponding to this concept. For the first of these acts we need imagination; for the second, understanding; for the third, judgment, which would be determinative judgment if we are dealing with an empirical concept. (FI 20: 220; 408)

Since the whole point of this passage is to provide a contrast with the notions of "mere reflection" and "merely reflective judgment," which

Kant is about to introduce, some attention to its main points is certainly called for. To begin with, even though Kant refers to three distinct "acts," it seems more reasonable to take him to be describing three irreducible requirements or conditions of such judgment, rather than a series of temporally successive discrete acts. Of these, the first two are quite clear, and so too are their connections with their respective faculties. Given the basic elements of Kantian epistemology, empirical cognition first of all requires that a manifold of intuition be apprehended together as constituting a manifold. In the language of the A-Deduction, it must be "run through and held together" (A99), and this task is appropriately assigned to the imagination. The second condition is that it be conceptualized, that is, brought to the "objective unity of apperception," and thereby thought under the concept of an object, which is obviously the work of the understanding.

In the case of the third condition (exhibition), however, neither its necessity nor its connection with the assigned faculty (judgment) is immediately apparent. To be sure, we have seen that it is absolutely essential for Kant that every concept (even pure ones) be exhibitable or presentable in intuition, but in the present case, the connection with intuition seems already to have been accounted for by the fact that what is conceptualized is just the apprehended manifold. In other words, here, as in the logical reflection analyzed in Chapter 1, the procedure works from the ground up, so to speak. Moreover, the faculty usually assigned the task of exhibiting or, what amounts to the same thing, schematizing concepts is the imagination rather than judgment, as Kant here seems to suggest.[6]

Nevertheless, I believe that we can understand what Kant is getting at here if we simply keep in mind the connection with determinative judgment.[7] First of all, even though the process of reflection is from the ground up, the imagination must already be operative at the perceptual level in the apprehension of the manifold. Second of all, as we saw in Chapter 1, if this apprehension is to provide the basis for a reflection that yields an empirical concept, it must present something "universal in itself," or, equivalently, the exhibition of an "as yet undetermined concept." For unless the imagination could perform this task, there would be no empirical concepts and therefore no determinative function of judgment. But while it is the imagination that produces the schemata that are to be recognized as exhibitions of what is thought in a reflected concept, it falls to judgment to recognize the actual fit between apprehended particular and concept. In other words, judgment is required in order to be able to take what is exhibited by the imagination as instantiating what is thought in a concept. Accordingly, in this sense at least, judgment is likewise itself deeply involved in exhibition.[8] Setting aside these terminological points, however, the basic thrust of this passage is clearly that the very possibility of a determinative judgment depends on a harmony or cooperation between understanding and imagination. For the recognition that what is thought in a concept is presented or exhibited in a corresponding intuition obviously presupposes not only that the understanding can produce such concepts, but also that the imagination can exhibit them.

Kant's own understanding of the interplay between imagination and understanding in all cognition is nicely, albeit metaphorically, expressed in a passage contained in a student's transcript of his lectures on logic. According to this transcript Kant states:

> Imagination and understanding are two friends who cannot do without one another but cannot stand one another either, for one always harms the other. The more universal the understanding is in its rules, the more perfect it is, but if it wants to consider things *in concreto* then [it] absolutely cannot do without the imagination. (LD-W 24: 710; 447)[9]

As the passage clearly indicates, the "friendship" between imagination and understanding is not without a certain tension, which results from the fact that they pull in opposite directions: the understanding toward universality and the imagination toward specificity. Accordingly, though the understanding requires the imagination to exhibit intuitively what is thought in its concept, and the imagination presumably needs the understanding to give it direction so that it can know what to exhibit, they nevertheless often work at cross purposes (and therefore "harm" one another). Although Kant does not spell it out, this presumably occurs either when the understanding in its endemic quest for universality produces a concept that is too general and indeterminate to be represented adequately *in concreto* by any particular instance, for example, the concept of a living thing, or when the particular imaginatively apprehended is too idiosyncratic or atypical to represent adequately what is thought in the concept, for example, the image of a three-legged dog.

If this is correct, it suggests that the general notion of a harmony or fit of the cognitive faculties may be taken in either a minimal or a maximal and ideal sense, with the latter allowing for degrees of approximation to this ideal. Harmony, minimally construed, occurs whenever there is any cognitive fit between concept and intuitive representation, that is, whenever the intuition is subsumable under the concept. In that sense, harmony is a necessary condition of cognition. By contrast, harmony, maximally or ideally construed, occurs when the fit between universal and particular is extremely close, that is, when the understanding's concept is not too indeterminate for the imagination and, conversely, the latter's image exhibits all of the essential features thought in the concept. In that case, we can think of the two faculties working together smoothly, like two well-meshed gears with little friction, and the subsumption accordingly proceeds without difficulty.

Kant turns to the question of the interplay of the two faculties (which he does not here describe as "friends") in "mere reflection" or a "merely reflective judgment" that does not issue in a determinate concept, and therefore in cognition, in the paragraph that immediately follows the cited passage from the First Introduction. He there states that "When we merely reflect on a perception we are not dealing with a determinate concept, but are dealing only with the general rule for reflecting on a perception for the sake of the understanding as a faculty of concepts" (FI 20: 220; 408).

Given the previous account of reflection leading to determination and Kant's present suggestion that the activity is for the sake of the understanding, the "rule" involved in "mere reflection" can only be to look for an intuitive content in what is perceived, which prior to and independently of any conceptualization or comparison with other perceptions, presents itself as yet containing something "universal in itself." The latter could also be characterized as a "schema," but not of an "as undetermined concept," since, *ex hypothesi,* no concept emerges from such reflection. Instead, it is a form that one might term "schema-like" or, perhaps, as the "schema of a schema," since it presents itself as if it were structured in accordance with a certain rule, though no particular rule can be specified.[10]

Reflection involves comparison, however, and since a comparison with other representations in order to find commonality is precluded by the nature of the reflection in question, Kant has to explain what is compared with what in such reflection. His answer, contained in the same paragraph, is that "In a merely reflective judgment imagination and understanding are considered as they must relate in general in the power of judgment, as compared with how they actually relate in the case of a given perception" (FI 20: 220; 408). In other words, in such a judgment, a comparison is made between the actual relationship of the faculties in question in the perception of a given object and their maximal or ideal relationship, in which the "two friends" work together in a frictionless manner. Or, as we are about to see, aesthetic comparison may also be understood as the act of ascertaining through feeling whether or not the form of an object reflected upon occasions a free harmony in mere reflection.

Kant himself strongly suggests this characterization of such comparison in the following passage, in which he attempts to link it for the first time with the harmony of the faculties, the form of the object reflected upon, and a new kind of purposiveness, which differs from the logical purposiveness previously considered:

> [I]f the form of an object given in empirical intuition is of such a character that the *apprehension,* in the imagination, of the object's manifold agrees

with the *exhibition* of a concept of the understanding (which concept this is being indeterminate), then imagination and understanding are – in mere reflection – in mutual harmony, a harmony that furthers the task of these faculties; and the object is perceived as purposive, [though] merely for judgment. Hence we then consider the purposiveness itself as merely subjective, since a determinate concept of the object is neither required nor produced by it, and the judgment itself is not a cognitive one. (FI 20: 220–1; 408)

As the text clearly indicates, a harmony in mere reflection is just the mental state in which the "two friends" serendipitously function smoothly together, rather than "harming" one another by working at cross purposes, as is usually the case. In terms of the analysis of Chapter 1, the imagination, under the general direction of the understanding, provides an apprehended content that presents itself as containing "something universal in itself," that is, something that appears as if it were the schema or exhibition of an "as yet undetermined concept," albeit no concept in particular. In such a state, which corresponds with the norm required for cognition without itself amounting to cognition, we might think of the understanding as "energized" to grasp the rule that seems to underlie this apprehended content, which, in turn, "inspires" the imagination to exhibit it as fully as possible. Accordingly, it is in this way that the two faculties reciprocally enhance one another's activity in an indeterminate manner.

The passage also indicates that it is the *form* of the object that occasions this entire process. Kant's conception of form as it relates to taste is a complex and controversial topic with which we shall be directly concerned in Chapter 6. For present purposes, however, it must suffice to note that, since it is the sensible data *qua* apprehended, that is, as synthesized by the imagination, which simulate the exhibition of a concept and thereby produce the harmony, this form cannot be construed as a determinate feature of the object that is, as it were, delivered to reflective judgment for its endorsement. Instead, the object as it presents itself in intuition should be viewed as occasioning the form or schema-like pattern produced by the imagination. Moreover, it is precisely in virtue of its ability to occasion the production of such a form that the object is deemed purposive for judgment.

Admittedly, like Kant's characterization of the imagination and understanding as "two friends," all of this remains highly metaphorical and, though perhaps suggestive, notoriously difficult to express in a precise way, much less evaluate. And we shall see that the same may also be said about Kant's other accounts of the harmony of the faculties, as it is operative in the judgment and experience of beauty.

Nevertheless, I believe that at least a beginning can be made in understanding Kant here, if we keep in mind the account of logical reflection sketched in Chapter 1 and referred to in the preceding pages. For the function attributed to the imagination in mere reflection is not that different from the one assigned to it in cognition or, equivalently, reflection leading to determination, namely, to present something "universal in itself" or exhibit an "as yet undetermined concept." The difference is only that in the mere reflection involved in a judgment of taste, the imagination does not exhibit the schema of a specific concept under which the object can be subsumed in a determinative cognitive judgment. Instead, it exhibits a pattern or order (form), which suggests an indeterminate number of possible schematizations (or conceptualizations), none of which is fully adequate, thereby occasioning further reflection or engagement with the object. Thus, it is in this way that the object presents itself in intuition, prior to any conceptualization, as if designed for our cognitive faculties, that is, as subjectively purposive.[11]

III

At this point in his exposition, Kant has introduced all of the essential features of his conception of the judgment of taste save one, namely, its aesthetic nature. To be sure, he describes the judgment resulting from this process of mere reflection as an "*aesthetic* judgment of reflection" (FI 20: 221; 409), in contrast to a teleological one, but the sense in which it is aesthetic has not yet been explained. This is the task of the next section (VIII), which is given the seemingly awkward title "On the Aesthetic of the Power of Judging" [*Von der Ästhetik des Beurteilungsvermögens*]. Moreover, in this context Kant introduces a new distinction, this time between two species of aesthetic judgment: those of reflection and those of sense.

What makes a judgment aesthetic is the fact that it is based on a feeling of pleasure or displeasure, which for Kant entails that it is noncognitive. Instead of a claim about an object, it is about the representational state of the subject in apprehending an object. This reflects Kant's consistently held and explicitly anti- Baumgartian view that feelings (pleasure and displeasure) have no cognitive function at all (not even with respect to the representation of the subject as appearance). Thus, he defines an aesthetic judgment in general (including both species) as "one whose predicate can never be cognition (i.e., concept of an object, though it may contain the subjective conditions for cognition as such)" (FI 20: 224; 412). This is because the determining ground of such a judgment is always the one "so-called sensation" that can never become a concept of an object, namely the feeling of pleasure and displeasure (FI 20: 224; 412–13). The reference to a "so-called sensation" expresses the point Kant makes elsewhere by distinguishing between sensations proper, such as those of color or sound, which constitute the "matter of empirical intuition," and the feelings of pleasure and displeasure. Although both are subjective in that they reflect the state of the subject, the former, but not the latter, may be referred to objects in cognitive judgments.[12]

Kant characterizes an aesthetic judgment of sense as one that is based on "a sensation that is connected directly with the feeling of pleasure and displeasure" (FI 20: 224; 413). In other words, it is a judgment about the agreeableness (or lack thereof) of the sensation produced by an experiential encounter with an object, say, the taste of wine. By contrast, an aesthetic judgment of reflection is described as one in which the determining ground is "the sensation brought about in the subject by the harmonious play of the two cognitive faculties . . . when, in the given representation, the imagination's ability to apprehend, and the understanding's ability to exhibit further each other" (FI 20: 224; 413).

In the latter case, Kant claims that the relation between these faculties "brings about, through its mere form, a sensation; and this sensation is the determining ground of a judgment, which is therefore called aesthetic, and amounts to a subjective purposiveness (without a concept) and hence is connected with the feeling of pleasure" (FI 20: 224; 413). Thus, whereas both species of aesthetic judgment are noncognitive because based on sensation, they are so in different ways. Those of sense may be said to bypass cognition altogether, since the sensation arises immediately from the perception, independently of any reflection on it. By contrast, in an aesthetic judgment of reflection, it is precisely the reflective act of comparison, which does involve reference to the cognitive faculties and their normative relation, that produces the sensation in question.

In his initial attempt to explain how a sensation or feeling of pleasure or displeasure might enter into an act of judgment, Kant notes that the relation between imagination and understanding in such an act can be considered in two ways: either objectively as belonging to cognition (Kant here refers to the transcendental schematism as an account of this objective relation) or subjectively, "insofar as one of these faculties furthers or hinders the other in one and the same representation and thereby affects one's *mental state,* so that here we consider the relation as one that *can be sensed"* (FI 20: 223; 411). In the latter case, of course, the judgment is aesthetic, since the relation is sensed (felt), rather than grasped conceptually. But it nevertheless remains reflective, since the pleasure stems from the harmonious relation of the cognitive faculties in an act of "mere reflection."

As already indicated, Kant also links the feeling of pleasure connected with such reflection to the representation of a subjective purposiveness. Indeed, in an effort to contrast his view with Baumgarten's analysis of the judgment of beauty as the sensible (and, therefore, confused) representation of perfection (which for Kant would count as objective purposiveness), he remarks that the representation of subjective purposiveness involved in the judgment of beauty is "even identical with the feeling of pleasure" (FI 20: 228; 418).[13] This remark, like many similar ones, is highly obscure and naturally gives rise to the questions of what Kant means by pleasure, and how he can identify it with a representation of subjective purposiveness.

With regard to the first question at least, Kant is somewhat helpful, since he provides a so-called transcendental definition of pleasure, which is found near the end of the remark attached to Section VIII. It reads:

> *Pleasure* is a mental *state* in which a representation is in harmony with itself [and] which is the basis either for merely preserving this state itself (for the state in which the mental faculties further one another in a representation preserves itself) or for producing the object of this representation. On the first alternative the judgment about the given representation is an aesthetic judgment of reflection; on the second, a pathological aesthetic judgment or a practical aesthetic judgment. (FI 20: 231–2; 419–20)

By characterizing this definition as "transcendental," Kant intended to underscore its complete generality, that is, its applicability to every kind of pleasure, no matter what its nature or source.[14] And in contrasting the pleasure that serves merely as the basis on which a harmonious mental state preserves itself with one through which it produces the object of the representation, he is clearly anticipating the important distinction drawn in the Analytic of the Beautiful between the disinterested pleasure of taste and other interested forms that are concerned with the existence of the object in which the pleasure is taken (which includes pleasure in both the agreeable and the good, here characterized as "pathological" and "practical pleasure," respectively).[15]

A seemingly peculiar feature of this account is that Kant presents this contrast not so much as one between different kinds of pleasure, all falling under the generic description of being a harmonious mental state, but rather as one between different types of *judgment* of pleasure, that is, of aesthetic judgment, each of which construes pleasure in a different way. Nevertheless, this characterization of pleasure in terms of the kind of judgment in which it enters not only accords with Kant's focus on aesthetic judgment (and particularly on how an aesthetic judgment of reflection differs from one of sense), but also points to a feature of his conception of pleasure that is crucial to his identification of the feeling of pleasure in the judgment of taste with the representation of a subjective purposiveness, namely, its intentionality.

Although the issue remains controversial, with texts pointing in both directions, I believe that the bulk of the evidence suggests that, in spite of his explicit denial of cognitive status to the feeling of pleasure or displeasure, Kant nonetheless held that the relationship between the free harmony of the faculties and the pleasure in the judgment of taste is intentional as well as causal.[16] In other words, the feeling of pleasure is not simply the effect of such a harmony (though it is that); it is also the very means through which one becomes aware of this harmony, albeit in a way that does not amount to cognition. Accordingly, in the section currently under consideration, Kant explicitly characterizes the relation between the faculties as one that *can be sensed* (FI 20: 223; 411); and he remarks that, although this sensation (of the relation) is not a sensible representation of an object, it does amount to a "sensible representation of the state of the subject who is affected by an act of that faculty [of judgment]" (FI 20: 223; 411–12).

Once the intentionality of the feeling in the judgment of taste is assumed, the identification of the pleasure connected with the free harmony with a representation of subjective purposiveness loses much of its mystery. The free harmony is itself subjectively purposive, since it involves the furtherance of the cognitive faculties involved therein, and the pleasure is precisely the sensation through which the subject becomes aware of it. The harmony, one might say, is feelingly apprehended, and this apprehension is, like the harmony, an inherently pleasurable mental state that endeavors to preserve itself. In fact, as we shall see in more detail later, it is this very mental state insofar as the subject is reflectively (yet aesthetically) aware of it.[17]

Conversely, if we deny the intentionality of feeling for Kant, we are left with the view that the pleasure of taste is merely the effect of the free harmony of the faculties. Since there can here be no question of an independent cognitive awareness of one's mental state, the pleasure on this view must be regarded as an inference-ticket, from which the free harmony is then inferred. But in that event, the judgment of taste loses the very aesthetic character on which Kant insists so strongly, becoming instead an empirical causal claim, and a rather problematic one at that.[18]

Finally, though the point is often obscured by the fact that Kant generally talks about pleasure and its connection with the harmonious relation of the cognitive faculties, the faculty that feels or senses this relation is termed "pleasure and *displeasure*" (emphasis mine). Moreover, the relation in question need not be harmonious, as is evident not only from Kant's characterization of the potential for conflict between the "two friends," but also from the previously cited passage in which he claims that the imagination and understanding can either further or *hinder* one another, and that in both cases this is felt. In short, by including the latter as something that can be felt in reflection, presumably with a sense of displeasure, Kant provides the basis for negative judgments of taste (including, but not necessarily limited to, judgments of ugliness). We shall return to this topic in Chapter 3, where I shall argue that the inclusion of space for such negative judgments is criterial for the adequacy of an interpretation of Kant's theory of taste.

IV

Whereas the question regarding judgments of taste in the First Introduction centered around the nature and possibility of an aesthetic judgment of reflection, that of the Second focuses instead on the nature and
possibility of an aesthetic representation of purposiveness. Since these
turn out to be equivalent problems, there is no incompatibility between
the two accounts, though there are significant differences in emphasis.

For present purposes, the key portions of the Second Introduction are
Sections VI and VII. In the first of these, Kant attempts to link the logical
purposiveness of nature, whose principle was "deduced" in the preceding section, with the feeling of pleasure by means of the principle that
"The attainment of an aim [*Absicht*] is always accompanied by a feeling of
pleasure" (KU 5: 187; 27). The claim is that the discovery of a contingent
orderliness in nature (one with respect to its empirical laws) necessarily
brings with it a feeling of pleasure. Here the *contingency* of the orderliness, the fact that, notwithstanding the transcendental principle of purposiveness, we have no grounds to expect it in a particular case, is the crucial factor in producing the pleasure.

In order to underscore the latter point, Kant notes that such a feeling
is not associated with the conformity of appearances to the transcendental laws of the understanding, since there is nothing contingent about
this. Similarly, he admits that there is no pleasure involved in the apparent organizability of nature in terms of genera and species. But he also
insists that there once was, and he explains the lack of pleasure currently
felt on the grounds that it has become so familiar to us that we no longer
take special notice of it, that is, we have lost sight of its contingency (KU
5: 187; 27).[19]

For the most part, Kant treats the existence of such pleasure in the discovery of a contingent orderliness or conformity of nature to the conditions of our comprehension as a fact that everyone will immediately acknowledge. But he also endeavors to explain it on the basis of the
previously cited principle that the attainment of an aim always brings with
it a feeling of pleasure. Moreover, after citing this principle, for which no
argument is given, Kant adds that "if the condition of attaining that aim
is an *a priori* representation, as it is here as a principle for reflective judgment as such, then the feeling of pleasure is also determined by a ground
which is *a priori* and valid for everyone" (KU 5: 187; 27).

By suggesting that the pleasure felt in discoveries of what are taken to
be instantiations of the contingent conformity of nature to our cognitive
needs has an *a priori* ground in the principle of reflective judgment, Kant
might be thought to be already referring to the pleasure of taste and the
a priori principle on which its claim to universal validity presumably rests.
Thus, Guyer takes Kant here to be preparing the way for the eventual

grounding of taste by appealing to the principle that "pleasure is always produced by the satisfaction of an objective," which, he states, Kant employs "as a lawlike and fundamental premise," albeit without supporting argumentation.[20] Moreover, given this premise, Kant, in Guyer's view, is committed to the project of showing that the pleasure of taste must likewise be connected with the attainment of an aim. Although Guyer dismisses this move insofar as it is an attempt to provide an *a priori* principle for aesthetic judgment (at least partly on the grounds that the principle in question is empirical)[21], he also states that what he characterizes as Kant's "general theory of pleasure" may be fruitfully used to interpret his theory of aesthetic response.[22] In fact, he provides a lengthy account of the harmony of the faculties and the pleasure taken therein on the basis of this very principle.[23]

Since our concern here is neither with Guyer's interpretation of Kant's theory of aesthetic response nor his view of the harmony of the faculties, we need not pursue these topics at present. Nevertheless, something must be said regarding Kant's alleged "principle" or psychological law to the effect that "pleasure is always produced by the satisfaction of an aim." To begin with, Guyer's formulation of this principle is highly ambiguous. On the one hand, it can be taken to mean that pleasure occurs *only* when an aim of some sort is satisfied, which would make such satisfaction a necessary condition of pleasure. On the other hand, it can be taken to mean that *every satisfaction of an aim* is attended with pleasure, which would make satisfaction merely a sufficient condition. By treating the principle as a lawlike claim that is intended to explain all pleasures, including the pleasure of taste, Guyer seems to be taking it in the former sense (or perhaps both). Not only, however, is such a "law" inherently implausible in its own right, but it is also difficult to square with the Kantian text.

It is inherently implausible because there seem to be clear cases of pleasure that are unconnected with the satisfaction of an aim, namely, those that are totally unexpected. Suppose, for example, I just happen to meet and converse with my favorite movie actress at a cocktail party. Not only did I not intend to meet her there, but I may never even have entertained the idea of meeting her at all. Such an encounter, one might say, was "beyond my wildest dreams." Nonetheless, this would hardly preclude the possibility of my taking pleasure in such an encounter, were it perchance to occur. Indeed, it might be claimed that some of life's greatest pleasures fall into this category.

Moreover, even setting aside the question of its plausibility as an account of the genesis of pleasure, Kant could not have understood the principle in the manner in which Guyer suggests because it is incompatible with his account of the very pleasure that is supposed to be explained, namely, the pleasure of taste. The defining feature of this pleasure for Kant is its disinterestedness; and even though this notion of a disinterested liking or pleasure is highly controversial and has not yet been considered (it is the topic of Chapter 4), it should at least be clear that a disinterested pleasure cannot be regarded as one taken in the satisfaction of an aim.[24] Thus, for Kant, the claim that the attainment of an aim is always connected with the feeling of pleasure must be taken in the weaker sense in which such attainment is merely a sufficient condition.[25]

This result, however, generates a fresh puzzle about the purpose of the discussion of pleasure in the discovery of a contingent orderliness in experience. On Guyer's reading this is no problem, since such pleasure is understood as an illustration of a general principle that also applies to the judgment of taste. But once this is denied, the entire discussion in Section VI seems to lose its point. Why, after all, should Kant introduce a kind of pleasure that is radically distinct from the pleasure of taste and attempt to link *it* with an *a priori* principle, when his real concern is with the pleasure of taste and its claim of an *a priori* grounding?

The key to the answer lies in the structure of the Second Introduction, specifically in the location of Section VI between the deduction of the logical or formal purposiveness of nature as an *a priori* principle of judgment in Section V and the preliminary discussion of judgments of taste as involving an aesthetic representation of purposiveness in Section VII. My suggestion, in other words, is that VI is to be taken as a transitional section, intended as a bridge between the initial discussion of logical or formal purposiveness by means of which Kant first connects judgment with an *a priori* principle of its own and the central concern with judgments of taste, which lay claim to a certain normativity (and therefore some kind of *a priori* grounding) in spite of their aesthetic nature. To this end, then, Kant attempts to show in Section VI how the representation of one kind of purposiveness, namely that which is manifested in certain successful cognitive projects, is connected with a feeling of pleasure, in order to prepare the ground for an account of how the representation of a very different kind of purposiveness (or at least a very different *representation* of purposiveness) is likewise connected with such a feeling.

Thus, whereas in Section VI the focus was on the pleasure felt in a purposiveness that is recognized in and through the successful completion of a cognitive activity, the new focus is on the connection between the feeling of pleasure and a representation of purposiveness that "precedes the cognition of an object and that we can connect directly with this representation [the perception of the object], even if we are not seeking to use the representation of the object for cognition" (KU 5: 189; 29). Kant attempts to link the latter type of representation of purposiveness with the feeling of pleasure by drawing a parallel between them. In essence, both are claimed to be subjective features of representations, which, unlike sensations, cannot become elements in the cognition of an object. And, apparently on the basis of this parallel, Kant concludes that, in the case of such purposiveness, "We call the object purposive only because its representation is directly connected with the feeling of pleasure, and this representation is an aesthetic representation of purposiveness" (KU 5: 189; 29).

At first glance at least, this might seem to be one of those notorious *non sequiturs* for which Kant is often criticized. After all, from the fact that pleasure and this form of purposiveness are both subjective in the sense indicated, it does not follow that the purposiveness (of the form specified) of an object "must be directly connected with the feeling of pleasure." Indeed, why need it have anything at all to do with pleasure?

Fortunately, further consideration suggests that Kant is not arguing in this manifestly invalid way. His point seems rather to be that, since the form of purposiveness described would, *ex hypothesi*, not enter into the cognition of an object, the only way in which it could be represented is aesthetically, that is, through a feeling of pleasure. In short, it is an instance of the ubiquitous Kantian strategy of argument by elimination. Assuming the dichotomy between conceptual and aesthetic modes of representation, and ruling out the former, the latter remains as the only viable alternative. But, as Kant himself recognizes, this does not take us very far, since the real question becomes "whether there is such a representation of purposiveness at all" (KU 5: 189; 29).

In endeavoring to explain the possibility of the latter, Kant appeals to the same considerations as he did in the First Introduction in his explication of an aesthetic judgment of reflection or "mere reflection." Once again, the pleasure is connected with the apprehension of the form of an object in intuition, without any appeal to a concept, with the pleasure arising from the harmonious play of the cognitive faculties in this apprehension (KU 5: 189–90; 29–30). Thus, with respect to the nature of aesthetic reflection and the elements involved therein, the discussion of the Second Introduction has nothing of substance to add to the richer, more detailed treatment of the First.

It does go beyond the First, however, in its exploration of the claim to normativity inherent in the judgment of taste. In the First Introduction, Kant's treatment of this topic is extremely cursory, consisting mainly in the postponement of any serious consideration of it until after the completion of the exposition of judgments of taste in the main body of the treatise.[26] By contrast, in the Second Introduction, Kant offers what amounts to a preview of his eventual analysis by indicating a partial analogy between judgments of taste and singular, empirical cognitive judgments. A judgment of taste, Kant now suggests, is like such an empirical judgment in that, even though it cannot lay claim to any *a priori* validity or objective necessity, it does claim to be valid for everyone. And, he continues in anticipation of a later account of the "logical peculiarities" of judgments of taste in the Deduction of Pure Aesthetic Judgments:

What is strange and different about a judgment of taste is only this: that what is to be connected with the representation of the object is not an empirical concept but a feeling of pleasure (hence no concept at all), though, just as if it were a predicate connected with cognition of the object, this feeling is nevertheless to be required of everyone. (KU 5: 191; 31)

Kant then goes on to suggest that the ground of this pleasure that may be required of everyone is to be found in "the universal, though subjective, condition of reflective judgments, namely the purposive harmony of an object (whether a product of nature or of art) with the mutual relation of the cognitive faculties (imagination and understanding) required for every empirical cognition" (KU 5: 191; 31). Thus, as he will do in more detail in both the Analytic of the Beautiful and the Deduction, Kant attempts to explicate the normativity of judgments of taste by linking them, in spite of their noncognitive nature, with the conditions of cognition. As we shall see, this attempted linkage is the source of much of the obscurity, as well as the interest, of Kant's account.

V

This obscurity is largely a feature of the Introductions, where the linkage of judgments of taste with the conditions of cognition appears to take the form of a simple identification of the transcendental principle of purposiveness with the *a priori* principle supposedly underlying judgments of taste. To be sure, statements suggesting a connection between natural beauty and the logical or formal purposiveness of nature are not lacking in the main body of the text. But they tend not to be found within the discussion of taste itself, and they do not claim that the principle of purposiveness is itself the principle of taste.

One such passage from the main text is part of the transition from a consideration of the beautiful to the sublime. By way of contrasting these two species of aesthetic judgment, Kant states that "Independent natural beauty reveals to us a technic of nature that allows us to present nature as a system in terms of laws whose principle we do not find anywhere in our understanding: the principle of a purposiveness directed to our use of judgment as regards appearances" (KU 5: 246; 99). In other words, the point here seems to be that instances of natural beauty provide a kind of support (which certainly cannot be regarded as "evidence") for the principle that judgment necessarily presupposes in its reflection on nature. In this respect, then, the discovery of natural beauty might be viewed as a kind of stimulus to scientific inquiry.[27]

Another passage connecting natural beauty with the transcendental principle of purposiveness is in the opening paragraph of the *Critique of Teleological Judgement,* where Kant is clearly attempting to contrast the kinds of purposiveness under discussion in the two basic divisions of the third *Critique,* and to indicate their respective connections with the transcendental principle. The claim here is that the purposiveness of nature in its particular laws gives one grounds to *expect* [my emphasis] that it might also contain some forms that are pleasing aesthetically. This is contrasted with the situation regarding teleological judgment, where the transcendental principle does not bring with it any corresponding expectations concerning the discovery of instances of objective purposiveness (KU 5: 359; 235).

Thus, in the one case, the experience of beauty is said to provide a kind of support to the transcendental principle (which hardly needs it, if the account of its deduction in Chapter 1 is correct), and in the other, it is the transcendental principle that provides a reason to expect that *some* natural forms may be beautiful. But in neither case is there any claim to the effect that the transcendental principle itself somehow grounds particular judgments of taste.

This is precisely what Kant does seem to claim, however, in both Introductions. Thus, in the discussion of teleological judgment in the First Introduction, Kant states with regard to aesthetic judgments (of reflection) that "Although they themselves are not possible *a priori,* yet *a priori* principles are given in the necessary idea of experience as a system, and these principles contain the concept of a formal purposiveness of nature for our judgment and reveal *a priori* the possibility of aesthetic judgments of reflection as judgments based on *a priori* principles" (FI 20: 232–3; 421–2). And later, in the lengthy section entitled "The Encyclopaedic Introduction of the Critique of Judgment into the System of the Critique of Pure Reason," where his concern is once again with the thesis that judgment must have its own transcendental principle, Kant writes with regard to the principle of purposiveness:

> Although this principle determines nothing regarding the particular natural forms, [and] their purposiveness must always be given [us] empirically, still the judgment about these forms, as a merely reflective judgment, acquires a claim to universality and necessity. It does so because in it the subjective purposiveness that a given representation has for judgment is referred to that *a priori* principle of judgment, the principle of the purposiveness of nature in its empirical lawfulness in general. Hence we will be able to regard aesthetic reflective judgments as resting on an *a priori* principle (even if not on a determinative one), and the faculty of judgment will, regarding these judgments, find itself entitled to a place in the critique of the higher pure cognitive faculties (FI 20: 243; 432–3).

Similarly, in the Second Introduction, after providing a sketchy account of the normativity of judgments of taste at the end of Section VII, Kant remarks that the possibility of such judgments presupposes an *a pri-*

ori principle, and that this is what makes them subject to a critique. Kant does not here identify the required principle, noting only that it cannot be either a cognitive one for the understanding or a practical one for the will (which means that it cannot be a determinative principle at all) (KU 5: 191–2; 31). In the next section, however, which is mainly devoted to a preliminary account of teleological judgments and their difference from aesthetic ones, he explicitly equates the principle underlying aesthetic judgment with "the principle of a formal purposiveness of nature, in terms of its particular (empirical) laws, for our cognitive faculty" (KU 5: 193; 33).

Kant's reasoning in these passages seems to be roughly the following: (1) We have seen that the inclusion of judgment in the "system" of higher cognitive faculties requires that it have its own *a priori* or transcendental principle. (2) We have also seen that the formal or logical purposiveness of nature is such a principle. (3) But judgments of taste, as merely reflective judgments, make a claim for universality and necessity. (4) If this claim is legitimate, it must rest on an *a priori* principle, and since the judgments are merely reflective (do not involve determination), it must be a principle that pertains to judgment in its reflective capacity. (5) Since the purposiveness of nature has already been shown to be such a principle, judgments of taste must be based on it (or at least they must be if their claims are to be warranted).

Additional impetus for this line of reasoning is also provided by the need, expressed in both Introductions, to establish an *a priori* connection between judgment, as the cognitive faculty that mediates between understanding and reason, and the feeling of pleasure and displeasure, which mediates between cognition and the faculty of desire or will in the overall system of mental faculties.[28] In short, both the concern to provide an *a priori* principle capable of licensing the normativity claim inherent in judgments of taste and the more general systematic concerns bearing on the place and function of a critique of judgment within the critical system seem to have led Kant to identify the principle of taste with the previously deduced principle of the purposiveness of nature.

Nevertheless, as many commentators have noted, such an identification is highly problematic at best. First, this line of reasoning is obviously fallacious, since it does not follow from the fact (assuming it is a fact) that the purposiveness of nature is the *a priori* principle of reflective judgment in its logical reflection (the project of applying logic to nature) that it is likewise the principle underlying its purely aesthetic reflection.[29] Second, whereas judgments of taste are concerned with the purposiveness for judgment of *particular* forms, prior to and independently of any comparison with other forms, the principle of logical or formal purposiveness is concerned only with the relation between diverse forms. Thus, it governs a completely different form of reflection than is operative in judgments of taste.[30] Third, the principle of logical or formal purposiveness was deduced as a principle of cognitive judgments, which, as such, have nothing to do with feeling. To be sure, we have seen that in Section VI of the Second Introduction, Kant does attempt to show that a feeling of pleasure is connected with the fulfillment of a cognitive aim, if that fulfillment is perceived as dependent on nature's contingent harmony with our cognitive requirements. But we also saw that such a pleasure is completely different from the disinterested pleasure of taste.[31] Fourth, the attempted grounding of aesthetic judgments in the principle of logical or formal purposiveness does not work, since the validity of the latter does not entail even the *possibility* of the validity of any instance of the former.[32] Finally, even if the validity of such a grounding be granted, it could account only for the possibility of judgments of *natural* beauty, leaving those of *artistic* beauty without any a priori basis.

The latter point has been emphasized by Guyer, who sees in Kant's association of the problem of taste with that of the systematicity of nature a major, even "fateful," confusion, which affects many aspects of his aesthetic theory, including his apparent tendency to privilege natural over artistic beauty and his formalism.[33] Neither of these, Guyer maintains, are warranted by Kant's account of aesthetic response (the harmony of the faculties), which he regards as the only viable part of Kant's theory of taste. According to Guyer, Kant's mistake lies in assuming (or at least suggesting) that the principle of aesthetic judgments must be one about *natural* objects of taste, rather than about the faculties of those who make judgments. He further claims that the only component of aesthetic judgment that is in any sense a priori is the claim of the agreement of everyone, and the only principle it presupposes is that of the similarity of cognitive faculties.[34]

Guyer certainly has grounds for complaint against Kant's procedure in these cited texts. He is also correct in noting that the problematic passages occur in contexts in which Kant is introducing a fresh distinction between aesthetic and teleological judgment, and that in so doing, he tends to ignore or set aside the previous distinction between logical reflection (involving a comparison of forms) and aesthetic reflection (concerned with a particular form).[35]

Nevertheless, we cannot follow him in his further claims about the principle of purposiveness (or, as he terms it, "systematicity") itself and the a priori dimension of judgments of taste. To begin with, this principle is not "about nature" except in a Pickwickian sense. As we saw in Chapter 1, it is a product of the heautonomy of judgment, and it dictates that we are to proceed in our investigation of nature *as if* it were organized for the benefit of judgment. This may seem like a small point, but it does suggest that the grounding of judgments of taste in this principle (were it warranted) would not commit Kant to the view that these judgments are about properties of natural objects. More importantly, Guyer is wrong in his account of the *a priori* dimension and principled nature of judgments of taste. To anticipate some of the central themes of the following chapters, judgments of taste express a *demand* for agreement, not (as Guyer suggests) an expectation of it, and, as such, they must rest on an *a priori* principle. Moreover, as we shall see in subsequent chapters, the assumption of shared cognitive faculties (though certainly vital to Kant's position) cannot itself be this principle, since that concerns merely the *quid facti* and not the *quid juris.*

A useful starting point for a discussion of this problem is provided by Klaus Düsing, who attempts to deal with it by distinguishing between the general principle of the purposiveness of nature for judgment and the concept of formal or logical purposiveness.[36] On his reading, the passages in which Kant seems to present the latter as the *a priori* principle underlying judgments of taste are to be taken as reflecting a certain carelessness on his part, specifically, a tendency simply to identify on occasion these two conceptions of purposiveness. In reality, however, it is really the former principle that underlies judgments of natural beauty. Düsing recognizes, of course, that this still leaves artistic beauty unexplained; but his response to that problem consists entirely in an appeal to a passage at the end of the First Introduction in which Kant remarks that "Our judging of artistic beauty will have to be considered afterwards, as a mere consequence of the same principles that underlie judgments about natural beauty" (FI 20: 251; 441).[37]

Düsing is correct both in distinguishing between a general principle of purposiveness and the principle of formal or logical purposiveness as a specific form thereof, and in pointing out that Kant sometimes misleadingly equates them. He is likewise correct in underscoring the significance of the passage linking judgments of artistic with those of natural beauty. But to stop at this point is to leave judgments of natural beauty, and, *a fortiori,* those of artistic beauty as well, unexplained. This is because it remains unclear how even a general principle of purposiveness could serve to license particular claims of taste (whether they concern natural or artistic beauty). And, unfortunately, Düsing has nothing to say on this issue.

Although the systematic treatment of this question is the concern of the second part of this study and particularly of Chapter 8, which deals with the Deduction, some preliminary conclusions can be reached at this point regarding the discussion in the Introductions. First, it is difficult to avoid the conclusion that in the passages in question (or at least in the latter two of them), Kant is guilty of a slide from the conclusion that judgment has an *a priori* principle for its investigation of nature to the claim that this very principle also grounds judgments of taste. What he should have said (and the first of the cited passages might be taken as claiming just this) is that the demonstration that judgment in its investigation of nature has an *a priori* principle unique to it raises the *possibility* that it also has one in its aesthetic capacity. In other words, the deduction of the principle of purposiveness serves as a prolegomena, or prelude, to a deduction of taste, but does not of itself constitute that deduction (either in whole or part).

Second, it should be clear from what has been said so far that the key to the normativity of judgments of taste must lie in the nature of *judgment* and not the nature of nature. In the first chapter we saw that Kant links the principle of logical purposiveness with the heautonomy of judgment. Thus, even though the principle refers to nature as the sphere of its application, it really consists in a demand imposed by reflective judgment on itself to proceed in its quest for empirical knowledge, as if nature were ordered in a manner that accords with the conditions of judgment. Moreover, in light of this, it seems highly significant that in a passage in the First Introduction in which he comments (albeit perfunctorily) on the claim of aesthetic judgments of reflection to universality and necessity, Kant explicitly links the principle underlying such judgments with the heautonomy of judgment. In fact, he does so on the by-now familiar grounds that here "judgment legislates neither to nature nor to freedom, but solely to itself" (FI 20: 225; 414).

Combining the discussions of heautonomy in the two Introductions indicates that the "legislations" of systematicity or logical purposiveness and of taste should be viewed as two species of heautonomy (presumably that of teleology being a third), that is, of reflective judgment legislating to itself regarding the conditions of its successful exercise. But if this is the case, it follows that the true relationship between formal or logical purposiveness and taste is not that the former is itself the principle of the latter; it is rather that the *principle* licensing the former (the conditions of a reflective use of judgment) is identical to the principle underlying the latter. Indeed, only on such a reading, which I hope to confirm in the second part of this study, does it become possible to preserve the essential link between judgments of taste and the general account of reflective judgment upon which Kant insists in both Introductions, without confusing the various forms of reflection between which Kant also took great pains to distinguish. As we shall also see in more detail in the second part of this study, this enables us to understand Kant's claim that judgments of artistic beauty are a consequence of the same principles that underlie judgments about natural beauty.

THE *QUID FACTI* AND THE *QUID JURIS* IN THE DOMAIN OF TASTE

THE ANALYTIC OF THE BEAUTIFUL AND THE
QUID FACTI

AN OVERVIEW

This part of the study is concerned with Kant's analysis of the nature and validity of judgments of taste, as treated in the Analytic of the Beautiful and the Deduction of Pure Aesthetic Judgments. Its organizing principle is that the distinction between the *quid facti* and the *quid juris*, which, as Dieter Henrich has shown, Kant took over from the so-called *Deduktion-schriften*, which were still widely used in his time to adjudicate various legal claims, is applicable to the *Critique of Judgment* as well as to the other *Critiques*.[1] More specifically, the claim is that the *quid facti* in the domain of taste concerns the question of whether a given judgment of taste is pure, while the *quid juris* is whether a judgment that meets the conditions of purity can make a rightful demand on the agreement of others. The latter question is obviously the concern of the Deduction; but I am also suggesting that the Analytic of the Beautiful deals with the former, by specifying the conditions that must be met by any judgment that purports to be pure.

The present chapter is intended as an introduction to this part as a whole, but particularly to the next four chapters, which deal respectively with the four "moments" of the Analytic of the Beautiful. It is divided into five parts. The first two discuss two general features of judgments of taste that are frequently downplayed, ignored, or, in the case of the second, denied in the literature: The first feature is the aesthetic nature of the judgment of taste, which is a presupposition of everything that follows; and the second is the fact that Kant's account allows for the possibility of negative as well as positive judgments of taste. The third part considers the official organization of the Analytic into four moments that correspond to the division of the table of logical functions in the first *Critique*.[2] Appealing mainly to the analysis of this table by Reinhard Brandt, it maintains that, when due allowance is made for the aesthetic nature of the judgment of taste, the four moments of the Analytic of the Beautiful may be seen to constitute genuine counterparts to the corresponding logical function and that, like their first *Critique* counterparts, their ordering constitutes a natural progression. The fourth part then contrasts this reading of the Analytic with the very different one proposed by Paul Guyer, who maintains that the organization on the basis of the table of logical functions "masks" rather than reveals the true structure of Kant's argument. Finally, the fifth part attempts to show that the Analytic, on the reading advocated here, may be said to provide a progressive determination of the *quid facti.*

I

In spite of its title, the Analytic of the Beautiful is concerned not with the nature of beauty *per se,* but rather with the *judgment* through which the beauty (or lack thereof) of a particular object of nature or art is appraised. Moreover, for Kant the decisive feature of such judgment is that it is *aesthetic.* Although this may seem obvious enough on the face of it, and was already emphasized in Chapter 2, it bears reemphasis, particularly since Kant devotes the first section of the first moment, which really forms an introduction to the Analytic of the Beautiful as a whole, to the elaboration of this point.

As Kant indicates in this opening section, the significance of the fact that judgments of taste are aesthetic is that it indicates that they are based on feeling. As such, they have a subjective source quite distinct from cognition, even the confused variety with which Baumgarten connected the determination of beauty. Accordingly, it is with the clear intent of distancing his view from the latter's conception of the aesthetic as confused conception that Kant writes:

> To apprehend a regular, purposive building with one's cognitive faculty (whether the representation is distinct or confused) is very different from being conscious of this representation with a sensation of liking. Here the representation is referred only to the subject, and indeed to his feeling of life [*Lebensgefühl*] under the name pleasure or displeasure, and this forms the basis of a very special faculty of discrimination and judgment [*Unterscheidungs-und Beurteilungsvermögen*]. This faculty does not contribute anything to cognition, but merely compares the given representation in the subject with the entire representational faculty of which the mind becomes conscious when it feels its own state. (KU 5: 204; 44)

The cryptic reference to a comparison of a representation with the entire representational faculty of the subject is clearly an allusion to the accounts of aesthetic reflection given in the Introductions, and it also points ahead to further developments of the topic that Kant will provide in the second and third moments. As we have already seen, this connection with reflection is crucial for Kant, since it opens up the possibility that judgments of taste may possess a grounded claim to normativity in spite of their merely aesthetic nature. But, as was the case in the First Introduction, that the judgment of taste involves reflection is only one side of the story; equally significant is the fact that it is based on feeling. Indeed, since Kant tends to argue *from,* rather than to, this thesis, whereas he does endeavor to explain how such judgments can nevertheless involve reflection, the aesthetic nature of the judgment of taste may be viewed as the most basic underlying presupposition of his whole account.[3] For if this were challenged, the whole subsequent argument of the Analytic of the Beautiful would lose its point.

With this in mind, several features of the cited passage call for further comment. The first is the characterization of the feeling in question as the "feeling of life" [*Lebensgefühl*]. Although there is no explicit indication of this in the account of pleasure in the First Introduction discussed in Chapter 2, it is hardly a new theme in Kant. In fact, expressions of it can be found in numerous versions of his lectures, where he refers, for example, to pleasure as the feeling of the promotion of life and displeasure as the feeling of the hindrance of life.[4] Underlying this characterization is the definition of life given in the *Critique of Practical Reason* as "the faculty of a being by which it acts according to the faculty of desire," with the latter being the "faculty such a being has of causing, through its ideas, the reality of the object of these ideas." In the same context, he defines pleasure as "the idea of the agreement of an object or an action with the subjective conditions of life" (KpV 5: 9n; 9–10). On the basis of texts such as these, it seems clear that Kant understands by pleasure and displeasure something like a sense of the increase or diminution of one's level of activity, particularly one's activity as a thinking being.[5] This also explains why, as we have already seen, Kant claims that a pleasurable mental state is one which the subject endeavors to preserve and an unpleasant state one which determines the subject to change its state.

The second major point is that feeling, so construed, is not a mere receptivity, but an active faculty, indeed a faculty of appraisal.[6] Kant indicates as much in the passage currently before us, when he remarks that such feeling provides the basis for a "very special faculty of discrimination and judgment," one which does not contribute anything to cognition. Presumably, what is judged or, better, appraised aesthetically through this faculty is the capacity of a representation to occasion an enhancement or diminution of one's cognitive faculties in their cooperative activity. This appraisal occurs in an act of (mere) reflection, which "compares the given representation in the subject with the entire representational faculty of which the mind becomes conscious when it feels its own state." Correlatively, the discrimination consists in the reception or acceptance of representations that are felt to enhance these powers in such an engagement and the exclusion (from its attention) or rejection of those that are felt to diminish them.

Kant gives clear expression to the connection between his view of pleasure and aesthetic appraisal in §12 of the Analytic of the Beautiful, when he remarks that "We *linger* [*weilen*] in our contemplation of the beautiful, because this contemplation reinforces and reproduces itself" (KU 5: 222; 68). By contrast, as he notes in the General Comment attached to the Analytic of the Beautiful, everything that manifests a stiff (almost mathematical) regularity runs counter to taste [*hat das Geschmack-widrige an sich*] and thereby has the opposite effect of boring us [*lange Weile macht*] (KU 5: 242–3; 93). Accordingly, whereas in the former case the contemplation of the object is a never-ceasing source of enjoyment, always disclosing new possibilities for the reciprocal engagement of the imagination and the understanding in their free play, in the latter case the aesthetic possibilities are soon exhausted (if they were present at all), and a feeling of dislike ensues.

It should also be at least noted at this point that this understanding of the feeling of pleasure and displeasure as a faculty of discrimination and appraisal serves to illuminate a feature of Kant's accounts of aesthetic judgment in the Introductions that otherwise seems mysterious, or at least arbitrary, namely, his insistence on a systematic linkage between judgment and feeling as the two "mediating" faculties.[7] Such a linkage is certainly required by Kant for systematic reasons, particularly for effecting the transition from nature to freedom (to be discussed in Chapter 9). But his attempt to introduce it by appealing to an analogy is, to say the least, unconvincing. The situation appears quite different, however, if feeling is itself regarded as a faculty of discrimination and appraisal, since it then becomes natural to link it with judgment. In fact, the two must be viewed as intimately linked in the judgment of taste; for whereas it is judgment that reflects, that is, compares, it is feeling that appraises the results of this reflective activity. This, as we have already seen, is why judgments of taste are characterized as aesthetic judgments of reflection.

It is likewise important to realize that the major reason that a judgment of taste is aesthetic is that what it appraises can only be determined aesthetically. This is because the result in question, namely, the affect or bearing of the representation of an object on one's cognitive faculties, insofar as they are engaged in an act of mere reflection, is something that can only be felt.[8] Moreover, this not only explains why we must attribute intentionality to aesthetic feeling (a point that was insisted on in Chapter 2), but it also provides the key to understanding Kant's repeated suggestion that feeling functions as, or like, a predicate in a judgment of taste.

Kant first compares feeling to a predicate in the Second Introduction, when he suggests that it functions in a judgment of taste, "just as if it were a predicate connected with the cognition of the object" (KU 5: 191; 31). Later, in the Deduction, he states that it serves "in the place of a predicate" (KU 5: 288; 152); and finally, in the same context, he remarks that the singularity of judgments of taste stems from the fact that they connect their predicate (the feeling) with a given singular representation, rather than with a concept (KU 5: 289; 154). Clearly, Kant does not intend us to understand that the feeling functions as a logical (not to mention a real) predicate, since the judgment of taste is noncognitive. The point is rather that the feeling serves as the vehicle through which we perceive the aptness or subjective purposiveness (or lack thereof) of a given representation for the proper exercise of our cognitive faculties. And, as such, it might be viewed as the aesthetic analogue of the "recognition in the concept" to which Kant refers in the A-Deduction.[9]

II

The second feature of Kant's account that needs to be emphasized at the very outset is that it is concerned with negative as well as positive judgments of taste. Indeed, one would expect this to be the case, since our basic intuitions about aesthetic valuations surely indicate that negative judgments must have the same status (as judgments of taste) and the same claim to validity as their positive counterparts. Otherwise, the point on which Kant insists in his discussion of the Antinomy of Taste, namely, that we can quarrel [*streiten*] about taste, though we cannot dispute about it (KU 5: 338; 210–11), would lose its sense.[10] Moreover, it should be sufficiently clear from what we have already seen in this chapter about the nature of the judgment of taste, as well as from the discussion in Chapter 2 of Kant's account of such judgments in the two Introductions, that he holds to such a view. Nevertheless, it bears emphasis at this point because it has been largely ignored by many commentators, including some of the more prominent recent English-language interpretations, and explicitly denied by others.[11]

Undoubtedly, one of the reasons for this reaction is Kant's relative lack of attention to the issue in the *Critique of Judgment* itself. For the most part, he there understandably focuses on positive assessments of beauty, although, as already indicated and as we shall see in more detail in subsequent chapters, he does not neglect negative judgments and aesthetic disliking completely. Nevertheless, the situation is quite different, if one considers the discussions of taste in other Kantian texts, including various versions of his lectures. In fact, Kant's concern with such judgments can be traced back at least to his important 1763 essay, "Attempt to Introduce the Concept of Negative Magnitudes into Philosophy." There, in accordance with the central theme of the essay, Kant characterized ugliness as a "negative beauty" (NG 2: 182; 221) the point being that it is a true negation and not merely the absence of beauty. In later texts we find what might be termed a three-valued "logic" of taste, wherein the dry or the dull [*trocken*], indicating a mere lack of aesthetic value, is placed between the positive and negative values of beauty and ugliness. For example, in a transcript of one of his lectures on metaphysics, Kant remarks: "That which pleases through mere intuition is *beautiful,* that which leaves me indifferent in intuition . . . is *non-beautiful;* that which displeases me in intuition is ugly" (MV 29: 1010; 480). Similarly, in another version, Kant indicates in connection with his discussion of taste that everything related to pleasure and displeasure involves a trichotomy (MD 28: 676; 378).[12]

Far from being surprising, such a three-valued scheme is likewise what one would expect, given the systematic importance that Kant consistently assigned after the 1763 essay to the distinction between a real and a merely logical opposition. The former is between contraries, which Kant symbolizes as + and -, and therefore allows for an intermediate, neutral condition = 0, whereas the latter, as between contradictories, does not. Since Kant regarded the opposition between both virtue and vice and the pleasant and the unpleasant (or agreeable and disagreeable) as instances of real rather than merely logical opposition, there is no reason to expect that he would not also characterize the opposition between the beautiful and the ugly in the same way.[13]

Admittedly, the situation is complicated by a certain ambiguity in Kant's understanding of the "non-beautiful." For example, on the one hand, he seems to have regarded the predicate *trocken* as functioning to exclude an object from aesthetic consideration altogether, rather than as characterizing a distinct aesthetic evaluation.[14] And though he reserves a logical space for the indifferent within the realm of feeling, he also seems to deny that anything could fill that space.[15] On the other hand, as we have already seen, Kant viewed stiff, quasi-mathematical regularities as occasioning a feeling of boredom, and therefore presumably an actual dislike, though we have no reason to assume that he would have regarded such objects as ugly.

These complications do not affect the main point, however, which is simply that Kant recognized a class of negative judgments of taste, which includes, but is not necessarily limited to, judgments of ugliness, and which have the same claim to normativity as their positive counterparts. Accordingly, I believe that it is a reasonable criterion of any interpretation of Kant's theory of taste that it be able to account for the possibility of negative judgments so construed. Moreover, in what follows, this shall emerge as a significant factor on more than one occasion.

III

Another major concern here is with the organization of the Analytic of the Beautiful on the basis of the organization of the table of the logical functions of judgment in the first *Critique.* For we shall see that an appreciation of this organization and the reasoning underlying it is essential to the establishment of the thesis that the Analytic is concerned with the *quid facti* in the domain of taste. Consequently, the intent of this section is to explicate and defend this organization by comparing it to that of the table of logical functions.

Let us begin, then, with a consideration of Kant's own account of the matter. It is contained in a footnote appended to the heading of the first moment, where he states:

> But we have to analyze judgments of taste in order to discover what is required for calling an object beautiful. I have used the logical functions of judging as a guide in finding the moments that judgment takes into consideration when it reflects (since even a judgment of taste still has reference to the understanding). I have examined the moment of quality first, because an aesthetic judgment about the beautiful is concerned with it first (KU 5: 203; 43).

The note consists of four sentences, each of which, but particularly the latter two, requires comment. The first, which provides us with the definition of taste as a faculty for estimating the beautiful, is directly relevant to the thesis of the first section of this chapter (the aesthetic nature of the judgment of taste). As already indicated, taste is the capacity to appraise the beauty (or lack thereof) of particular objects (or their representations) by means of feeling. As such, it may also be described as a capacity for aesthetic discrimination.

The second sentence indicates that the goal of the analysis of judgments of taste (and therefore of the Analytic of the Beautiful) is to uncover the factors relevant to such an appraisal or discrimination. At first glance, this might be thought to conflict with the claim that the goal is to determine the conditions under which a given judgment of taste can be pure. In addition, it might be argued against such a reading that it is only in the third moment that Kant deals explicitly with the distinction between pure and impure judgments of taste.[16] Nevertheless, since it is clearly Kant's position that it is only the pure judgment of taste that is concerned with the beauty (or lack thereof) of an object, an account of the conditions required for calling an object beautiful would at the same time be an account of the necessary conditions for calling a judgment of taste pure. Accordingly, there is no incompatibility between Kant's own characterization of the task of the Analytic and the characterization given here.

It is only in the third sentence of the note that Kant gets to the main point, namely, the reason for organizing the Analytic on the basis of the table of logical functions. Here the obvious question is why such a table, which is concerned with the logical functions exercised in cognitive judgments and their propositional expressions, should be of any relevance to the determination of the conditions of explicitly noncognitive, aesthetic appraisals or discriminations. Granted, that since a claim of taste is an evaluative judgment, it has a determinate propositional form ("x is beautiful"), and as such it must have features corresponding to the logical functions, namely, a quantity, quality, relation, and modality. But it is far from obvious that this should be of any systematic significance in uncovering the factors relevant to the determination of beauty or, equivalently, the purity of a judgment of taste

Confining ourselves to the note, it seems clear that the key to Kant's answer lies in the reference to the "moments that judgment takes into consideration when it reflects," as well as the immediately ensuing parenthetical remark that "even a judgment of taste still has reference to the understanding." In other words, it is the *reflective* nature of the judgment of taste, which, in turn, involves a reference to the understanding, that underlies the appeal to the logical functions. This suggests that there is a close connection in Kant's mind between these functions and the act of reflection, and it is just this connection that needs to be clarified.

As we saw in Chapter 1 of this study, the connection between reflection and the logical functions is a central theme in the work of Béatrice Longuenesse; and even though she does not explicitly concern herself with judgments of taste, I believe that the main thrust of her analysis is directly germane to the point at issue. Of particular relevance in this regard is Longuenesse's thesis that logical reflection aims at the formation of concepts that are combinable in judgments, which in her terms means that such reflection operates in the service of the "capacity to judge," that is, the logical functions, which constitute the forms in which this capacity is exercised. The connection between such reflection and the logical functions is not direct, however, since it is mediated by the concepts of comparison to which Kant refers in the Amphiboly chapter and which play a large role in Longuenesse's reading of Kant. As Kant puts it in the key passage from that chapter:

> Before constructing any objective judgment we compare the concepts to find in them *identity* (of many representations under one concept) with a view to *universal* judgments, *difference* with a view to *particular* judgments, *agreement* with a view to *affirmative* judgments, *opposition* with a view to *negative* judgments, etc. (A262/B317-8)

According to this passage, there is a direct correlation between the concepts of reflection (identity and difference and the moments of quantity) on the one hand, and the concepts of agreement and opposition and the moments of quality, on the other. And even though Kant does not complete the picture by connecting the remaining concepts of reflection (inner and outer, matter and form) with the moments of relation and modality, the "etc." clearly indicates he assumed that the correlation could be extended to these as well.[17] Moreover, since these concepts of reflection directly govern the "universalizing comparison," analyzed in Chapter 1, which involves empirical schemata to be reflected as concepts that are combinable in "objective judgments," it follows that this reflection is subject to conditions imposed by the logical functions of judgment. In other words, logical reflection aims at meeting the conditions necessary for the making of judgments of the forms specified in the table of logical functions; and it does so by reflecting in light of the concepts of comparison.

This may help to explain why the logical functions are relevant to logical reflection; but it does not suffice to account for their relevance to judgments of taste, where the goal is not cognition, and concepts of comparison are clearly not operative. Nevertheless, the relevance of these functions to the analysis of the judgment of taste can be brought out, if we keep in mind the account sketched in Chapter 2 of the reflective nature of such judgments. For we saw there that this reflection consists in a comparison between the relation of the cognitive faculties in their free engagement with a given object or its representation and the ideal, frictionless harmony, which maximally facilitates cognition. Consequently, even though the actual appraisal is made aesthetically, that is, through feeling, the reflection or comparison underlying this appraisal involves an essential reference to the conditions of cognition. Moreover, this would seem to provide ample justification for a turn to the logical functions in an effort to uncover the factors to which reflection appeals in the assessment of aesthetic value, which, as I have suggested, are also the factors on the basis of which the purity of a judgment of taste is determined.

If this organization is to prove truly useful for the purposes intended, however, it must indicate something significant about the connection between the moments of the pure judgment of taste. Indeed, one might expect that it reflect a natural progression of these moments, analogous to, though different from, the progression in the first *Critique*. But far from being obvious, this is precisely what is denied by Guyer, who instead sees the official organization of the Analytic (beginning with disinterestedness – the moment of quality) as masking the real structure of Kant's argument.[18] And, of course, Guyer is far from alone in his negative evaluation of the organization of the Analytic of the Beautiful.[19] Consequently, we shall take up the question of whether there is any such progression, and this first of all requires a consideration of Kant's remark in the last sentence of the note that he will begin with the moment of quality rather than quantity because it is that with which a judgment of taste is first concerned.

Clearly, in order to adjudicate this issue, it is absolutely essential to have in view an understanding of the reasoning underlying the determination and ordering of the functions of judgment in the first *Critique*. Moreover, this is itself a highly complex and controversial topic that has been the subject of some debate in the recent literature. Fortunately, however, it is not necessary to enter here into the details of this debate, since for our present limited purposes we can safely rely largely on the account of Reinhard Brandt.[20] What is of particular interest to us here is Brandt's focus on Kant's remark that modality is a peculiar function in that "it contributes nothing to the content of the judgment (for, besides quantity, quality, and relation, there is nothing that constitutes the content of a judgment), but concerns only the value of the copula in relation to thought in general" (A74/B99–100).

Saving the discussion of modality for later, the first point to note is the claim that the functions of quantity, quality and relation, in that order, exhaust the *content* [my emphasis] of the judgment.[21] Since Kant is here concerned with delineating the formal features of judgment as such, the latter term cannot have its usual meaning, according to which it is contrasted with *form*. Instead, it must be understood as referring to the structural features requisite for a fully formed cognitive or logical judgment. Thus, to claim that the first three functions exhaust the content of a judgment is to claim that they are jointly both necessary and sufficient to generate such a judgment.

According to Brandt, the reason for beginning with quantity is that judgment is discursive cognition or cognition through concepts, and concepts are general representations, which refer to a plurality of items. Consequently, the first thing to be determined is whether the predicate concept is taken to refer to all, some, or only one of the items falling under the subject concept, that is, the quantity of the judgment. Quality comes next in Brandt's account, because any judgment, *qua* judgment, essentially involves either an assertion or a negation (the complications caused by the infinite judgment being left out of the preliminary account).[22] But quite apart from the details of Brandt's analysis, it seems clear that the quality of a judgment, as here construed, presupposes its quantity, since the affirmation or negation concerns a quantified subject.

In addition, relation is required to link the items in the judgment, which in the most basic form (categorical judgment) are the subject and predicate concepts, and in the more complex forms (hypothetical and disjunctive judgments) are themselves judgments. Moreover, given these, we have all of the elements required for a judgment, as Brandt illustrates by appealing to the (nonmodalized) judgment: "All bodies are divisible." Here we find a universally quantified subject, an affirmatively qualified copula, and a predicate related to the subject, which exhausts what can be said of the content of this judgment.[23]

By contrast, modality only enters the story later, since it presupposes a fully formed judgment. Consequently, what it adds is not part of the content of the judgment, but rather an indication of how the assertion or negation ("the value of the copula") is taken with respect to "thought in general." In other words, it is concerned with what might be termed the epistemic value of the judgment, that is, whether it is to be taken as merely problematic, as assertoric, or as apodeictic. And while this is obviously essential for determining the connection between the judgment and the remainder of the body of knowledge, it does not enter into a consideration of the nature of the judgment as such.[24]

Returning to the third *Critique,* I think that it is possible to provide an analogous line of reasoning regarding the order and nature of the moments relevant to the analysis of the judgment of taste. This order will not amount to a deductive chain of inferences, but it should provide a rational progression, which is all that is required to justify the appeal to the first *Critique's* table as the organizing principle for the Analytic in the third.[25]

To begin with, since the judgment is aesthetic, it is based on feeling rather than concepts, so this must be the primary factor to be considered. Now, feeling may be considered either with regard to its quantity (strength) or its quality (kind), but clearly it is the latter that is crucial in determining what is distinctive about a judgment of beauty. Consequently, given its aesthetic nature, it is appropriate for Kant to claim in the note that "an aesthetic judgment about the beautiful is concerned with it [quality] first."[26] Moreover, we shall see (*pace* Guyer) that this appropriateness is reinforced by the fact that the quality of the feeling (its disinterestedness) is the key to the determination of the quantity of the judgment (its subjective universality).

For the present, however, we need only note that a consideration of quantity naturally comes next on the grounds that an aesthetic judgment is a *judgment,* and therefore necessarily has a scope. But, once again, since it is an *aesthetic* judgment, its scope or quantity cannot be understood according to the model of the logical quantity of a cognitive judgment about objects ("All S are P"), but must rather concern the sphere of judging subjects to whom the feeling is applicable. In short, as Kant argues in the second moment, the universality of a judgment of taste, as an aesthetic judgment, can only be a subjective universality.

Furthermore, even though the judgment of taste has a subjective basis and cannot be quantified over objects, it expresses an evaluation of an object or its representation. Consequently, since it is not the feeling that is appraised, but rather an object or its representation by means of a feeling, the judgment presupposes some relation between the subject's feeling and the nature of the object. Once again, however, the relation here differs markedly from its logical counterpart, since it holds between the feeling of the judging subject and the object judged, rather than between the subject of the (categorical) judgment and what is predicated of it. And, of course, there could be no aesthetic counterpart of the combination of judgments (the hypothetical and disjunctive forms).

This brings us to the function of modality; and if the parallelism holds true, the judgment of taste must not only have a modality, but one that does not add to the "content" of the judgment. Beginning with the latter point, it seems that the first three moments exhaust what is claimed in a judgment of taste in a manner analogous to the way in which the corresponding functions exhaust the content of a cognitive judgment. Thus, if a judgment of taste is to count as a pure judgment, that is, a judgment of beauty, the feeling through which the object is appraised must have both a certain quality (disinterestedness) and a subjectively universal quantity or scope. In addition, assuming that Kant's analysis is correct, the feeling must also be related to the estimation of the form of the object. The latter is, of course, a controversial matter, which must be decided in the course of the analysis (Chapter 6); but for present purposes, we need only note that this exhausts what is claimed in a pure judgment of taste. What then of its modality? As we shall see in more detail shortly, rather than introducing an additional factor to the claim itself, it concerns the bearing of this claim on the judgment of others. In short, it attaches to what might be termed the "evaluative force" of the claim.[27]

IV

Although this sketch of the structure of the Analytic of the Beautiful certainly does not of itself suffice to show that it is concerned with the determination of the *quid facti* in the domain of taste, or even that there is such a thing, it does put us in a position to address this issue. But rather than approaching it directly, it may prove useful to take a somewhat circuitous course and first contrast the reading I have suggested with the radically different view of Paul Guyer regarding the organization of the Analytic. This, then, will be the concern of the present section, and in the fifth (and last) I shall turn directly to the issue of the connection between the Analytic of the Beautiful and the *quid facti*.

As already indicated, Guyer not only dismisses the organization of the Analytic on the basis of the logical table from the first *Critique* as an anachronism stemming from Kant's earlier adherence to the rationalist view of beauty as perfection confusedly conceived, but he also suggests that it masks the real structure of the argument. In particular, he rejects any attempt to read the Analytic as a progressive argument in which succeeding moments build on the preceding ones. At the heart of this critical treatment is his dismissal as a *non sequitur* of the inference from disinterestedness to universality with which Kant begins the second moment. Instead, Guyer locates the true beginning of the Analytic in the universality claim of the second moment.[28]

He further contends that the second and fourth moments, on the one hand, and the first and third, on the other, "constitute two functionally distinct groups of criteria."[29] The former (universality and necessity) are analytic criteria for distinguishing a judgment of taste from a merely first-person report of a response to an object; whereas the latter (disinterestedness and purposiveness of form)[30] are the "justificatory criteria," stating the "facts" on the basis of which the claim of universality and necessity is supposedly made. But since Guyer also denies that the second and fourth moments impose distinct conditions on the judgments of taste, his view comes down to the claim that there is really only a single analytic criterion, which, like the general criterion for the *a priori*, may be expressed in terms of either universality or necessity.[31] Moreover, on this point at least, Guyer's reading appears to have become the standard one.[32]

Since I intend to treat the disinterestedness thesis in Chapter 4 and to analyze and defend Kant's inference from disinterestedness to universality in Chapter 5, I can at present do nothing more than issue a promissory note on that score. Nevertheless, we have already seen why it is appropriate for Kant to begin the Analytic of the Beautiful with a discussion of the moment of quality, and we are in a position to say something about the relation between the second and the fourth moments, which is clearly the major issue.

To begin with, it must be admitted that Guyer's reading, which denies any significant difference between the claims of the second and fourth moments, has a number of things in its favor. First, as Guyer himself points out, Kant uses very similar language in the two places. For example, already in the second moment he speaks of the judgment of taste as requiring [*ansinnen*] everyone to like the object (KU 5: 213–14; 57), and even of demanding agreement (KU 5: 214; 58). He is likewise correct in noting that the fourth moment does not impose a distinct condition on [the content of] a judgment of taste, though, as I shall argue, he draws the wrong conclusion from this.

In addition, the great difference between the nature of the universality that Kant attributes to judgments of taste and the logical universality that pertains to cognitive judgments makes an application of the sharp distinction between the second and fourth moments, which seems perfectly in order in the case of cognitive judgments, appear highly problematic in the case of judgments of taste. For if, as Kant insists, the "subjective universality" of judgments of taste (also termed "universal communicability") concerns the complete sphere of judging subjects rather than the set of objects falling under a predicate-concept, then it seems virtually indistinguishable from the putative necessity of such judgments, which likewise applies to the complete sphere of judging subjects. In fact, since Kant famously insists on the equivalence of necessity and universality as the criteria of the *a priori* (B4), and since, as we shall see, he treats judgments of taste as being themselves *a priori*, or at least as resting on an *a priori* principle, it might even be argued that regarding the second and fourth moments as presenting functionally equivalent analytic criteria offers the most plausible reading of the text.[33]

Moreover, since Guyer himself insists on the point, it hardly suffices as a defense of the actual organization of the Analytic to note that such a reading requires abandoning any significant parallel between the organization of the table of logical functions of judgment and that of the moments of the judgment of taste. Nevertheless, I also think it fair to say that if, in spite of the factors that appear to support Guyer's reading, it can be shown that a plausible reading can be given to the Analytic of the Beautiful on the assumption of a significant parallelism with the organization of the table of logical functions, then such a reading is to be preferred, since it corresponds with Kant's express intent.

In attempting to sketch such a reading, the first point to note is that the subjective universality (or universal communicability) of one's feeling is part of what one *means* in judging an object beautiful. As Kant remarks at the beginning of the second moment, "this claim to universal validity belongs so essentially to a judgment by which we declare something to be *beautiful* that it would not occur to anyone to use this term without thinking of universal validity" (KU 5: 214; 57). In other words, the universal "quantity" of one's liking or disliking, like the disinterestedness from which it supposedly follows, and the formal purposiveness that follows from it, is an essential ingredient in the pure judgment of taste, one without which the possibility of this judgment-type cannot be conceived. Consequently, it too belongs to the "content" of the judgment.

Additional evidence that Kant viewed the universality of judgments of taste in this way, that is, as belonging to the intrinsic content of the judgment itself, is provided by his discussion of the topic in various versions of his anthropology lectures. Thus, in the lectures from the winter of 1777–8, while speaking of the properties of taste, Kant remarks, "[T]hat it is universal lies already in the explication of taste" (Anthro P 25: 788). Moreover, in the lectures from the winter of 1781–2, Kant explicitly contrasts the universality built into a judgment of taste, which distinguishes it from a judgment of the agreeable, with the demand placed on others for agreement. Whereas Kant suggests that the former lies in the nature of the thing [*Natur der Sache*] and can be judged *a priori*, he says of the latter: "[T]he necessity that men must *agree* in this [a judgment of taste] cannot be claimed on the basis of reason, but we must rather consult experience" (Mensch 25: 1097). Although Kant certainly abandoned the view that the demand for universal agreement regarding a judgment of taste must be based on experience, he retained the idea that the universality of such judgment lies "in the nature of the thing."[34]

What, then, are we to make of the fourth moment, particularly as contrasted with the second? When first raising this issue, I suggested that the specific contribution of modality to a judgment of taste is to attribute to it an evaluative force. This attribution takes the form of a claim on the agreement of others and may be seen as a genuine analogue of the epistemic value registered in the modalization of a cognitive judgment or, as Kant puts it, "the value of the copula in relation to thought in general." An obvious difference is that cognitive judgments allow for three modalities, and judgments of taste only one; but I do not think that this marks an essential difference in *how* this modality is understood. In any event, I would now like to expand a bit on this suggestion, in the hope of convincing the reader that there is, indeed, a distinct modal function in pure judgments of taste or, equivalently, that their necessity is not simply to be equated with their universality.

Putting the matter in terms of Kant's language from the first *Critique*, one might say that the judgment of taste already has, in virtue of its very nature, a relation to "feeling in general," since it claims not to be based on a merely private feeling (like the agreeable), but rather on one that is universally shareable in virtue of its disinterestedness. Thus, as we have seen, an aesthetic judgment that did not involve such a relation simply would not count as a judgment of taste. But it is one thing to view a feeling-type in this way (as not merely private) and another to hold up one's particular judgment as normative for others. Although closely related, they remain analytically distinct aspects of a judgment of taste.

The distinction can perhaps be clarified by considering it in light of Kant's claim in §19 of the B-Deduction that objective validity pertains to every [cognitive] judgment in virtue of its "logical form." As was noted in the analysis of this characterization of judgment in Chapter 1, Kant does not mean by this that every cognitive judgment (*qua* judgment) is true, but rather that it makes a claim to truth or has a truth value. To be sure, Kant does not regard objective validity as itself one of the logical functions of judgment, and it is certainly not equivalent to the function of universality; so in this respect, the parallelism with the subjective universality or universal communicability of judgments of taste breaks down. Kant does take it as criterial for judgment, however, since it provides the basis for distinguishing between a judgment and a mere association of the same representations, which has no truth value. Moreover, so construed, the objective validity of a cognitive judgment is quite distinct from its modality, which, as we have seen, concerns merely the "value of the copula in relation to thought in general" (A74/B99–100).

Appealing to the analogy with this defining feature of a cognitive judgment, one might claim that just as every cognitive judgment possesses an objective validity that distinguishes it as a judgment from mere association, so, too, every judgment of taste possesses a subjective universality that belongs to it intrinsically and distinguishes it from a mere judgment of agreeableness. And, continuing with the analogy, this subjective universality must likewise be distinguished from the modality of judgments of taste, understood as an implicit demand placed on the agreement of others with one's evaluation. In this way, then, the modality of judgments of taste may be regarded as a genuine analogue to its logical counterpart, since it likewise stands apart from the other moments (including universality) in not forming part of the content of the judgment.

V

If the preceding analysis is correct, it undermines a basic premise of Guyer's proposed reorganization of the Analytic of the Beautiful (the essential equivalence of the second and fourth moments), and with it the claim that its four moments are to be divided into two categories: the first and third offering "justificatory" and the second and fourth "analytic" criteria. Instead, it suggests an organizational structure that parallels that of the table of logical functions of judgment in the first *Critique,* with the first three moments defining the "content" of pure judgments of taste and the fourth standing apart and concerned with the evaluative force of such judgments.

Moreover, though it certainly does not make the case (this being a major goal of the next four chapters), the preceding analysis does at least give further credence to the view that the ordering of the moments of the Analytic of the Beautiful on the basis of the logical functions reflects a unified and progressive account of the factors involved in judgments of beauty or, equivalently, of the conditions under which a judgment of taste is deemed pure. Even granting this, however, one may still wonder what it has to do with the *quid facti*. And since Kant himself makes no explicit reference to the topic, either in or in connection with the Analytic of the Beautiful, we must consider what he has to say about it elsewhere.

In addition to the famous formulation at the beginning of the Transcendental Deduction in the first *Critique* (A84/B116), perhaps the most helpful of Kant's discussions of the distinction is in a *Reflexion* in which he writes: "The *quaestio facti* is in what manner one has first come into possession of a concept; the *quaestio juris,* with what right one possesses and uses it" (R 5636 18: 267).[35] The concern of the *quid* or *quaestio facti* is thus with the mode of origination of a concept. More specifically, it is with whether a concept has an *a priori* or an empirical origin. The underlying assumption is that the former mode of origination is at least a necessary condition for any non-empirical use of a concept; and in the *Critique of Pure Reason* it is the so-called Metaphysical Deduction that supposedly establishes such an origin for the pure concepts of the understanding by deriving them from the logical functions of judgment.[36] Accordingly, it is in the Metaphysical Deduction that the *quid facti* is addressed in the first *Critique,* while the questions of the right and the restrictions on the use of these concepts are reserved for the Transcendental Deduction.[37]

Applying this account of the *quid facti–quid juris* contrast in the first *Critique* to the third, one would expect that the Analytic of the Beautiful in the latter, which supposedly corresponds to the Metaphysical Deduction in the former, is likewise concerned with a question of origin. Moreover, this is precisely what we find, albeit with one significant difference, which stems from the fact that the judgment-form being analyzed is aesthetic rather than cognitive. As such, the concern is with the origin of the *feeling* underlying a judgment of taste, rather than of a concept on which the judgment is based. To anticipate once again the results of the Analytic, the feeling must not be based on an interest; it must stem from the free harmony of the faculties, and it must be occasioned by the purposiveness of the form of an object.

It is clear that each of these factors relates to the question of origin, albeit in different ways. The first relates to the feeling as a form of appraisal and concerns the basis or determining ground of this appraisal. By ruling out any interest as a possible basis, it is a merely negative condition, but it nonetheless serves as the *conditio sine qua non* of the purity of a judgment of taste. The second concerns the subjective source of the feeling in the nature of our cognitive faculties, which underlies its universality, and the third its objective correlate or occasion. Together they define what might be termed the "purity conditions" of the feeling in the judgment of taste and therefore of the judgment of taste as well.

Interestingly enough, what Guyer terms the "justificatory criteria" (the first and third moments) fall squarely under the *quid facti* on this reading, rather than, as his label suggests, the *quid juris*. Nevertheless, it is permissible to term them "justificatory" under two conditions. First, it must be kept in mind that what they supposedly justify is the claim that a given judgment of taste is pure (which is perfectly compatible with Guyer's account of these moments). Second, for the reasons previously given, the same status or function must also be assigned to the second moment. Granted, the latter hardly seems to follow from the idea of universality, which, as such, has nothing to do with origin. But the connection becomes apparent once it is noted that in this moment, Kant introduces the free harmony of the faculties as the subjective source of the pleasure of taste.

This brings us, once again, to the anomalous fourth moment, or modality, which might seem to pose something of a dilemma for the interpretation advocated here. On the one hand, the emphasis that has been placed on its difference from the other moments appears to call into question its connection with the *quid facti*. For if, as I have repeatedly claimed, this moment does not add anything further to the *content* of a judgment of taste, then it becomes unclear how it could contribute to the *quid facti*. On the other hand, if, as seems reasonable, one appeals to what this moment does in fact add to the discussion, namely, the idea of a common sense as the ultimate presupposition of a pure judgment of taste, then we do have a new condition that may plausibly be related to the *quid facti,* since it is a matter of origin. In that case, however, it appears difficult to retain the view that, unlike the other moments, it adds nothing to the content of a pure judgment of taste, which was essential to the distinction between the second and fourth moments.

Finally, to complicate matters further, we shall see that in the fourth moment, Kant not only argues for the necessity of presupposing a common sense as a condition of the possibility of pure judgments of taste, but he also (in §21) advances an epistemological argument in justification of his making such a presupposition. And this argument, which is frequently taken as a proto-deduction or "first deduction," certainly appears to concern the *quid juris,* rather than merely the *quid facti.*

Since these problems are the central concern of Chapter 7, I shall here merely state the main points on which my response to them turns, saving the more detailed discussion for later. First, even though the idea of a common sense clearly pertains to the *quid facti,* this does not entail that it adds anything new to the content of a pure judgment of taste. Its function instead is to provide a unifying focus, through which the elements of a pure judgment of taste that have been analyzed separately in the first three moments are brought together into a whole. As Kant puts it at the very end of this moment, the task of the Analytic had been only "to analyze the faculty of taste into its elements and to unite these ultimately in the idea of a common sense" (KU 5: 240; 90).[38] Second, I shall try to show that the argument of §21 need not be taken as a proto-deduction of judgments of taste, but may be viewed instead as an attempt to show that cognition itself requires the presupposition of something like a common sense. Although this obviously would not count as a deduction of taste, it is of direct relevance to an eventual deduction because it shows that what initially seems problematic, namely, the very idea of a common sense, is, in fact, required as a condition of ordinary cognitive judgments.[39]

THE DISINTERESTEDNESS OF THE PURE
JUDGMENT OF TASTE

As already noted, the first moment of the Analytic of the Beautiful deals with the quality of the feeling in a pure judgment of taste, and this quality is said to lie in its being devoid of all interest or, more simply, disinterested. In introducing this thesis, Kant claims that "Everyone has to admit that if a judgment about beauty is mingled with the least interest then it is very partial and not a pure judgment of taste" (KU 5: 205; 46). The phrase "everyone has to admit" suggests that Kant took himself to be appealing to a view widely shared by his contemporaries, which he then used as a nonproblematic starting point for his account of taste. Recent work, however, has made it clear that this is not the case. In spite of being anticipated to some extent by theorists, such as Shaftesbury and Hutcheson, the view that the judgment or experience of beauty was disinterested, at least in the broad sense in which Kant understood this, was far from the prevailing opinion of aestheticians of Kant's time in either Great Britain or Germany.[1]

In addition to being novel, Kant's conception of disinterestedness has also seemed to many to be highly problematic. The heart of the difficulty lies in the connection between interest and existence, which is built into the initial definition of interest as "the liking we connect with the representation of an object's existence" (KU 5: 204; 45). This entails that a disinterested liking, which is what the liking for the beautiful is supposed to be, must be independent of any concern for the existence of the object of that liking. Moreover, this is precisely what Kant claims, noting that the question of whether a given object is beautiful is quite distinct from the question of whether one cares for the existence of things of that kind. At issue is, rather, "how we judge it in our mere contemplation of it (intuition or reflection)" (KU 5: 204; 45). And, by way of reaffirming the point, he remarks at the end of the section that "In order to play the judge in matters of taste, we must not be in the least biased in favor of the thing's existence but must be wholly indifferent about it" (KU 5: 205; 46).

This account raises at least three major questions. The first is whether a disinterested liking or pleasure is possible at all, particularly given Kant's subsequent characterization of pleasure as the "consciousness of a representation's causality directed at the subject's state so as to *keep* him in that state" (KU 5: 220; 65). Since any pleasure thus involves an endeavor to maintain itself, it might seem that it must likewise involve an interest in the continued existence of whatever is responsible for producing this state in the first place.[2] Secondly, even if the possibility of a disinterested liking be conceded, the claim that the liking for the beautiful is of this nature seems quite dubious. Surely, one who delights in the beauty of works of art is also pleased by the fact that such works (as well as such institutions as museums where they can be viewed) exist.[3] Finally, there is the question of the consistency of Kant's overall position. How can he insist within the Analytic of the Beautiful that judgments of taste are not only not based on an interest but also "of themselves do not even give rise to any interest" (KU 5: 205n; 46), while later arguing not merely for an empirical but also for an intellectual interest in the beautiful?

Since I shall deal with the last question in some detail in the third part of this study, I do not intend to consider it any further at this point. Instead, I shall focus exclusively on the first two, or, more precisely, on the second, since we shall see that the answer to it provides the basis for an answer to the first as well. The underlying assumption, which can only be confirmed retrospectively by the results of the analysis as a whole, is that disinterestedness matters because it is the *conditio sine qua non* of the purity of taste.[4] Here "pure" has both the negative sense of being purely or merely a judgment of taste, that is, a merely aesthetic judgment based on feeling rather than a concept, and the positive sense of having an *a priori* or normative component. A judgment of taste must be pure in both senses if it is to be able to make a valid demand on the agreement of others, while still preserving its aesthetic character.

This chapter is divided into four parts. Since Kant's insistence on disinterestedness can be understood only in light of his conception of interest, the first part explicates the latter conception by considering Kant's major discussions of it in his writings on moral philosophy. The second and third parts use these results to analyze Kant's argument for the disinterestedness of the pure judgment of taste. In light of this analysis, the fourth part then addresses the objections I have noted. A major goal is to show that, contrary to initial appearances, the disinterestedness thesis, properly understood, accommodates our basic intuitions about interest in the existence and accessibility of objects deemed beautiful.

I

Although there are numerous references to the interests of reason (both speculative and practical) in the first *Critique*, the concept of interest is imported into the third *Critique* from Kant's moral theory, particularly the account of moral motivation and agency.[5] Moreover, we shall see that, while there is no incompatibility between the various accounts of interest (and the lack thereof), there are significant differences in emphasis that can be explained in terms of the quite different roles that the concept is assigned in moral and aesthetic theory.[6]

Kant introduces the concept in a note in the *Groundwork*, in which he contrasts inclination and interest as two species of the dependence that characterize a finite or "contingently determinable" rational will, that is, one that does not always choose what is "objectively necessary" (Gr 4: 414n; 81). The former is defined as "the dependence of the faculty of desire on feelings," which, as such, always indicates a need, and the latter as the dependence of such a will on principles of reason. Since Kant goes on to assert that the concept of interest applies only to a dependent will, that is, one "which is not in itself always in conformity to reason," it would seem that by "principles of reason" he means subjective principles or maxims, which may or may not conform to the requirements of the categorical imperative. In any event, the main idea is that simply having a desire or inclination (even a strong one) is not yet to have an interest. The latter requires, in addition, some kind of rational endorsement of the desire, a "contingent determination of the will." In other words, as rational agents, we don't simply have interests; rather, we *take* an interest in something through a rational endorsement. Correlatively, a desire or inclination only becomes an interest, that is, a reason to act or, equivalently, an incentive [*Triebfeder*], insofar as it is rationally endorsed. Accordingly, the concept of interest is an essential ingredient in Kant's conception of rational agency, providing one of the ways in which he refers to the spontaneity of the agent.[7]

Kant clarifies this connection between interest and rational agency in a later note in the *Groundwork*, in which he characterizes an interest simply as "that by which reason becomes practical" (Gr 4: 460n; 128). And in light of this, he explicitly affirms what was already implicit in the earlier passage, namely, that nonrational beings do not have interests (although they do have desires or sensuous impulses). Consequently, our ability to have (or take) interests (like, we shall see, our capacity to take a *dis*interested delight in beauty) defines our middling state as finite, sensuously affected, yet also rational, beings, distinct from both the brutes and the deity.

Kant's main concern in both notes, however, is not simply to insist that interests do not derive directly from desires or inclinations, requiring in addition an exercise of practical spontaneity, but rather to introduce the even more radical idea that not all interests stem from desires or inclinations in even this indirect way. Thus, it becomes crucial for Kant to distinguish between two quite distinct types of interest: a "pathological" or empirical interest based on antecedent desires or inclination, and a "practical" or "pure" interest. The latter would amount to an incentive or reason to act that is independent of any desire or need stemming from our sensuous nature and would alone count as a moral interest.[8]

Kant returns to this topic in the *Critique of Practical Reason* in the chapter "On the Incentives of Pure Practical Reason." As the chapter heading indicates, the concern is specifically with the question of how pure practical reason, the faculty that is the source of the moral law, can also motivate. The general answer is that it does so by generating in the minds of finite rational agents a feeling of respect for the law, and this feeling gives moral considerations their motivating force.[9] Within the context of this discussion, Kant returns to the concept of interest, stating that it arises from the concept of an incentive; that it can only be attributed to rational beings; and that "it signifies an *incentive* of the will insofar as it is *represented by reason*" (KpV 5: 79; 83).

The latter phrase marks a significant clarification of the initial formulations in the *Groundwork*, since it suggests that the role of reason common to all interests involves the conceptual representation of a possible state of affairs to be actualized through volition (which is why nonrational animals do not have interests). Similarly, Kant's remark a few lines later that the concept of a maxim is itself based on the concept of interest is likewise a refinement of the *Groundwork's* account (with its ambiguous reference to "principles of reason"), since it indicates that finite rational beings form maxims on the basis of their interests, rather than the reverse, as the earlier account seemed to suggest. Nevertheless, setting aside these details, the account in the second *Critique* is essentially the same as that of the *Groundwork*. For common to both is the understanding of an interest in general as that which moves a rational agent to act, and, therefore, the recognition of the need to isolate and establish the possibility of a pure or moral interest, without which there would be no specifically moral reasons to act, that is, no moral incentive.

From the perspective of the third *Critique*, however, the most notable feature of these discussions of interest is their lack of any explicit reference to existence, which, as we have seen, is precisely the basis on which Kant contrasts interested liking in all its forms with the disinterested liking for the beautiful. Thus, the third *Critique* lumps together precisely what Kant endeavored to distinguish in his major antecedent writings on moral theory, while these writings remain silent regarding the point that he later (in the third *Critique*) emphasizes. This anomaly does not indicate any significant change or inconsistency on Kant's part, however, since it can easily be explained in terms of the radically different concerns of the contrasting discussions of interest.

In order to make this clear and to gain a unified view of Kant's conception of interest, it is useful to consider a passage from the Introduction to the *Metaphysics of Morals* that is subsequent to both the second and third *Critiques* and that may be read as an attempt to connect them. As in the third *Critique,* Kant here focuses on the concept of pleasure, distinguishing a *practical pleasure,* by which is meant one that is necessarily connected with desire for an object, from a merely contemplative pleasure or *inactive delight,* which is not so connected with desire.[10] More simply, the contrast is between a desire-related and a desire-independent pleasure. The latter is identified with the pleasure of taste; and though Kant does not explicitly characterize it as disinterested, he does say that, since it is not necessarily connected with the desire for an object, it is not "at bottom [*im Grunde*] a pleasure in the existence of the object of a representation but is attached only to the representation by itself" (MS 6: 212; 41).

Following the teachings of the second *Critique,* Kant also insists that practical or desire-related pleasure comes in two forms, depending on whether the pleasure is cause or effect of the desire. Pleasure, insofar as it is a cause of desire, is ordinary sensuous pleasure, and the ensuing desire, if habitual, is inclination. Correlatively, if one adopts a general rule connecting such pleasure with the will (faculty of desire), then one has an interest of inclination in whatever satisfies that desire. Thus, to say that I have an inclination for martinis is to say that I have an ongoing desire for them resulting from the fact that I have frequently found their consumption pleasurable. And if I make it my maxim to consume them with some regularity, then I have not merely an inclination but an *interest* (of inclination). By contrast, if the desire or, more properly, the *faculty* of desire, is the cause of the pleasure, then the pleasure is intellectual, since it stems from the faculty of desire or rational will itself. Pleasure in the existence of moral goodness would be of this nature and the ensuing interest an "interest of reason" (MS 6: 212; 41).

Although there is much of importance in this cryptic text, what is of greatest immediate relevance is the connection of both kinds of pleasure (and interest) with volition, since this is what enables us to understand the third *Critique*'s emphasis on the connection between interest and existence. In fact, Kant explicitly affirms such a connection at the very beginning of his discussion in the third *Critique,* stating that an interested liking "always refers at once to our faculty of desire, either as its determining ground or at least as necessarily connected with that determining ground" (KU 5: 204; 45). Presumably, the second disjunct refers to a liking for the morally good based on respect for the moral law.

The main point, however, is that just as all intentional actions aim at some end (a point on which Kant insists in the *Metaphysics of Morals*),[11] so the interests on which these actions are based, whether their source be sensuous inclination or pure moral considerations, are in the realization of the state of affairs projected as the end of the action. But to be interested in the realization of a state of affairs is to be concerned with existence. Consequently, having an interest in something necessarily involves desiring its existence, and this holds true regardless of the nature of this interest.

This, then, is the background of the third *Critique*'s characterization of interest in terms of a liking for (or pleasure in) existence. What is liked is not the mere existence of some object or state of affairs *per se*, but rather its contribution to the attainment of some desired end.[12] What the third *Critique* adds to this story is the radically new idea that there can be a liking that is *not* so connected with the representation of the existence of the object of that liking (in the language of the *Metaphysics of Morals,* one that is a "merely contemplative pleasure or *inactive delight*"), and that the liking for the beautiful fits this description.

II

Given this conception of interest, Kant's ostensible strategy in the first moment of the Analytic of the Beautiful is to determine the peculiar quality of the liking for the beautiful by contrasting it with the interested likings for the agreeable and the good. As such, his procedure has been aptly characterized as a *via negativa*.[13] It is clear, however, that of itself this is insufficient to establish the disinterestedness of the liking for the beautiful. For even granting the interested nature of the other two species of liking and the essential difference between them and the liking for the beautiful, it by no means follows that the latter is disinterested. In order to establish this on the basis of its difference from the likings for the agreeable and the good, it must also be shown that the latter two exhaust the species of interest. Otherwise the possibility remains open that the liking for the beautiful is connected either with a unique aesthetic interest or with some other unspecified interest distinct from that of the agreeable and the good. Strangely enough, Kant does not argue explicitly for this latter thesis, though he clearly recognizes the problem (see KU 5: 205; 46). Accordingly, we shall have to make the argument for him on the basis of the materials he provides. But before that can be attempted, it is first necessary to consider his accounts of the agreeable and the good.

Kant defines the agreeable at the beginning of §3 as "*what the senses like in sensation*" (KU 5: 205; 46). The relation to sensation is clearly intended to contrast with reflection; but rather than develop the contrast between these as he did in the First Introduction, Kant devotes the bulk of this brief section to a discussion of the quite different topic of psychological hedonism. Indeed, it is only in the last paragraph that he gets to the point at issue: the connection between the liking for the agreeable and interest. This connection, he claims,

> is already obvious from the fact that, by mean of sensation, the judgment [of agreeableness] arouses a desire for objects of that kind, so that the lik-

ing presupposes something other than my mere judgment about the object: it presupposes that I have referred the existence of the object to my state insofar as that state is affected by such an object. That is why we say of the agreeable not merely that we *like* it but that it *gratifies* us [*es vergnügt*]. When I speak of the agreeable, I am not granting mere approval [*Beifall*]: the agreeable produces an inclination (KU 5: 207; 48).

There are three points to be noted here. First, we have the claim that the pleasure in the agreeable precedes the desire, rather than the reverse. This anticipates the distinction drawn in the *Metaphysics of Morals* between the two species of practical pleasure, which correspond to two ways in which pleasure and desire can be related (as cause and effect of each other). Only in the case of intellectual pleasure (which is equivalent to a liking for the morally good) does the desire precede the pleasure, and then it is not really desire *per se* but rather, as we have seen, the *faculty* of desire (the will) that is the source of the liking. Conversely, in the case of sensuous desire (for the agreeable), pleasure functions as the source of desire in the perfectly ordinary sense that we desire something precisely because it produces pleasure. Second, the reference to "objects of that kind" reflects the connection between interest and rational representation, that is, a concept of the *kind* of thing one finds agreeable. Although it may be a particular martini that I find agreeable on a particular occasion, this quality will be attributed to every other similarly constituted martini on relevantly similar occasions, because it is expected that they will produce similar pleasant sensations. And this expectation is based on a concept of the kind of thing a martini is. Third, as based on sensation, the liking for the agreeable rests on a causal relationship between the object of one's liking and oneself. The object is deemed agreeable precisely because it produces a pleasant sensation. Furthermore, since such a relationship depends upon the existence of the object of that liking, it is clear that the liking for the agreeable is necessarily connected with existence and, therefore, with interest.

In §4 Kant explores the liking for the good and contrasts it briefly with that for the beautiful. As in the previous case, a considerable portion of the discussion is devoted to a side issue (the difference between the agreeable and the good); but there is also the additional complication of having to distinguish between two species of good (the useful or instrumentally good and the intrinsically or morally good) and showing that each is necessarily connected with an interest.

The starting point is the definition of the good in general as "what, by means of reason, we like through its mere concept" (KU 5: 207; 48). If we like something merely as a means to some end, we regard it as useful or instrumentally good; and if we like it for its own sake, we view it as intrinsically [*an sich*] good. Common to both forms is the connection of the liking with a concept of "what sort of thing the object is supposed to be" [*was der Gegenstand für ein Ding sein solle*] (KU 5: 207; 49), that is, the idea of a purpose it serves (either indirectly as means or directly through itself).

Kant also suggests that this distinguishes the liking for the good (in both forms) from the liking for the beautiful, which does not require a determinate concept of the object and the purpose it serves. Instead, we are told that the latter is based on a reflection regarding an object, which supposedly leads to "some concept or other" [*irgend einem Begriffe*], it being indeterminate which one (KU 5: 207; 49). And, Kant remarks, this dependence on reflection likewise suffices to distinguish the liking for the beautiful from the sensation-based liking for the agreeable.

The reference to reflection points back to the initial account of judgments of beauty as aesthetic judgments of reflection in the First Introduction and forward to the subsequent moments of the Analytic of the Beautiful. What is of immediate concern, however, is the connection of the liking for the good with the concept of a purpose, since this provides the basis for the conclusion that such liking concerns the existence of its object and is thereby connected with an interest. Moreover, Kant insists that, far from being an exception to this, the morally good carries with it the highest interest: "For the good is the object of the will (a faculty of desire that is determined by reason). But to will something and to have a liking for its existence, i.e., to take an interest in it, are identical" (KU 5: 209; 51).

Although this passage is crucial for an understanding of Kant's conception of interest, it requires some qualification. The problem is that the assertion of an equivalence between willing x, liking the existence of x, and taking an interest in x, is too strong, since one may like the existence of and, therefore, take an interest in many things that one merely *wishes* to exist but does not actually *will* to exist, that is, endeavor to bring about. Nevertheless, this does not change anything essential, since, as Kant remarks in the *Metaphysics of Morals,* even a wish is an action of the faculty of desire, albeit one without issue (MS 6: 213; 42). Accordingly, Kant's point can be reformulated as follows: The liking for x concerns the existence of x, and is therefore connected with interest, just in case x is a possible object of the faculty of desire, whether it be actually willed or merely wished for.

III

As already noted, however, it by no means follows from the fact that the liking for the beautiful is distinct from that for the agreeable and the good and that the latter two are necessarily connected with an interest, that this liking is genuinely disinterested. This would follow only if it could also be shown that the agreeable and the good exhaust the species of interest. Thus, one would expect to find an explicit argument for this in §5, where the conclusions from the preceding analysis are supposedly drawn. We find instead, however, that Kant there argues for the quite different thesis that the agreeable, the good, and the beautiful constitute three different species of liking, since they "designate three different relations that representations have to the feeling of pleasure and displeasure" (KU 5: 209–10; 52). But whatever merits this argument may have, it certainly cannot show that the liking for the beautiful must be disinterested.

Nevertheless, Kant does provide us with the resources for arriving at the desired result. The essential points are the already emphasized connection of all interest with the faculty of desire, and the fact that there are only two different ways in which a pleasure (and an interest is a pleasure in the existence of something) can be related to the faculty of desire of a rational agent: either as the ground or as the product thereof. These correspond to the two species of practical (volition-related) pleasure distinguished in the *Metaphysics of Morals*, as well as to the distinction between the agreeable and the morally good drawn in the third *Critique*. Nor is the instrumentally good an exception to this. Since the latter is not liked for itself, but solely on the basis of the end it serves, such a liking must be subsumed under either the agreeable or the morally good (depending on the nature of the end). Thus, it follows from Kant's analysis that all interests fall into one of the above two categories; and since the liking for the beautiful has been shown to be distinct from both, it follows that it must be disinterested.

Given the connection between interest and the faculty of desire or will, the same result can also be derived directly from Kant's motivational dualism. As is clear from *Groundwork* I, Kant holds that all incentives or reasons to act stem from either duty or inclination, with the latter understood in a broad sense to include any stimulus to action that stems from our sensuous, as opposed to our rational, nature.[14] But as the generic sources of reasons to act, these would also be the sources of corresponding interests. For as Kant notes in the *Critique of Practical Reason*, "From the concept of an incentive comes that of an *interest*," which, as we have seen, is there defined as "an incentive of the will insofar as it is represented by reason" (KpV 5: 79; 83). Consequently, there should be precisely as many types of interest as there are species of incentive for finite rational agents, namely two.

These considerations also seem to underlie the argument in §5, particularly Kant's claim that of the three kinds of liking, only that for the beautiful is *free* as well as disinterested (KU 5: 210; 52). Indeed, it is free precisely because it is disinterested. In characterizing the liking for the beautiful as "free," Kant is not, of course, suggesting that one can freely decide whether or not to find a particular object beautiful. The point is rather that this liking, in contrast to the liking for both the agreeable and the good, is not compelled by any factors extrinsic to the act of contemplation itself, that is, "by any interest, whether of sense or of reason" (KU 5: 210; 52). In the case of the agreeable, the extrinsic factor is our sensuous nature and, therefore, ultimately the laws of nature; in the case of the good, it is the moral law which "compels" approval (if not obedience).

Finally, Kant spells out this notion of a free (because interest-independent) liking in terms of the presence or absence of a need. All interest, he tells us, either presupposes or gives rise to a need, "and because interest is the basis that determines approval, it makes the judgment about the object unfree" (KU 5: 210; 52). Clearly, Kant is here using the term "need" [*Bedürfniss*] in a much broader sense than usual. Typically, Kant connects needs with our sensuous nature, the basic idea being that this nature is the source of needs that often conflict with moral requirements. Here, by contrast, the suggestion is that there is also a need stemming from pure practical reason, and that it is the source of the lack of freedom with respect to moral commands. As is clear from the context, however, "need" here signifies merely the rational necessity of obedience, and not some kind of psychological exigency, "For where the moral law speaks we are objectively no longer free to select what we must do" (KU 5: 210; 52). That the liking for the beautiful is independent of this moral need, as well as any need arising from our sensuous nature, is both the meaning of its disinterestedness and the ground of the autonomy of the pure judgment of taste.

IV

Although this analysis may help fill in the gaps in Kant's argument and show how the disinterestedness thesis follows from his basic assumptions regarding interest, it obviously does little or nothing to make this thesis plausible in its own right. For when all is said and done, we are still left with the simple question of how someone who takes pleasure in beauty can be indifferent to the existence of the objects that are the source of this pleasure.

The short answer is that one cannot be indifferent, but that, appearances to the contrary, the disinterestedness thesis does not really require that one be. At least there is nothing in the considerations underlying this thesis that entails any such untoward consequence. As a first step in showing this, let us consider the explication [*Erklärung*] of taste as "the ability to judge an object, or a way of representing it, by means of a liking or disliking *devoid of all interest*" [*ohne alles Interesse*] (KU 5: 211; 53), which Kant presents as the conclusion to the first moment.

This explication indicates that the disinterestedness thesis concerns the quality of the liking (or disliking) *by means of which* an object is deemed beautiful (or nonbeautiful).[15] In other words, it is the determination of aesthetic value that must be independent of interest, because any such dependence would make this determination subserve some other value, thereby undermining both the autonomy and the purity of taste. Moreover, Kant had already made this clear in the previously cited passage from §2, when he remarked that "Everyone has to admit that if a judgment about beauty is mingled [*mengt*] with the least interest then it is very partial and not a pure judgment of taste" (KU 5: 205; 46). And, by way of announcing his strategy for the remainder of the first moment, he remarks at the end of this section that the best way to elucidate this claim is to contrast the "pure, disinterested liking that occurs in a judgment of taste" with a liking connected with interest" (KU 5: 205; 46).

Up to this point, Kant's position seems reasonably unproblematic. A liking based, even in part, on an antecedent interest would not yield a pure judgment of taste. This much, at least, it seems reasonable to claim with Kant that "everyone has to admit." The real difficulties begin, however, with the notorious note appended to the latter claim, in which Kant states that judgments of taste are not only not based on an interest, but also, in contradistinction to pure moral judgments, do not of themselves even give rise to one. This leads to the question of the connection between the being-based-on and giving-rise-to an interest distinction and the forementioned condition of the purity of a judgment of taste. The usual reading is to take this condition as applying only to the first disjunct. Thus, commentators tend to admit that Kant is on relatively solid ground in ruling out the possibility that judgments of taste are *based on* an interest, since this is clearly incompatible with their purity. But they then proceed to point out that this provides no warrant for denying the apparently obvious fact that the experience of beauty can, and frequently does, give rise to a genuinely aesthetic interest. Consequently, it is argued that in rejecting the latter possibility, Kant must be deeply confused, perhaps as a result of his mistaken belief that it is only in society that one can become interested in the beautiful.[16]

We need to assume that Kant is confused, however, only if it is also assumed that giving rise to an interest can have nothing to do with the grounds of a judgment. Moreover, the fact that Kant did not believe this to be necessarily true is indicated in the very note under question, through the contrast of judgments of taste with pure moral judgments. The latter, Kant contends, though *disinterested,* that is, not based on an interest, are nevertheless *interesting,* that is, give rise to an interest, which seems closely related to the claim in §4 that, as the object of a will determined by reason, the morally good "carries with it the highest interest" (KU 5: 209; 51).

That pure moral judgments give rise to an interest or, equivalently, that the morally good (which is determined by a pure moral judgment) carries with it an interest, is not simply an incidental feature of our moral experience. On the contrary, it is a necessary condition of the moral law's claim upon us. For unless the law carried with it an incentive, and therefore an interest, it would be merely a theoretical proposition about the mode of behavior of some putative perfectly rational beings, and in no way a practical, that is, action-guiding principle for finite, imperfectly rational agents such as ourselves. In short, it is only because the law generates an interest that pure reason can be practical. But this entails that its capacity to give rise to an interest is at least partly constitutive of our "liking" for it, which Kant terms "respect."

This suggests that Kant added the troublesome requirement that judgments of taste not give rise to an interest in order to distinguish them from pure moral judgments. More importantly, it also suggests that his reason for doing so is to underscore the point that giving rise to an interest cannot be a condition of the liking for the beautiful itself (as it is for the morally good). If it were, the purely contemplative nature of this liking would be lost, and with it all pretense of purity, since it would have to be connected with volition. Furthermore, if this analysis is correct, it creates the space for a distinction between a liking that incidentally gives rise to an interest and one whose very nature depends on its doing so.

Admittedly, Kant does not explicitly draw such a distinction, though he certainly seems to hint at it in the previously cited passage from the *Metaphysics of Morals,* where he states that the pleasure of taste is not "at bottom" a pleasure in the existence of an object. By introducing this qualification, Kant appears to be suggesting that the pleasure of taste may, without sacrificing its disinterested character, involve a liking for the existence of an object in an incidental way. But whether or not this captures Kant's intent in this passage, the fact remains that some such distinction is perfectly compatible with his overall conception of interest.

Finally, with this distinction in place, there is nothing to prevent Kant from acknowledging that a liking for the beautiful may produce an interest (construed as a liking for existence) in many of the ways noted in the literature. In short, someone with taste can, without detriment to the disinterested nature of the judgment itself, and therefore its purity, take pleasure in the fact that beautiful objects exist, that there are institutions such as museums that provide ready access to these objects, and the like. What is precluded is merely that such interest serves as part of the determining ground of the liking itself. But clearly it does not, since the fact that one derives pleasure from visiting museums is not the reason that one appreciates the beauty of the works it contains. On the contrary, it is precisely because the experience of beauty is inherently pleasurable (apart from any interest) that the latter (interested) pleasure arises.

Although this answers the second question regarding the disinterestedness thesis posed at the beginning of the chapter, namely how a liking for the beautiful may be viewed as disinterested, it might still be argued that it is inadequate inasmuch as it appears to leave the first question unaddressed. The latter, it will be recalled, involved a general worry about the possibility of a disinterested liking as such, on the grounds that since every pleasure involves an endeavor to preserve itself, it must likewise involve an interest in the continued existence of whatever is responsible for this state. And it seems of little avail to argue that the liking for the beautiful fits the description, if the very idea of a disinterested liking turns out to be incoherent.

The short and obvious retort to this line of objection is that the fact that pleasure in the beautiful fits this description already shows that the idea of a disinterested pleasure is not incoherent. At least it does so if we add the noncontroversial premise that there is such a thing as pleasure in the beautiful, together with the admittedly more controversial result of the argument of the first moment that this pleasure is distinct from that of both the agreeable and the good. Moreover, we shall see in Chapter 13 that a similar claim is likewise made about the sublime, which is also based on an aesthetic judgment of reflection.[17]

Given the preceding analysis of interest, however, it is also possible to respond to the objection in a somewhat more direct manner. Here it is essential to keep in mind that according to the conception of interest with which Kant operates, what makes a liking (or pleasure) interested is its connection with some aim or desire distinct from the liking itself.[18] Furthermore, as the preceding analysis indicates, the latter is the case only if the liking either involves the satisfaction of an antecedent desire (as with the liking for the agreeable) or gives rise to an interest that is at least partly constitutive of the liking (as with the liking for the morally good). Consequently, merely endeavoring to remain in a pleasurable mental state does not of itself make this liking interested, in Kant's sense. This would follow only if the endeavor were itself (at least partly) constitutive of the liking. But this is clearly not the case. For we endeavor to remain in a mental state because it is pleasurable; it is not pleasurable because we endeavor to remain in it.

5

SUBJECTIVE UNIVERSALITY, THE UNIVERSAL VOICE, AND THE HARMONY OF THE FACULTIES

The second moment has the dual task of explicating the "quantity" of judgments of taste, which Kant characterizes as a universality that is not based on concepts, and uncovering the subjective ground of such universality. The latter, as we have already seen, is located in the harmony (or lack thereof) of the imagination and understanding in their free play. Although Kant does not refer explicitly to *pure* judgments of taste within this moment, it is clear that he has them in mind, since, among judgments of taste, these are the ones that are thought to involve universality. Since the lack of a concept is a direct consequence of the aesthetic nature of such judgments, it is not really argued for again here. Nevertheless, we shall see that it plays a crucial role in both the explication of the universality thesis and the determination of the subjective ground of this universality.

The present chapter follows the structure of Kant's argument in the second moment and is composed of four parts, each one corresponding to a section of this moment. The first part analyzes the highly controversial derivation of the universality claim from the interest-independence affirmed in the first moment (§6). The second examines Kant's attempt to confirm the thesis that judgments of beauty necessarily involve such a claim through a comparison with the agreeable and the good (§7). The third considers Kant's account of the merely subjective nature of the universality in question, its connection with the idea of a universal voice, and the problem of erroneous judgments of taste that arises from the introduction of this idea (§8). Finally, the fourth discusses Kant's purported "key to the critique of taste," by means of which he grounds the universal communicability of judgments of taste in the harmony of the faculties in free play (§9). As already noted in Chapter 3, the latter constitutes the contribution of the second moment to the determination of the *quid facti*. Consequently, it will be a major focus of attention in this chapter.

I

Kant begins the second moment by declaring straight out that the explication of the beautiful as the object of a universal liking not based on concepts "can be inferred from the preceding explication of it as object of a liking devoid of all interest" (KU 5: 211; 53). This inference has come under sharp attack, however, particularly from Paul Guyer. In order to facilitate an adjudication of the issues involved, I shall first cite the argument in full; then present the gist of Guyer's criticisms, which may be taken as representative of the critical response; and then attempt to defend the argument against these criticisms. The argument goes as follows:

> For if someone likes something and is conscious that he himself does so without any interest, then he cannot help judging that it must contain a basis for being liked [that holds] for everyone [*das kann derselbe nicht anders als so beurtheilen, dass es ein Grund des Wohlgefallens für jedermann enthalten müsse*]. He must believe that he is justified in requiring [*zuzumuthen*] a similar liking from everyone because he cannot discover, underlying this liking, any private conditions, on which only he might be dependent, so that he must regard it as based on what he can presuppose in everyone else as well. He cannot discover such private conditions because his liking is not based on any inclination he has (nor any other considered interest whatever): rather, the judging person feels completely *free* as regards the liking he accords the object. Hence he will talk about the beautiful as if beauty were a characteristic of the object and the judgment were logical . . . even though in fact the judgment is only aesthetic and refers the object's representation merely to the subject. He will talk in this way because the judgment does resemble a logical judgment inasmuch as we may presuppose it to be valid for everyone. (KU 5: 211; 53–4)

Guyer dismisses this alleged "deduction" of universality from disinterestedness as a *non sequitur* on the familiar grounds of a neglected alternative. And, as a final twist of the knife, he raises the specter of something like an is–ought confusion. As he puts it:

> From the fact that a delight is not caused by any interest or desire, it does not follow that it is valid for everyone. It might be entirely accidental or based on some other kind of merely private condition. Universality cannot be deduced from disinterestedness alone, nor does it follow that in requiring disinterestedness of a pleasure one is requiring that it be universal; one may simply be requiring a source other than interest, quite apart from any consideration of intersubjective validity at all. Indeed, one might maintain that unless the requirement of disinterestedness is already a normative requirement for intersubjective acceptability, trying to deduce such a requirement from disinterestedness confuses a factual matter with a normative requirement.[1]

Before responding to this critique, which underlies Guyer's already discussed reconstruction of the Analytic, it is instructive to consider briefly the extremely guarded nature of Kant's language in the passage in question. Rather than speaking simply of a logical inference from disinterestedness to universality, Kant seems to be making a psychological claim concerning the mind-set of someone who takes something to be beautiful on the basis of a putatively disinterested liking. Thus, he uses locutions such as "he cannot help judging," "he must believe that he is justified," "he must regard it as based," and so forth, in order to describe this mind-set. This could be taken as an indication of Kant's own doubts about the cogency of the inference in question, which might seem to support Guyer's critique. Or, alternatively, it could be viewed as an expression of skepticism regarding the possibility of determining with certainty that a given liking really is disinterested. In the latter case, the doubt would not concern the hypothetical inference itself, but the determination of the truth of the antecedent.[2]

Although it is impossible to decide the matter with any certainty, I believe it highly likely that Kant had *both* of these caveats in mind, and that the recognition of this is essential to a proper interpretation, not only of the second moment but also of the Analytic of the Beautiful as a whole. The reason for the second caveat seems clear and largely explains Kant's previously noted skepticism about the possibility of determining whether a given judgment of taste is pure. We shall be returning to this point later in this and in subsequent chapters. For the present, however, the first caveat must be the focus of attention. Why, we may well ask, would Kant begin the second moment with an argument he knew to be dubious, and then use it to derive the essential features of his conception of taste?

The answer I propose is that Kant did not view the argument as dubious, but rather as merely preliminary and therefore as insufficient. Consequently, it is this insufficiency that Kant's guarded language is (at least in part) designed to express. The argument's function, on this reading, is merely to build a bridge from disinterestedness to the normative concerns of the Analytic and Deduction. In order to fulfill this bridging function, the inference from disinterestedness to universality must be viewed as a reasonable and natural one, but not necessarily as one that must be simply accepted as it stands. What makes the inference problematic is the peculiar nature of this putative universality: its independence from concepts. Kant underscores this in the second half of §6, and it leads to the characterization of the universality as "subjective" (KU 5: 212; 54).

My suggestion, then, is that Kant fully realized that the notion of such a nonconceptual, feeling-based universality is inherently problematic, and that before it can be accepted he must offer a coherent account of the conditions of its possibility.[3] Lacking this, we have merely the conditional: The independence of interest of the liking in a judgment of beauty entails a claim of universality, assuming that such a universality is even possible. But since this is still quite removed from Guyer's claim that Kant simply based his key move to universality on a *non sequitur,* it remains necessary to respond to his objection. For if it holds, Kant's argument clearly lacks even the conditional validity that seems required, if it is to serve the modest, introductory function here assigned to it.

In formulating this response, the first step is to note that once moral interest is ruled out as a possible ground of the liking for the beautiful, as it already is by the argument of the first moment and the stipulated aesthetic nature of judgments of taste, it follows that interest-independence is at least a *necessary* condition for any universality claim regarding such a liking. For, clearly, such a claim cannot be based on any merely private interest (a point which even Guyer concedes), and the only non- private interest available (moral interest) has already been eliminated.[4] Consequently, the question reduces to whether the negative feature of not being grounded in an interest is also a *sufficient* condition for claiming universality for one's liking (again assuming that such a universality is possible). Why can't a liking be disinterested (in the sense indicated in Chapter 4) and yet be of merely private validity, lacking any basis for assuming that it could be shared by others?

This, in essence, is Guyer's question and, at first glance at least, it seems to be a perfectly reasonable one. Let us, then, pursue the matter further by asking on what such a putatively disinterested, yet nonuniversally projectable, liking could be based. Unfortunately, Guyer's suggestions on this score are not particularly informative. As we have seen, he tells us merely that "It might be entirely accidental, or based on some other kind of merely private condition." Surely, if this supposedly neglected alternative is to be viewed as a viable one, we need to learn much more about what it involves than Guyer tells us.

More importantly, the suggestions that he does offer, vague as they may be, are only examples of disinterested liking by stipulation, and therefore beg the question against Kant. Apparently, what he has in mind is some personal idiosyncrasy or quirk, which might lead one, for example, to like (or dislike) all paintings containing a certain shade of red. Such an aesthetic response is surely possible (indeed, it is all too common), and could no doubt be attributed to a host of different contingent factors: physiological, environmental, cultural, and so forth. Moreover, as such, it obviously has no claim to universality. Nevertheless, granting all of this, the question remains: Is such a response *disinterested,* given Kant's account of interest?

The answer, I think, is clearly negative. For all of the examples of nonuniversally projectable likings that Guyer adduces (as well as any others that one might add) fall under the general rubric of the agreeable. Consequently, it seems difficult to avoid the conclusion that the "merely private condition" to which Guyer obliquely refers must be characterized as an inclination in the broad sense, that is, some kind of desire or aversion connected with our sensuous nature.[5] But this, in turn, suggests that an idiosyncratic liking could be due only to an idiosyncratic inclination of some sort and therefore to an idiosyncratic interest. There is nothing in Kant's account that rules out such interests, and their possibility may, in fact, be part of the reason for the dubitability of any assumption of disinterestedness.

Admittedly, showing the inadequacy of Guyer's alleged counterexamples is not equivalent to demonstrating the positive thesis that the interest-independence of a judgment of taste is sufficient as well as necessary for its claim to universality. Nevertheless, it does strongly suggest that the lack of universality of a putative judgment of taste is *always* to be explained on the basis of an underlying interest; and this is equivalent to the thesis in question.

Finally, given these considerations, the remaining portion of Guyer's objection to the move from disinterestedness to universality, namely, that Kant either already builds a normative sense into the idea of disinterestedness (which would make the move to universality trivial) or that he conflates factual with normative matters, can be dealt with expeditiously. Certainly, Guyer is correct in suggesting that disinterestedness is fundamentally a factual matter, even though it is also a necessary condition of the purity of a judgment of taste. For whether or not one's liking for an object depends on an interest is a question of psychological fact, and this is not undermined by the epistemological thesis that any claim of interest-independence is dubitable. Similarly, he is correct in noting that universality, as Kant here construes it, is a normative notion, since it involves the idea of universal validity. Nevertheless, far from either assuming such validity in the first place or attempting to derive it from a purely factual premise, Kant is not at this point making any claim for universal validity at all. In fact, he could not do so for the very reasons already noted.

How, then, are we take Kant's argument in §6? My suggestion is that it be viewed as an analytic argument, similar in both form and spirit to the claim that if I take myself as free, then I also take myself as under the moral law, which constitutes the first and essential part of the "Reciprocity Thesis," that is, the thesis that "freedom and unconditional practical law reciprocally imply each other" (KpV 5: 29; 29–30). That argument is analytic and hypothetical, since it does not pretend to establish either that we are free or that we are subject to the moral law, but merely that insofar as we regard ourselves as free, we are also rationally constrained to regard ourselves as subject to the moral law.[6] Similarly, the present claim is that if I regard my liking as free (in the sense indicated in §5), then I am likewise constrained to assume that it must have *some* intersubjectively valid ground. But this inference may turn out to be illusory if no such ground is forthcoming, and this cannot be decided unless it can first be determined what such a ground (assuming its possibility) would be like. The latter is the major concern of the remainder of the second moment, but before turning to that topic we must consider the contributions of §7 and §8, which jointly play an important transitional role.

II

§7 contains a relatively straightforward attempt to support the claim that judgments of taste do, in fact, inherently involve a universality claim. It likewise constitutes a virtually new beginning, since after deducing the putative universality of such judgments from their disinterestedness, Kant now appeals directly to what we would now call the "logic" of judgments of beauty. Just as in the first moment he attempted to articulate what is distinctive about the "quality" of the liking for the beautiful (its disinterestedness) by comparing it with the liking for the agreeable and the good, so he now uses the same terms of comparison to contrast the scope or "quantity" of their respective claims.

In reality, however, except for a final sentence in which Kant acknowledges that judgments about the good also involve a "rightful" claim of universal validity, albeit one that is based on a concept (KU 5: 213; 56), the entire discussion is devoted to a contrast between claims for the beautiful and the agreeable. Moreover, in drawing this contrast, Kant not only equates the universality of the former with its universal validity (a normative notion), but he also asserts that this claim is connected with a demand on others for agreement with one's assessment. Thus, Kant brings into the discussion of the second moment considerations that more properly pertain to the fourth, which, as has been already noted, undoubtedly contributes to the tendency prevalent in the literature to regard these two moments as making virtually the same point.

To begin with, Kant takes it as noncontroversial that claims about the agreeable make no pretence to universal validity. "Everyone acknowledges," he remarks, "that his judgment, which he bases on a private feeling and by which he says that he likes some object, is by the same token confined to his own person" (KU 5: 212; 55). In short, it is generally admitted that, in spite of a widespread *de facto* agreement about some objects, there is no genuine normativity in such matters. Consequently, in the case of the agreeable, a dispute about taste is logically out of order, amounting (although Kant does not put it this way) to a kind of category mistake.

Appealing again to linguistic usage, Kant further contends that the situation with regard to judgments of beauty is quite different. Here it is the expression "It is beautiful for me" that is out of order, a misuse of terms, as it were. For, as Kant puts it, if someone declares something to be beautiful, "then he requires the same liking from others; he then judges not just for himself but for everyone, and speaks of beauty as if it were a property of things" (KU 5: 212; 55–6).

Of course, this latter way of speaking about beauty is likewise in a sense out of order, since beauty is not such an objective property. Kant's point, however, is that the language of beauty (as contrasted with that of the agreeable) is inherently normative, involving censure and demand. In fact, anticipating the later discussion of the significance of taste, Kant even suggests that the demand extends from agreement about the aesthetic value of a particular object to the possession of taste. Thus, taste itself becomes something that one ought to have (KU 5: 213; 56).[7]

Strictly speaking, however, to claim that a liking for the beautiful purports to be universally valid, since it supposedly stems from a condition that is not private but common to all, is not equivalent to claiming that a judgment of beauty places a demand on others that they agree with one's assessment. In spite of its presumption of normativity, I have suggested in Chapter 3 and shall reiterate in Chapter Seven that the former pertains to the "content" of the judgment of taste, constituting an essential part of what one means when one claims to find something beautiful. The latter, by contrast, concerns the evaluative force or bearing on others of the *already formed judgment,* and is thus not itself part of its content.

Nevertheless, it must once again be acknowledged that these two features or "moments" are closely related. For not only is such putative universality a necessary condition for requiring the agreement of others; it is also a short step from asserting it through one's judgment to requiring or demanding such agreement. Consequently, it is easy to see why Kant would conflate these notions, particularly when he is concerned to contrast the normative language of beauty with that of the agreeable. But this does not require us to follow him in this conflation; and, as I shall try to show, it is possible to reconstruct the argument in a manner that enables us to avoid doing so.

III

The task of §8 is to examine more carefully the peculiar species of universality that pertains to judgments of taste by contrasting it with the familiar, conceptually based, universality operative in cognitive judgments. What we need to know first of all is what a merely subjective, nonconceptually based universality would be like, and only then will we be in a position to investigate the conditions of its possibility. Accordingly, Kant begins §8 by noting the unique nature of this special kind of universality and its significance for the transcendental philosopher. Reflecting directly on the line of thought that led to the original idea of a critique of taste, Kant remarks: "This universality requires a major effort on his [the transcendental philosopher's] part if he is to discover its origin, but it compensates him for this by revealing to him a property of our cognitive faculty which without this analysis would have remained unknown" (KU 5: 213; 57).[8]

Nevertheless, rather than turning directly to the task at hand, namely, an examination of the nature of this universality, Kant devotes a lengthy paragraph to a reiteration of the result already attained in the preceding section, that is, to making it clear "that this claim to universal validity belongs so essentially to a judgment by which we declare something to be *beautiful* that it would not occur to anyone to use this term without thinking of universal validity" (KU 5: 214; 57). This passage, which was previously cited in Chapter 3, is a significant text for the interpretation advocated here; for it suggests that Kant does, in fact, view the claim of universal validity as part of the "content," that is, as an inherent structural feature of a pure judgment of taste, which, as such, is distinguishable from its modality.

Once again, however, though his proper concern at this point is merely with the former, Kant interjects the latter into the story as well. Thus, in contrasting judgments of the agreeable (here connected with the "taste of sense") and judgments of beauty (connected with the "taste of reflection"), Kant asserts that the former are generally construed as merely private [*Privaturtheile*], whereas the latter are "put forward as having general validity [*gemeingültige*] (as being public [*publike*])" (KU 5: 214; 57). And given this distinction, which Kant presents as embedded in our ordinary, prephilosophical understanding, he proceeds to remark that whereas in the case of the former, people generally do not require the agreement of others, even though there is often a fairly widespread *de facto* agreement, in the case of the latter, there is an acceptance of the principle that agreement is to be demanded, even though there may be great disagreement regarding particular instances. As Kant puts it, "What the people who make these judgments [judgments of beauty] dispute about is not whether such a claim is possible; they are merely unable to agree, in particular cases, on the correct way to apply this ability" (KU 5: 214; 58).

Having established to his satisfaction that judgments of beauty, as ordinarily construed, make a universality claim, which he continues to equate with the demand for agreement, Kant finally turns in the third paragraph of §8 to the analysis of this peculiar species of universality. He begins by noting that a universality not resting on concepts of the object cannot be a logical universality at all, but can only be an aesthetic one, which he further claims must be subjective rather than objective (KU 5: 214; 58).

As we have already seen, however, this aesthetic universality differs from the familiar logical variety in more than its subjectivity or reference to the sphere of judging subjects. For whereas the latter does truly concern the *quantity* of a judgment, the former is clearly a matter of its *validity*, which again is a normative notion and, as such, quite distinct from the notion of quantity. Thus, the propositions "All men are mortal," "Some men are mortal," and "Socrates is mortal" have different logical quantities, but they are nonetheless all equally universally valid. In fact, Kant insists that all judgments of taste have the same logical quantity, namely singularity (not universality). The paradigm is the judgment: "This rose is beautiful"; and its generalization "All roses are beautiful" is, according to Kant, no longer really an aesthetic judgment, "but . . . a logical judgment based on an aesthetic one" (KU 5: 215; 59).

Kant characterizes this subjective or aesthetic universality first as "general validity" [*Gemeingültigkeit*], and then as "subjective universal validity" (KU 5: 214–15; 58). By the latter is understood the validity of a feeling with respect to the entire sphere of judging subjects, as contrasted with the objective validity of a predicate with respect to the entire sphere of objects falling under the subject-concept. And appealing to that contrast, Kant suggests that "if the judgment is valid for everything contained under a given concept, then it is also valid for everyone who represents an object by this concept" (KU 5: 215; 58).

The latter is presumably an attempt to bring together the quite distinct notions of logical universality and universal validity. But if this is so, it is clearly unsuccessful. For singular and particular cognitive judgments, which relate a predicate merely to one or to some of the objects falling under the subject-concept, likewise assume the validity of these judgments for everyone who applies the predicate to the appropriate sphere of objects falling under that concept. Thus, contrary to Kant's apparent suggestion, there is no direct correlation between the two types of universality.

Nevertheless, neither this nor the previously noted conflation of the moments of universality and necessity prove fatal to Kant's analysis, nor even to his attempt to structure the Analytic of the Beautiful on the basis of the table of logical functions from the first *Critique*. For one thing, we have seen that it is possible (indeed necessary) to distinguish between the claims of the second and fourth moments, even though Kant fails to do so consistently. For another, Kant's central point that judgments of beauty inherently involve a universality claim for a feeling remains in place, even though this species of universality is further removed from the logical variety than some of Kant's remarks and the projected parallelism of the moments of logical and aesthetic judgments might suggest. Throughout this section, Kant is obviously struggling for a way to characterize this universality that preserves both the aesthetic nature of the judgment and the subjectivity that is inseparable from it. Moreover, he does in fact arrive at a more adequate way of doing so with the appeal to the idea of a "universal voice" [*allgemeine Stimme*].

As is clear from the manner in which Kant uses it, the idea of a universal voice functions as the aesthetic analogue of Rousseau's general will; that is to say, it serves as the postulated source of the putative universality of a judgment of taste.[9] Thus, Kant remarks that even though our liking for the beautiful is not based on a concept, but is instead the result of a direct perception ("just as if . . . it depended on that sensation"), yet, "if we then call the object beautiful, we believe we have a universal voice, and lay claim to the agreement of everyone" (KU 5: 216; 59–60). The operative term here is "believe." Since Kant is still concerned merely with an analytic connection between a claim of taste and the assumption of universality, there is no inference from the fact that one believes that one is speaking with a universal voice to the conclusion that one's liking for something amounts to anything more than a merely personal preference. Like Rousseau's general will, the universal voice does not err, since it constitutes the very norm of correctness.[10] But also as in Rousseau, there is no assurance that one actually is speaking with such a voice. Kant expresses this complex point by suggesting that the universal voice is merely "postulated" in a judgment of taste and that it is "only an idea" (KU 5: 216; 60). By characterizing it as an idea, Kant underscores the purely normative status of this conception; and by stating that it is postulated in a judgment of taste, he indicates that such a judgment presupposes or postulates the condition of its own possibility.[11]

This, in turn, gives rise to two essential questions: the possible ground for such an idea, and, since the universal voice is always correct, the explanation of the possibility of erroneous judgments of taste. Kant begins his consideration of the first question in §9, but deals briefly with the second at the end of §8. Kant's discussion of the latter topic is extremely cryptic, and we are not yet in a position to deal with the issue systematically. Nevertheless, the text is of considerable importance, since it is one of Kant's few explicit discussions of what might be termed the epistemology of taste. The relevant text goes as follows:

> Whether someone who believes he is making a judgment of taste is in fact judging in conformity with that idea [of a universal voice] may be uncertain; but by using the term beauty he indicates that he is at least referring his judging to that idea, and hence that he intends it to be a judgment of taste [*das es ein Geschmacksurtheil sein solle*]. For himself, however, he can obtain certainty on this point [*davon*], by merely being conscious that he is separating whatever belongs to the agreeable and the good from the liking that remains to him after that. It is only for this that he counts on every-

one's assent, and he would under these conditions be justified in this claim, if only he did not often [*öfter*] fail to observe these conditions and so make an erroneous judgment of taste. (KU 5: 216; 60).

For present purposes, the crucial question raised by this passage is the referent of *"davon."* In fact, Ted Cohen has suggested that there are four possible referents of the term, each of which is consistent with the grammar of the sentence. According to him these are: (1) intending to make (or "lay down") a judgment of taste, (2) actually making (or "laying down") such a judgment, (3) referring one's judgment to the idea of a universal voice, or (4) judging in conformity with the idea of a universal voice.[12] Since attempting to make a judgment of taste and referring one's judgment to the idea of a universal voice are basically equivalent (Kant has been arguing that such a reference is implicit in a claim of taste), and actually making such a judgment and judging in conformity with the idea are likewise equivalent, the basic interpretive options can be reduced to two: trying to make or actually succeeding in making a judgment of taste. Nevertheless, this still leaves us with a significant ambiguity, which requires some resolution at this point.

Perhaps the most natural reading of the passage is that what one is certain of is merely the intention of making a judgment of taste (which entails the reference of one's judging to the idea of a universal voice). Since this leaves open the possibility that one has not, in fact, succeeded, an erroneous judgment of taste is an erroneous second-order judgment that one has actually made a first-order judgment of taste.

Apparently counting against this reading, however, is the claim that the certainty in question is supposedly arrived at through a consciousness that one has, in effect, filtered out of one's liking everything that pertains to the agreeable and the good, leaving as residue nothing but the disinterested liking for the beautiful. Since this makes it difficult to see what room is left for error regarding the nature of one's judgment, it suggests that the certainty concerns the fact that one has actually made a judgment of taste or, equivalently, judged in conformity with the idea of a universal voice. According to on this reading, then, the only remaining question, and therefore the locus of any possible uncertainty, is whether the judgment of taste is correct. I truly judge (by taste) x to be beautiful, but I may simply be wrong.

Setting aside the fact that it conflicts with the interpretation offered here, this second reading involves at least two serious (if not fatal) difficulties. First, it undermines the analogy between the universal voice and Rousseau's general will, which clearly seems intended by the text, since it entails that a judgment in conformity with this idea might be incorrect (which could never be said of a judgment in conformity with the general will). Second, it conflicts with what Kant himself says in the Deduction, where, as we shall see in more detail later, he emphasizes the extreme difficulty, if not the impossibility, of determining what this reading suggests we can be fully certain about.[13]

Although I can hardly claim to be able to resolve definitively all of the textual difficulties that arise at this point, I do think that considerable light can be shed on the problem by the introduction of the distinction between a judgment of taste *simpliciter* and a *pure* judgment. Moreover, since this distinction is one on which Kant himself insists (even though he does not appeal to it here), such a procedure seems unobjectionable.

To begin with, this distinction enables us to disambiguate the text in question by taking it to be saying that we can be certain about having made a judgment of taste and, perhaps even of having tried to have made a pure judgment, but we can never be certain that we have succeeded in making the latter. Accordingly, my consciousness of having separated out from my liking everything pertaining to the agreeable and the good concerns merely the *attempt* to make a pure judgment of taste. Being a sincere and discriminating lover of the beautiful, I make every effort to do this, because I recognize that it is a necessary condition of the conformity of my judgment to the universal voice. But, alas, I can never be certain that I have succeeded. For no matter how careful I may have been, there always remains the possibility either that my judgment has been corrupted by some quirky and unnoticed liking (perhaps of the kind suggested by Guyer in his critique of the argument of §6), or that I have simply failed to abstract completely from the factors that I believe myself to have set aside. In either not very unlikely event, I have certainly made a judgment of taste (a claim of liking or disliking based on feeling) and have attempted to make a pure judgment, but I have simply failed with regard to the latter. Accordingly, the error is not, as Cohen suggests, in falsely believing that I have made a judgment of taste at all (it's difficult to conceive how one can be confused about that), but in claiming that my *de facto* judgment is pure.

This reading can be further bolstered by the obvious parallel with the Kantian account of morality. As is well known, Kant insists that the categorical imperative requires that we act not only according to, but also from, duty, that is, that the moral necessity of an act be the sole (or at least sufficient) ground for its performance. Notoriously, however, Kant also insists that we can never be certain that we have actually acted from duty alone; for no matter how conscientious we may be, the possibility always remains open that we were moved to act by some underlying inclination, rather than the pure thought of duty.[14] Analogously, then, we may (indeed, should) strive for aesthetic purity, which involves the sincere effort to abstract from all extraneous, that is, interested, grounds of liking, even though we can never be certain that we have succeeded in attaining it.[15] Moreover, as I shall argue in more detail later in this study, it is precisely such a view that is required by Kant's overall theory.

IV

According to its heading, §9 is concerned with the question of whether in a judgment of taste, the feeling of pleasure precedes the judging of the object or the judging precedes the pleasure. At first sight this might seem like a puzzling question, which stands in no essential connection with the preceding account. Nevertheless, a little reflection makes it apparent that it is really concerned with the sought for ground of the pleasure that is claimed in the judgment of taste to be universally valid. Indeed, Kant immediately underscores the point by telling us that the solution of this problem constitutes nothing less than "the key to the critique of taste" (KU 5: 216; 61).

The reason that it is the key is given in the succeeding paragraph, which is reminiscent of the famous appeal to the Copernican analogy in the formulation of the problem of *a priori* knowledge in the Preface to the second edition of the *Critique of Pure Reason*. There Kant had argued that an explication of the possibility of *a priori* knowledge is not forthcoming on the assumption that our knowledge must conform to objects, since any such knowledge would have to be based on a prior experience of the objects; but it is readily explicable on the contrary assumption that objects conform to our knowledge of them (or, more precisely, to the conditions of such knowledge) (Bxvi-xvii).[16] Now, in reasoning that closely parallels this, he argues:

> If the pleasure in the given object came first, and our judgment of taste were to attribute only the pleasure's universal communicability [*allgemeine Mittheilbarkeit*] to the representation of the object, then this procedure would be self-contradictory. For that kind of pleasure would be none other than mere agreeableness in the sensation, so that by its very nature it could have only private validity, because it would depend directly on the representation by which the object is *given*. (KU 5: 216–7; 61)

This paragraph marks the initial appearance in the text of the expression "universal communicability," which, together with its variants, plays a large role in the remainder of the Analytic and the Deduction. In the present context at least, it has the normative sense of being universally attributable or shareable, and it thus functions as a close synonym of "subjective universal validity."[17] Consequently, it is what must be accounted for if one is to account for the universality claim built into the judgment of taste. Moreover, it seems reasonable to assume that Kant's choice of this expression at this crucial turn in his analysis is not unrelated to his appeal to the idea of a universal voice in the preceding section. To claim to speak with a universal voice is precisely to claim that one's judgment is universally shareable in the sense that it appeals to a subjective condition that is accessible to all. And the concern of §9 is to uncover this condition.

The text currently before us proceeds toward this end by eliminating one putative explanation of the possibility of judgments of taste and affirming what is taken (without argument) to be the only remaining alternative. The assumption to be eliminated is that the pleasure in the object (for which universality is being claimed) precedes the judging of the object. As already suggested, this is the aesthetic analogue of the anti-Copernican notion that our knowledge must conform to objects. It fails because *that* kind of pleasure (one arising directly from a sensation of an object) would be merely a pleasure in the agreeable, and would therefore have only private validity. Consequently, the attempt to account for the universality claim implicit in a [pure] judgment of taste in this manner would be "self-contradictory" (or, more precisely, self-defeating), since the condition under which the pleasure (according to this hypothesis) is produced is incompatible with any claim to universality.

Given this result, one would expect (following the Copernican analogy) that the next claim would be that the judgment must somehow precede the pleasure, which would then lead to an investigation of what such judgment must be like if it is to yield the desired result. We shall see that this is, in fact, precisely how Kant proceeds in the bulk of §9 and the remainder of the Analytic of the Beautiful. But rather than completing the present line of argument in this way, he begins the next paragraph by concluding:

> Hence it must be the capacity for being universally communicated [*allgemeine Mittheilungsfähigkeit*][18] of the mental state, in the given representation, which underlies the judgment of taste as its subjective condition, and the pleasure in the object must be its consequence. (KU 5: 217; 61)

This is undoubtedly among the most puzzling statements in the *Critique of Judgment*, and it raises at least two exegetical problems. The first is to explain how the pleasure of taste can be the *result* of the judgment, when (since the judgment is aesthetic) it is also supposed to be its basis or condition.[19] The second, and more serious, problem is to explain how, as the text seems to indicate, the pleasure of taste can be the result of the very universal communicability of the mental state in the judgment. Since the universally communicable mental state is presumably itself pleasurable (at least in the case of positive judgments of beauty), this seems to commit Kant to the view that the pleasure of taste must be in the universal communicability of the pleasure of taste, which seems hopelessly circular, to say the least.

The standard device for dealing with the first problem is to draw a distinction between the act of "judging the object" (*die Beurtheilung des Gegenstandes*) and the "judgment of taste" (*Geschmacksurtheil*) proper.[20] Given this distinction, one can say that the judging, by which is understood the supposedly disinterested act of reflection or contemplation, precedes the pleasure, but the latter precedes, and provides the basis for, the actual judgment or verdict. Although it conflicts with Kant's language in the passage in question (he refers to the judgment of taste as preceding the pleasure), some such distinction seems called for, and it does provide a solution to the first problem. Unfortunately, however, it does not suffice to resolve the second, since we are still left with the paradoxical thesis that the pleasure of taste, which is claimed in the judgment of taste proper to be universally communicable, is produced by the universal communicability of the very pleasure that arises in the act of judging.

Perhaps the most elaborate treatment of both problems to be found in the literature is Paul Guyer's. Guyer sees in the argument of §9 as a whole a theory of aesthetic response according to which such a response consists of two logically distinct acts of reflection: first, an act of "mere reflection," in which the pleasure is felt, and second, an act of aesthetic judgment proper, in which the cause of the pleasure is attributed to the harmony of the faculties.[21] He also recognizes, however, that the passage currently under consideration (as well as a later passage)[22] is plainly incompatible with any such reading. The problem, as already noted, lies in the apparent implication that the universal communicability of the mental state in judging the object (which Guyer identifies with "mere reflection") is itself the source of the pleasure. Not only does Guyer find this incompatible with the theory of aesthetic response he attributes to Kant, but he also finds it to be "obviously absurd."[23]

In view of this analysis, Guyer quite naturally sees his exegetical task to be to provide an explanation of the presence of such an absurdity in the text, rather than to offer a philosophical justification of it. Moreover, he suggests two possibilities for such an explanation. The first is that the offending passage may be a remnant of Kant's earlier anthropological view that the pleasure of taste is directly related to universal communicability, which somehow found its way into the text of the third *Critique* in spite of the fact that he had abandoned this view many years earlier.[24] Surprisingly, Guyer proposes this as a possibility even though, later in this very section, Kant explicitly denies that pleasure in the ability to communicate one's mental state could account for the pleasure of taste. To be sure, Kant does not deny the existence of a pleasure in universal communicability, but merely the possibility of appealing to it in order to explain the necessity connected with the judgment of taste, since it is based on the merely empirical assumption of a natural propensity [*Hang*] to sociability (KU 5: 218; 62–3).[25] Nevertheless, Kant would have to have been confused indeed to have made such a mistake. Guyer's second and "less speculative" proposal is that Kant may simply have confused the two senses of reflection ("simple reflection" and "reflective judgment") to which he allegedly appeals in his theory of aesthetic response.[26] Once again, however, this explanation does not do much credit to the author of the third *Critique*.

Hannah Ginsborg's interpretation of the notorious third paragraph of §9 stands opposed to Guyer's at virtually every point. Not only does she deny any need to distinguish between two acts of reflection, but she also accepts at face value and defends Kant's claim that the pleasure in a judgment of taste is in the universal validity of the mental state. On her reading, this claim is circular but not viciously so, since the judgment of taste is "a formal and self-referential judgment that claims, not the universal validity of an antecedently given feeling of pleasure, but rather its own universal validity with respect to the object."[27] In other words, a judgment of taste is really a judgment about the normativity of one's own mental state with respect to the object deemed beautiful, and the demand for agreement implicit in such a judgment is simply the demand that this normativity be recognized by others.[28]

Apart from the issue of the relation between the claims of the second and fourth moments, this raises the obvious question of what such a self-referential judgment has to do with pleasure. Ginsborg's answer turns on an appeal to Kant's own previously cited characterization of pleasure in §10 as "the consciousness of a representation's causality directed at a subject's state so as to *keep* him in that state" (KU 5: 220; 65). Her suggestion is that the pleasure of taste is due to the "self- grounding character of one's mental state in representing an object," where what makes it self-grounding is its very normativity. I remain in that mental state because I recognize that I ought to be in it, and this is inherently pleasurable.[29]

There are several things to be said in favor of Ginsborg's deeply suggestive reading. First, it attempts to makes sense of the text as it stands, which is certainly a major desideratum for any interpretation. Second, it seems to capture much of what Kant was getting at with his appeal to the idea of a universal voice, since, as we have seen, to take oneself to be speaking with such a voice is just to take one's mental state as subjectively universal. Third, it suggests a simpler, more unified picture of reflection than Guyer's two-acts view. Finally, it avoids attributing to Kant the thesis that what the judgment of taste demands (or predicts) of others is that they have qualitatively identical feelings in response to the same objects. As we shall see later in this study, this is a questionable consequence of Guyer's reading, which he then uses as a basis for his critique of the Deduction.

Nevertheless, I think that Ginsborg goes too far when she affirms that a judgment of taste is essentially *about* its own normativity, and that the pleasure of taste is a pleasure in this normativity. In addition to the inherent implausibility of such a view of judgments of taste, which I believe remains in spite of all her efforts to convince us otherwise, at least four major considerations speak against her reading as an interpretation of Kant's intent in §9.

The first is the simple fact that it commits Kant to a *non sequitur.* As we have seen, Kant (following the Copernican analogy) asks whether the feeling of pleasure precedes the act of reflection or the reverse. Since on the former hypothesis we cannot explain how judgments of taste could have universal communicability, the obvious inference is that we should adopt the latter. But it certainly does not follow from the rejection of the first alternative either that we must view the judgment of taste as self-referential (as distinct from simply being reflective) or that the pleasure of taste is a pleasure *in* the universal communicability of a (pleasurable) mental state. Thus, even though Kant presents it as such, it remains difficult to see how the thesis she attributes to Kant can be regarded as an inference from what precedes it in the text.

The second problem with Ginsborg's reading is its apparent lack of accord with the main drift of the overall argument in §9. The incongruity of the claim that she endeavors to defend with this argument was already pointed out by Guyer, and it is not clear that she does very much to address that issue. She does, of course, contend that her reading provides the promised "key," but her procedure still seems to be a case of the tail wagging the dog.

The third problem is that her account of the pleasure of taste seems to deprive this pleasure of its disinterested nature. To be sure, Ginsborg explicitly denies this and regards it as a virtue of her interpretation that it can account for such disinterestedness. Appealing to the distinction drawn in the First Introduction between the pleasure in the good that is mediated by the faculty of desire and the pleasure of taste that is not (FI 20: 206–7; 395–6), which she correctly takes as an anticipation of the later distinction between interested and disinterested pleasure, Ginsborg insists that the pleasure of taste, on her reading, is disinterested because it involves self-perpetuation without mediation by desire.[30] It should be clear from the argument of the previous chapter that the pleasure of taste must have some such character, if it is to count as disinterested. The problem, however, is whether this can be said of a purported pleasure in the universal communicability of one's mental state. Counting against this is the previously noted fact that in §9, Kant explicitly links the pleasure in universal communicability with the predisposition to society, which certainly makes it interested, according to his criterion.[31]

Finally, the fourth problem concerns the question of negative judgments of taste to which I have already alluded on several occasions. If anything is clear about Ginsborg's reading, it is that she does not allow room for such judgments. For if the pleasure of taste is literally in the universal communicability of one's pleasure, then there is no place for an analogous universally communicable displeasure, since universal communicability is itself a source of pleasure. In fact, Ginsborg readily acknowledges this point, arguing in response that Kant does not really want to allow for such judgments, at least not as *pure* judgments of taste.[32]

In view of the analysis of Chapter 3, where it was suggested that an ability to account for the possibility of negative judgments is criterial for the adequacy of an interpretation of Kant's theory of taste, this claim cannot be accepted. Admittedly, however, insisting on this point in the present instance brings with it problems of its own, since it requires us to agree with Guyer in rejecting the literal meaning of the problematic first sentence in the third paragraph of §9. Nevertheless, unlike Guyer, I do not think that this requires us to assume either that Kant mysteriously reverted to an earlier view at a key point in his argument or confused two distinct acts of reflection. The explanation may be simpler and more charitable to Kant, though clearly not totally exculpatory.

The problem, as I see it, stems from Kant's apparent attempt to combine two distinct claims in the passage in question: (1) that the (subjective) universality of the liking affirmed in a judgment of beauty must be based on the universal communicability of the mental state; and (2) that the latter derives its universal communicability from its connection with a universally communicable act of judging or reflection, which, in turn, explains why this judging must (logically) precede the pleasure. Unfortunately, instead of making these points separately, Kant runs them together in the claim that "it must be the universal communicability of the mental state, in the given representation, which underlies the judgment of taste as its subjective condition, and the pleasure in the object must be its consequence." In reality, however, all that is required to rectify matters is to substitute "a universally communicable mental state" for "the universal communicability of the mental state." In addition to removing much of the air of paradox surrounding the text, this would allow room for the possibility of negative judgments of taste; for there is nothing inherently problematic in a universally communicable mental state of displeasure (as opposed to a displeasure in its very communicability).[33]

Furthermore, with this in place, the remainder of the argument in §9 proceeds fairly smoothly. Its goal is to locate a universally communicable mental state that can serve as both the source of the disinterested pleasure of taste and the ground of its universal communicability; and the essential premise is that "Nothing can be universally communicated except cognition and representation, insofar as it pertains [*gehört*] to cognition" (KU 5: 217; 61). Since we are dealing with an *aesthetic* judgment, the first alternative is ruled out. Consequently, the concern is to show that the representation involved in aesthetic reflection does "pertain to cognition," even though the judgment itself is noncognitive.

Kant does this by connecting such representation with the relation of the cognitive faculties (imagination and understanding) in their "free play." As is already clear from the preliminary account of judgments of taste in the First Introduction, though not itself *amounting to* cognition, this relation *pertains to* cognition, since the harmonious interworking of imagination and understanding is a necessary subjective condition of it. All that Kant now adds to this story is that the indispensability for cognition of the harmony of the faculties is the ground of its universal communicability. For, as he puts it:

> [W]e are conscious that this subjective relation suitable for cognition in general must hold just as much for everyone, and hence be just as universally communicable, as any determinate cognition, since cognition always rests on that relation as its subjective condition. (KU 5: 218; 62)

The essential idea here is that of a subjective condition of cognition, which is to be contrasted with the familiar objective conditions of the first *Critique,* for example, space, time, and the categories. The latter conditions are objective or, perhaps better, objectifying, in the sense that they constitute the very form or framework of objectivity. A subjective condition, on the other hand, would be one that is somehow necessarily involved in representation, but does not determine the objects represented, not even these objects considered as phenomena. We have seen from our consideration of Kant's treatment of logical purposiveness that conditions of reflection are subjective conditions in this sense. But the harmonious relation of the imagination and the understanding in reflection on a given representation is likewise a subjective condition, since it is a condition of the successful functioning of judgment but does not determine the nature of the objects judged about. Moreover, as such, it applies universally to the sphere of judging subjects, which is just Kant's point.

Although the matter remains highly controversial, I believe that if Kant's conception of the harmony of the faculties and its significance for judgments of taste is to be understood properly, it is essential to distinguish between this harmony of the faculties and their free play.[34] As already indicated, "free play" refers to the relation between the imagination and understanding in the act of "mere reflection," that is, the "free" reflection operative in a judgment of taste, which, as the explication of the first moment indicates, can issue in either a disinterested liking or disliking. These two possibilities stem from the fact that such reflection can either succeed or fail to produce a harmonious relation of the faculties. In the former case, the mental state is pleasurable and the object occasioning this harmonious relation deemed beautiful. In the latter case, however, the outcome of the free play is a state of *dis*harmomy, where the faculties hinder rather than help one another in their reciprocal tasks, thereby producing a mental state of disinterested displeasure and a negative judgment of taste. As Kant puts it elsewhere, "To judge an object by taste is to judge whether freedom in the play of the imagination harmonizes or clashes with the lawfulness of the understanding" (Anthro 7: 241; 109).

Moreover, just as there can be a free play without harmony, so there can also be a harmony without free play. This occurs in ordinary cognitive judgments, but particularly in judgments of perfection. For in the latter case, the harmony is based on a determinate concept of the object (of what sort of thing it is supposed to be), which leaves no scope for the free activity of the imagination. And though the consciousness of such a lawful, conceptually determined harmony may be pleasurable, it is not the pleasure of taste.[35]

Having thus traced the subjective universality or universal communicability affirmed in a judgment of taste to the harmony of the faculties in free play as its only conceivable source, one might think that Kant is finally ready to deal with the nature of the demand for agreement that such judgments make, that is, their putative necessity. But after noting this problem, he suggests that he must delay consideration of it until it can be determined: "whether and how aesthetic judgments are possible *a priori*" (KU 5: 218; 63). This way of putting the issue reflects Kant's tendency on occasion to treat the question of whether such judgments have an *a priori* ground as equivalent to the question of whether they are themselves *a priori*. In any event, rather than dealing with that question in either form, he devotes the remainder of §9 to the discussion of the allegedly "lesser question" of "how we become conscious, in a judgment of taste, of a reciprocal subjective harmony between the cognitive faculties" (KU 5: 218; 63). More precisely, the issue is whether we do so aesthetically, through a sensation, or intellectually, "through consciousness of the intentional activity by which we bring these faculties into play" (KU 5: 219; 63).

Since the judgment of taste is an aesthetic judgment, it is clear that the answer will be the former. Nevertheless, the discussion, which may be viewed as a transition of sorts to the third moment, is not redundant; for it tells us what exactly is being sensed, namely, "the quickening [*Belebung*] of the two faculties (imagination and understanding) to an activity that is indeterminate but, as a result of the prompting of the given representation, nevertheless accordant [*einhelliger*]: the activity required for cognition in general" (KU 5: 219; 63). In other words, what the mind senses or, better, feels, is the interplay of its cognitive faculties in the apprehension of an object. This interplay is "free" insofar as it is not directed by a determinate concept, but it is still guided by the general conditions of cognition. Moreover, Kant concludes, precisely because this feeling has reference to the latter, we must consider it valid "for everyone who is so constituted as to judge by means of understanding and the senses in combination (in other words, for all human beings)" (KU 5: 219; 64).

With this, Kant completes the task of the second moment, which, as we have seen, is to link the universality postulated in a judgment of taste, its inherent claim to speak with a universal voice, to the free play of the faculties, and to the feeling (a disinterested liking or disliking) through which this play is manifest aesthetically. This state or condition of free play of the cognitive faculties is thus seen to be a necessary condition of the possibility of a pure judgment of taste, and establishing this is the contribution of the second moment to the overall project of the Analytic of the Beautiful: the determination of the *quid facti* in the realm of taste. Insofar as this is accomplished in §9, it is justly characterized as the "key to the critique of taste."

BEAUTY, PURPOSIVENESS, AND FORM

Following the "guiding thread" of the table of judgments in the *Critique of Pure Reason*, the third moment in the Analytic of the Beautiful is that of relation. Unlike the logical functions of relation or the relational categories, however, the relation in question is between the judging subject and the object judged and/or its representation. Thus, for the first time in the Analytic, the aesthetic object, which up to this point has been largely left out of the picture, becomes an explicit focus of attention.[1]

Nevertheless, it is clear from both the inclusion of this discussion in the moment of relation and the emphasis placed on the *representation* of the object that the concern is not with the inherent nature of such an object, not even considered as phenomenon, but rather with the object *qua* represented, that is, apprehended in mere reflection, and its aesthetic, and therefore noncognitive and nonpractical, relation to the subject. Although it is never explicitly formulated as such, the basic question underlying the discussion is how we are to characterize this relation, such that it can account for the possibility of a universally communicable pleasure in the harmony of the faculties. Thus, as I shall try to show, the third moment presupposes and builds upon the results of the second in much the same way as the latter presupposes and builds upon the results of the first.

It is also in this context that Kant introduces the essential, yet deeply problematic, notions of a "purposiveness without purpose" and "form" (including both a "form of purposiveness" and a "purposiveness of form") into the analysis of taste. These come together in the explication of the beautiful offered at the end of the third moment: "*Beauty* is an object's *form of purposiveness* insofar as it is perceived in the object *without the representation of a purpose*" (KU 5: 236; 84). Accordingly, much of the present chapter will be devoted to the attempt to explicate these notions and the complex relationships between them.

This does not, however, exhaust the significance of the third moment. For it is also here that the concern with the nature of a *pure* judgment of taste and the conditions of its possibility, which I have argued is implicit in the Analytic from the beginning, becomes fully explicit. Moreover, since this leads Kant to introduce a number of fresh distinctions, it greatly complicates the discussion and helps to make the third moment, with its eight sections, not only the longest but also the most complex of the four.

The following attempt to analyze the intricate, sometimes meandering, and often confusing line of argument of this moment is divided into four parts. The first considers the definitions of the key terms "purpose," "purposiveness," and "pleasure," and the introduction of the conception of a purposiveness without a purpose in §10. The second analyzes Kant's argument that the latter, or its equivalent (the form of purposiveness), is the determining ground of the (pure) judgment of taste (§11), and the subsequent account of the peculiar pleasure of taste as a pleasure in such purposiveness (§12). Together, then, these two parts deal with the portion of the third moment that directly concerns the explication of the beautiful just noted.

The third part examines the contrast between pure judgments of taste (based on the purposiveness of the form of an object and/or its representation) and impure judgments that are based on extrinsic sensible factors such as charm and emotion (§13–§14). It is here that the vexing question of Kant's "formalism" initially arises. We shall see that even though Kant's analysis does not justify the highly restrictive type of formalism that he appears to advocate in these sections, it does support the general thesis that only formal features of an object or its representation are capable of occasioning the harmony of the faculties.

Finally, the fourth part of this chapter discusses the three sections (§15–§17) in which taste is both contrasted with, and related to, conceptual representation. Here the focal point will be Kant's effort in §16 to show how, in spite of the irreducibility of the aesthetic representation of purposiveness to any representation of perfection affirmed in §15, taste can nevertheless combine with conceptual representation to form a complex, only partly aesthetic, type of judgment, which is still a judgment of beauty in a broad sense.

I

The definitions of basic terms, which Kant offers in §10, is perhaps one of the more graphic examples of his oft-noted penchant for being technical without being precise. Moreover, the attempt to collate them with the definitions and accounts of similar terms and conceptions given in the Introductions, so as to arrive at a uniform set of definitions, has proven to be a daunting, if not hopeless, task.[2]

The goal of §10, clearly enough, is to provide a generic account of purposiveness [*Zweckmässigkeit Überhaupt*], which can then form the basis for an understanding of the specific mode of purposiveness relevant to judgments of taste. But since this conception presupposes that of an end or purpose [*Zweck*],[3] Kant actually begins with the latter term. Setting aside everything empirical (specifically the feeling of pleasure), and considering only the "transcendental," that is, generic, attributes, he defines "purpose" as "the object of a concept insofar as we regard this concept as the object's cause (the real ground of its possibility)" (KU 5: 220; 64–5).[4] In other words, a purpose in the broadest sense is the product of an intentional causality, one which presupposes a concept of what the thing is meant to be.[5] Accordingly, as Kant notes, the representation of the effect precedes and is the determining ground of the cause.

This generic definition of "purpose" contains nothing new and of itself raises no problems. The same cannot be said, however, of the definition of "purposiveness," which is apparently derived from it. In sharp contrast to the accounts in the Introductions, where purposiveness is connected primarily with nature and attributed to objects and-or their relations, Kant here defines it as "the causality that a *concept* has with regard to its *object*" (KU 5: 220; 65). And without any further explanation, he equates this with purposive form (*forma finalis*). Thus, purposiveness is now treated as the property of a *concept*, specifically, the property of having causality with regard to its object (a purpose). Presumably, to have such causality is to have purposive form.

Moreover, to confuse matters further, after having identified pleasure as the empirical factor to be set aside in the definition of "purpose," Kant ends the first paragraph of §10 by defining it. And, like the definition of "purposiveness," this definition appears to differ (at least superficially) from what he says elsewhere on the topic. As he now defines the term:

> Consciousness of a representation's causality directed at the subject's state so as to *keep* him in that state, may here designate generally what we call pleasure; whereas displeasure is that representation which contains the ground that determines [the subject to change] the state [consisting] of [certain] representations into their own opposite (i.e., to keep them away or remove them). (KU 5: 220; 65)

We saw in Chapter 2 that in the First Introduction, Kant characterized pleasure in general as "a mental state in which a representation is in harmony with itself." This, then, led to a distinction between the kind of pleasure in which this harmony was the basis merely for preserving the state itself and the kind in which it produces a desire for the object (or object-type) that occasioned the feeling (FI 20: 230–31; 420). Although Kant did not there develop the point, it was noted that the former kind is to be identified with the disinterested pleasure of taste and the latter with the interested pleasure in either the agreeable or the good.

We further saw in Chapter 3, in considering the aesthetic nature of the judgment of taste articulated in the very first section of the Analytic of the Beautiful, that pleasure and displeasure are to be understood in connection with a subject's feeling of life or *Lebensgefühl*. And by considering this and other texts, it was suggested that the feelings of pleasure and displeasure be viewed respectively as a sense of the increase or diminution of one's level of activity, particularly as a thinking being.

If, as seems reasonable, we assume that a mental state in which a representation is in harmony with itself is also one in which there is an increase in a subject's level of activity and *vice versa*, there appears to be no serious conflict between the first two accounts. Nor should it be objected that the first speaks of preservation and the second of increase, since the (harmonious) state of increased vitality is precisely what the subject endeavors to preserve.

The definition currently before us, however, seems to differ from the preceding accounts, particularly that of the First Introduction, in at least two nontrivial respects. First, by locating pleasure in the "Consciousness of a representation's causality," and so forth, Kant appears to make the pleasure consist in the *awareness* of the causal power of a representation to preserve a (presumably harmonious) mental state, rather than in the mental state itself. Second, by connecting this awareness with the causal power to preserve the mental state, he also seems to make the preservation of the state the ground of the pleasure, rather than (as the earlier formulations suggest) merely the consequence thereof. And quite apart from the question of its compatibility with what Kant says about pleasure elsewhere, the latter seems quite problematic, since one would assume that a subject endeavors to preserve a state because it is pleasurable, not that the preservation is what makes the state pleasurable.

The key to the resolution of the first apparent discrepancy lies in the previously emphasized intentionality of the feeling of pleasure. Although the definition in the First Introduction makes no reference to consciousness, we saw in Chapter 2 that Kant connected the contrast between two kinds of pleasure (disinterested and interested) with the distinction between two kinds of *judgment* of pleasure. And from this it was inferred that, in spite of its noncognitive nature, a pleasure (or displeasure) for Kant is more than a "raw feel"; that it involves a mode of awareness of one's mental state, which, in turn, underlies the possibility of an aesthetic judgment, understood as a judgment or evaluation made by means of or through the feeling itself, rather than one about its causal ancestry.[6] Moreover, essentially the same view is present in §1 of the published text; since, as we have also seen, Kant there emphasizes the status of the feeling of pleasure as a special faculty of judgment or discrimination , which, as such, necessarily involves a certain intentionality.[7] Consequently, rather than conflicting with the previous accounts, by including a reference to consciousness, the definition of pleasure in §10 merely makes fully explicit what was implicitly the case all along.

In order to understand the second apparent discrepancy, it is necessary to realize that Kant included a reference to causality in the present characterization of pleasure to suggest a connection with the preceding definition of purposiveness as "the causality that a *concept* has with regard to its *object.*" This connection, in turn, must be viewed in light of the ultimate goal of the analysis, which, as in both Introductions, is to link the pleasure of taste with an aesthetic awareness of purposiveness. If this is kept in mind, it is possible to give the passage a more charitable reading, according to which it does not commit Kant to the highly counterintuitive view that pleasure consists in the awareness of the causal power of a representation to keep one in a mental state (or in its actual keeping one in such a state, for that matter). According to this reading, it is our *liking* for the representation (and the object occasioning it) that stems from our consciousness of its capacity to keep us in a mental state; but it has this capacity only because the state itself (not the causal power of the representation to preserve it) is inherently pleasurable, which induces the subject to endeavor to remain in it.[8]

As already noted, however, this whole discussion of pleasure must be seen in light of Kant's basic goal, which is to link pleasure to purposiveness, particularly the purposiveness without purpose that is presumably operative in the judgment of taste. But before this can be accomplished, the latter notion must itself be introduced and explicated. This is the task of the second paragraph of §10.

Kant begins by returning to the underlying notion of a purpose, this time relating it specifically to a will. The latter is defined, in familiar enough fashion, as the faculty of desire insofar as it can be determined only by concepts, which, in turn, is equated with acting in conformity with the representation of a purpose. Consequently, to have a will is to have the capacity to set purposes for oneself; correlatively, a purpose is an object of volition, something consciously intended, which certainly accords with the previous account. Turning to the adjectival form, Kant then remarks that we can also term an object, mental state, or action [*Handlung*] "purposive" [*zweckmässig*]; indeed, he suggests that we can do so "even if their possibility does not necessarily presuppose the representation of a purpose." What is required is merely that we can grasp the explanation of their possibility only by deriving it from a will. Finally, Kant concludes from this that we can perceive in objects and note, "if only by reflection," a "purposiveness as to form [*Zweckmässigkeit der Form nach*] . . . without basing it on a purpose (as the matter of the *nexus finalis*)" (KU 5: 220; 65).

We shall see that this delineation of the sphere of purposiveness (objects, mental states, and actions) is crucial for understanding the connection between purposiveness and the judgment of taste. The immediate problem, however, is that neither the initial characterization of purposiveness in terms of the causality of a concept nor the present one does very much to make this connection intelligible. Indeed, these two accounts do not even seem compatible with each other (not to mention Kant's other accounts). For whereas in the first paragraph purposiveness was attributed to the causality of a *concept*, it is now predicated of certain *products*. And these products (which presumably include mental states and actions as well as objects) need not be viewed as actually produced by a conceptually governed causality. All that is required for the attribution of purposiveness to such products is that they can be explained or conceived only on the assumption that they are based on such a causality, that is, "on a will that would have so arranged them in accordance with the representation of a certain rule." Moreover, it is this latter conception that supposedly legitimates the concept of a purposiveness without a purpose, which comes into play whenever something exhibits purposiveness by the stated criterion, though we do not actually posit the causes of its "form" (i.e., its organization or structure) in a will (which would make it a purpose) (KU 5: 220; 65).

The reference to how the possibility of something must be conceived (presumably by beings with our form of understanding) strongly suggests that Kant is here making a belated attempt to link the discussion of a purposiveness without purpose not merely to pleasure but also to the analysis of reflective judgment contained in the Introductions. Nevertheless, there are at least two problems with such an attempt. The first is simply that it is not clear how this definition makes the applicability of purposiveness to mental states and actions any more intelligible than the initial one. Certainly, insofar as they are intentional, both may be viewed as "purposive" within the terms of Kant's definition; but *qua* intentional, their purposiveness is *with* purpose. And of a nonintentionally produced mental state or a nonintentional action, it simply does not seem to make sense to claim that "we can grasp the explanation of its possibility only by deriving it from a will."

The second problem is that *all* purposiveness is "without purpose" in the sense noted, simply in virtue of the fact that it is posited by reflective judgment. For something is "purposive" (or exhibits purposiveness) by this criterion just in case we can account for its possibility only by regarding it as the product of an intentional causality or design. But, as we have seen in the first part of this study, judgment in its reflective capacity is *never* warranted in moving from the purely subjective necessity of conceiving of the possibility of something in this way (e.g., the systematic ordering of nature or the structure of organic beings) to the assertion of an actual intention or purpose. In other words, for reflective judgment, it is *always* a matter of how we are constrained to conceive of the possibility of something, rather than of how it is really possible, since a judgment affirming the latter, that is, an actual purpose, would be determinative. Consequently, for reflective judgment it is always a matter of a purposiveness without purpose; so the distinction between a purposiveness without and one with a purpose seems to reduce to the contrast between a purposiveness posited by reflective judgment and one posited by determinative judgment (which necessarily involves a purpose), rather than one that falls within the sphere of reflective judgment itself.

II

Not surprisingly, these difficulties or obscurities in the definitions in §10 cause problems for the interpretation and evaluation of the argument in §11, where Kant attempts to relate these definitions to the analysis of the judgment of taste presented in the first two moments. The basic claim, articulated in the heading, is that "A Judgment of Taste Is Based on Nothing but the *Form of Purposiveness* of an Object (or of the Way of Representing It)" (KU 5: 221; 66). Since this anticipates the explication of the beautiful given at the end of the third moment (*"Beauty* is an object's form of purposiveness insofar as it is perceived in the object *without the representation of a purpose"*), the section is obviously the key one in the moment, at least from a systematic point of view. And, as such, it clearly deserves close scrutiny.

As usual, Kant's argument is by elimination, with the elimination concerning possible grounds for the liking affirmed in a judgment of taste. Translating considerations derived from the first moment into the language of purpose, Kant argues first that, as disinterested, the liking cannot be based on a "subjective purpose." Although Kant does not explain what he means by this, he presumably has in mind some object in which one is interested on subjective or desire-based grounds, that is, something agreeable.[9] Then he claims that it also cannot be based on the "representation of an objective purpose," which he identifies with a concept of the good. The latter is ruled out because of the aesthetic nature of the judgment, which precludes it from being based on a concept. Instead, referring back to the account of the harmony of the faculties in §9, Kant suggests that "it involves merely the relation of the representational powers to each other, so far as they are determined by a representation" (KU 5: 221; 66). Finally, after ruling out these two kinds of purposes, and with them any appeal to either the agreeable or the good, he concludes:

> [T]he basis that determines a judgment of taste can be nothing but the subjective purposiveness in the representation of an object, without any purpose (whether objective or subjective), and hence the mere form of purposiveness, insofar as we are conscious of it, in the representation by which an object is *given.* (KU 5: 221; 66)

Like the move from disinterestedness to universality at the beginning of the second moment, this argument initially appears quite problematic. For the conclusion that a judgment of taste must be based on a subjective *purposiveness,* as previously described, hardly seems to be entailed by the premises that it must be based on neither a subjective nor an objective *purpose.* Why, one might ask, need a judgment of taste have *anything* to do with purposiveness at all?

The argument evidently assumes that it must, and ruling out the two kinds of purposes (which are supposedly exhaustive), it then in effect concludes that it can only be based on a purposiveness *without* purpose, with that understood in terms of the definition in §10 as the mere "form of purposiveness." But to assume that the category of purposiveness must in some way be involved (with or without a definite purpose) does seem to beg the question. Moreover, even assuming *some* connection between taste and purposiveness, it is not clear why judgments of taste must involve the mere "form of purposiveness" as introduced in §10.[10] This question seems particularly pressing, since it is this connection of the judgment of taste with form that leads directly to Kant's much criticized formalism. Finally, there is the still unresolved problem of how this conception of purposiveness is to be related to mental states and actions (as well as objects).

Saving a discussion of Kant's aesthetic formalism for the next section, I shall attempt to deal with the other problems here. Although the first mentioned of these problems (why any purposiveness at all?) is the most fundamental, I shall begin with a discussion of the second (why the form of purposiveness?) since it is largely exegetical, and a successful resolution of it will put us in a better position to deal with the first, while this, as we shall see, leads directly to the third (why purposiveness of mental states and actions as well as objects?).

To begin with, insofar as Kant distinguishes in §11 between a subjective purposiveness and a subjective purpose, the former must be viewed as at least a species of purposiveness without purpose. Thus, even though Kant uses the expression "subjective purposiveness" elsewhere in a way that is compatible with such purposiveness being based on a definite purpose, this cannot be the case here.[11] Moreover, since Kant will argue in §15 that any determination of an *objective* purposiveness presupposes the concept of some purpose that an object is to serve (KU 5: 227; 73), it follows that there is no place in the Kantian scheme for the notion of an objective purposiveness without purpose.[12] And this, in turn, entails that, at least within the confines of the third moment, "subjective purposiveness" and "purposiveness without purpose" are equivalent expressions, which is precisely how Kant treats them in §11.

Furthermore, since we have seen that for Kant to regard something as purposive without assigning a definite purpose to it is basically to view it as if intended (by a will), it is not a significant stretch to equate being sub-jectively purposive with exhibiting the "form of purposiveness," in the sense of seeming as if designed.[13] Consequently, making due allowances for Kant's fluid terminology and the frustrating obscurity of his definitions, it does seem reasonable to conclude that *if* a judgment of taste is based on a subjective purposiveness, this may also be described as being based on the mere form of purposiveness, which, again, is exactly what §11 affirms.[14]

We thus return to the original and fundamental question: Why must we assume that a (pure) judgment of taste is based on purposiveness in any sense at all? The key to this, I suggest, is to recognize that §11 con-tains an elaboration (in the new set of terms introduced in §10) of the results achieved in §9. In other words, we must keep in mind that, as the language of §11 indicates, purposiveness is introduced in the context of an analysis of a universally communicable pleasure in a mental state of free harmony occasioned by reflection on an object. This enables us to understand not only why purposiveness is involved but also why it is pred-icable of mental states and actions as well as objects (and the aesthetic representation thereof), which was our third problem.

First, given this analysis, together with Kant's treatment of judgments of taste in the Introductions, it seems reasonable to characterize the men-tal state of free harmony as itself "subjectively purposive." In fact, this state is the primary locus of purposiveness in the analysis of taste, since it pro-vides the actual determining ground of the judgment of taste.[15] What makes such a mental state subjectively purposive, however, is not that "we can grasp the explanation of its possibility only by deriving it from a will," but rather that it enhances the reciprocal activity of the imagination and understanding. Moreover, it does this in virtue of a structural feature of the state termed "harmony" or "attunement," which is itself "without pur-pose," since (in the state of free play) it does not aim at a determinate cognition. Granted, this may not mesh neatly with §10's generic account of purposiveness, since we have seen that, if taken literally, this is not ap-plicable to (nonvoluntary) mental states; nevertheless, it is obviously what Kant had in mind in that section when he included mental states in the scope of a purposiveness without purpose.

Second, a similar claim can be made about the "act" [*Handlung*] of free play through which the harmonious mental state is produced, which is presumably why Kant included acts or actions under the rubric of pur-posiveness without purpose in the first place. In fact, the distinction be-tween the purposiveness of the mental state and that of the act really amounts to the distinction between the product and the process by which it is brought about. Once again, however, it is crucial that the act be one of free play; for if it is governed by a determinate concept, then its out-come is a cognition, that is, an actual purpose rather than a merely pur-posive relation.

This brings us, then, to the last of the three items that supposedly fall under the rubric of purposiveness without purpose, namely objects. Although the last to be discussed here, it is the first listed by Kant. Indeed, it might seem that it is the most important, since it alone involves a connection between the judging subject and some property of the object, which is supposedly the concern of the third moment to establish. Clearly, it is the one closest to the express terms of Kant's definition in §10, since (unlike the mental state of free harmony and the act of free play through which it is produced) it does appear reasonable to say of an object whose representation occasions such a harmony in a perceiver that it seems as if it were designed, just as one says this of the logical purposiveness of nature featured in the Introductions.

Nevertheless, in my judgment, it would be going too far to conclude from this analysis that with the purposiveness of the object of taste, Kant grants to beauty the status of a property of certain objects, of being, as McDowell puts it, part of the "fabric of the world."[16] Although some of what Kant says here and elsewhere, particularly the distinction between the beautiful and the sublime drawn in §30 (to be discussed in Chapter 8) and the account of the intimations of nature's moral purposiveness that are presumably supplied by natural beauties (which will be the central topic of Chapter 10), certainly suggests an objectivist view of at least natural beauty, it seems clear that Kant took his account of the aesthetic, and therefore noncognitive, nature of the judgment of taste to entail the subjectivity of beauty.

Although he does not deny that this is how Kant understood his own theory, it has been argued by Karl Ameriks that Kant *ought* to have regarded beauty as an objective feature of things, more specifically as a causal property analogous to secondary qualities on the Lockean picture. Ameriks's view, which he characterizes as a "mild revisionism," rests on two main claims: (1) The actual arguments that Kant provides for the subjectivity thesis are not sufficient to establish it; and (2) Kant would have been better off adhering to an objectivist view, since it provides a surer, nonparadoxical basis for addressing his main concern, namely, the universal validity of judgments of beauty.[17]

I shall comment briefly on each of these in turn; but before addressing the issues directly, it may be useful to point out that there is something peculiarly anachronistic in Ameriks's revisionary proposal. For certainly Kant was well aware of the fact that regarding judgments of beauty as objective and in some sense conceptual would provide the easiest way to justify their claim to universal validity. He had, after all, the Baumgartian view as a model for such an objectivist account of beauty. But it is only in light of his rejection of such a view that the problem of taste arose for Kant. In other words, the problem for Kant is precisely how judgments that are aesthetic, and therefore merely subjective, can nonetheless demand universal agreement.

If the initial premise were denied, there might very well have been an account of the validity of judgments of beauty roughly along the lines of Baumgarten's; but there would have been no "critique of taste" and, *a fortiori*, no critique of judgment either. Consequently, to suggest, as Ameriks does, that Kant ought to have regarded judgments of taste as objective is to suggest that the whole project of the *Critique of Aesthetic Judgment* rests on a mistake. Now this, of course, may be correct; in fact, I emphasized in Chapter 3 that Kant tends to argue more from than to the aesthetic (and therefore subjective) nature of the judgment of taste. And this naturally suggests the possibility that he may be subject to a radical critique from an objectivist perspective, for example, the Hegelian.[18] But leaving that very large issue aside, my present point is only that it would be seriously misleading to regard Ameriks's proposed reconstruction as merely a "mild revision," a kind of friendly amendment to the orthodox Kantian theory![19]

Moreover, it is possible to grant much of what Ameriks says about the nondecisiveness of some of Kant's arguments for the subjectivity of taste without drawing his revisionary conclusions. In particular, one can accept his point that arguments from the nonconceptual nature or the non-demonstrability of judgments of beauty could easily be applied to claims about secondary qualities. And since Kant is notoriously unclear about the status of secondary qualities (sometimes apparently viewing them as purely subjective and sometimes, in a more Lockean manner, as having a foundation in the primary qualities of things), it could be maintained on the basis of these considerations that beauty is just as subjective or objective as the latter. But in neither case, Ameriks argues, does it warrant assigning it a special kind of subjectivity, different from that of secondary qualities, and requiring a special kind of deduction.[20]

As Ameriks is well aware, however, Kant's main ground for denying objectivity to judgments of beauty is their connection with pleasure. Since, as we have seen, the feeling of pleasure, unlike other "objective" sensations, involves no reference to an object, but merely to a sentient subject and its states, Kant concludes that judgments made on the basis of this faculty must be lacking in objectivity. Against this Ameriks argues that "the fact that the kind of taste Kant is discussing requires discrimination *by* something subjective does not entail that *what* is discriminated should be called subjective."[21] This may be true; but in my view it misses the point. For it is not merely that discriminations of taste are made by something subjective (which applies to both gustatory and aesthetic taste) that makes judgments of taste irredeemably subjective; it is rather that what is *discriminated* is a state of the subject (a mental state of harmony or discord) of which one can become aware only through feeling.[22]

In addition to undermining the aesthetic nature of the judgment of taste, Ameriks's proposal also threatens its normativity, insofar as it effectively makes it into a causal judgment about the properties, or complexes thereof, that tend to produce a certain kind of pleasurable response in "normal" human beings under certain circumstances. Admittedly, this may seem paradoxical, since Ameriks introduces his proposal precisely in order to account for such normativity. As Ginsborg points out in her critique of objectivist views of taste, however, Ameriks's proposal bears a striking resemblance to Burke's view, which Kant dismisses in the General Remark on the Exposition of Aesthetic Reflective Judgments on the grounds that such a "physiological" approach cannot account for the demand for agreement built into a claim of taste (KU 5: 277–8; 137–40).[23]

Moreover, Kant himself explicitly rejects any merely causal model for the pleasure of taste in §12, which is given the somewhat incongruous heading: "A Judgment of Taste Rests on A Priori Grounds" (KU 5: 221; 67). The point is that this model is incompatible with the *a priori* grounding presumably required for a judgment of taste, since causal relations among objects of experience can be known only *a posteriori*.

The bulk of §12 is, however, devoted not to this topic but to the central issue of the connection between the purposiveness in the judgment of taste and pleasure. The analysis turns on an analogy between the pleasure of taste and moral feeling, the latter having been introduced into the discussion because it appears to be an exception to the principle that causal relations are cognizable only *a posteriori*. Kant denies that this is, in fact, an exception on the dual grounds that it is a matter of intelligible, rather than empirical, causality, and, more importantly for present purposes, because what follows from "the idea of the moral as cause" [*der Idee des Sittlichen als Ursache*] is not the feeling of respect *per se*, but rather the determination of the will. This feeling then enters the causal story only because the "mental state of a will determined by something or other [*eines irgend wodurch bestimmten Willens*] is itself already a feeling of pleasure and is identical with it" (KU 5: 222; 67). In other words, the moral feeling of respect is not to be regarded as a psychological state incidentally produced by the consciousness of the obligatory power of the moral law, but rather as the affective side of that very consciousness.

It is this latter point that provides the basis for the analogy of the pleasure of taste with moral feeling. Just as moral feeling is not to be thought of as caused by the determination of the will through the moral law, but is instead an ingredient in the consciousness of such a determination, so, in the case of the contemplative judgment of taste, "The very consciousness of a merely formal purposiveness in the play of the subject's cognitive faculties . . . is that pleasure" (KU 5: 222; 68).[24] Thus, the pleasure of taste, which purports to be universally communicable, is claimed to be nothing more than the affective awareness of this purposiveness, which again implies its intentionality. Correlatively, the mental state is not purposive because it produces pleasure (which would make purposiveness into a causal property of certain mental states), but is rather pleasurable because it is purposive. Moreover, this is precisely what one would expect, given the priority of the judging to the feeling affirmed in §9 as the key to the critique of taste.

Causality is, however, not left completely out of the story. Appealing to the definition of pleasure given in §10, Kant claims that the pleasure in the beautiful does exercise a causality; namely, it preserves the representative state of the subject and the activity of the cognitive faculties involved therein. In fact, it does so without any further aim beyond its own self-maintenance. Accordingly, Kant notes, "We *linger* in our contemplation of the beautiful, because this contemplation reinforces and reproduces itself" (KU 5: 222; 68). By denying any further aim to this pleasurable consciousness of the purposiveness of the mental state of free harmony, Kant is once again underscoring the disinterested nature of the liking for the beautiful. But unlike Ginsborg's account in terms of the self-referentiality of the pleasure of taste, this does not preclude the possibility of negative judgments of taste involving a universally communicable displeasure. In the latter case, the endeavor of the mental state to preserve itself in its free play is frustrated, and instead of lingering in contemplation, the activity is abandoned.

III

Having introduced the notion of a form of purposiveness and connected it with the pleasure of taste, Kant is ready to explicate the underlying conception of form and to connect it explicitly with a pure judgment of taste. This is the task of §13–§14, where Kant introduces his notorious formalist thesis that a pure judgment of taste attends exclusively to the form of the object or its representation. Such judgments are distinguished from the impure or empirical variety, which are either conditioned by or based on such factors as charm and emotion. An additional noteworthy feature of these sections is Kant's sharp change of tone in the presentation of his claims. Whereas in the first two moments, Kant often wrote as if he were presenting generally acceptable views (even though we have seen that this was not the case with regard to disinterestedness), he now seems to take pains to point out that he is going against the consensus. Thus, while insisting on a sharp distinction between beauty and charm, he notes that this is widely ignored (KU 5: 223; 69). He further admits that "most people" will declare a mere color or tone to be "beautiful in themselves" (KU 5: 224; 70); but he then proceeds to argue that they are either simply wrong or correct for the wrong reasons. In short, Kant here seems to be taking the offensive, arguing explicitly for a nonstandard position, one which, as we shall see, is based on a deeply problematic conception of form.

The problem can be clarified by noting the distinction, emphasized by Guyer, between a *form of purposiveness* and a *purposiveness of form*.[25] In the preceding section we were concerned exclusively with the former notion. As we have seen, "form" here has the sense of *mere* form; so the operative contrast is between merely seeming purposive or being purposive-like, which occurs when this purposiveness is not connected with a determinate purpose, and actually being purposive or manifesting a purpose. As we have also seen, the object of a pure judgment of taste (or its representation) is deemed purposive in this sense insofar as it occasions the harmonious (and purposive) mental state that is the source of the universally communicable pleasure of taste. And this seems to suggest that it is sufficient that an object (or its representation) be capable of occasioning such a state for the form of purposiveness to be attributed to it.

By contrast, "purposiveness of form" refers, as the phrase indicates, to the purposive nature of the *form* of an object. Consequently, it seems to be a species of genuine purposiveness, albeit one that somehow pertains merely to the form of an object (or its representation), as opposed to its "matter," that is, its sensible content. Moreover, we see here the source of the twofold problem posed by these sections. First, since the form of purposiveness is clearly not equivalent to the purposiveness of form, Kant owes us an argument, which he never provides, for the sudden move in §13 from the former to the latter. Second, Kant seems to take the latter to entail a highly restrictive aesthetic formalism, which not only is implausible in its own right but also stands in apparent contradiction to his later characterization of beauty as the expression of aesthetic ideas.

Although I believe that such criticism is not entirely unwarranted, I also think that there is a defensible core to Kant's formalism and that it cannot be dismissed as the result of an illicit slide of the kind Guyer suggests. At the very least, I shall argue, Kant's account of the harmony of the faculties entails a certain conception of form as the condition of this harmony, and that this, in turn, explains the move from the form of purposiveness to the purposiveness of form. And in Chapter 12 I shall further argue that, properly construed, Kant's focus on form in the Analytic of the Beautiful is perfectly compatible with his later characterization of beauty in terms of the expression of aesthetic ideas (KU 5: 320; 199). Our present problem, however, is that Kant does not limit himself to this acceptable conception in the Analytic. Instead, as Guyer and others have noted, he identifies aesthetic form with spatiotemporal structure, that is, perceptual or cognitive form, and it is this identification that leads to the highly restrictive formalism.[26]

The official thesis of §13 is that a pure judgment of taste is independent of both charm and emotion. But since emotion [*Rührung*] is not discussed at all in this section and only briefly at the end of §14 (where it is connected with the sublime), the focus is entirely on the rejection of charm, both as the criterion of, and an ingredient in, beauty. The initial reason offered for this rejection is one that is already familiar to us, namely, that a liking for charm is really a liking for the agreeable, and thus based on an interest, which undermines any claim to universal validity.

In the second paragraph of §13, however, Kant goes beyond this and affirms that beauty is properly concerned only with form, whereas charm concerns matter. Thus, a judgment of taste based on charm is one in which "the matter of the liking is passed off as the form." On the basis of this, in the third paragraph Kant defines a *pure judgment of taste* negatively as one that is not influenced by charm (or emotion), and positively as one whose determining ground is "merely the purposiveness of form" (KU 5: 223; 69). Here, then, is the locus of the fateful shift to a new notion of form, one which supposedly functions as the sole determinant of aesthetic worth.[27]

Nevertheless, §13 does not really tell us what is meant by either "form" or "matter" in this context. We learn this first in §14, where the latter is clearly equated with sensation (or what is given in sensation) and the former apparently with spatiotemporal organization. The dominant theme in this section is the correlation between the pure–empirical and the matter–form distinctions. Thus, Kant remarks that only pure aesthetic judgments, since they are formal, are properly judgments of taste, whereas the empirical variety, also characterized as "material aesthetic judgments," are reducible to judgments about the agreeable. Naturally, judgments based on charm or emotion are assigned to the latter category (KU 5: 223-4; 69).

Kant's major concern in §14 is to defend this formalist thesis against possible objections, and it is in the course of this defense that we first come to see what it involves. The major objection that he addresses concerns the belief, attributed to "most people," that "a mere color, such as the green color of a lawn, or a mere tone (as distinct from sound or noise) as, for example, that of a violin" are beautiful in themselves. This is seen as a potential objection or, better, counterexample, to Kant's view because both the color and the tone "seem to be based merely on the matter of representations, i.e., solely on sensation" (KU 5: 224; 70). But instead of simply denying that mere colors and tones can by themselves count as beauties, Kant seems to suggest that they may indeed be considered as such insofar as they are pure, since this already involves form, rather than merely matter or sensation. According to this view, then, where most people go wrong is not in assuming that mere colors or tones can be beautiful, but rather in misconstruing the grounds of this beauty, regarding it as a question of matter or sensation rather than form.

I have said that Kant *seems* to affirm this, rather than simply dismissing the notion that colors or tones of themselves have any claim to beauty because there is a notorious difficulty regarding the text. The core of the problem concerns the question of Kant's adherence to Euler's theory of colors and sounds as vibrations of the ether in uniform temporal sequence and of air, respectively. Kant remarks that if we accept this theory, together with the assumption, "which I do not doubt at all" [*Woran ich doch gar nicht zweifle*] that

> the mind perceives not only by sense, the effect that these vibrations have on the excitement of the organ, but also, by reflection, the regular play of the impressions (and hence the form in the connection of different representations), then color and tone would not be mere sensations but would already be the formal determination of the manifold in these, in which case they could even by themselves be considered beauties. (KU 5: 224; 70–1)

The clause "which I do not doubt at all" refers to the assumption that some reflection is involved even in the perception of colors and tones. This assumption would seem to be entailed by Euler's theory, and it is the locus of the textual problem. As Wilhelm Windelband, the editor of the third *Critique* for the *Akademie Ausgabe*, points out, this formulation first appears in the third edition, where it replaces "which, however, I doubt very much" [*woran ich doch gar sehr zweifle*] that appeared in the first two.[28] Thus, the question becomes whether Kant changed his mind on this fundamental point or merely corrected a misprint in the earlier editions. Unfortunately, the evidence does not point unambiguously either way. On the one hand, there are texts in which Kant clearly expresses his basic agreement with Euler's theory, while, on the other hand, in a passage in the *Anthropology*, he seems to favor an alternative theory in the case of sight.[29] And, to make matters even more confusing, Kant expresses a certain ambivalence on the question within the *Critique of Judgment* itself.[30]

Nevertheless, all things considered, it seems reasonable to assume that Kant accepted Euler's theory or, at the very least, took it as a serious possibility; and this required him likewise to take seriously the possibility that reflection is involved in the sensation of mere colors and tone.[31] At the same time, however, Kant also insists on limiting this to what is "pure" in a simple kind of sensation, by which he understood its "uniformity, undisturbed and uninterrupted by any alien sensation" (KU 5: 224; 71). Consequently, it is the uniformity that pertains to form; while the fact that it can be appreciated in reflection in abstraction from the particular quality of the sensation is apparently what allows such uniformity to be considered beautiful, rather than merely agreeable. This is contrasted with so-called mixed colors, which not being simple, presumably lack the uniformity on the basis of which an appreciation of mere form in abstraction from the matter of sensation is possible.[32]

After this cryptic, yet revealing, discussion of color, Kant devotes the rest of §14 to the reiteration and clarification of his view that beauty properly concerns only form and that charm stands in at best a tenuous relationship with the beautiful. On the one hand, he insists that it is a "vulgar error," harmful to "genuine, uncorrupted, solid taste," to consider charm as actually contributing to the beauty of an object. On the other hand, he concedes that charm may have a kind of auxiliary role to play by awakening interest when taste is not yet cultivated (KU 5: 225; 71). The main import of this portion of the section, however, lies in what Kant has to say about the arts. Thus, he remarks that in all visual arts, insofar as they are fine arts, *design* [*Zeichnung*] is alone what is essential, whereas features, such as colors that illuminate the outline, belong to charm and therefore can make the object vivid to sense, but not beautiful. Moreover, Kant reduces the form of sensible objects (of both outer and inner sense to either *shape* or *play* [*Gestalt, oder Spiel*]. Although he does not define the former, his emphasis on design indicates that he means by it spatial configuration,[33] while with regard to the latter, he distinguishes between a play of shapes in space (as in dance and mimetic art) and a mere play of sensations in time. Kant admits that in both cases charms may be added, but he insists that in the former case it is *design* and in the latter *composition* that are alone the proper object of a pure judgment of taste (KU 5: 225; 71–2).

This is as clear an illustration as one could wish of a restricted formalism in Guyer's sense, that is, one that equates form with the spatial or temporal organization of objects, actions, or, in the case of music, series of sounds.[34] As Guyer correctly notes, this formalism arises from a straightforward application of the first *Critique*'s conception of perceptual form to the object of aesthetic evaluation.[35] Just as spatiotemporal ordering and the content given in sensation were characterized in the Transcendental Aesthetic respectively as the form and matter of perception or empirical intuition, so now this same ordering or organization is regarded as the unique "formal," beauty-making feature of objects, and sensible content is viewed as the "matter," capable only of "charming," that is, producing a feeling of agreeableness lacking any claim to universality. That such a formalism is restrictive, indeed, unduly so, is evidenced by the fact that it precludes, from the realm of taste proper, features that are usually (and rightly) thought to be integral to the beauty of works of art. For example, in painting, this thesis would apparently rule out such features as the arrangement of the colors and in music, instrumentation, both of which must be assigned to mere charm, according to the Kantian schema.[36] Moreover, as Guyer points out, Kant's appeal to pure colors hardly helps matters, since it is precisely the complex arrangement of colors (or tones) that one would like to think of as potentially beautiful.[37]

In calling attention to this formalism, Guyer also insists that it is not required by the harmony of the faculties, which for him constitutes the essence of Kant's theory of aesthetic response.[38] Indeed, for him the form of purposiveness stands for little more than a placeholder for whatever is capable of occasioning such harmony.[39] Now, insofar as we have seen that the form of purposiveness was introduced into the story precisely to account for this harmony, there seems to be some truth to this analysis. Nevertheless, I believe that Guyer goes too far, since Kant's account of the harmony of the faculties does require a connection with form, if not the conception of form derived from the Transcendental Aesthetic.[40]

The connection with form follows directly from the reflective nature of the judgment of taste.[41] What is decisive here is that the harmony of the faculties is a harmony in mere reflection, which means that the product of the imagination's apprehension seems suitable for the exhibition of a concept (although no concept in particular). But, clearly, only an arrangement or ordering of sensible content, that is, an organized manifold of some sort, and not an isolated sensation, is capable of fulfilling that function.[42] In other words, only such an arrangement could serve as a possible subject for reflection, and such an arrangement of sensible data, as contrasted with the data themselves, certainly counts as "form" in Kant's sense. Indeed, this is precisely Kant's point in the cited passage concerning color; for there, it will be recalled, the key factor was that color perception (at least according to Euler's theory), necessarily involves an element of reflection, in contrast to mere sensation, and it was this reflection that was correlated with form.

It should also be clear that form, construed as a possible subject matter for reflection, may include, but need not be limited to, spatiotemporal configuration.[43] What is required is merely some kind of diversity for the imagination to unify in its apprehension and present for reflection. Although it is admittedly difficult to see how this could be found in the simple, uniform colors to which Kant refers, there is no reason that it could not be provided by an arrangement of contrasting colors as well as shapes. For instance, the set of paintings by Josef Albers, cited by Guyer as a counterexample to Kant's formalism on the grounds that their aesthetic value stems from their confluence of colors rather than their rigid geometrical form, could easily be brought under this nonrestrictive conception of form.[44]

This likewise accords with the preliminary account of aesthetic form, given in Chapter 2 in connection with the discussion of Kant's treatments of judgments of taste in the Introductions. There, it will be recalled, I suggested that "form" referred primarily to the ordering or arrangement of an object's features as they are taken up by the imagination, so that the question becomes whether this ordering or arrangement (form) simulates the exhibition of a concept. On this view, a beautiful object is one which provides the materials for such an ordering by the imagination, and one which does this may be said to possess a "subjective formal purposiveness" or a "purposiveness of form." This is a nonrestrictive conception of form; but it is not a trivial one, since not every object meets this condition.[45]

Another text supporting this broader interpretation of form is §67 of the *Anthropology*. In an explanation of the nature of taste, Kant there writes:

> But in *taste* . . . that is, in aesthetic judgment – what produces the pleasure in the object is not the *sensation* immediately (the material element in our idea of the object). It is rather the way in which free (productive) imagination arranges this matter inventively [*durch Dichtung zusammenpaart*] – that is, the *form;* for only form can lay claim to a universal rule for the feeling of pleasure. We can expect no such universal rule from sensations, which can differ greatly, as the subjects differ in the aptitude of their senses. (Anthro 7: 240–1; 108)

Here again, form is explicitly identified with the arrangement of the sensible material produced by the imagination in its apprehension of the object (rather than with any structural feature of the object apprehended), and once again there is no indication that this arrangement is limited to spatiotemporal configuration. Against this it might be objected that a reference to the latter is implicit in the connection between form and universality, as opposed to sensations which can make no such claim. Indeed, it is precisely the need to account for universality that apparently underlies Kant's tendency to conflate perceptual and aesthetic form in the third moment.[46] But even if Kant at times may have thought that it was, it really is not necessary to identify form with spatiotemporal configuration in order to account for the universality of a pure judgment of taste.[47] For, as we have seen in connection with the analysis of the second moment, what is required for such universality is merely a universally communicable mental state. Moreover, a state of free harmony of the cognitive faculties is such a state, since in harmonizing with each other, the imagination and understanding accord with the condition of cognition, and since (on pain of skepticism) this condition must likewise be regarded as universally communicable. What we now learn is that only the "form" of the representation of an object can provide the basis for such a harmony because only this form can provide the subject matter for the act of reflection in which a free harmony occurs. As we have already seen, however, any arrangement of the sensible data apprehended that is capable of occasioning and sustaining reflection counts as "form" in this sense, and this is not limited to spatiotemporal ordering.[48]

What, then, of the charge that Kant is guilty of a slide from the form of purposiveness to the purposiveness of form? Or perhaps that he simply equated the two? As the preceding analysis shows, they are clearly two distinct conceptions, and it cannot be denied that Kant moves from one to the other without any explanation of the terminological shift, just as if he regarded them as synonymous. Nevertheless, given this analysis of purposive form, the procedure is not as egregious as it first appears. For what this analysis shows is that the object (or representation thereof) that occasions the free harmony of the faculties falls successively under both descriptions. It falls under the first insofar as it is introduced (in §11) as the occasion of this free harmony. It is brought under the second when we learn (§13–§14) that it functions in this manner in virtue of its purposive form. In short, an object of aesthetic appraisal exhibits the form of purposiveness just in case it has a purposive form. Moreover, this result survives the rejection of Kant's ill-advised, restrictively formalistic, account of such form.

Parenthetically, it is interesting to note that form in this extended sense is also the basis for judgments of ugliness. A sensation of itself may be agreeable or disagreeable, but it cannot be beautiful or ugly because a bare sensation cannot provide a basis for the reflection through which both beauty and ugliness are determined. Otherwise expressed, the lack of form or the "formlessness" underlying a negative judgment of taste is itself a species of form (albeit a displeasing one), since it supplies material for reflection. Nevertheless, we cannot simply identify the ugly with such formlessness, since Kant connects the sublime with the latter, and he certainly did not wish to regard the sublime as a species of the ugly. As we shall see when we come to the sublime, however, this particular type of formlessness is again a species of form, since it occasions a kind of reflection, albeit one that is distinct from that of the judgment of taste.

IV

Whereas §13 and §14 were concerned with the determination of the condition of the purity of a judgment of taste, which they located in purposive form as opposed to sensible matter, the last three sections of the third moment refocus on the aesthetic nature of such judgments. Thus, the same purposive form, which is apprehended aesthetically through feeling, is now contrasted with conceptual content (in the form of a concept of what the object is meant to be [*sein soll*]), which is grasped cognitively. At the most superficial level, the basic idea is that just as sensible matter (in the guise of charm and emotion) can undermine the purity of a judgment of taste, if it is made either a condition of, or an ingredient in, the evaluation, so, too, the introduction of conceptual content can produce the same result. In reality, however, the full story turns out to be much more complex and interesting. For Kant holds that the conceptual component can enter into a positive relation to taste in a way that sensible factors, such as charm and emotion, cannot. Moreover, this asymmetry leads, in turn, to the necessity of distinguishing between an impure judgment of taste and a judgment of beauty that is not purely a judgment of taste. Although Kant does not draw this distinction in so many words, we shall see that it underlies his whole analysis in these sections.

In §15, Kant provides the basis for what follows by emphasizing the complete independence of the judgment of taste as such from the concept of perfection. This independence does not come as a surprise, since it is a direct consequence of the aesthetic nature of the judgment of taste on which Kant has insisted from the very beginning. Nevertheless, Kant apparently thought it important to emphasize it at this point in order to avoid a possible confusion between his conception of purposive form, now also labeled "subjective formal purposiveness," and the Baumgartian perfectionist view of beauty, which appeals to an "objective," that is, conceptually based, purposiveness (KU 5: 228; 74). In particular, it must be distinguished from a thing's "qualitative perfection," understood as the harmony of its manifold (set of properties) with the concept of the thing, that is, "with *what sort of thing it is meant to be*" [*was es für ein Ding sein solle*] (KU 5: 227; 74).[49] The basic difference, of course, is that the Kantian subjective formal purposiveness, as a purposiveness *without purpose*, does not rest on a concept at all, much less on one of what sort of thing the object of a pure judgment of taste is meant to be. Accordingly, beauty cannot be conceived, as it is by the Baumgartians, as perfection confusedly represented. On the contrary, from Kant's standpoint, such a view completely misconstrues the transcendental nature of the distinction between sensibility and understanding, and, as a consequence, fails to recognize the aesthetic nature of the judgment of taste.[50]

In §16, however, Kant appears to make a significant retreat from this sharp separation between the judgment of taste (as purely aesthetic) and any judgment of perfection. For he there introduces a distinction between two kinds of beauty: free and dependent or adherent [*anhängende*] beauty (*pulchritudo vaga* and *pulchritudo adhaerens*).[51] Free beauty, we are told, does not presuppose a concept of what the object is meant to be, whereas adherent beauty does presuppose such a concept, "as well as the object's perfection in terms of that concept." Consequently, the latter species of beauty "is adherent to a concept (i.e., it is conditioned beauty) and as such is attributed to objects that fall under the concept of a particular purpose" (KU 5: 229; 76).

Moreover, Kant further indicates that this contrast cuts across the distinction between natural and artistic beauty. Thus, as examples of free beauty he cites flowers, various birds, and many crustaceans of the sea, as well as designs *à la grecque,* the foliage on borders or on wall paper, and all music not set to words [*ohne Text*] (KU 5: 229; 76–7). And later in the same section, Kant also includes in the category of adherent beauty such items as human beings, horses, and buildings, as well as any kind of representative art, all of which supposedly presuppose a concept of what the object is meant to be.[52] The basic point here is that this concept functions as an external, that is, extra-aesthetic, constraint or condition on what may properly be deemed beautiful. So, for example, Kant suggests that much decoration might be added to a building, were it not for the fact that it functions as a church, or, that a human figure might be embellished with all sorts of designs (he here has in mind the Maori tattoos), were it not a human figure (KU 5: 530; 77). In such cases, then, purely aesthetic value seems to be trumped by other considerations, which may, but need not be, moral.

This whole account raises many questions that have been discussed in the literature. Among these are: Why are animals such as crustaceans included in one category and horses and human beings in the other? What does Kant mean here by "representation," and how does it relate to the governing notion of presupposing a concept of what the thing is meant to be? Does Kant's location of representative art (however that may be understood) in the category of merely adherent beauty commit him to the view that foliage on borders is somehow aesthetically superior to the works of Michelangelo or Shakespeare? Is the distinction best described as holding between two kinds of beauty, as the opening portions of the text clearly suggest, or is it rather between two ways of judging beauty, as Kant's closing remarks indicate? And if the latter, does it follow that any potential object of aesthetic appraisal may be evaluated in either manner?[53] Clearly, however, the major puzzle is simply how, given the thesis of the third moment, together with his unambiguous pronouncements in §15, can Kant regard judgments of adherent beauty as judgments of beauty at all? Or, putting it in the object mode, how can he regard adherent beauties as properly beautiful, since in their case the perceived purposiveness is clearly subservient to a purpose?[54]

The whole question of the relation between free and adherent beauty will be taken up again in Chapter 12 in connection with an analysis of Kant's views on fine art. But here our attention must be confined mainly to the last and most important of the aforementioned problems, since it directly concerns the compatibility of Kant's conception of a merely adherent beauty with the basic principles of his theory of taste, and particularly the thesis of the third moment. Once this is resolved, it should be possible to say something (at least in a preliminary way) about some of these problems, saving the issues that bear specifically on fine art (such as the nature of representation) for Chapter 12.

The major point is that rather than attempting (unsuccessfully) to impose constraints on the pure judgment of taste beyond those derivable from the harmony of the faculties alone, as Guyer has suggested, Kant is here indicating how taste can enter into more complex forms of evaluation in which it plays a subordinate role without compromising its inherent purity.[55] As Martin Gammon has pointed out, Kant supplies the model for such a combination, and therefore for understanding the possibility of a merely adherent beauty at the end of §14, where he introduces under the label "*parerga*" extrinsic factors, such as picture frames, draperies on statues, and colonnades around buildings.[56]

For present purposes, the essential point about such *parerga* is that insofar as they increase the liking for the basic object of aesthetic evaluation, they do so in virtue of their form (KU 5: 226; 72). In other words, such "parergonal objects" are deemed beautiful in their own right by means of a pure judgment of taste; but this beauty is nonetheless conditioned by the larger whole in which these objects play a subordinate role. Thus, a picture frame might be quite beautiful, if considered by itself, yet totally inappropriate as a frame, if it detracted from the appreciation of the painting which it frames. Moreover, even though Kant does not use the expression in this context, it is clear that the beauty of the frame may be said to be adherent to its function.

Given this, we can see that what Kant does in §16, with his conception of adherent beauty, is to apply this idea of aesthetic supplementation or enhancement to a whole, which is no longer purely aesthetic but is instead governed by a concept of what the object is meant to be. Just as in the case of the picture frame, the fact that it serves a purpose constrains or conditions, but does not undermine, its aesthetic value, so too, the beauty of a building that serves as a church is constrained by its function; but this function does not become the determining ground of the aesthetic liking itself. If the latter were the case, the judgment of adherent beauty would, indeed, become a judgment of perfection, and its aesthetic quality would be lost. This does not occur, however, when the aesthetic evaluation is subordinated to a more complex one, of which it forms only a part. To be sure, this more complex evaluation is no longer *purely* a judgment of taste, but this does not undermine the *purity* of the taste component itself. As is the case with "free beauties" (so called because they are free from such constraints), the underlying norm for taste as such remains purposiveness of form, rather than perfection. Consequently, there is no contradiction with §15 or, more generally, with the overall thrust of the argument of the third moment.

This reading not only removes the threat of contradiction and accords with Kant's own analyses of his examples of adherent beauty, but it also provides a basis for dealing with some of the other objections and puzzles that have been noted. First, we can reject Guyer's charge that Kant is attempting to smuggle in substantive restrictions on taste that do not follow from the doctrine of the harmony of the faculties. Since the restrictions Kant is introducing do not apply to taste itself, but rather to its use in connection with certain purposes, his objection simply misses the point. Second, we can see why Kant classifies some animals, such as crustaceans, in the category of free beauties and others, such as horses, in the category of adherent beauty. The point is simply that in the former case we do not usually associate such natural forms with any purpose with which we might combine their aesthetic estimation, whereas in the latter case we clearly do. Thus, our evaluation of horses is so closely connected with the purposes for which we use them that it is difficult, if not impossible, to separate a purely aesthetic estimation from this larger picture. The example of flowers, which Kant describes as free, natural beauties, is interesting in this regard because, as he indicates, they do serve objective purposes as the reproductive organs of plants. Kant also points out, however, that hardly anyone but the botanist knows what sort of function a flower is supposed to fulfill, and even the botanist, while recognizing it, is easily able to abstract from this in making a pure judgment of taste (KU 5: 229; 76).

This latter point also bears on the problem that Kant seems unsure as to whether the distinction he has in mind is between kinds of beauty or kinds of judgment about beauty. In fact, though Kant does present the distinction in both ways, neither is quite correct. The proper contrast is between two ways in which the beauty of an object (which as such is always the object of a pure judgment of taste) is to be considered: either solely in its own terms, or as an ingredient in a larger whole, which involves the thought of the purpose served by the object. The implication is that in some cases, it is either very difficult to abstract from this purpose, as in the case of horses, or somehow impermissible or inappropriate, as in the cases of human beings.

Furthermore, in this context it is noteworthy that Kant concludes his discussion in §16 by pointing out that the distinction between free and adherent beauty provides a tool for the analysis and resolution of aesthetic disagreements. When he initially considered such disagreements, the question turned on whether the evaluation was based on purposiveness of form or mere charm and/or emotion. Although the normativity of taste cannot be grounded prior to the Deduction, it was already clear at that point that the purity of a judgment of taste is at least the *sine qua non* of any claim to speak with a universal voice. Now, by contrast, Kant suggests that if one party to an aesthetic disagreement is making a judgment of free and the other of adherent beauty, both may be correct in their evaluations. To be sure, he also says that the former is making a pure and the latter an "applied" [*angewandtes*] judgment of taste (KU 5: 231; 78). Nevertheless, an applied judgment of taste (whatever that may be) is clearly not the same as an impure one (even though it is not purely a judgment of taste). And this, again, underscores the asymmetry between taste's relation to charm or the merely agreeable on the one hand and to perfection or the good on the other. Whereas the former poses a direct threat to the purity, and hence normativity, of taste, the latter simply imposes limits on its hegemony.

Finally, it will be noticed that, though I have supposedly been concerned with both §16 and §17, I have focused the discussion exclusively on the former. This is because from the standpoint of Kant's theory of taste, the latter section, which is concerned with the human figure as the ideal of beauty, does not add anything of decisive significance. From that standpoint, the beauty of a human being is simply another type of adherent beauty. The difference is that unlike the other forms of adherent beauty discussed in §16, that to which the beauty of the human figure adheres is the rational idea of morality. As Kant puts it, what is properly "ideal" in the human figure "consists in the expression of the moral" (KU 5: 235; 83). And this is what makes it impermissible rather than, as with the other types of adherent beauty, merely psychologically difficult, to view the beauty of the human figure apart from the concept of "what sort of thing it is meant to be." For the very same reason, Kant's discussion of this unique ideal points ahead to the connection of taste and the experience of beauty with morality, which is the concern of the third part of this study; but it does not really contribute anything further to the theory of taste itself.[57]

THE MODALITY OF TASTE AND
THE *SENSUS COMMUNIS*

The fourth moment of the Analytic of the Beautiful is concerned with the modality of a pure judgment of taste, specifically the necessity claim or demand for agreement that is made in connection with a judgment purporting to be pure. It was argued in Chapter 3 that the modality of the pure judgment of taste, like that of logical judgments, is unique among the moments in that it does not contribute anything to the content of the judgment, but concerns instead its bearing on the judgment of others, or what might be termed its evaluative force. Thus, the content of a pure judgment of taste is completely determined by its disinterestedness, its subjective universality based on a free harmony of the faculties, and its basis in the form of the object or its representation. Since these exhaust the conditions under which a given judgment of taste can be pure, they also determine the distinct elements of the *quid facti*. What the fourth moment analyzes is the demand for the agreement of others made by a judgment possessing these features.

Its basic claim is that this demand presupposes the idea of a common sense [*Gemeinsinn*], an idea which combines within itself all of the factors analyzed separately in the first three moments, and which therefore functions as the supreme condition of the possibility of a pure judgment of taste. As already noted in Chapter 3, Kant himself makes this point at the end of §22, when he remarks that the task up to this point has been merely "to analyze the faculty of taste into its elements, and to unite these ultimately in the idea of a common sense" (KU 5: 240; 90). And, as was also there noted, for this very reason the fourth moment, like the first three, pertains to the *quid facti;* though it also differs from them in that, rather than an additional condition, it provides a unifying focus for the conditions that must be met, if a judgment of taste is to be pure.

Admittedly, however, this picture, with its neat division of labor, appears to be called into question by Kant's procedure in the fourth moment. For after moving in the familiar regressive fashion in the first three sections, from a consideration of the nature of the necessity claim connected with the pure judgment of taste to the idea of a common sense as its necessary condition, Kant suddenly appears to shift his concern in §21 to that of providing a transcendental grounding for the principle of common sense itself by linking it to cognition and its necessary conditions. In other words, Kant seems to have turned, already within the Analytic of the Beautiful, from an analytic or regressive to a synthetic or progressive procedure, and, therefore, from the *quid facti* to the *quid juris*. Moreover, this has quite understandably led many commentators to assume that he is here offering a "first deduction" of the principle of taste, which is later supplemented (or replaced) by the official Deduction.[1]

Nevertheless, two features of Kant's account call into question this assumption and provide at least indirect support for the alternative reading advocated here. First, we shall see that the so-called deduction of §21 turns out to be manifestly inadequate as a deduction of a common sense, construed as the principle of taste; though it contains a line of argument that is at least plausible, if taken instead as an attempt to show that we have grounds to assume something like an epistemic common sense as a condition of the universal communicability of cognition. Second, in the second half of §22, Kant poses a series of questions regarding common sense and taste, which are extremely perplexing, if not unintelligible, on the assumption that he has just provided a deduction of the principle of taste, but are perfectly in order and deeply suggestive if one abandons that assumption.

In light of these considerations, then, the major goal of the present chapter is to integrate the argument of the fourth moment into the interpretive framework of the *quid facti* as specified in Chapter 3. It is divided into three parts. The first traces the basic argument leading to the idea of a common sense as the ground or condition of the demand for agreement affirmed in a pure judgment of taste (§18–§20). The second analyzes the argument of §21. As already suggested, its aim is to show that though the argument is unsuccessful if taken as a deduction of the principle of taste, it becomes plausible if understood in strictly epistemological terms. It also attempts to show that, on the latter reading, the argument of §21 for the necessity of presupposing a common sense, though not itself part of the deduction of taste, nonetheless serves a twofold function: First, it provides grounds for postulating a cognitive capacity that is a necessary (though not a sufficient) condition of the possibility of taste; second, it removes a worry generated by the account of the conditions of a pure judgment of taste that the very idea of a common sense, as Kant here understands it, might be incoherent. Finally, the third part analyzes §22, including the questions posed in its second paragraph, in light of the preceding account of §21. It suggests that, for the most part, §22 should be seen as a continuation of the discussion of the main topic of the fourth moment, from which §21 is something of a digression (albeit an important one), and that the questions posed in its second paragraph point forward to the connection between taste and morality, rather than backward to the argument of §21.

I

We have seen that, in spite of the similarity of function, the modality of aesthetic judgments, like their quantity, differs markedly from that of cognitive judgments. Whereas the modality of the latter concerns the nature of the connection of the representations united in the judgment (whether they are thought as belonging together problematically, assertorically, or apodeictically),[2] that of aesthetic judgments concerns the connection of the representations with *feeling*. Thus, Kant begins §18 by noting that for every representation there is at least the *possibility* of its connection with pleasure; that to call something agreeable is to claim that it *actually* gives rise to pleasure; and that to think of something as beautiful is to assume a *necessary* reference to liking (KU 5: 236; 85). Although Kant does not bother to indicate it at this point, it seems clear that precisely the same analysis is applicable to the connection with displeasure or disliking. Accordingly, one may say of any representation that it is a possible source of displeasure; that to call something disagreeable is to claim that it actually occasions such a negative feeling; and, finally, that to call something ugly is to assert that it has a necessary connection to displeasure or disliking.

Kant, however, is interested only in the last of these aesthetic modalities, which, as we shall see, he does later present in a way that includes the negative as well as the positive form. But the first order of business is to distinguish the kind of necessity affirmed in a claim of taste from both the theoretical, objective necessity involved in *a priori* knowledge claims and the practical, objective necessity of moral commands. Like the corresponding universality, the necessity affirmed in a pure judgment of taste is subjective, since it relates to a feeling. Kant himself characterizes it as *exemplary*, which is glossed as "a necessity of the assent of *everyone* to a judgment that is regarded as an example of a universal rule that we are unable to state" (KU 5: 237; 85). In other words, when I take myself to be making a pure judgment of taste (whether positive or negative), I am claiming to have judged an object as it ought to be judged, and this is the basis for my demand for the agreement of others.[3] Moreover, I make this claim because I assume that my judgment instantiates a universal rule, which, since the judgment is aesthetic rather than cognitive (based on a feeling rather than a concept), cannot be stated.

The idea that one has judged an object as it ought to be judged also helps to bring out more clearly the difference between the second and fourth moments. For, once again, the former concerns the "quantity" of the feeling, that is, the idea that it is a universally shareable, rather than a merely private, one, which is part of what is meant by claiming that the liking is for the beautiful (as opposed to the agreeable); and this is quite distinct from the claim that, in a particular case, one's evaluation is as it ought to be.

When I first discussed this difference in Chapter 3, I attempted to illustrate it by means of a parallelism between the subjective universality or universal communicability that is intrinsic to a judgment of taste, and that distinguishes its "logic" from that of a judgment of agreeableness, and the objective validity that is criterial for a cognitive judgment, since it serves to distinguish a judgment from the mere association of the same representations. In both cases, we have features that are intrinsic to and criterial for judgment, and that seem to resemble closely modality insofar as they involve a normative element; yet we also saw that, in both cases, they must be sharply distinguished from the latter. Now, in light of the account of exemplary necessity, we are in a position to illustrate the same distinction by means of a comparison with moral judgments, which may even be more to the point, since the notion of universality is operative in both cases.

To begin with, claims regarding the moral goodness (or badness) of acts, characters, or states of affairs are, in virtue of their logic, inherently universal. Thus, as Kant repeatedly points out, it is incoherent to claim that something is "right for me," but not also right for any other rational agent under relevantly similar circumstances. This is nothing more than what is usually called the "universality of reasons." But such universality, which, in Kant's terms, is part of the "content" of a moral judgment, is certainly distinct from the claim that one has judged as one ought to have judged, that is, has based one's evaluation on the proper principle. The latter is determined by the categorical imperative, which asks only whether a maxim is consistent with itself when made into a universal law.[4]

The major difference between judgments of taste and moral judgments is that, in the case of the former, the rule grounding the judgment cannot be stated. Although a direct consequence of the aesthetic, noncognitive nature of the judgment, it is easily subject to misunderstanding. Since, as we shall see, the goal of the Deduction is precisely to formulate and ground the normative principle of taste, there is a sense in which the rule must be statable; otherwise there would be no point to a critique of taste. Thus, what Kant is denying is simply that the rule in question can function as an objective principle stating necessary and/or sufficient conditions of beauty; for in that case, the judgment would be either objective and cognitive or morally practical.

Continuing his analysis of this exemplary necessity, Kant points out in §19 that it is not only subjective but also conditional [*bedingt*].[5] Specifically, it is conditional upon the correct subsumption of the instance (the particular appraisal) under the unstatable rule. Since we believe that we have in this rule a ground that is common to all, we "solicit" [*wirbt um*] the assent of all to our evaluation. Indeed, Kant suggests that if (*per impossibile*) we could be certain of the correctness of our subsumption, we could actually count on this universal assent (KU 5: 237; 86).[6] Clearly, the latter cannot be his considered view, since a *de facto* universal agreement would depend on *everyone* (not merely oneself) making the correct subsumption; but this does not affect the main point that one's demand for the agreement of others is conditional upon the correctness of one's subsumption under an unstatable rule.

In the next section (§20), Kant identifies this mysterious, unstatable rule, which serves as the condition or ground of the demand for universal agreement implicit in the pure judgment of taste, with the idea of a common sense. This, therefore, marks the first appearance of this conception, which is initially defined as "the effect arising from the free play of our cognitive faculties" (KU 5: 238; 87). The argument for the necessity of presupposing a common sense, so construed, is typically succinct and by elimination. The underlying premise is that the claim of an exemplary necessity, like any necessity claim, must rest on some principle. The issue is therefore what kind of principle could underwrite such a subjective necessity. Given the nature of the judgment in question, Kant reasons that it must be one that determines what is liked or *disliked* [emphasis mine] by means of feeling, rather than concepts, yet at the same time with universal validity. This formulation is significant, since it shows that the principle underlying a pure judgment of taste must account for negative as well as positive judgments. But the major point is Kant's conclusion that such a principle can only be regarded as a common sense [*nur als ein Gemeinsinn angesehen werden*] (KU 5:238; 87). In other words, a common sense is presented as the only conceivable candidate for the required principle, because it is the only faculty capable of combining the features of being a sense and being able to support claims of universal validity.

It is important to recognize that the idea of a common sense, as it emerges here, is designed to provide precisely what the first three moments of the Analytic revealed to be necessary for the possibility of a pure judgment of taste. Thus, the "effect arising from the free play of our cognitive faculties" may be characterized as a disinterested liking (or disliking), which, in virtue of its subjective source (in the free play of the cognitive faculties), is attributable to all judging subjects, and which is occasioned by the form of the object or its representation. In this respect, Kant's procedure may be compared with the central argument of Part I of the *Prolegomena*. There, it will be recalled, Kant was concerned to uncover the condition under which mathematical knowledge could be both synthetic and *a priori* (a seemingly impossible combination). The answer provided was that such knowledge is possible only on the assumption of an underlying pure or *a priori* intuition (a likewise seemingly impossible combination), which is claimed to be possible, however, just in case this intuition contains nothing but a pure form of sensibility.[7] What now needs explaining is something that seems equally paradoxical, namely, a *feeling* (something inherently private), which is connected with a claim of universal communicability. Thus, the idea of a common sense, as the only condition under which such a claim regarding a mere feeling is possible, plays precisely the same role in the case of taste as that of a pure intuition does in the case of mathematics.

Against this claim for such a parallelism it might be objected that "common sense" or *sensus communis* is a familiar philosophical expression with a long, albeit extremely complex, history, whereas "pure intuition" is a term of art, expressly introduced by Kant to resolve a problem that he took himself to be the first to have fully recognized.[8] But even though Kant here helps himself to a familiar philosophical notion, he clearly does not take himself to be using it in a familiar way. This much is evident from his explicit distinction of it from the common understanding [*gemeine Verstand*], which, he notes, is also referred to as a "common sense" [*Gemeinsinn*] (KU 5: 238; 87). Indeed, given Kant's well-known disparagement in the *Prolegomena* of the attempt of the Scottish "common sense" philosophers to answer Hume by appealing to the "*gemeinen Menschenverstand*,"[9] one would hardly expect him to appeal to a variant of that notion to resolve an analogous transcendental problem regarding taste.[10] On the contrary, the emphasis in the conception of common sense to which Kant here appeals is on the fact that it is a *sense*. More specifically, it is a sense (or feeling) for what is universally communicable, which can also be assumed to be universally shared. Otherwise expressed, it is a shared capacity to feel what may be universally shareable.[11] Given Kant's analysis in the preceding moments, an effect of the free play of the cognitive faculties falls under this generic conception of a common sense; but the central point is that only such a conception is capable of resolving the problem posed by the analysis of the conditions of taste. Consequently, it is a common sense in this sense that must be presupposed, if a pure judgment of taste is to be possible.

II

With this understanding of Kant's project in mind, we are in a position to examine the argument of §21, which, as previously noted, is usually taken as an attempted deduction of common sense as a principle of taste. Admittedly, such a reading is strongly suggested by the text. Kant, after all, moves directly from the claim that the idea of a common sense is necessarily presupposed in a putatively pure judgment of taste in §20 to a consideration of the question of whether we have grounds for presupposing a common sense in §21. Moreover, unless we are explicitly told otherwise, it certainly seems reasonable to assume that the same thing is understood by a common sense in both sections. Indeed, we shall see that the idea of a common sense to which Kant appeals in §21 fits the general description of what is required according to §20, namely, a shared sense for what is universally shareable or communicable.

Nevertheless, though perhaps the most natural one, such a reading is not actually required. For it is also possible to take the argument of §21 as an attempt to ground or, more precisely, show the reasonableness of postulating, a strictly cognitive conception of common sense. Such an endeavor would not constitute part of a deduction of taste, understood as a *sensus communis aestheticus,* but it would bear on an eventual deduction in the two ways noted previously: namely, by providing grounds for presupposing what turns out to be a necessary condition of the possibility of taste, and by alleviating a worry, generated by the apparently paradoxical nature of the faculty to which Kant is appealing, that the very idea of a common sense might be incoherent or an impossible fiction. Moreover, if the latter were part of Kant's concern, it would also support the previously suggested parallelism with the *Prolegomena's* appeal to a pure intuition to account for the possibility of cognition that is both synthetic and *a priori*.

Since both readings are possible, the choice between them must turn on the question of which, all things considered, makes better sense of the text. And this can be determined only by a close consideration of the argument, which is compressed into a single paragraph in the text, but may be broken down into roughly the following steps:

1. Cognitions and judgments, together with their accompanying convictions [propositional attitudes] must be universally communicable. This is a condition of claiming agreement with an object; consequently, its denial leads to skepticism (sentence one).

2. This entails that the mental state required for cognition in general, that is, the "attunement" [*Stimmung*] of the cognitive faculties, which is that "proportion" [*Proportion*] suitable for turning representations into cognitions, must also be universally communicable. Again, to deny this would be to open the door for skepticism, since this attunement is the subjective condition of cognition (sentence two).

3. This attunement actually occurs whenever the perception of a given object puts the imagination into play, which, in turn, sets the understanding into action; but this attunement varies in proportion to differences in the occasioning objects (sentences three and four).

4. Nevertheless, there must be one optimal attunement, that is, one in which the inner relation is most conducive to the mutual quickening of the cognitive faculties with a view to cognition in general; and this attunement can be determined (recognized) only by feeling (since the alternative – concepts – is ruled out) (sentence five).

5. Moreover, both this attunement and the feeling of it in connection with a given representation must likewise be universally communicable (sentence six).

6. But the universal communicability of this feeling presupposes a common sense (sentence six).

7. Consequently, we do have a basis for assuming a common sense, without relying on psychological observation, as a necessary condition of the universal communicability of our cognition, which must itself be presupposed if skepticism is to be avoided (sentence six).

As should be clear from these steps, the argument attempts to establish the necessity of presupposing a common sense on the basis of epistemological premises that do not make any explicit reference to the nature of taste. The claim is that the price of denying this presupposition is skepticism concerning cognition, rather than merely taste. In fact, there is not a single reference to taste in the entire section. Consequently, the argument poses two basic questions, which must be addressed by any interpretation: (1) whether it, in fact, succeeds in showing that the denial of a common sense entails a skepticism regarding cognition; and (2) if so, what, if anything, does this have to do with taste?

Clearly, the first two steps, which are generally viewed as fairly nonproblematic, relate directly merely to the former question.[12] The first contains a capsule analysis of objectivity reminiscent of the *Prolegomena's* identification of objective validity and necessary universality (for everyone).[13] Put simply, the basic idea is that universal communicability is a condition of objective validity, understood in traditional terms as "agreement with an object," in the sense that it is a condition of distinguishing between "x seems to me to be the case" and "x is the case." Accordingly, to deny the universal communicability of cognitions is to deny the possibility of drawing this distinction, which is precisely what the skeptic claims. As is appropriate, Kant does not here attempt to refute such a skepticism, but simply to point out that it is the price one must pay for denying this universal communicability.

The second step extends this analysis from cognitions to their subjective condition or underlying mental state, which is characterized as that "attunement" or "proportion" of the cognitive faculties requisite for cognition in general. What Kant seems to have in mind here is the relation-

ship between imagination and understanding that allows for the subsumption of what is given in intuition and apprehended through the
imagination under the concepts of the understanding. Clearly, unless our
qualitatively similar intuitions could be subsumed under the same concepts, the universal communicability of our cognitions would be impossible, and we could not distinguish between what merely seems to be the
case under certain private conditions and what actually is the case. Thus,
once again, the door would be open to skepticism.

Problems begin, however, with the next two steps, where Kant first introduces a distinction between various degrees or proportions of attunement, which is a function of differences in the objects apprehended, and
then suggests that one such attunement must be "optimal" [*die zuträglich-
ste*] for the purpose of cognition in general. Since Kant claims that this
optimal attunement can be determined only through feeling, rather than
concepts, and since this leads to the identification of this feeling with
common sense (step 6), via the assertion of its universal communicability (step 5), it is also here that the crucial link with taste must be made
for any reading that sees in the argument an attempted deduction of the
principle of taste.

Kant's argument, according to this generally accepted reading, continues roughly as follows. (1) By the "optimal attunement" is to be understood that which is most conducive to the free harmony of the faculties, which we have already seen is the source of the pleasure of taste. In
other words, it is the *aesthetically* optimal attunement (a reading which is
certainly suggested by Kant's reference in this context to the mutual
"quickening" [*Belebung*] of the cognitive faculties).[14] (2) The feeling
through which this is apprehended is taste, and this feeling must be universally communicable because the free harmony is. (3) But this universally communicable feeling presupposes a common sense; indeed, it presupposes a common sense precisely as defined in §20, namely, "the effect
arising from the free play of our cognitive faculties." (4) Consequently,
common sense, so construed, must be presupposed as a necessary condition of *cognition*, or, more precisely, it must be presupposed if skepticism is to be avoided.

Admittedly, it would be nice if this argument, or some variant thereof,
were successful; for it would provide a transcendental grounding for taste
by linking it directly to the conditions of cognition, which is precisely
what Kant claims is required in §9. Granted, it would not satisfy the radical skeptic, who denies the reality of knowledge, but that need not seriously trouble the aesthetician, who is not concerned with global worries
regarding skepticism. Unfortunately, however, there are at least two major problems with such an argument besides the fact that it does not answer the skeptic.

The first and most obvious difficulty concerns the move from the cognitive to the aesthetic, particularly given Kant's efforts to keep them apart through his critique of the Baumgartian conception of beauty as perfection confusedly perceived. Thus, one might wonder why the universal communicability of one's mental state should entail (or have anything to do with) the communicability of a feeling associated with that state, or even why there must be such a feeling in the first place.[15] More generally, one might question why the common sense that the argument claims must be presupposed as a condition of the universal communicability of *cognition* should have anything to do with the one that supposedly must be presupposed as a condition of *taste*. As Anthony Savile has noted, "To assume the existence of an *aesthetic* common sense on that basis is precisely to beg the very question at issue."[16]

The second problem is just the converse of the first, and concerns the implications of the argument for cognition. As we have seen, Kant's explicit conclusion (step 7) is that if skepticism is to be avoided, a common sense must be presupposed as a condition of the universal communicability of our cognition. Now if this cognitively necessary common sense is identified with the common sense that, according to §20, must be presupposed as a condition of taste, that is, the aesthetic common sense (which is what the reading of the argument as a deduction of the latter requires), then it follows that the aesthetic common sense or taste must itself be presupposed as a condition of cognition.

To attribute such a view to Kant is in itself highly implausible, though something resembling it is to be found in Hume.[17] It becomes completely impossible, however, if one keeps in mind that the common sense at issue in the case of taste is the effect of the *free play* [emphasis mine] of the cognitive faculties. There is simply no way in which a feeling resulting from the noncognitive condition of free play could serve as a condition of cognition. Consequently, if read as an attempted deduction of common sense as a condition of taste, the conclusion of §21 is not merely unconvincing; it is incoherent.[18]

With these problems in mind, let us now consider how the argument of §21 fares on the assumption that it is not intended as a deduction of common sense as a condition of taste, but merely as an attempt to show that cognition requires the assumption of something like a common sense in its own right.[19] The aim here is not to defend this argument in all its details, since that would take us well beyond our present concerns, but simply to demonstrate its plausibility, given Kant's basic epistemological commitments. Of course, implicit in this procedure is the assumption that the purpose of an argument for the necessity of presupposing an explicitly cognitive version of common sense is to give some support to the idea that a pure judgment of taste may *likewise* be thought to be grounded in a common sense, albeit not a cognitive one.

Clearly, nothing more need be said about the first two steps of the argument, since, as we have already seen, they are concerned with the conditions of cognition. The first question that arises, thus, concerns the supposed variation in the proportion or degree of attunement that is supposedly a function of differences in the occasioning objects (step 3). On a straightforwardly epistemological reading, this can be taken to mean merely that some intuited manifolds are easier to bring under (empirical) concepts than others.[20] The degree of difficulty here would depend both on the nature of the object, which provides the intuitive content to be conceptualized, and the intellectual resources of the subject doing the conceptualizing. Thus, as we saw in Chapter 1, Kant's savage is unable to integrate his apprehension of a house into his fund of empirical knowledge because he lacks both the concept and the schema, whereas we have no difficulty in doing so. Similarly, on this reading, the optimal attunement (step 4) would be that proportion which maximally facilitates cognition or, equivalently, in which the "two friends" work together without their customary friction. Presumably, this would occur when intuitive content and conceptual rule seem, as it were, particularly made for each other.

This brings us to the claim (also in step 4) that this optimal attunement can be determined only by feeling. As we have seen, this is the real basis for the turn to taste on the standard reading, and the reason adduced for it in the text is that this attunement cannot be determined by concepts (which, by elimination, supposedly leaves feeling). But if one keeps in mind that the appeal to feeling is made on the basis of the impossibility of appealing to concepts, this does not invalidate the purely epistemological reading, since it can be readily understood in terms of the account of judgment offered in the first *Critique*.[21]

As we have seen, Kant there defines judgment as the "faculty of subsuming under rules, that is, of distinguishing whether something does or does not stand under a given rule" (A132/B171); and he further claims that there can be no rules for judgment, so conceived. The latter is the case because the assumption that rules are necessary to determine whether something falls under a rule (and keep in mind that concepts are rules) leads to an infinite regress. But it follows from this that the subsumability of an intuition under a concept must be immediately seen, that is, "felt." And this is why Kant insists that judgment (unlike understanding) is a "peculiar talent, which can be practised only and cannot be taught" (A133/B172).

The interpretive suggestion, then, is that the common sense appealed to in §21 as a condition of cognition is to be identified with the "peculiar talent" referred to in the first *Critique*, rather than with the "effect of the free play of the cognitive powers" postulated in §20 as a condition of a pure judgment of taste. In other words, by "common sense" in §21, we must understand not taste *per se*, but rather the faculty for immediately seeing (without appeal to rules, and therefore through "feeling") whether, and how fully, a given intuited manifold accords with a particular concept, that is, judgment. This is not to be identified with the *"sensus communis logicus"* of §40, however, since Kant is quite clear that the latter is equivalent to the common human understanding [*gemeinen Menschenverstand*] (KU 5: 295n: 162), whereas what he is concerned with in §21 is more properly characterized as a "common sense" [*Gemeinsinn*].[22]

Moreover, given this interpretation of common sense in §21, the remainder of the argument proceeds fairly smoothly. For it is certainly reasonable to claim that both the attunement of the cognitive faculties and the "feeling" for it (the capacity to judge) must be universally communicable, at least if skepticism is to be avoided (step 5). And since this clearly presupposes a common sense (step 6), Kant can plausibly claim to have shown that there are epistemic, nonpsychological grounds for assuming a common sense (step 7).

As already indicated, such a line of argument would help to clear a logical space for the kind of common sense in which Kant is interested at this point by showing that the very idea of such a sense is not incoherent. Equally important, it provides grounds, taken entirely from an analysis of cognition, for postulating a capacity that is a necessary condition of taste, understood as a *sensus communis aestheticus*. For without the "peculiar talent" to recognize a fit between imagination and understanding under the conditions of cognition, a capacity to do so when the faculties are in free play would remain a completely inexplicable mystery. Otherwise expressed, if one could not sense the accord of an intuited manifold with a particular concept, it is difficult to see how one could sense its accord with the conditions of the exhibition of concepts in general, though no concept in particular, which is supposedly what occurs in a judgment of taste. And this makes the common sense of §21 into a necessary, though not a sufficient, condition of taste.

Finally, if this argument as I have sketched it still seems something less than fully convincing, it should be kept in mind that Kant here claims merely to have shown that we have grounds for assuming a common sense. No doubt, he was well aware that anything approaching an adequate demonstration of this thesis would require much more in the way of argument; but it also seems clear that such an effort would be inappropriate in the present context, since the main concern, after all, is still with taste.[23] All things considered, then, it seems reasonable to assume that, rather than being taken as an unsuccessful deduction of the principle of taste, the argument of §21 is best seen as something of a digression from the central line of argument of the Analytic of the Beautiful, though one that is not without significance both for this argument and for the subsequent Deduction.

III

In addition to making sense of the argument of §21 and its function within the overall project of the Analytic of the Beautiful, the interpretation sketched in the preceding section also helps to remove some of the mystery from the discussion of common sense in §22, particularly in its second and concluding paragraph. But before turning to that we must look briefly at the first paragraph of this section, which is basically a continuation of the discussion of the modality of a pure judgment of taste and its connection with the idea of a common sense that was interrupted by the argument of §21. Since this will lead us to a consideration of the diverse ways in which Kant seems to construe the notion of a common sense, this should also prove helpful for an understanding of the more problematic second paragraph.

The basic theme of the first paragraph in §22 is expressed in the heading attached to the section as a whole: "The necessity of the universal assent that we think in a judgment of taste is a subjective necessity that we represent as objective by presupposing a common sense" (KU 5: 239; 89). In claiming that in a judgment of taste we represent the subjective necessity as objective, Kant is not suggesting that such a judgment involves a subreption, that is, an illicit substitution of an objective for a subjective principle.[24] The point is rather that the judgment contains an "ought" or demand for agreement that is comparable to the demand contained in a judgment that is putatively grounded in an objective principle, namely, a cognitive or moral claim.

Since the warrant for this demand is supplied by the presupposed common sense, Kant claims that the latter functions as a merely ideal norm [*blosse idealische Norm*]; and in the beginning of the second paragraph he further characterizes this norm as "indeterminate" [*unbestimmte*] (KU 5: 239; 89). Presumably, the ideality of this norm stems from the fact that it dictates how everyone *ought* to judge, rather than predicting how they will in fact judge, and in this respect it is analogous to the categorical imperative. In addition to the fact that it requires merely an agreement in judgment and not an action (or omission), it differs from the latter with respect to its indeterminateness, which, as we have seen, means that there are no determinate criteria for its instantiation, that is to say, there is no universalizability test, or analogue thereof, for taste.

Although this account of the normative function of common sense seem clear enough by itself, it is sometimes claimed that Kant's overall discussion of common sense is deeply ambiguous, since he appears to take the notion in at least three distinct senses.[25] Thus, even setting aside the complexities caused by its appearance in §21, we note that it is first characterized in §20 as both a feeling and a principle, whereas in §22 it is declared to be a norm. And to make matters even more confusing, in the second paragraph of §22, and again in §40, it is equated with the faculty of taste itself. Finally, in the latter place it is also again characterized as a feeling, albeit in slightly different terms than in §20. In the former case, it is described as the feeling produced by the free play of the cognitive faculties, and in the latter, as the "effect that mere reflection has on the mind" (KU 5: 295; 162).

Since free play refers to the state of the cognitive faculties in aesthetic reflection, the two latter characterizations are equivalent; and since, as a principle, common sense is clearly supposed to function normatively, there is no difficulty identifying principle and norm. Nevertheless, this still leaves us with the three manifestly distinct characterizations of common sense as feeling, principle or norm, and faculty.

Of these, it is clear that the connection with feeling is fundamental, since it leads directly to the presupposed condition of a pure judgment of taste as a common sense. It is also clear that the key to the connection between common sense, construed as a feeling, and the other characterizations lies in Kant's conception of feeling as a faculty of discrimination and appraisal, discussed in Chapter 3. For understood as the faculty for the discrimination of the beautiful and the nonbeautiful on the basis of the effect of an object or its representation on the cognitive faculties in free play, "common sense" is simply another name for taste. Thus, one should not be surprised by their identification or the characterization of taste in the heading to §40 as a "kind of *sensus communis*" (KU 5: 293; 159).

Furthermore, insofar as it purports to be a "universal sense" that judges validly for all, common sense is, or at least takes itself to be, a norm or principle. And, as such, it underwrites the claim to speak with a "universal voice." In §40, Kant makes this point by suggesting that taste may be defined as the "capacity to judge that which makes our feeling in a given representation *universally communicable* without mediation of a concept" (KU 5: 295; 162).[26] But far from contradicting its other roles as feeling and faculty, this normative function of common sense is their necessary complement. For it is only because the idea of a common sense serves as an ideal norm that the demand for universal agreement associated with the aesthetic discrimination of taste is even conceivable. Consequently, these three characterizations reflect the complexity rather than the incoherence of the idea of a common sense, a complexity that is required if, as Kant maintains, it is truly to unite in itself the elements considered separately in the first three moments of the Analytic.

In light of these considerations, let us now turn to the puzzling second paragraph of §22. The paragraph is puzzling because, after supposedly establishing the necessity of presupposing a common sense as a condition of cognition in §21, and affirming its function as an ideal norm with respect to taste in the first paragraph of §22, Kant suddenly asks:

But is there in fact such a common sense, as a constitutive principle of the possibility of experience, or is there a still higher principle of reason that makes it only a regulative principle for us [in order] to bring forth in us for higher purposes, a common sense in the first place? In other words, is taste an original and natural faculty, or is taste only the idea of a faculty yet to be acquired and [therefore] artificial, so that a judgment of taste with its requirement for universal assent is in fact only a demand of reason to produce such agreement in the way we sense? In the latter case the *ought*, i.e., the objective necessity that everyone's feeling flow along with the particular feeling of each person, would signify only that there is a possibility of attaining such agreement; and the judgment of taste would only offer an example of the application of this principle. These questions we neither wish to nor can investigate at this point. For the present our task is only to analyze the faculty of taste into its elements and unite these ultimately in the idea of a common sense. (KU 5: 239–40; 89–90)

If, as is generally done, one takes the argument of §21 as an attempt (successful or otherwise) to provide a deduction of the common sense introduced in §20 as the principle of taste by linking it with cognition and the conditions of its universal communicability, then one can hardly regard the question of whether or not common sense is a constitutive principle of the possibility of experience as open.[27] At least one cannot do so without also assuming that Kant suddenly changed his mind about his main argument. For if one accepts that argument, so construed, then common sense clearly is a constitutive condition. Similarly, it is also difficult to see how it could have merely regulative status, or that taste, viewed as a "kind of *sensus communis*," could, like judgment, be anything but "an original and natural faculty," which may be practiced and developed, but cannot be learned or acquired. If, however, one takes the argument of §21 in the way suggested in the preceding section of this chapter, that is, as concerned merely with providing grounds that justify the assumption of a cognitive common sense, then all of these questions about a *sensus communis aestheticus* remain on the table. Indeed, nothing said in §21 could provide a sufficient basis to answer them. And this would explain why Kant says that he is neither willing nor able to address them at present, that is, within the confines of the Analytic of the Beautiful.

Why, then, according to the alternative reading suggested here, does Kant bother to introduce these questions at this point? The basic answer is clearly that he is providing an anticipatory hint of the connection between taste and morality, which we shall see to be the deepest theme of the *Critique of Aesthetic Judgment* as a whole. On this point at least, there seems to be general agreement among the commentators; but a discussion of this issue must be postponed until the third part of this study, where this connection will be the main focus of concern.

There is, however, one feature of this paragraph that does call for a brief comment at the present time, since it is sometimes thought to bear directly on the deduction of the principle of taste, which is our next topic. This is the suggestion, connected with the idea that common sense might be merely a regulative principle and taste an artificial and yet-to-be-acquired faculty, that the "ought" expressed in a judgment of taste reflects a demand of reason to produce unanimity in our way of sensing, and that it signifies merely the possibility of attaining such agreement. If, as is sometimes done, one assumes that for Kant the ultimate grounding of taste is moral, then it is natural to assume that Kant is here hinting at the fact that the "ought" of taste, that is, the demand for universal agreement, is somehow derived from the "ought" of morality.[28]

Although this particular text, together with many others on the subject of the connection between taste and morality, certainly suggests the possibility of such a reading, I believe that it misrepresents Kant's actual position. As I shall argue in more detail later, it is necessary to distinguish between two distinct "oughts" involved with taste. One, the only one considered so far, is the demand for agreement connected with the claim of taste. It is this ought that presupposes a common sense, and it is quite independent of morality. The second ought connected with taste is the demand to acquire the faculty itself, that is, to develop and refine one's ability to distinguish the beautiful from the merely charming, and so forth. This is the ought to which Kant is alluding in the passage currently under consideration, and it is connected with morality. Granted, the demand for agreement with one's putatively pure judgment of taste only makes sense on the assumption that those of whom the agreement is demanded possess the requisite capacity to make the appropriate discriminations, and in this respect, the two oughts are related. Nevertheless, in view of its merely conditional and ideal status, it hardly follows from this that the legitimacy of the first ought is dependent on that of the second, any more than, say, the legitimacy of the claim that one's judgment reflects the general will depends on its being acknowledged as such by others. On the contrary, we shall see that the legitimacy of the second ought, that is, the morally based demand to develop taste, presupposes that of the first. For only if a pure judgment of taste involves a legitimate demand for the agreement of others can there be a compelling moral interest to develop the capacity to make such judgments. Accordingly, it is to this issue, which concerns the deduction of the principle of taste, that we now turn.

THE DEDUCTION OF PURE JUDGMENTS
OF TASTE

Having completed our analysis of the Analytic of the Beautiful, viewed as an effort to uncover the conditions under which a judgment of taste can be pure, we are now in a position to consider Kant's attempt to ground the normativity of such judgments. This is the task of the Deduction, which, as noted previously, deals with the *quid juris*, the question of right, just as the Analytic dealt with the *quid facti*, or question of fact.

Although the entirety of §30–§54, which includes Kant's discussion of fine art and genius, falls under the general heading "Deduction of Pure Aesthetic Judgments," it is generally agreed that the actual deduction is contained in §30–§39, and these are the sections to be discussed in the present chapter.[1] Basically, I shall argue that Kant succeeds in the relatively modest task that he sets for himself in these sections, namely, to ground the right to demand agreement regarding such judgments by showing that it is derived from a subjective principle of judgment that is itself transcendentally grounded. This result is relatively modest, since it applies only to *pure* judgments of taste, and since it turns out that we are never in a position to determine with certainty whether a given judgment of taste is pure.

The chapter is divided into seven parts. The first deals with the opening section (§30), where Kant limits the scope of the Deduction to judgments of natural beauty, explicitly excluding judgments of the sublime and (by implication) those of artistic beauty as well. The second part discusses the goal, method, and structure of the Deduction as these are articulated in §31–§34. Following Kant's own claim in §34, I conclude that the argument consists of two main steps: one which formulates the *a priori* principle underlying pure judgments of taste (§35), and the other which provides this principle with a transcendental grounding (§38). These, together with the transitional sections (§36–§7), which attempt to connect the problem of a deduction of taste with the general critical problem of the synthetic *a priori*, are the concerns of parts three through five. The last two parts deal with some of the major criticisms that have been directed against the Deduction in the recent literature. The sixth examines the critiques of Paul Guyer and Anthony Savile, and the seventh the frequently voiced objection that Kant's argument, if it proves anything at all, proves too much because it entails that everything is beautiful.

I

Kant entitles the section as a whole a "Deduction of Pure Aesthetic Judgments" rather than merely one of pure judgments of taste because, in theory at least, it should cover judgments of sublimity as well as beauty, since, as he argues in the Analytic of the Sublime, these likewise involve a demand for universal agreement, which entails that they stand in need of justification. In reality, however, Kant spends the entire first section (§30) arguing that a special deduction is required only for judgments regarding the beautiful in nature, excluding thereby both judgments of the sublime and of artistic beauty.

All of this seems somewhat mysterious, and the mystery is only partially removed by the explanation offered. In the case of the sublime, this explanation turns on the distinction between a deduction *per se* and one that is distinct from an exposition.[2] Thus, Kant does not deny that judgments of sublimity require a deduction, but merely that they require one that is distinct from their exposition. In their case, the exposition is already the deduction, while this is not true of judgments regarding natural beauty.[3]

Kant offers two reasons for this differential treatment, only one of which is initially helpful. First, we are told that since natural objects judged sublime present themselves aesthetically as formless and unpurposive, sublimity, properly speaking, is predicated not of objects of nature but of ourselves, that is, of our "way of thinking" [*Denkungsart*] or its foundation in human nature (KU 5: 280; 142). In other words, the object deemed sublime is, in effect, merely the occasion for the purposive relation of the faculties (imagination and reason) involved in its estimation, and it is this relation and what it indicates about our supersensible nature or vocation that is the true locus of sublimity. As Kant had already put it in the Analytic of the Sublime, sublimity is only attributed to the object by a "certain subreption" (KU 5: 257; 114). In the case of natural beauty, however, the contrary is true. There, the object and, more generally, nature, since it provides such objects, presents itself as purposive for judgment. Accordingly, it does not make sense to say that the object is only improperly deemed beautiful, and that true beauty lies in ourselves.[4]

The second reason reflects the positive outcome of the Analytic of the Sublime. The key point, to which we shall return in Chapter 13 when we take up the topic of the sublime, is that the subjective purposiveness of the relation of the cognitive faculties is there claimed to be purposive for the will (defined as the faculty of purposes [*Vermögen der Zwecke*]), which is it-self governed by an *a priori* principle (the moral law). Put simply, Kant's claim is that the exposition of the concept of the sublime is sufficient to ground the demand for universal agreement because it shows that such judgments, though attributable to reflective judgment, are based on the *a priori* and objectively valid principle of morality (KU 5: 280; 142–3).[5] But since the Analytic of the Beautiful did not issue in a comparable re-sult, a separate deduction, distinct from the exposition, is there required.

The second of these reasons is genuinely helpful, since it not only ex-plains why a separate deduction is not needed in the case of the sublime, whereas it is required for the beautiful, but it also indicates what a de-duction of the latter must provide, namely, an *a priori* principle sufficient to ground the demand for universal agreement connected with a claim of taste. Nevertheless, this still leaves unexplained the force of the first of the reasons advanced, and why, unless it be sheer oversight, Kant omits any reference to judgments of artistic beauty.

With regard to the latter problem, it is sometimes suggested that Kant excludes judgments of artistic beauty from consideration because of their presumed lack of purity.[6] In support of such a reading, one might appeal to the curious summary remark at the end of §30, where Kant concludes that "the only deduction we will have to attempt is that of judgments of taste, i.e., judgments about the beauty in natural things; that will suffice for a complete solution of the problem for the whole faculty of aesthetic judgment" (KU 5: 280; 143). Since Kant obviously thought that judg-ments of artistic beauty were judgments of taste, one might infer from this, as well as what he says elsewhere, that he did not think that they were *pure* judgments of taste, and that this is why he excluded them from con-sideration at this point.

Although the premise that the Deduction is concerned only with pure judgments of taste is undoubtedly correct, there are at least three reasons that such an explanation of Kant's omission of artistic beauty must be re-jected. First, in spite of their apparent exclusion in the cited passage and the paucity of examples of aesthetic evaluations given in the text, it is clear that Kant does view the Deduction as concerned with artistic as well as natural beauty.[7] Second, as we have seen, in §16 he explicitly includes examples of artistic beauty among the "free beauties," which are para-digmatically objects of pure judgments of taste. Third, and most impor-tantly, we have also seen that, even in the case of judgments of adherent beauty, which are not *purely* judgments of taste, the taste component is still "pure," that is, concerned with the purposiveness of the form of the object. Thus, even if it were assumed (for the sake of argument) that all artistic beauty is adherent rather than free, and therefore that the deter-mination of such beauty is never entirely a matter of taste, it would not follow that they do not fall within the scope of the Deduction.[8]

Unfortunately, given the cryptic nature of Kant's remarks on the subject, a perfectly satisfactory solution to these problems may be too much to hope for. Nevertheless, I believe it possible to arrive at a plausible account of the major considerations underlying both the first reason for excluding the sublime and the omission of a reference to artistic beauty from the scope of the Deduction. This requires that we go beyond the text of §30, however, and consider Kant's remarks in this section about the purposiveness of natural forms in connection with his comments on the subject in the Introductions, as well as his account of the task of a transcendental deduction in the first *Critique.*

To begin with, in underscoring the difference between the beautiful in nature and the sublime, Kant not only emphasizes the former's connection with purposive form, but he also suggests that this raises all sorts of questions about nature's purposiveness that do not naturally arise in the case of the sublime (nor, presumably, in that of artistic beauty, either). These turn out to be teleological questions about the cause of this purposiveness, for example, how we are to explain "why nature has so extravagantly spread beauty everywhere," including places like the bottom of the ocean, where, Kant notes, it is unlikely to be observed by the human eye (KU 5: 279; 142). Moreover, this close linkage of natural beauty with the "real" or "objective" purposiveness of nature reflects a central theme of both Introductions. Thus, in the First Introduction, where the concept of a "technic of nature" functions as a veritable organizing principle, Kant explicitly links taste with this "technic" (FI 20: 220–1; 407–8), and he lumps aesthetic together with teleological judgments as judgments "about the purposiveness of nature" (FI 20: 241; 430). Similarly, we have seen that in the Second Introduction, the section devoted to the preliminary analysis of the judgment of taste is entitled "On the Aesthetic Representation of the Purposiveness of Nature" (KU 5: 188; 28). All of this suggests, then, that in spite of the sharp distinction between aesthetic and teleological judgment, Kant saw judgments of natural beauty as standing in a close connection with, indeed even giving rise to, questions about the purposiveness of nature.[9]

Insofar as the concern is merely to justify a right to demand agreement, this should have no bearing on the question of whether a separate deduction is required. But if one keeps in mind that the task of a transcendental deduction, as Kant formulates it in the first *Critique,* includes not merely justifying a rightful claim to knowledge, but also determining the limits of this claim, then the situation looks rather different.[10] For this suggests that the reason that only judgments regarding the beautiful in nature require a separate deduction has nothing to do with the nature of taste, or any fundamental difference between judgments of natural and artistic beauty, and everything to do with the fact that only the former immediately raise issues that lead judgment beyond its proper limits, namely, to questions about the purposiveness of nature and its supersensible ground.

Admittedly, apart from a brief comment at the end of the remark to §38 (KU 5: 291; 156), Kant does not address such questions within the confines of the Deduction, though we shall see that he does deal with them later in connection with the discussion of the relationship between taste and morality. Nevertheless, it seems reasonable to assume that Kant took himself to have shown in the Deduction that such questions were precluded from an account of taste itself (in contrast to one of its relationship with morality) in virtue of the subjective nature of its grounding principle (which again distinguishes it from the sublime). According to this reading, then, Kant may be taken to be suggesting that, just as the Transcendental Deduction of the first *Critique* denies the legitimacy of a theoretical use of the categories with regard to noumena (while keeping open the possibility of a practical use in connection with morality) by showing that their objective validity extends only to what is given in accordance with our forms of sensible intuition (space and time), so, too, the Deduction of taste, by means of the subjective nature of its principle, rules out any direct application to noumena of its "category," the purposiveness of nature, while again leaving room for a practical use in connection with morality.

Finally, if this or something like it reflects Kant's thinking on the topic, it becomes clear why he does not refer to judgments of artistic beauty at this point. As is the case with the sublime, the point is not that such judgments do not require a deduction at all, but instead that they do not require a *separate* deduction. The reason for this, however, is not that their exposition already is their deduction; it is rather that they do not need one that is distinct from the deduction provided for judgments of natural beauty. The deduction of the latter suffices for both species of beauty because judgments of artistic beauty neither require a distinct principle nor raise any distinct problems regarding the purposiveness of nature. In fact, Kant makes the connection quite clear at the end of the First Introduction, when, in a previously cited passage, he remarks that "Our judging of artistic beauty will have to be considered afterwards, as a mere consequence of the same principles that underlie judgments about natural beauty" (FI 20: 251; 441). Regrettably, however, he did not reiterate this point at the beginning of the Deduction.

II

Having thus delimited the scope of the Deduction, Kant's next preliminary task is to determine precisely what is to be established and to describe the method to be used. Both of these are accomplished in §31, though its heading indicates that it is concerned only with the latter. As Kant here informs us, what must be demonstrated is "merely the *univer-*

sal validity, for the faculty of judgment as such, of a *singular* judgment that expresses the subjective purposiveness of an empirical representation of the form of an object" (KU 5: 280–1; 143–4). Since this corresponds precisely to the pure judgment of taste as expounded in the Analytic of the Beautiful, this characterization is hardly surprising. And neither is it surprising that Kant tells us in the same section that such a judgment possesses a twofold logical peculiarity: a universality, which is not of the logical variety, since it is that of a singular judgment; and a necessity, which, like all necessity, rests on an *a priori* ground, but whose ground does not allow for the possibility of proof because it is merely subjective. Once again, this corresponds to what we have already learned in the Analytic of the Beautiful. For this very reason, however, it *is* surprising to find Kant now claiming:

> If we resolve these logical peculiarities, which distinguish a judgment of taste from all cognitive judgments, we shall have done all that is needed in order to deduce this strange ability we have, provided that at the outset we abstract from all content of the judgment, i.e., from the feeling of pleasure, and merely compare the aesthetic form with the form of objective judgments as prescribed by logic. (KU 5: 281; 144)

Given the sharp distinction between the *quid facti* and the quid *juris* that has been insisted on here, not to mention the division of labor between an analytic (or exposition) of the judgment of taste and its deduction (or legitimation) to which Kant himself appeals in §30, one would hardly expect Kant to say that a "resolution" [*Auflösung*] of these peculiarities suffices for a deduction of the judgment-type possessing them. After all, was not such a resolution supposedly already accomplished in the Analytic of the Beautiful, through the appeal to the harmony of the faculties and the idea of a common sense? More importantly, as Jens Kulenkampff has suggested, does not such a procedure effectively reduce Kant's so-called deduction to a "second analytic"?[11]

Kulenkampff here raises an important objection, one that can be adequately addressed only through an analysis of the structure of the Deduction. But even apart from such an analysis, it should be clear that a "resolution" that is to suffice as a deduction must do more than merely uncover necessary conditions of the possibility of judgments possessing the peculiarities in question. It must also demonstrate that such judgments are themselves possible, which entails that the conditions obtain and that the claims made by such judgments are valid. Moreover, this requires showing both that these judgments rest on an *a priori* principle capable of warranting these claims and that this principle is itself transcendentally grounded in the conditions of knowledge.

As already noted, this is precisely the direction in which Kant is heading; but before we take up the central issue of the principle of taste and its deduction, it should prove instructive to look briefly at Kant's account of the peculiarities discussed in §32–§33. For though these correspond to the initial accounts in the Analytic of the Beautiful, the formulations are markedly different, and these differences are not without significance for the proposed deduction of the principle of taste.

The first peculiarity of a (pure)[12] judgment of taste is located in what might be termed its *as if objectivity,* that is, its analogy to an ordinary cognitive judgment regarding a particular object. As Kant puts it, "A judgment of taste determines an object in respect of our liking (beauty) [but] makes a claim to the agreement of *everyone's,* as if it were an objective judgment" (KU 5: 281; 145). This *as if objectivity* might seem to differ from the subjective universality of the second moment, but it really serves to underscore what is peculiar in the latter. There is nothing peculiar in a *cognitive* judgment making a universality claim; but that an *aesthetic* judgment might do so, that is, present itself as possessing the semantic force of a cognitive one, is seemingly paradoxical and therefore requires explanation.

A similar analysis applies to the second peculiarity of a pure judgment of taste, which might be called its *as if mere subjectivity.* In Kant's terms, "A judgment of taste is not at all determinable through grounds of proof, just as if it were merely *subjective*" (KU 5: 284; 147). This negative formulation does not make any reference to the necessity affirmed in the fourth moment; but, like the preceding, it does call attention to what is problematic in the exposition of this judgment-type given in the Analytic of the Beautiful. Again, there is nothing noteworthy in denying the possibility of proof for a judgment claiming merely a subjective or private validity, such as one regarding agreeableness. On the contrary, this is just what one would expect. But that this is denied in the case of a judgment making a necessity claim, that is, one demanding universal agreement, is indeed peculiar, since it seems to undermine the very conditions under which such a claim could be justified. Thus, this feature likewise points to the necessity of some kind of transcendental account.

In each case, then, Kant reformulates the result of the corresponding moment in the Analytic of the Beautiful in such a way as to make clear just what it is in the "logic" of a pure judgment of taste that calls for a distinct transcendental grounding. Moreover, in so doing, he is clearly attempting to convince the reader that the problem he is posing constitutes an aesthetic analogue of the quintessentially critical problem of the possibility of the synthetic *a priori.* In fact, we shall see that he later proceeds even further along this path, and explicitly identifies the problem with which the Deduction is concerned as a species of this general problem. We shall also see that this identification is misleading, since it ignores the deep disanalogy due to the aesthetic nature of the pure judgment of taste.

Nevertheless, this does not detract from the analysis of these peculiarities, which serves precisely to emphasize this nature.

Beyond this, there is one additional feature found in these sections that is germane to the Deduction, and therefore worthy of comment at this time. This is the appeal to the autonomy of taste, which is first introduced in §31 as an "autonomy as it were" [*gleichsam . . . einer Autonomie*] (KU 5: 281; 144). By referring to it merely as an "as it were" autonomy, Kant is clearly attempting to distinguish what he here has in mind both from the conception of autonomy appealed to in his moral theory and the heautonomy of judgment of the Introductions. His point is simply that in a judgment of taste, one must appeal to one's own resources (taste) and not consider the judgment of others, since what others (even the supposed experts) think about the aesthetic value of a particular natural object or work of art cannot be a determinant of one's own taste.[13]

In §32, autonomy, so construed, is further equated with apriority. The idea here is that in judging whether or not something is beautiful, one does not "grope around [*herumzutappen*] among other people's judgments," which would supposedly constitute a kind of empiricism, as well as a heteronomy of taste; rather, we demand that a subject "pronounce his judgment *a priori*" (KU 5: 282; 145).[14] Although Kant's point is certainly clear enough, his terminology seems somewhat forced, since *a priori* here obviously cannot mean independently of experience, but rather precisely on the basis of one's own "experience."[15]

Kant attempts to illustrate this thesis by means of the interesting example of the young poet who stubbornly (yet apparently mistakenly) insists on the beauty of his own creation in the face of the adverse judgment of audience and friends alike. Only later, Kant tells us, when his taste is sharpened, will he voluntarily [*freiwillig*] depart from his earlier assessment, that is, depart on the basis of his own taste, rather than merely in order to gain the approval of his critics (KU 5: 282; 145–6).

This example is interesting because it apparently uses an instance of *bad* (or mistaken) taste to illustrate the principle of the autonomy of taste. By appealing to his own taste, the young poet is proceeding according to the rules of the game. His judgment is presumably disinterested (at least insofar as it is not based on the desire to gain the approval of others-as a critic-if not as a poet), and yet, as Kant's account undeniably implies, it is nonetheless erroneous.[16] Clearly, this raises further interesting questions about erroneous judgments of taste; but from the point of view of the Deduction, the essential point is that autonomy turns out to be merely a necessary, and not also a sufficient, condition of the legitimacy of a claim of taste. Moreover, this once again points us in the direction of a second-order normative principle as the sought-for sufficient condition governing the proper use of this "as it were" autonomy.

In §34, Kant finally makes this explicit. Operating with the familiar dichotomy between objective and subjective principles, he first denies the possibility of an objective principle [*Princip*] of taste, and then argues that this does not preclude a subjective one. The former, which would be a principle [*Grundsatz*] through which the beauty of an object could be determined by subsuming the concept of the object under it, is ruled out on the familiar grounds that judgments of taste are aesthetic. Accordingly, Kant seconds Hume's observation that though critics can reason more plausibly than cooks, they nevertheless share the same fate, namely, that they cannot expect agreement to come from the force of their proofs, "but only from the subject's reflection on his own state (of pleasure or displeasure), all precepts and rules being rejected" (KU 5: 285–6; 149).[17] But, in opposition to Hume, Kant also insists that this does not preclude a subjective principle, by which he understands one that governs this very reflection of a subject on his or her own state. In fact, he concludes that insofar as the critique of taste has a transcendental dimension, its task is precisely "to set forth [*entwickeln*] and justify [*rechtfertigen*] the subjective principle of taste as an *a priori* principle of the faculty of judgment" (KU 5: 286; 150). We can see from this that the actual deduction must consist of two steps: one in which the subjective principle of taste is "set forth" or explicated, and the other in which it is grounded.

III

Kant identifies the required subjective principle in the heading of §35 as the "faculty of judgment as such" [*Urteilskraft überhaupt*] (KU 5: 286; 150). Apart from a brief concluding paragraph, which merely reiterates the previously made point that the discovery of the principle legitimating judgments of taste can be based only on a consideration of the logical form of such judgments, that is, the very peculiarities just discussed, the section consists of a single dense paragraph. But in view of its systematic significance, it requires a detailed consideration.

To begin with, it is important to note that the entire discussion is formulated in terms of the language of subsumption, which reflects the first *Critique*'s characterization of judgment as "the faculty of subsuming under rules, that is, of distinguishing whether something does or does not stand under a given rule" (A132/B171). The problem, however, is that Kant formulated this conception of judgment with cognitive judgments in mind; and in such judgments a general concept is either already given or acquired through a process of reflection. But in the case of an aesthetic judgment there is, *ex hypothesi*, no concept, either given or acquired through judgmental activity, under which the representation of the object of the judgment could be subsumed. Consequently, it is difficult to see how judgment, understood as the faculty of subsumption, could conceivably provide, much less itself constitute, the sought-for subjective principle of taste.

This, in turn, suggests that the question of the possibility of judgments with the logical peculiarities that have been shown to belong to judgments of taste can be reformulated as that of the possibility of a purely aesthetic (nonconceptual) subsumption. And once again, at a crucial point in the argument, Kant turns to what he alleges to be the only condition under which such a subsumption is possible, namely, that it must be under the "subjective formal condition of judgment as such," which is identified with the faculty of judgment itself (KU 5: 287; 151). In other words, in a judgment of taste it is the faculty of judgment itself that plays the role assigned to a concept in a cognitive judgment; so the representation of the object is subsumed under this faculty, which therefore serves as the subjective principle of such judgments. But what does it mean to subsume a representation under a cognitive faculty in general and under judgment in particular? Unless a clear sense can be given to such "subsumption," Kant's solution must remain a purely verbal one, without any power to explicate the normativity of taste.

Before attempting to provide a positive answer to this question, it must be reemphasized that the principle in question is not to be identified with the transcendental principle of reflective judgment, namely, the logical purposiveness of nature or systematicity, discussed in the two Introductions. Such a reminder is necessary because, as we saw in Chapter 2, Kant does identify the latter with the principle of taste in the Introductions, though we also saw that such an identification cannot be taken at face value.[18]

Nevertheless, it is also the case that Kant's account of the transcendental grounding of the principle of logical purposiveness or systematicity is crucial for understanding his claim that in a judgment of taste, the representation of the object is subsumed under the faculty of judgment itself. Although Kant does not here mention the term, the essential point is once again that the autonomy of judgment takes the form of a "heautonomy."

As we saw in the first part of this study, the term "heautonomy" expresses the idea that judgment in its reflection legislates merely to itself and not to nature (or freedom). Thus, even though logical purposiveness or systematicity turns out to be a necessary condition of the coherence of our empirical knowledge, it is not a condition that we are entitled to declare must be met by nature. The necessity is instead a purely subjective one to presuppose such purposiveness. This makes the principle merely regulative rather than constitutive; but it also indicates how and why judgment might be regarded as the source of its own normativity and therefore serve as principle to itself. The latter is the case because what judgment presupposes in its reflection is nothing other than the conditions of the possibility of its successful activity. Consequently, these conditions are normative for judgment in its cognitive reflection, just as normativity in general for Kant is rooted in the conditions of the successful or coherent activity of the faculty in question.[19]

Much the same story applies to judgments of taste, with the significant qualification that, since they are not cognitive, judgment here serves directly as principle for itself, without providing a distinct principle under which the data are subsumed. Moreover, since the general business of judgment is subsumption, this entails that in a judgment of taste, representations are subsumed under the condition[s] of subsumption and that is what must be meant by the "subjective formal condition of judgment as such." This condition is merely subjective or heautonomous because, like that of the logical purposiveness of nature, it is a constraint on judgment's capacity to perform its characteristic subsumptive activity, rather than on what might be encountered in experience. Similarly, it is *formal* because it is a constraint on the form of what is apprehended insofar as it allows for the possibility of subsumption (its subjective purposiveness for judgment). And since subsumption requires that what is given in sensible intuition and apprehended through the imagination be brought under concepts of the understanding, this condition turns out to be nothing other than the harmonious interplay of the imagination and the understanding in their respective activities.

This notion of the harmony or attunement of the imagination and understanding is obviously not a fresh contribution of the Deduction. Indeed, we have seen that it was the centerpiece of the preliminary discussion of judgments of taste in both Introductions, and loomed large in §9 and §21 of the Analytic of the Beautiful as well. What is new here, apart from some details, is that the connection between this harmony and the subsumptive activity of judgment is made fully explicit, and this connection proves to be key to the normativity of this harmony for judgment and, therefore, for taste. For what Kant now argues is that the judgment of taste, by which we must understand not the verdict ("this x is beautiful") but the act of aesthetic estimation that issues in the verdict, consists in "the subsumption of the very imagination under the condition [which must be met] for the understanding to proceed in general from intuition to concepts" (KU 5: 287; 151). Moreover, since, given Kant's account of judgment, this condition can only be a certain organization or coherence in what is imaginatively reproduced (in the apprehension of the manifold), such that it is suitable to being brought under a concept or rule, it is equivalent to subsumability.

In explicating this point, Kant describes the activity of the imagination in its free play (its aesthetic apprehension unconstrained by concepts) in deeply suggestive fashion as "schematizing without a concept" (KU 5:

287; 151). The importance of this notion can be appreciated in light of the considerations advanced in Chapter 1 regarding the conditions of empirical concept formation. Following the suggestion of Longuenesse, it was there argued that the comparison leading to the formation of such concepts is itself concerned with schemata, understood as patterns or rules governing apprehension, rather than with the impressions or images of an empiricistic account. Consequently, the possibility of generating schemata (apprehension-rules) antecedently to the concepts they schematize was seen to be a necessary condition of the possibility of the "universalizing comparison" through which the concepts themselves are formed. And it follows from this that if the imagination could not "schematize without a concept," it could not schematize at all.[20]

Nevertheless, the schematization without a concept performed by the imagination in its free play differs from that required for cognition in that it does not issue in the exhibition of a determinate concept. What it yields instead is rather what might be described as the exhibition of the form of a concept in general (but not any concept in particular). Moreover, for this very reason, taste requires something more than (as well as different from) the mere subsumability that suffices for cognition. Since in its free play the imagination does not provide the understanding with the exhibition of a determinate concept, its harmony with the latter can consist only in stimulating it (and *vice versa*). Thus, as we have already seen, in an engagement with the beautiful, the "two friends" each proceed on their own paths, without the customary interference or friction between them; yet they do so in such a way that each spontaneously promotes the activity of the other. Or, as Kant now puts it, they "reciprocally quicken each other" (KU 5: 287; 151).

Although Kant himself is notoriously unclear regarding the mechanics of this reciprocal quickening, the basic idea is presumably that the imagination in its free play stimulates the understanding by occasioning it to entertain fresh conceptual possibilities, while, conversely, the imagination, under the general direction of the understanding, strives to conceive new patterns of order. In any event, the important thing about this mutually beneficial activity is that it is immediately felt, and this feeling is the basis for the verdict of taste that the object occasioning the activity is beautiful (or not beautiful, if the "two friends" hinder rather than enhance one another). And, on this basis, Kant concludes that taste, as a subjective power of judgment [*subjective Urteilskraft*] does indeed contain a principle of subsumption, not of intuitions under concepts (which would make it objective), "but, rather, one of the faculty of intuitions or exhibitions (i.e., the imagination) under the faculty of concepts (i.e., the understanding) insofar as the imagination *in its freedom* harmonizes with the understanding *in its lawfulness*" (KU 5: 287; 151).

IV

This, then, completes the first step of the Deduction, which, as we have seen, attempts to "set forth . . . the subjective principle of taste as an *a priori* principle of the faculty of judgment." Clearly, the argument rests squarely upon the account of reflective judgment and aesthetic judgments of reflection provided in the Introductions, as well as the analysis of the pure judgment of taste in the Analytic of the Beautiful. Thus, even though it is a logical extension of what precedes it, and therefore consistent with the basic principles of Kant's analysis, it can hardly be regarded as persuasive independently of its connection with the Kantian theories of reflective judgment and taste. Moreover, even if all of this is granted, the argument is still not complete, since it remains necessary to ground this principle itself, that is, to establish the normativity of the norm. Kant attempts to do this in §38; but since this is separated from the preceding by two transitional sections (§36–§37), which attempt to relate the project of a deduction of taste to the general critical project of grounding synthetic *a priori* judgments, I shall here briefly consider these, saving an examination of the actual deduction of the principle for the next section.

Kant's basic concern in these transitional sections seems to be to convince the reader (and perhaps himself) that, in spite of its aesthetic nature, a judgment of taste involves a synthetic *a priori* claim, and thus falls within the purview of transcendental philosophy. As I suggested earlier, the claim for syntheticity seems highly artificial, given the noncognitive nature of such judgments. Judgments of taste, Kant reasons, must be synthetic because they cannot be analytic, "for they go beyond the concept of the object, and even beyond the intuition of the object, and add as a predicate to this intuition something that is not even cognition: namely a feeling of pleasure (or displeasure)" (KU 5: 288; 153). One might think that the more natural conclusion to draw is that since such judgments have a feeling rather than a concept as predicate, they can be *neither* analytic nor synthetic (that distinction being intended to apply only to cognitive judgments).[21]

The claim about the *a priori* nature of judgments of taste is at once of greater importance and more problematic. In fact, Kant himself seems to signal his recognition of its problematic nature by qualifying the straightforward claim that such judgments are *a priori* with the parenthetical remark: "or want to be considered" as such (KU 5: 289; 153).[22] Although we have already seen that at one point Kant suggests that the apriority of judgments of taste rests on the fact that they claim to speak for others "without being allowed to wait for other people's consent" (KU 5: 288; 153), his considered view is that it rests on their claim to necessity, that is, on the demand made on others for agreement with one's own feeling.[23]

Against this Lewis White Beck has argued, however, that this claim to necessity does not suffice to make judgments of taste *a priori*, since ordinary empirical judgments (judgments of experience) make an analogous demand, without thereby ceasing to be merely *a posteriori*. Working with the analogy between judgments of experience (as characterized in the *Prolegomena*) and judgments of taste suggested by Kant himself, Beck insists that this necessity claim requires merely that such judgments, like judgments of experience, rest on an *a priori* principle, not that they be themselves *a priori*.[24]

Insofar as we take judgments of taste to be analogous to judgments of experience, Beck is certainly correct. But the emphasis on necessity suggests that Kant may also have had in mind the analogy with moral judgments. And here he seems to be on stronger ground, since first-order moral claims, such as "one should never lie," are both based on an *a priori* principle and purport to be themselves *a priori*. Nevertheless, setting that aside and granting that Kant does tend to run together considerations bearing on first-order judgments of taste with those bearing on the *a priori* principle, the fact remains that Kant's main concern in these transitional sections is clearly with the latter. Moreover, there are two aspects of Kant's discussion of the apriority of the principle of taste in these sections that are worthy of comment, since they are directly germane to the interpretation of this principle sketched in the prior section.

The first occurs within the context of Kant's attempt (§36) to explain how aesthetic, in contrast to theoretical or cognitive judgments, can lay claim to necessity, which is equivalent to showing how they can involve an *a priori* principle. As he points out, this requires showing how such a principle may be involved when judgment does not, as in the latter case, merely have to subsume given data under objective concepts of the understanding in order to be subject to a law, "but where it is, subjectively object to itself as well as law" [*sie sich selbst subjectiv Gegenstand sowohl als Gesetz ist*] (KU 5: 288; 153).

Although it really adds nothing new, this formulation of what one might call the normative structure of a judgment of taste is notable for its focus on the reflexive nature of such judgments. Judgment is here a law to itself in the sense that the "subjective formal condition of judgment as such" takes the place of a pure concept of the understanding (the lesson of §35). It is subjective *object* to itself in the sense that the reflection involves the conformity (or lack thereof) of the relation of the cognitive faculties in the aesthetic engagement with an object. Thus, in claiming that x is beautiful, I am claiming that my representation of x is purposive for judgment in the way previously discussed; so the judgment is about the suitability for judgment of a given object or its representation. Once again, then, it is a matter of the *heautonomy* of judgment, its normativity for itself, rather than for nature or freedom.[25]

The second noteworthy aspect of Kant's discussion in these sections is his attempt to explain (§37) "What is Actually Asserted *A Priori* about an Object in a Judgment of Taste" (KU 5: 289; 154). After noting that with the exception of moral feeling, which is not really comparable to the pleasure of taste since it is based on a determinate law, we cannot connect *a priori* a feeling of pleasure or displeasure with any representation, Kant concludes that, in a judgment of taste, "[I]t is not the pleasure, but the *universal validity of this pleasure*, perceived as connected in the mind with our mere judging of an object, that we represent *a priori* as [a] universal rule valid for everyone" (KU 5: 289; 154).

Although he thinks that the main point is clear enough, Guyer complains that there is nonetheless a certain clumsiness (actually a redundancy) in Kant's manner of expression here, "for claiming universal validity for a pleasure attributed to mere estimation [Guyer's rendering of *Beurtheilung*] is indeed representing it as a valid rule for everyone, that is, supposing that any subject ought to feel pleasure in a given object."[26] This complaint suggests that Kant's point is not as clear to Guyer as he maintains, however, since it indicates a confusion of levels on his part, for which Kant's somewhat misleading language regarding apriority in these sections may be at least partly responsible. There would indeed be a certain clumsiness if Kant were here making a claim about first-order judgments of taste, since the qualifying clause "but the universal validity of this pleasure" (which Kant himself emphasizes) would be out of place. But there is none if the claim is taken to refer to the second-order principle of taste. So construed, the claim is that the principle (or universal rule) for judgment is just the universal validity, that is, the normativity or exemplary necessity, of the pleasure felt in connection with the mere judging of an object. It is, then, this rule, which is really equivalent to the subjective principle of taste presented in §35, that underlies and licenses first-order judgments of taste. And, of course, it is also this rule that requires a deduction or justification.

V

The justification of the subjective principle of taste articulated in §35 is the task of §38, which is appropriately entitled "Deduction of Judgments of Taste." Although one might not think so on the basis of the discussions in the secondary literature, this deduction is relatively simple and straightforward, at least when compared with the two versions of the Transcendental Deduction in the first *Critique*. Moreover, Kant himself notes this fact in the remark attached to the argument (KU 5: 290; 156). The actual deduction consists of three sentences, each of which may be considered as a distinct step in the argument, though the second sentence may itself be broken down into two substeps. I shall first cite the steps and then comment on each in turn:

1. If it is granted that in a pure judgment of taste our liking for the object is connected with the mere judging of its form, then this liking is nothing but its subjective purposiveness for judgment, which we sense as connected in the mind with the representation of the object.

2. Now, since with regard to the formal rules of judging apart from all matter (whether sensation or concept), judgment [*Urteilskraft*] can be directed only to the subjective conditions of the employment of judgment in general (which is restricted neither to a particular mode of sense nor a particular concept of the understanding), and hence to that subjective factor [*dasjenige Subjective*] that can be presupposed in all men (as is required for possible cognition in general), so it must be allowable to assume that the agreement of a representation with these conditions of judgment is valid for everyone *a priori*.

3. That is to say, the pleasure or subjective purposiveness of a representation for the relation of the cognitive faculties engaged in the judgment of a sensible object in general can with right be required of everyone (KU 5: 289–90; 155).

Since the first of these steps is essentially a restatement of the main result of the third moment of the Analytic of the Beautiful, it is not a fresh contribution of the Deduction. Nevertheless, it is vital to the success of the overall argument, since it provides the bridge linking the liking (or disliking) demanded of others in a pure judgment of taste to the subjective conditions of judgment. More precisely, it links the required feeling to the purposiveness for judgment of the representation of an object, and it is this purposiveness that is understood in terms of the conditions of judgment. Beyond its role in the Deduction, this step is also noteworthy for the light it sheds on Kant's alleged formalism. For here "form" clearly refers to form for judgment, which means a capacity to occasion a harmonious interplay of the cognitive faculties, rather than merely a spatiotemporal form.

The second step, which, as noted, may be broken down into two substeps, constitutes the real nerve of the argument. The major problem with the first of these substeps is exegetical, namely how to understand the "formal rules of judging" [*der formalen Regeln der Beurteilung*] to which Kant here refers. Since the judging at issue is clearly of the aesthetic variety, and since we have been told repeatedly that such judging has no rules (formal or otherwise), it is not immediately obvious what he has in mind. The claim embodied in this substep becomes intelligible, however, if we take the "rules" to be the norm or principle required for the judgment of aesthetic form. According to this reading, then, Kant is claiming simply that we must look to the "subjective conditions of the employment of the faculty of judgment as such" in order to locate this principle. Moreover, this is just what one would expect, given the thesis of §35 that the principle of taste can be only the "subjective formal condition of judgment as such." Thus, what the first substep really does is to make it explicit that it is this very principle that is to be legitimated.

The actual legitimation or deduction of the principle, such as it is, occurs in the second substep. It consists essentially in the bare assertion that we may presuppose that these same conditions of judgment apply to everyone, on the grounds that they are also conditions of cognition. From this it is then inferred that we are entitled to assume that a representation's conformity with this condition (or conditions), that is, its "subjective purposiveness for judgment," will be valid for everyone.

Finally, the third step completes the deduction by transferring the entitlement claim from the conformity of a representation to the subjective conditions of judgment to the pleasure through which such conformity is felt (and, one might add, to the displeasure through which a lack of conformity is felt). This last move is necessary to ground the right to demand agreement, which is what has been at issue all along.

The crux of the argument appears to be a principle of the form: If x is subjectively purposive for me, then it must be subjectively purposive for everyone. This seems a reasonable-enough claim, given the connection between subjective purposiveness and the conditions of judgment built into the very definition of such purposiveness, and the fact that the cost of denying the universality of these conditions would be a radical skepticism that would undermine any form of rational communication. Moreover, Kant himself indicates that this is basically what he had in mind, both in a footnote attached to §38, where he states that the initial thing that must be granted is that "in all people the subjective conditions of this faculty [judgment] are the same" (KU 5: 290n; 155), and in the subsequent comment, where, by way of explaining why the deduction (meaning thereby the argument of §38) is "so easy," he tells us that it asserts only that "we are justified in presupposing universally . . . the same subjective conditions of the faculty of judgment that we find in ourselves" (KU 5: 290; 156).

In spite of some superficial similarities, this argument is quite different from that of §21.[27] As we have seen, that argument begins with the assumption of the universal communicability of cognition and of the attunement of the cognitive faculties that it requires. From there it moves to the necessity of presupposing a common sense, construed as a shared capacity for recognizing (without rules and therefore through "feeling"), the optimal attunement of the cognitive faculties required for cognition in general. As I claimed in my analysis of §21, this shared capacity is best understood as the faculty of judgment, as characterized in the first *Critique*, and therefore has nothing directly to do with taste. Here, by contrast, the connection between taste and the conditions of cognition or judgment, which remains mysterious in §21, is assumed from the start as the result of the argument of §35 that the faculty of judgment itself (in the form of the conditions of its successful operation) provides the sought-for subjective principle of taste. Given this, the "deduction" of §38 then affirms the universal validity of this *principle* of taste on the grounds that it is also a condition of cognition. Thus, though taste is grounded indirectly in the conditions of cognition by showing that its governing principle has that status, there is no suggestion (as there is in §21 when read as a deduction of the principle of taste) that taste is itself such a condition.

This difference notwithstanding, the argument of §21, at least as interpreted in Chapter 7, nevertheless provides an essential precondition of the present deduction. Its major relevance is to the third step, where, as already noted, Kant extends the entitlement claim from the conformity (or lack thereof) of a given representation to the subjective conditions of judgment to the feeling through which this is apprehended aesthetically. Against this extension it might be objected that the relatively nonproblematic claim that we must assume the universality of the subjective conditions of cognition and of what conforms or fails to conform to these conditions (at least if we wish to avoid a radical epistemological skepticism) does not automatically extend to any feeling bearing on these conditions. Indeed, it does not follow that we need assume any such feeling at all (much less one that is universally attributable).

The response, based on the suggested reading of §21, is that cognition itself presupposes a common sense [*Gemeinsinn*], understood as a universally valid "feeling" through which the conformity of universal and particular is immediately apprehended in judgment. But if this is the case, and if, as Kant now argues, taste, which he later characterizes as a "kind of *sensus communis*" (KU 5: 293; 159), is likewise a feeling directed to the conformity of given representations with these same conditions, then it does seem reasonable to assume the universal validity of this feeling as well. Conversely, if this initial connection between feeling and cognition (through judgment) is denied, then the claim that we are entitled to assume the universal validity of the feeling connected with the judgment of taste does indeed remain problematic and ungrounded.

In order to evaluate this argument, it is obviously crucial to become clear about what it purports to accomplish. As already noted, the avowed goal is merely to "set forth and justify the subjective principle of taste as an *a priori* principle of the faculty of judgment," and if one accepts the basic Kantian account of judgment and the results of the Analytic of the Beautiful, it can plausibly be claimed to have accomplished this task. But to ground the subjective principle of taste or, what amounts to the same thing, a *sensus communis aestheticus,* is not yet to justify the demand for agreement in any particular case. For, as Kant himself points out in the footnote to §38, the latter also requires that "the judgment has taken into consideration merely this relation [of the cognitive faculties] (and hence the *formal condition* of the faculty of judgment) and is pure, i.e., mingled neither with concepts of the object nor with sensations as the judgment's determining grounds" (KU 5: 290n; 155).

Although the terminology is not used, Kant here clearly distinguishes between the *quid juris* and the *quid facti*, connects the latter with the question of purity, and suggests that both are required to legitimize any given judgment of taste. In other words, in order rightfully to demand the agreement of others to one's aesthetic assessment of an object of nature or art, one must be assured both that pure judgments of taste are normative (because they have an *a priori* warrant) and that one's judgment is, in fact, pure. Moreover, this accords perfectly with Kant's famous opening statement in the Transcendental Deduction of the first *Critique* that "Jurists, when speaking of rights and claims, distinguish in a legal action the question of right *(quid juris)* from the question of fact *(quid facti);* and they demand that both be proved" (A84/B116).

Kant also notes, however, that precisely because the judgment of taste is based on feeling rather than concepts, determining the correctness of the subsumption "involves unavoidable difficulties" and "may easily be illusory" (KU 5: 290–1; 156). In fact, even though he does not say it in so many words, the clear implication of Kant's analysis is that we can *never* be certain in any instance that we have made the correct subsumption, that is, that one's judgment is based solely on the relation of the faculties in free play.[28] We can, of course, take pains to abstract from charm, emotion, and the like, and presumably the need to do this is part of what Kant is hinting at in §22 with the oblique reference to taste (identified with the *sensus communis*) as a regulative rather than a constitutive principle. But though we may be required to strive toward this ideal of aesthetic purity, we can never be certain that we have attained it, just as in the moral realm we can never be sure that we have acted from duty alone.

What is particularly noteworthy here is simply that Kant does not seem to have been at all disturbed by this result. On the contrary, he remarks in the footnote that "even if a mistake be made on the latter point, this amounts to nothing but an incorrect application, in a particular case, of an authority given to us by a law, and in no way annuls the authority" (KU 5: 290n; 155). Moreover, he makes essentially the same point in the comment attached to §38, insisting that problems concerning the correctness of subsumption, which also occur, though in a lesser degree, in cognitive judgments, do not affect the legitimacy of the "*principle* [emphasis mine] of judging validly for everyone from subjective grounds" (KU 5: 291; 156).

Clearly, then, Kant's position is that the Deduction establishes merely the *quid juris*, and that this stands regardless of the difficulties involved in the determination of the *quid facti.* Indeed, it stands even if (as I believe to be the case for Kant) we can never be certain in a particular instance that the conditions of a pure judgment of taste have been met. For we at least know through the Analytic what these conditions are and that they are attainable by beings such as ourselves. In short, we know that (and on what basis) such a thing as a pure judgment of taste is possible and that it has normative force.

This is, indeed, a weaker conclusion than many have assumed to be required for a genuine deduction of taste. The contrasting view, argued most forcefully by Guyer, is that any such deduction must ground the right to expect (albeit under ideal conditions) agreement in particular claims of taste. And by this criterion the argument obviously fails. I shall consider Guyer's criticisms in some detail in the next section; but before turning to that, two brief comments about the significance of the Deduction according to the reading suggested here are in order.

The first is that, though relatively modest when compared to the claims of the Transcendental Deduction in the first *Critique,* the conclusion here attributed to the Deduction is far from trivial. For if sound, it establishes something that is frequently denied, namely, that there is normativity in the domain of taste, and that this normativity is based on a principle unique to judgment. Consequently, judgments of taste are reducible neither to judgments of agreeableness, which lack normativity altogether (the empiricism of taste), nor to judgments of perfection, whose normativity is based on a principle extrinsic to taste (the rationalism of taste).[29] Moreover, since this is tantamount to establishing the autonomy of taste, such a result would seem to provide ample justification for a separate critique of the faculty of taste.

The second and final point is that this outcome is also the best that could be expected, given Kant's analysis of the nature of taste. For if, as Kant consistently maintains, judgments of taste are aesthetic, then any normativity pertaining to them must govern feeling, and this already precludes the possibility of a rule or decision procedure for determining whether any particular judgment conforms to this norm. Indeed, as I hope should be clear by now, the interest of Kant's theory of taste consists largely in the fact that it attempts to preserve a space for normativity without denying the aesthetic nature of judgments of taste. And, as suggested earlier, though different from, this is nonetheless analogous to the problem of the synthetic *a priori.*

VI

Having completed an analysis and interpretation of the Deduction, we are now in a position to consider in more detail some of the critiques of its argument that have been already noted in passing. In the present section I shall examine two of the more interesting and influential of these in the recent literature: those of Paul Guyer and Anthony Savile. These critiques are based on readings of the Deduction that share some common ground, but nonetheless differ from each other in interesting ways, as well as from the interpretation offered here. At the very least, this should provide some indication of the wide variety of ways in which Kant's terse argument has been construed.

A. *Guyer.* Apart from the insistence that its argument is independent of the appeal to morality, Guyer's interpretation of the Deduction differs at virtually every point from the one advocated here.[30] To begin with, on his reading, it is concerned with the licensing of an expectation of agreement rather than a demand. More specifically, its aim is to justify "the epistemological presumption of claiming to know about the subjective states of others."[31] And from this he concludes reasonably enough that, in order to succeed, the Deduction must show not merely that we have a general authorization to lay claim to the agreement of others (on the assumption that the proper subsumption has been performed) but also that we are justified in attributing specific feelings to particular individuals in particular circumstance. Echoing Hume's remark that the problem [of a standard of taste] becomes pressing "when critics come to particulars," he insists that "Kant's own analysis of aesthetic judgment requires that his deduction come to particulars."[32]

Given this reading, Guyer has little difficulty showing that the need to "come to particulars" opens up a fatal gap in Kant's argument. Although he characterizes this gap in a number of ways, the main point is simply that the universal ascription of a general capacity for cognition or judgment, that is, a capacity for unifying manifolds through concepts or subsuming intuitions under them, does not entail an analogous universal capacity for responding (through feeling) when this unification (or subsumption)[33] is brought about without any concepts. Consequently, it does not entail that everyone will respond to the same unification in the same way, which means that the argument from the universality of the conditions of cognition cannot ground the universality of the aesthetic response.[34]

This alleged gap is, however, entirely the result of Guyer's assumption regarding what a successful deduction of taste must accomplish. To be sure, any such deduction must begin with particulars, since a judgment of taste is necessarily singular. But it hardly follows from this that it must "come to particulars" in the sense Guyer intends. On the contrary, if we keep in mind the sharp distinction between the *quid juris* and the *quid facti*, it becomes clear that what is required is the legitimation of a general principle of taste, and that such a principle retains its validity even if it turns out that one can never determine with certainty that a given judgment accords with it. For, as Kant had already indicated in §19, the latter is conditional on the correctness of the subsumption under the indeterminate norm.

Interestingly enough, at one point Guyer himself entertains, albeit halfheartedly, the possibility that the Deduction makes a weaker claim than the one he imputes to it. On this alternative reading, which is based on the suggestion in §22 that common sense might be a regulative rather than a constitutive principle, the Deduction is seen as an attempt to prove merely that anyone could find an object beautiful, as distinct from the claim that (under proper circumstances) everyone will.[35] This alternative deduction, which is explicitly modeled on that of regulative ideas in the Appendix to the Dialectic in the first Critique, begins with the postulation of the universal communicability of knowledge as a "necessary maxim of reason." The idea here is that such communicability may greatly enhance our capacity to extend our empirical knowledge, even though it is not a constitutive condition of its possibility. From this it supposedly follows that there could be an injunction to maximize such communicability, which is then "extended to the case of taste by the argument that the conditions of the communicability of taste are the same as those of the communicability of knowledge in general."[36]

Since Guyer neither defends such an argument nor attributes it to Kant, a lengthy examination of it would be pointless. Nevertheless, a brief inspection may help to shed some additional light on the basic assumptions underlying his reading of the Deduction. What Guyer is clearly trying to accomplish with his avowedly "speculative" reformulation is to express what he takes to be the logic of Kant's actual argument in the language of regulative, rather than constitutive, principles. Thus, whereas the latter, on his view, assumes without warrant that universal communicability is a necessary condition of knowledge and then infers from this (again without warrant) the universal communicability of the aesthetic response (identified with the common sense of §21), the regulative version of the story apparently infers from the maxim to maximize the universal communicability of knowledge that one should also strive to maximize the universal communicability of the aesthetic response or, more simply, agreement in the realm of taste. On this reading, then, aesthetic response is (or ought to be) guided by the regulative idea that a consensus in taste is in principle attainable.

In proceeding in this manner, Guyer is evidently attempting to impose the first Critique's model of a transcendental deduction on that of the third. Since the deduction of the categories, which treats them as constitutive principles, does not seem to work, he turns naturally to the deduction of regulative principles. It is difficult to see, however, how this reformulation helps to avoid the fatal gap, which Guyer insists undermines Kant's actual argument. For this gap supposedly concerns the move from the conditions of knowledge to those of aesthetic response, and this move remains essential to the regulative version he sketches. In other words, if the direct move from the universal communicability of knowledge to that of the aesthetic response is invalid (as I agree with Guyer it is), then so, too, is the move from the regulative demand to maximize the former to the demand to do the same for the latter. In fact, in order to justify such a move it is necessary to presuppose that the development of taste is somehow itself a condition of knowledge or its universal communicability (for why else ought one to acquire it?); but this remains as implausible now as it was when initially considered in the examination of §21.[37] Moreover, this, of itself, should give one pause before accepting Guyer's reading of the Deduction in either its constitutive or its regulative forms.

B. Savile. Savile begins his analysis of Kant's attempt to justify judgments of taste virtually at the point at which Guyer's ends.[38] Thus, he concurs with Guyer that the purely epistemological argument fails to establish the legitimacy of such judgments on the grounds that pleasure in the harmony of the cognitive faculties under conditions of cognitive constraint, which is the most that a focus on the shared conditions of cognition can show, is not transferable to aesthetic judgment in which, ex hypothesi, these constraints do not apply. In short, there is no direct transition from the cognitive to the aesthetic.[39] Unlike Guyer, however, Savile builds his critique around the problem of erroneous judgments of taste, as exemplified by Kant's own example of the young poet. As we have seen, this poet made an "autonomous" judgment of taste, since he relied on his own feeling rather than accepting the verdict of the critics, but his judgment is nonetheless incorrect. According to Savile, what this supposedly shows is that "judgments that are unimpeachably judgments of taste," for example, that of the young poet, need not embody a legitimate claim to universal consent.[40]

This conclusion is certainly correct. But rather than recognizing that it raises no problems for Kant, since the Deduction is only supposed to apply to *pure* judgments of taste, Savile regards it as pointing to a major difficulty, albeit one that can be overcome by adopting the suggestion of §22 that common sense or taste is not a natural faculty (since that would supposedly make an erroneous judgment of taste totally inexplicable). Thus, like Guyer before him, Savile turns to the alternative conception of common sense or taste as a faculty that needs to be acquired. But he differs from Guyer in that he takes this seriously, and sees it as the key to Kant's actual legitimation project. As a first step in this reconstruction, he notes that this enables us to read the official deduction (§38) as applying only to those who have already acquired taste. In other words, the judgment "x is beautiful" makes a claim about universal agreement only within the community of those with taste. Given this scope limitation, the young poet is not a counterexample, since he has not yet acquired taste, even though he made a perfectly proper judgment of taste.[41] Moreover, Savile suggests that this also explains why Kant thought that the deduction was so easy, since the real work now becomes to explain why we ought to develop taste, a claim that is not even meaningful on the assumption that taste is a natural faculty.[42]

In introducing the requirement to develop taste (which for Guyer is only part of his "speculative" alternative reading) into the actual Kantian legitimation project, Savile occupies common ground with those interpreters who look for a moral foundation for taste. He differs from them, however, in attempting to provide a grounding for the claim that one ought to develop taste that is independent of morality. Eschewing, like Guyer, any specifically moral considerations, Savile insists that the "ought" in question is that of good (external) reasons.[43] In other words, what Kant must show is that there are good reasons, applying to each of us, to develop this faculty. Moreover, he maintains that this is precisely what Kant was attempting to do, albeit not very successfully, in §41–§42, which deal respectively with the empirical and intellectual interest in the beautiful.

We cannot here rehearse the reasons for Savile's dissatisfaction with these arguments. What is important is merely his claim that they point to a lacuna in the overall argument, which, according to him, Kant himself recognized and endeavored to fill in the later portions of the text. The suggested lacuna is the very one on which Guyer also insists, namely, the need to extend the argument to particulars. For Savile, it is not enough to learn that we ought to develop taste (whether for reasons of social coherence or on other grounds), since this entails merely that we ought to develop the capacity to take pleasure in some objects or other, or perhaps even the same objects (if the claim is based on the need for social cohesiveness). What is needed, he thinks, is a more focused ought, one which entails that there are some objects, namely beautiful ones, in which one ought to take pleasure.[44] This is because only such an ought is sufficient to ground the demand to take pleasure in a particular object that is connected with a judgment of taste and that has been the concern of the legitimization project from the beginning.

In what is clearly the most speculative and interesting part of his reconstruction, Savile maintains that Kant not only recognized this demand but also succeeded fairly well in meeting it with his doctrine of aesthetic ideas. Very roughly, the claim is that the fact that an object expresses aesthetic ideas is at once a reason that one ought to be engaged with it and a ground for claiming it beautiful. Thus, the doctrine of aesthetic ideas provides the bridge linking the general demand to acquire taste to the specific demand to take pleasure in particular objects, that is, those that express aesthetic ideas.[45]

We shall consider both Kant's account of a quasi-obligation to develop taste and his doctrine of aesthetic ideas in the third and fourth parts of this study. But quite independently of these considerations, it should already be apparent that, in spite of its suggestiveness and subtlety at many points, Savile's analysis is fatally flawed. As was the case with Guyer, the problem lies in the underlying assumption that what Kant is trying to do (or at least ought to be trying) is to ground the legitimacy of particular claims of taste, rather than merely the judgment-type (the pure judgment of taste), as defined by the conditions laid out in the Analytic of the Beautiful. In fact, Kant could not have taken up the former task without abandoning the view that the necessity involved in a judgment of taste is not amenable to proof, which, as we have seen, is one of the two peculiarities of taste, the "resolution" of which is supposed to constitute the Deduction. Consequently, if, as Savile maintains, showing that there are some objects in which one ought to take pleasure were part of the task of the Deduction, it could succeed only by undermining one of its basic premises.[46]

VII

Perhaps the most persistent and widespread criticism of Kant's deduction of taste is that if it proves anything at all, it proves too much, namely, that every object must be judged beautiful. This line of criticism follows naturally from the consideration of Kant's attempt to link the grounds of judgments of taste with the conditions of cognition, a linkage that itself seems necessary in order to connect such judgments with an *a priori* principle of judgment and thereby provide them with some sort of normativity. For if, as Kant suggests, the harmony of the faculties constitutes a necessary subjective condition of cognition, which must therefore occur in all cognition, and if the ability to occasion such a harmony is a sufficient condition for judging an object beautiful, then it would seem that every object of possible experience must be judged beautiful, simply in virtue of conforming to this condition.[47] Moreover, such a result seems to be implicit in much of what Kant has to say on the subject. Consider, for example, §39, which serves as a kind of appendix to the Deduction. As Kant there puts it with regard to the pleasure of taste:

> This pleasure must of necessity rest on the same conditions for everyone, because they are subjective conditions for the possibility of cognition as such, and because the proportion between these cognitive faculties that is required for taste is also required for the sound and common understanding that we may presuppose in everyone. (KU 5: 292–3; 159)

One possible approach to the problem, which has been proposed in the literature, is to accept the apparent implication of passages such as this one that according to Kant's view, everything is indeed beautiful and to deny that this involves any absurdity. Insofar as proponents of this position also deny the possibility of negative judgments of taste, their views have already been addressed in Chapter 3.[48] But since the view with which we are presently concerned goes beyond this denial and maintains that Kant *should not* have allowed for the possibility of negative judgments on the grounds that his theory quite reasonably entails that everything is beautiful, it calls for a separate consideration.

One interpreter who takes this line is Theodore Gracyk, who attempts to defend the "everything is beautiful" thesis by appealing to the first *Critique's* contrast between the objective and subjective time-orders. According to Gracyk, this distinction opens up the possibility that a work of art might be beautiful and yet its beauty not appreciated due to the failure on the part of a perceiver to realize sufficient unity in the subjective time-order on a given occasion.[49] Unfortunately, the imposition of the first *Critique's* distinction between time-orders on the third *Critique's* account of the judgment of taste is not very convincing, particularly since judgments of taste (except possibly in the case of music) do not seem to have anything to do with time-orders. Even if we were to accept this analysis, however, the most that it shows is how there might be a failure to recognize an object's beauty under certain conditions, and this is still a long way from defending the claim that *every* object is beautiful, if judged correctly.

Of greater interest is the approach of Reinhard Brandt.[50] Although he acknowledges that Kant recognizes the reality of judgments of the form "x is not beautiful" or "x is ugly," Brandt denies that they are universally communicable and, therefore, pure judgments of taste, on the familiar grounds that such communicability pertains only to the mental state of free harmony. But Brandt goes beyond this merely negative point and argues that Kant had good reasons, stemming from the relation between taste and morality, for not admitting negative judgments of taste.

Brandt's analysis focuses on the Dialectic, where, like Crawford and other advocates of the view that the true foundation of taste for Kant is moral, he locates the core of the deduction. His basic point is separable from this, however, since it turns on Kant's own claim that natural beauty provides indications of the moral purposiveness of nature. According to his reading, this of itself commits Kant to the thesis that everything (or at least everything in nature) must be beautiful and that the failure to appreciate the beauty of certain things in nature is to be attributed to a lack of taste, which, as §22 suggests, may be a faculty that is acquired, rather than natural. And in support of this reading, he cites in a footnote a passage from a transcript of the anthropology lectures of 1784–5, where Kant is reported as reasoning:

Can something ugly [*eine Hässlichkeit*] possibly be produced in nature as a product thereof? No. For if we had an *extended* [*ausgebreitete*] knowledge of its purposes, if we knew the uses of all its members, then *nothing* that is produced according to the rules of nature would appear ugly but truly beautiful; for in the course of nature everything is beautiful. Ugliness is merely relative in comparison with others. If we notice the regularity [*Regelmässigkeit*] then even the ugly is regular [*regelmässig*]. (Anthro M 25: 1378)[51]

We shall be concerned with the way in which natural beauty provides an indication of nature's moral purposiveness and its significance for morality in Part III of this study (particularly Chapter 10). Even prior to considering this topic, however, it should be noted, first, that such a view does not require that *everything* in nature provide indications of this purposiveness, and, second, that not being beautiful is not equivalent to being ugly. Granted, if nature were primarily ugly and presented us with only rare specimens of beauty, the pure, morally based interest in natural beauty with which Kant is concerned would probably not arise. But such an interest is perfectly compatible with much (indeed most) of nature not being perceived as beautiful, which, again, is not equivalent to its being ugly.

Since Brandt only refers to this passage in a note, it would be unfair to suggest that it is central to his argument. Nevertheless, it is also important to realize that texts such as these do not support the claim that for Kant, everything in nature (leaving aside works of fine art or artifacts) is beautiful in the *aesthetic sense*. On the contrary, in this passage (and others like it), Kant is clearly concerned with the question of teleology or objective purposiveness, rather than taste, which, as we have seen, is a matter of subjective purposiveness. But to claim that everything is beautiful (in the aesthetic sense) because it is purposive in an objective (moral) sense, or even regular, would be to undermine the entire basis of Kant's theory of taste. Consequently, if Kant's theory of taste is to be rescued, it must be shown that it does not entail that everything is beautiful, when evaluated aesthetically by means of a pure judgment of taste.

The usual initial move for those who acknowledge this point is to appeal to Kant's notion of the "proportionate attunement" [*proportionirte Stimmung*] of the cognitive faculties referred to in §9 (KU 5: 219; 64) or, more simply, their proportion [*Proportion*] to which Kant refers in §21 and again in §39. In particular, the claim in §21 that the attunement of the cognitive faculties varies in proportion, with this variation being a function of the nature of the object, and that "there must be one attunement in which this inner relation is most conducive to the (mutual) quickening of the two mental faculties with a view to cognition . . . in general" (KU 5: 238; 88) has been thought to provide a way out of the difficulty. The idea here is that not every object, but merely those that occasion this maximal attunement or proportion, are properly deemed beautiful.[52]

Against this it is frequently argued, however, that such a move only rescues Kant from the "everything is beautiful" problem at the cost of undermining the ability of the Deduction to establish the universality and necessity of judgments of taste. For if one emphasizes the differences in proportion, and, therefore, in aesthetic response, occasioned by different objects, then the close link with the conditions of cognition is broken, and with it any ground for asserting that an attunement felt by one person must be felt by others as well. And from this it is then inferred that any interpretation of the Deduction is confronted with a stark dilemma: Either accept the apparent absurdity that everything is beautiful or abandon the attempt to show that judgments of taste can possess the normativity claimed for them.[53]

In an attempt to address this dilemma, to which I think the "everything is beautiful" objection reduces, I shall consider each horn in turn. And, finally, by way of putting it into a broader framework, I shall also suggest that there is an illuminating parallel between this problem and its solution and one that is sometimes thought to arise regarding the Transcendental Deduction in the first *Critique*.

With regard to the first horn, the account of Kant's theory of taste sketched in the preceding chapters should have made it reasonably clear that he is not committed to the view that an object is judged beautiful simply in virtue of conforming to the conditions of cognition. The main point here is that subsumability under, or agreement with, "the subjective conditions for the possibility of cognition as such," referred to in §39, is merely a necessary and not also a sufficient condition for something to be judged beautiful. In order for the latter to be warranted, an object must not simply conform to, or harmonize with, these conditions; it must do so in a certain way, namely in free play, that is, in an act of aesthetic appraisal, which involves a suspension of our ordinary cognitive concerns with classification and explanation, as well as our sensuous and moral interests as rational agents.

Accordingly, it is crucial to become clear about the difference between the two ways in which an object (or, more properly, its representation) can harmonize (or fail to harmonize) with the subjective conditions of judgment. Fortunately, since this is largely a matter or reviewing ground already covered, it is possible to be relatively brief. To begin with, in the case of cognition, the question is whether what is given in sensible intuition and apprehended through the imaginative synthesis is subsumable under a determinate empirical concept (or concepts). Moreover, this, in turn, is a matter of discovering in the apprehended object relevant similarities to other objects, which makes possible its classification as an instance of a kind or an exemplification of a law. Indeed, we have seen in the first part of this study that the principle of the logical purposiveness of nature or systematicity provides judgment with a license in its reflection on nature to presuppose that such uniformity is there to be found, if one looks hard enough for it.

Aesthetic reflection, by contrast, is not at all concerned with the comparison of the object reflected upon with other objects because its aim is neither to classify the object under a determinate concept nor to explain it by bringing it under a covering law. It rather focuses on the object in its uniqueness or sheer singularity, not as an instance of kind, but, as it were, itself a kind. And since the content of such reflection cannot involve a comparison with other objects for the purpose of cognition, it can only be (as Kant indicates in the First Introduction) a comparison of its intuitive representation with the conditions of cognition themselves.[54]

Once again, then, the question is whether the object presents itself in intuition, that is, in its immediacy, apart from any comparison with other objects, as purposive for the workings of judgment. As we have seen, this may be said of an object just in case its intuitive representation simulates the exhibition of a concept, or, equivalently, that its "form" as apprehended immediately suggests a rule-governedness, albeit no rule in particular (for the latter would necessarily involve comparison with other objects and an appeal to determinate concepts). In that case, as Carl Posy has put it, the experience of the object "invites the application of a concept" (though, again, no concept in particular); and since the application of a concept requires the contribution of both the imagination and the understanding, such an "invitation" leads to the "mutual quickening" of these faculties in their free play.[55] That is why Kant remarks at the end of §12 that "We *linger* [*weilen*] in our contemplation of the beautiful because this contemplation reinforces and reproduces itself" (KU 5: 222; 67). This is to be contrasted with the normal experience of a good cognitive fit, wherein the mind "lingers" no longer than is necessary to grasp the fit, and where the object given in intuition might be said to "invite" or "demand" the application of a specific concept (or concepts) precisely because it provides a particularly apt illustration of what it is to be an object of a certain kind.

Given such an account of the experience of beauty and its difference from cognition, it should be clear that not every object is beautiful, and that no object is beautiful merely in virtue of its conformity to the subjective conditions of cognition (or judgment). On the contrary, an object is deemed beautiful precisely because of its effect on the mind in a reflection in which the normal concerns of cognition are suspended. Moreover, in light of this, we can easily understand Kant's talk of a differential in the degree of "attunement" or the "proportion" of the cognitive faculties. This attunement (in contrast to a cognitive fit) is something that is felt only in mere reflection, and pertains to the extent to which a given object is felt to "invite the application" of a concept," or, equivalently, promote the "mutual quickening" of the cognitive faculties in their free play.

Here (as in the case of cognition) there is certainly room for differences in the degree of attunement, as well as for the experience of something that is positively unappealing or disinviting to the mind in its mere reflection, that is, the ugly, yet which is itself fully cognizable (though not, of course, as ugly).

The avoidability of the second horn of the dilemma is largely a function of what one takes the goal of the Deduction to be. Clearly, if with Guyer and many others one takes it to be to ground an expectation (or reasoned prediction) of a particular response to a particular object of nature or work of art, then an account of taste such as the one I have sketched makes this horn unavoidable. For differences in aesthetic response stemming from differences in the attunement of the faculties would seem to undermine any basis for expecting (not to mention demanding) agreement.

If, however, one interprets the Deduction in the manner suggested here, namely as grounding the possibility and the normativity of the pure judgment of taste in the "subjective principle of the faculty of judgment as such" (§35), which is itself shown to be normative for all human beings (§38), then the objection seems to lose much of its force. To be sure, I cannot say that others *ought* to agree with my aesthetic assessment of an object any more than I can expect (or predict) that they will; but this is only because I cannot be sure in any given case that my judgment of taste is pure.

Against this it might be objected that there can still be disagreement or conflict between pure judgments of taste, particularly if, as was suggested, such judgments are based on something beyond the mere conformity of a representation with the conditions of cognition. In fact, we have already noted that Kant himself insists in the Dialectic of Aesthetic Judgment that one can quarrel about taste, even though one cannot dispute about it. And if this is the case, it seems to follow that one would not be justified in demanding the agreement of others even if (*per impossibile*) one could be certain that one had made a pure judgment of taste.

Although this objection may be a perfectly natural one to raise at this point, I believe that it can be answered in terms of Kant's account of taste. At bottom the issue comes down to the question of whether a pure judgment of taste can be erroneous; for if it cannot then, clearly, there cannot be a conflict between *pure* judgments.[56] When this question was first taken up in Chapter 6 in connection with an analysis of the idea of a universal voice, it was suggested that Kant introduced the latter conception as the aesthetic analogue of Rousseau's general will. And from this it was inferred that while one may certainly be mistaken in assuming in a given judgment of taste that one is truly speaking with a universal voice, insofar as one is, one's judgment (like the dictates of the general will) cannot err. Moreover, since it was also argued that actually speaking with a universal voice is equivalent to making a pure judgment of taste, it likewise follows that a pure judgment of taste cannot err. Consequently, errors in taste (such as that exemplified by the young poet) are to be seen as cases of mistaking one's *de facto* judgment of taste for a pure judgment.

Admittedly, of itself, this hardly resolves the problem, since it concerns merely a conceptual claim made with respect to the idea of a universal voice postulated in a judgment of taste purporting to be pure. But when this is combined with the results of the Deduction as analyzed here, things look rather different. For even though the Deduction on this reading is limited to pure judgments of taste, it establishes the *possibility* as well as the normativity of such judgments. In other words, by showing that a pure judgment of taste (as explicated in the Analytic of the Beautiful) is based on a subjective principle intrinsic to judgment, which we are rationally constrained to recognize as valid for all human beings, Kant also shows that the pure judgment of taste is not a mere chimera or "phantom of the brain."[57] And this remains true even though such a judgment may, in fact, be as rare as an action motivated by the pure thought of duty alone.

Moreover, the success of the deduction, so construed, is not undermined by the fact that the attunement of the faculties on which a pure judgment of taste is based is not equivalent to the one required for cognition and, therefore, occasioned by every cognizable object. For this lack of equivalence, which provides the basis for the second horn of the dilemma, does not concern the norm itself, but merely the difficulty of subsuming a particular instance under it. And as Kant himself points out in the previously cited note to §38 that is intended to clarify the intent of the Deduction, a mistake regarding the latter "amounts to nothing but an incorrect application, in a particular case, of an authority given to us by a law, and in no way annuls the authority" (KU 5: 290; 155). Once again, it is only this authority, which suffices to establish the possibility of a pure judgment of taste, with which Kant is concerned in the Deduction on the reading advocated here.

Finally, it may prove instructive to compare briefly this "everything is beautiful" objection and the sketched response to it with an analogous objection that has been raised against the Transcendental Deduction of the first *Critique* by C. I. Lewis and Norman Kemp Smith, among others. Like the one presently before us, this objection holds that if Kant's deduction proves anything at all, it proves too much. Specifically, the charge is that in showing that everything must conform to the categories, it rules out the very possibility of discordant, nonobjective "experiences." As Lewis puts it in his provocative question, "Did the sage of Königsburg have no dreams?"[58]

The basic response to this line of objection has been provided by Lewis White Beck and may be broken down into two steps.[59] The first consists in pointing out that the principle of apperception affirms merely that "It must be *possible* [my emphasis] for the 'I think' to accompany all my representations" (B131), not that it actually does so on every occasion. It thus asserts the necessity of a possibility. The "I" of apperception actually accompanies these representations [intuitions] only insofar as one explicitly brings them to the "objective unity of self-consciousness" through judgment. Moreover, it is only insofar as representations are brought to this unity that they are subsumed under the categories. Thus, room is left in the Kantian scheme for intuitions that are not brought under the categories (though not for those that cannot be brought). To be sure, these unapperceived representations (intuitions) remain "nothing to me," cognitively speaking, but they may nonetheless influence my behavior.[60]

The second step is to insist that being thus brought to the objective unity of self-consciousness, and thereby also brought under the categories, is merely a necessary and not also a sufficient condition for referring representations to a public, objective world distinct from the self. In addition to being referred to objects in this sense, these "apperceived" representations can also be taken to refer merely to the subject and to characterize how things appear to a particular subject under given conditions. To be sure, in spite of Kant's apparent disclaimer in the *Prolegomena,* such a connection or relation of representations is likewise subject to the categories (as the Transcendental Deduction requires). But this does not of itself make them into "objective representations" in a strong sense. For, as "concepts of an object in general," the categories provide the normative principles on the basis of which the distinction between the subjective or merely private and the objective is drawn *within possible experience.* Consequently, in being brought under the categories, sensible data become, as it were, candidates for inclusion in an objective spatiotemporal order, but not necessarily members thereof.

Admittedly, much more would be required to defend these claims in a remotely adequate manner. Nevertheless, this should suffice to indicate that a similar two-step response is applicable to the "everything is beautiful" problem. First, just as a given representation must not only be such that it conforms to the possibility of the 'I think,' but must actually be accompanied by an 'I think,' if it is to amount to cognition, so, in the aesthetic case, if an object or its representation is to be deemed beautiful, it must not merely accord with the subjective conditions of cognition; it must do so in a particular manner, namely in mere reflection.

Second, just as being referred to the transcendental conditions of experience (the objective unity of apperception and the categories) merely makes a representation a candidate for objectivity, rather than a representation of an objective state of affairs, so, in the case of taste, being referred (in mere reflection) to the subjective conditions of judgment makes an object or its representation merely into a candidate for aesthetic evaluation, rather than actually beautiful. For, as has been noted repeatedly, the object could either harmonize or clash with these conditions, just as in the case of cognition it can refer either to the public objective world of phenomena or merely to the way in which that world appears to a particular subject under particular conditions. Thus, Kant's transcendental account has room for both nonobjective representations (including dreams) and aesthetic encounters with the nonbeautiful.

THE MORAL AND SYSTEMATIC SIGNIFICANCE OF TASTE

REFLECTIVE JUDGMENT AND THE TRANSITION FROM NATURE TO FREEDOM

The focus of the preceding part of this study was on the claim to normativity inherent in the pure judgment of taste. It was argued, first, that the Analytic of the Beautiful addresses the *quid facti* by determining the conditions under which a judgment of taste can be pure and, second, that the Deduction resolves the *quid juris* by showing that, on the one hand, a pure judgment of taste makes a rightful demand for agreement but that, on the other hand, it is impossible to determine with certainty whether any given judgment of taste is pure. Although Kant makes passing allusions to the issue, particularly in §17 and §22, my discussion abstracted from the whole question of the connection between taste and morality, which for many interpreters is the key to the grounding of the normativity of taste itself.[1] This was done in order to show that, contrary to these interpreters, the grounding of the pure judgment of taste is independent of any connection taste may have with morality.

It should not be inferred from this, however, that the connection with morality is merely a side issue, peripheral to the main business of the *Critique of Aesthetic Judgment*. On the contrary, we shall see that this connection lies at the very heart of Kant's project, though it presupposes, and therefore cannot help to ground, the normativity of the pure judgment of taste. In fact, one might even go so far as to say that the grounding of the normativity of the pure judgment of taste may itself be seen as the first step in the connection of taste with morality, rather than, as is frequently done, viewing the latter as the final stage in the legitimization of the former.

Moreover, it should be noted at this point that, in spite of our numerous disagreements, many of which have been underscored in the first two parts of this study, on this fundamental issue I am in complete agreement with Paul Guyer. As he succinctly puts the matter in a statement of the main thesis of his recent book, "Taste can serve moral autonomy only if morality can also recognize aesthetic autonomy."[2] Although he formulates the issue in terms of the autonomy of taste and I tend to put it in terms of normativity, this does not indicate a substantive difference between us. For as we have seen, the peculiar form of autonomy attributed to the pure judgment of taste, namely heautonomy, is both a necessary and sufficient condition of its normativity. Accordingly, the question becomes how taste, in virtue of its "heautonomy," can, in Guyer's terms, "serve moral autonomy."

In explaining just how this comes about, however, my account will once again differ from Guyer's in several respects. To anticipate, I shall argue that some relatively neglected features of Kant's moral theory, namely, the conceptions of radical evil and an indirect duty, are absolutely essential to understanding the connections between taste and the experience of beauty and morality. In addition, I shall claim that the cultivation of taste and the experience of beauty contribute to the development of morality in two distinct (though related) ways: The first, which is limited to natural beauty, is by giving rise to an intellectual interest in the beauties of nature insofar as they provide an intimation of nature's moral purposiveness; the second, which applies to both natural and artistic beauty, is by symbolizing the morally good. These will be among the concerns of Chapters 10 and 11 respectively.

Although we shall see in Chapter 11 that the intimation natural beauties provide of nature's moral purposiveness must itself be understood in terms of the symbolization of morality (through their expression of aesthetic ideas), the protomoralizing function it serves differs from that of other modes of symbolization and can be fulfilled only by natural beauties. Whereas the latter serve mainly to wean us from an excessive attachment to our sensuous interests and egocentric involvements with the world, the former provides a kind of moral encouragement that helps to strengthen our wavering commitment to morally required ends. And in this way, then, we shall see that Kant is able to privilege natural beauty from the moral point of view, while at the same time preserving a potentially moralizing function for artistic beauty as well.

Nevertheless, in order to understand why either such moral encouragement or a weaning from the sensuous and egocentric is required for autonomous moral agents, such as ourselves, we must consider Kant's discussion in the Second Introduction of the "immense gulf" between nature and freedom and of the necessity of a "transition" [*Übergang*] from our manner of thinking about the former to our manner of thinking about the latter. Accordingly, this is the subject matter of the present chapter, which is intended as an introduction to the third part as a whole and is divided into five parts.[3] The first provides a brief overview of Kant's various accounts of the nature of, and need for, an *Übergang* from nature to freedom in texts prior to the *Critique of Judgment* (including the First Introduction). The second analyzes the problem as spelled out in Section II of the Second Introduction and discusses its connections with both

Kant's moral theory and the conception of logical purposiveness treated in Chapter 1. Finally, parts three through five consider various aspects of the solution as adumbrated in Section IX of the Second Introduction.

I

Prior to the Second Introduction, where it occupies pride of place, there are four texts from the critical period in which Kant either refers explicitly to an *Übergang* from nature to freedom (or its equivalent) or poses the problem to which it is the apparent solution. As we shall see, however, in none of these is the discussion more than peripheral to the main topic, and Kant is not very clear about how this *Übergang* is to be understood, or even about the precise nature of the problem in question.

The first of these texts is from the introductory discussion of the transcendental ideas in the Transcendental Dialectic in the first *Critique*. As Kant there remarks in passing, "concepts of reason [transcendental ideas] may perhaps make possible a transition from the concepts of nature to the practical concepts, and in that way may give support to the moral ideas themselves, bringing them into connection with the speculative cognition of reason" (A339/B386). Since beyond stating that we can expect further explanation in the sequel [*dem Vefolg*], Kant has nothing more to say about the transition at this point, it is difficult to determine exactly what he had in mind, and therefore where in the *Critique* to locate this sequel. Nevertheless, there are only two places fitting this general description, though in neither of them does Kant refer explicitly to an *Übergang*.

One, suggested by Heinz Heimsoeth, is that Kant is referring to the discussion of the treatment of the idea of freedom in the Third Antinomy and its resolution.[4] Since Kant there introduces transcendental freedom in a theoretical context as a cosmological idea, that is, as the idea of an undetermined cause or ground of the world as a whole, and then later moves to a discussion of its role in the conception of the practical freedom of the human will, his procedure may be described as involving a transition (brought about by a transcendental idea) from a concept of nature to a practical concept. Moreover, since the idea in question, namely freedom, is central to morality as Kant conceives it, this transition may also be described as giving support to moral ideas by connecting them with the speculative cognition of reason.[5]

The other possibility, which has been suggested by Klaus Düsing, is that Kant is looking ahead to the discussion of the highest good in the Canon of Pure Reason, specifically his account of the purposive unity of things, which supposedly unites practical with speculative reason (A815/B843–A816/B344).[6] For in view of his reintroduction of the ideas of God, immortality, and freedom in the Canon in connection with the concept of the highest good, Kant's procedure there may also be described as an attempt to give support for moral ideas by linking them to these speculative ones, thereby producing a kind of unification of theoretical and practical reason. Although this unification is likewise brought about by the ideas themselves (this time mainly those of God and immortality), it should be noted that it is seriously at odds with Kant's fully developed moral theory, since it is based on the assumption that belief in the objective reality of the ideas of God and immortality are necessary in order to have an incentive to morality. As Kant there succinctly puts it, "Without a God and without a world invisible to us now but hoped for, the glorious ideas of morality are indeed objects of approval and admiration, but not springs of purpose and action" (A813/B841).[7]

On balance, I favor the latter reading, since the problem it addresses is somewhat closer to the one with which Kant eventually connects the need for an *Übergang* in the third *Critique*. Nevertheless, it must be emphasized that on either interpretation, there remain significant differences between the first and third *Critiques* in the understanding of both the nature and the necessity of the transition. Indeed, I believe that these differences are so great that it is highly misleading to regard the passing mention of an *Übergang* in the first *Critique* as an anticipation of the problem with which Kant became centrally concerned in the third. In part, this is due to the change in Kant's views on moral motivation brought about by his "discovery" of the principle of the autonomy of the will as the true foundation of morality.[8] Of even greater relevance to our present concerns, however, are the facts that in the third *Critique* the *Übergang* is attributed to judgment's concept of the purposiveness of nature, rather than to ideas of reason, and only in the Second Introduction is it appealed to in order to bridge a supposed "immense gulf" between the domains of the concepts of nature and freedom.

In the Preface to the *Critique of Practical Reason*, Kant again refers in passing to an *Übergang*, this time from the theoretical to the practical use of the categories (here described as "concepts of reason") (KpV 5: 7; 7). Although Kant's "fully critical" views on moral motivation are now in place, his analysis of the problem and its proposed solution is still quite far from that of the third *Critique*. The problem itself, as Kant now defines it, is that of grounding a practical use (with respect to noumena) of concepts, which in the first *Critique* were limited to phenomena. In short, it is a matter of resolving an apparent contradiction between the two *Critiques* (or, more precisely, between the first *Critique* and the *Groundwork*), which had been alleged by his critics, rather than of providing some kind of unifying bridge between the theoretical and practical "standpoints."[9] Moreover, Kant seems to regard this *Übergang* as accomplished by the *Critique of Practical Reason* itself, through its justification of a practical use for the "category" of freedom. Finally, it is also noteworthy that Kant here appears to deny what he will shortly thereafter take to be a major problem requiring a separate critique, namely, that there are any "gaps" [*Lücken*] in the "critical system of speculative reason." On the contrary, he here insists that this system is "complete in its design" (KpV 5: 7; 7).

Although the term does not appear, Kant's first actual discussion of the problem for which an *Übergang* will be appealed to as the solution is to be found in the conclusion of his essay of 1788: "On the Use of Teleological Principles in Philosophy." Since this was written in the same year as the appearance of the second *Critique*, Kant's mature moral theory is likewise in place. Thus, there is no longer talk of finding an incentive for morality through the theoretical use of reason, and therefore of effecting the transition in that way. Instead, morality is now understood as a "pure doctrine of purposes" [*reine Zweckslehre*], and the problem is understood to concern the possibility of the realization of these purposes in the world.

This possibility, Kant suggests, must be accounted for if the objective reality of the morally prescribed purposes is to be secured. As we shall see shortly, this is precisely how the problem is presented in the Second Introduction to the *Critique of Judgment*. Moreover, in accordance with the main theme of the essay (the philosophical uses of the teleological principle), the task is assigned to teleology, which must concern itself both with the final causes given in the world and the "suitability of the supreme cause of the world to a totality of all purposes as its effect" (GTP 8: 182–3). Unfortunately, however, Kant gives no indication of how teleology (or the "teleological principle") is supposed to accomplish this goal.

The problem of an *Übergang* appears in yet another guise in Section XI of the First Introduction, which is characterized as the "Encyclopaedic Introduction of the Critique of Judgment into the System of the Critique of Pure Reason" (FI 20: 241; 431). This section, which follows the accounts of the various forms of purposiveness and reflective judgment, marks a return to the central theme of the First Introduction: the integration of the critique of judgment into the "system of the critique of pure reason." As we have already seen in the first part of this study, this integration depends on demonstrating that judgment, like understanding and reason, has its own *a priori* principle (the purposiveness of nature), even though, as a principle of reflective rather than determinative judgment, it does not ground a distinct part of the system of philosophical knowledge. In the language of the Second Introduction, it does not have a separate domain [*Gebiet*] in which it is legislative. In spite of this lack of a domain, however, we have also seen that Kant claims that judgment's principle of purposiveness functions as the *a priori* principle governing judgments of taste (at least concerning objects of nature). Moreover, on this basis he concludes provisionally that if the critique of taste has a transcendental aim (something that can only be established in the work itself, presumably through a deduction of the principle of taste), then it "fills a gap [*Lücke*] in the system of our cognitive faculties, and hence opens up a striking . . . prospect of a complete system of all the mental faculties, insofar as in being determined they are referred not just to the sensible but also to the supersensible" (FI 20: 244; 434).

After a series of tables spelling out the systematic connections between the various faculties, principles, and products,[10] Kant turns in the penultimate paragraph of this section to the question of how judgment fills this presumed gap in the system. It is in this context that he introduces the notion of an *Übergang*, by way of a summary of the main results of this "encyclopaedic introduction." As he here describes the system and the place of judgment therein:

> Thus we find a system of the mental faculties in their relation to nature and to freedom, each having its own *determinative a priori* principles and hence constituting the two parts of philosophy (theoretical and practical) as a doctrinal system, as well as a transition [*Übergang*] by means of judgment, which connects the two parts through a principle of its own. This transition is from the *sensible* substrate of theoretical philosophy to the *intelligible* substrate of practical philosophy; [it is made] through the critique of a faculty (judgment) that serves only for this connection. Hence this faculty cannot on its own provide any cognition or contribute anything whatever to doctrine; but its judgments – called *aesthetic* judgments (whose principles are merely subjective), since they differ from all those that are called *logical*, i.e., from those (whether theoretical or practical) whose principles must be objective – are of so special a kind that they refer sensible intuitions to an idea of nature in which [nature's] lawfulness is beyond [our] understanding unless [we] relate nature to a supersensible substrate. (FI 20: 246–7; 436)

Several points in this dense passage call for comment. To begin with, by the "sensible substrate of theoretical philosophy" Kant presumably means the highest conditions of the possibility of objects as appearances, that is, the sensible "real ground" of nature, rather than something "supersensible" (i.e., merely intelligible).[11] Thus, in the First Analogy, Kant characterizes time as the substrate (or permanent form) of inner intuition, and argues that there must be found in appearances "the substrate which represents time in general" (A182/B224–5). Similarly, in the *Prolegomena* Kant refers to space (the "mere universal form of intuition") as the "substrate of all intuitions determinable to particular objects" (Pro 4: 322; 68–9). Correlatively, the "intelligible substrate of practical philosophy" is the idea of freedom, which in the second *Critique* Kant characterizes as the "*ratio essendi* of the moral law" (KpV 5: 4n; 4). Accordingly, the *Übergang* may be appropriately described as from nature (or the conditions of the possibility of cognition thereof) to freedom, as the condition of practical philosophy and, indeed, of the practical use of reason.

It is also noteworthy that the *Übergang* is said to occur through a *critique* of judgment, rather than through judgment itself, though it is made on the basis of that faculty's peculiar principle[s], as they are operative in aesthetic judgments. The latter point suggests a sharp contrast with the standpoint of "On the Use of Teleological Principles in Philosophy," since, as we have just seen, Kant there emphasizes the role of teleology in effecting the *Übergang*, but not a word is said about taste or the beautiful. Nevertheless, the difference on this point between the two nearly contemporaneous texts appears somewhat less severe, if one keeps in mind that the principle of taste that is here referred to (but not named) is just that of the purposiveness of nature. For it is this principle that refers "sensible intuitions to an idea of nature in which [nature's] lawfulness is beyond our understanding unless we relate nature to a supersensible substrate." In other words, the mediating role assigned to judgment and uncovered by the critique of that faculty is here made to depend on the claim (common to both Introductions) that the principle of the purposiveness of nature is itself the *a priori* principle underlying and licensing judgments of taste. And, as we have already seen, this claim is not only highly problematic in its own right but also at variance with the account of taste and its principle that Kant provides in the Deduction.

Perhaps a more significant difference between the account of the *Übergang* in the First Introduction and the problem as posed in "On the Use of Teleological Principles in Philosophy" is that the former makes no reference to the specifically moral problem emphasized in the latter. Instead, the problem is presented as if it were a purely systematic one, that of filling a "gap" in the critical system, rather than one that has anything specifically to do with morality. Moreover, as we are about to see, this presentation of the problem and Kant's failure to provide an explanation of how the *Übergang* is actually brought about are the two main ways in which the account of the First Introduction differs from that of the Second.

II

In the Second Introduction, the problem requiring an *Übergang* for its solution is no longer characterized as that of filling a "gap" in the critical system, but rather of bridging a gulf, indeed, an "immense gulf" [*unübersehbare Kluft*] between what happens according to the laws of nature and what ought to happen according to laws of freedom (KU 5: 175; 13). This subtle shift in formulation reflects a sharpening of the problem, which Kant now poses in terms of a set of geopolitical metaphors that supplant the idea of system as the leitmotif of the Second Introduction. Thus, understanding and reason are described as each having its separate domain [*Gebiet*] or legislation (theoretical and practical, respectively), so that the field of philosophy is divided into two domains (nature and freedom). This is, of course, the same duality through which Kant introduced the problem of finding a systematic place (and hence a principle) for judgment in the First Introduction. But rather than appealing to judgment at this point, he now focuses on the difficulties inherent in the sharp separation between these two domains.

Expressed in terms of the geopolitical metaphors, the initial complicating factor is that, on the one hand, these two legislations are over a single territory [*Boden*], namely, the sum total of objects of possible experience, while, on the other hand, neither of these legislations is supposed to interfere with the other. Thus, the laws of nature stemming from the understanding determine what is the case, and the laws of freedom derived from reason dictate what ought to be; and these two orders must be viewed as being compatible without one being reducible to the other, that is, without forming a single domain. This irreducibility is essential because the idea of a "reduction" of what is to what ought to be (of nature to freedom) would be nonsensical for Kant, whereas the more familiar reduction in the other direction yields a naturalistic form of compatibilism that would undermine genuine freedom, and therefore morality.[12]

Although the latter does not constitute an insuperable problem for Kant, since, as he reminds us, the resolution of the Third Antinomy established at least the conceivability (logical possibility) of the coexistence of these two legislations and their corresponding faculties in the same subject, this is not the end of the story. For this critical resolution of the freedom–nature problem seems to create a new difficulty, namely, accounting for the compatibility of the *effects* of the two kinds of legislation in the sensible world. Kant thinks that the compatibility of the legislations themselves is assured by the transcendental distinction, which assigns one of them to objects considered as they appear (the sensible) and the other to objects considered as they are in themselves (the supersensible). But this only makes it seem even more mysterious how the *products* of these legislations, which presumably all manifest themselves in the sensible world, are to be brought together. In other words, the problem is to understand how the laws of nature, which govern what *does* happen, can accommodate morality's demands regarding what *ought* to happen.

Although he does not refer to it explicitly, Kant here seems to have in mind the Leibnizian conception of a preestablished harmony between the realms of nature and grace.[13] In any event, some such conception would be required to provide a theoretical solution to the problem. But it is just the possibility of such a solution that is precluded by the results of the first two *Critiques*, which denied the possibility of any theoretical knowledge of the supersensible and allowed for the attribution of merely a practical reality to the ideas thereof. And it is in view of the impossibility of such a solution that Kant concludes:

> Hence an immense gulf is fixed between the domain of the concept of nature, the sensible, and the domain of the concept of freedom, the super-

sensible, so that no transition from the sensible to the supersensible is possible (and hence by means of the theoretical use of reason), just as if they were two different worlds, the first of which cannot have any influence on the second. (KU 5: 175–6/14–15)

One might wonder what, from the Kantian standpoint at least, would be wrong with such a two-world picture, which preserves the integrity of each "world" or "standpoint." The answer, as Kant proceeds to tell us, is that "the second *is* to have an influence on the first, i.e., the concept of freedom is to actualize in the world of sense the purpose enjoined by its laws" (KU 5: 176; 15). At issue here is a central, though frequently overlooked, feature of Kant's moral theory, namely, the idea that the moral law dictates the pursuit of certain ends. These include the ethical ends of one's own perfection and the happiness of others, as well as the moral-political or juridical ends of a lawful [*rechtlich*] condition, that is, civil society under a republican constitution, and a condition of perpetual peace between states.[14] More generally, there is the requirement to work for the advancement of the highest good on earth, which is best seen as a totalizing concept encompassing all universally valid ends, rather than as a distinct end.[15] As we shall see, Kant introduces the conception of the highest good as the final purpose [*Endzweck*] of creation into the discussion in the last section of the Second Introduction, where he also sketches the critical solution to the problem of the *Übergang*.

For present purposes, however, the main point is the moral necessity of presupposing the *possibility* of realizing or, better, promoting, the ends (whatever they may be) dictated by the moral law.[16] It is not that success must be guaranteed, but merely that it not be precluded; for one cannot rationally act in pursuit of an end, the promotion of which is taken to be impossible. Moreover, since the arena in which these ends are to be realized or promoted is the sensible world, it follows that a moral agent must presuppose a certain amenability of nature and its lawful order to our moral projects. As Kant puts the matter at the end of Section II:

> Hence it must be possible to think of nature as being such that the lawfulness in its form will harmonize with at least the possibility of the purposes that we are to achieve in nature according to laws of freedom. So there must after all be a ground *uniting* the supersensible that underlies nature and the supersensible that the concept of freedom contains practically, even though the concept of this ground does not reach cognition of it either theoretically or practically, and hence does not have a domain of its own, though it does make possible the transition from our way of thinking in terms of principles of nature to our way of thinking in terms of principles of freedom (KU 5: 176; 15)

Perhaps the most striking feature of this passage is its focus on *the way of thinking* about nature in relation to our moral projects. Thus, the requisite *Übergang* is not from nature to freedom *per se,* but from our way of thinking [*Denkungsart*] about the former (in terms of laws of nature) to our way of thinking about the latter (in terms of moral laws). Since the problem as here formulated is essentially a practical one confronting the moral agent who conscientiously endeavors to further the ends dictated by the moral law, rather than a systematic one, as it appeared to be for Kant in the First Introduction, or a "speculative" problem, as it later became for some of Kant's idealistic successors, it might seem strange that Kant expresses it in this way instead of in straightforwardly ontological terms.[17] Nevertheless, it is precisely because it is a practical problem that Kant formulates it in terms of our manner of thinking of nature. For what is crucial from the "practical point of view" is how an agent must conceive of nature in order to pursue rationally the ends dictated by morality. In fact, unless it is possible to think of nature as amenable to the realization of moral requirements, morality itself, or at least a significant portion thereof, would have to be rejected as a "phantom of the brain."[18] As we shall see later, the idea of the supersensible ground of nature is brought into the picture because it is only by reference to such a ground that nature's harmony with morality can even be thought.

In order to understand the relevance of the problem Kant is posing to the project of the third *Critique,* as well as to the solution he will propose, it is instructive to note its close parallelism with the epistemological problem discussed in Chapter 1. It was there emphasized that there are two distinct transcendental problems regarding cognition. The first, which is dealt with in the Transcendental Deduction of the first *Critique,* concerns the necessity of the conformity of appearances to the pure concepts of the understanding. It was also suggested that this deduction can be viewed as an attempt to exorcize the specter of transcendental chaos (or disorder at the Transcendental level) in the guise of the dreaded possibility that "Appearances might . . . be so constituted that the understanding should not find them to be in accordance with the conditions of its unity" (A90/B123). The Transcendental Deduction removes this possibility by showing its incompatibility with the conditions of the unity of apperception.

It was also noted, however, that this result only establishes the lawfulness of nature in a formal and very general sense (its conformity to the transcendental laws of the understanding). Consequently, the possibility still remains open that the order of nature is such that it is not cognizable by the human mind. This second specter, which arises from the demise of its transcendental counterpart, was characterized as that of empirical chaos (or disorder at the empirical level). In this context, it was further suggested that the goal of the deduction of the principle of logical purposiveness is to exorcize this second specter, which it attempts to do not by demonstrating that nature must be purposive, but rather by showing that in the pursuit of empirical knowledge we are constrained to approach it as if it were purposive. Thus, judgment, unlike understanding, legislates not to nature but to itself. What it governs is our "way of thinking" about nature, insofar as we are engaged in the project of empirical enquiry.

The present suggestion, then, is that the nature–freedom problem in Kant may likewise be analyzed at both the transcendental and empirical–anthropological levels, which raises the possibility, to be explored in the next section, that reflective judgment and its principle might likewise provide the basis of the solution at the latter level.[19] At the transcendental level, the question is whether free agency is compatible with the causality of nature (the transcendental principle of causality), and this question is answered positively by means of the resolution of the Third Antinomy. At the empirical–anthropological level, the question becomes whether the ends dictated by the "laws of freedom" (moral laws) are realizable in the sensible world, that is, in the empirical order of nature. Thus, whereas the empirical-level epistemological worry is whether there is a humanly cognizable order of nature at all, the parallel practical worry is whether this order is such as to allow for the realization of moral demands. For all that we could know *a priori*, this order might be such as to frustrate the promotion of moral goals, the attainment of anything approaching a kingdom of ends among human beings. In other words, the question is whether what is required by (moral) theory is achievable in practice (in the "real world").

This question is anthropological as well as empirical because it is precisely human nature in its empirical character that appears to present the greatest obstacle posed by nature to the attainment of the ends dictated by morality. For, as Kant famously claims, the most distinctive feature of this nature is the propensity to discord or "unsociable sociability" [*ungesellige Geselligkeit*], which, on the one hand, leads human beings to seek the society of others, and, on the other hand, generates conflicts which make the social condition untenable.[20]

In his sketch of a teleological view of history in §83 of the *Critique of Judgment*, Kant spells out at least part of what he meant by this by suggesting that the passions of ambition, lust for power, and greed, particularly on the part of those who rule, make war inevitable and therefore appear to stand in the way of the attainment of the morally required end of perpetual peace (KU 5: 432–3; 320). Elsewhere, he refers to destructive passions, such as the desire for vengeance, and the manias for honor, domination, and possession, all of which work contrary to the ends of pure practical reason (Anthro 7: 270–4; 137–40).[21] Accordingly, there is an obvious conflict between what, on Kant's view, morality requires of human beings and the dismal view of human nature provided by his anthropology. And, given this conflict, it is easy to see why Kant would insist on the moral necessity of being able to think of [human] nature "as being such that the lawfulness in its form will harmonize with at least the possibility of the purposes that we are to achieve in nature according to laws of freedom." If we could not regard nature (particularly human nature) in this way, our moral life would indeed be as chaotic as our theoretical life would be without the assumption of a cognizable order of nature. Moreover, in both cases the problem is the threat posed by particularity to universal and necessary ends.

III

Section IX of the Second Introduction is entitled "How Judgment Connects the Legislations of the Understanding and of Reason" (KU 5: 195; 35). It thus purports to provide the solution to the problem posed in Section II. But before turning to the proposed solution, Kant reformulates the problem in sharpened form. Referring once again to a "great gulf" [grosse Kluft], now described as separating the supersensible (in the subject) from appearances, Kant notes that such a gulf would prevent any effect of the legislation of each (under its own basic laws) on the other, thereby making it impossible to throw a bridge [Brücke] from one domain to the other. He also maintains, however, that such an implication cannot be accepted. For though there can be no question of the sensible determining the supersensible in the subject (presumably, that would amount to what is, i.e., human nature in its empirical character, determining what morally ought to be), the reverse is possible, at least with regard to the "consequences that the concept of freedom has in nature." Indeed, he insists that "this possibility [the supersensible in us determining the sensible] is contained in the very concept of a causality through freedom, whose effect is to be brought about in the world in conformity with formal laws of freedom" (KU 5: 195; 36).

The main difference between this and the initial formulation of the problem lies in the emphasis placed on freedom as a mode of causality, in contrast to the "laws of freedom," that is, the principles of morality. The idea that we must regard our moral projects as realizable in the sensible world is still in place. In fact, as already indicated, Kant expands upon it by introducing the concept of the final end [Endzweck], later to be identified with the highest good, as the effect at which the laws of freedom direct us to aim. Moreover, Kant now says that it is specifically in the nature of the subject as a sensible being that we must presuppose the condition under which this end is realizable (KU 5: 196; 36). Thus, the focus is directed to human nature as the main arena in which the moral struggle occurs and the ends of morality are to be realized. Nevertheless, the major emphasis is on the efficacy of our free causality (this causality itself being taken as a fact) *vis-à-vis* the obstacles to its morally required ends put in its way by human nature. Expressed in terms that Kant uses elsewhere, what is at issue is not the *autonomy* of the human will (which is just that of pure practical reason), but rather its *autocracy*, that is, the actual capacity of the will to attain the ends dictated by the laws of freedom.[22] For it is only with respect to this capacity that one can speak meaningfully of "obstacles" or "hindrances" to the exercise of freedom posed by our natural constitution as beings in the world of sense.

In a note appended to this discussion, Kant responds to a criticism raised by Ulrich, Rehberg, and perhaps others against just this aspect of his theory of freedom, namely, its apparent assumption of a causal relation between freedom and nature.[23] The basic and predictable objection is that, given the phenomenal-noumenal distinction, Kant has no business speaking about nature as either putting obstacles in the way of freedom or of furthering its ends, since this would mean that the phenomenal somehow influences or affects the noumenal.[24] Against this, Kant responds that he is not assuming any direct relation (whether it be one of furtherance or hindrance) between nature and freedom, but rather between nature as appearance and the *effects* of freedom in the sensible world, which are likewise appearances. Accordingly, at issue is the question of the compatibility of the phenomenal effects of freedom, which at one point Kant identifies with the "appearance of the final purpose in the world of sense" (KU 5: 196; 36), with the order of nature (including human nature) governed by empirical laws. By way of underscoring the latter point, Kant notes that even the causality of freedom is that of a natural cause (the human being as subject to the laws of nature); so that what is properly intelligible, that is, not part of the sensible world, is merely the determining ground of this causality (KU 5: 195–6n; 36).[25]

It is therefore with respect to thought of the phenomenal effects of freedom (and their supersensible ground) that we must understand the function of reflective judgment and its "category," the purposiveness of nature in providing the practically necessary *Übergang* between nature and freedom. As one might expect in view of the parallelism between the theoretical and the practical problems outlined in the preceding section, the claim will be that what judgment does by means of the concept of purposiveness is to presuppose the necessary condition for the efficacy in the sensible world of a morally directed freedom or, equivalently, the actualization of the final purpose. Moreover, judgment purportedly does this "without regard to the practical" (KU 5: 196; 36). In other words, the purposiveness that judgment attributes to nature is not itself a moral purposiveness, at least not initially, but merely the general accord with our cognitive requirements that reflective judgment must presuppose as a condition of its own activity. Otherwise judgment would already be subservient to morality, and could therefore hardly serve to make possible a transition to it from what is initially regarded as a completely amoral nature.

In the second paragraph of Section IX, Kant attempts to spell out this mediating function of judgment by relating it to the idea of a supersensible substrate, which, as we have seen, figured prominently in the parallel discussion in the First Introduction. Referring to the basic result of the first *Critique,* Kant remarks that the fact that the understanding gives laws to nature *a priori* proves that we can know nature only as appearance. This result points to a supersensible substrate of nature (the need to assume some purely intelligible ground of appearance), but it leaves this substrate completely *undetermined.* In the terms of the first *Critique,* the thing as it is in itself is thought by the pure understanding as a merely "transcendental object = x," about which nothing positive can be said.[26] By contrast, Kant claims that "Judgment, through its *a priori* principle of judging nature in terms of possible particular laws of nature, provides nature's supersensible substrate (within as well as outside us) with *determinability* by the *intellectual faculty.*" Finally, completing his account of the contributions of the cognitive faculties, he notes that reason, "through its *a priori* practical law, gives this same substrate *determination*" (KU 5: 196; 37).

Kant's main point in this paragraph is therefore that judgment makes possible an *Übergang* precisely by making *determinable* that which the understanding in its theoretical legislation leaves indeterminate and reason determines through its practical legislation, namely, the supersensible substrate of nature (within as well as outside us). Consequently, if we are to make any sense of this, it is obviously necessary to become clear about the following questions: First, what is meant by providing "*determinability by the intellectual faculty,*" particularly with respect to this still mysterious supersensible substrate? Second, why is it that *judgment,* and judgment alone, can do this? Third, in what sense is this a necessary precondition for reason's determination? Fourth, how does this relate to the problem of an *Übergang,* which is itself said to be necessary for the actualization of the ends of freedom in the sensible world? And, finally, what is the role of taste in this complex story?

With regard to the first point, the account certainly suggests that determinability is provided by the intellectual faculty through the introduction of some conceptual content into the thought of what was previously taken as a mere = x. In other words, it renders it thinkable in a positive manner, though not yet knowable. This occurs just in case it can be shown that we are constrained (due to the very nature of our faculties) to think of this = x in a certain way, even though this way of thinking cannot count as knowledge. Moreover, judgment's concept of the purposiveness of nature meets these conditions perfectly. First, it has reference to the supersensible substrate of nature, rather than simply to nature as appearance, since it concerns the necessity of thinking of appearances as having their *ground* in an understanding, though not ours.[27] In other words, to think of nature as purposive (in the logical sense considered in Chapter 1) is just to consider it as ordered in a certain way (for the benefit of our cognitive faculties), and this entails the thought (though not the knowledge) of some underlying source of this order, which, since it does not itself appear, must be regarded as supersensible.

It also seems clear that only judgment or, more precisely, reflective judgment, among the cognitive faculties, is capable of producing such a thought. Certainly, understanding cannot do so, since its function is merely to explicate appearances in terms of their transcendental and empirical laws. And (pure practical) reason does not do so either, since it supplies practical *determination* through the moral law, rather than mere *determinability*. But this is just what reflective judgment does by introducing its concept of the purposiveness of nature as a presupposition of the investigation of nature, which, as merely subjectively necessary, does not involve the claim that nature really is purposive. In fact, one could claim that it is precisely the function of reflective judgment to provide determinability that does not amount to determination. As the very term suggests, the latter is the task of determinative judgment, though the sphere of its determination is limited to possible experience, and therefore does not reach the supersensible.

The questions of the connection of this determinabilty provided by reflective judgment with the problem of an *Übergang* and the realization of morally required ends in the sensible world are more complex, and require a consideration of the different roles of teleological and aesthetic judgment. These will be the concerns of the final two sections of this chapter. In order to understand Kant's position with respect to both teleological and aesthetic judgment, however, it is important to keep in mind his characterization of the *Übergang* as concerned with the "way of thinking" discussed in the preceding section. Once again, what is required is some basis for thinking about the sensible world as amenable to the morally required ends, which is equivalent to thinking about it or, more properly, its supersensible substrate, as morally purposive. Since such a conception has no basis in our purely theoretical understanding of nature and its empirical laws, particularly when one includes in this the dismal account of human nature provided by anthropology, there is indeed a "great gulf" between the view of nature that science provides and the one that morality requires. Moreover, insofar as it introduces the general concept of purposiveness, reflective judgment may be said to make the thought of nature (or its substrate) morally determinable, since it prepares the way for thinking about it as morally purposive without itself imposing moral categories in a determinate manner.

IV

Since our concern here is specifically with the moral significance of taste, and therefore the role of aesthetic judgment in effecting an *Übergang*, it is not possible to discuss the function of teleological judgment in more than a cursory manner. Nevertheless, even a brief overview of the major points of Kant's position as contained in the Critique of Teleological Judgment should help in understanding the former, particularly since we shall see that the two accounts converge at a crucial point.

Although for the most part the Critique of Teleological Judgment is concerned with what Kant terms "intrinsic purposiveness," that is, the purposive organization exhibited by living organisms, it also discusses an "extrinsic purposiveness," which, as the name suggests, is the purposiveness of some natural products with respect to others, that is, their suitability as means for the ends or purposes of other living (intrinsically purposive) beings.[28] In fact, starting with §82 of the Appendix, the latter form of purposiveness becomes the main focus of concern. What is important for Kant about such purposiveness is that it leads to the question of whether nature as a whole might be thought as purposive, not in the sense of logical purposiveness considered in Chapter 1, but rather as a system of real purposes, working together for the attainment of a universal end.

The latter is possible, Kant suggests, only if there is some species that could be regarded as the "ultimate purpose" [*letzter Zweck*] of nature, which would be one for whose benefit everything else in nature may be thought of as means. Not surprisingly, Kant concludes that the only possible candidate for such a favored species is humankind; and this is justified on the grounds that man "is the only being on earth who can form a concept of purposes and use his reason to form an aggregate of purposively structured things into a system of purposes" (KU 5: 426–7; 314).

The question, which is taken up in §83, therefore becomes what nature's ultimate purpose with respect to humankind could be, assuming that there is one. Kant thinks that it must be either some end that nature itself essentially provides for us through its beneficence or a special capacity, given to us by nature, for the pursuit of our own freely chosen ends. The former is termed happiness and the latter culture [*Cultur*]. Kant rules out happiness on several grounds, including the indeterminacy of our idea of happiness; the obvious fact that nature does not seem to have made us its special favorites in this regard (witness plague, famine, frost, other predatory animals and the like); and, most interestingly, "man's own absurd natural predispositions," which render us incapable of true and lasting contentment (KU 5: 430; 318). And this naturally leaves culture as the only remaining alternative.

All of this is still purely hypothetical, however, since it is based on the assumption that nature has an ultimate purpose and therefore may be viewed by reflective judgment as a teleological system. But such an assumption can be justified only on the condition that humankind (the only conceivable candidate for the ultimate purpose of nature) has "the understanding and will to give both nature and himself reference to a purpose that can be independent of nature, self-sufficient, and a final purpose" (KU 5: 431; 318). In other words, humankind may be viewed as the ultimate purpose of nature [*letzter Zweck*] just in case it is intended for a higher and final purpose [*Endzweck*], which is not to be sought within nature itself, and which can only be moral.

Kant will later (§84) identify this final purpose with the existence of rational beings under moral laws, which leads to a discussion of the highest good and the physicotheological and moral proofs of the existence of God (the topics of the final sections of the Critique of Teleological Judgment). Our concern, however, is only with the implications of the subsumption of the teleological under the moral perspective for the understanding of culture and the teleological role Kant assigns to it. Clearly, since it is directly related to freedom, understood as the capacity to set ends, culture is a good *prima facie* candidate for a purpose of nature that could subserve some final moral purpose transcending nature. Nevertheless, before such a status can be assigned to culture, further specification of the way in which it is here being understood and an account of how it could (indirectly) serve a moralizing purpose are required.

In addressing these questions, Kant distinguishes between two types of culture: the culture of skill [*Geschicklichkeit*] and the culture of discipline [*Zucht*]. As the label suggests, the former is the capacity to attain the purposes that humankind collectively sets for itself, whatever they may be. Although Kant suggests that the development of such a capacity is essential to our moral vocation, he also points out that it is not of itself sufficient, since it does not involve the discrimination among possible ends. In fact, echoing Rousseau, Kant notes that the development of culture in this sense leads inevitably to inequality, oppression, the attachment to luxuries, and all of the social and political evils that follow therefrom, including the greatest of all such evils, war.

Against Rousseau, however, he also suggests that all of the "glittering misery" produced by the advancement of the culture of skill leads indirectly but inevitably to the development of republican institutions and international relations conducive to perpetual peace (KU 5: 432–3; 320). Thus, even this form of culture is viewed by Kant as contributing to the realization of morally necessary ends, albeit in a manner that operates behind the backs, as it were, of the agents in question. This is, of course, what is often and aptly called Kant's conception of the "cunning of nature," which is a central theme of his well-known historical and political essays, including *Perpetual Peace*.[29]

The culture of discipline is characterized as the "liberation of the will from the despotism of desires" (KU 5: 432; 319). Although Kant thus defines this form of culture in explicitly negative terms, he immediately signals its importance for the moral life. For, as he indicates, this "despotism" is one to which we all too freely subject ourselves, allowing "ourselves to be fettered by the impulses that nature gave us only as guides so that we would not neglect . . . our animal characteristics, whereas in fact we are free enough to tighten or slacken, to lengthen or shorten them, as the purposes of reason require" (KU 5: 432; 319). Accordingly, it is clear that it is to this despotism that we must look to find the source of those self-imposed obstacles and hindrances to the realization of morally required ends noted earlier.

As Kant makes clear when he returns to a consideration of this form of culture at the end of §83, he sees it expressed positively in the pursuit of ends which, while not themselves moral, are nonetheless independent of sensuous desire, namely aesthetic and intellectual ones. And, once again, this is marked by a partial agreement and a partial disagreement with Rousseau. In particular, Kant agrees with Rousseau that, of itself, the development of such interests and propensities makes humanity merely civilized [*gesittet*] rather than moral [*sittlich*]. But he differs from Rousseau in placing a positive value on the former. Thus, appealing again to the presumed purposiveness of nature, he contends that this civilizing process performs an essential educational function, since it "makes us receptive to purposes higher than those that nature itself can provide." Finally, continuing this line of thought, he concludes that the fine arts and sciences help to prepare humankind "for a sovereignty in which reason alone is to dominate . . . and so let us feel a hidden aptitude within us for higher purposes" (KU 5: 433–4; 321).

The upshot of §83 is therefore that, in spite of our "absurd natural predispositions," reflective judgment in its teleological form provides grounds (that fall well short of proof) for thinking about human nature as amenable to morality; and by this means, it helps to bring about the required *Übergang* in our way of thinking. It does so through a teleological analysis of culture, which suggests both that these predispositions and the "tyranny of desire" to which they give rise may be viewed as indirectly fostering morally required ends, and that this tyranny may at least be mitigated by something like an aesthetic education.

The latter point is of greatest interest to us here, since it indicates that the teleological picture of human nature and history sketched in the *Critique of Judgment* actually culminates in an account of the function of taste as helping to bring about the required transformation of human nature. In short, teleology leads to aesthetics. Conversely, we shall see in Chapter 10 that the appreciation of natural beauty leads to a morally teleological view of external nature and therefore aids in the determinability of the "supersensible without." Thus, in this respect, aesthetics leads to [moral] teleology. Moreover, as we shall further see in Chapter 11, the change effected in human nature by the development of taste concerns not merely our way of thinking but, even more fundamentally, our way of feeling and evaluating. But before turning to these topics, we must return to Section IX of the Second Introduction, in order to consider what Kant has to say there about the connection between taste and the *Übergang* from nature to freedom.

V

Kant's actual discussion in this section of the function of taste with respect to the *Übergang* is extremely cryptic and perplexing, even by Kantian standards. It is contained entirely within the last paragraph, which is devoted as a whole to a review of the "higher" faculties of the soul, meaning thereby those with a certain kind of autonomy. Kant's concern here, as in the corresponding portion of the First Introduction, is to spell out in tabular form the systematic connections between the three general faculties of the mind and the corresponding cognitive faculties, their governing principles, and their spheres of application. The portion that concerns us here consists of the following two sentences:

> Judgment's concept of a purposiveness of nature still belongs to the concepts of nature, but only as a regulative principle of the cognitive faculty, even though the aesthetic judgment about certain objects (of nature or art) that prompts [*veranlasst*] this concept of purposiveness is a constitutive principle with respect to the feeling of pleasure or displeasure. The spontaneity in the play of the cognitive faculties, whose harmony with each other contains the ground of this pleasure, makes that concept of purposiveness suitable for mediating the connection of the domain of the concept of nature with that of the concept of freedom, as regards freedom's consequences, inasmuch as this harmony also promotes the mind's receptivity to moral feeling. (KU 5: 197; 37–8)

Even though the first of these sentences does not directly concern the question of an *Übergang*, it contains some noteworthy points. To begin with, there is the previously discussed attempt, characteristic of both Introductions, to link taste with the purposiveness of nature. Unlike other such texts (including the table that follows the paragraph), however, Kant does not here suggest that the purposiveness of nature is itself the principle of taste. Instead, he states that it is the aesthetic *judgment* that is the *constitutive principle* with respect to the feeling of pleasure or displeasure, and that the judgment merely "prompts" this concept of purposiveness. The attribution of constitutive status to the aesthetic judgment with respect to feeling clearly reflects Kant's systematic thesis (common to both

Introductions) that it is the function of judgment to legislate to feeling. But it also calls to mind the account in §35, where Kant maintains that it is the faculty of judgment itself that serves as the subjective principle of taste and that underlies the demand for universal agreement.

Somewhat more perplexing is the claim that aesthetic judgments of both nature and art prompt (or occasion) the concept of the purposiveness of nature. To be sure, there is nothing surprising in the suggestion that judgments of natural beauty might do this. For Kant himself emphasizes in the Deduction, when contrasting natural beauty and the sublime, that the discovery of natural beauties inevitably raises all sorts of teleological questions. For example, he asks, "How are we to explain why nature has so extravagantly spread beauty everywhere, even at the bottom of the ocean, where the human eye . . . rarely penetrates?" (KU 5: 279; 142). Indeed, as we saw in Chapter 8, this is one of the reasons that such judgments require a deduction distinct from their exposition. But since these considerations clearly do not apply to beautiful works of art, the question naturally arises: In what sense might judgments of artistic beauty (or the beautiful works themselves) be said to prompt the thought of the purposiveness of nature?

There are, as far as I can see, only two possible answers to this question, neither of which is fully satisfactory. One is to appeal to Kant's account of genius as a means for overcoming what has seemed to some to be too rigid a dichotomy between natural and artistic beauty.[30] Since Kant characterizes fine art as the art of genius and suggests that for genius it is nature (within the subject) that gives the rule to art (see KU 5: 307; 175, and 309; 177), it might be argued that what artistic beauty occasions is the thought of the purposiveness of nature within (or its supersensible substrate), just as natural beauty gives rise to the thought of the purposiveness of external nature. We shall return to some of the issues concerning the relation between artistic and natural beauty and the connection of the former with the conception of genius in Chapter 12. For the present, however, two brief comments must suffice. First, Kant uses "nature" in a number of distinct senses, and it is by no means clear that his use of it with respect to genius (to reflect the unconscious, prerational sources of the genius's creative powers) was really seen by Kant as equivalent to the sense of "nature" he connects with the thought of purposiveness.[31] Second, if he did view these as equivalent, then his subsequent denial that artistic beauty can awaken a pure intellectual interest (to be discussed in Chapter 10) is, indeed, puzzling.

The second possible reading of Kant's claim that artistic beauty somehow prompts the thought of the purposiveness of nature turns on what is supposedly common to the two species of beauty, namely, a purposiveness of form. If one combines this with Kant's claim that beautiful art must look to us like nature (though we are conscious of it as art) (KU 5:

306; 174), it might be argued that the appreciation of beautiful form in works of art leads one to contemplate forms in nature, which, in turn, occasions the thought of nature's purposiveness. This has the advantage over the first possible reading of being compatible with the sharp distinction between artistic and natural beauty drawn in connection with the question of interest, but it seems less than compelling as a psychological claim. Artistic beauty may, in fact, lead one to contemplate nature in this way; nevertheless, there is no reason to assume that it must, or even that it generally does so.

Though the second sentence is more directly germane to the question of the nature and significance of an *Übergang*, it also introduces further complexities. The sentence may be broken down into at least three subclaims, each of which requires separate consideration. First, there is the claim that the harmony resulting from the spontaneity in the play of the cognitive faculties promotes the mind's receptivity to moral feeling. Second, there is the suggestion that this promotion concerns the phenomenal effects of freedom. Finally, there is the contention that, because of the latter, the concept of the purposiveness of nature, which is itself merely alluded to rather than mentioned in the sentence, is suitable as a mediator between the respective domains of the concepts of nature and freedom.

The initial puzzle posed by the first claim concerns the significance of the term "spontaneity." By emphasizing that it is the *spontaneity* in the play of the cognitive faculties that is responsible for the result in question, Kant certainly seems to indicate that he is referring to the intelligible ground or substrate in the subject (the supersensible within), which accords with the teaching of the first *Critique* that the understanding and imagination, in contrast to the receptivity of sensibility, are spontaneous.[32] But since Kant refers to the pleasure arising from the harmony, it is also possible to take him as merely reiterating his standard thesis that the pleasure of taste results from the free harmony of the imagination and understanding. On this reading, then, the reference to spontaneity serves merely to underscore the point that not every harmony of the imagination and understanding, but only one that is "free," that is, not conceptually constrained, engenders the feeling in question. In fact, I suspect that Kant wished to make both points at once. The latter is what one would expect, given the argument of the Analytic; but, as we shall see in Chapter 11, the former is strongly suggested by Kant's argument in the Dialectic, where he asserts that the judgment of taste is ultimately grounded in reason's indeterminate concept of the supersensible (KU 5: 340; 212), indeed, in what may be considered the "supersensible substrate of humanity" (KU 5: 340; 213).

Of greater immediate relevance, however, is the claim that the harmony resulting from the spontaneous play of the cognitive faculties "promotes the mind's receptivity to moral feeling." In order to understand this, we need to turn to the discussion of moral feeling in the *Metaphysics of Morals,* rather than to the better-known account of respect in the *Critique of Practical Reason.* In the Introduction to the *Doctrine of Virtue,* which is the second part of the former work, Kant lists moral feeling, together with conscience, love of one's neighbor, and respect for oneself or self-esteem as concepts of what is presupposed on the part of feeling [*Aesthetische Vorbegriffe*] by the mind's receptivity to concepts of duty in general (MS 6: 399; 200). Kant characterizes these as both moral endowments [*Beschaffenheiten*] and mental predispositions [*Gemütsanlagen*]. He also claims that, as subjective preconditions of morality or, more precisely, "conditions of receptiveness to the concept of duty," we cannot be said to have a duty to acquire them. Kant denies, perhaps somewhat optimistically, that anyone is actually totally devoid of these endowments, which, in contemporary terms, would amount to being a complete sociopath. But his main point is that if someone were devoid of them, moral claims could have no motivational force, which is what makes it erroneous to speak of an obligation to possess them (MS 6: 399; 201).

Kant here defines moral feeling as "the susceptibility [*Empfänglichkeit*] to feel pleasure or displeasure merely from being aware that our actions are consistent with or contrary to the law of duty" (MS 6: 399; 201). To be sure, the pleasure or displeasure is not the reason to act as morality requires. That is to say, we do not obey the categorical imperative because we think that doing so will produce a pleasurable outcome and failure to so the opposite. Nor is moral feeling a sensible means for "perceiving" what is morally required. In fact, Kant explicitly denies that it is to be called a moral *sense* (MS 6: 400; 201). It is, rather, the affective dimension of our recognition of duty, a dimension that accounts for the motivational force of moral requirements by providing the grounds for what Kant terms a pure moral interest and what many contemporary philosophers would call a "proattitude" toward morality. In short, moral feeling is the name given by Kant to our responsiveness to moral requirements. Thus, if (*per impossibile,* according to Kant) one were totally devoid of such feeling, these requirements would not possess any motivational force. Presumably, one might still recognize their "objective necessity" in a purely theoretical fashion, but they would have no "subjective necessity" or practical import because they would not be taken as sources of reasons to act.

Even though Kant denies that we can be said to have a duty to acquire such feeling in the first place, he suggests that it is appropriate to speak of an obligation to *cultivate* and to strengthen the feeling that we do have (MS 6: 399–400; 201).[33] Kant does not here indicate why this is the case, but it seems clear that he viewed the cultivation of such a feeling as essential to the formation of a virtuous character. For the greater one's responsiveness to moral requirements, the easier it is to resist the temptations stemming from interests connected with our sensuous nature and, therefore, the greater one's self-mastery or autocracy. Moreover, this enables us to appreciate the significance of Kant's claim that the free harmony of the faculties involved in the experience of beauty promotes the mind's responsiveness to moral feeling. Indeed, it follows from this account of moral feeling that, if it is the case that the free harmony promotes such responsiveness, then it does have a significant moralizing function.

The examination of this claim, however, and a full consideration of the moralizing functions of taste must be reserved for the next two chapters, where we shall consider Kant's actual discussion of these topics in the body of the *Critique of Aesthetic Judgment*. For the present, our concern is with the second of the forementioned claims in the sentence currently under consideration, namely, that the promotion of moral feeling concerns the phenomenal effects of freedom. There are, I think, two distinct senses in which this may be taken. First, as Kant himself indicates in his discussion of moral feeling, this feeling results from the affection of inner sense by the representation of the moral law (MS 6: 399; 201). In short, it is a matter of sensibility, albeit moral sensibility, and, as such, pertains to the phenomenal. Moreover, since its cause is not itself something phenomenal, but rather the consciousness of the authority of the law, which is inseparable from the consciousness of freedom, any enhancement of this feeling may be appropriately described as a phenomenal effect of freedom.

The second sense in which this claim may be taken is less obvious, though more significant, since it takes us to the heart of Kant's complex theory of virtue. The basic idea, which Kant develops in a number of places, is that, in spite of the struggle between duty and inclination that is usually seen as constituting the moral life for Kant, the actual demeanor of the genuinely virtuous person is one of cheerfulness rather than moroseness.[34] In short, virtue wears a happy face. This is because such a person is simply not subject to temptations, at least not to most of those that torment the rest of us; and this relative freedom from temptation enables one to remain cheerful in the performance of duty, since one is not consumed by the thought of the necessity of sacrificing some great personal good. Moreover, since this cheerfulness, which is manifest outwardly as well as inwardly, is itself a consequence of the cultivation of moral feeling as explicated, it too may be viewed as a phenomenal effect of freedom.

This, then, brings us to third and final claim to be discussed, namely, the suitability of the concept of the purposiveness of nature as a mediator between the domains of the concepts of nature and freedom. Since the preceding considerations did not involve any reference to this concept, it might well be viewed as a gratuitous appeal to it on Kant's part, perhaps one driven more by the architectonic considerations underlying the argument of both Introductions than by any genuine connection between such purposiveness and the *Übergang* supposedly effected by taste. Nevertheless, I think that we can understand Kant's basic point if we keep in mind that, at least in the case of natural beauty, the purposiveness (of form) is the objective correlate of the harmony of the faculties. Furthermore, if we take seriously the idea that the appreciation of artistic beauty leads one to contemplate forms in nature (and therefore their purposiveness), the account might even be extended to artistic beauty as well. In any event, if the promotion or enhancement of the mind's receptivity to moral feeling may be characterized as effecting a transition from nature to freedom, as I think it clearly can, and if it is the purposiveness of nature that occasions this harmony, then it does seem reasonable to claim that the concept of purposiveness plays a mediating role. But this is as much as can be learned from the Introduction. In order to gain a fuller understanding of Kant's views on the moral significance of taste, it is necessary to proceed to an examination of the texts to which what has been considered so far is intended to serve as an introduction.

BEAUTY, DUTY, AND INTEREST

THE MORAL SIGNIFICANCE OF NATURAL BEAUTY

It was suggested in Chapter 9 that the cultivation of taste and the experience of beauty contribute to the development of morality, and therefore help to bring about the required transition from nature to freedom, in two distinct ways: One is by giving rise to an intellectual interest in natural beauty in virtue of the fact that such beauty appears to provide an intimation of nature's moral purposiveness; the other, which applies to both natural and artistic beauty, is by helping to wean us from an excessive attachment to sensuous interests and egocentric involvements with the world, as a result of which it may be said to symbolize morality. The first of these is the subject matter of the present chapter.

In addition to the previously discussed sections II and IX of the Second Introduction, a key text in laying the foundation for Kant's account of the connection between taste and morality is §40. Of particular significance in this regard is Kant's claim that taste has more of a right to be considered a *sensus communis* than the common human understanding, because it involves a capacity in mere reflection to abstract from private factors and evaluate the formal features of a representation from a universalistic standpoint (KU 5: 293–4; 160). Clearly, already implicit in this characterization are the analogies with moral reflection and decision that make taste suitable both as a preparation for and as a symbol of morality. In other words, the very features that entitle taste to be described as a *sensus communis* are those that ground its connection with morality.

This, in turn, naturally calls to mind the cryptic questions that Kant raises (without answering) in the second paragraph of §22, where he asks whether common sense is a constitutive principle of the possibility of experience (which seems to be the view suggested by the argument of §21) or, alternatively, whether there is "a still higher principle of reason that makes it only a regulative principle for us to bring forth in us, or higher purposes, a common sense in the first place?" (KU 5: 240; 90). As we shall see, Kant's general answer is that taste, as a "kind of *sensus communis*," is indeed a capacity that we are in some sense required to cultivate (if not possess in the first place), and that the higher principle of reason underlying this requirement is the moral law.

Our immediate concern, however, is with the oft-cited reflection with which Kant concludes the discussion of §40:

> If we could assume that the mere universal communicability as such of our feeling must already carry with it an interest for us (something we are, however, not justified in inferring from the character of a merely reflective power of judgment), then we could explain how it is that we require from everyone as a duty, as it were [*gleichsam*], the feeling in a judgment of taste. (KU 5:296/162)

This is naturally a central text for those interpreters who maintain that the grounding of taste for Kant turns ultimately on its relation to morality, since it suggests that it is precisely by means of establishing a connection with moral interest that the demand for universal agreement necessarily connected with the pure judgment of taste can be justified.[1] In other words, by identifying the "feeling in a judgment of taste" to which Kant refers with the particular aesthetic response, and the mysterious "duty, as it were," with the demand for agreement built into a judgment of taste, these interpreters view this passage (together with a parallel claim in §59 regarding beauty as a symbol of morality to be discussed in Chapter 11) as steps in an extended, and (at this point) still incomplete deduction.

Since it has already been argued in Part II of this study that the deduction is in fact completed in §38 (§39 constituting an appendix), such a reading obviously cannot be accepted here. But this creates the need to provide alternative accounts of both the "feeling in the judgment of taste" and the "duty, as it were." To anticipate, I shall assume that the feeling refers to the general capacity for aesthetic response, that is, taste, and that the duty, as it were, is to develop this faculty as a condition of the possibility of taking a purely intellectual interest in natural beauty. As noted, this interest is based on the fact that natural beauty appears to provide a sign of nature's moral purposiveness. Consequently, the task is to show how and why this provides the basis for a duty, as it were (to be identified as an indirect duty), to take an interest in natural beauty and therefore to develop the capacity (taste) required to appreciate it in the first place.

These, then, are the concerns of the present chapter, which largely takes the form of a commentary on sections §41 and §42 and is divided into four parts. The first deals with the issue of the compatibility of such an interest with the disinterestedness of the pure judgment of taste. The second considers the dichotomy between an empirical and an intellectual interest in the beautiful, in terms of which Kant sets up his problem. It also examines his rejection of a particular form of the former, namely, an interest in universal communicability based on an inclination for society, as a suitable vehicle for the transition. The third analyzes Kant's account of the moral significance of an intellectual interest and of why it is limited to natural beauty. Finally, the fourth and major section considers this duty, as it were, which it explicates in light of some of the factors introduced in Chapter 9.

I

When the concept of disinterestedness was introduced in Chapter 4, the main focus was on the question of how, given the obvious fact that lovers of the beautiful seem interested in the existence of works of great art, as well as in the museums, theaters, concert halls and the like where they are exhibited or performed, Kant can maintain not only that pure judgments of taste are not based on an antecedent interest (which seems plausible enough), but also (and more problematically) that, of themselves, they do not even give rise to an interest. The question of the compatibility of this seemingly counterintuitive thesis with the claim presently under consideration that such judgments (or the experience of beauty) may nonetheless be connected with an interest was thus postponed for future consideration. Clearly, however, the time of reckoning has arrived; so something must be said about this further complication in Kant's account.

Kant offers his general explanation at the beginning of §41, where he writes:

> That a judgment of taste by which we declare something to be beautiful must not have an interest *as its determining ground* has been established sufficiently above. But it does not follow from this that, after the judgment has been made as a pure aesthetic one, an interest cannot be connected with it. This connection, however, must always be only indirect. In other words, we must think of taste as first of all connected with something else, so that with the liking of mere reflection on an object there can be connected, in addition, a pleasure *in the existence* of the object (and all interest consists in pleasure in the existence of an object). (KU 5: 296; 163)

At least at first glance, this explanation appears only to confuse matters further. For by denying merely that an interest can serve as the determining ground of a judgment of taste, thereby omitting the claim that it cannot give rise to one either, it might seem that Kant here significantly weakens the disinterestedness thesis as initially formulated. Or, even worse, since the initial denial that judgments of taste give rise to an interest was intended precisely to distinguish such judgments from moral judgments, whereas the present claim seems to be that it is their connection with an interest that (at least in part) grounds their connection with morality, it might appear that Kant is guilty of an outright contradiction.

Nevertheless, there is neither a contradiction between these two texts nor even a weakening of the initial thesis. To begin with, being brought into connection with morality does not undermine the generic difference between moral and aesthetic judgments. On the contrary, as was noted in Chapter 9, it is precisely the original independence of taste from morality (which is one aspect of its autonomy) that makes it possible subsequently to connect them, and that enables taste to aid in effecting the required transition. The transition, after all, is supposedly from concepts of nature to concepts of freedom, the sensible to the intelligible; and (as was noted in Chapter 9) taste could hardly aid in this if, as many of Kant's contemporaries assumed, the beautiful were itself fundamentally akin to the morally good, which, in Kantian terms, would mean that taste (as the capacity to judge the beautiful) already lies on the intelligible side of the divide.

Second, and equally important, Kant never denies unqualifiedly that judgments of taste can give rise to an interest. He denies only that they can do so "of themselves." Moreover, the latter denial is preserved in the passage presently under consideration, even though it does not refer to it explicitly. In fact, already in the note Kant had alluded to at least part of his later account by intimating that an interest does attach to having taste in society. Thus, rather than contradicting the initial account of disinterestedness, the new account complements it by specifying the condition under which disinterested judgments of taste (or the capacity for such judgments) can be connected with an interest. As our text indicates, this condition is merely that the connection be indirect. In other words, the connection between the disinterested liking for the beautiful expressed in a judgment of taste and an interested pleasure in the *existence* of the objects deemed beautiful must be mediated by "something else" (a "third thing," if you will), which, if it is to account for an interest in the beautiful, presumably must itself be (or involve) an interest.

Even setting aside for the moment the reference to universal communicability, however, the situation is further complicated by Kant's suggestion in §40 that the problem is not simply to explain how the liking of taste (or its universal communicability) could "carry with it an interest," but why it *must* [*müsse*] do so. Consequently, Kant is concerned to ground a necessary connection between some still-unspecified interest and the disinterested pleasure of taste. Moreover, given the definition of interest as "pleasure in the existence of an object" (KU 5:296; 163),[2] this necessary connection must be between the pleasure of taste (or its universal communicability) and a further pleasure in the existence of the objects deemed beautiful. Accordingly, the question becomes which among the human likings and interests are capable of being brought into a necessary connection with the disinterested liking of taste.

Clearly, the underlying assumption is that only such a connection is capable of accounting for a putative duty, as it were, to take an interest in the existence of beautiful objects and, by extension, to develop the capacity to appreciate their beauty in the first place, namely taste. Equally, clearly, to establish such a duty, as it were, requires showing that the development of the latter interest contributes significantly to morality or, more specifically, to the transition from nature to freedom. Thus, it is to this issue that we now turn.

II

In setting up the problem in §41, Kant suggests that the sought-for "something else" with which the disinterested liking for the beautiful can be conjoined could either be something empirical, identified with "an inclination inherent in human nature," or something intellectual, which he characterizes as "the will's property of being determinable *a priori* by reason." Since both of these involve the liking for the existence of an object, Kant claims that both are capable of providing "the foundation for an interest in something that we have already come to like on its own account and without regard to any interest whatsoever" (KU 5: 296; 163).

By indicating that the options are either an empirical, inclination-based interest or an intellectual, morally based one, Kant is clearly assuming the previously discussed dichotomy between the agreeable and the good as the two species of interest. As we have seen in Chapter 4, it is this very dichotomy that underlies Kant's otherwise puzzling inference that the liking for the beautiful must be disinterested because it is distinct from both of these interested likings. Similarly, he now uses the same dichotomy as the basis for a typical argument by elimination. We would expect that such an argument will purport to show that the empirical interest is inadequate to the task at hand, leaving us with the intellectual interest as the only viable candidate. In other words, we are to conclude that the necessary connection in question (between the disinterested liking for the beautiful and an interested pleasure in the existence of beautiful objects) is possible, just in case the latter is of the intellectual variety.

Although the argument does follow this schema, it does so only roughly. For rather than arguing in general against the suitability of *any* empirical, inclination-based interest (though his argument certainly has such a general implication), Kant focuses exclusively on a particular interest of this sort, namely, the previously discussed interest in the universal communicability of our liking for the beautiful, which is supposedly based on our sociability or natural propensity [*Hang*] for society. Since Kant obviously attaches great importance to the universal communicability of taste, and since the view under consideration bases the interest in such communicability on something that Kant himself regards as deeply rooted in human nature, namely sociability, one would naturally expect to find him sympathetic to it. In fact, it bears an obvious kinship to his own earlier view, according to which the pleasure of taste is itself based on its universal communicability.[3] Thus, it seems that Kant's strategy is to offer what he takes to be the strongest case for an empirically based interest in the existence of beautiful objects, the implication being that the demonstration of its inadequacy suffices to eliminate the entire class of such interests.

At first glance, however, it might appear that this strategy backfires because of the *prima facie* plausibility of the view presented. Reduced to its essentials, the basic argument is that, as inherently social beings, we necessarily take an interest in the universal communicability of our evaluations and feelings, as well as our thoughts, and this translates into an interest in the development of taste, defined as a "capacity to judge [*Beurteilungsvermögen*] whatever allows us to communicate even our *feeling* to everyone else" (KU 5: 297; 163). Consequently, our interest in taste and in the existence of beautiful objects is a function of our underlying interest in universal communicability, which, in turn, is derived from our propensity to society or sociability. Moreover, in language reminiscent of the duty, as it were, of §40, this line of argument is supported by the reflection that a "regard for universal communicability is something that everyone expects and demands from everyone else, on the basis, as it were, of an original contract dictated by [our] very humanity" (KU 5:297; 164).[4] All of this seems relatively straightforward, and it certainly accords with the basic principles of Kantian anthropology. Why, then, we may ask, does Kant reject this line of argument or, more properly, set it aside as irrelevant?

If we are to understand Kant at this point, it is essential to see that his quarrel is not with the sketched argument itself (indeed, it seems clear that he found it unobjectionable as a bit of anthropological reasoning[5]), but with the use to which it is supposedly being put. Once again, we must recall that the concern is not simply to find some human liking or interest that can function as a third thing connecting the disinterested liking of taste with a further pleasure in the existence of beautiful objects; it is, rather, to connect taste with an interest capable of yielding the grounds for a duty, as it were, to take an interest in the existence of beautiful objects and, *a fortiori*, to develop taste as the capacity to take such an interest. But this, in turn, requires showing how the disinterested liking of taste can be brought into connection with moral interest, thereby helping to bring about the required transition from nature to freedom.

Kant unambiguously signals his true opinion of the matter in the final paragraph of §41, where he remarks that the reason for dismissing such an empirically based interest is its irrelevance to his present concern, which, as he now describes it, is only with "what may have reference *a priori*, even if only indirectly, to a judgment of taste." The reason the latter is important, he tells us, is that if even in this [indirect] form such a connection with interest should be discovered, "then taste would reveal a transition of our judgmental faculty [*Beurteilungsvermögens*] from sense enjoyment to moral feeling" (KU 5: 297; 164). Moreover, Kant continues, "not only would we then have better guidance in using taste purposively," but it [taste or our judgmental faculty] would also be presented as "a mediating link in the chain of the human *a priori* powers . . . on which all legislation must depend" (KU 5: 298; 164).

All of this makes it abundantly clear that Kant's real reason for dismissing an empirical interest in the beautiful is its unsuitability for the systematic-practical task of mediating between nature and freedom. The most obvious and basic reason for this unsuitability lies in what may be described as the two-fold conditionality of such an interest. First, it is based on an assumed inclination for society inherent in human nature. Once again, the problem is not with the assumption that there is such an inclination (Kant would hardly want to doubt that), but rather stems from the fact that no inclination, not even one inherent in human nature, could support a necessity claim. Second, as connected with the social inclination, an interest in the universal communicability of one's feeling would be operative only in society, which means that it would lack true universality. In short, the interest in question lacks both the necessity and universality that is required to ground a duty, or even, as it turns out in this case, a mere duty, as it were.[6]

Although this is clearly Kant's more-or-less official reason for rejecting the interest in universal communicability as the "third thing" with which taste must be connected in order to serve as mediator, it is not the only one suggested by the text of §41. A second reason, which remains more or less implicit, is that this interest in communicability is only tangentially related to taste, and even more tangentially to the existence of beautiful objects, which is presumably the basic interest to be explained. To be sure, Kant does remark, in support of the thesis, that it is only in society that an interest in beauty arises, and this is certainly entailed by the operative premise that this interest is based on the universal communicability of our feelings. Nevertheless, in principle at least, ugly objects could provide an equally viable occasion for communication, since human beings can obviously unite on the basis of their dislikings as well as their likings. Consequently, this account in terms of universal communicability does not seem to entail a necessary function for the experience of *beauty*.

Moreover, even though Kant does not discuss the ugly in this context, he effectively acknowledges the main point in his brief anthropological-historical sketch of the development of an interest in beauty and universal communicability contained in the third paragraph of §41. Thus, he admits that the desired socializing role was originally played by charms (rather than beautiful objects), as examples of which Kant cites dyes used by native peoples (the Caribs and the Iroquois) to paint themselves and natural objects, such as flowers, sea shells, and beautifully colored feathers. These, then, were the initial objects of the socially based interest. Only later, Kant continues, was this interest in mere charm supplemented by one in beautiful forms, where the liking is independent of any gratification. And, finally, he remarks, "when civilization has reached its peak, it makes this communication almost the principle activity of refined inclination, and sensations are valued only to the extent that they are universally communicable" (KU 5: 297; 164).

A final reason for rejecting this interest in universal communicability lies in the potentially morally corrosive effects of its unbridled development. This line of thought, which is implicit in the passage regarding civilization at its peak, is connected with an essentially Rousseauian culture-critique that runs as a subtext throughout the entire discussion of the interests indirectly connected with the beautiful.[7] For if one recalls that in §83 Kant characterizes the most advanced stage of civilization as a "glittering misery" [glänzende Elend] because it involves the development of insatiable inclinations (KU 5: 432–33; 320–21), it becomes evident that he did not regard this later development, which involves a debilitating aestheticism, as an unambiguously good thing. Seen from the standpoint of Kant's moral psychology, this can be viewed as an illustration of the general principle of the unreliability of inclination and of the interests based upon them, even potentially beneficial ones such as the interest in universal communicability. Clearly, this is what Kant had in mind, when in summing up his views on this interest at the end of §41, he writes:

> This much we can surely say about empirical interest in objects of taste and in taste itself: in such an interest taste caters to inclination, and no matter how refined this inclination may be, still the interest will also easily fuse with all the [other] inclinations and passions that reach their greatest variety and highest degree in society; and if our interest in the beautiful is based on these, then it can provide only a very ambiguous transition from the agreeable to the good. (KU 5: 298; 164–5).

Given this result, the question thus becomes whether the so-far neglected member of the dichotomy, namely an intellectual, morally based interest, might provide a less ambiguous or dubious transition, perhaps even one capable of yielding a duty, as it were, to take an interest in both "objects of taste and taste itself." This is the concern of §42, where, as Kant suggests, he will consider taste "in its purity" (KU 5: 298; 165), that is, independently of any inclination-based interest with which it may be contingently conjoined under certain conditions.

III

Kant begins his consideration of this new question by referring to the debate between upholders of the more-or-less orthodox enlightenment belief in an intrinsic connection between the love of beauty and moral goodness and the proponents of the Rousseauian thesis that "virtuosi of taste" are as a rule morally corrupt. In apparent agreement with the latter, he concludes not only that a feeling for the beautiful differs in kind from moral feeling (which is not particularly controversial), but also, and more significantly, that we cannot assume an inner affinity [innere Affinität] between interest in the beautiful per se and moral interest.

Nevertheless, rather than simply siding with the Rousseauian view, which would effectively undermine the whole project of connecting taste with morality in a positive way, Kant attempts to mediate the dispute by limiting the scope of its critique to artistic beauty, thereby leaving open the possibility of a connection between a moral interest and an interest in natural beauty.[8] Thus, in partial agreement with the more orthodox enlightenment view, he states:

> I do maintain that to take a direct interest in the beauty of nature (not merely to have the taste needed to judge it) is always a mark of a good soul; and that, if this interest is habitual, if it readily associates itself with the contemplation of nature, this indicates at least a mental attunement [Gemüthsstimmung] favorable to moral feeling. (KU 5: 298–9; 165–6)

Kant also insists, however, that the interest be in beauty rather than charm and that it must be thought to pertain to nature rather than to art.[9] Indeed, with regard to the latter point, he notes that if one were deceived into believing that something was a natural beauty and later recognized it to be artificial, then any direct interest (although not necessarily the aesthetic evaluation) would disappear. Moreover, Kant presents this conclusion not merely as his own opinion but as the considered view of all those who have cultivated their moral feeling (KU 5: 297; 166). Accordingly, he takes his main task to be to account for this moral superiority of natural over artistic beauty, which cannot be a matter of purely aesthetic ranking.

It is by way of explaining this presumed superiority that Kant links the intellectual interest in natural beauty with the problem of a gap between nature and freedom. He begins by focusing on the parallel between aesthetic and moral judgments and their corresponding capacities. Both are concerned with forms (forms of objects in the one case and forms of maxims in the other); both involve a liking that is made into a law for everyone; and, finally, neither is based on an antecedent interest. They differ in that the aesthetic judgment is based on feeling and the moral on concepts and, more significantly for present purposes, on the fact that the moral, but not the aesthetic, judgment of itself gives rise to an interest.

As we saw in Chapter 9, the basic moral interest is in the objective reality of our moral ideas, that is, in the realizability in nature of our moral projects. We also saw that it is precisely this interest that underlies the need to bridge the "immense gulf" between the realms of nature and freedom. Now, however, in attempt to connect this interest with taste and an intellectual interest in natural beauty, Kant characterizes the interest more specifically as being "that nature should at least show a trace or give a hint that it contains some basis or other [*irgend einen Grund*] for us to assume in its products a lawful harmony with that liking of ours which is independent of all interest" (KU 5: 300; 167).

Kant's reasoning here seems to be roughly the following: Since, as moral agents, we necessarily take a direct interest in the realization of morally required ends, and since it is nature that supplies the enabling conditions for the realization of these ends, this interest must also attach to any trace or hint that nature reveals of its harmony with these ends. Kant could not, of course, claim straightaway that natural beauties do in fact provide such traces and hints, since that would amount to a dogmatic teleological claim that goes well beyond the scope of reflective judgment. The claim, instead, is that it is reasonable to assume that morally well disposed agents will naturally take them as doing so and, therefore, also take a direct interest in the beautiful in nature.

This claim is based on a twofold analogy between nature's presentation of beautiful forms (its aesthetic purposiveness) and the moral purposiveness in which we are interested. First, it is a form of purposiveness in the sense of being a mode in which nature appears to favor us. Here Kant's idea appears to be that the only way in which we can comprehend this favoring is by somehow connecting it to our moral vocation (KU 5: 301; 168).[10] Second, like moral purposiveness, it produces a universally communicable liking that is quite distinct from one produced through the satisfaction of any of the ends of inclination. Together, they suggest (but hardly entail) that any conscientious moral agent with the capacity to appreciate such purposiveness, that is, anyone with taste, will view any manifestation of it as an indication of nature's moral purposiveness and take an interest in it on that basis. Conversely, someone without a well-developed moral interest will not take any additional interest in such signs, even if that person has the taste to appreciate natural beauty aesthetically. And from this, Kant concludes that "If someone is directly interested in the beauty of nature, we have cause to suppose that he has at least a predisposition to a good moral attitude" (KU 5: 300–1; 167).

IV

It is, however, one thing to claim that an interest in natural beauty is an indicator (of undetermined reliability) of a predisposition to morality, or even of a good moral character, and quite another to claim that one ought to develop such an interest. Accordingly, even granting that taste is itself a necessary condition of the interest, it does not follow that we have anything like a duty to develop taste. In order to establish this, it is necessary to show how taste and the intellectual interest ensuing from it can themselves help to bridge the gap between nature and freedom by bringing about a transition from sense enjoyment to moral feeling.[11] For only on this basis can it be claimed that taking such an interest is something that one ought to do.

Unfortunately, Kant does not provide any argument for this, and thus he does not really redeem the promissory note at the end of §40, namely, to explain "how it is that we require from everyone as a duty, as it were, the feeling in a judgment of taste" (KU 5: 296; 162). Instead, he ends the discussion of interest in §42 by simply asserting that we do in fact require others to take a direct interest in natural beauty (with the emphasis placed on its being natural). As evidence for this purportedly factual claim, he notes only that "[W]e consider someone's way of thinking to be coarse and ignoble if he has no *feeling* for beautiful nature (which is what we call the receptivity for an interest in contemplating nature) and sticks to the enjoyments of mere sense that he gets from meals or the bottle" (KU 5: 303; 169–70). This may very well be true as an observation, but it hardly constitutes a justification of this requirement or an explanation of its grounds.

Nevertheless, it does seem possible to sketch such an argument on the basis of the materials that Kant has provided, both in the *Critique of Judgment* and in his writings on moral theory. This sketch should explain both the grounds for requiring such an interest and the reason for characterizing it merely as a duty, as it were, rather than as a full-fledged duty. Once again, the basic idea is the necessity of being able to think of nature as amenable to our morally required ends, as, so to speak, "on our side." As we saw in the preceding section, natural beauties are deemed valuable precisely because they provide hints or traces (not amounting to evidence, much less proof) of nature's moral purposiveness. The question thus becomes the *practical* significance of these hints or traces; and the basic Kantian answer seems to be that they are morally beneficial insofar as they help to strengthen our otherwise wavering commitment to morally required ends. Consequently, it is incumbent upon us as moral agents to take an interest in these hints and traces and, *a fortiori*, to develop the capacity to do so, namely taste.

Baldly stated, however, this claim poses as many problems as it resolves. For though it seems relatively clear that some confidence that "nature is on our side" is a necessary condition of the possibility of the moral life for Kant, it hardly follows that an *aesthetic appreciation* of mere hints or traces of such purposiveness is likewise a necessary condition. In fact, the view that one need rely upon any such extrinsic factors seems to run counter to the central Kantian doctrines of the autonomy of the will and the sufficiency of the duty motive. Certainly, the Kantian moral agent does not stand in need of them in order to have an incentive [*Triebfeder*] to be moral. Why, then, should they be necessary in order to strengthen one's commitment to do what duty requires?

The issue is a complicated one, the exploration of which leads us, at least briefly, down some of the less frequently trodden paths of Kant's moral theory and moral psychology. The starting point is the contrast between the autonomy and the autocracy of the will discussed in Chapter 9. Clearly, the need to strengthen one's moral commitment concerns autocracy rather than autonomy. That is to say, it is not a matter of having a reason to act that stems from one's rational will, rather than one's sensuous nature, but of the strength of will to remain firmly committed to the morally dictated ends in the face of competing inclinations.

Equally significant is the fact that, on the Kantian picture, the hindrances and obstacles to the performance of duty against which the will must struggle, that is, temptations, are essentially self-imposed. In other words, moral strength is required not to preserve the self from inclinations and desires stemming from an "alien" sensuous nature, but rather to combat competing ends that the will freely sets for itself. Thus, the struggle between freedom and nature on the Kantian picture is really the struggle of freedom with itself. And this is what preserves the connection between this struggle and the conception of autonomous agency.

In order to understand why there should be such a dialectical struggle, however, we must appeal to Kant's notorious doctrine of radical evil. Although the point is often overlooked, it is crucial to keep in mind that by such evil, Kant does not mean extreme evil, which for him takes the form of wickedness [*Bösartigkeit*], but rather an ineliminable susceptibility to temptation that characterizes even the best of us and that provides the ultimate basis for all immoral actions.[12] In other words, Kant, like Marx after him, construed the term "radical" in its etymological sense as indicating root.[13] Thus, by "radical evil" is to be understood the root of all evil, which for Kant lies in freedom (rather than mere nature). This susceptibility applies to both narrow and wide duties, but it is particularly dangerous in the case of the latter.[14] Since such duties require merely the adoption of a maxim committing oneself to the pursuit of a certain end, say, alleviating the suffering of others, rather than the performance of specific acts, it is all too easy to become diverted, for example, to let other, prudential considerations outweigh the claim of someone in need of help. Indeed, the temptation to do so is greatly increased by the fact that, on most occasions at least, there is no guilt or demerit (but simply a lack of moral worth) in the neglect of an opportunity to offer such help.[15]

It is, then, against the backdrop of this conception of radical evil that we must understand the general need for a strengthening of one's commitment to morally required ends, as well as the compatibility of this need with the doctrine of autonomy. A good illustration of this line of thought, which I have discussed elsewhere, is provided by Kant's puzzling claim that there is "an indirect duty to cultivate the compassionate natural (aesthetic [ästhetische]) feelings in us, and to make use of them as so many means to sympathy based on moral principles and the feeling appropriate to them" (MS 6: 457; 251).[16] Since this is analogous to the claim that there is a duty, as it were, to take an interest in natural beauty and to develop the capacity to take such an interest, I shall approach the latter through a consideration of the former.

What is initially puzzling about Kant's claim is the suggestion that there is a morally sanctioned requirement (an indirect duty) to cultivate the natural feeling of sympathy, which is supposedly accomplished by visiting scenes of human misery, such as hospitals, debtors' prisons, and the like. Why, one might ask, should a presumably autonomous moral agent need to cultivate and make use of such a feeling, when the pure thought of duty is at hand and, of itself, supposedly sufficient to give one an overriding reason to help others in need? And how can such natural feelings serve as means to a "sympathy based on moral principles"? Indeed, this puzzlement is only increased by Kant's remark at the end of this brief discussion that the feeling of sympathy is "one of the impulses that nature has implanted in us to do what the representation of duty alone would not accomplish" (MS 6: 457; 251). To be sure, Kant here refers to what the representation of duty alone "*would* not accomplish" [*nicht ausrichten würde*], rather than what it *could* not accomplish, which would clearly contradict the principle of the sufficiency of the duty motive. Nevertheless, some account of what it is that the duty motive alone would not accomplish and how its supplementation by the natural feeling of sympathy could preserve the purity of moral motivation are certainly called for at this point.

In my original discussion of this problem, I argued that the cultivation of the natural feeling of sympathy is intended to fulfill a twofold function.[17] On the one hand, it increases our awareness of (and sensitivity to) the true suffering of others, and, therefore, our awareness of occasions for beneficent action; on the other, it makes us more capable of being moved to action by such suffering. The first part of this claim is relatively unproblematic. In order to help others in anything more than a random way, one must be aware that they are in need of help, and the cultivation of sympathetic feelings aids in this awareness by lengthening our moral antennae, so to speak. And since the thought of duty alone clearly does not enable us to recognize the occasions when beneficent action is truly needed, sympathetic feeling (an appreciation of the suffering or true needs of others) therefore accomplishes what the pure thought of duty does not.

The second part is far from unproblematic, however, since by suggesting that the cultivation of sympathetic feeling is necessary (or even useful) for increasing our capacity to be moved to act on moral grounds by the suffering of others, it reintroduces the specter of heteronomy and the loss of the purity of moral motivation that occasioned our puzzlement in the first place. For why, it must be asked, need a virtuous Kantian moral agent feel sympathy for those in distress, once the duty to help them is recognized? Indeed, would not the inclusion of such a feeling in an agent's motivational set deprive the beneficent act of all moral worth? At least that seems to be the clear implication of the famous account of moral worth in the *Groundwork*.[18]

It is in addressing this latter issue that the doctrine of radical evil, understood as an ineliminable susceptibility to temptation, and the associated conception of the moral struggle as one of freedom with itself must be brought into the story. To begin with, since this general susceptibility to temptation (as contrasted with actually being tempted by something) affects even the best of us, it follows that even the virtuous need to be on guard against it. Thus arises the need for what Kant sometimes (somewhat misleadingly) calls a "counterweight" to the claims of the self-regarding inclinations, which take the form of temptations.[19] What is crucial to keep in mind, however, is that the feeling of sympathy does not serve as a counterweight by either replacing or directly propping up the duty motive (which would entail the impurity of the will). Rather, it functions *indirectly* by providing a reason to act beneficently, namely, the recognition of genuine suffering, that counters the reasons stemming from my sensuous nature, which lead me to grant a higher priority to the satisfaction of my own desires. In short, the feeling of sympathy functions as a weapon against the propensity to evil, rather than as a directly motivating factor. Consequently, it is, as such, a weapon that it enables us to do "what the thought of duty alone would not accomplish."

In order to appreciate fully the need for such a weapon, it is also necessary to keep in mind that the duty in question (beneficence) is imperfect or of wide obligation. As already indicated, it is with regard to such duties that the struggle with the propensity to evil is the greatest, since it is all too easy to find reasons to avoid performing any given action falling under a duty of this sort. This seems to be especially true with regard to beneficence, however, since without a keen recognition of the needs of others that one is in a position to ameliorate, one quite naturally places priority on the satisfaction of one's own desires. Consequently, the sympathetic apprehension of the suffering of others prompts one to abandon an excessively egocentric perspective, and in this respect may be characterized as a moral facilitator.

Finally, it is precisely because it functions as such a facilitator that Kant characterizes the obligation to develop one's sympathetic feelings as merely an "indirect duty," rather than a full-fledged one. Although the concept of an indirect duty does not appear to have a place in Kant's official taxonomy of the types of duty, he appeals to it fairly frequently in his writings on moral theory, particularly with regard to the cultivation of one's own happiness. Thus, in the *Groundwork*, the *Critique of Practical Reason*, and the *Metaphysics of Morals*, Kant insists that, though it is absurd to speak of a duty to cultivate one's own happiness, we do have an indirect duty to do so. Moreover, in all three texts he explicitly connects this indirect duty with the need to ward off temptation.[20] Appealing to this model, then, an indirect duty may be described as a maxim or course of action that, while not of itself obligatory, may become such if it serves to lessen significantly or remove self-imposed obstacles to the fulfillment of one's genuine or direct duties. And, as I have tried to argue, the cultivation of sympathetic feelings falls under that description.

Given this, the present suggestion, which is admittedly somewhat speculative, is that similar considerations apply, *mutatis mutandis*, to the development of an appreciation of the indications of nature's moral purposiveness provided by beautiful natural objects. To be sure, these indications do not fulfill the epistemological function of making us aware of occasions for moral activity that we might otherwise not notice. In this respect, the analogy with the cultivation of our sympathetic feelings does not apply. Nevertheless, our awareness of these indications does also serve as a "counterweight" to the tendency to ignore occasions for dutiful action, albeit in a somewhat different way than our sympathetic feelings. Whereas the latter do so by reinforcing our sense of the genuine needs of others and, therefore, of their (nonjuridical) moral claims upon us, the former does so by reinforcing the sense that nature is on our side and, therefore, that our moral efforts will not be in vain. Here the temptation to be counteracted is to succumb to the thought of the futility of moral effort, which is arguably one the prime ways in which radically evil moral agents, such as ourselves, tend to evade the claims of duty, especially those that do not appear to be easily fulfillable. Accordingly, this thought must constantly be struggled against, and it is here that these traces and hints of nature's moral purposiveness enter into the moral life. They do so by helping to reinforce our all-too-tenuous commitment to the ends that are also duties and ultimately to the highest good.[21]

If this is correct, it also enables us to see why we have here merely a duty, as it were, which I take to be equivalent to an indirect duty, rather than a genuine or direct duty. It cannot be a direct duty because the development of an appreciation of nature's traces and hints of its moral purposiveness, like the cultivation of one's sympathetic feelings, is neither itself a morally necessary end nor a necessary means to the attainment of one. One could, after all, have a good will and yet totally lack the capacity or opportunity to appreciate natural beauty. For these reasons I think that the capacity to appreciate natural beauty, like the capacity to sympathize with the plight of others, is best characterized as a moral facilitator. Moreover, once again, it is precisely because of humanity's inherent propensity to evil that such a facilitator is required.

Finally, the preceding analysis may be compared with Kant's brief discussion of the proper attitude toward natural beauty in *The Doctrine of Virtue*, which forms part of an "episodic section," dealing with a supposed "amphiboly in moral concepts of reflection, taking what is man's duty to himself for a duty to other beings" (MS 6: 442; 237). Kant's basic point in this section is that our supposed duties to nonrational animals are really duties to oneself, which by an "amphiboly" are transposed into duties to animate nature. With respect to inanimate nature, however, Kant thinks that the question of duty arises only in the case of beautiful objects. And here he claims that a propensity to the wanton destruction of what is beautiful in inanimate nature, a *"spiritus destructionis,"* is, in fact, contrary to our duty to ourselves. The express reason is that

> It weakens or uproots that feeling in man which though not of itself moral, is still a disposition [*Stimmung*] of sensibility that greatly promotes morality or at least prepares the way for it: the disposition, namely, to love something (e.g. beautiful crystal formations, the indescribable beauty of plants) even apart from any intention to use it. (MS 6: 443; 237)

Although Kant now speaks of a genuine duty to oneself rather than merely of a duty, as it were, or indirect duty, it clearly remains a matter of moral facilitation. What is at issue is something that is not inherently moral (since it pertains to sensibility and is merely aesthetic), but that nonetheless plays a significant morally preparatory role. Presumably, Kant can speak here of an actual duty because of its purely negative nature. Rather than the positive requirement to develop the capacity for the kind of feeling in question, which for the reasons already given could amount to nothing more than an indirect duty, the obligation is merely to refrain from the wanton destruction of natural beauties. And this, like acts of self-abuse, can be prohibited because of the morally pernicious nature of the propensity for such destruction. Once again, however, this duty must itself be understood against the backdrop of the underlying conception of radical evil. This is not only because the very need for an aesthetic "preparation" for morality presupposes such evil, but also because the propensity to destroy beautiful things, or the *"spiritus destructionis,"* which is what must be guarded against, is itself a symptom of radical evil.

The reason that Kant proposes in support of this duty is likewise worthy of note. In view of the central argument of this chapter, one would expect him to have claimed that the propensity to the wanton destruction of inanimate natural beauty is morally pernicious precisely because such destruction deprives us of much-needed indications of nature's moral purposiveness. Instead, he strikes a somewhat different chord, involving a different sense of moral facilitation. For what is actually described as facilitating morality (without being itself moral) is the act of loving something apart from any intention to use it, that is, disinterestedly. This is certainly compatible with, but it also differs in at least two significant ways from, the facilitation of morality through the development of an intellectual interest in natural beauty. First, as Kant makes clear, such an interest arises from an explicitly moral concern, and therefore is in the service of a moral commitment that is already assumed to be in place, whereas the love with which Kant is now concerned is itself merely aesthetic and functions only as a preparation for morality. Thus, it does not presuppose any prior moral commitment. Second, and equally important, this second mode of moral facilitation, unlike the first, is applicable to artistic as well as natural beauty, since the disinterested love of each kind of beauty is capable of playing a morally preparatory role.

Far from undermining the argument of the present chapter, however, this supports the claim that there are two distinct ways in which beauty serves morality and helps to effect the transition from nature to freedom. It is therefore to the second of these ways, in virtue of which beauty serves as a symbol of morality, that we now turn.

THE ANTINOMY OF TASTE AND BEAUTY AS A SYMBOL OF MORALITY

Our present concern is with Kant's conception of beauty as a symbol of morality and its significance for both taste and morality. But since the section in which Kant articulates this doctrine (§59) constitutes the completion of the Dialectic of Aesthetic Judgment, it will be necessary to consider the argument of the Dialectic in some detail. This will not amount to a digression from the main purpose of this portion of our study, however, since we shall see that the problem Kant takes up in the Dialectic (the formulation and resolution of an antinomy of taste) is itself intimately related to the general problem of the systematic and moral significance of taste. In particular, it marks a return to themes set forth in Section IX of the Second Introduction, which were discussed in Chapter 9.

The chapter is divided into six parts. The first analyzes Kant's account of the nature of the antinomy of taste and tries to show that, contrary to some interpretations, he is there concerned with a genuine and fresh problem. The second and third parts deal with the account of the resolution of the antinomy in §57 and the comments attached to that section. The former discusses what might be termed the "formal" resolution through the clarification of the sense of "concept" appealed to by both parties, and the latter the problematic and much-criticized appeal to the supersensible that Kant makes on the basis of this resolution. The fourth part analyzes the actual account of beauty as a symbol of morality, which it interprets in light of Kant's conception of aesthetic ideas. The fifth part marks a return to the question of moral significance by considering how an engagement with the beautiful (both natural and artistic) constitutes a preparation for morality in virtue of symbolizing it. Finally, the sixth part revisits the issue of the deduction of taste by arguing that a key passage in §59 is not to be read (as it frequently is) as claiming that it is this very symbolization of morality that grounds the legitimacy of the pure judgment of taste.

I

There can be such a thing as a dialectic of aesthetic judgment only if there is a genuine antinomy, that is, a conflict between two equally necessary but apparently contradictory propositions, each of which is a valid consequence of a generally accepted principle of aesthetic judgment. Kant puts the issue at the beginning of his discussion of the antinomy by noting that if the faculty of aesthetic judgment is to be dialectical it must "be rationalizing" [*vernünftelnd sein*], by which he means that its principles must claim universality on *a priori* grounds (KU 5: 337; 209).[1] Thus, only a clash between such principles could constitute an antinomy.

Given this, Kant quickly rules out the possibility of an antinomy between first-order aesthetic judgments, whether they be aesthetic judgments of sense regarding the agreeable or of taste regarding the beautiful.[2] The former is obvious, since there is no incompatibility between claims regarding agreeableness. One and the same thing might very well seem agreeable to someone and highly disagreeable to someone else (or even to the same person at different times), without any threat of contradiction. For, as we have seen, such "judgments" claim no more than a merely private validity.

This is not the case with judgments of taste, however, since two judgments regarding the same x of the form "x is beautiful" and "x is not beautiful" do genuinely conflict. Nevertheless, Kant suggests that, insofar as each person relies on his or her own taste, such a conflict does not assume antinomial status, since no one attempts to make one's judgment into a universal rule (KU 5: 337; 209). At first glance this might seem to conflict with the claim of the Analytic that in making a judgment of taste one purports to be speaking with a universal voice; but I take Kant's point to be that one must acknowledge that the other likewise purports to be speaking with such a voice, so that both are really relying merely on their own taste. Consequently, there is no conflict of principles, since the opposing judgments may be seen as conflicting applications of the same principle, namely, that one must rely on one's own taste.[3]

It follows that if there is to be such a thing as a dialectic of taste, it must be one concerning the critique of taste, that is, the second-order principles underlying the first-order judgments of taste. Moreover, Kant suggests that such a conflict, amounting to a genuine antinomy, would cast doubt on the "lawfulness" [*Gesetzmässigkeit*] of the faculty of aesthetic judgment and thus of its very possibility (KU 5: 335; 210). In other words, Kant highlights the potential significance of an antinomy of taste by raising the specter of a hopeless skepticism regarding taste, a euthanasia of pure taste, if you will, analogous to the specter raised in the Dialectic of the first *Critique* concerning the theoretical use of reason.[4]

After thus specifying the conditions to be met by an antinomy of taste and indicating its potential significance for a critique of taste (§55), Kant begins the search for such an antinomy by considering two widely shared assumptions or "commonplaces" [*Gemeinörter*], which may be regarded as second-order principles of taste (§56): "*Everyone has his own taste*" and "*There is no disputing about taste*" (KU 5: 338; 210). Of themselves, however, these hardly constitute an antinomial conflict, since they are perfectly compatible. As an expression of aesthetic subjectivism or relativism, the former entails that any putative "dispute" over taste is at bottom nothing more than a clash of personal preferences (perfectly analogous to one regarding the agreeable) for which neither side can produce any justifying grounds. And this is tantamount to claiming that there is no disputing about taste.

Nevertheless, Kant notes that, in virtue of its ambiguity, the second leaves room for a third principle, or qualified version of the second, which, though not in common use, is both widely accepted and incompatible with the first, namely, "One can quarrel [*streiten*] about taste (though one cannot dispute [*disputiren*] about it)" (KU 5: 238; 211). This new principle is compatible with the original commonplace it replaces because the conditions for a quarrel are weaker than those for a dispute. The former requires merely the assumption that there is something like a fact of the matter, that is, a right and a wrong view. This suffices to make the disagreement genuine, even though there may be no available means to resolve it definitively. The latter, by contrast, requires a determinate decision procedure or proof by means of which the dispute can be definitively decided. In Kant's terms, this means that it is assumed that the judgment is based on objective concepts that can serve as grounds of proof. Moreover, as Kant points out, even the weaker view clashes with the first commonplace, since the latter explicitly denies that there is anything like a fact of the matter regarding taste.

We thus arrive at a conflict concerning the conditions of the possibility of a judgment of taste, and it is here that Kant locates the antinomy. Since it denies that there is anything like a fact of the matter regarding taste, the subjectivistic position is committed to the denial that judgments of taste are based on any objective grounds or concepts. Conversely, the position that maintains that we can even so much as quarrel about taste is committed to the assumption that there are justifying grounds (or concepts) for judgments of taste, even if we are not in a position to appeal to them in order to adjudicate disputes. Thus, the thesis asserts that "A judgment of taste is not based on concepts; for otherwise one could dispute about it (decide by means of proofs)"; while the antithesis maintains that "A judgment of taste is based on concepts; for otherwise, regardless of the variation among such judgments, one could not even so much as quarrel about them (lay claim to other people's necessary assent to one's judgment)" (KU 5: 338–9; 211).

Although, as it stands, this does not have the developed structure of the better-known antinomies from the first *Critique*, wherein each side argues for its case apogogically through a *reductio* of the opposing view, it can easily be given such a form. So construed, the argument for the thesis proceeds as follows:

1. Assume the opposite: Judgments of taste are based on concepts.
2. It follows from this that it must be possible to dispute about taste.
3. But this is impossible.
4. Therefore, judgments of taste are not based on concepts.

This argument has the appropriate *reductio* form and is clearly valid (it may be formulated as a *modus tollens*: c-> d; not-d; therefore, not-c). It also appeals to the premise accepted by the opponent that there can be no disputing about taste. Although the thesis does not refer explicitly to the claim of the antithesis that one can quarrel about taste (as opposed to disputing about it), it can be taken as maintaining that this distinction is specious, since that which would suffice to account for the possibility of the former (a concept) would suffice for the latter as well. Otherwise expressed, it holds that one cannot maintain *both* that there is no disputing taste (but merely quarreling) *and* that judgments of taste are based on concepts. Since this is precisely what is denied by the antithesis, it is also obviously the problematic point. Nevertheless, as Kant will go on to show, it follows from a natural understanding of what is meant by a *concept*, namely, a determinate set of marks that provides a rule or decision procedure for the recognition of what falls under it. In fact, given this conception of a concept, it may be seen as an exemplification of the analytic principle: If there is a ground, there must be a consequent.

Appropriately formulated, the argument for the antithesis goes as follows:

1. Assume the opposite: Judgments of taste are not based on concepts.
2. It follows from this that we could not even quarrel about taste.
3. But we do quarrel about taste.
4. Therefore, judgments of taste are based on concepts.

Once again, the argument has a *reductio* form and is formally valid (the *modus tollens* is: not-c -> not-q; q; therefore, c). Here the essential premise, which is also shared by the thesis, is that unless a judgment of taste were based on a concept (had some objective ground), we could not even quarrel about taste. This can also be expressed as the principle that if there is so much as a fact of the matter (which is a condition of the possibility of a quarrel), it must be based on some concept that serves as ground. Of itself, this seems unproblematic, since it may be taken as a logical version of the principle of sufficient reason (if there is a conclusion there must be a premise capable of grounding it).[5] What is problematic, however, since it directly contradicts the thesis, is the assumption (underlying step three) that there can be something like a fact of the matter, *sans* a decision procedure capable of determining it, even *in principle*. The latter qualification is crucial, for in order to generate the antinomy with which Kant is concerned, the antithesis must be committed to the view that it is in principle impossible to adjudicate conflicting claims about taste through some decision procedure, not simply that it is very difficult to do so or would require great expertise).[6] And this likewise turns on a certain view of a concept as a ground.

II

Kant lays out the essential features of his resolution of this antinomy in the very first paragraph of §57, where he writes:

> There is only one way for us to eliminate the conflict between the mentioned principles, on which we base all our judgments of taste (and which are nothing but the two peculiarities of a judgment of taste that were set out in the Analytic): We must show that the concept to which we refer the object in such judgments is understood in different senses in those two maxims of the faculty of aesthetic judgment, and show that it is necessary for our transcendental faculty of judgment to adopt both these senses (or points of view in judging) but that even the illusion arising from our confusion of the two is natural and hence unavoidable. (KU 5: 339; 211)

Embedded in this programmatic statement are four major points: (1) the identification of the two parties to the dispute with the two peculiarities of the judgment of taste discussed in the Analytic and the Deduction; (2) that the only possible way to resolve the conflict is by showing that the concept to which the object is supposedly referred in a judgment of taste is understood differently by the two parties; (3) that it is likewise necessary to show that both "maxims" or "points of view" are required; (4) that the illusion arising from the confusion of the two senses of the concept is "natural and hence unavoidable."

Assuming the identification of the thesis and antithesis with the two peculiarities of the judgment of taste analyzed in the Analytic and the Deduction, it is not surprising that Kant suggests both are required. For these peculiarities have been shown to reflect constitutive features of the judgment of taste on the basis of which it is distinguished from all cognitive judgments as well as evaluative judgments of the agreeable and the good. Thus, point three seems to follow unproblematically from one. Nevertheless, point one itself is puzzling for at least two reasons. First, it is by no means obvious that the thesis and antithesis are equivalent to these two peculiarities. Second, if they are, the whole argument of the antinomy seems threatened by redundancy, since we saw in Chapter 8 that it was precisely the self-proclaimed task of the Deduction to "resolve" these peculiarities. Thus, if the argument of the Deduction is successful, as Kant presumably thought it was, one wonders what work is left for the antinomy to accomplish.

Further questions concerning Kant's efforts to relate the antinomy to the treatment of the antinomies in the first *Critique* are also raised by two and four. At the heart of the problem is Kant's quick move from a formal resolution of the conflict through the disambiguation of the "concept" supposedly underlying the judgment of taste to the introduction of the apparatus of transcendental idealism. To anticipate, Kant argues that the appearance of a contradiction can be removed by recognizing that the thesis is really denying merely that judgments of taste are based on a *determinate* concept and that the antithesis, properly construed, maintains that they must be based on an *indeterminate* one. But he then proceeds to identify this indeterminate concept with reason's concept of a supersensible substrate (in its various permutations); and this move has been greeted with suspicion by commentators (most notably Guyer), who see Kant's argument at this point as driven by architectonic considerations having nothing directly to do with the analysis of taste.[7] Moreover, any such suspicion is further fueled by the fourth point, which involves Kant's attempt to relate his present account to the first-*Critique* doctrine of transcendental illusion.

Because of these complexities, it is convenient to divide the discussion of the resolution of the antinomy into two parts. Accordingly, I shall consider Kant's treatment of points one and two in the present section, which basically deals with the formal resolution of the antinomy, and the move to the supersensible and the illusion that is supposed to be inevitably connected with it in the next.

With regard to the first point, we must keep in mind that Kant characterizes these peculiarities in different ways within the Deduction. Thus, in his first explicit reference to them in §31, he basically identifies them with the claims of the second and fourth moments of the Analytic respectively, namely, "the universality of a singular judgment, as opposed to a logical universality based on concepts," and a "necessity that does not depend on any *a priori* bases of proof" (KU 5: 281; 144). As we have already seen, however, in his actual discussion of these peculiarities, Kant characterizes them in terms of an "as if objectivity" and an "as if subjectivity," respectively. In virtue of the former, the judgment of taste is said to make a claim to everyone's assent, "as if it were an objective judgment" (KU 5: 281; 145), and in virtue of the latter, it is not determined by any basis of proof, "just as if it were merely subjective" (KU 5: 284; 147).

The latter formulations go some way toward linking these peculiarities with the antithesis and thesis positions, respectively. For the antithesis assumes the objectivity of judgments of taste (that there is something like a fact of the matter), from which it infers that they must be based on concepts, whereas the thesis assumes their subjectivity, from which it infers that they cannot be based on concepts.[8] Nevertheless, significant differences still remain between the peculiarities and the two sides in the antinomial conflict. The thesis, after all, does not simply assert that the judgment of taste has a feature analogous to that of a merely subjective claim; it asserts that it has merely a subjective basis, in spite of the fact that it makes a claim to universality. Similarly, the antithesis asserts not as-if objectivity, but actual objectivity, and it does so even though the judgment is not capable of proof.

Even granting these complications, however, I believe that such considerations help us to understand what Kant may have had in mind. In spite of his express language, I take Kant's point not to be that the thesis and antithesis are each to be simply equated with one of the two peculiarities, but rather that the former are derived from the latter by a process of absolutization. In other words, the antinomy is generated through the inflation of what is initially merely a moment or aspect of the judgment of taste into a free-standing principle that expresses the whole truth regarding taste. Or, expressed in terms of the first *Critique*, what has happened is that these peculiarities are converted into principles of reason (governing the judgment of taste), much as the categories are supposedly converted into ideas of reason by being related to the thought of the unconditioned.[9]

We shall return to this issue in connection with a discussion of the fourth of the noted points (the naturalness and inevitability of the illusion). For the present, however, our concern is with the second of the two problems raised by Kant's apparent identification of the thesis and antithesis with the two peculiarities, namely, the question of redundancy. Simply put, the problem is that Kant had already described the method of the Deduction as "resolving" the twofold peculiarity of the judgment of taste (KU 5: 281; 144). But, given the forementioned identification, it appears that he is attempting to do precisely the same thing with respect to the antinomy. This characterization of his procedure also lends support to the widely shared view that in the Dialectic, Kant is still concerned with the problem of providing a deduction, or, in Guyer's version, that he is attempting an additional deduction for the benefit of those who may not have been satisfied with the official one.[10]

The fact that Kant returns to these peculiarities does not, however, mean that he is still concerned with the deduction of the principle of taste. For the question he now addresses is a fresh one, namely, whether these two equally essential moments of the judgment of taste, let us call them its subjective and its objective poles, are mutually compatible. This issue was not posed within either the Analytic or the Deduction because it arises only when the two are inflated or converted into distinct free-standing principles, each claiming to provide a complete account of the grounds of the judgment of taste. And this is the work of reason in its endemic quest for the unconditioned.[11] Once this occurs it becomes natural to ask if the "moment" of subjectivity is sufficient to preclude any conceptual basis capable of grounding the judgment of taste's claim to intersubjective validity, and if the "moment" of objectivity entails that such a judgment must have a conceptual basis capable of yielding grounds for a proof.

Admittedly, we have already noted that Kant does claim that, if unresolved, the Antinomy of Taste would undermine the results of the Deduction. Nevertheless, this hardly makes the resolution itself a deduction. In fact, all that the resolution claims to show is that, properly construed, the two "maxims" are compatible, that even though they point in opposite directions there is no real contradiction between them. Since this is merely a necessary, not also a sufficient condition of the intersubjective validity of the judgment of taste, it cannot constitute a deduction.

The point may be illustrated by a brief consideration of Kant's comment on the significance of the antinomy concerning the highest good in the second *Critique*. Prior to offering his "critical resolution," which, as always, involves an appeal to transcendental idealism, Kant remarks:

> Since . . . the furthering of the highest good . . . is an *a priori* necessary object of our will and is inseparably related to the moral law, the impossibility of the highest good must prove the falsity of the moral law also. If, therefore, the highest good is impossible according to practical rules, then the moral law which commands that it be furthered must be fantastic, directed to empty imaginary ends, and consequently inherently false (KpV 5: 113–14; 120)

Although Kant here graphically illustrates what is at stake in this antinomy, which threatens the possibility of the highest good, namely, the denial of the moral law, it hardly follows that its resolution is to be taken as a deduction of the moral law that either supplants or supplements the notorious appeal to the fact of reason in the Analytic.[12] For assuming that the obligation to pursue the highest good follows from the moral law, it likewise follows that the denial of the possibility of the former entails the fictive nature of the latter (a valid law cannot require the impossible); but it does not follow from this that the possibility of the highest good suffices to establish the validity of the moral law (since the former is merely a necessary and not also a sufficient condition of the latter).

The conclusion to be drawn is that in both the second and third *Critiques*, the resolution of the antinomy is to be seen as an attempt to remove an obstacle to the acceptance of the principle in question (the principle of morality in the former and the principle of taste in the latter), rather than as an attempt to provide an independent justification of that principle.[13] Nor should it be objected at this point that such a result conflicts with the first *Critique* model, where Kant does claim that the antinomy yields an indirect proof of transcendental idealism that complements the direct proof of the Aesthetic. This is perfectly correct but beside the point, for a proof of idealism is one thing and the deduction of an *a priori* principle quite another. Moreover, we shall see that the resolution of the present antinomy likewise leads to idealism, so that in this respect it (like that of the second *Critique*) conforms to this model.[14]

This brings us, then, to the second major point in the opening paragraph of §57, namely, the methodological claim that the only way to resolve the antinomy is to show that the notion of a concept is understood differently in the thesis and antithesis. This may not be obviously the *only* conceivable way to adjudicate the dispute, but it is certainly *a* way. For if the party that maintains and the party that denies that judgments of taste are based on a concept do not mean the same thing by "concept," then there is no direct contradiction between them. Not only may each side be reasoning correctly from its particular understanding of concepts, but each of these understandings may itself be at least partially correct. And this, of course, is precisely what Kant wants to claim.

Although Kant never says so explicitly, since the concept in question is the one to which one supposedly refers in making a judgment of taste, it seems reasonable to identify it with the concept of the beautiful.[15] Consequently, the questions become what kind of a concept is this concept of the beautiful, and how is it understood by the two parties to the antinomial dispute.

Beginning with the second question, it is clear that the thesis position conceives it in terms of the model of an ordinary concept of a kind, that is, a *repraesentatio generalis* that defines a class of objects falling under it. Thus, as we have seen, it assumes that the concept must be one that provides a rule or decision procedure for determining whether or not a given object falls under the concept. Since such a rule is precisely what Kant means by a schema, it follows that the thesis assumes that the concept of the beautiful must be schematizable or, as Kant tends to put it in the third *Critique*, exhibitable in intuition.[16] This is not to say that the thesis position assumes that we have such a concept of the beautiful; on the contrary, it explicitly denies this. The key point, however, is that it is precisely because it assumes that this is what the concept of the beautiful would have to be like, if it were to serve as the ground for a judgment of taste, that this position denies that such a judgment is based on a concept. And in doing so, it also denies that we have such a concept.

Conversely, the antithesis must assume that we have a concept of the beautiful, since it insists that the question of whether or not something is beautiful is a genuine one bearing on the nature of the object (we can quarrel about taste). Does it then appeal to the same conception of a concept as does the thesis? The answer seems to be yes and no. Clearly, it does so insofar as it takes itself as the direct contradictory of the thesis (which it must do if it is to make use of an apogogic mode of proof). Otherwise, there would not be even the appearance of an antinomy. But insofar as it claims merely that there is something like a fact of the matter regarding beauty, and not that it is decidable (even in principle) in any given case, it does not actually require such a "thick" conception of a concept. In fact, since "concept" for the antithesis position serves merely as a placeholder for whatever it is that grounds the validity (or lack thereof) of particular judgments of taste, it needs to understand by "the beautiful" nothing more than a (to us) unknown ground of claims of taste. Accordingly, if it accepts the thesis's view of concepts in general and the concept of the beautiful in particular (presumably because it assumes that all concepts must be of this nature), it says more than it needs to say, indeed, more than it knows to be the case.[17]

Given this state of affairs, Kant's formal resolution consists essentially in disambiguating the term "concept," so as to remove the appearance of contradiction between the two positions. This is accomplished by distinguishing between concepts that are determined or determinable and those that are not. Since to determine a concept is to provide it with a corresponding sensible intuition, this amounts to a distinction between concepts that can be provided with such an intuition and those that cannot. Kant suggests that concepts of the understanding (by which he presumably means both pure and empirical concepts) are of the former kind, and as an example of the latter he cites reason's transcendental concept of the supersensible underlying the sensible intuition through which the former is determined. And of the latter he adds that it cannot be further determined theoretically (KU 5: 339; 212).

This distinction gives Kant all that he needs for a formal resolution of the antinomy that combines features of the resolutions of both the mathematical and the dynamical antinomies in the first *Critique*. First, the contradiction disappears, because insofar as both sides understand the concept putatively involved in the judgment of taste in the former sense, they are mere contraries rather than contradictories. And, as such, they simply ignore the possibility that the concept might be of the latter kind. Second, even this contrariety can be removed by reformulating the thesis to read that the judgment of taste is not based on a *determinate* concept and the antithesis that it is based on an *indeterminate* one (KU 5: 340–1; 213). For, so revised, it is clear that the thesis and antithesis may both be true, which is just what Kant wishes to claim.

III

As already noted, Kant does not rest content with this merely formal resolution. Instead, he proceeds to identify the indeterminate and indeterminable concept required to avoid the contradiction with the concept of a supersensible substrate. To be sure, in his initial appeal to it, Kant refers to it as "one such concept" [*Ein dergleichen Begriff*] (KU 5: 340; 212), suggesting that it is merely a candidate for the required concept; but without anything in the way of additional argument, he proceeds as if it were obvious that it is the only candidate.

To make things even more confusing, Kant characterizes this supersensible in diverse ways. Thus, he describes it initially as "reason's pure concept of the supersensible underlying the object (as well as underlying the judging subject) as an object of sense and hence as an appearance" (KU 5: 340; 212); and later in the same section, he refers to what purports to be the same concept both as "the supersensible substrate of humanity" (KU 5: 340; 213) and as the "supersensible substrate of appearances" (KU 5: 341; 213). Since these correspond to the "supersensible without" and the "supersensible within" of the Second Introduction, the claim seems to be that the resolution of the antinomy leads to the supersensible in both senses.[18]

The basic problem, however, is understanding why it involves an appeal to the supersensible in *any* sense. As already indicated, Guyer, among others, treats this sudden appeal to a concept of the supersensible and the idealism that seems inseparable from it with considerable suspicion. Reduced to its essentials, Guyer's major complaint is that the concept of a supersensible ground (in whatever form it may take) is not the only indeterminate concept that we have. Also falling into that category is the concept of the harmony of the faculties, which, he insists, "is clearly not identical with the concept of any supersensible object."[19] Instead, he suggests it is either an epistemological concept of the conditions under which a manifold of intuition can be united or a psychological concept of the mental state in which this unity is felt to obtain. By contrast, the concept of the supersensible, for Guyer, is an ontological concept, referring to the to-us unknown constitution of empirical objects and subjects as things in themselves.[20]

Given this, Guyer concludes unsurprisingly that the indeterminate concept of the harmony of the faculties is the one Kant should have appealed to at this point. Consequently, on Guyer's reading, Kant's introduction, instead of the concept of a mysterious supersensible ground, is to be viewed as the result of either excess zeal in relating the current discussion to his beloved architectonic or a misguided effort to answer the skeptic (who is presumably not satisfied with the argument of the Deduction) by providing a metaphysical grounding for taste in the supersensible.[21]

Having already argued that the Dialectic of Taste is not to be viewed as an attempt to replicate or supplant the Deduction, I see no need to deal any further with the second of the possibilities offered by Guyer. Suffice it to say that since the deduction of the principle of taste stands on its own (or at least was thought to do so by Kant), there is no need to provide it with any additional metaphysical support. Indeed, the attempt to provide such support would obviously run up against the familiar critical strictures regarding the limits of knowledge.

Nevertheless, this still leaves in place Guyer's main complaint regarding the legitimacy of Kant's move to the supersensible at all; and here it must be admitted that this complaint seems to have at least *prima facie* plausibility. Kant does appear to assume without argument that the concept of a supersensible ground (in its various forms) is the only one fitting the description, and this does lead directly to the importation into the discussion of transcendental idealism in a way that seems intended to parallel the manner in which it is brought into the discussion of the antinomies in the first *Critique*.

Consequently, it becomes necessary to determine whether the turn to the supersensible at this point is motivated by the underlying theory of taste (which is precisely what Guyer denies) or whether it may be dismissed as nothing more than an unwarranted attempt to link the discussion of taste with the official architectonic. Since a positive answer to this question would render idle Guyer's suggestion that all that is required is the indeterminate concept of the harmony of the faculties, I shall proceed directly to that issue, without stopping to consider his essentially empiricistic account in its own terms.[22]

As a first step in understanding Kant's move to the supersensible, it should be noted that the concept in question must not simply be indeterminate (which is all that Guyer focuses on) but *indeterminable*. But in order to avoid misunderstanding on this point, it is important not to confuse the present discussion with the account of determination and determinability in Chapter 9 in connection with Section IX of the Second Introduction. There, it will be recalled, it was a matter of making *conceptually* determinable (by the "intellectual faculty") the thought of the supersensible substrate of nature. For the theoretical faculty (understanding), this substrate is viewed merely as the completely indeterminate thought of a something = x; determinability, in the sense of a conceptual content not amounting to cognition, is then provided by reflective judgment with its concept of purposiveness, which, in turn, prepares the way for a practical determination through reason. Thus, reflective judgment was seen to play an essential mediating role in the *Übergang* from nature to freedom.

The present concern, by contrast, is with the determination (or lack thereof) of a concept by providing it with a corresponding intuition or, equivalently, by exhibiting it in intuition. Thus, both merely indeterminate and actually indeterminable concepts may be said to be "unexhibited." The difference is that in the former case, exhibition remains possible (and necessary if the concept is to yield cognition of an object, i.e., not be empty), whereas in the latter, it is ruled out in principle. But a concept fitting the latter description is by definition an idea of reason. In fact, in the first of two comments attached to §57, Kant defines such ideas as "indemonstrable concepts of reason" (where "indemonstrable" means unexhibitable), in contrast to aesthetic ideas, which are defined as "inexponible representations of the imagination" (KU 5: 342; 215).

We shall deal with the important topic of aesthetic ideas later in this chapter and in Chapter 12. For present purposes, however, the main point is that an indeterminable concept is an idea of reason and that such a concept is required for the resolution of the antinomy, since a merely indeterminate (but determinable) concept would hold open the possibility of proof (through its determination). Otherwise expressed, only such a "concept" could be viewed as having the normative standing required to ground the possibility of genuine disagreement, while at the same time precluding the possibility of the determination needed to provide a rule capable of yielding a decision procedure for disputes about taste.

Ideas of reason may also be regarded as concepts of a supersensible ground or substrate.[23] That this holds for transcendental ideas follows directly from Kant's account of their formation through the extension of categories to the unconditioned. As he argues in the first part of the Transcendental Dialectic, such an extension results naturally from the application of the illusory principle of reason: "[I]f the conditioned is given, the whole series of conditions . . . a series which is therefore itself unconditioned – is likewise given, that is, contained in the object and its connection" (A307–8/B364).[24] Since the unconditioned which reason posits in accordance with this principle in its endemic quest for totality or closure is both itself supersensible and the ultimate ground of the sensibly conditioned, to form such an idea of reason is just to form the concept of a supersensible ground or substrate of the sensible (which, as such, is always conditioned). For example, the idea of the soul is thought as the unconditioned ground of the appearances of inner sense, and the idea of God (the *ens realissimus*) as the unconditioned ground of all things (things in general).

A similar analysis also applies to other ideas of reason, for example, moral ones, each of which may be described as the concept of a maximum or unconditioned totality (and therefore supersensible) that functions as an archetype grounding and conditioning the estimation of its ectypal approximations. A case in point is Kant's example of the idea of a constitution as "*the greatest possible human freedom* in accordance with laws by which *the freedom of each is made to be consistent with that of all others*"

(A316/B373). As Kant notes, this idea of a maximization of freedom under universal laws is never realized concretely in the sensible world, but it nonetheless functions as a valid archetype grounding judgments regarding existing political arrangements.[25] Thus, if, as I have argued, an indeterminable concept is an idea of reason, it follows that it is also the concept of such a supersensible ground or substrate, which is just what Kant maintains is required for the resolution of the antinomy.

As is so often the case in Kant interpretation, however, the resolution of one problem leads immediately to another, for in the preceding section the indeterminable concept in question was identified with the concept of the beautiful. This seemed a reasonable inference to draw, since it is difficult to think of another concept capable of playing the role assigned to it in the resolution of the antinomy. The problem, however, is that the concept of the beautiful appears an unlikely candidate for an idea of reason since beauty, unlike, say, the ideas of the soul and God, supposedly pertains to sensible objects, rather than to something supersensible or transcendent. In fact, we have seen that the beauty of an object attaches to the manner in which it presents itself in sensible intuition, apart from any conceptualization. Consequently, it is far from obvious that the concept of the beautiful qualifies as an idea of reason that leads us inevitably from something sensible to its supersensible ground or substrate. Moreover, if it does not qualify for this status, it becomes difficult to see why such ideas are in any way involved in the judgment of taste; and this once again calls into question Kant's resolution of the antinomy.

In response to such a line of objection, it may first be noted that, given Kant's taxonomy of representations, there is nothing else for the concept of the beautiful to be besides an idea.[26] Clearly, it is not a sensation or intuition, and treating it as a concept of the understanding (either empirical or pure) is ruled out by its indeterminability. Consequently, one might claim that it qualifies as an idea virtually by default.

Nevertheless, if this were all there was to be said in favor of the hypothesis that the concept of the beautiful is an idea of reason, it would not be worth a second thought. Fortunately, however, this is not the case. Let us consider the explication of the beautiful offered at the end of the third moment of the Analytic: "Beauty is an object's form of *purposiveness* insofar as it is perceived in the object *without the representation of a purpose*" (KU 5: 236; 84). Though each of the moments terminates in what Kant describes as an "explication of the beautiful," this is the only one that relates to the *object* judged beautiful (as opposed to the liking or judgment through which an object's beauty is determined). Consequently, it deserves to be privileged in an investigation of the nature of the concept of the beautiful for Kant. Moreover, if the indeterminable concept is equated with the beautiful, so conceived, the argument of §57 appears in a different light.

To begin with, the form of purposiveness, understood as "mere form," that is, as purposiveness without purpose, has at least as strong a claim to be the concept required to resolve the antinomy as Guyer's harmony of the faculties. Since it is a characterization of the beautiful, it can plausibly function as the ground of a judgment of taste: An object is deemed beautiful just in case it exhibits the form of purposiveness. Furthermore, such a concept is not merely indeterminate but indeterminable. For to determine it would involve the introduction of a definite purpose, which is precisely what is precluded. And for this reason, it also can be said to account for the possibility of a quarrel regarding taste, while precluding the possibility of a dispute. There are, after all, no applicable rules or criteria for determining whether or not a given object exhibits the form of purposiveness in its mere apprehension, which is precisely what would be required if it were to function as a determinate concept capable of resolving disputes.

The concept can likewise lay claim to being an idea of reason, or at least to involve such an idea. After all, in the first *Critique*, purposiveness in general and the closely connected notion of systematicity, which corresponds to the formal or logical purposiveness of the third *Critique*, are explicitly treated as ideas because they reflect the unity of reason, which is just that of a system, that is, an ordered whole governed by a unifying principle.[27] In fact, Kant there says of purposive unity that the idea of such unity is inseparably bound up with the very nature of our reason" (A695/B723). To be sure, in the third *Critique*, purposiveness is attributed to reflective judgment as its unique *a priori* principle or "category." But even here the connection with reason is not denied.

The basic point is one with which we are already familiar from the discussion in Chapter 6 of Kant's definitions of purpose and purposiveness in §10.[28] As we saw there, to view an object as a purpose is to consider it as the product of an intelligent causality, that is, of a rational will aiming at a determinate end. Correlatively, to view it as purposive (but without attributing to it a definite purpose) is to consider it as if it were the product of such a causality, even though we cannot know it to be such. But to think of it in this way is to attribute its "form," that is, its purposive or designlike appearance, to a supersensible ground or substrate. Consequently, assuming that beauty, construed as the form of purposiveness, is the indeterminable concept that Kant has in mind in §57, the introduction of the supersensible is perfectly appropriate.

This reading also makes it possible to remove the appearance of a conflict between the appeal to the supersensible in §57 and the affirmation of what Kant terms the "idealism of purposiveness" in §58. Since by such "idealism" Kant means essentially the denial that natural beauty indicates any real purposiveness on the part of nature (or its author), it is sometimes thought that he here takes back much of what was claimed about the reference to the supersensible in the preceding section.[29] In fact, most of the section is devoted to the offering of naturalistic, that is, mechanistic, explanations of the production of natural phenomena such as crystal formations that are often judged beautiful. In addition to linking the antinomy of taste explicitly with transcendental idealism, Kant's intent in this curious section seems to be partly to block unwarranted ventures into a dogmatic teleology occasioned by reflection on the diverse beauties of nature and partly to underscore the autonomy of taste and its principle. Thus, echoing themes from the Analytic and the Deduction, Kant insists that "beauty is not a characteristic of the object considered in its own right" [*für sich betrachtet*] (KU 5: 347; 221), and that it is "we who receive nature with favor, not nature that favors us" (KU 5: 350; 224). Kant is here appealing to the by-now familiar Copernican principle that if the standard of beauty is sought in nature (or the intention of the artist) rather than in ourselves, that is, if we must conform our judgment to the object, rather than the object to our manner of judgment, then the universality and necessity of the pure judgment of taste (what he here terms the "rationalism of taste") would be lost.

None of this conflicts with §57, however, if we take the indeterminable concept to be that of the form of purposiveness. To the contrary, the form of purposiveness entails the idealism of purposiveness as Kant construes it. For to say of an object that it exhibits such a form is not to attribute to it a determinate property that it possesses in its own right, but merely to assert that it seems as if designed with our cognitive capacities in mind (though we have no grounds for assuming that it really was). In short, by "form" is here again to be understood "mere form," which carries with it no ontological implications. Similarly, it is "we who receive nature with favor" because it is we who place a value on it (and art) in judging it to conform to our own heautonomous norm.

Finally, this subjectification of purposiveness, which is really nothing more than its relativization to reflective judgment, does not render otiose the appeal to the idea of the supersensible. For this is likewise a matter of how we view nature, insofar as we take it to exhibit the form of purposiveness in objects deemed beautiful. Since to claim that nature exhibits such forms is to claim that it appears (aesthetically) as if designed for us, one cannot entertain this thought without referring to the idea of a designer, and, therefore, to that of a supersensible substrate of nature. Moreover, it is precisely because it occasions such a thought that the experience of natural beauty serves to facilitate the transition "from our way of thinking in terms of principles of nature to our way of thinking in terms of principles of freedom" (KU 5: 176; 15).

Similar considerations also apply to the other dimension of the supersensible, namely, the "supersensible within" or, as Kant here terms it, "the supersensible substrate of humanity." The key to Kant's position lies in the previously cited claim in the Second Introduction that

> The spontaneity in the play of the cognitive faculties, whose harmony with each other contains the ground of this pleasure, makes that concept of purposiveness suitable for mediating the connection of the domain of the concept of nature with that of the concept of freedom, as regards freedom's consequences, inasmuch as this harmony also promotes the mind's receptivity to moral feeling. (KU 5: 197; 37–8).

When first considering this sentence in Chapter 9, I focused on the reference to the spontaneity in the play of the cognitive faculties. The suggestion was that at least part of what Kant was doing there was indicating the connection between this spontaneity and freedom. It is not that Kant intended either to identify such spontaneity with freedom or to claim that it somehow entailed it. It was, rather, to suggest that the thought of this spontaneity (though not of itself that of freedom) points to something supersensible in us, that is, something that cannot be explained naturalistically, which, on the basis of our consciousness of the moral law, is subsequently determinable from a practical point of view as freedom. In short, it gives determinability to the supersensible within in a manner paralleling the way in which the concept of purposiveness gives determinability to the supersensible without.[30]

This, then, is surely part of what Kant has in mind in §57, when he connects the resolution of the antinomy with the idea of a supersensible within, but it is not all. Of equal or perhaps even greater importance, since it directly concerns the promotion of the mind's receptivity to moral feeling, is the disinterested nature of the liking arising from the free harmony of the cognitive faculties. As we shall see in more detail later in this chapter, the independence of this liking from any sensuous interest both points to a capacity of those with taste to transcend an attachment to the purely sensuous enjoyment of the agreeable (which is a necessary, though not a sufficient, condition of an attachment to the morally good) and enables the cultivation of taste to serve as a preparation to morality.

For the present, however, our concern is with the fourth and last of the claims made at the beginning of §57, namely, that the illusion that arises from the confusion of the two senses of the concept appealed to by the thesis and antithesis in the antinomy of taste is "natural and unavoidable." In claiming this, Kant is clearly attempting to link this antinomy to the doctrine of transcendental illusion that underlies the entire Transcendental Dialectic in the first *Critique*. Reduced to its essentials, this doctrine holds that in following its own prescriptive law of seeking the totality of conditions for a given conditioned (which we may think of as a quest for complete explanation or closure), reason naturally and inevitably assumes that this totality and, therefore, the unconditioned is itself "given" in the sense of being accessible (in principle) to thought.[31] This assumption is natural because reason makes it in the ordinary course of seeking conditions; and it is inevitable because reason cannot coherently seek conditions without assuming that they are there to be found. At the same time, however, Kant also insists that it is illusory, since it assumes that what holds true in the logical sphere (the necessity of a complete set of premises for any conclusion) also holds of reality. In fact, in the Transcendental Dialectic, Kant argues that all of the errors of traditional metaphysics arise from being taken in by this illusion. He further claims that, since it is inevitable, this illusion cannot be eliminated, not even by a critique of pure reason. What such a critique can do, however, is enable one to avoid being deceived by it, and thus avoid the fallacious inferences of traditional metaphysics.[32]

Admittedly, this line of thought is not obviously transferable to the antinomy of taste, which does not seem to involve any metaphysical inferences of the kind dismissed as illusory in the first *Critique*. Moreover, Kant does precious little to spell out the connection he has in mind. Instead, he baldly asserts that by showing that the two sides are compatible, the resolution of the antinomy will also make comprehensible why the illusion is natural and unavoidable to human reason, and why it remains after the resolution, even though it ceases to deceive us (KU 5: 340; 213).

Nevertheless, the overall discussion of the antinomy does offer two clues on the basis of which it seems possible to reconstruct Kant's underlying line of thought. First, as we have already seen, at the very beginning of §57 he indicates that the supposedly natural and unavoidable illusion arises from a confusion of two senses of the concept to which we refer the object in the judgment of taste (KU 5: 339; 211). Second, in the second comment attached to §57, while discussing the antinomies in all three *Critiques*, Kant indicates that the antinomy of taste is really an antinomy of *reason* [my emphasis] concerning the faculty of aesthetic judgment and, as such, stems from reason's demand of the unconditioned for a given conditioned (KU 5: 345; 218).

Beginning with the latter point, what represents the "conditioned" here is the particular aesthetic evaluation: "This object is beautiful" (or not beautiful). Thus, to say that reason demands the "unconditioned" for the given conditioned is to say that it demands the complete and sufficient ground for the determination of the judgment (the aesthetic analogue of the sufficient set of premises presupposed by the conclusion in a logical judgment or syllogism).[33] But this ground is to be found only in the concept to which the object is referred in the judgment. Accordingly, the underlying assumption, shared by both sides, is that if there is something like a fact of the matter regarding taste, that is, something conditioned in the forementioned sense, then there must be a concept serving as its ultimate ground. Moreover, since serving as such a ground is thought to involve providing the complete set of conditions requisite for the determination of the judgment, it follows that this concept is naturally and inevitably taken as fully determinate.

Once one introduces the distinction between determinate and indeterminate and indeterminable concepts, the illusion supposedly loses its grip on us, since we can then see that the inference from "There must be a concept as underlying ground" to "This concept must be determinate and, as such, provide a rule for resolving disputes regarding taste" is fallacious. Nevertheless, the underlying illusion remains in place, since it continues to be natural to view all concepts in this way, that is, as concepts of the understanding.

Finally, since we have seen that an indeterminable concept is an idea of reason and that the latter is the concept of a supersensible substrate, and since the supersensible (according to the critical theory of sensibility) must be understood as qualitatively distinct from everything sensible, it follows that the distinction between the two kinds of concept necessary to avoid being deceived by the illusion and, therefore, resolving the antinomy, depends crucially upon the transcendental distinction between the sensible and the supersensible. But this distinction is equivalent to the distinction between things considered as they appear (the sensible) and things considered as they are in themselves or, equivalently, as some "pure understanding" might think them (the supersensible), which is the essence of transcendental idealism.[34] Thus, Kant can legitimately claim, as he does in §58, that the resolution of the antinomy, like those of the other two *Critiques*, leads ultimately to transcendental idealism.[35]

IV

If the preceding analysis is correct, it follows that Kant's resolution of the antinomy by means of an appeal to the indeterminable concept of the supersensible is neither a desperate attempt to bolster the original deduction of taste nor a mere exercise in architectonics. As suggested at the beginning of the chapter, it is, instead, an attempt to lay the foundation for the account of beauty as the symbol of morality in §59. As was also suggested, the latter is the culmination not only of the Dialectic but also of the Critique of Aesthetic Judgment as a whole, since it provides the richest account of how beauty (both natural and artistic) mediates between nature and freedom.

Kant begins his account of this symbolization with a discussion of the by-now familiar topic of exhibition, particularly the exhibition of ideas of reason. Once again, the underlying principle is that concepts of the understanding can be directly exhibited in intuition or schematized, whereas ideas of reason, because of their distance from everything sensible, cannot. But rather than concluding from this that ideas cannot be exhibited in any sense, Kant now suggests that they can be indirectly exhibited by means of symbols, with the latter functionally defined as intuitions that exhibit a conceptual content in an indirect fashion by means of an analogy (KU 5: 351–2; 226–7).

Although the basic thesis that ideas of reason (including the moral law) both require and are capable of some kind of indirect exhibition or analogue of schematization is already to be found in the first two *Critiques*, its characterization as a symbolic exhibition and its connection with reflective judgment are contributions of the third.[36] According to this account, what is directly presented [*darstellt*] in a case of indirect exhibition or "symbolic *hypotyposis*" is not the idea to be symbolized but some other (schematizable) concept. The representation of the object, which is the sensible realization of this latter concept, then functions as the symbolic exhibition of the initial (unschematizable) idea just in case judgment's reflection on it is formally analogous to the form of reflection on the original idea (KU 5: 351; 226). As Kant indicates, this procedure involves a double function of judgment (one quasi-determinative and the other reflective). In the first, judgment applies the concept to be symbolized to the object of a sensible intuition, and in the second it applies the rule for reflecting on the former object to the thought of an entirely different object, which supposedly corresponds to the original idea (KU 5: 352; 227).

Kant illustrates this by the examples of a constitutional monarchy governed by the rule of law, which is symbolized by an animate body, and a monarchy governed by an individual will, which is symbolized by a handmill. The point is that even though there is no resemblance between these two types of institution and the two types of physical object, there is one between the nature of our reflection on each. Thus, in reflecting on an animate body, one necessarily appeals to the idea of a purposive, organic connection between the parts, which is supposedly also appropriate to the thought of the *modus operandi* of a constitutional monarchy. By contrast, a handmill suggests the thought of a mere machine, which supposedly captures metaphorically the functioning of a despotic government.

The key to this account of symbolization is the idea of a formally analogous reflection, which in the examples cited seems to concern the manner in which the relationship between the whole and its parts is conceived. More generally, the analogy concerns the rule or organizing principle that governs reflection on the sensible and intellectual objects, respectively. When these rules of reflection are sufficiently analogous, the former may serve as a symbol of the latter.[37] Consequently, to claim that beauty symbolizes morality is to claim that there is a sufficiently significant isomorphism between reflection on the beautiful and moral reflection so that the former activity may be regarded as a sensuously directed analogue of the latter.[38]

To leave it at that, however, is to ignore an essential difference between the two types of reflection, which Kant's cryptic account of symbolization glosses over. This difference stems from the purely aesthetic nature of the judgment of taste, that is, from the fact that, unlike moral judgment or reflection, a judgment of taste is not based on a determinate concept.[39] For this suggests an important question with which Kant does not deal explicitly, namely, how can the mere reflection on a sensible intuition, which *ex hypothesi* is not governed by a determinate concept, be viewed as formally analogous to the explicitly rule-governed reflection on the corresponding intellectual object? This question does not arise in the case of Kant's examples, since they each involve a reflection based on determinate concepts (of a handmill and an organism), whereas this is precisely what is supposedly lacking in the mere reflection of taste.[40]

The answer, I shall try to show, lies in Kant's conception of aesthetic ideas, which he first introduces in §49 in connection with the discussion of genius, and returns to in the first comment added to §57 in connection with the introduction of the concept of the supersensible.[41] Thus, even though Kant does not refer to it explicitly in §59, I am suggesting that this conception is central to the understanding of his account of how beauty symbolizes morality and, therefore, of the mediating function of the beautiful.[42]

Kant initially defines an aesthetic idea as "a representation of the imagination which prompts much thought, but to which no determinate thought whatsoever, i.e., no *concept*, can be adequate, so that no language can express it completely and allow us to grasp it" (KU 5: 314; 182). Later he characterizes such ideas as "inexponible [*inexponible*] representations of the imagination (in its free play)" (KU 5: 343; 217). Since to expound an intuition means to bring it under concepts, an inexponible intuition is just one that cannot be completely determined conceptually. Thus, aesthetic ideas may be described as intuitions produced by the imagination in its free play that cannot be brought under concepts, at least not completely. In both places Kant contrasts them with rational ideas or ideas of reason, understood in the usual manner as "concepts to which no *intuition* (representation of the imagination) can correspond" (KU 5: 314; 182) or, more simply, as "indemonstrable concepts of reason" (KU 5: 342; 215), where to demonstrate means to exhibit a concept in intuition.

For present purposes, however, our main concern is with the two reasons Kant offers for characterizing these products of the imagination as "ideas." The first may be termed their quasi-schematizing function. As Kant initially puts it, "[T]hey do at least strive toward something that lies beyond the bounds of experience, and hence try to approach an exhibition of rational concepts (intellectual ideas), which gives to the latter the semblance [*Anschein*] of objective reality" (KU 5: 314; 182). The second reason may be described as their transcendent pretensions. Kant puts the point by stating that, though they are inner intuitions, they share with ideas of reason the feature of not being completely determinable by a concept (of the understanding) (KU 5: 314; 182–3). The latter is because they either attempt to depict something explicitly supersensible (such as the poet's depiction of heaven, hell, eternity, creation, and the like) or they emulate ideas of reason in striving for a maximum, that is, for a completeness in the representation of something sensible "for which no example can be found in nature." As examples of this emulation, Kant offers poetic depictions of such things as "death, envy and all the other vices, as well as love, fame, etc." (KU 5: 314; 183).[43]

Kant clearly indicates that the second of these two reasons for calling these inner intuitions "ideas" is the main one (KU 5: 314; 182)\, but he neglects to point out that this is because it is presupposed by the first. In other words, aesthetic ideas may serve as indirect exhibitions of their rational counterparts precisely because they necessarily involve a striving toward transcendence, either in the sense of endeavoring to depict something inherently supersensible or of attempting to approximate imaginatively the completeness or totality that is thought in the idea but not attainable in experience. Moreover, for our purposes, this turns out to be the crucial point; for it is precisely by means of aesthetic ideas that indirectly exhibit ideas of reason (in virtue of their analogous ways of gesturing to the supersensible) that beauty (both natural and artistic) functions aesthetically, that is, apart from a determinate concept, as a symbol of morality.

In an effort to substantiate this claim, I shall here consider briefly some of the details of Kant's account of such ideas, saving a fuller discussion (which includes their connection with genius) for Chapter 12. To begin with, Kant connects the formation of aesthetic ideas with the productive capacity of the imagination. The imagination in its freedom (from the laws of association) links the thought of something supersensible with a wealth of sensible representations or images, which does not amount to a logical expansion of the concept (through additional predicates), but does constitute an "aesthetic expansion," through the connection of the core concept (say, that of God or eternity) with these sensible representations that call to mind related or associated thoughts. These, in turn, may be said to "prompt much thought" (presumably concerning the concept in question), and therefore lead to an expansion of the mind, albeit in an indeterminate manner (KU 5: 315; 183).[44]

Significantly, Kant terms these supplementary representations involved in the aesthetic expansion of a rational idea "aesthetic attributes," thereby indicating both their analogy to, and difference from, the logical attributes through which a concept is supposedly expanded in a logical, that is, cognitive, synthetic judgment. As examples of such "attributes," he cites Jupiter's eagle with the bolt of lightning in its craw, which is supposedly an attribute of the king of heaven, and the peacock, which serves as an attribute of heaven's stately queen (KU 5: 315; 183). Unlike logical attributes, these are not taken to refer to actual properties of what is supposedly represented or exhibited through them, namely, the sublimity and greatness of creation (the actual content of the thought). Nevertheless, Kant suggests that they function to expand the mind's thought of the latter in ways that cannot be captured in language (KU 5: 315; 183). As he later puts it, they enable us to add to the thought (the pure rational idea) "much that is ineffable" (KU 5: 316; 185).

Kant also indicates that these aesthetic attributes "yield [*geben*] an aesthetic idea, which serves the rational idea as a "substitute for a logical exhibition" (KU 5: 315; 183). The claim that they "yield" an aesthetic idea suggests that such ideas are to be viewed as collections of aesthetic attributes. As we shall see in more detail in Chapter 12, however, aesthetic ideas are no more to be conceived as mere collections of such attributes than ordinary concepts are to be conceived as mere collections of logical attributes or marks. In both cases, a rule or ordering principle is required, though in the case of aesthetic ideas it remains indeterminate. Thus, by an aesthetic idea may be understood an indeterminately, that is, aesthetically, ordered set of aesthetic attributes.[45] Since this order is indeterminate, the rule unifying the components of an aesthetic idea obviously cannot be precisely defined. Nevertheless, one might think of it as something like a principle for the selection and organization of aesthetic attributes, such that they constitute a meaningful and aesthetically pleasing whole.

More important for present purposes is the claim that aesthetic ideas serve rational ideas as a "substitute for a logical exhibition." This follows directly from the first of the forementioned reasons for calling them ideas, and it entails that they function as symbols in the sense indicated in §59. Indeed, such ideas fit perfectly our functional definition of a symbol as an intuition that exhibits a conceptual content in an indirect fashion by means of an analogy. The point is not that all such symbols are aesthetic ideas but, rather, that these ideas constitute a significant subset of possible symbols of rational ideas, namely, those that express or exhibit the corresponding idea independently of a determinate concept. Consequently, this explains how the beautiful (by means of aesthetic ideas) may be said to symbolize ideas of reason.

Before proceeding further, however, it is essential to keep in mind that this analysis applies to *natural* as well as to artistic beauty. The application to natural beauty might seem problematic in view of the explicit connection between such ideas and genius, which is the centerpiece of Kant's analysis of fine art. But in a perplexing though much-discussed passage at the beginning of his account of the specific forms of fine art, Kant proclaims that "We may in general call beauty (whether natural or artistic) the *expression* of aesthetic ideas" (KU 5: 320; 189). We shall consider how natural beauty may be said to express aesthetic ideas shortly, and the broader questions of why the expression of aesthetic ideas should be viewed as criterial for beauty and its compatibility with the formalism of the third moment will be among the central concerns of Chapter 12. For present purposes, we need only note that Kant does view natural beauty as expressing aesthetic ideas, which means that an account of symbolization in light of the latter would be applicable to both species of beauty.

Nevertheless, this does not suffice to explain how the beautiful (whether natural or artistic) symbolizes *morality*. Clearly, if one were simply to identify all rational ideas with moral ideas, this would follow as a matter of course, since in symbolizing any rational idea the beautiful would also be symbolizing morality. But it is highly doubtful that this is what Kant intended.[46] To begin with, some of his own examples of rational ideas that are supposedly symbolized aesthetically, namely envy and other vices, hell, eternity, and so forth, speak against any such facile identification. Admittedly, all of these ideas might be said to relate to morality in a broad sense, though in the case of other ideas, for example, the infinite, the connection would be more tenuous. Even if we were to assume for the sake of argument, however, that all rational ideas have *some* relation to morality, this would still not give Kant all that he needs. For though he begins §59 referring to the beautiful simply as a symbol of morality, he later makes clear that he intends this to mean that it symbolizes the morally good [*Sittlich-Guten*] (KU 5: 353; 228). But it remains far from obvious how an aesthetic idea, symbolizing, say, envy, may thereby be claimed to be symbolizing something morally good, not to mention *the* morally good itself.[47]

One possible way out of this difficulty is simply to deny that *everything* beautiful symbolizes the morally good. On this reading, though everything beautiful expresses aesthetic ideas, only some beautiful objects would express ideas of moral goodness, and therefore only those objects could be said to symbolize morality in the appropriate sense.[48] In addition to the already cited examples of aesthetic ideas and the rational ideas they purportedly symbolize, at least some support for such a view is provided by Kant's reflections on artistic beauty. Thus, after distinguishing between art that, in virtue of its purposive form, attunes the spirit to ideas and art that, by aiming at mere enjoyment through the matter of sensation (charm and emotion), eventually enervates the spirit and produces disgust with the object formerly liked, Kant writes:

> Unless we connect the fine arts, closely or remotely, with moral ideas, which alone carry with them an independent liking, the second of the two alternatives just mentioned is their ultimate fate. They serve in that case only for our diversion, which we need all the more in proportion as we use it to dispel the mind's dissatisfaction with itself, with the result that we increase still further our uselessness and dissatisfaction with ourselves. For the first

of the two alternatives, it is generally the beauties of nature that are most beneficial, if we are habituated early to observe, judge, and admire them. (KU 5: 326; 196)

Assuming that Kant is here referring to works of fine art that are appropriately deemed beautiful, rather than to putative works that aim merely at enjoyment, the clear implication of this passage seems to be that such works may, but need not, express aesthetically any moral ideas. Otherwise there would be no need to bring them into connection (either closely or remotely) with such ideas in order to avoid the deleterious consequences indicated. But if to symbolize morality is to express moral ideas aesthetically, that is, in the form of aesthetic ideas, then it apparently follows that not all beauty, at least not all artistic beauty, symbolizes morality.

Nevertheless, in spite of passages such as this and the apparent disparagement of the moral significance of fine art considered in Chapter 10, it seems implausible to attribute this view to Kant. For the claim of §59 is that the beautiful as such symbolizes the morally good (not simply that some beautiful objects do so), and the same conclusion seems to be required by the underlying assumption of an isomorphism between reflection on the beautiful and on the morally good. Again, this isomorphism must apply to *all* reflection on the beautiful (both natural and artistic), not merely to the subset of beautiful objects that exhibit or express moral ideas. Consequently, it seems that we must either abandon the hypothesis that beauty's symbolization of morality is to be understood in terms of its expression of aesthetic ideas or explain how, on the basis of this conception of aesthetic ideas, it can symbolize morality without expressing moral ideas.

Although Kant never deals explicitly with this problem, I believe that his accounts of aesthetic ideas and the symbolization process (cryptic and incomplete as they may be) provide what is needed for a positive resolution. Once again, the key point is that aesthetic ideas involve a striving toward transcendence or a gesturing to the supersensible, either through the depiction of something inherently supersensible (for example, God, freedom, or immortality) or through their endeavor to express a totality or completeness that exceeds what is exhibitable in experience. Moreover, it is in virtue of this formal feature, which pertains to aesthetic ideas as such, that they "serve as a substitute for a logical exhibition" and therefore as a symbol. In other words, in expanding the mind and "prompting much thought," (albeit of an indeterminate kind) aesthetic ideas lead the mind of someone engaged in the contemplation of beauty from something sensible to the supersensible.

Given this, the claim is simply that it is in virtue of the same formal feature through which aesthetic ideas symbolize ideas of reason that they also symbolize morality, *whether or not the particular ideas they evoke are di-*

rectly related to morality. This is because such reflection is formally isomorphic with reflection on the morally good, particularly if we understand by the latter what the second *Critique* terms the "object of pure practical reason," that is, the objective or end of moral endeavor, which thought in its completeness or totality is the highest good in the world.[49] For though reflection on such an object starts with something sensible, since it concerns an end that is to be realized in the world, it necessarily proceeds to the supersensible idea of its completion, which can never be exhibited in experience, and from this to the supersensible conditions of its realization (the postulated ideas of God, freedom, and immortality).

Admittedly, this yields a purely formal and, indeed, minimalist conception of how the beautiful symbolizes morality. Nevertheless, such a conception seems unavoidable if, as Kant presumably intends, we are to preserve its application to *all* reflection on the beautiful and, therefore, to both natural and artistic beauty.[50] Moreover, Kant clearly indicates his own adherence to a formalistic analysis of the relation between reflection on the beautiful and on the morally good when he attempts to summarize the basic similarities (and differences) between them in terms of four main points: (1) Both involve a direct liking (although the liking for the beautiful is based on reflection on an intuition and that for the good on a concept). (2) Both likings are independent of interest (although, again, the liking for the morally good directly gives rise to one). (3) Both involve the harmony of freedom with law (in the case of the judgment of taste it is the harmony of the imagination in its freedom with the lawfulness of the understanding, and in the case of the moral judgment, the harmony of the free will with itself according to laws of reason). (4) Both involve the thought of universal validity (in the case of the beautiful this is not determinable through any universal concept, whereas in the case of the morally good it is so determinable) (KU 5: 354; 229).

To the extent to which the symbolic relation between the beautiful and the morally good is based on these factors, it is unquestionably formal; but it should not be inferred from this that it therefore has nothing to do with aesthetic ideas.[51] For even though there is no reference to aesthetic ideas on the list (nor anywhere in §59 for that matter), they remain an essential presupposition of the whole account. This is clear from the first point of comparison: the fact that the liking for the beautiful is based on reflection on an intuition and that for the good on a concept. Recall that, in our initial discussion of the symbolic relation, it was suggested that an appeal to aesthetic ideas is necessary precisely in order to understand how there could be an isomorphism between a reflection based on an intuition and one on a concept. Thus, if this is correct, it follows that Kant cannot spell out the formal analogy between these two qualitatively distinct species of liking without appealing (at least implicitly) to his doctrine of aesthetic ideas.

Moreover, it must be emphasized that this formalistic account, which is required in order to understand how all beauty can be claimed to symbolize morality, does not preclude the possibility that some beautiful objects may also symbolize morality in a secondary but more substantive sense. Presumably, this occurs when, in addition to occasioning a form of reflection isomorphic with reflection on the morally good, they also evoke (through their aesthetic attributes) specific moral ideas.

The latter point is suggested by Kant's previously cited remarks about the beauty of fine art, but it is perhaps best illustrated by his account of natural beauty. This account is connected with Kant's previously noted claim that natural (as well as artistic) beauty expresses aesthetic ideas. Thus, we revisit this passage, this time citing Kant's claim in its entirety:

> We may in general call beauty (whether natural or artistic) the *expression* of aesthetic ideas; the difference is that in the case of beautiful art the aesthetic idea must be prompted by a concept of the object, whereas in the case of beautiful nature, mere reflection on a given intuition, without a concept of what the object is intended to be [*sein soll*], is sufficient for arousing and communicating the idea of which the object is regarded as the *expression*. (KU 5: 320; 189)[52]

For present purposes at least, the main interest of this passage lies in the way in which natural beauty is said to express aesthetic ideas, namely, through a mere reflection on the intuition of an object, apart from any concept of some purpose the object might serve (which would render the ensuing judgment teleological rather than aesthetic). And of particular significance in this regard is that such reflection is deemed sufficient to communicate an idea expressed by the object reflected upon.

The reference to communication seems to take us beyond the purely formal isomorphism that applies to reflection on the beautiful as such and suggests the idea of some specifically moral content that might also be communicated symbolically through aesthetic ideas. Moreover, though I cannot be certain that this is what Kant had in mind, our previous discussion of an intellectual interest in natural beauty suggests at least one significant candidate for a specifically moral idea that might be evoked by an engagement with natural beauty, namely, nature's moral purposiveness. For since all natural beauty is based on an object's exhibition of the form of purposiveness, and since to attribute such a form to an object is to view it as if designed with our cognitive capacities in mind, it follows that reflection on natural beauty naturally evokes the distinct but related thought of nature's moral purposiveness. In this sense, then, all natural beauty may be said to express or symbolize the same rational idea; and, as we saw in Chapter 10, this is the basis of the "duty, as it were," to take an intellectual interest in such beauty. Presumably, then, this is at least part of what Kant meant when, in commenting on the kinship between aesthetic and moral feeling, he refers mysteriously to that "cipher through which nature speaks to us figuratively in its beautiful forms" (KU 5: 301; 168).[53]

In addition to nature's moral purposiveness, there seems to be no reason why natural beauties cannot also express or symbolize other, more specific, moral ideas in a manner analogous to that of beautiful works of art. In fact, Kant claims precisely this for the charms of beautiful nature, which, he suggests, often seem fused with beautiful form, and which "contain, as it were, a language through which nature speaks to us and which seems to have a higher meaning" (KU 5: 302; 169). And, in an attempt to illustrate this by means of colors, Kant remarks:

> Thus a lily's white color seems to attune the mind to ideas of innocence, and the seven colors [of the spectrum], from red to violet, [similarly seem to attune it, respectively, to the ideas of] sublimity, (2) courage, (3) candor, (4) friendliness, (5) modesty, (6) constancy, and (7) tenderness. (KU 5: 302; 169)[54]

Unfortunately, apart from suggesting immediately after this remark that a bird's song "proclaims his joyfulness and contentment with existence," and a somewhat similar statement concerning trees, landscapes, and colors at the end of §59 (KU 5: 354; 230), this is really all that Kant has to say explicitly on the topic. Nevertheless, putting this together with our previous results, it suggests a fairly complex picture in which natural beauty symbolizes morality at three levels: First, there is the purely formal level of reflective isomorphism that it shares with artistic beauty; second, there is its expression of the idea of nature's moral purposiveness, which is the main superiority it holds over artistic beauty; and third is the capacity of some natural beauties, likewise possessed by some artistic beauties, to express aesthetically particular moral ideas. But, of course, at none of these levels is it a matter of assigning determinate purposes [Absichten] to nature (or its author), since that is incompatible with the idealism of purposiveness on which Kant insisted in §58.[55]

Finally, if this picture is basically correct, it enables us to understand how Kant could both privilege natural beauty from a moral point of view (as he undoubtedly did) yet not totally deny moral significance to artistic beauty (which he apparently did not intend to do).[56] Expressed in terms of Kant's distinction between the different dimensions of the supersensible, the point would be that, since its manner of symbolizing morality involves the idea of nature's moral purposiveness, natural beauty may be said to bring about a transition to the supersensible without as well as within, while an engagement with artistic beauty promotes primarily a transition to the supersensible within.[57]

V

After this lengthy consideration of the antinomy and its resolution, we are finally in a position to return to the question posed at the beginning of this chapter, namely, how does beauty (both natural and artistic) contribute to morality in virtue of symbolizing it? The short answer, of which there are intimations scattered throughout the text, is that it does so by providing a pleasing propaedeutic to, or preparation for, the serious business of morality that is not already of itself moral.[58]

Kant had already given an indication of this propaedeutic function in the "General Comment on the Exposition of Aesthetic Reflective Judgments," prior to the "official" account of symbolization, when he remarked that "The beautiful prepares us for loving something, even nature, without interest" (KU 5: 267; 127).[59] And this, in turn, calls to mind the passage from the *Metaphysics of Morals* cited at the end of Chapter 10. Perhaps his clearest statement of this point, however, is at the end of §59, where from the fact that beauty symbolizes the morally good he concludes:

> Taste enables us, as it were, to make the transition from sensible charm to a habitual moral interest without making too violent a leap; for taste presents the imagination as admitting, even in its freedom, of determination that is purposive for the understanding, and it teaches us to like even objects of sense freely, even apart from sensible charm. (KU 5:354; 230)

The main reason for taste's capacity to effect such a transition should be apparent from the preceding analysis of the reflective isomorphism between the beautiful and the morally good. Insofar as reflection on the beautiful necessarily involves a transition to the supersensible, it mirrors the basic movement of moral reflection. In other words, it is not that taste contributes to the transition (and, therefore, to morality) because it symbolizes morality, but rather that it symbolizes morality because it already of itself (independently of morality) involves a transition from the sensible to the supersensible. As Kant puts the point in connection with his discussion of interest and a presumed link between beauty and an accompanying moral idea, "[I]t is not this link that interests us directly, but rather the beauty's own characteristic of qualifying for such a link, which therefore belongs to it intrinsically" (KU 5: 302; 168–9). Applying this to the present context, we can say that it is precisely by means of its intrinsic characteristic, through which it qualifies as such a link, that beauty symbolizes morality. Indeed, as Guyer has emphasized, it is only on this basis that the autonomy of taste can be reconciled with its moral significance.[60]

Moreover, as we have already seen, though the transition effected through reflection on the beautiful is not itself a transition to morality, it does facilitate that transition. It does so because it involves, on the one hand, an attempt to set aside all interests or likings stemming from one's sensuous nature (the agreeable) and, on the other, the adoption of a universalistic standpoint that is at least analogous to the standpoint taken by the autonomous moral agent as a legislative member of a kingdom of ends. In other words, it involves both a distancing from the sensuous side of the self through a liking that is not sensuously based because it is "free" (though it does refer to a sensible object), and the thought of oneself as a member of an ideal community subject to a universally valid norm.

The latter feature of Kant's account, which has been largely neglected till now (though it was alluded to at the beginning of Chapter 10), is intimately connected with his characterization of taste as a *sensus communis* in §22 and §40. In insisting in the latter place that taste (the *sensus communis aestheticus*) has more of a right to that honorific title than the common human understanding (or *sensus communis logicus*), Kant focuses on the universalism inherent in the judgment of taste. Thus, he notes that he is there taking *sensus communis* to refer to "the idea of a public sense [*gemeinschaftlichen Sinnes*],[61] i.e., a capacity to judge that in reflecting takes account *(a priori)*, in our thought, of everyone else's way of representing, in order *as it were* to compare our own judgment with human reason in general" (KU 5: 293; 160). And, in further clarifying this process, Kant remarks that "we compare our judgment not so much with the actual as with the merely possible judgment of others"; and, finally, he adds significantly that this is accomplished by "abstracting from the limitations that happen to attach to our own judging," which we do by "leaving out as much as possible whatever is matter, i.e., sensation, in the representational state, and by paying attention solely to the formal features of our representation or our representational state" (KU 5: 294; 160). As already noted, the process of aesthetic reflection here described is not equivalent to moral reflection; but it is formally analogous to it. Moreover, for this very reason it provides a valuable preparation for morality.[62]

Once again, however, it must be emphasized that the fact that the beautiful symbolizes morality in the manner here described qualifies it merely as a *preparation* for morality. In other words, it does not elevate taste into either an ingredient in morality itself or a necessary condition of a good will. Consequently, though Kant does not himself make the point, the requirement to appreciate beauty and to develop the capacity to do so, that is, taste, must be seen as a matter of moral facilitation and, therefore, merely as a duty, as it were, or indirect duty. A good will obviously requires the kind of distancing from sensuous interest that taste involves, but Kant certainly would not wish to claim that this aesthetic distancing is either necessary or sufficient for moral distancing. The former would have to be rejected because it rules out the possibility of a good will for those who simply lack the physical capacities or opportunity to appreciate beauty, the latter because it would require attributing such a will to the aesthete. Nevertheless, keeping in mind the background doctrine of radical evil, it does seem reasonable to claim that by helping to wean us from too great an attachment to sensuous satisfaction, and by providing an alternative standard of evaluation that appeals to our higher cognitive powers and to the judgment of others, the appreciation of beauty can play a significant, albeit auxiliary, role in the moral life.[63]

VI

This, then, brings us to the final issue before us in this part of the study, namely, the connection of this account of the beautiful as a symbol of the morally good with the justificatory project of the Deduction. In spite of everything that has been said up to this point about the division of labor, it might be argued that this account is rendered moot by Kant's own express words in §59, where he states:

> Now I say: the beautiful is the symbol of the morally good; and also that only in this respect [*in dieser Rücksicht*] (a relation [*einer Beziehung*] which is natural to everyone and which everyone also requires from others as a duty), does it please with a claim to the assent of everyone, whereby the mind at the same time becomes conscious of a certain ennoblement and elevation above the mere receptivity of a pleasure through sense impressions and values the worth of others also according to a similar maxim of the faculty of judgment. (KU 5: 353; 228)[64]

Kant is sometimes thought to be claiming here that it is only because the beautiful symbolizes the morally good that the pleasure of taste can be demanded (as a duty) from everyone. According to this reading, then, the demand of taste (the aesthetic "ought") is reduced to the straightforwardly moral demand to be sensitive to symbols of morality and, ultimately, to be morally sensitive.[65]

Nevertheless, this passage is hardly unambiguous. For though it can certainly be read in this way, it can equally well be taken as affirming virtually the opposite thesis, namely, that it is precisely because the beautiful pleases in a way that permits the pure judgment of taste to lay claim to the assent of everyone that it symbolizes morality. In other words, on this alternative reading, what underlies the demand for universal agreement in a pure judgment of taste, and therefore accounts for its normativity, is not an antecedent connection with morality, but rather the form of reflection it involves, one which, as we have seen, includes a distancing from sensuous interests, a harmony of freedom and lawfulness, and the adoption of a universalistic perspective, and so forth. Furthermore, it is in virtue of this very form of reflection, one which is "natural to everyone" and which brings with it a consciousness of a "certain ennoblement" and of the value of the worth of others, and so forth, that the beautiful symbolizes the morally good. And from the fact that the beautiful symbolizes the morally good it follows that we have a duty (in light of the preceding, Kant should have said "duty, as it were" or indirect duty) to attend to the beautiful, since it is precisely the isomorphism between reflection on the beautiful and on the morally good that qualifies the former as a preparation for morality.

Moreover, given the preceding analysis of reflective isomorphism, there seems little doubt about which reading we should prefer. For just as the beautiful does not effect a transition from the sensible to the supersensible because it symbolizes morality, but rather symbolizes morality because it effects such a transition, so, too, the pure judgment of taste does not make a valid demand on others because it symbolizes morality, but rather it is because of the "purity" underlying the validity of its demand that it symbolizes morality. Consequently, only the latter reading preserves the autonomy of taste in the sense of its irreducibility to either the agreeable or the good, while still accounting for its connection with morality as a symbol. Indeed, we might ask how the beautiful could possibly serve as a symbol of morality unless the legitimacy of its demands were assumed independently of this function.[66]

IV

PARERGA TO THE THEORY OF TASTE

FINE ART AND GENIUS

Apart from the treatment of aesthetic and teleological judgment in a single work, perhaps the strangest feature of the *Critique of Judgment*, at least to the post-Hegelian reader for whom "aesthetics" and "philosophy of art" are virtual synonyms, is the fact that it is only near the very end of the portion dealing with aesthetic judgment (§43 to be exact) that Kant turns to the topic of fine art. To be sure, we do not find here the first reference to art and artistic beauty. On the contrary, we have seen that references to them are scattered throughout the Analytic of the Beautiful and the Deduction. And we have also seen that in the sections lying between the Deduction and the discussion of fine art, Kant argues that only natural and not artistic beauty is capable of being connected with an intellectual, morally based interest. Nevertheless, as has been frequently noted in the literature, the whole discussion of fine art and its connection with genius has an episodic character about it that makes it difficult to integrate into the overall argument of the work.[1]

As far as the doctrine of genius is concerned, this is hardly surprising, since Kant's fundamental concern is with the nature of aesthetic *judgment*, not artistic production. In other words, his is what is often termed a "reception aesthetic," rather than a "creation aesthetic."[2] In fact, as we have seen, it is a reception aesthetic in which it is assumed from the start that the same principles govern judgments of both natural and artistic beauty. And given this assumption, together with the systematic importance for Kant of the connection between natural beauty and the purposiveness of nature, it is to be expected that he would privilege natural beauty within his theory of taste.

Even when he turns to the nature of artistic production and its relation to genius, however, Kant continues to be oriented toward the judgment of taste.[3] Thus, his basic concern may be described as accounting for the possibility of a pure judgment of taste regarding fine art. As we shall see, this leads to a question concerning the possibility of a work of fine art itself, the solution to which is provided by the theory of genius.[4] This new problematic is rooted in a tension that has remained dormant up to this point between the general claim that a pure judgment of taste involves an appreciation of purposiveness without purpose (or the mere form of purposiveness) and the requirement that in judging artistic beauty one must be conscious of it as art, that is, as embodying the conscious intent of the artist. As Kant puts it at the beginning of §45, "In a product of fine art we must become conscious that it is art rather than nature, and yet the purposiveness in its form must seem as free from all constraint of chosen rules as if it were a product of mere nature" (KU 5: 306; 173).

It is because I take Kant's account of fine art and genius as intended primarily to resolve this problem (and secondarily to show that, contrary to the initial impression created by the argument of §42, fine art is not without moral significance) that I have characterized this account as "parergonal" to his theory of taste.[5] This is not to suggest, however, that this account is without any real importance or interest; it is merely that its importance and interest remain extrinsic to the theory of taste itself. Like the account of reflective judgment and logical purposiveness discussed in Chapter 1, this account (together with that of the sublime offered in Chapter 13) serves to frame Kant's theory of taste, rather than constituting an essential part of it.[6]

This general viewpoint underlies the orientation of the present chapter. Rather than attempting to provide a complete account of Kant's views on fine art, which would require a book-length study in its own right, I shall focus on a set of problems that arise from Kant's attempt to connect his views on fine art and genius with his underlying theory of taste. Accordingly, the first two of the five sections into which this chapter is divided will be concerned, respectively, with what I take to be the foundational question concerning the conditions presupposed by a pure judgment of artistic beauty and the conception of genius as the key to its resolution. Sections three and four will then deal with two issues that concern the compatibility of central aspects of Kant's account of fine art with the claims of the Analytic of the Beautiful: One is the question of the compatibility of the account of beauty in terms of the expression of aesthetic ideas with the formalism of the third moment of the Analytic. The other, which requires an analysis of the nature of artistic representation in Kant, concerns the compatibility of his account of fine art with the contrast between free and adherent beauty discussed in Chapter 6. As we shall see, this is a problem because Kant's account of fine art seems to suggest that all judgments of artistic beauty are "logically conditioned," which, in turn, appears to be equivalent to claiming that all artistic beauty is merely adherent. Thus, it becomes necessary to revisit the free-adherent beauty distinction in light of Kant's later discussion of fine art. Finally, there is a question about the internal consistency of Kant's account of artistic creation, which I shall discuss briefly in the fifth section. The main problem here is that Kant appears to suggest both that genius is necessary for the production of fine art (§46) and that taste without genius is sufficient (§50).

I

Kant begins his account of fine art (§43) in scholastic fashion by attempting a definition by genus and species. First, the genus art is contrasted with nature as doing [*Tun*], to acting [*handeln*], or operating [*Wirken*]. The basic idea, which governs everything that follows, is that art, as distinguished from nature, is conceived as the product of conscious human intent and skill. In order to be regarded as a work of art, an object must be assumed to have been deliberately created for the sake of some end. Thus, the elaborate hives produced by bees do not count as works of art because they are produced instinctively, rather than consciously. Second, within the realm of such human products and activities, art is further distinguished both from science, as a practical from a theoretical ability, and from mere craft [*Handwerk*].

Interestingly enough, Kant suggests two quite distinct grounds for the latter distinction. One is whether the activity is inherently satisfying, so that it may be undertaken for its own sake, or whether it is disagreeable in its own right and therefore only undertaken as a means to an end (payment). An obvious problem with this way of drawing the art–craft distinction is its arbitrariness, since the same activity can be viewed as highly meaningful and satisfying by one person and as disagreeable and burdensome by another. This does not affect Kant's second way of drawing it, however, which is in terms of the degree of talent required (KU 5: 304; 171). Accordingly, even though Kant himself does not offer a complete definition, art in general may be defined as an intentional activity of human beings that aims at the production of certain objects and that requires a significant degree of specialized skill or talent of some sort. Correlatively, the products of such activity are works of art.

Art so defined, however, is obviously not equivalent to *fine* art [*schöne Kunst*], which is alone the concern of taste. Thus, in an effort to arrive at the required definition, Kant first divides all art into *mechanical* and *aesthetic*, the difference lying in the nature of the end intended. The former aims at making a possible object actual in a way that answers to our cognition of that object; the latter aims simply at arousing pleasure. In other words, whereas the former intends the production of something that is useful for some determinate purpose, the goal of the latter is to produce something that is immediately enjoyable in its own right. This includes both agreeable and fine art, which are distinguished on the basis of the means to which they appeal in order to arouse pleasure. As one would expect from the discussion in the Analytic of the Beautiful, the former aims at arousing pleasure through mere sensations, whereas the latter aims at producing pleasure accompanying representations that are *"ways of cognizing"* [*Erkenntnissarten*] (KU 5: 305; 172).

Assuming that by the latter expression Kant means reflection, the contrast between merely agreeable and fine art amounts to the distinction between art that arouses pleasure directly through sensation and art that occasions a pleasure in reflection. Moreover, Kant confirms this reading at the end of section §44 when, after suggesting that the very concept of the universal communicability of a pleasure carries with it the thought that it must be a pleasure of reflection (rather than sensation), he remarks that the "standard" [*Richtmass*] for fine art "is the reflective faculty of judgment and not sensation" [*Sinnesempfindung*] (KU 5: 306; 173). Since by "standard" Kant here clearly understands the normative ground, principle, or source of the validity of judgments of fine art, this amounts to an application to such judgments of the central claim of the Deduction that the principle of taste is the "subjective formal condition of judgment as such" (KU 5: 287; 151).[7] Thus, this application might be characterized as Kant's much-belated "deduction" of judgments of fine art.

Another noteworthy feature of this section is Kant's emphasis on the socializing function of fine art, although this function is simply affirmed rather than either really explicated or argued for. Thus, after a paragraph devoted to the merely agreeable arts, in which he suggests that some of them, for example, table music [*Tafelmusik*], may themselves fulfill a socializing function by "fostering the free flow of conversation," in spite of the fact that they aim merely at momentary enjoyment, (KU 5: 305; 173), Kant remarks by way of contrast that "Fine art . . . is a way of representing that is purposive on its own and that furthers, even though without a purpose, the culture of our mental powers for social communication" (KU 5: 306; 173). In claiming that fine art is "purposive on its own" [*für sich selbst zweckmässig*], Kant is claiming that it (unlike merely agreeable art) produces purposive forms (material for reflection); and in stating that the enhancement of our capacity for social communication is attained "without a purpose," he seems to be suggesting that this is the effect of the art, though not the intention of the artist.

Kant's serious discussion of fine art begins, however, with §45, which is given the significant heading "Fine Art is an Art insofar as it Seems at the Same Time to be Nature" (KU 5: 306; 173). This heading indicates one-half of the problem of conceptualizing the possibility of fine art, namely, that it must *seem* like nature. The other and equally significant requirement, which Kant perhaps here omits because of its obviousness, is that we must be conscious of it as art (KU 5: 306; 174). Although this may be too obvious to include in the heading, it is not the trivial point that it must *be art*, but rather the substantive claim that we must be *conscious* of it as such. As Kant makes clear, this is because such a consciousness is a precondition of its evaluation as beautiful or, equivalently, as fine art. For unless we were aware of it as the product of a conscious intent, we could not begin to appreciate it as art. Moreover, in light of this twofold requirement, Kant draws a contrast with natural beauty, the latter being regarded as beautiful only if it also looks like art (KU 5: 306; 174).

Although this contrast has a paradoxical ring to it, it is important to recognize that there is nothing paradoxical in this account of natural beauty, at least nothing beyond the underlying conception of a purposiveness without purpose that applies to the beautiful as such. In fact, the requirement that such beauty look like art amounts to nothing more than that it exhibit the form of purposiveness, which certainly can be understood independently of any appeal to conscious intent. The case is quite different with regard to fine art, however, because here the two requirements do seem to be in tension with each other. That the object appear to us as if it were natural, even though we are conscious of it as a product of art, places a demand upon the object that is not easily met, even if this demand is not strictly self-contradictory.[8] Thus, there seems to be a hitherto unnoticed problem about the conditions of the possibility of an object of fine art.

Viewed in isolation, the first requirement (that we be conscious of the object as art) is somewhat suggestive of Arthur Danto's well-known account of the nature of art.[9] Appealing to Andy Warhol's *Brillo Box* as a paradigm case, Danto suggests that the question of what makes something a work of [fine] art cannot be answered by reference to any observable properties of the object. For in terms of such properties, it is indistinguishable from an ordinary Brillo box that one finds in a store; and the same may be said of Duchamp's urinal and the like. What makes these works of art, then, on Danto's view, is their "aboutness"; that is to say, they endeavor to make a statement (for Danto a reflexive, theoretical statement) about the nature of art itself, and for one to regard them as works of art is just to view them in this light (as objects susceptible of interpretation).[10]

Similarly, for Kant, to be conscious of something as art is to take it as the product of a conscious intent on the part of the artist and, therefore, as involving an "aboutness" or intentionality that likewise makes it subject to interpretation. Moreover, although Danto poses the issue in terms of the distinction between an object of art and an ordinary commercial product (an artifact, in Kant's sense), whereas Kant tends to see the relevant contrast as between a product of art and a natural object, he would seem to be in agreement with Danto that the difference cannot be drawn (at least not always) in terms of manifest properties.[11]

Nevertheless, the second requirement (that the work of art seem like nature), which for Kant is clearly the most important one, differentiates his view sharply from one such as Danto's. The latter requirement is more important for Kant because it is the condition for distinguishing fine art from other forms of art (presumably including ordinary Brillo boxes and urinals), rather than from nature, and it is also for this reason that it differs so greatly from Danto's view. For it means that in order to be recognized as *fine* art, more is required than that one merely be conscious of it as involving "aboutness" and being subject to interpretation. This, after all, could be said about a philosophical treatise, a mathematical proof, and perhaps even an ancient artifact excavated at an archaeological cite whose use remains unknown, if not an ordinary Brillo box, none of which would be judged works of fine art.[12] In order to count as the latter, Kant insists that it must also please in a certain way, namely, in mere estimation [*in der blossen Beurteilung*] or reflection independently of a concept.

It is therefore in light of this constitutive feature of a pure judgment of taste that we must understand the requirement that a work of art seem like nature. Clearly, this does not mean that it must seem *to be* nature in the sense of a faithful copy or representation.[13] It is, rather, that it must seem natural in the sense of being spontaneous, unstudied, or, as Kant puts it, "unintentional" [*unabsichtlich*] (KU 5: 174; 307), that is, as if it were a product of mere nature rather than art.[14] Equally clearly, however, it cannot be a matter of seeming as if not designed simply because it is *badly* designed. In order to be judged beautiful, the object must be subjectively purposive for judgment; that is, it must occasion a harmony of the faculties in free play, and this could not occur if it were badly designed. Consequently, the requirement is that the object appear "natural" or undesigned *in its very purposiveness,* and it must do so even though we know it to be a product of art. Only in this way can it please independently of a concept (as well as a sensation), that is, in a way that preserves the freedom of the imagination. Conversely, if our liking for an object were based on a concept of it (of what it should be), then this liking would stem from its suitability for a specific purpose, which, in Kant's terms, means that we would like it as mechanical rather than as fine art.

Thus, as already noted, the air of paradox arises from putting together these two requirements. It entails that in viewing something as a work of fine art, we must take it as an intentional product, executed in accordance with a plan (be conscious of it as art), while, at the same time, it must look to us as if precisely the opposite were the case, that is, as if it were mere nature. The former condition is requisite for being able to take it as a work of art at all, and therefore as even a potential candidate for aesthetic evaluation; the latter is necessary for actually making such an evaluation and therefore for treating it as fine art.

In order to clarify the precise nature of this apparent paradox and its significance for Kant's theory of fine art, a brief comparison with the concept of a natural purpose [*Naturzweck*], which is the central concept of the Critique of Teleological Judgment and which is supposedly applicable to organic beings, may be of help.[15] In explicating this concept in the Analytic of Teleological Judgment, Kant emphasizes that it imposes a twofold requirement on anything falling under it: On the one hand, such an entity must be conceivable only as a purpose; that is, its form or structure (the interrelation of its parts) must be such that it can be understood only in terms of an idea of the whole; while, on the other hand, it must be regarded as a product of *nature* rather than art.[16]

Here it is important to realize that there is nothing problematic in either requirement considered by itself. This is obvious in the case of the second, since we encounter countless objects meeting this requirement every day. But in spite of the seemingly paradoxical nature of the language in which it is formulated, the same holds for the first requirement as well, which applies paradigmatically to products of art, particularly machines. For it is characteristic of a machine that the idea of the whole governs the arrangement of the parts (and even their status as parts), and these, therefore, can be understood only in terms of their contribution to the functioning of the whole. Moreover, we can easily conceive the possibility of entities fitting this description. We do so by regarding them as products of human art or intention; and, setting aside some possible puzzle cases, we tend to have no difficulty inferring from their existence the activity of an intelligent being as cause. In fact, the latter is a perfectly ordinary piece of causal reasoning, based on analogy, and issuing in a fully determinative judgment that does not require the assumption of any special teleological principle.

A problem does arise, however, when these two requirements are combined and applied to one and the same entity. For the second requirement precludes what, according to the first, would be the appropriate causal explanation, namely, an intelligent agent acting purposively in light of an idea of the effect to be produced. More specifically, the problem is to preserve what we might term the "*Zweck*-condition," when the entity to which it is being applied is also known to be a product of nature (the "*Natur*-condition"). And far from being sanguine about the possibility of doing this, Kant entertains the possibility that the very thought of a natural purpose may be self-contradictory (KU 5: 270; 249).[17]

It is, therefore, hardly surprising that, in his endeavor to characterize such an entity, Kant resorts to seemingly paradoxical formulations. Thus, in what he describes as a "provisional" formulation of this requirement in §64, he stipulates that a thing counts as a *natural* [my emphasis] purpose (rather than merely as a purpose) "if it is *both cause and effect of itself*" (though in a twofold sense) (KU 5: 370; 249). As his subsequent illustration by appeal to the example of a tree indicates, this twofold sense refers to the tree *qua* species and *qua* individual. But what is particularly noteworthy here is that this peculiar mode of causality (being at once both cause and effect of itself), which in traditional ontology is usually predicated only of God (*causa sui*), is now used to model the tree's epigenetic properties of reproduction, growth, and, more generally, the mutual dependence of the parts on one another and on the whole.[18]

Kant attempts to clarify further this conception of a natural purpose as both cause and effect of itself in the next section (§65), which supposedly provides his definitive treatment of the topic. Reduced to essentials, the problem, as he now defines it, is to explain how one can preserve the thought that the idea of the whole determines the structure and interrelations of the various parts without also assuming that it is the cause (which would make the entity a product of art, rather than nature).

The basic answer is that we must conceive of such an entity not simply as organized but as *self-organizing* (KU 5: 374; 253). This supposedly preserves a significant role for the *idea* of the whole, albeit a radically transformed one, since it now functions merely as a ground of our cognition of the form of the object and its systematic unity [*Erkenntnissgrund*], rather than as an actual cause (KU 5: 373; 252). Moreover, in developing the contrast between such a self-organizing being and a machine, which is organized and produced by an external cause, Kant attributes to the former a formative force, indeed, a "self-propagating formative force" [*eine sich fortpflanzende bildende Kraft*], as opposed to the mere motive force [*bewegende Kraft*] attributed to the components of the latter (5: 374; 253).[19] And echoing Hume of the *Dialogues Concerning Natural Religion*, whose influence is apparent throughout this entire discussion, Kant concludes that such a conception of causality is *sui generis*, bearing merely a "remote analogy" with our familiar causality in terms of purposes (KU 5: 375; 255).[20]

Since organisms are presumably just such self-organizing, self-regulating beings, Kant uses this analysis to ground his two-part claim that, on the one hand, a teleological mode of reflection (one governed by the idea of the whole) is indispensable for an understanding of organisms and that, on the other, this involves merely a reflective use of judgment, which therefore does not posit purposes as actual causes. Our concern, however, is not with Kant's account of biological explanation, but rather with the light that his analysis of the concept of a natural purpose and the conditions of its possibility sheds on the concept of a work of fine art and the conditions of its possibility. And here we find an interesting and perhaps unexpected result, namely, that these two conceptions are virtual mirror images of each other. Just as we have seen that the problem in the conception of the possibility of a work of fine art is to conceive how an object can seem "natural," in the sense of appearing as if *not designed*, even though it is known to be a product of art (and therefore designed); so we now learn that the problem in the conception of the possibility of a natural purpose is to understand how an object can continue to be conceived in light of the idea of purpose (or as if it were a work of art), in spite of the fact that it is known to be a product of nature.

The crucial point is that in both cases we are led to a significant revision in our ordinary understanding of causal efficacy. Thus, as we have just seen, the analysis of the concept of a natural purpose led to the conclusion that we can conceive of the possibility of such beings only by viewing them as self-organizing, a mode of production that is *sui generis* and, that Kant takes pains to point out, bears only a remote analogy to our ordinary causality in terms of purposes. Similarly, as we are about to see, in order to conceive of the possibility of a work of fine art, we are likewise required to assume a unique productive force, namely that of genius.

Before turning to that topic, however, it must be reemphasized that it is precisely the problem of accounting for the possibility of the production of a work of fine art (one which seems like nature, though we are conscious of it as art) that leads Kant from an exclusive focus on the question of taste (or a "reception aesthetic") to a concern with artistic production (or a "creation aesthetic"). Consequently, it is only in light of this problem that we can understand the systematic function of Kant's discussion of fine art within the Critique of Aesthetic Judgment. It belongs there insofar as the problem naturally arises from a reflection on the differences between judgments of natural and artistic beauty; but, as already noted, for this very reason it remains parergonal to the theory of taste.

II

Kant begins his discussion of genius (§46) with a preliminary definition, which he seems to regard as expressing the received (or at least widely accepted) understanding of the term: "*Genius* is the talent (natural endowment) that gives the rule to art." But since talent is understood as an innate productive capacity that itself belongs to nature (the nature of the subject), he further suggests that genius may also be defined as "the innate mental predisposition [*Gemütsanlage*] (*ingenium*) *through which* nature gives the rule to art" (KU 5: 307; 174).[21] From the point of view of the preceding analysis, what is most interesting about this definition in its second form is that it suggests a direct solution to the puzzle concerning the creation of fine art. Such art can *seem* like nature, even though we are conscious of it as art, precisely because it *is* a product of nature (the nature of the artist).[22] Moreover, though Kant does not put the point in quite this way, he does claim that it follows from this definition that the "fine arts must necessarily be considered arts of genius" (KU 5: 307; 175).

The argument for this claim consists of four steps, which, in typical fashion, are condensed into a single paragraph. First, Kant reminds us

that art presupposes rules on the basis of which a product must be produced if it is to count as art. Presumably, this applies to all art (not simply to fine art) and serves to distinguish a work of art from a product of
nature. Second, he likewise reminds us that, in the case of fine art, a judgment about its beauty cannot be based on any rule that has a *concept* as its
determining ground. This is because a judgment based on a concept of
the object would no longer be a judgment of taste (or, more precisely, it
would not be a pure judgment of taste). Together, then, these first two
steps summarize the results of the preceding analysis of the constraints
on a judgment of artistic beauty (we must be conscious of it as art, i.e., as
produced in accordance with a rule or plan, though it must seem like nature). The decisive move is made in the third step, where Kant says simply that "fine art cannot itself devise [*ausdenken*] the rule by which it is to
bring about its product." And from this he concludes in the fourth step:

> Since, however, a product can never be called art unless it is preceded by a
> rule, it must be nature in the subject (and through the attunement of his
> faculties) that gives the rule to art; in other words, fine art is possible only
> as the product of genius. (KU 5: 307; 175)

The third step is decisive because it marks the point at which Kant
shifts from a consideration of the conditions of the judgment of artistic
beauty to a consideration of the conditions of its creation. Unfortunately,
as it stands, the argument seems far from convincing. The initial problem concerns the meaning of the claim that "fine art cannot devise the
rule." Since a *work* of fine art is obviously not the sort of thing that could
devise a rule, this must refer to the artist *qua* producer of such a work. But
since it is also obvious that there must be a sense in which the artist is the
author of the rule (where else could it come from?), the claim that it is
"nature in the subject" that is the source of the rule must be understood
as an elliptical way of stating that the rule in question cannot be one that
is consciously adopted and applied by the artist by means of a delibera-
tive process.[23]

In that case, however, the claim appears to be a gross *non sequitur*. For
nothing about the *source* of the rule that must underlie a work of fine art
(as a condition of its being art) seems to be entailed by the negative requirement that the *judgment* regarding this work cannot be based on a
concept (presumably this very rule). On the contrary, all that appears to
be necessary is that the artist possess the requisite skill to disguise the underlying rule or organizing principle of the work, so as to make it "seem
like nature" in the sense previously discussed. Moreover, if this is the case,
then the conclusion that the source of the rule must lie in the "nature"
of the subject likewise does not follow, at least not if the term is understood to refer to something other than conscious intent.

Nevertheless, things are not as hopeless as they may at first appear. A crucial feature of Kant's account, which was neglected in the sketch of his argument, is the reference to the attunement of the faculties of the artist as the source of the rule (with this attunement identified as the "nature in the subject"). This suggests that what is essential to artistic creation is a powerful imagination, albeit one that spontaneously harmonizes with the requirements of the understanding.[24]

Such a claim also seems to be a reasonable inference from the analysis of the conditions of a judgment of artistic beauty. For if the rule or organizing principle of a work of art were derived from the understanding of the artist, that is, if it were consciously adopted in the manner of a formula or blueprint dictating how to proceed, then the imagination of the artist would lose its freedom; it would be constrained by the concept which it would presumably be its task to exhibit in the work. In that case, however, the imagination of someone contemplating the work would likewise be constrained, which would again prevent a free harmony of the faculties, and thus the pleasure of taste. In other words, Kant's main point in the paragraph under discussion seems to be that there is an important correlation between the free harmony of the faculties required for the creation of fine art and that which is required for its proper enjoyment. And this, as we shall see, is a view that runs throughout Kant's entire discussion of fine art.[25]

In fact, this conception underlies the four conclusions which Kant proceeds to draw from his provisional account of genius (KU 5: 307–8; 175–6). The first is that *originality*, understood as a capacity for producing something for which no determinate rule can be given, and which therefore cannot be learned by following rules, is the foremost property of genius. Originality, so conceived, is clearly a capacity of the productive imagination. But since, Kant notes pointedly, there is such a thing as original nonsense, originality of itself is not sufficient for genius. Thus, Kant includes as a second condition that a work of genius must be *exemplary*, that is, it must serve as a model or norm for others as a basis of both inspiration (for subsequent geniuses) and judgment (for those with taste).[26] This clearly implies that a work of genius must accord with the requirements of the understanding, since otherwise it could not function normatively in these ways.

The third conclusion, namely that "Genius itself cannot describe or indicate scientifically how it brings about its products, and it is rather as *nature* that it gives the rule" (KU 5: 308; 175), is somewhat more problematic, since it seems to rule out the very possibility of geniuses in science. Nevertheless, it too is a consequence of the primacy given to the imagination, that "blind though indispensable function of the soul, without which we would have no cognition at all, but of which we are seldom even conscious" (A78/B104). The same may also be said about Kant's fourth and final conclusion, namely, that in the case of genius nature prescribes the rule to art and not to science, which merely makes explicit what is already implicit in the third. In other words, there are no geniuses in science, according to the received definition of genius, precisely because genius is understood primarily in terms of an imaginative capacity (albeit one constrained by understanding), rather than a powerful intellect.[27]

In presenting this preliminary account of genius, Kant suggests that he will discuss its adequacy in the next section (§47), and he even entitles the latter "Elucidation and Confirmation of the Above Explication of Genius." In reality, however, this section is devoted to a further exploration of some of the consequences of the initial definition, rather than to anything that might be regarded as its confirmation.

These consequences include a delimitation of the sphere of genius to exclude whatever can be attained through learning (which again rules out science); the tantalizing suggestion that, unlike science, fine art, as based on genius, has natural limits, which Kant thinks have in all likelihood been reached long ago (which is sometimes thought to foreshadow the "end of art" thesis of Hegel).[28] In addition, §48 contains an account of how works of genius function as models for later artists,[29] as well as important discussions of the relationships between natural and artistic beauty, on the one hand, and genius and taste, on the other. Thus, it is only in §49, entitled "On the Faculties of the Mind which Constitute Genius," that Kant attempts to provide his promised confirmation; and it is also in this context that he introduces the conception of aesthetic ideas.

Kant does not, however, begin §49 with a consideration of either aesthetic ideas or genius. Instead, he introduces a new conception, namely *spirit* [*Geist*], which is intimately related to both.[30] Spirit, in the aesthetic sense in which it is here used, is described as the "animating principle in the mind" (KU 5: 313; 181–2). Moreover, Kant states that the material [*Stoff*] that spirit uses to animate is precisely what gives to the mental faculties a "purposive momentum, i.e., imparts to them a play which is such that it sustains itself on its own and even strengthens the faculties for such play" (KU 5: 313; 182). In other words, what spirit produces, or, better, occasions by means of this material, is just the pleasurable mental state that obtains in an engagement with beauty. And since Kant goes on to identify this "material" with aesthetic ideas, it follows that these ideas are the source (or, in Aristotelian terms, the "material cause") of the pleasure of taste.[31]

We saw in Chapter 11 that Kant initially defines an aesthetic idea as a "representation of the imagination which prompts much thought, but to which no determinate thought whatsoever, i.e., no *concept*, can be adequate, so that no language can express it completely and allow us to grasp it" (KU 5: 314; 182). Since the concern there was to show both that and how such ideas make it possible for beauty to symbolize morality, the focus was on what was termed their quasi-schematizing function of providing indirect exhibitions, and therefore symbols, of rational ideas.

Although this function must still be kept in mind, our present concern is more with the connection of these ideas with the productive capacity of the imagination. This basic connection is already apparent in the definition; but Kant proceeds to relate aesthetic ideas more specifically to the imagination's productive capacity, which he describes as a power to create "as it were, another nature out of the material that actual nature gives it" (KU 5: 314; 182). It does this, Kant suggests, by processing the material that nature provides, that is, the data of sensible intuition, "into something quite different, namely, into something that surpasses nature" (KU 5: 314; 182). What the imagination fashions in this way are just aesthetic ideas, and, as we saw in Chapter 11, they "surpass nature" by providing indirect exhibitions of the supersensible.

We also saw that the components of aesthetic ideas are termed "aesthetic attributes," understood as imaginative representations associated with a core rational concept, which provide an "aesthetic expansion" of that concept and thereby "prompt much thought."[32] Once again, the basic idea is that such "attributes" may be said to enrich a given concept by relating it to certain supplemental representations in a way that is analogous to, though distinct from, the logical expansion of a concept that occurs through the addition of logical attributes (real predicates) in a synthetic judgment. To return to one of Kant's examples, Jupiter's eagle with the bolt of lightning in its craw functions as an aesthetic attribute by enriching the essentially rational thought of the sublimity and greatness of creation by means of a suggestive image. Another example Kant provides is from a poem of Frederick the Great, in which the king supposedly enlivens the rational idea of a cosmopolitan attitude, even at the end of life, by connecting it with the thought of the recollection of the pleasures of a fair summer's day, a recollection which is prompted by a serene evening (KU 5: 184; 316). In both cases, the image would seem to function as a metaphor for what is actually thought in the concept, and it is by so doing that it enlivens the mind in its contemplation of the concept.

As was already noted in Chapter 11, however, though it is composed of such aesthetic attributes, an aesthetic idea is more than a collection thereof. These attributes constitute what we might term the "matter" of an aesthetic idea, but equally essential to such an idea is its "form." By the latter is to be understood the organization or unity of these attributes, that in virtue of which they constitute a single aesthetic idea, in contrast, say, to a random "heap" of disconnected images. Thus, to say that such an idea, like its logical counterpart, requires a form as well as a matter is to say that it must possess a certain inner coherence or rule-governedness, an organic unity, if you will, albeit one that cannot be specified in a determinate manner. Moreover, it is in virtue of the latter that aesthetic ideas are universally communicable.

In light of this conception of an aesthetic idea, Kant returns near the end of §49 to the analysis of genius, which he now suggests "consists in the happy relation [of the imagination and understanding] – one that no science can teach and that cannot be learned by any diligence – allowing us, first, to discover ideas for a given concept, and, second, to hit upon a way of *expressing* these ideas that enables us to communicate to others, as accompanying a concept, the mental attunement that those ideas produce" (KU 5: 317; 185–6). And, Kant continues, the latter talent is what is properly termed spirit:

> For in order to express what is ineffable in the mental state accompanying a certain representation and to make it universally communicable . . . we need an ability to apprehend the imagination's rapidly passing play and to unite it in a concept that can be communicated without the constraint of rules (a concept that on that very account is original, while at the same time it reveals a new rule that could not have been inferred from any earlier principles or examples). (KU 5: 317; 186)

As this indicates, genius consists in a twofold capacity, which Kant describes both as discovering and expressing [aesthetic] ideas and as apprehending "the imagination's rapidly passing play" and uniting it in a concept. In spite of the obvious terminological differences, I believe that we should regard these descriptions as essentially equivalent. In both cases, the first conjunct refers to the selection of aesthetic attributes (which are "discovered" or "apprehended" by the imagination) and the second to their unification in an aesthetic idea (the "concept") through which an indeterminate thought is expressed. Moreover, both aspects of this activity involve the imagination in its free play, though in a way that accords with the requirements of the understanding for coherence and communicability; for it is only if these requirements are met that the product of this free play can be something more than "original nonsense."

Having thus "fleshed out" the conception of genius by connecting it to aesthetic ideas, Kant is finally in a position to revisit the initial definition of genius and the provisional conclusions derived therefrom in §46. His goal is clearly to confirm the basic thrust of this account and at the same time to make comprehensible what initially seemed problematic, namely, the appeal to the "nature" of the creative artist and its compatibility with the requirement of universal communicability that remains criterial for taste.

To this end, he first formulates four conclusions, which may be seen as partially revised versions of the ones originally drawn: (1) Genius is a talent for art rather than science. (2) As an artistic talent, it presupposes a determinate concept of the purpose to be achieved (and therefore understanding), as well as an indeterminate representation of the "material," that is, an intuition through which the concept is to be expressed – thus a relation of imagination of understanding. (3) Since this exhibition occurs primarily by way of aesthetic ideas, it concerns the imagination in its freedom from rules, "though still as purposive for exhibiting the given concept." (4) The "unstudied, unintentional" nature of the subjective purposiveness involved in the free harmony of the imagination with the lawfulness of the understanding (which, as we have seen, is precisely what makes a work of fine art seem like nature), "presupposes such a proportion and attunement of these faculties as cannot be brought about by any compliance with rules . . . but . . . only by the subject's nature" (KU 5: 317–18; 186). And, finally, on the basis of these "presuppositions," Kant offers his definitive characterization of genius as the "exemplary originality of the subject's natural endowment in the *free* use of his cognitive faculties" (KU 5: 318; 186).

Clearly, where these conclusions go beyond the ones initially drawn in §46 is in bringing aesthetic ideas into the picture. Equally clearly, the conception of such ideas is intended to supply the key to understanding the exemplary originality of a product of genius that is reaffirmed in the final definition. Once again, the originality consists primarily in the invention or discovery of the aesthetic attributes to express the underlying thought, that is, the conscious intent or purport of the work (which itself presupposes understanding), while the exemplarity derives largely from the cohesive unification of these attributes in an aesthetic idea or cluster thereof. This mode of unification, which might be said to define the style of an artist, is, then, the indeterminate but intuitively recognizable "rule," which is imitated by members of that artist's school or circle of followers and that inspires subsequent geniuses to produce their own exemplary creations.[33]

Most importantly, however, we also gain a somewhat deeper understanding of the sense of "nature" that is supposedly involved in the creative process. The basic idea is that the genius has not only the capacity to invent the appropriate attributes and unify them into a cohesive, aesthetically pleasing whole, but also the capacity to grasp the aptness of this creation (the aesthetic idea or cluster thereof) to express symbolically or metaphorically the underlying idea of the work. Since this aptness is something that the genius must, in the last analysis, simply feel or see, no rule can be given for it, which again means that it cannot be taught or acquired but is, rather, an innate talent stemming directly from the genius's nature. Consequently, by "nature" in this context we must understand not simply the sheer imaginative power of the genius, but also the ability to recognize (without appealing to determinate concepts or rules) the "harmony" between the products of the imagination in its freedom and the contents of the understanding.[34] Presumably, then, this is what Kant means by the "proportion and attunement" of the faculties that are characteristic of genius. The genius, on this view, is someone who is blessed with the unteachable ability to produce coherent imaginative associations (aesthetic ideas) that are particularly suited to express an underlying thought.

Finally, if this is correct, we find an interesting and perhaps unexpected parallel between genius and judgment.[35] For as has been noted on several occasions in this study, Kant insists already in the first *Critique* that there can be no rules for judgment, that it comes down to a matter of simply being able to see (or perhaps in light of our analysis of common sense *feel*) that a particular instance falls under a rule. Thus, it seems that at least one of the essential ingredients in genius must be a particularly acute form of judgment, one directed specifically at the fit between aesthetic and rational ideas. We shall return to the question of the components of genius in the last section of this chapter, in connection with the discussion of the relationship between genius and taste.

III

Our immediate concern, however, is with two important issues regarding aesthetic ideas that arise as a result of their connection with genius. The first, which was already touched upon in Chapter 11, is the claim that natural (as well as artistic) beauty is to be understood as the expression of aesthetic ideas. The second is the reconciliation of this general thesis about beauty as the expression of aesthetic ideas with the formalism of the third moment of the Analytic of the Beautiful.

In our previous discussion of the first issue, the emphasis was on the significance of the thesis that natural beauty expresses aesthetic ideas for the claim that beauty symbolizes morality. If, as seems clearly the case, Kant thought that *all* beauty symbolizes morality, and if, as I have argued, this symbolization must be understood in terms of the expression of aesthetic ideas, then Kant is committed to the thesis that natural beauty expresses these ideas as well. Thus, Kant's own explicit affirmation of this in §51 constituted a welcome confirmation of the previous analysis of how beauty symbolizes morality.

Nevertheless, some account of how this is possible and what it really means seems in order, particularly since, as we have just seen, Kant initially introduces aesthetic ideas in the context of his analysis of genius. As a first step in clarifying Kant's position, it should noted that there is no contradiction between his account of genius and the conception of natural beauty as expressing aesthetic ideas. A contradiction would arise only if genius were taken to be a necessary condition for the production of aesthetic ideas, but Kant is not committed to any such thesis. On the contrary, it seems quite clear that even within the domain of fine art, he did not want to claim that every expression of an aesthetic idea in a work of art is a sign of genius. For example, in spite of his well-known admiration for Frederick the Great, it is doubtful that Kant regarded him as a poetic genius! Kant's point is, rather, that a genius is someone who, for the reasons noted in the previous section, is extraordinarily good at producing and expressing aesthetic ideas, which does not preclude lesser talents from also producing them.[36] Indeed, as we shall see later in this chapter, at one point Kant even denies that a work of art need be rich in such ideas in order to be beautiful.

Moreover, since an aesthetic idea is defined as much by what it *does* ("prompt much thought," albeit of an indeterminate kind) as by what it *is* (an intuition of the imagination to which no determinate concept can be adequate), there is no inherent reason that such a representation must be occasioned by a product of art rather than nature. As we have already seen, the difference between the two modes of production of aesthetic ideas is merely that in the case of beautiful art, the idea is prompted by a concept of the object, whereas in the case of natural beauty, "mere reflection on a given intuition . . . is sufficient for arousing and communicating the idea of which that object is regarded as the *expression*" (KU 5: 320; 189). To claim that in the case of beautiful art the aesthetic idea is prompted by a concept of the object is, in effect, to claim that we must be conscious of it as art; and this requirement obviously does not apply to natural beauty. Nevertheless, this does not prevent the intuitive representation of a natural object (or scene) from having a comparable effect on the play of our cognitive faculties in mere reflection, thereby "prompting much thought."

In fact, this is just what is meant by the claim that the object is subjectively purposive for judgment or, equivalently, that it exhibits the "form of purposiveness."[37] In earlier discussions of this conception of purposiveness, the emphasis was placed on the notion that the object appears "as if designed" for our cognitive faculties, which we can now take to be equivalent to the claim that it "seems like art." But since the faculties for which the object seems as if designed are *cognitive*, the latter can only mean that it arouses and communicates some thought (again of an indeterminate kind) of that which the object is viewed as expressing. Indeed, given the nature of art as essentially communicative, we might ask how else something in nature could be said to seem like art.[38] Consequently, looking at Kant's account of the judgment of natural beauty as a whole, it seems reasonable to conclude that the claim that such beauty, like that of fine art, consists in the expression of aesthetic ideas merely makes explicit an important dimension that is there implicitly all along, rather than constituting a fresh and paradoxical point of departure.

Similar considerations also enable us to deal with our second problem in this section, namely the compatibility of the characterization of beauty in terms of the expression of aesthetic ideas with the claim of the Analytic that beauty is to be understood solely in terms of the purposiveness of the *form* of the object.[39] When the issue of Kant's aesthetic formalism was first taken up in Chapter 6, I noted (in agreement with Guyer) that there is indeed a slide in §13 from an understanding of the beautiful as exhibiting the form of purposiveness to an understanding of it as consisting merely in the purposiveness of the form of an object. But appealing to Guyer's distinction between a restrictive formalism (where "form" refers merely to spatiotemporal structure) and a broader, nonrestrictive sense (which includes things like the arrangement of colors in painting or instrumentation in music), I argued that Kant's conception of the harmony of the faculties in free play does entail a formalism of the latter sort. The basic claim was that the connection with form follows directly from the reflective nature of the judgment of taste. Since the harmony of the faculties must be one in "mere reflection," the sensible data must provide something on which to reflect, and this can only consist in a certain order or arrangement, which counts as "form" in Kant's sense. For only such an order or arrangement of the sensible data (*qua* apprehended by the imagination) could be suitable for the exhibition of a concept (though no concept in particular). Consequently, only an engagement with form could occasion a free harmony of the faculties.

Furthermore, it seems clear that there is no conflict between a formalism in this broad, nonrestrictive (yet nontrivial) sense and the expression of aesthetic ideas.[40] On the contrary, given the preceding analysis of these ideas, it is apparent that they themselves require a form as a necessary condition of their expression and communication. Confining ourselves for the present to those produced and exhibited by genius, the form is just the unity or coherence given to a collection of aesthetic attributes by the genius in virtue of which it becomes a communicable aesthetic idea. As we have seen, it is precisely this coherence that distinguishes the exemplary product of genius from "original nonsense," and it is by bringing this unity to the products of the imagination that the genius both brings the latter into harmony with his or her own understanding and makes it communicable to others. Thus, Kant's "expressionism" not only is compatible with his "formalism" but also presupposes it, since the form serves as the necessary vehicle for the expression.[41]

It is equally the case, however, that there can be no aesthetically pleasing form apart from the expression of aesthetic ideas. For, as we have also seen, form pleases in mere reflection by setting both the imagination and the understanding into a purposive, self-sustaining play, and it can only do this by "prompting much thought," that is, by expressing aesthetic ideas. In short, purposive form and the expression of aesthetic ideas are strictly correlative notions for Kant. Just as there can be no successful expression and communication of these ideas without form, so there can be no aesthetically pleasing form apart from the expression of ideas.[42]

Although Kant never makes this reciprocity of form and expression fully explicit, he gives ample indication that it underlies his analysis of beauty. Consider, for example, a previously cited passage from §42 concerning natural beauty. In defending his claim of a kinship between an interest in natural beauty and moral feeling, Kant there refers enigmatically to that "cipher through which nature speaks to us figuratively in its beautiful forms" (KU 5: 301; 168). Since, as we have seen, this "cipher" signifies the aesthetic ideas by means of which natural beauty symbolizes morality, this passage can only be read as asserting that it is through its beautiful forms that nature expresses aesthetic ideas and thereby "speaks to us." Similarly, in his discussion of the comparative aesthetic value of the fine arts, Kant says of music:

> [J]ust as modulation is, as it were, a universal language of sensations that every human being can understand, so the art of music [*Tonkunst*] employs this language all by itself in its full force, namely, as a language of affects; in this way it communicates to everyone, according to the law of association, the aesthetic ideas that we naturally connect with such affects. But since these aesthetic ideas are not concepts, not determinate thoughts, the *form* [my emphasis] of the arrangement of these sensations (harmony and melody), which takes the place of the form of a language, only serves to *express* [my emphasis], by means of a proportioned attunement of the sensations, the aesthetic idea of a coherent whole of an unspeakable wealth of thought, and to express it in conformity with a certain theme that is the prevalent affect in the piece. (KU 5: 328–9; 199)

Kant could hardly have been clearer than he is in this passage about the correlation between form and expression in music. And since Kant ranks music lowest of the arts in terms of its capacity to express aesthetic ideas, it indicates that what holds of music must also hold of other art forms, which likewise please on the basis of form but are presumably richer in their expressive capacity.[43] Thus, just as we concluded that the claim that natural beauty consists in the expression of aesthetic ideas is a matter of making explicit something that was implicit all along, so I think it can be claimed that the doctrine of aesthetic ideas, though it does not appear in the Analytic of the Beautiful, is a necessary complement to the formalism that Kant there affirms. Indeed, I think that, with some justification, one might compare the relation between the formalism of the Analytic and the later appeal to aesthetic ideas with the relation between the first and second formulations of the categorical imperative in the *Groundwork*. In both works it is a matter of two formulations of a norm, one emphasizing the form and the other the content, with each formulation yielding equivalent results.[44] The main difference is that in the *Ground-work* Kant makes the equivalence between these formulations fully explicit, whereas in the third *Critique* the task is left to the reader.

IV

Our next problem likewise arises from the appearance of a conflict between Kant's account of fine art and the third moment of the Analytic of the Beautiful. At issue is the compatibility of this later account with the distinction drawn in §16 between free and adherent beauty. As we saw in Chapter 6, this distinction is quite problematic in its own right, apart from any consideration of its relation to later portions of the text. The major problem at that point was how judgments of adherent beauty (whether natural or artistic) could be viewed as judgments of taste at all, since by definition they presuppose a concept of what the object is meant to be and therefore its perfection. Following the lead of Martin Gammon, it was suggested that the key to resolving the puzzle lies in the recognition of the parergonal status of adherent beauty. On this view, the beauty of an adherently beautiful object (say, a picture frame) is recognized by a pure judgment of taste (in which the concept of the object's perfection is not involved); but the overall assessment of the object is nevertheless conditioned by this concept. Otherwise expressed, a judgment of adherent beauty is not *purely* a judgment of taste, though the taste component within the complex evaluation itself remains *pure*. In this way, then, the conception of an adherent beauty (or the judgment thereof) was seen to be compatible with the formalism of the third moment (which concerned merely the pure judgment of taste).

Since the focus in Chapter 6 was on the generic features of Kant's theory of taste, the discussion largely ignored the fact that Kant presents the free-adherent beauty distinction as applying unproblematically to artistic as well as to natural beauty. Recall that as examples of free artistic beauties he cites such things as designs *à la grecque*, the foliage on borders or on wallpaper, and music not set to words. The defining characteristic of all of them, what makes them free beauties, Kant suggests, is that they "mean [*bedeuten*] nothing on their own: they represent nothing, no object under a determinate concept" (KU 5: 229; 77). By contrast, the beauty of a building such as a house or church is said to be merely adherent, since it presupposes a concept of what the object is meant to be and thus of its perfection (KU 5: 230; 77).

In its application to fine art, however, this contrast between free and adherent beauty poses at least two major questions beyond the ones dealt with in Chapter 6. The first concerns Kant's understanding of "representation" as it applies to art and its relation to the supposedly generic condition of adherent beauty, namely, that it presupposes a concept of what an object is meant to be. Simply put, the question is whether we are to understand "representing x" as equivalent to or as entailed by "presupposing [or falling under] a concept of what x is meant to be." For if this is the case, it would (at the very least) require the abandonment of the ordinary understanding of artistic representation as depiction or portrayal.[45] The second question stems from the examples themselves, particularly those of free beauty, all of which, except for music not set to words (which Kant himself does not value very highly), seem fairly trivial. This fact, together with Kant's definitions, seems to suggest that virtually all of what we commonly regard as great art falls into the merely adherent category. And this naturally raises the question of whether Kant really wished to hold this seemingly paradoxical position.

These questions internal to §16 assume even greater significance when viewed in connection with what Kant has to say about fine art in §48. For in the latter section, artistic beauty is defined as a "*beautiful representation of a thing*," in contrast to a natural beauty, which is simply a "*beautiful thing*" (KU 5: 311; 179). Moreover, the situation is further complicated by the fact that Kant goes on to claim that the judgment of the beauty of a work of art, in contrast to that of natural beauty, must be based on a concept of what the object is meant to be, and is therefore inseparable from an assessment of the thing's perfection (KU 5: 311; 179).

In a manner reminiscent of the discussion of adherent natural beauty in §16 and §17, Kant now notes that in certain cases of natural beauty, specifically animate objects such as human beings or horses, we must likewise attend to their "objective purposiveness" (which is equivalent to their perfection), and he concludes from this that in such cases "the judgment is no longer purely aesthetic, no longer a mere judgment of taste" (KU 5: 311: 179). Since, as he now puts it, we are then no longer judging nature "as it appears as art" (which is supposedly what occurs in a pure judgment of natural beauty), "but insofar as it actually is art (though superhuman art)," it turns out that what we are actually doing is making a teleological judgment, which "serves the aesthetic one as a foundation and condition that it must take into account" (KU 5: 311–12; 179–80). Moreover, Kant goes on to add, this may also be characterized as a "logically conditioned aesthetic judgment," since "we have to look beyond the mere form and toward a concept" (KU 5: 312; 180).

Although Kant himself does not make the connection explicit, this conception of a logically conditioned aesthetic judgment seems equivalent to what he had previously termed a judgment of adherent beauty. In both cases, the properly aesthetic assessment is conditioned by a concept of some purpose that the object is thought to serve, that is, a concept of what the object is meant to be, or its perfection. It is, of course, also this feature that makes the judgment at least partly teleological. For present purposes, however, what is most noteworthy about this account of a logically conditioned aesthetic judgment is that, apart from the reference to teleology, everything that Kant says here about this special type of natural beauty (or judgment thereof) appears to apply to all artistic beauty as he had just defined it. Indeed, having been told that all judgment of artistic beauty presupposes a concept of what the object is meant to be, it is difficult to avoid the conclusion that all such judgments must be regarded as logically conditioned and therefore as merely adherent in terms of the language of §16. Once again, Kant does not say this in so many words, but it seems to be an unavoidable implication of his account in §48.[46]

In that event, however, there appear to be at least two serious inconsistencies between the accounts of artistic beauty in §16 and §48. The first is that in the former place, Kant affirms that what he there terms free artistic beauties "represent nothing," whereas in the latter, he builds a reference to representation into the very definition of artistic beauty as a "*beautiful representation of a thing*." Clearly, either "representation" is to be understood differently in these two places or there is a direct contradiction between them. The second apparent inconsistency, as we have just seen, is that whereas in §16 at least some artistic beauties were regarded as free, it seems that according to the criteria of §48, all artistic beauty must be classified as adherent. Once again, either something different is meant by a "logically conditioned aesthetic judgment" in §48 than was meant by a "judgment of adherent beauty" in §16 or we have another direct contradiction.

Moreover, quite apart from these contradictions, if one of the problems with the first account was that it allowed room for only relatively trivial forms of art (such as designs *à la grecque*) in the class of free beauties, it is only exacerbated by the second, since it apparently precludes even these. Thus, either we must explain how being classified as a merely adherent beauty does not affect the aesthetic value placed on a work of art or we must seriously question the application of the concept of adherent beauty (or a logically conditioned aesthetic judgment) to fine art.

In the remainder of this section I shall attempt to deal with these problems in the order listed, beginning with the meaning of "representation" in art. Unfortunately, here as in so many other cases, Kant's explicit treatments of the topic are not particularly helpful. Not only does he fail to provide anything like a definition or statement of how he proposes to use the term, but he also uses it in quite distinct, though related, senses without stopping to apprise the reader of this fact.[47] As I shall try to show, however, by considering more carefully than has been done so far the contexts in which the term appears in §16 and §48, it is possible to save Kant from the charge of contradicting himself, though not that of excessive ambiguity.

A reference to "representation" occurs three times in §16. The first is in connection with the examples of free artistic beauties already mentioned (designs *à la grecque,* the foliage on borders or on wallpaper, and music not set to words, etc.). As previously noted, Kant says of such works of art that they "mean [*bedeuten*] nothing on their own: they represent nothing, no object under a determinate concept" (KU 5: 229; 77). In the next paragraph, after stating that when free beauty is judged according to mere form the judgment of taste is pure, he proceeds to add: "Here we presuppose no concept of any purpose for which the manifold is to serve the given object," and which the latter should therefore represent (KU 5: 229–30; 77).[48] Finally, in giving examples of adherent beauty, which are conditioned by a concept of what the object is meant to be, Kant first refers to a church and then to the figure of a man, of which he says that it

> could be embellished with all sorts of curlicues and light but regular lines, as the New Zealanders do with their tattoos, if only it were not the figure of a human being. And this figure [*dieser*] might have had much more delicate features and a facial structure with a softer and more likable outline, if only it were not meant to represent a man, and a warrior at that. (KU 5: 230; 77)

In the first of these passages, "representation" seems to have its familiar aesthetic sense of "depiction" or "portrayal." Thus, when Kant claims that free beauties of the type designated "represent nothing," he appears primarily to be denying that they signify anything, that they refer beyond themselves to something that they depict, either on the basis of perceptual similarities, conventional symbols, or some combination thereof. Simply put, they represent nothing in the sense that they are not "about" anything beyond themselves, as, for example, a painting depicting a historical or mythological event would be about that which it depicts. And for this reason, such beauties do not presuppose a concept of what their object is "meant to be" (e.g., a depiction of the Battle of Waterloo).

By contrast, it is clear that "representation" cannot be understood in this way in the other two passages. In the second, an object (presumably a work of art) is characterized as not representing a *purpose* [my emphasis]. If to "represent a purpose" means anything, it must be an elliptical way of saying that some object is an excellent specimen of a kind in the sense that it exemplifies the peculiar perfection of that kind.[49] In that case, of course, it likewise presupposes a concept of what the object is "meant to be," albeit in a very different sense than the first example, since it is now a matter of what it is *good for,* rather than what it *depicts.* Moreover, though the issue is complicated by the fact that it appears to concern the artistic decoration of a natural object (a human being) rather than a product of art in the usual sense, much the same can be said of the third example.[50] Here the crucial point is that the body to be decorated is that of a man, and even a warrior. Consequently, this determines both what it "represents" and what it is "meant to be," which, in turn, imposes extra-aesthetic constraints on what constitutes appropriate decoration.[51]

These examples from §16 therefore present us with two distinct senses of "representation," correlated with corresponding senses of what an object is "meant to be." I shall call them, respectively, the *depictive* and *exemplative* senses of representation and the *intentional* and *teleological* senses of what something is "meant to be."[52] The first pair of correlatives are obviously applicable only to works of art, whereas the second pair are applicable both to works of art and natural objects, though primarily to the latter. Unfortunately, Kant himself fails to distinguish these different senses of his key terms, but given these distinctions, we are in a position to address our first question: the compatibility of the distinction drawn in §16 between two kinds of artistic beauty, only one of which involves a representation of an object (in either of these two senses), with the definition in §48 of artistic beauty as a *"beautiful representation of a thing."*

An examination of §48 suggests that Kant there takes representation primarily in the depictive sense. Thus, he points out that the "superiority" of fine art to natural beauty consists in the fact that, within limits, it can depict [*beschreiben*] beautifully things that in nature we would dislike or find ugly (KU 5: 312; 180). The limitation from the side of the object is provided by the disgusting, which is claimed to be the only "kind of ugliness that cannot be represented in conformity with nature without obliterating all aesthetic liking and hence artistic beauty" (KU 5: 312; 180). The expression "conformity with nature" clearly indicates that "represented" is here taken in its depictive sense.[53]

In the next to the last paragraph of §48, however, Kant writes: "Let this suffice for the beautiful representation of an object, which is actually only the form of the concept's exhibition, the form by which this concept is universally communicated" (KU 5: 312; 180). Since it is in the very next section that he introduces the conception of aesthetic ideas, we can view this passage as part of a somewhat clumsy transition on Kant's part to this topic. The transition is clumsy (indeed misleading) because Kant appears to introduce a completely new sense of "representation," without informing the reader of this fact.

Nevertheless, setting that problem aside, this new conception of representation as expression (of aesthetic ideas) seems initially promising, since, given Kant's subsequent account of aesthetic ideas, it is presumably applicable to *all* artistic beauty, including the examples of free beauties from §16, which presumably are nonrepresentative in both of the senses previously designated. After all, even designs *à la grecque* must express such ideas according to Kant's subsequent account, if they are to be judged beautiful. Thus, if this is what Kant means by a *"beautiful representation of a thing,"* then even such designs (and other free beauties) may be said to "represent" in this extended sense, without any contradiction with what was claimed in §16.

Unfortunately, taking "representation" as equivalent to "expression" (where a work of art represents x just in case it expresses an aesthetic idea suitable for the symbolic representation of the rational concept of x) does not give us what we need or, rather, it gives us too much. For since natural as well as artistic beauty consists in the expression of aesthetic ideas, *all* beauty (including the natural variety) "represents" in this sense. Consequently, it does not provide a means for understanding the distinction between a *"beautiful thing"* and a *"beautiful representation of a thing,"* on which Kant's entire account of fine art is supposedly based.

In view of these considerations, there appears to be only one way left to render Kant's accounts of representation in §16 and §48 consistent with each other, namely, to focus on the contrast between a *beautiful thing* and *beautiful representation of a thing.* Although much of what Kant says about beautiful representations of things in §48 suggests the depictive sense of representation, the contrast itself need not be understood as requiring that sense. In fact, even setting aside the connection of representation with exhibition, Kant's overall account of fine art, including at least some of what he has to say about it in §48, strongly suggests a quite different understanding of the term, one which allows us to distinguish between what a work of art *depicts* (if, indeed, it depicts anything at all) and what it *represents.*

Central to Kant's account of fine art, in §48 and elsewhere, is the previously noted claim that in order to judge the beauty of a work of art it is necessary to have a concept of the "kind of thing the object is meant to be" (KU 5: 311; 179). This phrase, I take it, refers primarily to the art-form or genre of a work, for example, a historical painting, a sonnet, or a symphony, in contrast to the particular thing it may depict (again, if it depicts anything). Otherwise expressed, it indicates the kind of work that it must be seen as being, if one is properly to assess its beauty. The basic claim, then, is that without *some* knowledge of this sort, which in many cases might be fairly minimal, one cannot begin to appreciate a work of art because one is not aware of what the artist is trying to do.

Obviously, such knowledge, which is too general to amount to anything like the "correct interpretation," could become much more fine grained, and presumably this could increase (or perhaps diminish) one's appreciation of a work.[54] Moreover, even though Kant does not characterize it as such, this is clearly a consequence of his underlying principle that in order to appreciate artistic beauty, one must be conscious of it as art. Basically, this means that the appreciation of a work of art presupposes the awareness of some purpose that the artist is intending to achieve through the work, which is, of course, not the case in the appreciation of natural beauty. Presumably, this is likewise why Kant claims that "when we judge artistic beauty we shall have to assess the thing's perfection as well," with "perfection" defined as the agreement of a thing with its purpose (KU 5: 311; 179).

The "kind of thing the object is meant to be" may also be viewed as what it represents in the aforementioned exemplative sense. In other words, what it represents is just the *kind* of work it is.[55] But even though this is an exemplative sense of representation, it is crucial to note that what is exemplified is different than in the previously discussed cases of adherent beauty. There it was a matter of some extra-aesthetic purpose that the work was intended to subserve, and that imposed extra-aesthetic constraints on what is appropriate. Here, by contrast, what is exemplified, and therefore represented, is just the art-form or genre itself, the kind of work it is seen as being by its audience. To be sure, this likewise imposes constraints on what is appropriate; but these are no longer extra-aesthetic, since they stem from the art-form itself and may be seen as involving the academic norms or standards of correctness for that form. And, of course, the genius typically violates these academic constraints, producing new rules in the process (though always thereby running the risk of producing merely "original nonsense").

If this is correct, it finally gives us what we were looking for, namely, a sense of representation that is applicable to all works of fine art, but not to natural beauties, since it is derived from an analysis of the nature of such art. For, clearly, even a *design à la grecque* is representative in this sense (there is something which the artist must be seen as trying to do), whereas a beautiful sunset is not. Admittedly, it cannot be shown conclusively that this is, in fact, what Kant had in mind. His cryptic discussions of artistic representation are simply too ambiguous to allow for any such conclusion. Consequently, the possibility remains open that he was simply confused on the matter (appealing to different senses of "representation" in different contexts to draw different contrasts). Nevertheless, I maintain that Kant *could* have meant this (given what he actually says); and, more importantly, it is how he must be read, if his various accounts of artistic representation are to be made consistent with one another.

This does not, however, resolve all of our problems. On the contrary, it might be argued that it only exacerbates what has been viewed as the central problem all along, namely, that the requirement that the assessment of artistic beauty presuppose a concept of the kind of thing the work is meant to be, which we have seen is necessary to appraise it as *art*, appears to render all artistic beauty (or at least the judgments thereof) adherent by the criteria of §16.

One strategy for dealing with this problem, which has been suggested by Donald Crawford, is to insist that the free-adherent beauty distinction is to be interpreted strictly in terms of different kinds of judgment of beauty, rather than between different kinds of beauty.[56] Since, as we have seen, this is one of the ways in which Kant characterizes the distinction, it certainly has some textual support. Thus, on this reading, one makes a "free" judgment of the beauty of an object (whether of nature or art) when one abstracts from one's concept of what it is meant to be (its purpose), and an "adherent" or "dependent" judgment when the latter enters into one's evaluation. And since there would seem to be no more intrinsic difficulty in abstracting from one's concept of what it is meant to be in appreciating a work of art than there is for the botanist in abstracting from his or her knowledge of the purpose of the flower in order to enjoy its beauty, it is perfectly possible to make free judgments of artistic beauty.

Nevertheless, this strategy suffers from two fatal flaws. First, as Crawford himself acknowledges, it fails to deal with those cases in which Kant clearly takes the distinction to apply to the kinds of objects rather than to the judgments about them. Second, and more important, it ignores the fact that the "abstraction" called for is from the very conditions under which something can be judged as a work of art. Consequently, it can hardly provide the basis for distinguishing between two different kinds of judgment of *artistic* beauty.

Although it is without explicit textual support, an alternative, and I believe more viable, strategy involves reformulating the free-adherent beauty distinction in light of the conception of aesthetic ideas. Such a reformulation, I shall try to show, has the twofold advantage of making it possible to draw a distinction within the sphere of fine art that is functionally equivalent to the original distinction, albeit expressed in somewhat different terms, and of avoiding the troublesome implication that virtually all great art falls within the category of merely adherent beauty.

Kant comes closest to formulating such a view explicitly in his discussion of sculpture and architecture, as the two species of plastic art in §51. The former is defined as the "art that exhibits concepts of things corporeally, as they *might exist in nature* (though . . . with a concern for aesthetic purposiveness)," and the latter as the "art of exhibiting concepts of things that are possible *only through art*" (KU 5: 322; 191). As species of fine art, both express aesthetic ideas. But, as Kant points out, in the case of architecture, "the main concern is what *use* is to be made of the artistic object, and this use is a condition to which the aesthetic ideas are confined." In the case of sculpture, however, "the main aim is the mere *expression* of aesthetic ideas" (KU 5: 322; 191). And, somewhat more expansively, he continues, "what is essential in a *work of architecture* is the product's adequacy for a certain use;" whereas a "mere *piece of sculpture,* made solely to be looked at, is meant to be liked on its own account" (KU 5: 322; 192).

Kant goes on to remark that the piece of sculpture is an imitation of nature (which certainly makes it representational in the depictive sense), but that the imitation, or "sensible truth," should not be carried to the point where it ceases to look like art (KU 5: 322; 192). But in spite of these latter claims, which would seem sufficient to make it a merely adherent beauty by the criteria given in §16, it is clear that Kant is treating the piece of sculpture as a free beauty. What is essential is that it is not meant to serve any extrinsic purpose, that it is liked purely for itself, in virtue of the aesthetic ideas it expresses. Moreover, the fact that it depicts something and that its appreciation presupposes a concept of the kind of thing it is meant to be has no bearing on this.

Correlatively, even though he does not use the terminology, there can be little doubt that Kant is here effectively saying that the beauty of works of architecture is merely adherent because their expression of aesthetic ideas is subservient to their functions as places of worship, residences, monuments, and the like.[57] In other words, the aesthetic evaluation of a work of architecture is subject to extra-aesthetic constraints, stemming from its intended function, while that of a piece of sculpture is not (or should not be). Consequently, I believe that this best captures the fundamental difference that Kant was aiming at through his distinction between free and adherent beauty.[58] First, it accords perfectly with the account of adherent beauty as parergonal offered in Chapter 6. Second, as the contrast between sculpture and architecture (which can easily be generalized) indicates, it can be applied within the sphere of fine art, while preserving the principle that all judgment of artistic beauty presupposes a concept of what kind of thing the object is meant to be. Finally, and perhaps most importantly, it makes it possible to regard great painting, sculpture, music, and literature, and so forth as free beauties, without denying their expressive content.[59]

V

Whereas the previous set of problems have all concerned in one way or another the relation between the Analytic of the Beautiful and Kant's account of fine art, our final problem involves a conflict within the latter account itself. The problem concerns Kant's conception of genius and its relation to taste in the production of fine art. As we have seen, Kant introduces the concept of genius in §46 in order to account for the possibility of something having the seemingly paradoxical features that his analysis showed must be attributed to a work of fine art: It must look to us like nature, although we are conscious of it as art. This led to the characterization of fine art as the art of genius and of the latter as the "innate mental predisposition (*ingenium*) *through which* nature gives the rule to art" (KU 5: 307; 174). We further saw that genius, so construed, was said to be a talent for the creation of fine art, rather than science (since it involves the production of something for which no determinate rule can be given), and that its defining feature is an "exemplary originality."

Later, after Kant introduces the conception of aesthetic ideas, we also learned that this exemplary originality is to be understood as the capacity to discover and express such ideas.

Throughout all this, genius, as a productive capacity, is explicitly contrasted with taste, which is characterized as "merely an ability to judge, not to produce" (KU 5: 313; 181). In fact, in this context, Kant goes as far as to claim that merely conforming to taste does not of itself qualify something as a work of fine art. This, we are told, is because all that taste requires is a pleasing form, and this can be given to products that are manifestly not works of fine art, such as tableware, moral treatises, and sermons (KU 5: 313; 181).

At the same time, however, there is another strand of thought at work, according to which taste is itself viewed as playing a role in the production as well as the appreciation of works of art. So construed, taste is seen as a necessary complement of genius and even, at one point, as the *conditio sine qua non* of a work of fine art. The first reference to taste as a productive faculty is found in the treatment of the ideal of beauty in §17, where Kant endeavors to explain why we regard some "products of taste as exemplary" (KU 5: 232; 79). More significantly, in §47, though he does not refer to taste, Kant seems to qualify his initial characterization of genius by claiming that fine art has as an essential condition "something mechanical," which can be formulated in terms of rules, and thus an "element of *academic correctness*" (KU 5: 310; 178). On this view, genius becomes only one of the elements necessary for the creation of fine art. It is said to be the source of the *material* for fine art, whereas "processing this material and giving it *form* requires a talent that is academically trained" (KU 5: 310; 178). Similarly, in the last paragraph of §48, after the previously cited passage in which he denies that taste is a productive capacity and suggests that the imposition of a pleasing, communicable form (which is attributed to taste) does not of itself make something into a work of fine art, Kant concludes that we frequently find a "would-be [*seinsollenden*] work of art that manifests genius without taste, or another that manifests taste without genius" (KU 5: 313; 181). The latter passage, in particular, strongly suggests what we might term the "complementarity view," according to which genius and taste are each necessary and jointly sufficient conditions of the creation of artistic beauty. Consequently, any product lacking either one would be merely a "would-be" work of fine art.

Finally, in §50, which is entitled "On the Combination of Taste with Genius in Products of Fine Art," Kant appears to move beyond the complementarity view to one in which primacy is given to taste over genius. Addressing the traditional question of whether genius or taste is more important in a work of fine art, he equates this with the question of whether imagination is to be valued more highly than judgment, and he comes down squarely on the side of the latter. Thus, Kant suggests that "insofar as a work shows genius, it deserves to be termed *inspired* [*geistreiche*], but that it deserves to be called *fine* art only insofar as it shows taste" (KU 5: 319; 188). Accordingly, taste (not genius) turns out to be the sole necessary condition for a work of fine art; and in light of this, Kant claims that in order for a work to be beautiful, "it is not strictly necessary that it be rich and original in ideas." All that is required, he now suggests, is that "the imagination in its freedom be commensurate with the lawfulness of the understanding," which presumably is the business of judgment (and therefore taste) to determine (KU 5: 319; 188).

The contradictions between these various accounts are palpable and have not escaped the attention of the commentators.[60] At times viewed merely as a judgmental capacity that plays no part in the creative process, taste is elsewhere elevated into a co-partner in that process, and at one point is made the chief and indispensable factor. Correlatively, genius, initially introduced in order to account for the very possibility of a work of fine art, is demoted first to a co-equal status with taste and/or academic discipline, and then to a mere subordinate, a kind of second-class citizen in the creative process, whose contribution apparently can be sacrificed without totally negating the beauty of the work. In addition, this shifting evaluation of the nature and role of genius goes together with the forementioned change in the significance attributed to its distinctive product, aesthetic ideas. To be sure, the latter does not amount to a strict contradiction, since to deny that a work need be rich and original in ideas is not to affirm that it may be altogether lacking in them. Once again, the poetry of Frederick the Great is a case in point. Nevertheless, it certainly appears to be a striking shift of emphasis, indeed, one which Kant seems to reverse at the beginning of the very next section with the new definition of beauty as the "expression of aesthetic ideas" (KU 5: 320; 189).

Anything approaching an adequate treatment of this topic would require a lengthy study of the development of Kant's conception of genius, which can be traced through the various sets of lectures on anthropology and the *Reflexionen* associated therewith, as well as by a comparison of his views with those of his contemporaries. As the work of scholars such as Schlapp and Tonelli indicates, such a study would show that the apparent inconsistencies in the account of genius and its relation to taste in the third *Critique* reflect tensions and ambiguities that are discernible in Kant's thoughts on the topic after the 70s.[61] Moreover, it is also clear that Kant was quite cognizant of contemporary discussions of the nature of genius and attempted to incorporate much of what he read into his own account, which no doubt explains at least some of the inconsistency noted.[62]

Nevertheless, setting aside questions of historical influence and development, the basic fact is that in the third *Critique*, Kant operates with two distinct conceptions of genius.[63] One, which I shall call the "thick" conception, is at work throughout most of the discussion of fine art. It is this conception that is characterized as an "exemplary originality" and that includes understanding and, indeed, judgment, together with an inventive imagination as essential components.[64] It is also genius in this sense that "gives the rule to art," thereby distinguishing genuine products of genius from "original nonsense."

At some points, however, and particularly in §50, Kant presents a "thin" conception of genius, according to which genius seems to be limited merely to an imaginative capacity, and therefore does not itself involve understanding, judgment, or taste. Consequently, in these places Kant emphasizes the necessity of "clipping the wings" of genius, of "disciplining and training" it through taste or judgment, lest the imagination in its "lawless freedom" produce nothing but original nonsense. Only by this means, he suggests, can aesthetic ideas be made "durable, fit for approval that is both lasting and universal, and fit for being followed by others and for an ever advancing culture" (KU 5: 318; 188).

The thin conception represents a recurrent strand in Kant's thought about genius, but its function in the third *Critique* is largely polemical. Consequently, Kant appeals to this conception when his concern is to underscore the dangers of flights of fancy unfettered by discipline and judgment.[65] By contrast, it is the thick conception that is required by Kant's account of fine art and aesthetic ideas, in short, by his "creation aesthetic." Thus, in spite of its obscurity and difficulty, I believe that it is this conception that must be attributed to Kant in the attempt to reconstruct his views on the nature of artistic beauty and the conditions of the possibility of its production.

THE SUBLIME

The modern interest in the sublime is generally thought to have been awakened by the appearance in 1674 of Nicolas Boileau's translation of the treatise *Peri Hypsous* [*On the Sublime*], which is traditionally attributed to Longinus.[1] Largely as a result of the influence of this treatise, the topic of the sublime assumed central significance in the aesthetic reflections in the eighteenth century. Although the reasons for this sudden emergence of interest are complex, clearly a major factor was that the sublime represented that which stood outside the sphere of the dominant neoclassical aesthetic, with its emphasis on form, rules, and clarity.[2] For, on the one hand, the sublime constituted a major challenge for proponents of this aesthetic, while, on the other hand, it provided a natural focal point for its critics.

Apart from Longinus's treatise itself and Boileau's commentary, both of which continued to be widely read, the most influential treatment of the subject in the second half of the eighteenth century was Edmund Burke's, *A Philosophical Enquiry into the Origin of Our Ideas of the Sublime and the Beautiful* (first edition 1757).[3] Adopting a psychophysiological approach, Burke attempted to provide both a description of the experiences of the sublime and the beautiful and a causal account of the genesis of these feelings. Moreover, in contrast to most previous theorists, he emphasized the radical distinction between the two feelings. Most importantly, the sublime, for Burke, involved terror as its "ruling principle."[4] But since the sublime, as such, is liked, he concluded from this that the feeling cannot consist in an actual terror (which he regarded as the most painful of all human emotions), but rather in one that is felt, as it were, at a distance and in safety.[5] And from this connection of the sublime with terror, he further concluded that the liking for it must not be described as a pleasure, but should instead be viewed as a *"delight."*[6]

Kant shared the interest of many of his contemporaries in the sublime, and his initial published discussion of it, *Observations on the Feeling of the Beautiful and Sublime* of 1764, antedated the appearance of the German translation of Burke's *Enquiry* by nine years. As the title suggests, this brief work consists more of a series of aperçus regarding the two feelings and their various objects and forms than a serious analysis of the concepts.[7] But scattered references to the sublime in his lectures on anthropology and some of the *Reflexionen* connected therewith indicate that Kant had an ongoing, albeit somewhat sporadic, interest in the topic.[8] Nevertheless, the inclusion of it in the *Critique of Judgment* seems to have been a last-minute decision, and Kant clearly viewed it as parergonal to the central systematic concerns of the work.[9] In fact, he characterized the theory of the sublime as "a mere appendix to our aesthetic judging of the purposiveness of nature" (KU 5: 246; 100).

Given the continued interest of both Kant himself and many of his potential readers in the subject, this apparent marginalization of the sublime in the third *Critique* seems somewhat puzzling. The puzzle becomes even greater when one considers the two respects in which the sublime (as Kant conceived it) seems to be directly germane to the central concerns of the *Critique of Judgment*. First, like judgments of taste, those of sublimity are claimed to be aesthetic judgments of reflection, which, as such, rest upon an *a priori* principle and make a demand for agreement. Second, according to the terms of Kant's own analysis, the sublime stands in an even more intimate relation to morality than does the beautiful. Consequently, one might very well expect that Kant would grant it at least "equal billing" with, if not superior status to, the beautiful, rather than the belated and relatively minor role he actually assigns to it.

Nevertheless, Kant's deeply ambivalent attitude toward the sublime becomes somewhat more understandable if one distinguishes the question of its intrinsic significance from that of its relation to the systematic or architectonic concerns of the third *Critique*. The former I take to be undeniable for the reasons noted, but at the same time there are essential features of the sublime, as Kant understood it, which made it difficult for him to integrate it fully into the framework of the *Critique of Judgment*.

This tension, then, between the Kantian sublime and the systematic principles on which the *Critique of Judgment* is structured will be a central theme of the present chapter, which is divided into nine parts. The first provides a brief overview of the textual evidence for the last-minute nature of Kant's inclusion of the Analytic of the Sublime, together with an attempt to explain this on the basis of the merely parergonal status granted to it. The second discusses Kant's account of the similarities and differences between the beautiful and the sublime in §23 and the account of the division of the latter into the mathematically and the dynamically sublime in §24. Parts three through five together deal with the mathematically sublime. The first of these discusses the nominal definitions of the sublime given in §25; the second, the "quantity" of the mathematically sublime in §26; and the third, its "quality" (or phenomenology) in §27. Part six analyzes the account of the dynamically sublime in §28; and part seven examines the argument of §29, which, I argue, functions as the "deduction" of the sublime in both its forms. Finally, the eighth and ninth parts serve as appendixes to the account of the sublime and are concerned respectively with its relations to fine art and to morality.

I

A striking feature of Kant's treatment of the sublime, which is indicative of the last-minute nature of its inclusion, is the paucity of references to it outside of the Analytic of the Sublime itself. This is particularly true of the Introductions, where one would expect to find significant preliminary discussions.[10] Thus, even though in the First Introduction Kant focuses on the problematic of an aesthetic judgment of reflection and the judgment of the sublime clearly falls into that category, he fails even to mention it in that context. In fact, the first mention of the sublime occurs late in this lengthy text, where it is characterized in passing as concerned with a "relative subjective purposiveness," which is contrasted with the "intrinsic subjective purposiveness" pertaining to the beautiful (FI 20: 249; 439). And in the very last section, devoted to an account of the divisions of the *Critique of Judgment*, Kant refers to a proposed "critique of *intellectual feeling* [*Geistesgefühl*]," which he provisionally calls "the ability to represent a sublimity in objects" (FI 20: 250; 440). Moreover, in sharp contrast to the form which the treatment of the sublime eventually took, Kant suggests that it will contain a separate deduction and, like the beautiful, be divided into an analytic and a dialectic (FI 20: 251; 441).[11]

Contrary to what one might expect in virtue of its later date of composition, the treatment of the sublime in the Second Introduction is even briefer and more perfunctory than in the First. In fact, it is there confined to a single brief paragraph appended to the discussion of the aesthetic representation of purposiveness in Section VII. After devoting the entire discussion to judgments of taste and their relationship to the purposiveness of the form of objects, Kant points out that pleasure arising from reflection on the forms of things does not always indicate a purposiveness of objects with regard to the reflective faculty of judgment. "[S]ometimes," he suggests, it "indicates a purposiveness of the subject with regard to objects in terms of their form, or even their lack of form [*Unform*], in conformity with the concept of freedom." Such judgments, he further tells us, "arise from an *intellectual* feeling and as such refer to the sublime" (KU 5: 192; 32). And this is all that Kant has to say about the sublime in the entire Second Introduction!

The situation is not much different in the main body of the *Critique of Judgment*, since apart from the Analytic of the Sublime, there are only six explicit references or clear allusions to the sublime.[12] The earliest (and the only one in the Analytic of the Beautiful) occurs at the end of §14, where Kant is concerned to illustrate by means of examples the thesis of §13 that the pure judgment of taste must be independent of both charm and emotion [*Rührung*]. As was noted in Chapter 6, the entire account up until the last brief paragraph focuses exclusively on the former. Only at the very end, in what gives every appearance of being an afterthought, does Kant define emotion as "a sensation where agreeableness is brought about only by means of a momentary inhibition of the vital force [*Lebenskraft*] followed by a stronger outpouring of it"; and he then adds that this does not pertain to beauty at all, but rather to sublimity [*Erhabenheit*] (KU 5: 226; 72).

The second reference to the sublime is the claim in §30 that the exposition given of judgments of the sublime was also their deduction (KU 5: 280; 142). Since that was discussed in some detail in Chapter 8, I have nothing further to say about it here. The next reference is in §39, where, in contrast to the official view of the sublime as involving an agitation or movement of the mind, which is expressed in §14 by its connection with emotion, Kant describes the pleasure in the sublime as one of "rationalizing contemplation" [*vernünftelden Contemplation*] (KU 5: 292; 158). The remaining references are in §49 and §52 and are incidental to the main concerns of these sections. But since they relate to the question of the connection between the sublime and fine art, they will be discussed in part VIII of this chapter.

Although it hardly seems necessary, further evidence of the last-minute nature of Kant's inclusion of the sublime is provided by the Analytic of the Sublime itself. This is indicated by both the extreme clumsiness of the way in which the account is integrated into the text and the relatively undeveloped, confusedly structured analysis (compared to that of the beautiful) provided of the sublime. To begin with, the entirety of Book II of the Analytic of Aesthetic Judgment, that is, all of the text from §23–§54, which includes the Deduction, the account of the empirical and intellectual interests in the beautiful, and the discussion of fine art and genius, is entitled "Analytic of the Sublime," even though only §23–§29 (and the "General Comment on the Exposition of Aesthetic Reflective Judgments," which follows §29) deal with the sublime.

In addition, the actual discussion of the sublime is both structurally and philosophically flawed by Kant's failure to correlate two distinct organizing principles: One is the same table of judgment-forms used to organize the Analytic of the Beautiful; the other is the distinction between the mathematically and dynamically sublime, which has no analogue in the case of the beautiful. The systematic combination of these principles would presumably require that each of the two species of the sublime be analyzed under each of the four headings of the table. What we find instead, however, is that the mathematically sublime is analyzed only under the first two headings (quantity and quality) and the dynamically sublime under the third (relation). Moreover, though the discussion of modality is listed under the mathematically sublime, it actually deals with both species.[13] Finally, Kant further complicates things in the General Comment by introducing a new form of the sublime (pertaining to mental states), which does not seem to fall within either of the two species distinguished in the Analytic.[14]

Nevertheless, it is one thing to point out the obvious and quite another to provide reasons for this cavalier treatment of the sublime. Thus, we return to the question with which we began, namely why, given its connection with both reflective judgment and morality (the two major themes of the third *Critique*), did Kant describe the theory of the sublime as a "mere appendix to our aesthetic judging of the purposiveness of nature"?

In my judgment, there are two main reasons for this view, the first of which is indicated by the phrase "purposiveness of nature." In spite of its intrinsic interest and moral significance, the sublime really stands outside the framework of an investigation of the purposiveness of nature in a way in which the beautiful (at least natural beauty) does not. For the purposiveness of nature (in both its purely aesthetic and moral dimensions) is epitomized by the thought that nature "favors us," which, morally speaking, means that we may assume its amenability to the realization of the ends required by pure practical reason. Thus, as we saw in Chapter 10, the experience of natural beauty opens us up to intimations of such purposiveness and thereby helps to effectuate the needed transition from nature to freedom. The sublime, by contrast, offers us a very different "aesthetic education," which corresponds to a different side of Kant's moral theory. For what the experience of the sublime evokes in us is precisely a sense of our independence of, and superiority to, nature (both the sheer magnitude and power of external nature without and our sensuous nature within). And as central as this is to Kant's overall moral theory, it stands in a somewhat uneasy tension with the main theme of the *Critique of Judgment*, which remains the positive relation between freedom and nature.[15]

The second reason, which bears more directly on the underlying theory of reflective judgment, is suggested by the previously cited passage from the Second Introduction, where Kant relates the intellectual feeling, whose intentional object is the sublime, with "the purposiveness of the subject with regard to objects in terms of their form, or even their lack of form, in conformity with the concept of freedom." The essential point here is the explicit disassociation of purposiveness and form, which contrasts sharply with Kant's insistence on the close connection between them in the Analytic of the Beautiful. For since purposiveness is now referred to the concept of freedom, rather than to that of nature, it no longer has anything to do with the form of its object or its representation.

Given this, it seems clear that anything approaching an adequate integration of the theory of the sublime into the *Critique of Judgment* would have required, among other things, an extensive revision of Kant's conceptions of a purely aesthetic judgment, reflection, and purposiveness. Consequently, it becomes understandable why Kant only included a discussion of the sublime at the last minute, and even then tended to downplay its significance. On the one hand, he came to realize that the sublime is too closely connected with his concern to ground a transcendental function for judgment and to establish a connection between aesthetic judgment and morality to be omitted altogether, while, on the other hand, he also saw that it differs too sharply from the liking for the beautiful to be easily contained within the analytic framework developed for the treatment of the latter (the original project of a critique of taste). In what follows, I shall attempt to show how these factors are reflected in Kant's actual treatment of the sublime.

II

Kant introduces the topic of the sublime in §23 with an account of the chief similarities and differences between it and the beautiful. The similarities, which are all listed in the first paragraph, consist of five main points. (1) Both are "liked for their own sake" (which presumably indicates their disinterestedness). (2) Both are based on a judgment of reflection, rather than either a mere judgment of sense or a logically determinative judgment, which distinguishes them from the agreeable, on the one hand, and the good, on the other. (3) As based on a reflective use of judgment, the liking in both cases is referred to concepts, though it is indeterminate as to which ones. (4) For the same reason, the liking in both cases is connected with a mere exhibition or faculty thereof (imagination), with the result that we regard this faculty (with respect to a given intuition) as harmonizing with and enhancing the faculty of concepts, which in order to make room for the sublime is characterized as either understanding or reason. (5) Again for the same reason, both kinds of judgment are singular (involve a given intuition), yet lay claim to universal validity, even though they concern merely the feeling of pleasure, rather than the cognition of an object (KU 5: 244; 97–8). In short, they both are aesthetic judgments of reflection and, as such, share the features essential to that species of judgment.[16]

As Kant proceeds to point out in the remainder of this section, however, they are very different kinds of aesthetic judgments of reflection. The first of the differences indicated concerns the previously noted connection with form. The beautiful in nature, Kant reminds us, always concerns an object's form, which he now tells us consists in its boundedness [*Begränzung*]. In other words, whatever is deemed beautiful must be apprehended as an ordered whole falling within determinate limits. The sublime, by contrast, can also be found (Kant does not say that it must be found) in a formless object and, therefore, in something unbounded. What is required is only that this unboundedness be also thought of as totality [*Totalität*] (KU 5: 244; 98). Although this account is presumably intended as an introduction to both forms of the sublime, it should be noted that the latter seems applicable only to the mathematically sublime.

From this, Kant infers that the beautiful is the exhibition of an indeterminate concept of the *understanding*, whereas the sublime exhibits an indeterminate concept of *reason* (KU 5: 244; 98). This dual reference to an indeterminate concept is obviously intended to underscore the point that in both cases it is a judgment of mere reflection, that is, one not issuing in cognition, which would require a determinate concept. Nevertheless, the indeterminateness is of two quite different sorts. For as was noted in Chapter 11, all concepts of the understanding are determinate (or at least *determinable*), whereas all ideas of reason are indeterminate and (theoretically) indeterminable. An indeterminable concept of the understanding would be one that is not schematizable, which means that it is merely the form of a concept, not an actual concept. Consequently, we must take Kant's point here to be that the beautiful is that which has the form of the exhibition of *some concept or other* (it being undetermined which one), and this is fully in accord with the accounts in the Introductions and the Analytic of the Beautiful considered in the first two parts of this study.

Clearly, the main point of interest here is the correlation of the beautiful with the understanding in virtue of its connection with form and boundedness or limitation, that is, finitude, and of the sublime with reason in virtue of its connection with the formless and the unbounded or infinite. Thus, the feeling of the sublime will be closely related to our sense of the infinite, which also helps to explain why Kant here suggests that our liking for it is connected with the representation of *quantity*, and that for the beautiful with the representation of *quality* (KU 5: 98; 244). Once again, however, this seems applicable primarily (if not exclusively) to the mathematically sublime.

Turning from the conceptual bases of these feelings to their psychological character, Kant further suggests (in agreement with Burke) that the likings for the beautiful and the sublime are completely different in kind. What he says here about the liking for the beautiful does not go significantly beyond what we have previously been told, but it is nonetheless important for understanding its differences from the sublime. The essential point is the direct connection of the liking for the beautiful with the feeling of the furtherance of life, which makes it immediately and unambiguously pleasurable; and from this, Kant infers that it is compatible with charm and the play of imagination.

By contrast, the liking for the sublime is characterized (in a Burkean vein) as one that arises only indirectly, on the basis of a disliking. Rather than being a feeling of the furtherance of life, this "spiritual feeling" is said to be "produced by a feeling of the momentary inhibition of vital forces [*Lebenskräfte*], followed immediately by an outpouring of them that is all the stronger." As such, it is an emotion [*Rührung*], and seems to involve seriousness rather than play in the reflective activity of the imagination. More precisely, it is a complex mental state in which the mind is not simply attracted to an object but "alternately always repelled as well." This also explains why it (unlike the beautiful) is incompatible with charm, which merely attracts and does not repel. Finally, Kant concludes from this, in partial agreement with Burke, that "the liking for the sublime contains not so much a positive pleasure as rather admiration and respect, and so should be called a negative pleasure" (KU 5: 245; 98).[17]

The final difference between the likings for the beautiful and the sublime concerns their connections with purposiveness. Lest its significance be missed, Kant describes this as "the intrinsic and most important distinction" between the two (KU 5: 245; 98). Given our previous considerations, such a characterization is hardly surprising, and neither is the fact that Kant presents this difference as the consequence of the quite distinct relations of the two species of reflective aesthetic liking with the form of an object (or the lack thereof). As Kant here puts it:

> (Independent [*die Selbständige*]) natural beauty carries with it a purposiveness in its form, by which the object seems as it were predetermined for our faculty of judgment, so that this beauty constitutes in itself an object of our liking. On the other hand, if something arouses in us, merely in apprehension and without any reasoning on our part, a feeling of the sublime, then it may indeed may appear, in its form, counterpurposive [*zweckwidrig*] for our faculty of judgment, incommensurate [*unangemessen*] with our power of exhibition, and as it were violent [*gewaltthätig*] to our imagination, and yet we judge it all the more sublime for that. (KU 5: 245; 98–9)

As we have seen repeatedly, the purposiveness of the beautiful is always that of *form*, understood as the suitability of an object in its mere apprehension for the harmonious interplay of the "two friends," the imagination and the understanding. Consequently, an object deemed beautiful is felt in its apprehension to be perfectly commensurate with the capacities of the imagination, to be, as it were, made for it in its cognitive function of exhibiting something "universal in itself" for the benefit of the understanding. For the same reason, it is also felt to be fully commensurate with the requirements of reflective judgment in its move from intuition to concept, which is precisely why it is liked in mere reflection. What we now learn is that the sublime (much like the ugly) presents itself as *counterpurposive* for the same reflective activity of judgment in virtue of its form (or, better, lack thereof), yet (unlike the ugly) the object is liked, that is, its effect on the mind is felt as purposive. Thus, if the paradox underlying Kant's account of the beautiful is that of a purposiveness without purpose, underlying the sublime is the seemingly even more paradoxical conception of a *counterpurposive purposiveness.*

Rather than providing at this point a much-needed analysis of what such a paradoxical mode of purposiveness might involve, however, Kant proceeds to emphasize that we express ourselves incorrectly when we claim that any particular object in nature is sublime. Since counterpurposiveness cannot, as such, be liked, and since what is properly termed sublime cannot be contained in any sensible form but concerns ideas of reason, Kant insists that true sublimity is to be found only in the mind, and all that may be said about an object is that it is suitable for exhibiting or evoking such sublimity. Moreover, in so characterizing the sublime, Kant also suggests that this points to another fundamental difference from the beautiful, since he remarks that "we may quite correctly call a great many natural objects beautiful" (KU 5: 245; 99) Later, in a frequently cited passage, Kant makes a similar point by suggesting that the respect for our own vocation or the idea of humanity within ourselves, which underlies the feeling of the sublime, is "by a certain subreption" attached to a natural object that makes the former "as it were, intuitable" (KU 5: 257; 114).

In these places, as well as in §30 of the Deduction, Kant seems to be suggesting a difference in ontological status between natural beauty and the sublime. Beauty, on this view, is a perceptible feature (at least for those with taste) of certain objects of phenomenal nature, whereas sublimity is only attributable to a natural object through a subreption. Such a view, however, seems difficult to reconcile with Kant's insistence on the "idealism of purposiveness" in §58 and, indeed, with the entire account of judgments of beauty as aesthetic and, therefore, noncognitive. Consequently, we need an explanation of the claim that one may properly predicate beauty of natural objects but cannot do the same with respect to the sublime. Since judgments of beauty and sublimity are both aesthetic judgments of reflection, does it not follow that both beauty and sublimity are "subjective" in the same sense and to the same degree?

As suggested in Chapter 6, when we first took up the question of the "objectivity" of beauty, the answer lies in the nature of the referent in these two species of aesthetic reflective judgment, that is, with what is actually liked or valued therein. In the case of judgments of taste, what is liked is the object itself as it presents itself in intuition, though it is liked in virtue of its purposiveness for judgment (its subjective purposiveness). By contrast, in the case of the sublime, the object as it appears is *disliked,* since it presents itself as *counterpurposive* for judgment in its reflection. Kant here gives as an example the vast, storm-swept ocean, the immediate sight of which is horrible (KU 5: 245; 99). The point, then, is that with the sublime, the liking arises *in spite of* the appearance of the object, not because of it. What is actually liked in the experience of the sublime is, rather, the feeling of one's supersensible nature that is occasioned by the perception of such objects as stormy oceans, snow covered mountains, or erupting volcanoes in those whose minds are already filled with "all sorts of ideas" (KU 5: 245–6; 99).[18] And as the true referent of this liking, it is also what is properly deemed sublime.

It is precisely at this point, however, that the deep tension between Kant's theory of the sublime (which, following Burke, emphasizes the moment of negativity) and the underlying account of reflective judgment reveals itself. For the purposiveness of the beautiful, like the logical purposiveness of nature discussed in the Introductions, is a purposiveness *for judgment* in its reflective capacity. Consequently, in both cases (and the same may be said of teleological judgment), it is a matter of the *heautonomy* of judgment, of judgment legislating to itself with respect to its reflective activity.[19]

Nevertheless, this can no longer be said about the judgment of the sublime. Although the judgment remains both aesthetic and reflective, the faculty here is clearly not functioning heautonomously. Instead of legislating merely to itself, in the experience of the sublime, judgment encounters something that conflicts with its own requirements, so that the assessment of reflective judgment as such, that is, as operating in accordance with its own principles, must be negative, issuing in a dislike for the object. That an engagement with the sublime is nonetheless aesthetically pleasing is, therefore, the great puzzle posed by the sublime for Kant's account of reflective judgment. And, as we shall see in more detail during the course of this chapter, his solution turns on the introduction of a "higher purposiveness" (KU 5: 246; 99), which concerns the mind as a whole, but particularly the aims of reason. As important as it may be for our sense of ourselves as autonomous rational agents, however, such a "higher purposiveness" clearly stands apart from the theory of reflective judgment and the purposiveness of nature that serves as its "category."

III

The first of the three sections devoted to the mathematically sublime (§25) is concerned with the nominal definition of the term "sublime." As such, it stands apart from the remaining sections, which deal respectively with the quantity and quality of the sublime, and constitutes a kind of introduction to the topic.[20] In the course of his discussion, Kant offers three such definitions, the first and most basic of which is the "*absolutely great.*" This is followed by the distinction between being great or large [*gross*] and being a magnitude or quantum [*eine Grösse*], and a further distinction between claiming *simply* [*schlechtweg*] that something is great and maintaining that it is absolutely great [*schlechthin gross*], that is, great beyond all comparison (*absolute, non comparative magnum*) (KU 5: 248; 103).

Kant deals quickly with the initial distinction, noting that what makes something a magnitude or quantum is that it contains a multiplicity of homogeneous parts constituting a unity. This can be determined merely by considering the thing itself, without any comparison with others. Conversely, the determination of *how great* something is (its magnitude) requires a reference to something else, itself a quantum, which serves as its measure (KU 5: 248; 103–4).

The main interest of this preliminary discussion lies, however, in the account of the simply great [*schlechtweg gross*] and its distinction from the absolutely great [*schlechthin gross*] or sublime. The interest stems from the fact that Kant not only uses the former as a point of departure to introduce the mathematically sublime under its initial definition or description, but also attributes to it some of the features that are likewise assigned to the genuinely sublime. Consequently, even though Kant does not explicitly characterize it as such, it actually functions as a kind of proto- or quasi-sublime.

In saying of something that it is "simply great" [*schlechtweg gross*], Kant suggests, it appears that one has no comparison in mind, at least none with an objective measure, since it is not determined how large the object is. Nevertheless, he remarks that such judgments lay claim to universal assent. In fact, he explicitly compares them with judgments of beauty, noting that both "demand everyone's assent, just as theoretical judgments do" (KU 5: 248; 104).

The problem thus becomes how to understand such a demand and its putative legitimating ground. In dealing with this issue, Kant first notes that by characterizing something as simply great, we are not merely making the trivial point that the object in question has some magnitude; we are, rather, implying that its magnitude is greater than that of many other objects of the same kind, even though this superiority is not assigned a determinate numerical value.[21] For example, in saying of the Empire State Building or of certain basketball or football players that they are simply great, one is saying that they stand out among the class of buildings or human beings in terms of their size. Moreover, we expect others to agree with our assessments in spite of their indeterminacy, which presupposes that we base our judgments on a standard that we presume to be the same for everyone. But since this standard is subjective and underlies our reflective judgment about magnitude, Kant concludes that it does not serve for a logical, that is, mathematically determinate, estimation of magnitude, but only for an aesthetic one (KU 5: 249; 104). As Kant indicates in §26, by an "aesthetic estimation of magnitude" he means one made "by the eye," that is, in immediate perception, as contrasted with one made on the basis of a process of measurement through numbers or algebraic signs. Consequently, Kant is here attributing a normative dimension to such "aesthetic" evaluations quite independently of the question of the sublime.

Kant further suggests that this subjective standard of quantitative assessment may be either empirical or "one given *a priori*" (KU 5: 249; 104). The former is unproblematic and includes indeterminate magnitudes, such as the average size of people one knows (in relation to which a professional basketball player may seem simply immense) or of animals of a certain kind, trees, houses, mountains, and so forth. The latter is somewhat puzzling, however, since none of the examples that Kant gives, namely, the magnitude of a certain virtue, of the civil liberty in a country, or of the correctness or incorrectness of some observation or measurement, is a matter of physical size. Nevertheless, it does seem possible to appreciate Kant's main point by noting that the kind of *a priori* standard to which he is here appealing is said to be based on "deficiencies of the judging subject," that is, "subjective conditions of an exhibition *in concreto*" (KU 5: 249; 104). This suggests that what Kant has in mind here are universally shared constraints on what can be represented or distinguished subjectively, constraints which are grounded in the very nature of our cognitive faculties, and in that sense "given *a priori*." In fact, we shall see that it is precisely such a constraint on what can be aesthetically comprehended that underlies Kant's account of the mathematically sublime.

Continuing his analysis of the simply great, Kant notes that the mere magnitude of an object, quite apart from any interest we might have in it, and even if it is regarded as formless, "can yet carry with it a liking that is universally communicable and hence involves consciousness of a subjective purposiveness in the use of our cognitive faculties" (KU 5: 249; 105). What is particularly noteworthy here is that, aside from the reference to a possible formlessness, the liking for the simply great (not yet the absolutely great or sublime) is described in precisely the same terms used in the first three moments of the Analytic of the Beautiful: It is a disinterested, universally communicable liking, involving a consciousness (i.e., feeling) of subjective purposiveness.

As one would expect, however, this possible formlessness is the key to the difference between the two likings, since because of it what is liked in the case of the simply great is not the object, but rather the "expansion of the imagination itself" (KU 5: 249; 105). Moreover, even though the object itself is not directly liked in virtue of being viewed (in a merely reflective, nonmathematically determinative judgment) as simply great, Kant claims that its representation is always connected with "a kind of respect" [*eine Art von Achtung*], just as we connect what we call simply small [*schlechtweg klein*] with a contempt [*eine Verachtung*] (KU 5: 249; 105).

Only after completing this analysis of the simply great does Kant turn to the absolutely great or sublime. The basic difference is that whereas the former is termed great in comparison to things of its kind (even the tallest human being seems puny in relation to a mountain), the latter is deemed great in every respect and beyond comparison. Since this is an explicitly noncomparative sense of greatness, it follows that no standard or measure of this greatness is to be found outside the thing itself (as was still the case with the simply great). But since the claim to greatness must be based on some standard or measure (otherwise it could not lay claim to universality), the latter must be located within the thing itself. In other words, the thing functions as its own standard, calling attention to its inherent greatness, a point which Kant makes cryptically by stating that "It is a magnitude that is equal only to itself" (KU 5: 250; 105).

From this bit of conceptual analysis, Kant draws two further consequences: (1) that the sublime is not to be sought in objects in nature, but only in ideas; (2) a second nominal definition of the sublime as that *"in comparison with which everything else is small"* (KU 5: 250; 105). It is clear that this second definition is logically equivalent to the first, since it is derived directly from an analysis of what is meant by saying that something is absolutely great. It is also clear from this why the sublime is not to be sought in objects of nature, for as Kant goes on to note:

> [N]othing in nature can be given, however large we may judge it, that could not, when considered in a different relation, be degraded all the way to the infinitely small, nor conversely anything so small that it could not, when compared with still smaller standards, be expanded for our imagination all the way to the magnitude of a world; telescopes have provided us with a wealth of material in support of the first point, microscopes in support of the second. (KU 5: 250; 106)

Given this result, we can also see why Kant characterizes his initial definitions of the sublime as nominal. For if nothing in nature can possibly fit the description expressed in these definitions, then the possibility arises that the sublime is a mere fiction or "phantom of the brain." But since Kant clearly did not hold such a view, it became incumbent upon him to explain what justifies the use of the term and what experiences underlie it. It is in addressing these questions that Kant turns to a transcendental investigation of the subjective sources of the feeling of the sublime in the nature of our cognitive faculties. Consequently, it is here that the relation between the imagination and reason assumes central importance.

Kant initially discusses this relation at the end of §25, immediately following the negative conclusion about the objective reality of the sublime. He states that the imagination, in its endeavor to picture to itself something absolutely great, "strives to progress toward infinity" [*ins Unendliche*] and, in so doing, necessarily places itself under the demand of reason for "absolute totality as a real idea." Although Kant is not very informative regarding the crucial question of why the imagination is subject (or subjects itself) to the demand of reason for absolute totality, I believe that it is possible to reconstruct the gist of his position on the basis of the materials provided in §25, particularly if we include the previous discussion of the simply great.

What requires explanation is why the imagination is concerned with the absolutely great in the first place; and the answer is to be found in the supposedly pleasing and purposive expansion it experiences in an engagement with the simply great. Given this result, it seems reasonable to assume that the thought of something *absolutely* great would hold forth the promise of an even greater expansion and, therefore, an even greater satisfaction. But, in sharp contrast to the previous experience, this endeavor necessarily leads the imagination to strive toward infinity, since, as we have seen, nothing finite can fit the description of being absolutely great. Thus, the imagination must assume increasingly larger measures *ad infinitum* in pursuit of its goal.

It is also the case that anything that is to count as absolutely great, or as "a magnitude equal only to itself," must be thought of as an absolute totality, as complete in itself. For anything less than such a totality may be thought a mere part of a larger whole, in which case it cannot be taken as absolutely great. Consequently, the imagination finds itself guided in its reflection by reason's idea of such a totality, and only by realizing it can it apprehend something absolutely great.[22]

The project is, of course, futile, and the inevitable failure brings with it a feeling of displeasure. At this point, however, Kant does not mention this displeasure. Instead, he notes that the inadequacy of the imagination in this endeavor "itself is the arousal in us of the feeling that we have within us a supersensible faculty." And he adds to this that the absolutely great is not to be located in a sensible object (which we already know), but rather lies in "the use that judgment makes naturally of certain objects" for the sake of the latter feeling, and in contrast with which "every other use is small" (KU 5: 250; 106).

Although it remains unclear in what sense judgment's *use* of an object may be described as either great or small (not to mention absolutely great), Kant seems to be suggesting that these terms are appropriate just in case the use serves to evoke or occasion the thought of the absolutely great and the feeling for the supersensible associated therewith. And from this he concludes that what is to be termed sublime is not the object but "the attunement of the mind [*Geistesstimmung*] through a certain representation that occupies reflective judgment" (KU 5: 250; 149). In other words, what is really sublime is the complex mental state (which includes a feeling for the supersensible) that arises from the futile endeavor of the imagination to realize intuitively the idea of the absolutely great.

Kant concludes §25 with yet another nominal definition or, as he now terms them, "formulas" of the sublime. According to this formula, *"Sublime is what even to be able to think proves that the mind has a power surpassing every standard of sense"* (KU 5: 250; 106). On the surface at least, this differs markedly from the first two in that, on the one hand, it fails to mention size or greatness, while, on the other, it makes an explicit reference to the mind and its supersensible capacities that is not to be found in the others. Nevertheless, it may be viewed as a consequence of the first two formulas. For it is precisely what is thought to be absolutely great or, equivalently, that in comparison with which everything else is small, that requires a supersensible capacity even to think it, since it involves reason's idea of absolute totality, which clearly surpasses "every standard of sense."

IV

Section 26 constitutes a virtual new beginning. Although the definitions offered in §25 are eventually brought into the story, the analysis of the mathematically sublime proceeds by way of a general examination of the nature of magnitude and its estimation. The results of this examination are then used to explicate the special case of the mathematically sublime with its gesture to the infinite. Underlying the entire discussion is the distinction between the "mathematical" or, as Kant also terms it, "logical," and "aesthetic" estimations of magnitude. The former consists in measurement on the basis of numerical concepts or their algebraic signs. It thus falls within the purview of determinative judgment. The latter, as we have already seen, is an estimation in mere intuition "by the eye" (KU 5: 251; 107), that is, through an immediate apprehension not based on the application of a determinate measure.[23]

The mathematical estimation of magnitude takes place through the familiar practice of measurement, but Kant points out that the latter is of itself neither sufficient nor even primary for the determination of magnitude. It is not sufficient because measurement in terms of numerical concepts (inches, meters, acres, etc.) presupposes a given unit of measure. To be told, for example, that Noah's Ark was three thousand cubits long is not particularly helpful, unless one also happens to know that a cubit is a unit of measure based roughly on the length of a human forearm. Correlatively, it is not primary because (on pain of an infinite regress) the basic unit of measure must itself be determined merely aesthetically.[24]

This sharp distinction between the mathematical and aesthetic estimations of magnitude leads directly to the concept of a maximum [*Grösstes*]. There can be no maximum for mathematical estimation for the same reason that there is no largest number, namely, the infinite extendability of the number series. But though there can be no largest number, there is a largest unit of measure. Kant here terms it the "absolute measure," and it is conditioned by the limits of the human imagination, that is, by what is subjectively possible to "take in in one intuition" (KU 5: 251; 108). Moreover, it is this (subjectively) absolute measure that brings with it the idea of the sublime and the emotion connected therewith, an emotion "which no mathematical estimation of magnitude by means of numbers can produce (except to the extent that the basic aesthetic measure is at the same time kept alive in the imagination") (KU 5: 251; 107–8).

Kant attempts to explicate this subjectively grounded maximum by means of a brief analysis of what is involved in the imagination's grasping or taking in a multiplicity of items in a single intuition. This process, which is the means by which the basic aesthetic measure is determined, involves two distinct acts of the imagination. Kant terms these *"apprehension"* [*Auffassung*] and *"comprehension"* [*Zusammenfassung*] (KU 5: 251; 108).[25] The former consists simply in taking an item up into empirical consciousness and poses no problems for the estimation of magnitude because it can be iterated indefinitely or, as Kant here puts it, "may progress to infinity" (KU 5: 251; 108).

This is not the case with comprehension, however, which, as the term suggests, involves a holding together of the apprehended items.[26] As the imagination progresses in its apprehension, this holding together or retaining before the mind all of the apprehended items becomes increasingly more difficult. Thus, at a certain point in the process, a kind of equilibrium is reached, the imagination losing as much on the one side (comprehension) as it gains on the other (apprehension). Moreover, it is this that determines the maximum that the mind can take in in a single intuition and therefore use as a basic unit of measure.

The latter point is illustrated by two examples that have been the source of a certain amount of confusion in the literature. The first is taken from a comment by Savary, which Kant offers as confirming his claim about comprehension.[27] According to Savary's account, in order to experience the full emotional effect of the magnitude of the Egyptian pyramids one must neither get too close nor stand too far away. If one is too far away, the apprehended parts are only perceived obscurely, with the result that they produce no aesthetic effect. Conversely, if one is too close, then some time is required to complete the apprehension from base to peak, with the result that the parts perceived first are extinguished in the imagination as the later one's are apprehended, so that the comprehension is never complete.

In virtue of what Kant had just said about comprehension, it might seem that he has here gotten things precisely backward. For if the breakdown of comprehension is of itself to be the source of the emotional effect of the perception of the pyramids, then it would appear that the proper thing to do in order to attain such an effect is to stand as closely as possible to them![28] But this only follows on the assumption that what Kant is trying to illustrate here is an experience of the mathematically sublime, rather than the more general point of the necessary interrelation of apprehension and comprehension in the aesthetic estimation of magnitude. The reference to the emotional effect of this magnitude does not require such an interpretation, however, since we have seen that the experience of something as simply great, though quite distinct from the absolutely great or sublime, nonetheless involves a pleasing expansion of the imagination. Moreover, an aesthetic experience of the pyramids as simply great in Kant's sense would arguably require perceiving them at a distance that allows for full comprehension as well as distinct apprehension.

Nevertheless, Kant does clearly suggest a genuine encounter with the sublime in the second illustration, which is that of the experience of a spectator on first entering St. Peter's. As Kant describes reports of this experience, the spectator is seized by a bewilderment [*Bestürzung*] or kind of perplexity [*Verlegenheit*], which is said to result from the feeling of the inadequacy of the imagination for the presentation of the idea of the whole. When the imagination, upon reaching its maximum of comprehension, strives to extend it, it finds that it sinks back into itself; but the initial negative feeling is then transformed into an emotional delight [*rührendes Wohlgefallen*]" (KU 5: 252; 108–9). As we have already seen, such a transformation of an initially negative effect on the imagination into a delight is the hallmark of the sublime.

Since the great pyramids and St. Peter's, like the examples from §49 and §52, are works of art, and since Kant maintains that the sublime in its purity is to be sought in "crude nature" rather than in products of art (KU 5: 252–3; 109), questions naturally arise regarding both the consistency of Kant's position and the legitimacy of his apparent exclusion of the sublime from the domain of art. As already indicated, however, in order to avoid a lengthy digression, I shall postpone a consideration of this topic until the eighth section.

For the present, our concern is with the concept of purposiveness as it pertains to the sublime. The characterization of one's initial experience upon entering St. Peter's reconfirms the previously noted point that an encounter with the sublime is *counterpurposive* for judgment in its reflection, and in this respect more akin to the ugly than the beautiful. At the same time, however, it is also clear that the sublime must in some sense be subjectively purposive if it is to be liked aesthetically. This, then, is the problem with which Kant must deal. It is not a completely new one, since it first arose as a consequence of Kant's initial discussion of the distinction between the sublime and beautiful in §23. But instead of discussing it there, he reserved his treatment of it for the second part of §26. This treatment begins with a formulation of the problem in its full extent:

> What is this subjective purposiveness, and how does it come to be pre-scribed as a standard, thereby providing a basis for a universally valid liking accompanying the mere estimation of magnitude – an estimation that has been pushed to the point where the ability of our imagination is inadequate to exhibit the concept of a magnitude? (KU 5: 253; 110)

Although there appear to be two distinct questions here, (1) the na-ture of the subjective purposiveness operative in the mathematically sub-lime and (2) how this purposiveness comes to be prescribed as a standard or norm, we shall see that they are intimately connected. For in explain-ing this unique form of subjective purposiveness, Kant also accounts for its normative function as the ground of the universality claim in the judg-ment of the sublime. Unfortunately, in order to demonstrate this, it is necessary to examine closely some of the murkier details of Kant's analy-sis of the mathematically sublime.

To begin with, this analysis presupposes the first *Critique*'s thesis that reason, in its theoretical capacity, demands a systematic unity or totality (closure) that can never be provided by the understanding.[29] Of equal importance to the argument, however, is the difference in the functions of the imagination in the mathematical or logical and the aesthetic esti-mations of magnitude, particularly as they bear on the thought of the in-finite.

According to Kant's account, in mathematical estimation, the imagi-nation operates under the direction of the numerical concepts of the un-derstanding, which it schematizes. Since its aim is measurement, this ac-tivity is purposive, but it is an objective purposiveness involving nothing that is liked by aesthetic judgment. Moreover, such estimation can pro-ceed unproblematically to infinity, without any strain on the imagination, because the unit of measurement or quantum given in intuition for which it is ultimately responsible is irrelevant to the process, and because there is never any need to comprehend the totality in a single intuition (a *comprehensio aesthetica*). Whether the counting proceeds on the basis of the decadic or tetradic systems, whether the unit of measurement be a foot, a rod, a German mile, or even the diameter of the earth makes no intrinsic difference, since all that the imagination need do is to appre-hend successively the items measured (or counted). And since there is no maximum governing apprehension, it can do this to infinity [*ins Un-endliche*] (KU 5: 253–4; 110–11).[30]

Appealing to the first *Critique*'s conception of theoretical reason, how-ever, Kant insists that in the estimation of magnitude, the mind does not simply follow the understanding in its endless iteration. It also "listens to the voice of reason within itself," and this voice "demands totality for all given magnitudes, even for those that we can never apprehend in their entirety, but do (in sensible intuition) estimate as given in their entirety." He further insists that with this demand for totality comes an additional requirement for which the understanding has no need, namely, "comprehension in *one* intuition, and *exhibition* of all the members of a progressively increasing numerical series." In fact, Kant suggests that reason does not even exempt the infinite of space and past time from this totalizing demand (KU 5: 254; 111).

This is a difficult as well as important passage, but I take Kant's main point to be that, even though it meets all our legitimate cognitive needs, the mathematical estimation of magnitude by the understanding, with its infinity of endless progression, is not fully satisfying to the mind as a whole. This is because of the forementioned "voice of reason" and its inherent demand for totality or closure, which, if attained, would give the mind a purely intellectual satisfaction that can never be provided by the understanding. In looking for such satisfaction, the mind necessarily seeks something that is the business of the imagination to produce, namely, the "comprehension in *one* intuition" or *comprehensio aesthetica* of all of the elements of a whole being considered. Such comprehension is necessary for the mind's attainment of this satisfaction because to estimate a whole (such as that of past time) as "given" in its entirety is just to view it as the object or correlate of such a comprehensive grasp. The understanding does not require this, however, since it only attempts to think the whole progressively and not comprehensively (all at once, as it were). In other words, it does not attempt to think it as given *as a whole*.

As Kant proceeds to indicate in the next paragraph, the problem for the imagination stems from the infinite nature of the whole of which a comprehensive grasp is sought. Appealing (albeit without calling attention to the fact) to the first two nominal definitions of the sublime, Kant notes that the infinite is "absolutely great," and that "Compared with it everything else . . . is small" (KU 5: 254; 111). Given these definitions, it might seem that Kant now has everything he needs to connect this attempt to provide intellectual satisfaction with the sublime. But instead of doing this (or even mentioning the sublime), he emphasizes the importance of a preliminary conclusion, namely, that "to be able even to think the infinite as *a whole* indicates a mental power that surpasses any standard of sense" (KU 5: 254; 111).

Kant's argument for this claim is both cryptic and illuminating. It turns on the incommensurability of the infinite or absolutely great with any finite unit of measure (which is what is meant by a "standard of sense"). This incommensurability is a consequence of the fact that to think the infinite as a whole, while using a standard of sense, "would require a comprehension yielding as a unity [unit of measure] a standard that would have a determinate relation to the infinite, one that could be stated in numbers; and this is impossible" (KU 5: 254; 111). In other words, the unit of measure on the basis of which the thought of an infinite whole could be attained on a standard of sense would have to be of a magnitude such that for some determinate n, n times that measure would yield the infinite whole, which is clearly impossible. Indeed, the problem here is precisely the same as the one diagnosed in the preceding section in connection with the imagination's futile attempt to grasp the absolutely great, namely, that nothing less than something that is itself absolutely great could serve as the unit of measure. And Kant concludes from this that

> If the human mind is nonetheless to be *able even to think* the given infinite without contradiction, it must have within itself a power that is supersensible, whose idea of a noumenon cannot be intuited but can yet be regarded as the substrate underlying what is mere appearance, namely, our intuition of the world. (KU 5: 254–5; 111)

Given Kant's premises, the first part of this conditional conclusion seems unobjectionable. *If* the infinite cannot be thought as a whole on the basis of a sensible standard, that is, if the thought presupposes a supersensible capacity, then, clearly, a mind capable of this thought must have such a capacity. The problem, however, is that this leaves completely open the question of whether the human mind is, indeed, capable of this thought. In fact, it might appear that, since the human intellect is finite, the preceding argument actually shows that this is impossible. Furthermore, even if we grant such a capacity to the human mind, it does not seem to follow that it need involve the idea of a noumenon as supersensible substrate of "our intuition of the world."

Kant here appears to assume that the fact that the mind has such a supersensible capacity follows from the very demand of reason to think the totality of sensible representation as given, and he thus focuses instead on the question of *how* it thinks it. But in view of his insistence in the first *Critique* on the connection between such totalities and transcendental illusion, this might seem to be a highly dubious assumption.

Such a conclusion would, however, be premature. For the transcendental illusion that Kant claims to uncover in the Dialectic of the first *Critique* does not concern the mere *thought* of an infinite totality as given, but rather the idea that such a totality can be given as a possible object of human cognition. Expressed in terms of the present discussion, Kant's position is that we may perfectly well think an infinite totality as given, though not as given for a human or, more generally, a finite, sensibly conditioned intellect. In fact, the illusion may even be described as the inference that whatever is given in the first sense is also given in the second.[31]

Although this may initially seem somewhat paradoxical, it is actually not a radical claim at all. For not only is the idea that something might be "given," that is, constitute an object, for an intellect other than the human, which can never be an object for us, perfectly intelligible in its own right, but it also was appealed to (at least tacitly) by virtually the entire philosophical tradition before Kant. That other, "more than human intellect," for which the infinite is thought to be given in its entirety, is the divine or, in Kant's terms, intuitive intellect.[32] To be sure, Kant emphasizes that we cannot know whether such an intellect is really possible, but he also insists that it can be thought without contradiction, which is all that is necessary for present purposes.[33] Thus, while we cannot actually think God's thoughts, we can perfectly well think without contradiction (though we cannot know) *that* God has certain thoughts that are beyond our capacity to attain. Clearly, prominent among these thoughts is the comprehensive grasp of an infinite totality.[34]

Moreover, to think this infinite totality as object for a divine or intuitive intellect is precisely to think it as noumenon.[35] Although we cannot *intuit* this noumenon (that would require intellectual intuition or, equivalently, an ability to think God's thoughts), we can perfectly well *think* it. In fact, since we take it as corresponding to the totality of the appearances, which we, in virtue of our finite intellects, apprehend only piecemeal and asymptotically, we think it "as the substrate underlying what is mere appearance, namely, our intuition of the world." Thus, in spite of its finitude, the human mind shows itself to have a supersensible capacity that is manifest in the thought of a noumenon as supersensible substrate of appearance. What is crucial for understanding the sublime, however, is that, even though this thought does not fulfill any genuine theoretical goal, merely entertaining it produces "an expansion of the mind that feels able to cross the barriers of sensibility with a different (practical) aim" (KU 5: 255; 112).

This is the first of two parenthetical references to the practical in §26. But instead of explaining what he means by it, Kant seems to change the subject, beginning the next paragraph with the abrupt claim: "Hence nature is sublime in those of its appearances whose intuition carries with it the idea of their infinity" (KU 5: 255; 112). Viewed as an inference from the preceding considerations, this appears to be something of a *non sequitur*, since no mention was there made of the sublime. In reality, however, it is nothing more than an application of the third nominal definition of the sublime from §25: "what even to be able to think proves that the mind has a power surpassing any standard of sense." Given this definition, together with the proposition that the infinite is that which, even being able to think, proves that the mind has a supersensible capacity, it clearly follows that nature is sublime in those of its appearances that have the forementioned feature.

At this point, however, one may ask how, since nothing in nature *is* infinite or absolutely great, can it contain appearances of this sort? The key to the answer lies in the activity of the imagination or, more precisely, in the failure of its activity. This failure has nothing to do with measurement or the mathematical estimation of magnitude, since we have seen that any object is measurable through iterative procedures based on number concepts (or their algebraic equivalents) and an arbitrarily chosen unit of measure. It concerns, rather, the aesthetic estimation that certain objects in nature occasion in virtue of their sheer magnitude. Confronted with such an object, the imagination finds itself stretched beyond its natural limits, unable to comprehend in a single intuition the magnitude that its appearance suggests. In other words, such objects present themselves to the imagination *as if* they were absolutely great. Consequently, in order to do justice to this imagined greatness, that is, to estimate it aesthetically, the imagination endeavors to produce a unit of measure adequate to the task. Given the nature of the infinite or absolutely great, however, the only such measure is the "absolute whole of nature"; and this is self-contradictory because it involves the thought of the "absolute totality of an endless progression" (KU 5: 255; 112).

Thus, even though nothing in nature really is infinite, Kant is suggesting that certain of its appearances have an effect on the mind comparable to one that (*per impossibile*) something that actually was infinite would have. That is to say, these appearances produce a sense of the inadequacy of the imagination (which has at its disposal merely a "standard of sense") to provide the necessary aesthetic measure. As we have already seen, however, this result, though initially displeasing, leads the mind (still obeying the "voice of reason") to the thought of the supersensible. As Kant here puts it:

> Hence that magnitude of a natural object to which the imagination fruitlessly applies its entire ability to comprehend must lead the concept of nature to a supersensible substrate (which underlies both nature and our ability to think), a substrate that is large beyond any standard of sense and hence makes us judge as *sublime* not so much the object as the mental attunement [*Gemütsstimmung*] in which we find ourselves when we estimate the object. (KU 5: 255–6; 112)

Kant proceeds to remind us that this "mental attunement" concerns the relationship between the imagination and reason, but it is also the same attunement that accounts for the subjective purposiveness of the mathematically sublime. For the disharmony of the imagination with its old friend the understanding, which is counterpurposive for judgment as such, turns out to be a harmony of the same imagination with its new acquaintance, reason, and this harmony is purposive for the mind as a whole.[36] This is because the imagination, through its very inadequacy, leads the mind to entertain reason's idea of a supersensible substrate, thereby producing the forementioned attunement, which, Kant further suggests, "conforms to and is compatible with the one that an influence by determinate (practical) ideas would produce on feeling" (KU 5: 256; 113).

Although this second reference to the practical is still merely parenthetical, it is essential for understanding the nature of the purposiveness that the mathematically sublime involves. To begin with, the influence that determinate practical ideas produce on feeling is just moral feeling. Thus, what Kant is claiming is that the feeling produced by the mental attunement involved in entertaining the idea of the supersensible occasioned by objects deemed mathematically sublime "conforms to and is compatible with" moral feeling. This is not, however, to say that it *is* moral feeling. On the contrary, it is a purely aesthetic response, lacking the motivating force or determination of the will that is the distinguishing feature of the latter.[37] Nevertheless, it is at least analogous to moral feeling, and this suffices to make it purposive for the mind as a whole, or, as Kant sometimes puts it, *"the whole vocation* of the mind" (KU 5: 259; 116), since it helps attune the mind to the uncompromising demands of morality.

Finally, it is crucial to keep in mind that this claim about a connection with moral feeling is made already about the *mathematically* sublime. Thus, even though the experience of this species of the sublime involves the use of reason in its purely theoretical capacity, it is not purposive for reason in this capacity, since it does not aid in cognition. Its purposiveness concerns, rather, practical reason or, better, the mind as a whole insofar as it is concerned with the practical.[38] We shall see that this is likewise true of the dynamically sublime. But before turning to that, it is necessary to examine some features of the phenomenology of the sublime sketched in §27, since this should help us better understand the analogy between the feeling of the mathematically sublime and moral feeling that Kant affirms in §26 with very little in the way of either argument or explanation.

V

Although §27 officially deals with the "quality" of the feeling of the sublime, it does not parallel the first moment of the Analytic of the Beautiful, since there is no reference to its disinterestedness.[39] Instead, Kant characterizes this quality as consisting "in its being a feeling, accompanying an object, of displeasure about our aesthetic power of judging, yet of a displeasure that we represent at the same time as purposive" (KU 5: 259; 116). Moreover, in analyzing this quality, Kant offers what I have characterized as a phenomenology of the feeling, the upshot of which is the demonstration of a significant analogy, though not an identity, between the feeling of the sublime and moral feeling as discussed in the second *Critique.*

This connection is apparent from the very beginning, where Kant introduces the conception of respect, defined as "the feeling that it is beyond our ability to attain an idea *that is a law for us*" (KU 5: 257; 114). This is to be contrasted with a "kind of respect" to which Kant had referred earlier in connection with the analysis of the simply great. Although Kant does not refer back to the earlier discussion, the clear implication is that the absolutely great or sublime stands to respect proper as the simply great stands to a "kind of respect."

As one would expect from the previous analysis, the "law" in question turns out to be reason's demand imposed on the imagination to comprehend every appearance that may be given in the intuition of a whole. As one would also expect, in spite of its greatest efforts to exhibit this idea of reason, the imagination fails, thereby meeting the inability condition specified in the definition of respect. Moreover, we are once again told that this very failure of the imagination demonstrates its limits (which are those of sensibility), thereby awakening in the mind a feeling of respect for its own (supersensible) capacities and vocation. And in light of this, Kant remarks in a passage that was previously cited in part:

> By a certain subreption (in which respect for the object is substituted for respect for the idea of humanity in ourselves [*unserem Subjecte*]) this respect is accorded an object of nature that, as it were, makes intuitable for us the superiority of the rational vocation [*Vernunftbestimmung*] of our cognitive faculties over the greatest power of sensibility. (KU 5: 257; 114)

Taken literally, it is difficult to see how respect (as here defined) for the idea of humanity in ourselves could subreptively become transformed into respect for an object in nature. But Kant's carefully qualified language suggests that he means that the object as it presents itself to the subject in mere reflection, that is, apart from any conceptually grounded project of measurement, virtually requires the subject (at least one with sufficient culture) [40] to view it as absolutely great, thereby engendering the aforementioned psychological effects. In other words, the experience of the mathematically sublime must rest ultimately on a sense of an object, as it were, imposing itself upon us for its estimation in virtue of its sheer magnitude. And from this it follows that even though it is our supersensible nature and vocation, rather than the objects themselves, that is truly sublime, only certain objects are capable of occasioning such a feeling. [41]

A second noteworthy feature of the passage is the unexplained reference to the "idea of humanity in ourselves" and its apparent connection with the "rational vocation of our cognitive faculties." Since the latter presumably concerns theoretical reason (the thought of a supersensible substrate), whereas the former is an explicitly practical notion, this suggests that we have another expression of the interrelationship of theoretical and practical reason in the experience of the mathematically sublime.

In order to understand this interrelationship, it is necessary to distinguish between the *source* and the *object* of the feeling of respect. According to Kant's account, the feeling derives from the sense of the superiority of our rational capacities over those of sensibility (we can think what the imagination cannot comprehend), that is, it derives from an (aesthetic) awareness of a purely theoretical ability. By contrast, the actual object of respect turns out to be the idea of humanity in ourselves, that is, the idea of our nature as autonomous moral agents, which is then subreptively transferred to the natural object that occasions the whole process.

The key question is, therefore, how the feeling of the superiority of *theoretical* reason to sensibility leads to respect for our *moral* autonomy. Since it clearly is not a matter of logical entailment (we cannot infer our moral autonomy from a theoretical capacity to think the supersensible), the most plausible answer is that it serves as a reminder of this autonomy. In other words, the sense of the superiority of theoretical reason to sensibility brought about by an encounter with the mathematically sublime reminds us of a similar superiority of practical reason. Thus, it is the *practical* superiority, which is equivalent to the autonomy of the will, or at least the idea thereof, that is the object of respect. Correlatively, it is by serving as such a reminder that the feeling is purposive for the "whole vocation of the mind," which is ultimately practical.[42]

We can also see from this that the feeling associated with the mathematically sublime "conforms to and is compatible with moral feeling," since it likewise involves a respect for something supersensible in virtue of its superiority over everything sensible. And the analogy between the two feelings is further suggested by their structural similarity. For both the feeling of respect as analyzed in the second *Critique* and the feeling of the sublime are characterized by an initial displeasure that yields to a subsequent pleasure. As we have seen, in the case of the sublime, the displeasure arises from the inadequacy of the imagination and the pleasure from the fact that this inadequacy serves as an indicator of the supersensible capacities and vocation of our mind (whence its purposiveness). In the case of respect as moral feeling, the displeasure (Kant actually terms it pain) derives from the humiliation resulting from the striking down of self-conceit through the recognition of the authority of the moral law (in the eyes of reason) over all of the claims based on self-love; whereas the positive side of the feeling, though distinguished sharply from pleasure, is connected with self-approbation [*Selbstbilligung*] as a moral agent.[43]

Nevertheless, it is equally important to keep in mind that the feeling for the sublime is merely analogous or, as Kant himself puts it, "similar" to moral feeling, and not identical to it.[44] Indeed, the difference is already apparent from the previously cited definition of respect as the "feeling that it is beyond our ability to attain an idea that is a law for us." Although respect, so conceived, clearly differs from the mere simulacrum of respect (or a "kind of respect") associated with the simply great, it can hardly be equated with the respect whose proper object is the moral law, and which serves as the sole incentive to morality. The latter has nothing to do with the attainment of an idea, but is concerned rather with the *determination of the will*.[45] Moreover, this is because the respect associated with the sublime, like the feeling for the beautiful, is merely an aesthetic response directed to one's mental state, and therefore without motivating force. Otherwise expressed, the complex liking for the sublime remains a *spectator's* emotion, not the feeling of an *agent* involved in moral deliberation and decision.[46] How it can nonetheless be of significance for morality is a further question, which will be discussed in the final part of this chapter.

VI

Kant's analysis of the dynamically sublime in §28 may be profitably compared with Burke's account of the sublime as such. As previously noted, the sublime for Burke has its sole foundation in terror. In fact, the ideas of vastness and infinity, which are at the very heart of the mathematically sublime for Kant, are connected by Burke with the sublime only insofar as they are also related to terror.[47] Moreover, the connection is much more intimate in the case of power. Burke begins his discussion of this notion by remarking that, besides those things that directly suggest the idea of danger, he knows of "nothing sublime which is not some modification of power."[48] And, shortly thereafter he adds, "That power derives all its sublimity from the terror with which it is generally accompanied."[49] Thus for Burke, terror, power, and sublimity constitute a closely related set of concepts.

Although Kant clearly did not countenance the reduction of the mathematically to the dynamically sublime, which was in effect carried out by Burke, he did incorporate many Burkean elements, particularly the essential role given to fear or terror, into his account of the dynamically sublime. This incorporation is not carried out without difficulty, however, and requires an extra level of complexity that is quite alien to Burke.

Kant begins straightforwardly enough by defining *might* (or power) [*Macht*] as "an ability that is superior to great obstacles,"[50] and *dominance* [*Gewalt*] as might, insofar as it is "superior to the resistance of something that itself possesses might." Given these distinctions, he then states that nature is *dynamically sublime* when, in an aesthetic judgment, we consider it "as a might that has no dominance over us" (KU 5: 260; 119). As it stands, this does not have the form of a definition of the dynamically sublime, but it does indicate that the latter essentially involves an aesthetic estimation of a great natural force or power, which is also felt to be resistible.

By thus building resistibility or lack of dominance into the characterization of the dynamically sublime, Kant might be thought to have broken decisively with the Burkean account. After all, we tend not to be terrorized by natural powers that we are capable of resisting. Nevertheless, Kant begins the second paragraph of §28 by claiming, in basic agreement with Burke, that in order to "judge nature as sublime dynamically, we must represent it as arousing fear" (KU 5: 260; 219).

Unfortunately, the brief argument in support of this claim fails to connect the element of fear with the lack of domination featured in the characterization of the dynamically sublime. Since concepts are ruled out by the aesthetic nature of the judgment, Kant claims that the only way in which a superiority over obstacles can be determined is by the magnitude of resistance. But, Kant continues, whatever we strive to resist is an evil (he should have said is thought to be evil), and it becomes an object of fear if we find that our ability to resist is no match for it. And from this Kant concludes that "nature can count as might, and so as dynamically sublime, for aesthetic judgment, only insofar as we consider it as an object of fear" (KU 5: 260; 119).

It is clear from the conclusion that this argument succeeds in connecting fear with the dynamically sublime only by identifying the latter with the superior might of nature, thereby ignoring the proviso that the might be without dominance (or at least felt to be such). Nevertheless, the next two steps in Kant's account may be seen as an attempt to fill in this obvious gap in the argument.

First, in essential agreement with Burke, Kant distinguishes between considering an object *fearful* [*furchtbar*] and actually being afraid of it. In order to occasion the feeling of sublimity, the object must present itself as fearful; but since this feeling is supposed to involve a disinterested liking, it is obviously incompatible with a state of fear, which would preclude the aesthetic distancing necessary for such an evaluation, not to mention the liking. As Kant succinctly puts it:

> Just as we cannot pass judgment on the beautiful if we are seized by inclination, so we cannot pass judgment at all on the sublime in nature, if we are afraid. For we flee from the sight of an object that scares us, and it is impossible to like terror that we take seriously. (KU 5: 261; 120)

This resolves part of the problem noted above, since it explains why the object deemed sublime is not felt to have dominance over us. There is no sense of dominance because there is no real fear of the object. One is fortunate enough to be viewing the thunderstorm, hurricane, or erupting volcano (all Kantian examples of the dynamically sublime) from a safe distance. Nevertheless, it resolves only part of the problem, and the least significant part at that. For the lack of dominance, which Kant introduced into his conception of the dynamically sublime, is supposed to pertain to the aesthetic judgment itself, and not simply be a consequence of the fact that the judgment is merely aesthetic. In other words, *both* the overwhelming power of the object, which can be measured aesthetically only by our inability to resist it, *and* the sense of one's superiority to this power must somehow be felt within the aesthetic judgment itself.[51]

The latter is not a problem for Burke because he did not build a sense of the lack of dominance of nature over the self into the very structure of the feeling of the sublime. Instead, he merely insisted that not being in an actual state of terror is a condition of having the feeling in the first place. But since Kant does build this in, he must go further than Burke and overcome the apparent contradiction generated by his initial account. Moreover, it seems clear that the only way in which he can do this is by showing that a subject can within one and the same aesthetic experience be aware both of an utter helplessness in the face of the power of nature and of an independence from this power. And this is precisely what Kant proceeds to do by distinguishing between the subject as natural and as moral being. Thus, as he goes on to note by way of drawing a comparison with the mathematically sublime, even though within the experience of the dynamically sublime we fully recognize our physical impotence as natural beings in the face of an irresistible natural force, we also become aware of a capacity to judge ourselves as independent of this same nature and, indeed, "of a superiority over nature that is the basis of a self-preservation [*Selbsterhaltung*] quite different in kind from the one that can be assailed and endangered by nature outside us" (KU 5: 261; 120–21).

The term "self-preservation" seems to have been chosen with Burke in mind, since the latter especially emphasized it as the idea underlying the passions of pain and danger, which, in turn, account for the feeling of terror that is essential to his account of the sublime.[52] At the same time, however, Kant is indicating that the kind of self-preservation he has in mind concerns the moral rather than the natural subject, the humanity in our nature rather than the imperfect human beings that we in fact are. And this is a conception that has no place in Burke's explicitly naturalistic account. Once again, then, the basic idea is that in the experience of the sublime, the self is aware of its independence of nature and of all its limitations and vulnerability as a merely natural being because it also becomes conscious of a capacity and a vocation that transcends nature. In the case of the mathematically sublime, this involved merely a sense of the intellectual superiority of reason over sensibility in the guise of the imagination, which serves as a reminder of our "higher vocation." Now, by contrast, in the face of the raw power of external nature, we become directly aware of our independence, as persons, from our entire nature as sensuous beings and, therefore, of our superiority to any power that threatens merely the latter.[53]

After having sketched this conception of the dynamically sublime, which might be fairly characterized as "semi-Burkean," Kant devotes most of the rest of §28 to responding to anticipated objections to his account. He suggests three such objections, of which I shall discuss only the first two, since the third is theological in nature and of more relevance to Kant's views on religion (and its distinction from superstition) than to his theory of the sublime.[54]

The first of these objections concerns what we might term the "safety condition." It alleges that insofar as the danger is perceived not to be genuine, the ensuing feeling of independence from, and superiority to, one's sensible nature may likewise turn out to be spurious. Although Kant does not use the terminology, his brief response to this line of objection effectively amounts to an appeal to the autocracy–autonomy distinction discussed in Chapter 9. The key point is that what we become conscious of aesthetically, that is, feel approvingly, in the experience of the dynamically sublime, is only the "vocation" [*Bestimmung*] of our faculty insofar as the predisposition [*Anlage*] to it lies in our nature. This is equivalent to our moral autonomy or self-legislative capacity, which is to be distinguished from the actual strength of will or autocracy required to fulfill the demands of this self-legislation. Thus, Kant insists, "there is truth in this [the former], no matter how conscious of his actual present impotence man may be when he extends his reflection thus far" (KU 5: 262; 121).[55]

The second possible objection that Kant takes up in §28 is that his account of the feeling of sublimity presupposes subtle reasoning on the part of the subject, and hence is too "high-flown" [*überschwenglich*] for a merely aesthetic judgment. Here Kant's basic response closely parallels what he says in §40 in anticipation of a similar objection concerning the appeal to a *sensus communis* in judgments of taste.[56] He agrees that the account may seem highly implausible, but insists that observation proves to the contrary "that even the commonest judging can be based on this principle, even though we are not always conscious of it" (KU 5: 262; 121). Thus, as he so often does, Kant here appeals to the "ordinary sound human understanding," albeit this time construing it as a capacity for aesthetic judgment. Nevertheless, the example that Kant chooses to illustrate the implicit adherence of the "commonest judging" to this principle is both surprising and noteworthy. In response to a rhetorical question concerning what kind of person is most admired, even by a savage, he writes:

> It is a person who is not terrified, not afraid, and hence does not yield to danger. . . . Even in a fully civilized society there remains this superior esteem for the warrior, except that we demand more of him . . . Hence, no matter how much people may dispute, when they compare the statesman with the general, as to which one deserves the superior respect, an aesthetic judgment decides in favor of the general. Even war has something sublime

about it, if it is carried on in an orderly way and with respect for the sanctity of the citizen's rights. . . . A prolonged peace, on the other hand, generally tends to make prevalent a merely commercial spirit, and along with it base selfishness, cowardice, and softness, and to debase the way of thinking of that people. (KU 5: 262–3; 121–2)

One oddity in this passage is that the illustration of the sublime that it provides does not fit the account of the dynamically sublime of which it is a part. The latter supposedly refers to terrifying natural objects, forces, or events, such as hurricanes, volcanic eruptions, and the like, while Kant is now talking about a human, cultural activity (war) and what one might term the frame of mind of those who engage in it.[57] This is only a minor problem, however, since, as we have seen, Kant argues repeatedly that the true locus of the sublime (whether mathematical or dynamical) is the self, rather than external nature. In fact, immediately before discussing the objections with which we are now concerned, Kant concludes his actual exposition of the dynamically sublime with the reminder that "[N]ature is here called sublime [*erhaben*] merely because it elevates [*erhebt*] our imagination, making it exhibit those cases where the mind can feel its own sublimity, which lies in its vocation and elevates it even above nature" (KU 5: 262; 121). And since we are now concerned with the demeanor of human beings in the face of great physical danger, the example certainly fits the "spirit," if not the "letter," of the account of the dynamically sublime.[58]

The major interest of the passage lies, however, in its apparent glorification or, perhaps better, "sublimification" of war. And, as such, it calls to mind numerous other passages in Kant, including one from §83 of the *Critique of Judgment* (discussed in Chapter 9), in which he considers the teleological role of war in leading, by a kind of "cunning of nature," to the eventual formation of republican institutions and perpetual peace.[59] Nevertheless, it is important to realize that this teleological function is irrelevant to the present context, since it certainly would not be recognized by the savage who admirers the warrior, and probably not by the members of "fully civilized society," who prefer the general to the statesman, either.[60]

For the understanding of the sublime, the essential point is that it is an *aesthetic judgment* that prefers the general to the statesman or, more generally, that admires the warrior for his courage. And since an aesthetic judgment is *not* a moral evaluation, it does not suggest a favorable moral verdict on war or those who wage it. What it does suggest is, rather, that an uninvolved spectator would feel that there is something uplifting or inspiring in the resolution with which a soldier faces death because it represents something that is essential to morality, namely, the valuation of something as higher than physical existence, even though the particular valuation in question may not be made on moral grounds or even concern a morally permissible end.[61] All of this is lost, however, if the judgment of the sublime is viewed as a kind of disguised or aesthetically determined moral judgment, which once again underscores the point that the feeling of the sublime is analogous to, but not identical with, moral feeling.

VII

As we saw in Chapter 8, Kant does not deny that the sublime requires a deduction, but merely that it needs one distinct from its exposition. Kant does not tell us where in this exposition, that is, in the Analytic of the Sublime, the deduction is to be found; but it seems clear that the only plausible candidate is its final section (§29), which deals with the modality of the sublime. Moreover, even though this section is officially included within the dynamically sublime, Kant speaks there of the sublime as such and evidently intended the account to cover both species.

The goal of the deduction of the sublime, like that of the beautiful, is to ground the demand for agreement connected with such judgments, which is equivalent to accounting for their modality. In the case of the beautiful, the deduction required going beyond the Analytic because of the connection of taste with the subjective conditions of judgment. More specifically, it was necessary both to demonstrate, by means of an analysis of the twofold peculiarity of the pure judgment of taste, that the principle of taste is nothing other than the "subjective formal condition of judgment as such" (KU 5: 287; 151) and to show that this condition applies universally. By contrast, in the case of the sublime, no such consideration of subjective conditions is required, since the Analytic of the Sublime itself supposedly shows that judgments of the sublime are grounded in something that we are already justified in presupposing in everyone (that is, something justified independently of a "critique of judgment"), namely, the predisposition to moral feeling.[62]

The situation is complicated, however, by a significant difference between the two species of aesthetic reflective judgment with respect to their modal claims. As Kant remarks at the very beginning of his discussion, "Beautiful nature contains innumerable things about which we do not hesitate to require [*ansinnen*] everyone's judgment to agree with our own, and we can expect [*erwarten*] such agreement without being wrong very often." But there is no comparable expectation regarding the sublime because in order to be open to the sublime, "not only must our faculty of aesthetic judgment be far more cultivated, but so must the cognitive faculties on which it is based" (KU 5: 264; 124). In other words, since sensitivity to the sublime requires a much greater degree of mental cultivation than the capacity to appreciate the beautiful (at least in nature), the modality of judgments of sublimity seems more problematic.[63]

At this point, one may begin to wonder what has happened to Kant's insistence in §28 that "even the commonest judgment" can judge on the basis of the principle underlying the feeling of the sublime. And this wonderment only increases as the result of Kant's evident endorsement of the principle that "In order for the mind to be attuned to the sublime, it must be receptive to ideas" (KU 5: 265; 124). Thus, appealing to Saussure's account of the "otherwise good and sensible Savoyard peasant," who did not hesitate to call anyone who likes glaciered mountains a fool, he notes that "It is a fact that what is called sublime by us, having been prepared through culture, comes across as merely repellent to a person who is uncultured and lacking in the development of moral ideas" (KU 5: 265; 124).

Although Kant does not attempt to square this with his earlier claim, it may be possible to do so by focusing on the special nature of that example. In other words, Kant's view may be that while even the savage is capable of a kind of rudimentary aesthetic appreciation of the frame of mind that lifts itself above the concern for merely sensuous existence, as it is suggested by the figure of the warrior, an actual aesthetic appreciation of threatening objects of nature, such as glaciered mountains, as sublime requires a considerable level of cultivation. Thus, even though the Savoyard peasant is certainly no savage, he does not have sufficient intellectual cultivation to develop a liking for what to him seems extremely dangerous and therefore repellent.

It is also important in this connection to note that what Kant actually claims in the earlier passage is not that "even the commonest judgment" appreciates the sublime, but rather that it is capable of judging on "the principle" that he claims to underlie judgments of the sublime (KU 5: 262; 121). Admittedly, Kant does not identify this principle, but it seems clear from the context that it involves the forementioned elevation of the mind above the concern for sensuous existence, the valuation of something as higher than life. And the universal admiration for the warrior does suggest that even the savage is capable of an aesthetic appreciation of that, albeit one that is lacking a consciousness of its ground.

Kant's own concern is not with this issue, however, but with the implications of the fact that a genuine appreciation of the sublime presupposes a considerable level of culture for the modal status of such judgments. His response is to insist that, although this makes no difference to the modality of the judgment itself, that is, no difference *de jure*, it does lead to what one might term a subjective difference in the way in which we, in fact, demand (or expect) agreement in the cases of the beautiful and the sublime. In short, it concerns the *quid facti* rather than the *quid juris*.

In support of this *de jure* claim, Kant first points out that it does not follow from the fact that a judgment about the sublime requires more culture than one about the beautiful that it is itself culturally determined, which he takes to mean that it is merely conventional and, therefore, without any normative force. Kant is certainly right about this, as any example from, say, higher mathematics would show. Nevertheless, it does not take him very far, since it obviously does not suffice to show that such judgments are *not* culturally conditioned or otherwise lacking in normative force.

The second and essential part of Kant's argument attempts to address this question. Unfortunately, it consists in little more than the bald assertion that, rather than being based on something arbitrary or merely conventional, a judgment about the sublime

> has its foundation in human nature; in something that, along with sound understanding [*gesunden Verstande*], *we may require and demand of everyone, namely, the predisposition [Anlage]* to the feeling for (practical) ideas, i.e., to moral feeling (KU 5: 265; 125).

Actually, this language of requirement and demand is somewhat out of place with regard to moral feeling, since, as we saw in Chapter 9, Kant denies that there could be an obligation to acquire such feeling on the grounds that it is a precondition of being a morally responsible agent in the first place. Nevertheless, this does not really affect his main point, which, as he later puts it, is simply that "we presuppose moral feeling in man" (KU 5: 266; 125). Suitably reformulated, then, the claim is that since we must presuppose moral feeling in everyone (as a condition of treating someone as a responsible moral agent), and since judgments of sublimity have their foundation in a predisposition to this feeling, it is legitimate to attribute necessity to such judgments. After all, even Kant's savage and the uncultivated Savoyard peasant supposedly have this predisposition, and so we may assume that with the appropriate cultivation they could come to appreciate the sublime.[64]

Although Kant does not tell us here why he feels entitled to assume that judgments of the sublime are, in fact, based on this moral predisposition, it seems apparent that he takes this result to have been established by the preceding analysis of the sublime. Clearly, this puts a lot of weight on the Analytic of the Sublime, particularly its anti-Burkean elements that appeal to our supersensible vocation, capacities, and the like. Nevertheless, I do not intend to pursue these matters any further here, since it would take us too far afield. Instead, I shall consider briefly two possible difficulties concerning the deduction that arise even on the assumption of the overall correctness of the analysis of the feeling of the sublime.

The first is the question of its applicability to the mathematically sublime. I have pointed out that in §29, Kant apparently intended his account of the modality of judgments of the sublime to apply to it as well as to the dynamically sublime. But whether it actually does so is another matter. Speaking against such applicability is the claim Kant makes early on that the purposiveness of the mathematically sublime (or of the mental agitation it produces) is to be understood with respect to the cognitive faculties, and that of the dynamically sublime with respect to the faculty of desire or will (KU 5: 247; 101). If only the latter species of sublimity relates to the will, then it might seem to follow that only it can have its foundation in the predisposition to moral feeling. And if this is so, then we must look elsewhere, presumably to theoretical reason and its requirements, in order to find the foundation for the mathematically sublime.

The answer to this problem clearly lies in the relation to the practical, which, as we have seen, Kant attempts to make already in connection with the mathematically sublime. Thus, even though the impossible demand placed on the imagination stems from reason's purely theoretic need for totality or closure, the peculiar form of mental "attunement" arising from the very failure of the imagination to meet this demand was not purposive for theoretical reason *per se*, but for what Kant calls the "whole vocation of the mind," which is ultimately practical. More importantly, we also saw that this attunement supposedly "conforms to and is compatible with the one that an influence of determinate (practical) ideas would produce on feeling" (KU 5: 256; 113). Since this influence is moral feeling, it turns out that the predisposition to moral feeling underlies the feeling for the mathematically, as well as for the dynamically, sublime. At least it does so if we accept Kant's analysis of the latter, which is all that I am claiming.

A second potential difficulty stems from the fact that in underscoring the difference between an aesthetic judgment of sublimity and a proper moral judgment, I emphasized that the feeling occasioned by an encounter with the sublime is merely analogous to, and not identical with, moral feeling. And if this is true, it might seem to "open up a gap" between the sublime and the disposition to moral feeling that threatens the deduction of the sublime in both its forms.[65] For if the former is merely analogous to the latter, it is not clear that the presupposition of a predisposition to the latter is sufficient to ground a warrant to demand the former, even if we factor in the additional assumption of a sufficient level of general culture and moral development.

There is no gap, however, because the deduction does not turn on the analogy between the two types of feeling. In fact, the analogy is merely the consequence rather than the ground of the liking for the sublime. Assuming the correctness of Kant's analysis, the reason one likes something deemed sublime (in spite of its manifest counterpurposiveness for our sensible cognition or interests as a sensible being) is that it brings with it an awareness of our supersensible nature and vocation, in short, of our moral autonomy. Consequently, it is the *ground* of this liking that both explains the analogy and licenses the demand for universal agreement. The underlying assumption is simply that one ought to like something that functions in this way, at least if one values appropriately one's moral autonomy.

In addition to the caveats regarding a predisposition to moral feeling and the requisite level of moral and cultural development, which are specific to the sublime, the conditions which Kant placed on the necessity claims of the judgment of taste are still in force. Thus, the judgment must be disinterested, based on the proper "subsumption" and the like. In short, it must be a *pure* judgment of the sublime, which, as such, meets all the conditions specified in the determination of the *quid facti.*

Apart from a passing reference to disinterestedness (KU 5: 247; 100), Kant does not discuss any of this in connection with the sublime, perhaps because he thought it too obvious. He does, however, discuss the issue of the purity of judgments of the sublime in connection with the sublime in art. Although this was first noted in the fourth part in connection with an analysis of the mathematically sublime, a discussion of it was postponed in order to keep the focus on the main lines of Kant's argument. But we are finally in a position to return to this topic, which remains a matter of some interest.

VIII

As we saw in the fourth part, the question of the connection of the sublime with fine art arises from Kant's attempt to illustrate his abstract account of the interplay of apprehension and comprehension, and the possible breakdown of the latter in the aesthetic estimation of magnitude, by appealing to the examples of the Egyptian pyramids and St. Peter's. Apart from an issue regarding the pyramids discussed earlier, the problem does not lie with the examples themselves, but rather with the fact that, immediately after citing them, Kant goes on to argue that purity in the judgments of the sublime is to be found not in art but in nature, indeed, in "crude nature," that is, nature insofar as it does not bring with it the thought of determinate purposes, and in it merely insofar as it contains magnitude (KU 5: 252–3; 109). Since both examples are obviously works of art rather than objects of crude nature, and since at least the second is clearly intended by Kant as an illustration of the sublime, he appears to be guilty of a blatant inconsistency. And, perhaps more importantly, it is sometimes claimed by critics who wish to find room for something like a genuinely "artistic sublime" that Kant's exclusion (or near exclusion) of the sublime from the domain of fine art indicates a serious deficiency in his account.[66]

In addressing this issue, I shall begin with a consideration of the question of purity, since it provides the grounds for Kant's seemingly problematic claims about the sublime and fine art. In the case of the sublime, unlike the beautiful, the threat to purity comes only from the intellectual and not the sensuous side. Precisely because the sublime is initially *displeasing*, it has no analogue to the seductive charms that tend to undermine the purity of a judgment of taste. Nevertheless, as in the case of the beautiful, the intellectual danger stems from teleology or the idea of a purpose, which destroys the purely aesthetic nature of the judgment. Thus, what turns out to be of paramount importance for the sublime is the preservation of its aesthetic nature.[67] As Kant puts it, a pure judgment about the sublime "must have no purpose whatsoever of the object as its determining ground, if it is to be aesthetic and not mingled with some judgment of understanding or of reason" (KU 5: 253; 109).

Consequently, in privileging crude nature in the pure judgment of sublimity, Kant is, above all, attempting to preserve its *aesthetic* character. On his view, this is necessarily compromised if any consideration of the purpose or perfection of the object enters the picture as part of the basis for one's liking. This is particularly difficult to avoid, however, when the object is a product of art rather than nature.[68] For though the consciousness of it as art may be necessary for the appreciation of the beauty of a work of art, it is an obstacle to the pure feeling of the sublime. And for this reason, I believe it neither an accident nor a sign of inconsistency on Kant's part that the discussion of the issue of purity follows directly upon the examples of the Egyptian pyramids and St. Peter's. Rather than to present unambiguous examples or paradigm cases of the sublime, Kant's intent is to warn the reader that these examples, which were probably chosen because of their familiarity as illustrations of the sublime, are *not* to be taken as paradigmatic, since the sublime is to be sought instead in crude nature, where one's liking can more easily remain uncontaminated by any thought of purpose. But to claim this is not to deny that one's first experience of St. Peter's, or of many other buildings for that matter, can have about it something of the sublime, which Kant clearly thought to be the case.[69]

In this connection, it is also important to note that Kant does not deny a place to the sublime in fine art, though, in contrast to most of contemporaries and, indeed, the whole tradition stemming from Longinus, he certainly tends to minimize it.[70] Apart from the text currently under discussion, Kant touches upon the topic in three other places in the *Critique of Judgment*. The first is in his introductory comparison of the sublime with the beautiful (§23), where he remarks parenthetically that he will consider the sublime only in natural objects, since the sublime in art is always limited by the conditions of agreement with nature (KU 5: 245; 98).[71] Although Kant does not explain what these conditions involve, the most natural reading is that the artistic depiction of the sublime must (if it is to be liked as such) provide a faithful rendering of the object, or at least serve to call that object to mind. In the terms introduced in the preceding chapter, it must "represent" in the depictive sense.

The second reference to the sublime in relation to fine art occurs in §49 and is purely incidental. It concerns the poem of Frederick the Great noted in Chapter 12 in connection with the discussion of aesthetic ideas. In commenting on a line in which Frederick compares the flowing of the rays of the sun on a beautiful morning to the flowing of serenity from virtue, Kant remarks that the consciousness of virtue produces, among other things, "a multitude of sublime and calming feelings" (KU 5: 316; 185). Here the sublime clearly has nothing to do with the poem itself, but merely with the psychological state attendant upon the consciousness of virtue.

Somewhat more germane to our topic, however, is the note appended to this passage, where, with reference to the famous inscription above the temple of Isis ("I am all that is, that was, and that will be, and no mortal has lifted my veil"), Kant remarks: "Perhaps nothing more sublime has ever been said, or a thought more sublimely expressed" (KU 5: 316n; 185).[72] Although it is not clear whether Kant regarded this inscription as itself a work of fine art, it most certainly is not a natural object. Moreover, it is noteworthy that Kant ascribes sublimity both to the thought itself and to its mode of expression.

The final reference to the topic of the sublime in fine art is in §52 in connection with a discussion of the combination of various art forms in one and the same product. Just as oratory may be combined with pictorial presentation in drama, poetry with music in song, and music with a play of figures in dance, and so forth, Kant notes that "the exhibition of the sublime may, insofar as it belongs to fine art, be combined with beauty in a *tragedy in verse,* in a *didactic poem,* or in an oration." He further notes that in such combinations, fine art is "even more artistic" [*noch künstlicher*], while at the same time expressing doubt that in at least some of these cases the resulting product is more beautiful, "given how great a variety of likings cross one another" (KU 5: 326; 195).

Here again, Kant acknowledges a place for the sublime in fine art, at least in connection with certain of what he terms the "arts of speech" [*redenden Künste*].[73] This restriction, together with the attribution of sublimity to the mode of expression of the inscription above the temple of Isis, strongly suggests that Kant is here, at least in part, appealing to the traditional rhetorical conception of the sublime as consisting essentially in an "elevated tone" or "high style," that is, a sublimity in the *manner* of artistic depiction, rather than in the object depicted.[74]

Leaving that aside for the moment, however, it seems clear that Kant's skeptical stance toward the aesthetic value of the artistic use of the sublime reflects not only his personal taste but also his essentially Burkean view of the radical distinction between the likings for the sublime and the beautiful. In endeavoring to combine a sublime style or manner of depiction with a tasteful presentation, the artist is, as it were, forced to satisfy two masters at once.[75]

In spite of its brevity, perhaps Kant's most illuminating treatment of the connection between the sublime and fine art is in the *Anthropology*. As he there puts it:

> The sublime is the counterpoise [*Gegengewicht*], but not the contrary [*Widerspiel*] of the beautiful. It is the counterpoise because our effort and attempt to rise to a grasp (*apprehensio*) of the object awakens in us a feeling of our own greatness and strength; but when the sublime is *described* or presented, its representation in thought [*Gedankenvorstellung*] can and must always be beautiful (Anthro 7: 243; 111).[76]

Unlike the previous passages from the *Critique*, Kant is here clearly concerned with the sublime as object of depiction, rather than as a mode of depicting. The claim is that though art can certainly depict what in crude nature would be viewed as sublime, in order to please aesthetically this depiction must conform to the norms of taste (i.e., be judged beautiful).[77] Otherwise expressed, from the standpoint of taste, which is the standpoint from which artistic depiction must be judged, the norms of beauty govern. Or, alternatively, in terms of the language used previously in connection with the beautiful, one might say that the sublime in art is parergonal to the beauty of the work. And if this is true, it follows that judgments of the sublime in art are inherently adherent.

This is not the whole story, however, since it may still be argued that, in addition to depicting something sublime, and depicting something sublimely (in the sublime manner), art can also *evoke* a sense of the sublime.[78] In fact, there are certain well-recognized *genres* of fine art, such as romantic sublime landscape painting or the Gothic novel, in which this seems to be precisely the intent.[79] Consequently, successful works in these *genres* are liked not merely because they tastefully depict something sublime (though, presumably, they must at least do this if they are to be liked as art); they also do so in such a way as to lead one to an experience of the sublime that is similar in kind to what might be had in "real life."[80]

Although this is clearly true, there is no reason to believe that Kant need deny it. Indeed, Kant himself suggests just such a possibility in his parenthetical remark that the readers of Saussure's travelogue received not only valuable instruction but a "soul stirring sensation" [*seelenerhebende Empfindung*] as well (KU 5: 265; 125). Even though the travelogue is not itself a work of fine art, Kant's point that the reader receives such a sensation as an added bonus could easily be applied to examples of fine art.

The question is only how such works are to be analyzed in terms of the Kantian theory, and at least the outlines of an answer can be provided on the basis of the preceding considerations. The essential point is that both their beauty and their sublimity must be viewed as merely adherent rather than free. The former is the case because if the aim is to produce a soul-stirring sensation, then the manner of depiction must conform to this condition, which is clearly extrinsic to taste, though not extra-aesthetic in a broad sense. And this may well have been part of what Kant had in mind when he expressed a certain skepticism about works of art that attempt to combine beauty with the sublime.

More importantly for present purposes, however, the sublime also loses its independence by being brought into connection with fine art. For if the work is to be liked for its beauty or artistic value, as well as the sublimity it supposedly depicts and/or evokes, then the depiction of the sublime is again subject to the constraints of taste. Conversely, if these constraints are ignored and the only concern is to evoke a feeling analogous to what one would experience in an authentic engagement with the sublime in nature, that is, a "pure" feeling of the sublime, then it is not at all clear that art is superior to nature. And if this is the case, then we can appreciate the appropriateness of Kant's privileging of nature in his Analytic of the Sublime, though, admittedly, it would have been nice if he had also said a bit more on the subject of the place of the sublime in fine art.

Finally, at least a brief word is called for regarding a topic that is sometimes discussed in connection with Kant's account of the sublime, namely, the expression of aesthetic ideas. We have seen that for Kant, all beauty (natural as well as artistic) consists in the end in the expression of aesthetic ideas, but some interpreters have suggested a particularly close connection between the expression of such ideas in art and the sublime.[81] And if the sublime can be thought of as itself expressing aesthetic ideas, then it presumably can also be brought into a far more intimate relationship to the beautiful than Kant's official account suggests.

A close connection between the sublime and the expression of aesthetic ideas is suggested by the fact that both involve a relationship between the imagination and *reason* (not merely the understanding). As we have seen, in expressing aesthetic ideas, the imagination gestures to, or symbolizes, the supersensible, and Kant seems to make much the same claim concerning the imagination's role in the experience of the sublime. For its function there is precisely to call attention to our supersensible nature and vocation, and their superiority to our merely sensible existence and capacities.

Although this is true as far as it goes, it ignores the deep differences between the actual operation of the imagination in the two cases. In the case of the beautiful and its expression of aesthetic ideas, the imagination points to the supersensible in virtue of its being, as it were, *too* rich for the understanding. It provides intuitions, which, because of their abundance of "aesthetic attributes," cannot be brought to concepts. Consequently, far from being counterpurposive, the imagination is, if anything, overly purposive. If there is any failure here, it is not of the imagination but of the understanding in virtue of its intrinsic limits. And it is this failure of the understanding to keep up with the imagination that grounds the latter's connection with reason. By contrast, in the case of the sublime, it is precisely the counterpurposiveness of the imagination, its *inability* to realize the demands of reason, that accounts for the manner in which it points to the supersensible. As Kant expresses it in a characterization of the sublime given in the General Comment, "[I]t [the sublime] is an object of (nature) *the representation of which determines the mind to think of nature's inability to attain to an exhibition of ideas*" (KU 5: 268; 127). In the last analysis, then, it is its essentially negative manner of presentation that decisively distinguishes the sublime from the beautiful with respect to the expression of the supersensible.[82]

IX

Our final topic is the moral significance of the sublime. Although this is potentially a large subject, much of the ground has already been covered. Thus, I shall be quite brief, focusing my attention on the major respects in which the moral significance of the sublime differs from that of the beautiful.

To begin with, that the sublime has such significance is evident from the account Kant gives of it. As grounded in the predisposition to moral feeling, and therefore to morality itself, it clearly stands in a much more intimate relation to morality than does the beautiful, whose foundation lies, rather, in the subjective conditions of judgment, which have nothing directly to do with morality.

Moreover, as Kant points out in the General Comment, if we attempt to judge the morally good aesthetically, "we must represent it not so much as beautiful but rather as sublime, so that it will arouse more a feeling of respect (which disdains charm) than one of love and familiar affection" (KU 5: 271; 132). And Kant seems to have followed his own advice, since in his moral writings, he remarks, for instance, that we attribute a "certain *sublimity* [my emphasis] and *dignity* to a person who fulfills all his duties" (Gr 4: 440; 107); and he refers to the "sublimity of our own nature (in its vocation)," which the idea of personality "places before our eyes" (KpV 5: 87; 91).[83]

Nevertheless, as I have insisted on repeatedly, it must also be kept in mind that the judgment of the sublime (like that of taste) is *aesthetic;* that the feeling is merely analogous to (not identical with) moral feeling; that the respect it involves is both causally and phenomenologically distinct from respect for the moral law; and, finally, that, as the examples of the warrior and war clearly indicate, a judgment of sublimity is neither equivalent to nor entails moral approval. More generally, it is crucial to Kant's moral theory to keep these two feelings apart, since the failure to do so would undermine the rational foundations of morality.

In fact, the sublime (like the beautiful) is viewed by Kant merely as a preparation for morality and is, therefore, without any *direct* moral significance. Consequently, if Kant were to have spoken of a duty to develop an appreciation for or an interest in the sublime (which he does not do), it could only have been an indirect duty or a "duty, as it were."

In spite of these similarities, however, the sublime differs from the beautiful both in the *way* in which it prepares us for morality and the aspect of the moral life for which it prepares us. Both of these differences are succinctly expressed in Kant's well-known dictum in the General Comment that "The beautiful prepares us for loving something, even nature, without interest; the sublime, for esteeming [*hochzuschätzen*] it even against our interest (of sense)" (KU 5: 267; 127). Since both such love and such esteem (or respect) are essential and irreducible elements of the moral life for Kant, the preparatory role played by each remains distinct.[84]

This distinctness and its foundation in the nature of morality is best expressed in an important *Reflexion* in which Kant states that while the cultivation of the feelings for both the beautiful and the sublime in nature is a preparation for moral feeling, the former functions with respect to imperfect and the latter with respect to perfect duties (R992 15: 437). Admittedly, if taken as a strict dichotomy, this may be something of an exaggeration, since each type of aesthetic feeling can be brought into connection with each type of duty. Nevertheless, it does point to an important difference in the morally preparatory functions of the beautiful and the sublime.

In Chapter 10 we examined the connection between an interest in natural beauty and imperfect duties, which are positive duties to realize (or at least promote) certain morally required ends. Such duties are classified as imperfect or as of wide obligation by Kant because they require merely a sincere commitment to these ends, rather than the performance (or omission) of particular actions. It was there argued that because the attainability of these morally required ends (particularly that of the happiness of others) requires the cooperation of nature, and because even the most virtuous among us are subject to the temptation to subordinate the pursuit of such ends to self-interest (which is what Kant means by "radical evil"), and, finally, because one of the major sources of such temptation is the idea of the futility of moral endeavor in the face of a hostile or, at best, amoral world, a sense that nature is "on our side," and therefore that the effort will not be in vain, plays an important facilitating role in the moral life. I further argued that natural beauty for Kant is morally significant precisely because it provides an intimation of nature's amenability to these ends, and that this underlies what amounts to an indirect duty both to take an interest in natural beauty and to develop the capacity (taste) required to appreciate it.

What the forementioned *Reflexion* suggests is that a parallel story may be told about the sublime and its connection with perfect or strict duties, which for Kant are basically negative duties to refrain from doing anything that is inconsistent with the humanity in either oneself or others.[85] A crucial feature in this story is the negative nature of perfect duties. Precisely because they are duties to refrain from performing certain acts (such as lying, breaking a promise, or taking one's own life), they do not require the cooperation of nature to attain some end. Thus, unlike many imperfect duties, their fulfillment is entirely "up to us," which means that the whole teleological dimension that is so important to imperfect duties does not come into play.[86]

Nevertheless, because we are finite, sensuously affected beings, the fulfillment of these duties requires the governance of our natural, sensible nature by our rational, supersensible nature as autonomous agents. To be sure, such governance, or autocracy, is also required for the fulfillment of imperfect duties, since it is the defining condition of a virtuous character. In the latter case, however, this governance or autocracy is not sufficient for the actual attainment of the morally required ends (since the cooperation of nature is usually also required); and since these duties are imperfect, therefore allowing for exceptions, the sacrifices they require are generally not as great as those that a perfect duty may necessitate, for example, of one's life.[87]

Since, as has been noted repeatedly, it is a merely aesthetic feeling, without any direct motivating force, an attunement to the sublime obviously does not itself enable one to make the sacrifices that morality, particularly perfect duties, may require.[88] Nor is it even a necessary condition for being able to do so, since there is no reason to believe, for example, that the "good and otherwise sensible" Savoyard peasant would be incapable of fulfilling his duty in trying circumstances. Nevertheless, the sublime is morally significant because it provides us with an aesthetic awareness of precisely what morality requires of us with respect to *all* duties, and of what is *sufficient* for the perfect duties that constitute the veritable foundation of the moral life for Kant. Otherwise expressed, the sublime puts us in touch (albeit merely aesthetically) with our "higher self"; and, as such, it may help to clear the ground, as it were, for genuine moral feeling and, therefore, like the sensitivity to natural beauty, though in a very different way, function as a moral facilitator.

Finally, in thus contrasting the quasi-moralizing functions of the beautiful and the sublime, we can see that together they encompass the complex moral relationship in which we stand to nature (including our own nature as sensuous beings). As moral agents, we both are in need of nature's cooperation for the realization of morally required ends and must demonstrate our independence of, and superiority to, the same nature as the source of temptations to ignore our duties. From the standpoint of Kant's moral theory, it is clearly the latter, which we might say reflects the Stoic side of this theory, that is fundamental. And this is also the side that comes immediately to mind when one thinks of Kant's "rigorism."

As we have here seen at length, however, from the standpoint of the *Critique of Judgment* as a whole (both aesthetic and teleological judgment), it is the former, which we might term the Aristotelian side of Kant's moral theory, that predominates because it alone involves a direct connection with the purposiveness of nature and, therefore, the conditions of reflective judgment. This is not to say that the governing idea of purposiveness stands in no connection with the sublime; but the purposiveness of nature with respect to this feeling is at best indirect, since it consists in nothing more than throwing us back upon ourselves and our "higher purposiveness" as autonomous moral agents. And this again is why, in spite of its significance for Kant's moral theory, the doctrine of the sublime remains "a mere appendix to our aesthetic judging of the purposiveness of nature."

NOTES

Introduction

1. See George Dickie, *The Century of Taste, The Philosophical Odyssey of Taste in the Eighteenth Century*. Although Dickie includes Kant in his survey of eighteenth-century theories of taste, his account is extremely dismissive. Not only does he view Kant's theory as vastly inferior to Hume's, which is, of course, arguable, but he also characterizes it as virtually unintelligible and highly confused. Now there is no doubt that much of Kant's account is obscure, particularly to the twentieth-century reader who lacks sufficient background in the first two *Critiques* and the historical context of Kant's thought. And though I do my best in this work to remove as much of this obscurity as possible, I am well aware of the fact that a good deal remains. In my view, however, the confusions which Dickie claims to find in Kant concerning fundamental points of doctrine lie mostly with him rather than Kant. For his discussion makes it all too evident that he has only the most superficial acquaintance with the Kantian texts. To note just a single point, Dickie stresses that Kant's theory of taste is grounded in his teleology, which he construes essentially as an antiquated set of metaphysical beliefs, rather than seeing both as grounded in Kant's underlying conception of reflective judgment (loc. cit., pp. 86–7). I hope that my accounts of these topics in the first two chapters of this book will show just how wrongheaded such a view is.
2. Hans-Georg Gadamer, *Truth and Method*, pp. 35–42.
3. Ibid., p. 38.
4. Ibid., p. 36.
5. Ibid., pp. 35–40.
6. For accounts of the development of Kant's views on taste and related topics, see Otto Schlapp, *Kants Lehre vom Genie und die Enstehung der 'Kritik der Urteilskraft'*; Paul Menzer, *Kants Ästhetik in ihrer Entwicklung*; Hans-Georg Juchem, *Die Entwicklung des Begriffs des schönen bei Kant;* and John H. Zammito, *The Genesis of Kant's Critique of Judgment*. In addition to the lectures and *Reflexionen* on anthropology, important discussions of issues bearing on aesthetics are also to be found in the lectures and *Reflexionen* on logic, and even those on metaphysics.
7. For a discussion of Kant's views on the social nature of taste in his early lec-

tures and *Reflexionen* as well as the *Critique of Judgment*, see Paul Guyer, "Pleasure and Society in Kant's Theory of Taste."

8. Taste is not mentioned in the Dissertation, but Kant does say that "moral philosophy, so far as it supplies first principles of moral judgment, is known only through the pure intellect and belongs to pure philosophy" (Diss 2: 396).

9. Kant is criticized by Gadamer for thus breaking with the humanistic tradition stemming from such thinkers as Vico and Shaftesbury, with its all-inclusive sense of community as encapsulated in the conception of a *sensus communis*, through his separation of taste from its broader connections with morality and cognition. According to Gadamer, this narrowing of the focus of taste (and with it the *sensus communis*) to the aesthetic led nineteenth-century hermeneutics into a subjectivistic dead end (*Truth and Method*, esp. pp. 34–55. For a defense of Kant against this critique from a hermeneutic point of view, see Rudolf Makkreel, *Imagination and Interpretation in Kant*, pp. 157–8. We shall see in the course of this study that Kant's critical theory of taste does, indeed, preserve a connection with both morality and cognition, albeit one that is indirect.

10. This is the name usually given to the period between 1770, the year of the publication of the Inaugural Dissertation, and 1781, the year of the appearance of the first edition of the *Critique of Pure Reason*, during which Kant published virtually nothing of a philosophical nature.

11. Kant, letter to Herz of June 7, 1771, Br 10: 117.

12. Kant, letter to Herz of February 21, 1772, Br 10: 124.

13. Although Kant retained this note in the second edition of the *Critique*, he made three notable additions, which reflect his changing views about the possibility of a place for an account of taste within the critical philosophy. First, between "their" and "sources" he added "most prominent," thereby qualifying the complete empiricism of taste insisted upon in the first edition. Second, Kant added "determinate" between "can never serve as" and "*a priori,*" thereby creating conceptual space for the merely reflective, yet *a priori*, rules to which he will later appeal in the third *Critique*. And finally, at the end of the note, he made the last sentence into a disjunct, which states that "either" one should desist from the Baumgartian use of the term [aesthetic], "or else to share the term with speculative philosophy and take aesthetics partly in a transcendental meaning, partly in a psychological meaning" (B35–6).

14. For Kant's initial view of the relation between the *Critique of Pure Reason* and the two-part metaphysics of nature and morals, see "The Architectonic of Pure Reason," A832/B860–A851/B879. Kant had already abandoned this schema in the *Groundwork of the Metaphysic of Morals* (1785), with his attempt to provide a distinct grounding for the categorical imperative as the fundamental principle of morality.

15. Kant's letter to Reinhold, December 28 and 31, 1787, Br 10: 514–15.

16. The *Enstehungsgeschichte* of the *Critique of Judgment*, that is, the story of how it emerged from the initially projected critique of taste, is a complex and interesting one, different versions of which have been advanced by scholars, such as Michel Souriau, *Le jugement réfléchissant dans la philosophie critique de Kant;* Gorgio Tonelli, "La formazione del testo della *Kritik der Urteilskraft,*"

pp. 423–48; and, more recently, by Zammito, *The Genesis of Kant's Critique of Judgment*.

17. A good indication of the haste with which Kant composed the *Critique of Judgment* and of his changing views during the period of its composition (roughly from September 1787 through 1789) is provided by the fact that he wrote two distinct introductions to the work. The earlier and far lengthier version was presumably composed before May 1789, and the later and more concise one, which is the published version, after the completion of the main body of the text. For a brief summary of the scholarly views on this issue, see Zammito, *The Genesis of Kant's Critique of Judgment*, pp. 3–8. On December 4, 1792, Kant sent to J. S. Beck a manuscript of the earlier Introduction, of which Beck published an abridged version in his selections with commentary from Kant's critical philosophy (*Erlaüternder Auszug aus den kritischen Schriften des Herrn Prof. Kant, auf Anrathen desselben*). In the letter accompanying the manuscript, Kant remarks to Beck that he rejected this earlier introduction simply because of its disproportionate length; but he adds that it still contains "much that contributes to a more complete insight into the purposiveness of nature" (Br 11: 381). In the first two chapters of this work, we shall see that the latter is certainly true, but that there remain significant differences between the two texts. As is customary, the earlier version will be here referred to as the "First Introduction" and the later as the "Second Introduction."

18. The latter view is quite common in the literature. For a particularly clear expression of it, see J. D. McFarland, "The Bogus Unity of the Kantian Philosophy," pp. 280–96.

19. My earlier works to which I am here referring are *Kant's Transcendental Idealism* (1983) and *Kant's Theory of Freedom* (1990).

20. For a detailed discussion of this topic, see Konrad Marc-Wogau, *Vier Studien zu Kants Kritik der Urteilskraft*, esp. pp. 44–213.

21. The key idea, as I now see it, is provided by what Kant terms the "heautonomy" of judgment in its reflection, that is, judgment's peculiar form of autonomy through which it legislates to itself rather than to nature. This gives rise to a new form of merely subjective universality, which underlies the third *Critique* as a whole. I discuss this conception of heautonomy, its significance, and its application to the various forms of reflection in the first two chapters, as well as later in the work.

22. I am referring specifically to Peter McLaughlin, *Kant's Critique of Teleology in Biological Explanation*. Other useful discussions of the topic are to be found in J. D. McFarland, *Kant's Concept of Teleology;* and Clark Zumbach, *The Transcendent Science*. But perhaps the most useful overall account of Kant's views on teleology is Klaus Düsing, *Die Teleologie in Kants Weltbegriff,* to which I refer at several points in this study.

23. For anyone who may be interested, I should also point out that I analyze the argument of the second main part of the *Critique of Teleological Judgment* (the Dialectic) in "Kant's Antinomy of Teleological Judgment," pp. 25–42.

24. Béatrice Longuenesse, *Kant and the Capacity to Judge*, pp. 163–6.

25. Here I differ from Robert Pippin, among others. In a recent paper ("The Significance of Taste," pp. 549–69), Pippin defines what he terms Kant's "basic

question" as that of the intersubjective validity of judgments of taste, but argues that Kant's broader reflections concerning the significance of taste, which amount largely to its significance for morality, are essential ingredients in his answer to this question. Together with many others who opt for this interpretive line, Pippin seems to have operated under the assumption that either these broader issues concerning the significance of taste are essential to the determination of its normativity or, as he puts it, "they are mere addenda, suggestive but vague speculations *am Rande* which Kant allowed himself once the basic question had been answered" (Pippin, loc. cit., p. 550). By contrast, my central claim is that these two issues must be kept distinct, but that this separation does not result in the marginalization of the latter. Indeed, if anything it is the so-called basic question that is marginalized, since the normativity of the pure judgment of taste turns out to be a condition of taste's moral and systematic significance.

26. See Jacques Derrida, *The Truth in Painting*, pp. 17–147. I was initially led to see the possible relevance of the conception of a parergon, to which Kant himself appeals in §14 of the *Critique of Judgment* by Martin Gammon in his incisive analysis of adherent beauty in "Kant: *parerga* and *pulchritudo adhaerens*," pp. 148–67. Kant also uses the term *Religion within the Boundaries of Mere Reason* in connection with the issues discussed in the General Remarks to each of the four parts, which he claims border on, but do not belong to, religion within the boundaries of pure reason (Re 6:52; 96).

27. See Gadamer, *Truth and Method*, p. 44.

Chapter 1. Reflective Judgment and the Purposiveness of Nature

1. A characteristic feature of Kant's position in the third *Critique* is the virtual equation of reason with practical reason or, more precisely, since for Kant there is only one reason, with the practical use of reason. Accordingly, in spite of its title, the major concern of the first *Critique* is with the understanding, which is alone normative (with respect to nature). For a discussion of this topic, see Reinhard Brandt, "The Deductions in the *Critique of Judgment*, pp. 177–87.

2. Béatrice Longuenesse, *Kant and the Capacity to Judge*.

3. Here, as elsewhere, I am translating *Vorstellung* by the usual English rendering "representation," rather than Pluhar's "presentation," because Kant himself indicates its equivalence to the Latin *repraesentatio*. (See A320/B376.)

4. In the *Jäsche Logic* §81, Kant characterizes these two powers of judgment in a similar way; but he also remarks that the product of the reflective power has only subjective validity, because the universal it derives from the particular is only an *empirical* universality, which is a mere analogue of the *logical* variety (or strict universality). (See JL 9: 131–2; 625.)

5. The question of the relation between the Appendix to the Dialectic of the first *Critique* and the two Introductions to the third has become a controversial issue in the literature. Thus, Rolf-Peter Horstmann has argued that the principle of systematicity to which Kant appeals in the former text is merely logical rather than transcendental, on the grounds that it has a merely regulative rather than constitutive status. In his view, then, when Kant affirms the tran-

scendental status of the principle of logical purposiveness in the Introductions to the third *Critique*, he is radically modifying his conception of the transcendental. (See Horstmann, "Why Must There Be a Transcendental Deduction in *Kant's Critique of Judgment*," pp. 157–76). This has been denied by Reinhard Brandt, who notes that the principle is already assigned a transcendental status and function in the first *Critique*, which it acquires as a result of being the successor of the concept of *convenientia* from the Inaugural Dissertation. (See note 1). I have argued against Horstmann and others for the transcendental status of the principle of systematicity in the Appendix, and discuss its relation to the two Introductions to the third *Critique* in "Is the *Critique of Judgment* 'Post-Critical'?" pp. 78–92. For an analysis and overview of the literature on the relation between these texts, see Helga Mertens, *Kommentar zur Ersten Enleitung in Kants Kritik der Urteilskraft*, pp. 33–46.

6. Longuenesse, *Kant and the Capacity to Judge*, pp. 163–6.
7. Ibid., p. 195.
8. Ibid., pp. 244 and 253. The expressions "pre-reflectively" and "post-reflectively" are my own.
9. See Kant, UE 8: 222–3, and Longuenesse, *Kant and the Capacity to Judge*, pp. 252–3.
10. See, for example, the First Introduction, where Kant claims that "Every *determinative* judgment is *logical*, because its predicate is a given objective concept (FI 20: 223; 412); and the *Jäsche Logic*, where Kant, in contrasting reflective and determinative judgment and the inferences appropriate to each, states that the former has only subjective validity and does not determine the object, implying thereby that determinative judgment does possess objective validity and determines the object (JL 9: 131–2; 625–6).
11. For Kant, the categorical form of judgment is fundamental, hypothetical and disjunctive judgments being regarded as combinations of categorical judgments, which is why most of his schematic accounts focus on the categorical variety. Nevertheless, he rejects the attempt of certain logicians, e.g., Wolff and his followers, to reduce the latter two to categorical judgments, since they rest on quite distinct "logical functions," or acts of thought. (See JL 9: 104–5; 601.) For a discussion of this issue, see Longuenesse, *Kant and the Capacity to Judge*, pp. 99–106.
12. I discuss this issue in *Kant's Transcendental Idealism*, pp. 73–8.
13. In his own copy of the first edition, Kant changes "appearances" to "intuitions." (See LB 23: 45.)
14. This, of course, applies only to cognitive or logical judgments, which are the only kind with which Kant is concerned in the first *Critique*.
15. I discuss this issue in *Kant's Transcendental Idealism*, pp. 72–3. For a similar view worked out in much more detail see Longuenesse, *Kant and the Capacity to Judge*, pp. 180–8.
16. On the terminological point, see Longuenesse, *Kant and the Capacity to Judge*, p. 7, where she suggests that the *Urteilskraft* of the Analytic of Principles of the first *Critique* and the third *Critique* as a whole is to be understood as the actualization of this capacity [*Vermögen*].
17. Kant makes a similar point in his metaphysics lectures in terms of compari-

son. As he there puts it, "Animals compare representations with one another, but they are not thereby conscious of whether they harmonize or conflict [*disharmoniren*]" (MM 29: 888; 257). In other words, they lack the capacity for apperception, which entails that they are incapable of grasping conceptual connections.

18. Longuenesse argues persuasively that "logical reflection" (or comparison) as Kant discusses it in the Amphiboly chapter must be understood in two senses: a narrow sense that concerns merely an analytic relation between concepts, and a broad sense which involves a consideration of the sensible conditions of the application of a concept. See *Kant and the Capacity to Judge*, pp. 131–4, 137–8. In what follows I shall be concerned with logical reflection in this broad sense, since it alone is relevant to the acquisition of empirical concepts.

19. As is customary, I am focusing on this version of Kant's logic lectures because it is the one that he authorized for publication. It should be kept in mind, however, that similar accounts are to be found elsewhere in Kant's *Nachlass*. (See, for example, LPö 24: 566; LBu 24: 654; LD-W 24: 753; 24: 908–10; R2685 16: 552; R2876 16: 555–6; R2878 16: 556.)

20. Here Kant differs fundamentally from empiricists such as Berkeley and Hume, for whom it is an axiom that all ideas or perceptions are by their very nature particular, and the problem is to explain how some of these can nonetheless function universally, that is, to designate an indefinite number of individuals. For Kant, by contrast, a concept is by its very nature general (*repraesentatio per notas communes*), though its use in a judgment may be singular. (See, for example, BL 24: 239–40; 191, 257–9; 205–7; WL 24: 908–9; 352; LD-W 24: 754–5; 487–8; JL 9: 91; 589.) Nevertheless, he shares with Locke the problem of explaining how universality can arise in the case of empirical concepts.

21. Kant remarks that the origin of concepts in regard to their *matter,* whether they be empirical, arbitrary, or intellectual, pertains to metaphysics (JL 9: 94; 592).

22. See Longuenesse, *Kant and the Capacity to Judge*, p. 116.

23. For a recent formulation of this criticism, see Hannah Ginsborg, "Lawfulness without a Law," p. 53. A similar point is raised by Robert B. Pippin, *Kant's Theory of Form*, pp. 112–14.

24. David Hume, *A Treatise of Human Nature*, Book I, Part I, Sec. VII, p. 20.

25. I take it that this is at least part of what Kant has in mind in the first part of his account of the "synthesis of recognition in the concept," A103–5.

26. Hume, *A Treatise of Human Nature*, Book I, Part I, Sec. VII, p. 21.

27. See Ginsborg, "Lawfulness without a Law," pp. 55–6.

28. Longuenesse, *Kant and the Capacity to Judge*, p. 116. The contrast between this comparison and that of an animal, which was noted by Kant in *Metaphysik Mongrovious* (see note 14) is my own, but I believe that it reflects the spirit of her position.

29. This is the main topic of chapters 5 and 6 of Longuenesse's book. See *Kant and the Capacity to Judge*, pp. 107–66.

30. Ibid., p. 116.

31. Ibid., p. 116, note 29.

32. Ibid.

33. This contrast between schema and concept is analogous to the well-known Leibnizian distinction between clear and distinct cognition. As Leibniz ex-

pressed this distinction from the time of its first appearance in the paper "Meditations on Knowledge, Truth, and "Ideas" of 1684 on, a clear cognition is one that suffices for the recognition of the thing represented, and therefore for distinguishing it from other similar things, whereas a distinct cognition is one that enables one to enumerate the marks on the basis of which such distinction is made. The difference is that for Leibniz, clear (but not distinct) cognition is based on "the simple evidence of the senses," whereas a Kantian schema is a rule governing apprehension by the imagination.

34. Longuenesse, *Kant and the Capacity to Judge*, p. 117.

35. Ibid., p. 118.

36. I am grateful to Hannah Ginsborg for calling my attention to obscurities in my treatment of this difficult issue in an earlier version of the manuscript. It goes without saying that the obscurities that remain are due to me alone.

37. Ibid., p. 117. See also pp. 116, 118, 122.

38. See Longuenesse, *Kant and the Capacity to Judge*, p. 118. Actually, she misquotes the text slightly, rendering Kant's *Gemeingültigkeit* [general validity] as *Gemeinschaft* [community], but this does not affect the main points.

39. In the first Critique, Kant makes this point with regard to the schemata of the categories by claiming that as a "mediating representation" or "third thing," the schema must be homogeneous with the category (and therefore pure or intellectual), as well as with appearance (which requires that it be sensible. (See A138/B177). At present, of course, we are concerned merely with the schemata of empirical concepts.

40. The citation is from Locke, *Essay Concerning Human Understanding*, Book III, Chap. 3, 11. See Longuenesse, *Kant and the Capacity to Judge*, p. 119.

41. Leibniz, *New Essays on Human Understanding*, Book III, Chapter 6, Sec. 13, p. 309.

42. A reading that emphasizes the idea that Kant's arguments regarding the purposiveness in nature in both Introductions are directed against Hume, and specifically his doubts concerning the grounds of induction, has been advocated recently by Juliet Floyd, "Heautonomy: Kant on Reflective Judgment and Systematicity," pp. 192–218. In my view this is correct, but only part of a larger story, in which Kant's relation to Leibniz likewise plays a significant role.

43. As Reinhard Brandt points out, these are equivalent to the "principles of convenience" to which Kant refers in §30 of the Inaugural Dissertation. (See "The Deductions in the *Critique of Judgment*, pp. 181–2.) These same maxims are also analyzed at greater length in the Appendix to the Transcendental Dialectic (A652/B680-A660/B688).

44. On Hegel's reading of this proposition, see Manfred Baum, "Kants Prinzip der Zweckmässigkeit und Hegels Realisierung des Begriffs," pp. 158–73. I discuss the issue in "Is the Critique of Judgment "Post-Critical"?"

45. See Guyer, "Reason and Reflective Judgment," pp. 17–43; and "Kant's Conception of Empirical Law," pp. 220–42.

46. The diversity of formulations and functions is emphasized by Guyer, who claims that Kant affirms both a "taxonomic" and an "explanatory" version of logical purposiveness (or systematicity) and that they are unrelated. See Guyer, *Kant and the Claims of Taste*, pp. 44–5.

47. Ginsborg, *The Role of Taste in Kant's Theory of Cognition*, p. 190.

48. See Pro 4: 297–302; 45–50.

49. Kant contrasts judgments of experience with judgments of perception in the *Logic* as well as the *Prolegomena*. (See JL 9: 114; 609–9.) For a discussion of the latter account, see Longuenesse, *Kant and the Capacity to Judge*, pp. 195–8. In earlier versions of his logic lectures, Kant used the expression "*Erfahrungs-Urteil*" [judgment of experience] as a synonym for a singular judgment or *judicium intuitivum*, which is contrasted with a *judicium discursivum*. (See BL 24: 237, 280.)

50. For the connection between judgment in its logical use and syllogistic reasoning, see Longuenesse, *Kant and the Capacity to Judge*, pp. 90–5.

51. Although Kant does not make the point here, in his discussion of the same issue in the first *Critique* he points out that this process of specification is ideally infinite, since it is always appropriate to search for further subspecies. (See A655–7/B683–6.)

52. The significance of Kant's use of the matter–form contrast in this context is emphasized by Longuenesse, who relates it to his discussion of the topic in the Amphiboly chapter. See Longuenesse, *Kant and the Capacity to Judge*, pp. 152–4.

53. In the *Jäsche Logic*, Kant defines the *highest* genus as that which is not a species and the *lowest* or *infima* species as that which is not a genus. But whereas it is necessary to assume a highest genus, the possibility of a lowest species is denied on the grounds of the generality of every concept (JL 9: 97; 595). In the *Critique of Pure Reason*, Kant identifies the highest genus as the "concept of an object in general," which is subdivided into the concepts of something and nothing (A290/B346). There, however, he is concerned with transcendental rather than empirical concepts.

54. It is noteworthy that in the *Logic*, Kant characterizes induction and analogy as merely "logical presumptions," since they lack the true necessity possessed by inferences of reason (JL 9: 133; 627).

55. See MAN 4: 469–70.

56. This is contrasted with the principle of practical purposiveness, by which Kant seems to mean the purposiveness or end-directedness of a free will. The latter is deemed metaphysical rather than transcendental on the grounds that the concept of the faculty of desire considered as a will is given empirically (KU 5: 182; 21). In this whole discussion, Kant is appealing to the parallelism between a metaphysics of nature and a metaphysics of morals, the former resulting from the application of the transcendental principles of the first *Critique* to the empirical concept of body (the movable in space), and the latter from the application of the categorical imperative (which applies to all finite rational agents) to the human faculty of desire, regarded as a sensuously affected will. Kant discusses the latter application in MS 6: 216–17; 44.

57. Admittedly, there is a tension in Kant's thought at this point, since, as Guyer notes, he appears to waver between the view that there might be no laws at all and that there might be laws that are not discoverable by the human mind. See Guyer, "Reason and Reflective Judgment," pp.36–8, and "Kant's Conception of Empirical Law," pp. 233–4. I am assuming, however, that the latter reflects Kant's considered opinion (or at least what he ought to have main-

tained), since the Second Analogy of itself entails that there must be causal laws of some sort (albeit not necessarily ones that can be recognized as such).

58. I discuss this issue in more detail in connection with what I term the "weak" interpretation of the Second Analogy in "Causality and Causal Law in Kant: A Critique of Michael Friedman," *Idealism and Freedom*, pp. 80–91.

59. See also FI 20: 209; 397–8.

60. In the *Treatise*, Book I, Part III, Sec. VI, p. 89 (with which, of course, Kant was not familiar), Hume formulates the principles as holding *"that instances, of which we have had no experience, must resemble those, of which have had experience, and that the course of nature continues always uniformly the same."* I have said "something like" this principle because, as formulated, it is hopelessly vague and I am not here concerned with the details of a correct formulation. For a discussion of some of the problems involved, see Barry Stroud, *Hume*, pp. 54ff.

61. See also KU 5: 404; 287.

62. The thesis that Kant's new transcendental principle involves an abandonment of original "critical" principles has been explicitly affirmed by Burkhard Tuschling, "The System of Transcendental Idealism," pp. 109–27, and "Intuitiver Verstand, absolute Identität, Idee," pp. 174–88. I criticize Tuschling's analysis in "Is the *Critique of Judgment* 'Post-Critical'?" pp. 78–92.

63. What Kant actually claims is that "To every rational being possessed of a will we must also lend the idea of freedom as the only one under which he can act" (Gr 4: 448). What follows is based on my analysis given in "We Can Act Only under the Idea of Freedom," pp. 39–50.

64. I analyze this in detail in *Kant's Theory of Freedom*, Chapter 13.

65. The term *heautonomy* derives from attaching the Greek definite article "he" to the pronoun "auto," which stands for either "self" or "itself." On this issue see Juliet Floyd, "Heautonomy: Kant on Reflective Judgment and Systematicity," p. 205.

66. At this point my analysis is very close to that of Juliet Floyd, who likewise sees Kant's appeal to heautonomy as at the heart of his answer to Hume. See "Heautonomy: Kant on Reflective Judgment and Systematicity," esp. pp. 206–14.

67. As is clear from the context, in which Kant refers to the *Critique of Judgment* and its conception of purposiveness, he is here using the expression "*Critique of Pure Reason*" in a broad sense to encompass the "Critical Philosophy" as a whole, rather than merely the work with that title.

Chapter 2. Reflection and Taste in the Introductions

1. See also FI 20: 220; 408, and FI 20: 225; 414. In the latter place, Kant refers to an act that judgment performs as merely reflective power of judgment [*als blos reflectirende Urteilskraft*].

2. I am here only in partial agreement with Longuenesse (see *Kant and the Capacity to Judge*, p. 164 and notes 46, 47). I agree with her basic thesis that aesthetic and teleological judgments are merely reflective and that "merely reflective" means nondeterminative, but not with the suggestion that there are three different types of merely reflective judgments, since the supposition of logical purposiveness (which she identifies as the third type) is not so

much a type of reflective judgment as a principle governing empirical judgments that are both reflective and determinative. I also think it somewhat misleading to characterize, as she does, aesthetic reflective judgments as instances of "reflection failing to reach determination under a concept." The suggestion of a failure is out of place here, since the free play of the faculties in such reflection does not aim at such determination, and where there is no aim there can be no failure.

3. This topic will be taken up again in Chapter 12, in connection with a comparison between a natural purpose [*Naturzweck*] and a work of fine art.

4. This difference is reflected in the different concerns of a critique of teleological and of aesthetic judgment. The aim of the former is primarily negative, that is, to limit the claims to merely reflective judgments. Conversely, the aim of the latter is mainly positive, that is, to show that such claims can have more than a merely private validity, which involves demonstrating that they are based on reflection. (See FI 20: 241; 430.)

5. In what follows I am explicitly excluding the form of reflection of which Kant suggests animals are capable, which was discussed in Chapter 1. As far as I can see, the only thing that this has in common with the other forms is that it involves a comparison of representations.

6. To make things even more confusing, in another place Kant attributes the ability to exhibit to the understanding (FI 20: 224; 413). In my view, the only way in which this claim may be understood is as an elliptical way of making the point that the task of the understanding is to produce exhibitable concepts.

7. My reading of this passage has been influenced by that of Helga Mertens, *Kommentar zur Ersten Einleitung in Kants Kritik der Urteilskraft*, pp. 119–20.

8. Note that in Second Introduction, Kant likewise describes the task of judgment as to "*exhibit* (*exhibere*) the concept," but he glosses that as "to place beside the concept an intuition corresponding to it" (KU 5: 192; 33). I take this gloss to be compatible with the reading I have given, since it suggests that "exhibit" might be taken in the sense of indicating or pointing out, rather than actually producing the corresponding intuition. The terminological problem is further compounded, however, by the fact that within the body of the *Critique* itself, Kant explicitly identifies the faculty [*Vermögen*] of the exhibition or presentation [*Darstellung*] of concepts with the faculty of apprehension, which is, of course, the imagination (KU 5: 279; 142).

9. In an earlier passage from the same transcription of the lectures, the same simile appears. Kant is there quoted as saying: "Taste is art. The understanding and imagination, which have to unite in this are like two friends, who cannot stand each other and yet cannot part from each other – for they live in perpetual strife and yet are mutually indispensable" (LD-W 24: 707; 445). This passage is cited by Dieter Henrich in his account of the harmony of the faculties (*Aesthetic Judgment and the Moral Image of the World*, p. 53). I have cited the later passage because it is somewhat more informative about the nature of the conflict.

10. In the Deduction, Kant talks about the imagination "schematizing without a concept" (KU 5: 287; 151). This will be discussed further in Chapter 8.

11. This is to be contrasted with both the logical or formal purposiveness of

nature (systematicity) and the real or objective purposiveness of teleological judgment. In the former case, the purposiveness is subjective and consists in seeming as if designed for the benefit of our cognitive faculties; but, as we have seen, this purposiveness is presupposed, rather than found, and concerns nature as a whole, that is, its orderability in terms of genera and species and empirical laws, rather than particular phenomena. In the latter case, the purposiveness does concern particular phenomena (organic beings), and they are conceived of as if designed; but here there is no thought of their appearing as if designed for our comprehension. On the contrary, it is we who have to adopt the idea of design in order to begin to comprehend their structure and behavior.

12. See, for example, FI 20: 221–22; 410; KU 5: 189; 29; and KU 5: 203–4; 44–5.

13. Later in the First Introduction, Kant makes the claim in a somewhat weaker form, asserting that the concept of the "formal but subjective purposiveness of objects" is "basically identical with the feeling of pleasure" (FI 20: 230; 419).

14. In a note attached to this passage, Kant indicates that in using the term "transcendental definition," he is following the procedure of mathematicians (FI 20: 230n.; 419). (See also KpV 5: 9n; 9–10.)

15. This will be the topic of Chapter 4.

16. I argue for this at length in my paper, "Pleasure and Harmony in Kant's Theory of Taste," pp. 466–83. A similar interpretation of pleasure was earlier advocated by Richard Aquila, "A New Look at Kant's Aesthetic Judgments," pp. 87–114. The major advocate of the opposed causal view is Guyer.

17. Kant affirms this in §12, where he states that "The very consciousness of a merely formal purposiveness in the play of the subject's cognitive faculties is that pleasure" (KU 5: 222; 68).

18. I argue that this is a consequence of Guyer's view in "Pleasure and Harmony in Kant's Theory of Taste," p. 473.

19. Kant does not here explicitly state that we have lost sight of the contingency of the orderability of nature into genera and species, but I take this to be a fair statement of what he actually means.

20. Guyer, *Kant and the Claims of Taste*, p. 81.

21. Ibid., p. 82.

22. Ibid., p. 83.

23. Ibid., pp. 84–110.

24. See Ralf Meerbote, "Reflection on Beauty," pp. 69–70.

25. Interestingly enough, the problem is recognized by Guyer, who poses this very objection. His reason for opting for the strong claim in spite of this seems to be the previously noted connection asserted by Kant between the pleasure in the fulfillment of a cognitive aim and the *a priori* principle of purposiveness. See *Kant and the Claims of Taste*, pp. 80–1.

26. See FI 20: 229; 418, and 238–9; 428.

27. This suggestion is made in commenting on this passage by John Zammito, *The Genesis of Kant's Critique of Judgment*, pp. 151–3.

28. See FI 20: 207–8; 395–6, and KU 5: 178–9; 17–18. In the latter text from the Second Introduction, Kant suggests that such a connection is required in order to explain how judgment might provide a transition from the domain of the concepts of nature (understanding) to that of the concepts of freedom

(reason). The possibility of such a transition bears on the moral significance of taste and will be the main focus of the third part of this study.

29. The conclusion would follow if one were to add the premise that reflective judgment can have only a single principle. Moreover, Kant does argue for the latter thesis in the First Introduction, where, reasoning hypothetically, he claims that "if there is to be a concept or rule that arises originally from the faculty of judgment itself, it would have to be a concept of things of *nature insofar as nature conforms to our faculty of judgment,"* which he then goes on to characterize as the "concept of experience *as a system in terms of empirical laws*" (FI 20: 202–3; 392). But it is clear from the context that the analysis concerns judgment defined as the faculty of subsumption and, thus, refers merely to its cognitive activity. Moreover, Kant characterizes the concept of experience as a system as a [*einer solcher*] concept of that sort, not *the* concept.

30. See Konrad Marc-Wogau, *Vier Studien zu Kants Kritik der Urteilskraft,* p. 37.

31. Although he does not refer to the notion of interest, a similar point is also made by Marc-Wogau, *Vier Studien zu Kants Kritik der Urteilskraft,* p. 38.

32. Again a similar point is made by Marc-Wogau, *Vier Studien zu Kants Kritik der Urteilskraft,* p. 39. I here emphasize the *possibility* of the validity of a judgment of taste because, as I shall argue in Chapter 8, Kant's actual deduction of the principle of taste likewise does not suffice to guarantee that any particular judgment of taste can lay claim to validity.

33. Guyer, *Kant and the Claims of Taste,* pp. 61–7.

34. Ibid., p. 63.

35. Ibid., pp. 61–2.

36. Klaus Düsing, *Die Teleologie in Kants Weltbegriff,* esp. pp. 81–5.

37. I shall return to this passage in Chapter 8 in connection with the analysis of the Deduction, which, at one point, Kant suggests is limited to natural beauty. (See KU 5: 280; 143.)

Chapter 3. The Analytic of the Beautiful and the *Quid Facti:* an Overview

1. Dieter Henrich, "Kant's Notion of a Deduction and the Methodological Background of the First *Critique,"* p. 32. Although Henrich claims that this model applies to the deductions in all three *Critiques,* he does not discuss that of the third.

2. In the first *Critique* the table is divided into four headings or "titles": quantity, quality, relation, and modality, each of which has three judgment forms (here termed "moments") falling under them. (See A70/B95.) In the third *Critique,* however, Kant retains only the four titles, but now terms them "moments." In what follows I shall ignore this terminological difference.

3. The centrality of the claim that judgments of taste are aesthetic is also emphasized by Crawford, *Kant's Aesthetic Theory,* pp. 35–6.

4. ML_2 28: 586; 346. See also ML_1 28: 247; 63; MM 29: 891; 259; Anthro F 25: 559; Anthro P 25: 786; Mensch 25: 1068; and R988 15: 432–3.

5. This also suggests an interesting parallel with Spinoza's account of pleasure and pain, which he connects with the transition of the mind (and body) from one state of perfection, or level of vitality, to another. Thus, Spinoza defines

pleasure [*Laetitia*] as *"that passion by which the Mind passes to a greater perfection,"* and pain or sorrow [*Tristitia*] as "that passion by which the Mind passes to a lesser perfection" (*Ethics*, Part IV, Prop. XI, Scholium.) I discuss Spinoza's conception of pleasure and pain and its connection with changes in levels of vitality in my *Benedict de Spinoza*, esp. pp. 135–40.

6. This is emphasized by Martin Gammon, "What is a Judgment of Taste?" (unpublished manuscript). I am indebted to Gammon's account for a number of the points in this section.

7. See FI 20: 207–8; 396, and KU 5: 177–8; 16–17.

8. Once again, I am indebted to Martin Gammon for this very important point about what he terms the "semantic content" of a judgment of taste. In his terms, a judgment of taste amounts to an appraisal of the "the 'aesthetic' bearing of this representation on our mental state *as the ground* of a feeling of pleasure or displeasure" ("What is a Judgment of Taste?").

9. See A103–110. Kant, of course, there refers to the "synthesis of recognition in the concept," which is the concluding portion of the "threefold synthesis," and we cannot talk of a synthesis in the case of the judgment of taste. Nevertheless, the recognitional role played by feeling in judgments of taste corresponds to the role played by concepts in cognitive judgments.

10. The Antinomy of Taste and the important distinction between quarreling and disputing that Kant introduces will be discussed in Chapter 11.

11. In the recent English-language literature, the one attempt at a systematic discussion is by Hud Hudson, "The Significance of an Analytic of the Ugly in Kant's Deduction of Pure Judgments of Taste," pp. 87–103. In the German literature, there is Christian Strub's, "Das Hässliche und die 'Kritik der ästhetischen Urteilskraft,'" pp. 416–46; Christel Fricke, *Kants Theorie des reinen Geschmacksurteils*, esp. pp. 48–52; and Christian Wenzel, *Das Problem der subjektiven Allgemeingültigkeit des Geschmacksurteils bei Kant*, pp. 76–80. Those who deny that Kant allows for negative judgments of taste include Brandt, "Zur Logik des ästhetischen Urteils," p. 28, and more expansively in "Die Schönheit der Kristalle und das Spiel der Erkenntniskräfte," pp. 19–57; Theodore A. Gracyk, "Sublimity, Ugliness, and Formlessness in Kant's Aesthetic Theory," pp. 49–56; and David Shier, "Why Kant Finds Nothing Ugly," pp. 412–18.

12. See also R1946 16: 1946; LPh 24: 364; LPö 24: 520; LD-W 24: 708; 445–6. Some of these references were provided by Strub, "Das Hässliche und die 'Kritik der ästhetischen Urteilskraft,'" p. 422, note 24.

13. For the case of pleasure, see Anthro 7: 320; 99, and R537 15: 236. For the opposition between virtue and vice, see MS 6: 384; 189.

14. This is noted by Strub, "Das Hässliche und die 'Kritik der ästhetischen Urteilskraft,'" p. 446.

15. See MD 28: 676; 378.

16. There is already a reference to the pure judgment of taste in the first moment in connection with the discussion of disinterestedness (KU 5: 205; 46), and we shall see that disinterestedness is viewed by Kant as a condition, indeed as the *sine qua non*, of the purity of a judgment of taste.

17. The latter, however, is a very problematic claim and has been challenged by Klaus Reich (*The Completeness of Kant's Table of Judgments*, pp. 92–100). For an illuminating discussion of the whole issue and an attempt to demonstrate

that the correlation between concepts of reflection and logical functions can be carried through all the functions, see Longuenesse, *Kant and the Capacity to Judge*, Chapter 6.

18. Guyer, *Kant and the Claims of Taste*, pp. 120–32.

19. To cite but two examples, virtually the same negative assessment is expressed by critics as diverse as Derrida, *The Truth in Painting*, pp. 68–9, and Dickie, *The Century of Taste*, p. 88.

20. Reinhard Brandt, *The Table of Judgments*. Brandt's reconstruction has been sharply criticized by Michael Wolff, *Die Vollständigkeit der kantischen Urteilstafel*. Although I find Wolff's detailed and rigorous account of the "completion proof," which focuses largely on Kant's cryptic analysis of discursive thinking as the exercise of the capacity to judge in the first section of the "Clue to the Discovery of all Pure Concepts of the Understanding" (A67/B92–A70/B94), both impressive and convincing, it is not as directly germane to our present concerns as Brandt's. Moreover, there is substantial agreement between them on the aspects of Kant's position that are of immediate concern, e.g., the peculiar status of modality.

21. According to Wolff, the nonmodal forms concern the "propositional content" (*Die Vollständigkeit der kantischen Urteilstafel*, p. 126). On the peculiarity of the sense of "content" here, see also Brandt, *The Table of Judgments*, p. 62, and Longuenesse, "The Divisions of the Transcendental Logic and the Leading Thread," p. 147.

22. Brandt, *The Table of Judgments*, p. 5. See also pp. 61–5.

23. Brandt, *The Table of Judgments*, pp. 5–6. See also pp. 120–1. At the heart of Wolff's criticism of Brandt is his attack on the latter's hermeneutical method, which he characterizes as involving a free reflection on this "model judgment," rather than an attempt to derive the functions from an analysis of the very nature of a discursive understanding. (See *Die Vollständigkeit der kantischen Urteilstafel*, pp. 184f.) Once again, however, this issue is of no concern to us here.

24. Brandt expresses the latter point by suggesting that what modality does is to "localize [the judgment] in the *methodos* of knowledge," and that it is essential to every judgment as "an epistemic judgment." Thus, in terms of the architectonic of the *Critique* he connects it to the Doctrine of Method. See *The Table of Judgments*, pp. 6, 70–1, 121. By contrast, Wolff interprets modality in terms of the different ways of valuing the quality (assertion or negation) of the propositional content of a judgment and connects it with the function of thought in a judgment in general. (See *Die Vollständigkeit der kantischen Urteilstafel*, pp. 147–8.) But again this difference of analysis need not concern us here, since they agree on the central point regarding the distinctness of modality.

25. We shall see in Chapter 13 that, with some modification, Kant also uses his first *Critique* table of logical functions to organize the Analytic of the Sublime. It is likewise noteworthy that he does not even attempt to structure the Analytic of Teleological Judgment in this way. But this, I think, can be explained by the fact that Kant is there concerned with a method of investigating certain products of nature and, to some extent, nature as a whole, rather than

with a certain kind of judgment claiming normativity. Thus, there is no comparable problem of "pure teleological judgment."

26. Admittedly, the situation is complicated by the fact that Kant begins the Analytic of the Sublime, which is also concerned with a species of aesthetic judgment, with a consideration of quantity rather than quality. As we shall see in Chapter Thirteen, however, quantity here refers neither to the strength of the feeling nor to the universal scope of the judgment (its subjective universality, which it shares with the judgment of beauty). Moreover, the explanation that Kant offers for this procedure is confusing, to say the least. Thus, he remarks that the reason for changing the order from the Analytic of the Beautiful was that he there considered quality first because the beautiful concerns the form of an object, whereas the sublime may be formless (KU 5: 247; 100–1). But clearly, this is not a reason to begin with quality, which has nothing directly to do with form. And, as I have already indicated, it is certainly not the reason that actually led Kant to organize the Analytic of the Beautiful in the way he did.

27. This is in agreement with Brandt, who suggests in a note that the gap between the first three headings and the fourth applies to the analysis of aesthetic judgments as well. He also claims that the modality of the latter refers to the agreement of all others in the complete judgment. (See Brandt, *The Table of Judgments*, p. 129, note 23.) Wolff, by contrast, does not discuss the connection between the logical functions and the moments of the Analytic of the Beautiful.

28. Guyer, *Kant and the Claims of Taste*, pp. 131–2.

29. Ibid., p. 123.

30. Echoing Meredith's translation, Guyer consistently refers to this as "form of finality."

31. Guyer, *Kant and the Claims of Taste*, pp. 160–4.

32. See, for example, Paul Crowther, *The Kantian Sublime*, p. 139; and Eva Schaper, "Taste, sublimity, and genius," pp. 373–4.

33. Brandt, in criticizing a similar reading by Jens Kulenkampff, admits, as he euphemistically puts it, that "Kant does not always present this distinction [between the universal validity of the second moment and the modality of the fourth] with brilliant clarity," but suggests that it is clearly present in the account of the sublime. (See *The Table of Judgments*, p. 129, note 23.)

34. See also Kant's lectures from the winter of 1788–9 (during which time he was already at work on the third *Critique*), wherein Kant defines taste as "the capacity to choose publicly [*gesellschafftlich*], or the capacity to judge according to everyone's sense," and goes on to state that "The saying 'Everyone has his own taste' is false; for with one's own taste the concept of taste comes to an end" [*aufhören*] (Anthro B 25: 1509). This certainly seems to imply that the "concept of taste" includes the universal nature of the judgment of taste.

35. See also MM 29: 764.

36. See B159.

37. The location of Kant's treatment of the *quaestio juris* in the Metaphysical Deduction has been noted by H. J. De Vleeschauwer, *La Déduction Transcendentale dans l'Oeuvre de Kant*, vol. 1, p. 171; vol. 2, pp. 144, 151; vol. 3, pp. 132,

465, 473. It is also affirmed by Wolff, *Die Vollständigkeit der kantischen Urteilstafel*, pp. 117–8, and Ian Proops, "The 'Question of Fact' in Kant's Deduction of the Categories" (unpublished manuscript).

38. Although he does not interpret the Analytic as I do in terms of the *quid facti–quid juris* distinction and the peculiar nature of the function of modality, the significance of this statement as an indication of the fact that the *sensus communis* does not add anything essentially new to the content of judgments of taste has been noted by Christian Wenzel, *Das Problem der subjektiven Allgemeingültigkeit des Geschmacksurteils bei Kant*, pp. 162–6.

39. In order to understand the last point, it is crucial to keep in mind that by a common sense Kant here means a *Gemeinsinn*, that is, literally a sense for what is common or shared, as well as one that is itself shared; and this is quite distinct from ordinary common sense, which for Kant means the common or ordinary human understanding [*gemeinen Menschenverstand*]. Unfortunately, both are rendered by "*sensus communis*" and are usually translated into English as "common sense," thereby causing considerable confusion. This will be discussed in more detail in Chapter 7.

Chapter 4. The Disinterestedness of the Pure Judgment of Taste

1. Two helpful accounts of this topic are Paul Guyer, *Kant and the Experience of Freedom*, pp. 48–93; and Martin Gammon, "The Origins and Significance of Kant's Theory of Aesthetic Disinterest" (unpublished manuscript).

2. This is noted by Guyer (*Kant and the Claims of Taste*, p. 182) as an argument against the disinterestedness of the pleasure of taste, but I assume that it could also be used as part of a generalized argument against any disinterested liking.

3. See Donald Crawford, *Kant's Aesthetic Theory*, pp. 50–4; Guyer, *Kant and the Claims of Taste*, p. 197; and Jens Kulenkampff, "The Objectivity of Taste," pp. 108–9. The latter maintains that there can be no such thing as a disinterested pleasure.

4. Here I differ sharply from Karl Ameriks, who argues for the marginalization of the concept of disinterestedness, particularly with regard to the deduction of judgments of beauty. (See "Kant and the Objectivity of Taste," esp. pp. 4–5.) In my view, this represents a failure to distinguish between the *quid facti* and the *quid juris*.

5. In the first *Critique*, see especially Section 3 of the Antinomy of Pure Reason (A462/B490–A476/B504).

6. The analysis of the concept of interest that follows is in broad agreement with the far lengthier and more detailed discussion provided by Guyer, *Kant and the Claims of Taste*, pp. 167–202. In particular, I am in agreement with his view that the account in the third *Critique* is misleading and needs to be reformulated in light of the discussions from Kant's works in moral theory. However, I place greater emphasis on the compatibility of the different accounts by suggesting that apparent differences are reconcilable once one allows for the different contexts and emphases of the discussions. And, as already indicated, I differ radically from Guyer on the role of the disinterestedness thesis in the overall argument of the Analytic of the Beautiful.

7. For my views on this topic see Allison, *Kant's Theory of Freedom*, pp. 89–90.

8. See also Gr 4: 431; 98–99, and 449; 117.

9. For my analysis of respect see *Kant's Theory of Freedom*, pp. 120–28.

10. This may be compared with the distinction between two kinds of pleasure in the passage from the First Introduction (FI 20: 230–32; 420) considered in Chapter 2.

11. See particularly MS 6: 385; 189–90.

12. This is noted by Martin Gammon, "The Origins and Significance of Kant's Theory of Aesthetic Disinterest." (See note 1).

13. See Jens Kulenkampff, *Kants Logik des ästhetischen Urteils*, p. 68

14. For my discussion of this issue, including the distinction between broad and narrow senses of inclination, see *Kant's Theory of Freedom*, pp. 108–9.

15. The inclusion of disliking is an indication of Kant's intent to make room for negative judgments of taste. In this regard it is also noteworthy that the examples cited in §2 are all cases of interested *disliking*.

16. The latter point is suggested by Crawford, *Kant's Aesthetic Theory*, p. 52.

17. Although Kant does not develop the point, it is noteworthy that in his previously discussed account of pleasure in the First Introduction, he characterizes pleasure in general as "a mental state in which a representation is in harmony with itself [and] which is the basis either for merely preserving this state itself (for the state in which the mental faculties further one another in a representation preserves itself) or for producing the object of this representation. On the first alternative the judgment about the given representation is an aesthetic judgment of reflection: on the second, a pathological aesthetic judgment or a practical aesthetic judgment" (FI 20: 231–2; 419–20). What this suggests is that a disinterested liking may be equated with one that provides the basis for an aesthetic judgment of *reflection*. And this can be understood in terms of the independence of any concept of what an object ought to be, which is the hallmark of the "mere reflection" involved in such judgments. In short, what makes both of these species of aesthetic judgment disinterested is their merely reflective character, since this involves an abstraction from any end (whether private or objective) that the object of the liking might subserve.

18. If the specifics of Kant's conception of interest are lost sight of (which I believe to be frequently the case), then it becomes easy to assume an analytic connection between a liking and an interest, which obviously leaves no conceptual space for a disinterested liking (or disliking). Accordingly, it may be useful to recall that for Kant, all animal likings or pleasures are without interest; although they are clearly not disinterested in the manner of the likings for the beautiful and the sublime, which are to be understood in terms of an independence from the interests that we have as sensuously conditioned rational beings.

Chapter 5. Subjective Universality, the Universal Voice, and the Harmony of the Faculties

1. Guyer, *Kant and the Claims of Taste*, p. 132.

2. Anthony Savile does notice this language and takes it as evidence for the first alternative. See *Aesthetic Reconstructions*, p. 119.

3. In this respect, the problem of an aesthetic universality parallels the problem concerning the possibility of a common sense [Gemeinsinn] to be discussed in Chapter 7. In fact, they are really two expressions of the same problem, which is not surprising if, as I have already suggested, the idea of a common sense does not add anything new to the analysis, but merely provides a point of unification for the results of the first three moments.

4. Kant later makes the point by stating that "All interest ruins a judgment of taste and deprives it of its impartiality" (KU 5: 223; 68).

5. Kant's official definition of inclination is a "habitual desire." See MS 6: 211; 9 and Anthro 7: 251; 119.) In Kant's Theory of Freedom, pp. 108–9, I distinguished between this more narrow, technical sense of the term and a broad sense that covers any stimulus to action that stems from our sensuous as opposed to our rational nature. It is clearly this broad sense that is operative here, although the focus has shifted from stimuli to action to grounds for liking or desiring.

6. For my analysis and defense of the "Reciprocity Thesis," see Kant's Theory of Freedom, pp. 201–13, and Idealism and Freedom, pp. 114–18.

7. In thus building universality into the concept of taste, Kant may be viewed as adhering to the prevalent eighteenth-century conception of taste as inherently social, a sensus communis, that is emphasized by Gadamer. See Introduction, note 3.

8. See also Kant's letter to Reinhold of December 28 and 31, 1787, Br 10: 513; 127.

9. See Kulenkampff, Kants Logik der ästhetischen Urteils, p. 194, note 26. For a different construal of the universal voice as an "ideal predictor," see Guyer, Kant and the Claims of Taste, pp. 146–7.

10. See Rousseau, The Social Contract, Book Two, Chap. Three, "Whether the General Will Can Err."

11. This point is noted by Walter Cerf, in his translation and edition of Kant's Analytic of the Beautiful, p. 91.

12. Ted Cohen, "Why Beauty is the Symbol of Morality," p. 223.

13. See especially the remark to §38, where Kant puts the issue in terms of subsumption. I shall discuss this matter again in Chapter 8, which deals with the deduction of the principle of taste.

14. See, for example, A552/B580n and MS 6: 447; 241. I discuss the issue in Kant's Theory of Freedom, pp. 176–7.

15. Interestingly, Cohen also appeals to the analogy with morality at this point, but comes to the opposite conclusion, suggesting that, precisely because it is subjective, beauty may afford a certainty that we cannot have in morality. See "Why Beauty is the Symbol of Morality," p. 227. I must admit, however, that I find this latter suggestion puzzling. Certainly, it is completely incompatible with what Kant says in the remark to §38. See KU 5: 290–1; 156.

16. I discuss this issue in Kant's Transcendental Idealism, pp. 26–34.

17. See Guyer, Kant and the Claims of Taste, pp. 282–3, 415; and Hannah Ginsborg, The Role of Taste in Kant's Theory of Cognition, pp. 21, 43. Kulenkampff, Kant's Logik des ästhetischen Urteils, pp. 80–1, 191, note 15, attempts to capture the normative force of allgemeine Mittelbarkeit by connecting it with the notion of verifiability rather than communicability in the usual sense [Kommunizierbarkeit].

18. Even though the meanings seem to be basically equivalent, this phrasing is to be contrasted with *allgemeine Mittheilbarkeit* of the preceding paragraph. Pluhar ignores this difference, translating both as "universal communicability." By contrast, Bernard renders *allgemeine Mittheilungsfähigkeit* as "universal capability of being communicated," and Meredith as "universal capacity for being communicated." Both of these may be grammatically correct, but they misstate Kant's point, since it is the capacity for being communicated universally that is at issue, not the universal capacity of being communicated.

19. This result was pointed to as an indication of the absurdity of Kant's view by Edward Bullough, "The Modern Conception of Aesthetics," 1907, reprinted in *Aesthetics: Lectures and Essays*, ed. E. M. Wilkinson, London: Bows and Bows, 1957, p. 52. The reference is taken from Crawford, *Kant's Aesthetic Theory*, p. 70.

20. See Crawford, *Kant's Aesthetic Theory*, p. 70.

21. Guyer, *Kant and the Claims of Taste*, pp. 110–19, 151–60.

22. The later passage that Guyer discusses is in the fourth paragraph of §9, where Kant claims (following Guyer's translation) that "The subjective universal communicability of the mode of representation in a judgment of taste, since it is to obtain without presupposing a determinate concept, can be nothing other than the mental state in the free play of imagination and understanding (so far as they harmonize with each other, as is requisite for a *cognition in general*")" (KU 5: 217–18; 62). On his reading of this passage, Kant is guilty of a "category mistake" in identifying a property of a mental state with that state itself (*Kant and the Claims of Taste*, p. 155). Guyer is correct in that the passage taken literally does make such a claim, the problem lying in the phrase "than the mental state" [*als der Gemüthszustand*]. It seems reasonably clear, however, that the point that Kant is trying to make here is that the subjective universal communicability in question can only pertain to the mental state. Thus, we need accuse Kant of nothing more serious than a grammatical lapse. Moreover, of the English translations, only Meredith renders the passage in Guyer's way. Bernard translates it as "can refer to nothing else than the state of mind," Pluhar as "that of the mental state," and Cerf as "can belong to nothing else than to the mental state." Unfortunately, of these, only Cerf bothers to inform the reader that he is departing from the literal sense of the German text.

23. Guyer, *Kant and the Claims of Taste*, p. 155.

24. Ibid., pp. 157–8.

25. As we shall see in Chapter 10, Kant takes up a version of this anthropologically based view in §41, in connection with a discussion of an empirical interest in the beautiful, and likewise criticizes it on similar grounds.

26. Guyer, *Kant and the Claims of Taste*, p. 158.

27. Ginsborg, "Reflective Judgment and Taste," p. 72. For the fullest account of Ginsborg's interpretation of §9, see "On the Key to Kant's Critique of Taste," pp. 290–313.

28. In a later essay, Ginsborg expresses this normativity claim by suggesting that to experience an object as beautiful is to take one's imagination to be functioning as it ought to function with respect to the object. See "Lawfulness without a Law," pp. 70–74.

29. Ginsborg, "Reflective Judgment and Taste," p. 73.

30. Ginsborg, *The Role of Taste in Kant's Theory of Cognition*, pp. 26–7.

31. The same, of course, applies to the claim in §41, where Kant links the pleasure in universal communicability with an empirical interest in the beautiful that arises only in society.

32. She has made this response to me in private correspondence and in draft versions of papers; but as of the time of my writing this, she has not yet made it in print.

33. One might object at this point that there may, in fact, be a such a thing as a displeasure in communicability, for example, in the case of a communicable disease. But any such displeasure would clearly be based on an interest and therefore quite distinct from the displeasure of taste.

34. One of the few recent commentators to emphasize the need to make this distinction is Christel Fricke, *Kants Theorie des reinen Geschmacksurteils,* p. 50, and "Explaining the Inexplicable," p. 59. At one point Ginsborg acknowledges the distinction, but then proceeds to remark that she will use the terms "free play" and "harmony" interchangeably unless otherwise indicated. See *The Role of Taste in Kant's Theory of Cognition,* p. 97.

35. See Kant's discussion in the "General Note" appended to the Analytic of the Beautiful, where he distinguishes between an objective and a subjective harmony of the faculties (KU 5: 241; 91–2). Only the latter is a "free harmony."

Chapter 6. Beauty, Purposiveness, and Form

1. On this general point I am in agreement with Guyer, who likewise sees a shift to the object as the essential feature of the third moment. (See Guyer, *Kant and the Claims of Taste,* pp. 207–11.) Nevertheless, as shall become clear in the course of this chapter, I disagree with his central contention that Kant is here attempting (without success) to introduce a set of constraints (in the manner of traditional aesthetics) on what objects (or features thereof) may be judged beautiful. The most important of these (according to Guyer) turn out to be the formalist constraint that only features pertaining to the spatiotemporal form of objects are relevant to the determination of beauty (which he terms a "restrictive formalism"). Instead of seeing Kant as engaged in any such project, my reading treats the main argument of this moment as a continuation of the regress to conditions of pure judgments of taste begun in the first moment. Moreover, though I agree with Guyer that Kant does introduce a restricted formalism that is both unwarranted in its own right and not required by his analysis of the harmony of the faculties, I shall argue that the latter does entail a nonrestrictive (yet nontrivial) kind of formalism.

2. The fullest discussion of this problem in the literature is by Marc-Wogau, *Vier Studien zu Kants Kritik der Urteilskraft,* esp. pp. 69–89. See also Giorgio Tonelli, "Von den verschiedenen Bedeutungen des Wortes Zweckmässigkeit in der Kritik der Urteilskraft," pp. 154–66.

3. Though *Zweck* is often most naturally translated as "end," I shall continue to follow Pluhar in rendering it as "purpose" to underscore its connection with the adjective *zweckmässig* ["purposive"] and the abstract noun *Zweckmässigkeit* ["purposiveness"].

4. See also KU 5: 408; 292.

5. As Guyer notes, in calling something an end we are making a claim about the kind of causality that produced it (*Kant and the Claims of Taste*, p. 212).

6. See Chapter 2, Part III.

7. See Chapter 3, Part I.

8. This reading also accords with the definitions of pleasure that Kant offers elsewhere. For example, in the *Anthropology*, pleasure (in the agreeable) is characterized as "what directly prompts me to *maintain* this [my] state (to remain in it)" (Anthro 7: 231). (See also MM 29: 890–1; 258–59.)

9. I am here following Christel Fricke, *Kants Theorie des reinen Geschmacksurteils*, p. 106. She notes that by a "subjective purpose" could be meant either something agreeable or a sensitive state of pleasure, but that the context calls for the former.

10. This is the basic objection of Fricke, who has provided the most detailed critique of Kant's argument in §11 in the literature (see *Kants Theorie des reinen Geschmacksurteils*, pp. 109–11). Starting with the distinction between two senses of a "subjective purpose" (see note 9), she denies that the disjunction to which Kant appeals is exhaustive on the grounds that the representation of the object that occasions the pleasure of taste is a subjective purposiveness *with* a (subjective) purpose in the first of these two senses, since it produces a pleasurable mental state. And, given this, she maintains that the only sense of a subjective purposiveness or purposiveness without purpose that Kant succeeds in establishing in §11 is one that is basically equivalent to not being an object of interest, which means that the argument has not really advanced significantly beyond that of the first moment. Her main point, however, is that the concept of a purposiveness without purpose that Kant introduces in §10 is that of a systematic organization or logical purposiveness borrowed from the Introductions. Accordingly, the argument of §11 fails on her view because it fails to connect purposiveness without purpose in *that sense* with the judgment of taste. I agree that no such connection is made; but, as the reading offered here should make clear, I deny that this is Kant's intent.

11. For example, in the First Introduction, Kant seems to use the expression "subjective purposiveness" to cover both the "material purposiveness" of the agreeable affirmed in an aesthetic judgment of sense and the "formal purposiveness" of the beautiful affirmed in an aesthetic judgment of reflection (FI 20: 224–5; 413–14). Since the former sense is correlated with a subjective purpose in the sense of the production of a pleasurable mental state, this means that it counts as a subjective purposiveness *with* purpose. This usage is noted by Fricke (see *Kants Theorie des reinen Geschmacksurteils*, p. 104).

12. Later in §15, when discussing the concept of perfection, Kant remarks that a "formal *objective* purposiveness" that lacks a purpose, which he equates with the "mere form of a perfection," is a "veritable contradiction" (KU 5: 228; 74). The contradiction arises because the concept of a perfection rests upon a concept of what the object is meant to be [*was es für ein Ding sein solle*] and therefore on a determinate purpose. It has been pointed out to me by Hannah Ginsborg, however, that since Kant connects teleological judgments with an objective purposiveness, the present denial of an objective purposiveness without purpose appears to conflict with my earlier claim that *all*

purposiveness (presumably including the objective purposiveness of teleological judgment) is without purpose for reflective judgment. The explanation, which she also suggested (although not in the same terms as I here formulate it), is that the notion of being "without purpose" is construed differently in the two contexts. In the earlier one, the focus was on reflective judgment, and the claim was that all purposiveness is without purpose for such judgment because, on the one hand, reflective judgment can account for its possibility only by regarding it as the product of an intentional causality or design, while, on the other hand, such judgment is never warranted in positing an actual intentional causality or purpose as its ground. By contrast, in the present case, when considering the concept of perfection (which is just that of an objective purposiveness), what Kant is ruling out as absurd is an objective purposiveness without purpose for *determinative judgment* on the grounds that the determination of any such purposiveness presupposes the concept of a purpose.

13. On this point see also the note attached to the explication of the beautiful at the end of the third moment (KU 5: 236; 84). Kant is there concerned with the problem of apparent counterexamples to his explication of beauty in terms of the exhibition of the form of purposiveness that might be provided by discovered artifacts, the specific purpose of which remains unknown, but which are not thereby judged beautiful. As he points out, the very fact that we regard such objects as artifacts shows that we are assuming that they were produced with some determinate purpose in mind (though we do not know which one), which is not the case in judgments of beauty.

14. In other words, I am denying Fricke's claim that the purposiveness without purpose or "form of purposiveness" of §10 need be read as referring uniquely to the subjective logical purposiveness of the Introductions, that is, some kind of systematic unity. (See note 10.)

15. See, for example, KU 5: 228; 75, where the determining ground is identified with an "accordance in the play of the mental faculties insofar as it can only be sensed," which is precisely the subjectively purposive mental state.

16. John McDowell, "Aesthetic value, objectivity, and the fabric of the world," pp. 1–16. McDowell is here expressing his own view, however, and not attempting to expound Kant.

17. See Karl Ameriks, "Kant and the Objectivity of Taste," pp. 3–17, and, in a more recent version, "New Views on Kant's Judgment of Taste," pp. 431–47.

18. See G. W. F. Hegel, *Aesthetics, Lectures on Fine Art,* esp. vol. 1, pp. 56–61. Hegel characterizes the *Critique of Judgment* as "the starting point for the true comprehension of the beauty of art" (p. 60). But he also insists that it is *only* the starting point because of the alleged necessity of overcoming Kant's inveterate subjectivism. In his analysis, Ameriks does not discuss the Hegelian critique and I do not propose to deal with it here, since it leads to considerations that would take us well beyond the scope of the present study.

19. It should be noted that Ameriks only adopts this line of argument in the second of the essays referred to in note 17.

20. See Ameriks, "Kant and the Objectivity of Taste," pp. 5–12, where he entertains and rejects three proposals for understanding the distinct subjectivity of taste.

21. Ibid., pp. 12–13.

22. Although judgments of beauty are not involved, there is an interesting parallel here to Kant's reference in the *Prolegomena* to such judgments as "the room is warm"; "the sugar is sweet"; "the wormwood repugnant," as examples of judgments of perception that could never become judgments of experience, that is, be made objectively valid, "because they refer merely to feeling – which everyone acknowledges to be merely subjective and which must therefore never be attributed to the object – and therefore can never become objective" (Pro 4: 299 and note; 52). Obviously, there are objective features of the world (including the neurophysiological condition of the sentient subject) to which one can appeal in order to explain such feelings. But I take Kant's point to be (at least in part) that these judgments are not about such states of the world.

23. See Ginsborg, "Kant on the Subjectivity of Taste," pp. 453–4. It should also be noted that in the same essay, Ginsborg proceeds to mount a general Kantian critique of objectivist conceptions of beauty (including those of McDowell and David Wiggins) on the grounds that they are incompatible with what Kant terms the "autonomy of taste," that is, the thesis that as aesthetic, judgments of beauty can be based only on firsthand experiences and not on secondhand reports and descriptions, even if given by reliable experts. As she nicely puts it, one can rely on one's guidebook to believe reliably that the Dada Hari Mosque in Ahmedabad is reddish gray, but not to determine that it is beautiful (loc. cit., p. 459). One might likewise claim that I must rely on my own (gustatory) taste to determine that sugar is sweet. For Ameriks's response to this line of argument, see his "New Views on Kant's Judgment of Taste," pp. 445–7. I shall take up the issue of the autonomy of taste in Chapter 8.

24. See also FI 20: 229; 418.

25. It should be noted, however, that since Guyer translates *Zweckmässigkeit* as "finality," rather than "purposiveness," he renders the contrast as between the "form of finality" and "finality of form," *Kant and the Claims of Taste*, p. 219.

26. The most thorough analysis of the problem is provided by Guyer, *Kant and the Claims of Taste*, pp. 211–37. See also Crawford, *Kant's Aesthetic Theory*, pp. 92–113; Zammito, *The Genesis of Kant's Critique of Judgment*, pp. 10–21. Basically, I accept Guyer's criticism of Kant's actual procedure, as well as his contention that such formalism is not entailed by the harmony of the faculties. Where I differ is in my attempt to link a legitimate notion of aesthetic form with the harmony of the faculties. Although there are intimations of such a view in Guyer, he does not really develop it.

27. There is an interesting parallel here with Kant's well-known analysis of moral worth in the *Groundwork*. As I have argued elsewhere (*Kant's Theory of Freedom*, pp. 111–18), it is essential to an understanding of this analysis that one distinguish between actions that are "*from* inclination," in the sense that an inclination serves as the "determining ground of the will," and those that are merely "*with* inclination," in the sense that the agent has a sensuous incentive to act in that way, though the actual determining ground is the thought of duty alone. In the present case, one might say that the judgment of beauty can be "with charm" (or emotion), in the sense that the object provides such

attractions in addition to its beauty, but not from them, since the pure judgment of taste abstracts from these features and considers the "beauty alone." Obviously, similar issues of "overdetermination" also arise at this point.

28. See Wilhelm Windelband's *Sachliche Erläuterungen*, KGS 5: 527–9.

29. For the former, see Fire 1: 378, and MAN 4: 519–20n; for the latter, see Anthro 7: 156; 35.

30. Compare the discussion in §42, where Kant does state that sensations of sight and sound do allow for reflection (KU 5: 302; 169), with the discussion in §51, where he expresses uncertainty on the matter (KU 5: 324; 193–4). The latter discussion is interesting because it bears directly on the question of whether purely instrumental music is to be classified as a fine or merely agreeable art.

31. For a thorough discussion of this issue, see Theodore E. Uehling, Jr., *The Notion of Form in Kant's Critique of Aesthetic Judgment*. A concise discussion, based largely in Windelband's editorial comments, is also provided by Pluhar in a note to his translation (p. 70).

32. What Kant claims is that in the case of mixed colors, "we lack a standard for judging whether we should call them pure or impure" (KU 5: 224–5; 71). For a discussion of the significance of abstraction and some of the difficulties it involves, see Guyer, *Kant and the Claims of Taste*, pp. 229, 248–55.

33. On this point, see Crawford, *Kant's Aesthetic Theory*, pp. 98–9. As Crawford notes, the word *Zeichnung* is used by Kant to refer to a drawing, sketch or design, understood as a presentation of figures or shapes by means of lines. And he also points to several places in which Kant explicitly asserts that figure and shape are the relevant features of aesthetic appraisal.

34. Guyer, *Kant and the Claims of Taste*, p. 222.

35. Guyer, *Kant and the Claims of Taste*, pp. 224–37. See also Zammito, *The Genesis of Kant's Critique of Judgment*, pp. 118–21.

36. See Guyer, *Kant and the Claims of Taste*, pp. 226–32; and Crawford, *Kant's Aesthetic Theory*, p. 110.

37. Guyer, *Kant and the Claims of Taste*, p. 232.

38. Ibid., pp. 209–10.

39. Ibid., p. 216.

40. The point has been noted by several commentators, including Ameriks, in his review of Guyer's *Kant and the Claims of Taste*, p. 245, and Paul Crowther, *The Kantian Sublime*, pp. 56–7.

41. Guyer, *Kant and the Claims of Taste*, p. 230, does come close to recognizing this, noting that the pleasure of taste requires reflection and not merely a physiological response. But he does not relate this specifically to the notion of form.

42. I am here setting aside the fact that for Kant, a sensation as such cannot even be apprehended. See the discussion of the synthesis of apprehension in the A-Deduction (A99). Although including this would strengthen the case, it would also involve bringing in a host of considerations that are not directly germane to an understanding of Kant's theory of taste.

43. Kenneth Rogerson has argued for the stronger thesis that Kant cannot hold that spatial configurations provide the basis for a judgment of beauty because such configurations are conceptually determinable and this conflicts with the nonconceptual nature of the judgment of taste. See *Kant's Aesthetics*, p. 160.

Although Rogerson certainly has a valid point here regarding the difference between Kant's formalism and contemporary, conceptually based versions thereof, I think that the complete exclusion of spatial configuration (and its temporal analogue) goes too far, since to preserve such configuration as a proper subject matter for a judgment of taste, we need only distinguish between its apprehension through the imagination and its conceptual determination. It is only the latter that is excluded from a pure judgment of taste, not the former.

44. Guyer, *Kant and the Claims of Taste*, p. 231.

45. This latter point is relevant to the objection that Kant's theory entails that every object is beautiful, which will be discussed in Chapter 8 in the context of the Deduction.

46. See, for example, KU 5: 224; 70.

47. This tendency to connect the universality claim of a pure judgment of taste with spatiotemporal form seems to be more of a holdover from the period of the *Inaugural Dissertation* than a direct application of the doctrine of the first *Critique*. As the *Reflexionen* dating roughly from 1769 through the early seventies show, Kant entertained in that period the possibility of grounding the universality claims of judgments of taste in the "laws of intuitive cognition," that is, spatiotemporal form. This entails not only a restrictive formalism in Guyer's sense but also that everything conforming to these laws, that is, everything given in space and time, must be beautiful. See, for example, *Reflexionen* 639 (15: 276–9), 646 (15: 284), 648 (15: 284), 653 (15: 289), 672 (15: 298), 683 (15: 304–5), 685 (15: 305), 701–2 (15: 310–11), 711 (15: 315–16), 715 (15: 317), 743 (15: 327), 764 (15: 333). For a discussion of some of these *Reflexionen* and a different view of Kant's formalism and its viability, see Mary J. Gregor, "Aesthetic Form and Sensory Content in the Critique of Judgment," pp. 185–99. Appealing mainly to the role of the mathematical principles, Gregor sketches a Kantian formalism that anticipates contemporary varieties and that has the consequence of making the determination of form in music and painting into an empirical matter, subject to determination by the "experts." In my view, however, the latter is clearly incompatible with Kant's views on the subjectivity of taste and beauty as has been discussed.

48. Since space and time for Kant are forms of outer and inner sense, respectively, it follows that any representation through outer sense will involve a spatial ordering, and all apprehension will involve a temporal succession, but the point is that these need not be the features of the representation on which reflection focuses.

49. Kant also distinguishes this qualitative perfection from a quantitative perfection, understood as the completeness of a thing as a thing of its kind (KU 5: 227; 74). As Kant notes, the latter presupposes the former and is, more properly, a concept of magnitude.

50. Kant mounts a similar critique of the Baumgartian view in the Comment appended to Sec. VIII of the First Introduction (FI 20: 226–9; 415–18).

51. Following the Latin, I shall here render Kant's *anhängende Schönheit* as "adherent beauty," rather than Pluhar's "accessory beauty," or the more familiar "dependent beauty."

52. Kulenkampff, *Kants Logik des äesthetischen Urteils*, p. 200, note 2, suggests an affinity between Kant's distinction between free and adherent beauty and Francis Hutcheson's contrast between "original and absolute," and "relative or comparative" beauty. But since by the latter Hutcheson understands merely beautiful imitation or depiction, it applies only to artistic beauty and is therefore hardly equivalent to Kant's distinction (as Kulenkampff acknowledges). See Francis Hutcheson, *An Inquiry into the Original of Our Ideas of Beauty and Virtue*, pp. 16–29, 39–45.

53. The best discussion in the literature of many of these issues is by Eva Schaper, *Studies in Kant's Aesthetics*, pp. 78–98.

54. See Schaper, *Studies in Kant's Aesthetics*, pp. 80–1; Guyer, *Kant and the Claims of Taste*, p. 246.

55. See Guyer, *Kant and the Claims of Taste*, pp. 237 and 253. But see also pp. 246–8, where he entertains, as a "speculative" proposal about Kant's intent, a view very close to the one advocated here.

56. See Martin Gammon, "Kant: *parerga* and *pulchritudo adhaerens*" pp. 148–67. Gammon suggests, and I think correctly, that Kant's accounts of adherent beauty and the ideal of beauty must be seen as examples of "parergonal accommodation." The point is to show how taste can be made subordinate to some higher authority without losing its purity by entering into a complex evaluation of an object that is only partly aesthetic.

57. Actually, a considerable portion of §17 is devoted to an account of what Kant terms the "standard idea" of the human figure, which he distinguishes from the ideal. The former is a kind of culturally conditioned generic image, which provides, as it were, the norm for the academic correctness of a depiction of the human figure, but not of its beauty.

Chapter 7. The Modality of Taste and the *Sensus Communis*

1. See Guyer, *Kant and the Claims of Taste*, pp. 279–307, and Ameriks, "How to Save Kant's Deduction of Taste," pp. 295–302.

2. See A74–6/B99–101.

3. This is to be contrasted with the superficially similar account of Hannah Ginsborg, who in "Lawfulness without a Law," pp. 70–4, explicates Kant's notion of exemplary necessity in terms of how the object ought to be perceived or how the imagination ought to function. The difference stems from the fact that she understands the imagination being "as it ought to be" to mean that there is a free harmony, which, of course, rules out the possibility of negative judgments. By contrast, I understand the idea of judging an object as it ought to be judged to mean merely that the evaluation is appropriate to the circumstances, which, again, allows for negative judgments based on a disinterested disliking grounded in the lack of harmony of the faculties. For my criticism of Ginsborg on this issue, see Chapter 5.

4. I discuss this conception of universality in *Idealism and Freedom*, Chapter 10.

5. The term *bedingt* can be translated either as "conditional" or "conditioned," and Kant wishes to claim both for the necessity affirmed in the pure judgment of taste. In the present context, however, the claim is that it is *conditional*

upon a proper subsumption, not that it is *conditioned by* some principle. In the latter sense, all necessity (even the unconditional variety) is conditioned. Since Kant moves in §20 to the idea of a common sense as the condition of this necessity, this can be a source of confusion. Unfortunately, it is exacerbated by most of the English translators, of whom only Cerf translates it here as "conditional," rather than as "conditioned."

6. The text says that we could count on it if only we could always be sure [*nur immer sicher wäre*] of the correctness of our subsumption; but I assume that he cannot have meant that we must *always* be sure in order to be certain in a given instance. Moreover, we shall see that Kant's position is that we can *never* have such certainty.

7. See Pro 4: 282–3; 30.

8. I say this even though the expression "form of sensibility" appears prior to the *Prolegomena* in the first edition of the first *Critique* and even in its Latinate form in the *Inaugural Dissertation*, since in these works as well it functions as a term of art, intended to express a view that is uniquely Kant's.

9. Pro 4: 259; 7.

10. Accordingly, Kant is criticized by Gadamer for abandoning the widely shared humanistic conception of the *sensus communis* and linking it narrowly to taste. See *Truth and Method*, p. 34.

11. The roots of this conception of a common sense can be traced back to Kant's earlier views regarding the social or communal nature of taste. For example, in the metaphysical lectures dated from the mid seventies he is cited as claiming that judgments of taste, which include judgments of ugliness as well as beauty, presuppose a "universal sense" [*allgemeine Sinn*], which is grounded in a "communal sense" [*gemeinschaftlichen Sinn*] that is valid for everyone and that arises from communal intercourse (ML$_1$ 28: 249; 65). Similarly, in the anthropology lectures from 1781–2 he refers to taste as the "universal sense" (Mensch 25: 1095).

12. For a somewhat different, more critical reading of these steps see Guyer, *Kant and the Claims of Taste*, pp. 288–94.

13. Pro 4: 298; 46.

14. See Guyer, *Kant and the Claims of Taste*, p. 286.

15. Ibid., pp. 287–8

16. See Anthony Savile, *Aesthetic Reconstructions*, pp 145–6, 185, who accuses Kant of trying to assimilate the cognitive and the aesthetic cases. See also Fricke, *Kants Theorie des reinen Geschmacksurteils*, p. 173.

17. See David Hume, *A Treatise of Human Nature*, Book I, Part III, Sec. VIII, p. 103: "Thus all probable reasoning is nothing but a species of sensation. 'Tis not solely in poetry and music, we must follow our taste and sentiment, but likewise in philosophy."

18. See Fricke, *Kants Theorie des reinen Geschmacksurteils*, p. 168.

19. In reconstructing this argument I am largely following the suggestion of Fricke, *Kants Theorie des reinen Geschmacksurteils*, pp. 168–71. Fricke, however, presents her analysis only as one possible reading of the text and does not suggest that it reflects Kant's actual intentions. Thus, she does not pose the problem of its connection with the deduction as I have done here.

20. Such a claim is obviously not applicable to *pure* concepts or the categories,

since the Transcendental Deduction supposedly assures us that everything given in sensibility must be subsumable under these.

21. At least indirect support for such a reading is provided by Kant's explicit assertion of a similar, though distinct, epistemic role for feeling in "What Does it Mean to Orient Oneself in Thinking?" There, feeling is initially assigned the function of making the fundamental differentiation between left and right, and therefore of orienting oneself in space, on the grounds that this cannot be done by means of concepts alone (WH 8: 134–5; 8–9). Although he does not relate it directly to the argument of §21 or interpret it in the manner suggested here, the importance of this account of feeling for the Analytic of the Beautiful is emphasized by Jean-François Lyotard, *Lessons on the Analytic of the Sublime*, esp. pp. 8–26. Lyotard's main point is that for Kant, the act of thinking is invariably connected with a sensation or feeling of one's own mental state.

22. The point is noted by Fricke, *Kants Theorie des reinen Geschmacksurteils*, p. 172, note 16. Actually, the expression *Gemeinsinn*, in contrast to *gemein Menschenverstand*, is fairly unusual in Kant. Apart from one place in which he is concerned with Mendelssohn's use of this and related terms (WH 8: 136; 10), the only occurrences outside of the third *Critique* that I have been able to find in the published writings are in Anthro 7: 139; 20; 169; 46; 219; 89; 329; 189. In the first of these, Kant is contrasting men of common sense with men of science, and suggests that the former are adept at dealing with rules applied *in concreto*, which is close to the suggested meaning to be given to the expression in §21. The second speculates about why the sound human understanding [*gesunden Menschenverstand*] is also called common sense. The third and fourth contrast *Gemeinsinn* with *Eigensinn* or *Privatsinn*. One of the sources of confusion on this point is that Kant uses both *Gemeinsinn* and *gemein Menschenverstand* and its variants to translate the Latin *sensus communis*.

23. As Fricke also points out, an additional virtue of this interpretation of common sense in §21 is that it sheds some light on what appears to be the highly contrived correlation of the higher cognitive faculty of judgment with the mental faculty of pleasure and pain in both Introductions. See *Kants Theorie des reinen Geschmacksurteils*, p. 171, note 14.

24. In the first *Critique* and elsewhere, Kant characterizes a "subreption" or a "transcendental subreption" as a metaphysical fallacy in which something merely subjective or regulative is mistakenly taken for something objective or constitutive. See, for example A509/B537, A538/B610–11, A791/B819.

25. See Crawford, *Kant's Aesthetic Theory*, pp. 128–30; Guyer, *Kant and the Claims of Taste*, pp. 280–2.

26. In R1872, 16: 145, Kant writes: "The capacity to choose what pleases the senses of everyone. *Facultas diiucandi per sensum communem.* Taste is the capacity to choose sensuously [*sinnlich*] and with universal validity. This has regard more to the form than the matter of sensibility." See also R1512 15: 836, R1930 16: 160, Anthro P 25: 788, and Mensch 25: 1095–7.

27. For a very different reading of this paragraph and view of the issues it raises, see Guyer, *Kant and the Claims of Taste*, pp. 297–307.

28. See Savile, *Aesthetic Reconstructions*, pp. 146–56. Savile, however, gives a quite sophisticated and useful analysis of the different senses of "ought" involved.

Chapter 8. The Deduction of Pure Judgments of Taste

1. In what follows, I shall use the uppercase "D" when referring to the text of the Deduction, and the lowercase when referring solely to the argument.

2. In the first *Critique*, Kant tells us that by exposition [*Erörterung*] he means "the clear, although not necessarily exhaustive representation of that which belongs to a concept" (B38).

3. It is perhaps noteworthy that this seems to reflect a late change of mind on Kant's part, since in the overview of the structure of the *Critique* given at the end of the First Introduction, he suggests that the discussion of the sublime will precisely parallel that of the beautiful, each consisting of two divisions, an analytic and a dialectic, and the former of two chapters, an exposition, and a deduction. (See FI 20: 251; 441.)

4. It is also important to keep in mind that this is not incompatible with the subjectivity of beauty affirmed in Chapter 6. For as was suggested there, the point at issue is not whether judgments of beauty are properly about (or refer to) objects in the world; it is rather whether the determining ground for such judgments is to be located in some discernible property possessed by the objects or in the mental state of a subject in an aesthetic engagement with an object. And Kant consistently affirms the latter view for the reasons previously noted. (See Chapter 6, Section II.) Accordingly, we might say that judgments of beauty are subjective only in the second sense (with regard to their ground, rather than their referent), whereas judgments of sublimity are subjective in both senses.

5. See also KU 5: 292; 158.

6. Such a view is suggested, but not explicitly argued for, by Claude MacMillan, "Kant's Deduction of Pure Aesthetic Judgments," pp. 43–54.

7. This is particularly clear from §32, where Kant discusses the taste of the young poet and the importance of classical models for the development of taste.

8. In Chapter 12 I shall argue that an analogue of the free-adherent beauty distinction applies to artistic beauty.

9. This connection is already suggested by Kant in his letter to Reinhold of December 28 and 31, 1787, which was discussed in the Introduction. As was there noted, Kant tells Reinhold that he is preparing a work to be entitled "Critique of Taste," which is to deal with teleology (Br 10: 514–15).

10. See, for example, Axvi and B148.

11. Jens Kulenkampff, *Kants Logik der ästhetischen Urteils*, esp. pp. 97–111.

12. Although Kant does not include the modifier "pure" in his account of the peculiarities, this must be implicit; for otherwise at least the first peculiarity would not arise.

13. Guyer, *Kant and the Claims of Taste*, pp. 272 argues that Kant's doctrine of autonomy places a strong and unrealizable condition on the Deduction, namely, that it must justify the imputation of specific feelings to others on specific occasions. I shall deal with this claim later in the chapter, when I discuss Guyer's criticism of Kant's argument.

14. This mere or random groping metaphor is a prevalent feature of the Preface to the second edition of the *Critique of Pure Reason*, where Kant introduces the idea of his Copernican or transcendental turn. See, for example, Bvii, xi, xiv,

xv, and also MAN 4: 478. In all these places, it is such groping that precedes and is to be replaced by science.

15. This aspect of Kant's conception of the autonomy of taste is emphasized by Hannah Ginsborg in her analysis of the subjectivity of taste. See Chapter 6, note 23.

16. On the example of the young poet, see Guyer, *Kant and the Claims of Taste*, p. 270; Savile, *Aesthetic Reconstructions*, pp. 152–3; and Ginsborg, "Kant on the Subjectivity of Taste," pp. 452–3.

17. See David Hume, "The Sceptic," p. 163.

18. See Chapter 2, Section V.

19. For example, it could be argued that the categorical imperative expresses the conditions of the coherent legislation of practical reason in choosing justifiable maxims, just as the categories, as rules for the determination of the unity of apperception, express the conditions of the possible use of the understanding.

20. On schematizing without a concept, see Fricke, *Kants Theorie des reinen Geschmacksurteils*, pp. 118–19.

21. Yet Lewis White Beck suggests that if one were to accept C. I. Lewis's claim that the Second Analogy is analytical of the "concept of objective event," it could similarly be argued that the definition of the beautiful based on the moment of quantity, viz., "The *beautiful* is that which apart from a concept pleases universally" (KU 5: 219; 64), entails that the judgment is analytic. See "On the Putative Apriority of Judgments of Taste," p. 168, note 7. Not accepting Lewis's claim, I am not tempted to go that route.

22. In R818 15: 365 Kant writes: "Taste is that in the faculty of sensible judgment which is similar to reason [*Vernunftähnliche*], since one can judge as it were [*gleichsam*] *a priori* what in general will be pleasing to others."

23. See Guyer, *Kant and the Claims of Taste*, pp. 165–6, on the two senses of apriority.

24. Beck, "On the Putative Apriority of Judgments of Taste," pp. 167–70.

25. In spite of similarities in formulation, it should be noted once again that my analysis differs from Ginsborg's in at least one fundamental respect. Whereas she maintains that the judgment of taste is reflexive in the sense of being literally about its own normativity (or universal communicability), which, as previously argued, precludes negative judgments of taste, on my reading, a pure judgment of taste is concerned with the suitability for judgment of a given object or its representation, which preserves both the heautonomy of taste and the possibility of negative judgments. For my discussion of Ginsborg's view, see Chapter 5, part IV.

26. Guyer, *Kant and the Claims of Taste*, p. 259.

27. For a very different view of the relation between these two arguments, see Guyer, *Kant and the Claims of Taste*, pp. 315–17. As already indicated, he views them as two distinct attempts at a deduction of the claims of taste. I shall offer a critique of Guyer's interpretation in the next section.

28. A possible objection to this interpretation is provided by the discussion of the idea of a universal voice in §8 of the Analytic. As we saw in Chapter 5, Kant there states that "Whether someone who believes he is making a judgment of taste is in fact judging in conformity with that idea may be uncertain; but

by using the term beauty he indicates that he is at least referring his judging to that idea, and hence that he intends it to be a judgment of taste. For himself, however, he can easily attain certainty on this point [*davon*], by merely being conscious that he is separating whatever belongs to the agreeable and the good from the liking that remains to him after that" (KU 5: 216; 60). Admittedly, this passage is ambiguous, but as I argued in Chapter 5, I think it reasonable to take Kant to be claiming that what we can be certain of by attending to our mental actions is whether we have *intended* to make a pure judgment of taste (since this requires abstraction from the agreeable, etc.), not that we have in fact succeeded. Otherwise expressed, we can be certain that we have made a judgment of taste, but not that we have made a *pure* judgment. Moreover, on any other reading, it is difficult, to say the least, to reconcile the claims of §8 and §38. As I shall try to show in the final section of this chapter, the connection between judging in conformity with the idea of a universal voice and making a pure judgment of taste is also highly relevant to the response to the notorious "everything is beautiful" objection to the Deduction.

29. In the recent literature, the readings of the Deduction closest to the one advocated here are by Claude MacMillan, "Kant's Deduction of Pure Aesthetic Judgments," pp. 43–54, and Christel Fricke, *Kants Theorie des reinen Geschmacksurteile*. On page 152, note 1, Fricke remarks that the deduction of the principle of taste is closer to that of the second than of the first *Critique*, since it consists in its legitimation against skeptical objections from the side of empiricism, rather than the proof of a validity claim. I am in general agreement with this, but would add that Kant's target here is not simply empiricism, since he is equally concerned to defend the legitimacy of the principle of taste against those who wish to ground judgments of taste in a principle of perfection, that is, rationalists such as Baumgarten and Meier.

30. For a fuller account of my overall disagreement with Guyer on the analysis of Kant's conception of taste, see my "Pleasure and Harmony in Kant's Theory of Taste," pp. 466–81.

31. Guyer, *Kant and the Claims of Taste*, p. 260.

32. Ibid., p. 272.

33. Actually, Guyer himself does not formulate the issue in terms of subsumption, and would probably object to doing so; but I am nonetheless taking the liberty of doing so in order to relate his account to the interpretation advanced here.

34. Guyer, *Kant and the Claims of Taste*, esp. pp. 318–22.

35. Ibid., p. 325. For my own, very different reading of Kant's suggestion in §22 that common sense might be a regulative idea, see part III of Chapter 7.

36. Ibid. pp. 326–7.

37. See part II of Chapter 7.

38. Anthony Savile, *Aesthetic Reconstructions*, pp. 99–191.

39. Ibid., pp. 145–6.

40. Ibid., p. 153.

41. Ibid., p. 154.

42. Ibid., p. 159.

43. Ibid., pp. 160–1.

44. Ibid., p. 169.

45. Savile is well aware that this appeal to aesthetic Ideas gives a primacy to artistic beauty, which clearly reflects his own priorities as a contemporary aesthetician. By way of completing his reconstruction of Kant's argument, however, he does appeal to the passage in which Kant states that "We may in general call beauty (whether natural or artistic) the *expression* of aesthetic Ideas" (5: 320; 189), and he attempts to provide an account of how natural objects may be thought to express such Ideas. See *Aesthetic Reconstructions,* pp. 179–85.

46. As we shall see in Chapter 11, it would conflict with the Dialectic of Aesthetic Judgment as well. For Kant there distinguishes between disputing about taste, which presupposes the availability of a decision procedure based on proofs, and merely quarreling about it, which assumes normativity but does not allow for any decision procedure (KU 5: 338–9; 210–11). Moreover, Kant argues that the resolution of the Antinomy turns on the claim that the latter is possible even though the former is not. Thus, the claim that there could be a justification of particular claims of taste would contradict the solution to the Antinomy as well as the premises of Deduction; for in both places Kant insists that a judgment of taste rests on a principle that is both normative and indeterminate.

47. See Hud Hudson, "The Significance of an Analytic of the Ugly in Kant's Deduction of Pure Judgments of Taste," p. 87, and Christel Fricke, *Kants Theorie des reinen Geschmacksurteils,* pp. 4–5.

48. See Chapter 3, note 11, for references to the literature on this topic.

49. Theodore A. Gracyk, "Sublimity, Ugliness, and Formlessness in Kant's Aesthetic Theory," pp. 49–56.

50. Reinhard Brandt, "Die Schönheit der Kristalle und das Spiel der Erkenntniskräfte," pp. 19–57, and "Zur Logik des ästhetischen Urteils," esp. pp. 239–45. A somewhat similar view is also advanced by Garrett Thompson, "Kant's Problems with Ugliness," pp. 107–15.

51. Brandt, "Die Schönheit der Kristalle und das Spiel der Erkenntniskräfte," p. 35, note 34. I have cited more of the passage than Brandt does in order to make clear that Kant is not here concerned with an *aesthetic* evaluation.

52. See, for example, Ameriks, "How to Save Kant's Deduction of Taste," pp. 299–300.

53. For formulations of this dilemma, see Guyer, *Kant and the Claims of Taste,* pp. 297; Ralf Meerbote, "Reflection on Beauty," pp. 81; and Christel Fricke, *Kants Theorie des reinen Geschmacksurteils,* p. 167.

54. See my discussion of this topic in Chapter 2.

55. Carl J. Posy, "Imagination and Judgment in the Critical Philosophy," p. 41.

56. In this connection it should be noted that at the end of his discussion of the distinction between free and adherent beauty, Kant himself analyzes aesthetic disagreement in terms of a conflict between a pure and an "applied" judgment of taste (KU 5: 231; 78).

57. See Gr 4: 445; 112, where Kant uses this language to characterize the possibility that the categorical imperative, which was shown in the analytic portions of the *Groundwork* to be the supreme principle of morality, might be empty or otherwise inapplicable to finite rational agents such as ourselves. I

have chosen this language to indicate once again the analogy with the situation regarding the categorical imperative, the *possibility* of which Kant purports to have established in the third and synthetic portion of the *Groundwork*, even though it remains impossible to determine whether any particular action actually conforms to its dictates (is not only according to, but from duty). In both cases, what is at stake is merely a possibility: in acting purely from duty in the one case, and in making a pure judgment of taste in the other.

58. C. I. Lewis, *Mind and the World Order,* p. 221. See also Norman Kemp Smith, *A Commentary on Kant's Critique of Pure Reason,* p. 222.

59. Lewis White Beck, "Did the Sage of Königsberg Have No Dreams?" pp. 38–60.

60. I discuss this issue in *Kant's Transcendental Idealism,* pp. 152–8.

Chapter 9. Reflective Judgment and the Transition from Nature to Freedom

1. Commentators who hold some version of this view include Crawford, *Kant's Aesthetic Theory;* Kenneth Rogerson, *Kant's Aesthetics;* Salim Kemal, *Kant and Fine Art;* Anthony Savile, *Aesthetic Reconstructions.*

2. Guyer, *Kant and the Experience of Freedom,* p. 19.

3. The issues discussed here are obviously also closely connected to Kant's treatment of the sublime; but for reasons to be made clear at that time, this will be considered in Chapter 13 as part of the "*parerga*" to the theory of taste.

4. This seems to be the view of Heinz Heimsoeth, *Transzendentale Dialektik,* p. 59. For my own views on the connections between the cosmological and practical conceptions of freedom, see *Kant's Theory of Freedom,* esp. pp. 25–8.

5. Of course, "speculative cognition" [*den spekulativen Erkenntnissen*] cannot here be understood as actual knowledge, since Kant denies that such knowledge is possible.

6. Düsing, *Die Teleologie in Kants Weltbegriff,* p. 103.

7. I discuss the salient features of Kant's moral theory *circa* 1781, which remains a form of heteronomy, in "The Concept of Freedom in Kant's 'Semi-Critical' Ethics," pp. 96–115, and in *Kant's Theory of Freedom,* Chapter 3.

8. I discuss this point in *Kant's Theory of Freedom,* pp. 66–70.

9. This line of criticism was expressed most forcefully by H. A. Pistorius in his review of the *Groundwork.* For a discussion of Pistorius's critique (as well as related criticisms) and Kant's response to them in the Preface of the second *Critique,* see Lewis White Beck, *A Commentary on Kant's Critique of Practical Reason,* pp. 58–61. I discuss Kant's response to Pistorius in *Kant's Theory of Freedom,* Chapter 2.

10. For example, judgment is connected with the feeling of pleasure and displeasure among the mental faculties, with the purposiveness of nature as its principle, and with art as its "product" (FI 20: 246; 435). The sudden reference to art at this point as the product of judgments based on the principle of purposiveness may initially seem mysterious; but Kant later makes it clear that he is here referring to the idea of the technic (purposiveness) of nature, rather than the principle of artistic beauty (FI 20: 251; 440–1).

11. I am here following Helga Mertens, *Kommentar zur ersten Einleitung in Kants Kritik der Urteilskraft*, p 203. An alternative interpretation, suggested by Düsing (*Die Teleologie in Kants Weltbegriff*, p. 105) is that it refers to the "theoretically not cognizable substrate of the sensible or nature"; but I believe that Mertens is correct in rejecting this reading on the grounds that it makes the substrate in question into something nonsensible. On the various senses Kant gives to the term "Substrat," see also Heimsoeth, *Transzententale Dialektik*, p. 441, note 52.

12. I discuss Kant's reasons for rejecting such a compatibilism, not all of which are based on ethical considerations, in *Kant's Theory of Freedom*, especially Chapters 2 and 4. Although I disagree with several aspects of his account, I subscribe to Allen Wood's characterization of Kant's complex views on freedom as the "compatibilism of compatibilism and incompatibilism." See his "Kant's Compatibilism," p. 74.

13. Kant connects this Leibnizian doctrine with this very problem at the end of his polemical essay against Eberhard, in connection with the previously discussed claim that the "Critique of Pure Reason might well be the true apology for Leibniz." (See UE 8: 250.) Since this essay was published in the same year as the third *Critique*, it seems reasonable to see here an attempt at a "critical" reappropriation of Leibnizian thought in the practical domain analogous to the one discussed in Chapter 1 of this study with reference to empirical knowledge.

14. For my discussion of obligatory moral ends, see *Idealism and Freedom*, Chapter 11. I also discuss perpetual peace as a morally necessary end and the teleological considerations it involves in "The Gulf between Nature and Freedom and Nature's Guarantee of Perpetual Peace," pp. 37–49.

15. On the highest good as a totalizing concept, see Re 6: 5; 58. For a discussion of this point, see Düsing, "Das Problem des höchsten Gutes in Kants praktischer Philosophie," pp. 32–3.

16. For an analysis of the tensions in Kant's accounts of the highest good as an end to be fully realized or as merely to be promoted, see John Silber, "Kant's Conception of the Highest Good as Immanent and Transcendent," pp. 469–92.

17. For a sharply contrasting discussion of this issue see Véronique Zanetti, "Teleology and the Freedom of the Self," pp. 47–63. In contrast to my reading, Zanetti suggests that it is precisely the ethical significance of the problem that requires that the *Übergang* be in more than merely a way of thinking, and she points to Schelling as the thinker who first brought this line of thought to its logical conclusion.

18. The moral, as opposed to the merely systematic, basis of the *Übergang* in the Second Introduction is emphasized by Düsing, *Die Teleologie in Kants Weltbegriff*, esp. pp. 108–15.

19. Kant dealt systematically with this problem some three years later in *On the Old Saw: that it May be Right in Theory but it Won't Work in Practice*, where he insists that "the pursuit of a certain effect of our will would be no duty if the effect were not also possible in experience (whether conceived as complete or as constantly approaching completion") (TP 8: 276; 42).

20. For Kant's account of unsocial sociability, see especially IAG 8: 20–21. The systematic significance of this conception for Kantian ethics has been explored recently by Allen W. Wood, "Unsociable Sociability," pp. 325–51.

21. See also the account of the vices of culture, which at their maximum become "diabolical vices" (Re 6: 27; 75).

22. For Kant's conception of autocracy and its distinction from autonomy, see MS 6: 383; 188 and MS Vor 23: 396, 398; Mor M II 29: 626; and Fort 20: 295. For my own discussion of the topic, see Kant's Theory of Freedom, pp. 164–5 and 245–6.

23. This is to be distinguished from the properly transcendental dimension of Kant's conception of freedom, viz., the idea of a free act as itself causally unconditioned. It is this that is thought in the transcendental idea of freedom.

24. For Ulrich and Rehberg as the likely sources for this objection, see E. G. Schulz, Rehbergs Opposition gegen Kants Ethik, pp. 132–3.

25. The significance that Kant attached to this line of objection is reflected in the fact that he formulates a similar response, albeit expressed, in somewhat different terms, in Re 6: 170n; 190.

26. This does, however, allow for the possibility of negative claims, such as that of the nonspatiotemporality of things considered as they are in themselves. For my most recent analysis of this issue, see Idealism and Freedom, Chapter 1.

27. See KU 5: 180; 19.

28. Expressed in traditional Aristotelian terms, the difference between these two forms of purposiveness corresponds to the difference between a formal and a final cause. Thus, in arguing for the intrinsic purposiveness of living beings, Kant insists on the necessity of presupposing an idea of the whole, a blueprint as it were, whereas in the case of extrinsic purposiveness, it is a matter of something being for the sake of something else. The fact that much of Kant's account of purposiveness is not really teleological since it is concerned with formal rather than final causality is emphasized by McLaughlin, Kant's Critique of Teleology in Biological Explanation, esp. pp 39–45.

29. For a discussion of Kant's conception of the "cunning of nature" (a phrase which he never uses), see Yirmiahu Yovel, Kant and the Philosophy of History, pp. 125–57.

30. For a recent statement of this view in connection with the issue of interest, see Jane Kneller, "The Interests of Disinterest," pp. 782–84.

31. This point is emphasized by G. Felicitas Munzel in her commentary on Kneller's paper, "The Privileged Status of Interest in Nature's Beautiful Forms," pp. 789–90.

32. See, for example, A51/B75, B172, and B157–8. I discuss Kant's conception of epistemic spontaneity in Kant's Theory of Freedom, Chapter 2 and Idealism and Freedom, Chapters 4, 7, and 9.

33. In the parallel account of the cultivation of conscience, Kant refers to an indirect duty (MS 6: 401; 202). I shall argue in Chapter 10 that this is also how we must understand a supposed obligation to cultivate one's moral feeling or, indeed, to take an interest in the beauties of nature.

34. Texts in which this is expressed include Re 6: 24n; 72–3; MS 6: 409 and

484–5; 209, 273–4; Anthro 7: 235–236; 103–4; and Mor M II 29: 617 and 639. I discuss this topic in *Kant's Theory of Freedom*, pp. 163–4. For further discussion of it, see Karl Ameriks, "Kant on the Good Will," pp. 45–65.

Chapter 10. Beauty, Duty, and Interest:
The Moral Significance of Natural Beauty

1. See Chapter 9, note 1.
2. It should be noted that Kant here characterizes interest in terms of a pleasure [*Lust*] in the existence of something rather than, as in the initial formulation, as a liking [*Wohlgefallen*] connected with the representation of the existence (or continued existence) of an object, (KU 5: 204; 45). Nevertheless, this does not create any major difficulties, since Kant consistently treats *Wohlgefallen* and *Lust* as equivalent in his discussions of aesthetic response.
3. For an account of this earlier view of Kant that is found in his *Reflexionen* and student notes from his lectures, see Guyer, "Pleasure and Society in Kant's Theory of Taste," esp. pp. 41–7. More recently, Guyer has argued that Kant is here referring to and criticizing the account of Marcus Herz, *Versuch über den Geschmack*, 1776, 2d ed. 1790. See *Kant and the Experience of Freedom*, pp. 241–8. Although I find this suggestion quite plausible, I do not think that it materially affects the points at issue.
4. See Hannah Arendt, *Lectures on Kant's Political Philosophy*, pp. 76–7.
5. Within the confines of the *Critique of Judgment*, see the "General Remark on the Exposition of Aesthetic Reflective Judgments," where Kant writes: "It is true that our liking both for the beautiful and for the sublime not only differs recognizably from other aesthetic judgments by being universally *communicable*, but by having this property it also acquires an interest in relation to society (where such communication may take place" (KU 5: 275; 136).
6. This argument is criticized by Anthony Savile, *Aesthetic Reconstructions*, pp. 162–3. Savile neglects, however, its connection with the transition issue.
7. In addition to the conception of unsociable sociability, this Rousseauian side of Kant is perhaps best in evidence in the account of the vices of culture. (See Re 6: 27; 75.) These vices are all said to be rooted in the corruption of the predisposition to humanity, which seems to be the Kantian analogue of Rousseau's *amour propre*.
8. Of particular interest in this regard is Kant's apparent siding with Henry Home (Lord Kames) against Rousseau on the moral benefits of the refinement of taste in the early anthropology lectures of winter 1772–3. In support of Home's position, Kant here distinguishes the refinement [*Verfeinerung*] of taste from its pampering [*Verzärtelung*]. See Anthro C 25: 188. And in a later version of these lectures (from the winter of 1784–5, he remarks that the beautiful serves to recommend the good (Anthro M 25: 1332).
9. Here Kant differs from Home, who explicitly refers to the culture of taste in the fine arts. See note 8.
10. This line of reasoning accords with Kant's claim in the Critique of Teleological Judgment discussed in Chapter 9 that humankind may be viewed as the ultimate purpose [*letzter Zweck*] of nature only if it is seen as having a final

purpose [*Endzweck*] that transcends nature and is moral. In other words, any assumed purposiveness of nature with respect to us is to be understood ultimately in moral terms.

11. For a critique of Kant's argument in §42 based on similar considerations, see Crawford, *Kant's Aesthetic Theory*, pp. 148–9. In contrast to Crawford, however, I take this to indicate that the argument has not yet been formulated, rather than that it simply fails. Accordingly, the argument advanced in the rest of this section may be read as a response to Crawford and other critics (including Guyer) who accept his line of criticism.

12. For my detailed discussions of this issue, see *Kant's Theory of Freedom*, pp. 146–61, and *Idealism and Freedom*, pp. 169–82.

13. See Karl Marx, Introduction to the "Contribution to the Critique of Hegel's Philosophy of Right," in Karl Marx, *Early Writings*, p. 52.

14. This may help to shed some light on Kant's curious remark that the cultivation of the feelings for the beautiful and the sublime provide preparation for the development of moral feeling, the former with respect to imperfect, the latter with respect to perfect duties. See R992 15: 437. I shall return to this issue in Chapter 13.

15. In MS 6: 384; 189, Kant characterizes the contrast between virtue and lack of virtue or moral weakness as one of logical opposition, and that between virtue and vice as real opposition. According to this view, the failure to act beneficently on a given occasion, unless it reflects a principled refusal to help others, manifests a simple lack of virtue rather than vice. For a discussion of this issue, see Thomas E. Hill, Jr., "Kant on Imperfect Duty and Supererogation," pp. 147–75.

16. See Allison, *Kant's Theory of Freedom*, pp. 167–8, and *Idealism and Freedom*, pp. 122–3.

17. See *Kant's Theory of Freedom*, pp 167–8.

18. A criticism along roughly these lines was raised by Marcia Baron against my initial analysis of this problem. See her "Freedom, frailty, and impurity," pp. 433–5. My discussion in *Idealism and Freedom*, pp.118–23, is a response to her criticisms.

19. The expression "counterweight," which Kant uses frequently is misleading because it suggests a very un-Kantian view of motivation as involving a clash between motives viewed as psychic forces rather than as reasons to act. As such, it conflicts with what I have termed Kant's "Incorporation Thesis." For my most recent discussion of this thesis and its connection with the present problem, see *Idealism and Freedom*, pp. 118–23.

20. See Gr 4: 399; 67; KpV 5: 93; 97, and MS 6: 388; 192–3.

21. Although the element of radical evil is not brought into the story, in the *Critique of Judgment*, Kant discusses the need for a reinforcement of one's commitment to the highest good in connection with the moral proof of the existence of God. Especially relevant in this regard is the discussion of the righteous atheist, of which Spinoza is cited as an example. (See KU 5: 451–3; 341–2.) Based on this account, it might be claimed that natural beauty plays a role for the morally committed (though still fallible because radically evil) agent that is similar in kind to the role played by a morally based belief in the

existence of God. In both cases it is a matter of reinforcing the belief that nature is "on our side," which, in turn, is a necessary condition of a full commitment to morally dictated ends.

Chapter 11. The Antinomy of Taste and Beauty as a Symbol of Morality

1. At the suggestion of an anonymous reader for Cambridge University Press, I am following Bernard in translating "*vernünftelnd sein*" as "be rationalizing," rather than Pluhar's "engage in reasoning," in order to capture the sense of speciousness suggested by the German term. In a note attached to this sentence, Kant remarks that by a rationalizing judgment [*vernünftelndes Urteil*] or *judiciam ratiocinans* he understands one that can proclaim itself to be universal and thus serve as major premise in a syllogism. This is distinguished from a "rational judgment" [*Vernunfturteil*] or *judicium ratiocinatum*, which may serve as the conclusion of a syllogism and thus has an *a priori* ground. Clearly, it is judgments of the former type that are capable of generating antinomies. (See also A311/B368.)

2. By presenting the alternatives as exhausted by the contrast between aesthetic judgments of sense and of taste, Kant is ignoring the second species of aesthetic judgments of reflection, namely the sublime, which is the subject of Chapter 13. Kant does not include a dialectic of the sublime in the third *Critique* and he does not tell us why. In his original sketch of the groundplan of the work, however, he does indicate a place for such a dialectic (FI 20: 251; 441).

3. For a contrasting view, see Guyer, *Kant and the Claims of Taste,* p. 332.

4. In A407/B434, Kant refers to the "*euthanasia* of pure reason" as the outcome of the antinomy if not resolved.

5. In his polemic with Eberhard, Kant distinguished sharply between logical and real or metaphysical versions of the Leibnizian principle of sufficient reason (the former applying to propositions and the latter to entities or events) and accused Eberhard of conflating them. See UE 8: 193–8).

6. I say the antinomy with which Kant is concerned because the assumption that judgments of taste are in principle decidable would generate an antinomial conflict with the thesis, albeit one which, like the mathematical antinomies of the first *Critique*, would have to be resolved by showing that both thesis and antithesis are false. Instead, we shall see that Kant attempts to model this antinomy after the dynamical ones, in which the resolution consists in showing that thesis and antithesis may both be true. Nevertheless, Kant does suggest the possibility of an alternate way of formulating the antinomy by opposing the view that the determining ground of a judgment of taste is mere agreeableness with the rationalist view that it is perfection (which presumably would entail that judgments of taste are in principle decidable) (KU 5: 341; 214). Although Kant does not tell us why he chose the dynamical rather than the mathematical model (even though the latter was also possible), the answer probably lies in his concern with linking the two sides in the conflict to the two peculiarities of the judgment of taste. Moreover, this strategy no doubt also made it easier for him to introduce the notion of an indeter-

minable concept, which, as we shall see, is the key to the systematic significance of the antinomy.

7. See Guyer, *Kant and the Claims of Taste,* pp. 337–45.

8. This should also be compared with the discussion of the antinomy in *Metaphysik Vigilantius* (K3), where Kant characterizes the first peculiarity as the fact that "One demands and presupposes that what we find beautiful as an object of taste, everyone else who has taste will also find beautiful"; and the second as the claim that "a judging person absolutely cannot determine whether something is beautiful otherwise than through his own judgment" (MV 29: 1011; 481–2).

9. On this latter point, see A408/B435-A415/B443, where Kant derives the cosmological ideas in this manner.

10. See Guyer, *Kant and the Claims of Taste,* pp. 345–50.

11. Kant indicates that this is what he has in mind in his second comment on §57, where he writes: "That there are three kinds of antinomy is due to this: There are three cognitive faculties; viz., understanding, judgment, and reason. Each of these (as a higher cognitive faculty) must have its *a priori* principles. Hence, insofar as reason passes judgment on these principles themselves and their use, it unrelentingly demands, for all of them, the unconditioned for the given conditioned" (KU 5: 345; 218). The key point here is that it is an antinomy of *reason* with respect to judgment and its principles, which entails that it concern a quest for the unconditioned. We shall return to this point in connection with the analysis of the necessary and inevitable illusion that is supposedly connected with the antinomy.

12. It should be noted, however, that Kant describes the resolution of the antinomy as a deduction of the concept of the highest good (KpV 5: 113; 119).

13. This is to be contrasted with the view of Reinhard Brandt, "Analytic/Dialectic," pp 186–7.

14. The same may also be said of the antinomy in the second *Critique.* See KpV 5: 114–15; 120–2.

15. This is noted by Mary Mothersill, "The Antinomy of Taste," p. 84.

16. I discuss how a schema functions as rule in *Kant's Transcendental Idealism,* Chapter 8. See also Chapter 1, Part II, of the present work for a discussion of the generation and function of empirical schemata.

17. In this respect, it is comparable to the antithesis position in the first *Critique,* where Kant notes that (like the thesis) it "says more than it knows" (A472/B500). With regard to the mathematical antinomies, this means that it goes beyond the negation of the finitistic position of the thesis (the world is nonfinite), which is what it knows or correctly infers, to the dogmatic assertion of the infinitistic position. Here, by contrast, the antithesis goes beyond what it knows (namely, that we can quarrel about taste and that this presupposes a concept) by implicitly agreeing with the thesis regarding the nature of the concept of the beautiful.

18. There is also the much-discussed passage at the end of the second comment to §57, where Kant remarks that the resolution of the antinomy has led to three ideas: "*first,* the idea of the supersensible in general, not further determined as the substrate of nature; *second,* the idea of the same supersensible as the principle of nature's subjective purposiveness for our cognitive fac-

ulty; *third,* the idea of the same supersensible as the principle of the purposes of freedom and of the harmony of these purposes with nature in the moral sphere" (KU 5: 346; 219–20). I take it that Kant is here referring to the progressive characterization of the supersensible substratum of nature discussed in Chapter 9 as first an undetermined = x, then as receiving determinability through judgment's concept of purposiveness, and finally as receiving determination through reason's *a priori* practical law. On the question of the identity of the three supersensibles, see Pluhar's introduction to his translation, pp. lxiv–lxv.

19. Guyer, *Kant and the Claims of Taste,* p. 340.

20. Ibid.

21. Ibid., pp. 345–50.

22. Although Guyer does indicate that the concept of the harmony of the faculties could be understood in either epistemological or psychological terms, neither of which presumably involves any appeal to the supersensible, he indicates his clear preference for the latter by equating it with the concept of a state of the empirical self. See *Kant and the Claims of Taste,* p. 342. Such a concept obviously involves no reference to the supersensible, but equally obviously it lacks the normative force required for the concept capable of resolving the antinomy. Understood epistemologically, as referring to the conditions of the unity of the manifold, the concept of the harmony of the faculties does have such force, but then the question arises whether it can be completely divorced from any reference to the supersensible. In fact, we shall see that, understood in the latter manner, the concept of the harmony of the faculties leads directly to the idea of a supersensible ground or substrate, though not, as Guyer seems to assume, by way of providing some kind of metaphysical explanation.

23. As we saw in Chapter 9, Kant uses the term "substrate" to refer to the highest ground or condition of something.

24. For a detailed discussion of this, see Grier, *Kant's Doctrine of Transcendental Illusion.*

25. A similar claim is made with regard to the idea of virtue (A315/B371–2), to which Kant refers in the third *Critique* as well.

26. See Kant's "*Stufenleiter,*" (A320/B376–7).

27. See, for example, A680/B708.

28. On this point, see also FI 20: 234; 423; and Chapter 6, note 12.

29. Guyer, *Kant and the Claims of Taste,* p. 349.

30. On this point see Düsing, *Die Teleologie in Kants Weltbegriff,* pp. 112–15.

31. See A307–8/B363–4 and A497–500/B525–28.

32. The contrast between the fallacious inferences of traditional metaphysics and the unavoidable illusion on which they are based is a focal point of Grier's analysis in *Kant's Doctrine of Transcendental Illusion.*

33. See A500/B528.

34. For the fullest statement of my recent views on this point, see *Idealism and Freedom,* Chapter 1.

35. In commenting on this analysis, an anonymous reader for Cambridge University Press questioned whether this really establishes transcendental idealism or merely the necessity of a concept (of the supersensible) that is compatible with

such idealism. The reader is certainly correct in suggesting that a concept of the supersensible is not of itself sufficient for transcendental idealism (Leibnizian rationalism is a case in point). What requires transcendental idealism, however, is not the concept of the supersensible but the qualitative distinction between the sensible and the supersensible (the transcendental distinction), and this is what the resolution of the antinomy requires with its distinction between the two types of concept.

36. Kant insists in all three *Critiques* that *at least* this much is necessary, if ideas are to have any regulative or even practical function. Thus, in the first *Critique*, he claims that the transcendental ideas each provide an "analogon of a schema" (A665/B693), in terms of which their regulative function is to be understood. Similarly, in the second *Critique*, he presents the view, already present in the *Groundwork*, that even the moral law must be thought according to an analogy (or "Typic") as a law of nature if it is to be genuinely action guiding. See KpV 5: 67–76; 70–80. Moreover, at one point in the latter work he contrasts a schema with a mere symbol (KpV 5: 70–1; 72); but he does not go on to provide an analysis of what this symbolization consists in.

37. Although the analogy goes both ways, the symbolization relation is asymmetrical, since the symbol, as exhibition of a concept (or idea), is always something sensible (or sensibly instantiable), while that which is symbolized can be something nonsensible. This is the answer to the question posed by Ted Cohen, who asked why should not a good will be taken as a symbol of a beautiful object. See "Why Beauty is a Symbol of Morality," p. 232.

38. This brief account is to be contrasted with the detailed and in many ways informative discussion of this topic by G. Felicitas Munzel, "'The Beautiful Is the Symbol of the Morally-Good,'" pp. 301–29. Although there is much of value in Munzel's paper, particularly in the discussion of Kant's use of analogy and symbol in various works, I believe that the account is vitiated by a failure to note a significant difference between the third-*Critique* account of symbolization and that found in other Kantian texts. As she quite correctly notes, the usual function of a symbol for Kant is to provide some sort of cognition by way of analogy of the purely intellectual object symbolized. Accordingly, she takes the function of the analogy with the beautiful to be to help determine, relative to us, the meaning of the idea of the morally good (*Sittlich-Gute*), and, on her account, it does so in virtue of the analogy in causality between the way in which the morally good and the beautiful are produced. As a direct consequence of this, she is led to conclude that only artistic beauty can symbolize the morally good because only in the case of artistic production do we find the requisite analogy with moral production (see esp. pp. 321–6). This result is, however, not only highly counterintuitive but also without textual support. Since Kant was so emphatic in linking an intellectual interest in beauty specifically with natural beauty, it is only reasonable to assume that if he had intended to limit the symbolic relation to artistic beauty, he would have said so.

In addition, this reading fails to help explain why Kant should claim that regarding the beautiful in this way (as symbol) is both natural for everyone and regarded as a duty (a topic which she fails to discuss). In my judgment, this reading is based on a twofold mistake: (1) a failure to recognize that

Kant's concern in §59 is not with attempting to augment our cognition of the morally good (the symbolized) but rather with underscoring the significance of its symbol (the beautiful); (2) the location of the analogy in the respective modes of causality necessary to produce the symbol and the symbolized, rather than in the form of reflection on each. Thus, Munzel may be correct in arguing against Guyer (p. 321, note 30) that the analogy Kant intends is between the morally good and a beautiful object, rather than between moral and aesthetic judgment *per se*, but she fails to note that the point of this analogy lies completely in the parallelism in the reflection on these two objects.

39. Kant does note this difference, however, in a passage devoted to a comparison of the two species of liking. Thus he remarks that though both likings are direct, in the case of morality our liking is based on a concept, but in the case of the beautiful merely on a reflection on an intuition (KU 5: 353–4; 229). We shall return to this passage later in the chapter.

40. This is also true of Kant's other significant discussion of symbolization or indirect representation of the supersensible in Fort 20: 279–80.

41. A connection between aesthetic ideas and beauty's symbolization of morality is noted by both A. C. Genova, Aesthetic Justification and Systematic Unity in Kant's Third Critique," p. 302; and Rudolf A. Makkreel, *Imagination and Interpretation in Kant,* pp. 122–29. Neither, however, relates this mode of symbolization to the problem.

42. Although he does not deal with this aspect of the topic, my account of the nature and function of aesthetic ideas has been influenced by the insightful discussion of Rudolf Lüthe, "Kants Lehre von den ästhetischen Ideen," pp. 65–74.

43. Although it is questionable whether some of these, e.g., death, really count as ideas in the Kantian sense, that is, involve the thought of a totality or completeness that can never be found in experience, it is noteworthy that the contrast between the two kinds of aesthetic ideas corresponds to the distinction between two types of ideas of reason noted earlier in this chapter, namely, between ideas that explicitly refer to something supersensible (such as the idea of transcendental freedom) and ideas (such as that of a perfect constitution or virtue) of which approximations may be found in experience.

44. This account of aesthetic ideas as prompting thought and leading, in an indeterminate manner, to the expansion of the mind, should be viewed in connection with Kant's conception of the free harmony of imagination and understanding as analyzed in Chapter 2 and subsequent chapters. Although Kant never makes the connection explicit, it would appear from this that aesthetic ideas provide the means for occasioning such harmony and, therefore, the pleasure of taste. In Chapter 12 I shall discuss the relationship between the account of the beauty in terms of the free harmony of the faculties and the purposiveness of form that is characteristic of the Analytic of the Beautiful and the later account in terms of the expression of aesthetic ideas.

45. I shall argue in Chapter 12 that it is by means of providing such an indeterminate rule or organizing principle that genius gives the rule to art.

46. Admittedly, however, Kant does seem to suggest this at some points. See, for example, the very last paragraph of the Critique of Aesthetic Judgment, where he defines taste as "at bottom a capacity to judge the sensible render-

ing [*Versinnlichung*] of moral ideas by means of a certain analogy in the reflection on both" (KU 5: 356; 232).

47. There is also a debate in the literature concerning what Kant here means by
the "morally good." The candidates include freedom (Guyer, *Kant and the Experience of Freedom*, p. 252); the idea of the supersensible ground at the basis
of morality (Crawford, *Kant's Aesthetic Theory*, p. 157); the realized object of
the will determined by pure practical reason (Munzel, "'The Beautiful is the
Symbol of the Morally-Good,'" pp. 317–20). For reasons to be given later, I
take the latter to be closest to the truth. The main point, however, is that the
problem I have sketched arises on whatever referent for this term one
chooses.

48. The requirement that everything beautiful expresses aesthetic ideas follows
from Kant's claim that "We may in general call beauty (whether natural or
artistic) the expression of aesthetic ideas" (KU 5: 320; 189). I discuss this passage both in this chapter and Chapter 12.

49. See KpV 5: 57–71; 59–74.

50. This point is worth emphasizing since it is often denied in the literature.
Thus, as already noted, Munzel denies that it applies to natural beauty (see
note 34), while Guyer denies that it applies to artistic beauty, "Nature, art,
and autonomy," p. 268.

51. A criticism along these lines was suggested by Christian Wenzel in a seminar
discussion.

52. Two interesting recent discussions of this passage are those of Anthony Savile, *Aesthetic Reconstructions*, pp. 180–3, and Christel Fricke, "Kants Theorie
der schönen Kunst," p. 689.

53. On this point, see Fricke, "Kants Theorie der schönen Kunst," p. 689.

54. Kant's assignment of the colors of the spectrum to charm rather than to
beauty is another expression of his doubts about whether colors or tones of
themselves can be considered beautiful. As we saw in Chapter 6, the issue
turns on whether or not their perception involves reflection (which would allow for the apprehension of form) or is nothing more than sensation.
Strangely enough, however, in this very passage where he treats colors as
charms that may be intimately connected with natural beauty but cannot
themselves be regarded as beautiful, he also notes that color sensation does
involve reflection and therefore the apprehension of form.

55. By the "idealism of purposiveness" Kant does not mean transcendental idealism, but rather the idea that we cannot explain the purposiveness exhibited in either natural or artistic beauty in terms of any actual intentions. The
connection between such idealism and the passage currently under consideration is suggested by Makkreel, *Imagination and Interpretation in Kant*,
pp. 126–7.

56. The diametrically opposed view is affirmed by Salim Kemal, who insists on
the moral superiority of fine art over natural beauty (*Kant and Fine Art*, esp.
pp. 14–21). For a trenchant critique of Kemal on this point, see Guyer, *Kant
and the Experience of Freedom*, pp. 271–4.

57. It should be noted here that even if, on the basis of Kant's conception of genius, one endeavors to narrow, or even deny altogether, the distinction between natural and artistic beauty, the point still holds. For genius must pre-

sumably be thought of in connection with the "supersensible within" or, as Kant also terms it, the "supersensible substrate of humanity." I have noted some of my reasons for rejecting the appeal to the doctrine of genius in an attempt to interpret away the sharp distinction between natural and artistic beauty in Chapter 9. For more on this topic, see Munzel, "The Privileged Status of Interest in Nature's Beautiful Forms," pp. 789–90.

58. On the preparatory function of the beautiful with regard to morality, see R806, where Kant states that "Beautiful objects and beautiful representations of objects wean the mind from the mere satisfaction of enjoyment and bring it closer to morality" (15: 354); and R993, where he claims that "The culture of taste is preparation [*Vorübung*] for morality" (15: 438). Since the distinction between a beautiful thing and a beautiful representation of a thing is precisely how Kant differentiates natural from artistic beauty in the third *Critique* (KU 5: 311; 179), the first of these texts is noteworthy because it indicates that Kant assigned this preparatory function to both artistic and natural beauty. Similar claims are also to be found scattered throughout the anthropology lectures. (See, for example, Mensch 25: 1096–8, 1102; Anthro M 25: 1325.)

59. This is contrasted with the sublime, which Kant claims prepares us for "esteeming it [nature] even against our interest" (KU 5: 267; 167). I shall discuss the sublime and its relation to the beautiful in Chapter 13.

60. See Guyer, *Kant and the Experience of Freedom*, p. 19.

61. I am here following Meredith in rendering "*gemeinschaftlichen*" as "public," rather than Pluhar's "sense shared by all," because it captures the point that it is a sense *for what is shareable*, i.e., universally communicable, as well as a shared capacity. For more on this issue, see the discussion of common sense in Chapter 7.

62. This line of reasoning also suggests that the cultivation of moral feeling (understood as a sensitivity to the force of moral requirements) should likewise function as a propaedeutic to the development of taste. Moreover, Kant claims precisely this at the very end of §60 (KU 5: 356; 20).

63. This, again, is to be contrasted with the views of Crawford, *Kant's Aesthetic Theory*, pp. 153–9. He takes the claim that the beautiful symbolizes morality, to mean (in part) that it expresses the idea at the basis of all morality and he takes this to ground a duty to be sensitive to and cultivate an interest in the basis of morality. In addition to (in my view) mistakenly linking this argument with the deduction of taste, Crawford neglects Kant's characterization of the requirement to develop taste and the ensuing feeling for beauty as a "duty, as it were."

64. The translation of this passage is my own and differs significantly from that of Pluhar.

65. This is the view of Crawford, *Kant's Aesthetic Theory*, p. 153, where he cites this very passage as evidence that Kant himself realized that the deduction of judgments of taste requires a linkage with morality to be completed.

66. Others making this point include Salim Kemal, "Aesthetic Necessity," p. 184; and A. C. Genova, "Aesthetic Justification and Systematic Unity in Kant's Third Critique," pp. 296–7.

Chapter 12. Fine Art and Genius

1. On this point, see Otto Schlapp, *Kants Lehre vom Genie und die Enstehung der 'Kritik der Urteilskraft,'* p.303, and John H. Zammito, *The Genesis of Kant's Critique of Judgment,* pp. 129–30. Schlapp cites both Hermann Cohen and Victor Basch as having reached similar conclusions.

2. See, for example, Rudolf Lüthe, "Kants Lehre von den ästhetischen Ideen," p. 66; and Zammito, *The Genesis of Kant's Critique of Judgment,* p. 131.

3. Recently, this point has been emphasized by Danielle Lories, "Génie et goût: complicité ou conflit?" esp. p. 564.

4. Here I am in partial agreement with Salim Kemal, who poses a problem similar to the one I pose and likewise sees Kant's conception of genius as the key to the solution. (See *Kant and Fine Art,* esp. pp. 35–40.) He takes his analysis in a completely different direction than I do, however, arguing for the superior importance of artistic to natural beauty on essentially moral grounds. Moreover, the problem as Kemal defines it seems to have more to do with the possibility of *pure* or *free* judgments of artistic beauty than with aesthetic judgments of artistic beauty in general or with the very possibility of works of fine art. This is because he construes it to lie chiefly in the apparent anomaly that "an object cannot be considered both beautiful and a work of art," since the recognition of something as a work of art requires the application of a concept to it, which supposedly makes an aesthetic judgment impossible (loc. cit., p. 36). Kemal fails to note that, so construed, the problem concerns merely the possibility of a free judgment of artistic beauty (or possibly free artistic beauties), which appears to be the direct consequence of his general neglect of the whole question of the free- adherent beauty distinction and its application to fine art. By contrast, the latter question will be a central concern of the present chapter.

5. This moral significance is emphasized not only by Kemal (*Kant and Fine Art*) but also by Crawford, who maintains that Kant's treatment of fine art is motivated primarily by his concern to show that artistic as well as natural beauty contribute to the transition from nature to freedom. See "Kant's Theory of Creative Imagination," pp. 151–78. I certainly agree that this is an important part of Kant's motivation for treating fine art, but it is by no means the whole of it. Moreover, as should become even clearer with the discussion of the sublime in Chapter 13, this is perfectly compatible with the account being "parergonal" in the sense here used.

6. I am here in basic agreement with Gadamer, who remarks that "the concept of taste loses its significance if the phenomenon of art steps into the foreground" (*Truth and Method,* p. 56).

7. For my discussion of this see Chapter 8, Part III.

8. Thus, Zammito refers to this as the "grounding paradox of art." See *The Genesis of Kant's Critique of Judgment,* p. 131. See also Kemal (in note 4).

9. A similar comparison is drawn by Christel Fricke, who argues that a work of fine art for Kant is to be understood as a semantic artifact, and on this basis she suggests that the Kantian conception is able to accommodate contemporary forms, such as minimal art, conceptual art, and anti-art. (See Fricke,

"Kants Theorie der schönen Kunst," pp. 674–89). My account differs from Fricke's primarily in its emphasis on the second aspect of Kant's definition of fine art (that it must seem like nature), which in my view sharply differentiates his conception from this prevalent contemporary view.

10. Arthur Danto, *Beyond the Brillo Box.* For Danto's more recent formulation of his views, see *After the End of Art.*

11. See, for example, Kant's discussion of a successful imitation of the "singing" of a nightingale (KU 5: 302; 169). Kant here suggests that once the ruse is discovered and one realizes that what one is hearing is art, rather than nature, not only all interest but even all aesthetic satisfaction is lost. This certainly suggests that, like Danto, Kant would acknowledge that an object of art and a natural object might be indiscernible in terms of observable properties and yet have quite distinct aesthetic significance. Of course, the conclusion that he draws from this is precisely the opposite of Danto's.

12. Kant himself cites an example of the third type in a note at the end of the third moment in order to indicate that this is not the sense of purposiveness without purpose or purposive form with which he is concerned (KU 5: 236n; 84).

13. Admittedly, however, Kant does sometimes seem to take it in this way. See, for example, Mensch 25: 1101, and Anthro B 25: 1511.

14. In a Reflexion (dated 1776–8), Kant characterizes the required quality as naïveté (R953 15: 422). For a discussion of this point see Schlapp, *Kants Lehre vom Genie und die Enstehung der 'Kritik der Urteilskraft,'* pp. 70–1; and Giorgio Tonelli, "Kant's Early Theory of Genius," Part II, p. 210.

15. As Tonelli points out, Kant was very much concerned with the analogies between beauty and living beings, genial ideas, and organisms in his early *Reflexionen.* (See "Kant's Early Theory of Genius," pp. 214–16.)

16. For a useful analysis of this concept, see McLaughlin, *Kant's Critique of Teleology in Biological Explanation,* esp. pp. 44–50.

17. See also KU 5: 396; 278, where the apparent contradiction is said to be between the natural necessity pertaining to the organism as a product of nature and its contingency with respect to the laws of nature stemming from its purposiveness.

18. See McLaughlin, *Kant's Critique of Teleology in Biological Explanation,* p. 46.

19. Motive force for Kant consists of the attractive and repulsive forces of matter. These are the forces to which primary appeal is made in mechanistic explanation. For Kant's account of these forces, see MAN 4: 496–523; 40–76.

20. See Hume, *Dialogues Concerning Natural Religion,* p. 218.

21. On possible sources for this definition, see Schlapp, *Kants Lehre vom Genie und die Enstehung der 'Kritik der Urteilskraft,'* pp. 305–19, and Tonelli, "Kant's Early Theory of Genius," pp. 219–20.

22. On this point see also Kemal, *Kant and Fine Art,* p. 40.

23. Here I appear to differ from Kemal, who suggests that the sense of "nature" here is to be understood in contrast to divine grace (*Kant and Fine Art,* p. 47). I must admit, however, that I fail to understand the relevance of that contrast to the point of issue.

24. Kant makes this clear in his discussion of genius in the *Anthropology,* where he states that "The realm of imagination is the proper domain of genius because

the imagination is creative and, being less subject than other faculties to the constraint of rules, more apt for originality" (Anthro 7: 224; 93).

25. This point is emphasized by Zammito, who suggests that the "architectonic intention" underlying Kant's account of genius "was to read the production of beauty in art as structurally homologous with the appreciation of beauty." (See *The Genesis of Kant's Critique of Judgment*, p. 143.)

26 In a transcription of his anthropology lectures from 1784–5, Kant is cited as claiming that the genius provides new rules, and as an example of a work of genius he refers to Michelangelo's design of St. Peter's (Anthro M 25: 1311).

27. On the question of Kant's denial of the possibility of scientific genius, see Schlapp, *Kants Lehre vom Genie*, pp. 314–16, and Tonelli, "Kant's Early Theory of Genius," pp. 126–9. According to Schlapp, Kant was the first important thinker to deny this, but he also notes that he is far from consistent on this score. The latter point is indeed correct. For example, after initially suggesting, in agreement with the teaching of the third *Critique*, that the term "genius" is properly applied only to artists (Anthro 7: 224; 93), Kant proceeds to characterize Leibniz and Newton as geniuses (Anthro 7: 227; 95). Kant's exclusion of great scientists from the category of genius, however, would seem more intended to circumscribe the domain of genius (given its roots in the imagination) than to minimize their intellectual contributions. Moreover, as Zammito emphasizes, there is a strong polemical thrust directed against the proto-romantic conception of genius associated with Herder and the *Sturm und Drang* running throughout Kant's entire discussion of the topic. (See *The Genesis of Kant's Critique of Judgment*, esp. pp. 139–40.)

28. On this issue see Zammito, *The Genesis of Kant's Critique of Judgment*, p. 141.

29. For an interesting account of a "dialectic of art history" based largely on this discussion, see Guyer, *Kant and the Experience of Freedom*, pp. 291–303. And for an alternative and nuanced discussion of the different relations in which genius stands to its various audiences, see Martin Gammon, "Exemplary Originality," pp. 563–92. Although of considerable interest, these topics are too far removed from the central focus of this chapter to take up here.

30. For a discussion of Kant's conception of spirit in the early *Reflexionen*, see Tonelli, "Kant's Early Theory of Genius," pp. 114–16. Tonelli notes that Kant sometimes virtually identifies spirit, understood as the principle of vivification, with genius, but that for the most part he treats it as pertaining to talent and as merely one ingredient (albeit an important one) in genius. The latter is, of course, the relationship in which they stand in the third *Critique*.

31. What Kant actually says is that the animating principle, namely spirit, is the ability to exhibit aesthetic ideas (KU 5: 313–14; 182), which, I take it, implies that they constitute the material referred to in the preceding paragraph. Elsewhere, Kant is somewhat more explicit, stating that it is spirit that provides the ideas, while taste limits them to the appropriate form (Anthro 7: 246; 113).

32. Crawford, *Kant's Aesthetic Theory*, p. 122, suggests that "aesthetic attribute" is the general term used by Kant to indicate what the artist presents.

33. For an interesting discussion of this topic, see Gammon, "Exemplary Originality," pp. 563–92.

34. See Lüthe, "Kants Lehre von den ästhetischen Ideen," p. 73.

35. See Tonelli, "Kant's Early Theory of Genius," pp. 127–8 for an account of the role of judgment in genial creation in Kant's early *Reflexionen*.

36. Presumably, this would correspond to Kant's distinction between genius and talent, which he draws in various ways in his early *Reflexionen*. On this point see Tonelli, "Kant's Early Theory of Genius," pp. 111–13.

37. The connection is noted by Anthony Savile, *Aesthetic Reconstructions*, p. 182. Savile is one of the few commentators who places great emphasis on Kant's claim that natural beauty consists in the expression of aesthetic ideas.

38. As Fricke points out, Arthur Danto, operating with an understanding of art in terms of communication, denies that one can properly talk about natural beauty on the grounds that it makes no sense to think of a natural object as having a semantic function. Thus, in this respect, the Kantian view differs significantly from Danto's ("Kants Theorie der schönen Kunst," p. 689).

39. For a clear statement of the incompatibility thesis, see D. W. Gotshalk, "Form and Expression in Kant's Aesthetics," pp. 250–60. Gotshalk argues that Kant has a formalist theory of natural beauty and an expressionist theory of artistic beauty, each of which is intended to account for the connection between that species of beauty and morality. This is, of course, diametrically opposed to the view argued for here, according to which the same subjective principle of taste determines both forms of beauty. Moreover, Gotshalk's reading has little textual support.

40. Guyer makes what I take to be essentially the same point in his own terms, when he suggests that "the theory of aesthetic ideas . . . must derive from Kant's own exploitation of the gap between the general idea of the harmony of the faculties and the particular formalist opinions of the third moment" (*Kant and the Claims of Taste*, p. 233). See also his "Formalism and the Theory of Expression in Kant's Aesthetics," pp. 46–70).

41. See KU 5: 313; 181, where Kant characterizes form as "only the vehicle of communication." The passage is also cited by Crawford in his account of the issue currently before us. See his *Kant's Aesthetic Theory*, p. 123.

42. For a very useful discussion of this issue, which has influenced my own, see Kenneth R. Rogerson, *Kant's Aesthetics*, pp. 156–65. My only significant disagreement with Rogerson concerns his claim that the doctrine of aesthetic ideas constitutes part of the deduction.

43. See, for example, Kant's remark about painting, KU 5: 330; 201.

44. See Gr 4: 436; 103–4. Of course, the situation is complicated by the fact that Kant asserts the equivalence of three formulae for the categorical imperative, and there does not appear to be any analogous third alternative in the case of the judgment of taste. Nevertheless, I do not think that this undermines the comparison. For an excellent discussion of the equivalence issue regarding the diverse formulae, see Onora O'Neill, *Constructions of Reason*, pp. 126–44.

45. This is emphasized by Eva Schaper, *Studies in Kant's Aesthetics*, pp. 78–98. As I noted in Chapter 6, Schaper provides the best discussion of these issues as they arise within the context of §16. At this point, however, it must be emphasized that she confines her analysis to that portion of text. Thus, she fails to pose the question of the relation of Kant's initial account of the free-ad-

herent beauty distinction to his later account of fine art, which is precisely the focus of my present concern.

46. A similar conclusion is reached by Crawford, *Kant's Aesthetic Theory*, p. 115, although his strategy for dealing with it differs from mine.

47. The unclarity in Kant's use of "representation" with regard to art is emphasized by Schaper, *Studies in Kant's Aesthetics*, p. 91.

48. The German text here reads: *"Es ist kein Begriff von irgend einem Zwecke, wozu das Mannigfaltige dem gegeben Objecte dienen und was dieses also vorstellen solle . . .* " and is ambiguous, if not ungrammatical. The major difficulty is the referent of the second relative clause beginning with *"was."* I am following all the existing English translations in taking this to refer back to the purpose, rather than to either the given object or the manifold, but grammatically, it should read *welchen*. For a discussion of this point, see Walter Cerf (editor and translator), *Analytic of the Beautiful*, note w, pp. 112–13.

49. See Schaper, *Studies in Kant's Aesthetics*, p. 88.

50. It is perhaps noteworthy at this point that Kant includes such things as the "art of dressing tastefully" within the scope of painting in the broad sense (KU 5: 323; 193).

51. In interpreting this passage, I have followed the reading of all four English translations, which take Kant to be referring to the body of a man. But since the text refers merely to a figure [*Gestalt*] and later back to it through the pronoun *"dieser,"* Kant may possibly be referring to a statue or figure of a man. Accordingly, I have modified Pluhar's translation of this passage to reflect this ambiguity. In the latter case, of course, it would be a work of art in the usual sense, and *both* senses of "representation" as noted would be applicable to it. It would be viewed as depicting a warrior and as exemplifying one, with the latter being the source of the extra-aesthetic constraints.

52. Of these terms I believe that only the archaic "exemplative" calls for comment. I have chosen it rather than the more familiar "exemplary" in order to avoid confusion with Kant's characterization of the products of genius. The latter term obviously connotes excellence of the highest order, a worthiness to be emulated. By contrast, exemplative, as I am using it, is applicable to something thoroughly mediocre, since it requires merely that it be viewed as an example of a thing of a certain kind.

53. This is further brought out by Kant's explanation of why the disgusting cannot be rendered in an aesthetically pleasing manner, namely, the impossibility of distinguishing the artistic representation of the object from one's sensation (KU 5: 312; 80). Moreover, in the same context Kant also excludes sculpture (but not painting) from any *direct* representation of ugly objects (not merely the disgusting) on the grounds that "in its products art is almost confused with nature" (KU 5: 312; 180). But in a student's transcript of his anthropology lectures from the winter of 1788–9 (or just at the time of the composition of the third *Critique*), Kant claims that only poetry can depict the ugly beautifully, thereby excluding painting as well as sculpture, on the grounds that a painting must seem near to nature if it is to be judged beautiful (Anthro B 25: 1510–11).

54. I emphasize the generality of the kind of knowledge that I have in mind in order to make it clear that Kant, on this reading, is not guilty of what has been

termed the "intentional fallacy," that is, the claim that it is possible to grasp the actual intention of the artist in producing a given work and that the value of the work is to be measured by the success of the artist in realizing this intention. For an overview of the literature on this "fallacy," pp. 515–17.

55. This sense of "representation" is suggested by Schaper, *Studies in Kant's Aesthetics,* p. 93. But since she is not concerned with the account in §48, she does not note that it is applicable to all works of fine art, in virtue of their being works of art.

56. Crawford, *Kant's Aesthetic Theory,* pp. 114–17.

57. These examples are taken from a longer list supplied by Kant (KU 5: 322; 191–2).

58. This clearly represents at least a significant strand of the distinction as Kant draws it in §16. A possible reason that Kant combines it with reference to representation and the concept of what a thing is meant to be (which, as we have seen, are the sources of all the difficulties), is that he attempted to incorporate Francis Hutcheson's distinction between "absolute" or "original" and "relative" or "comparative" beauty. By the former, Hutcheson understood "that Beauty which we perceive in Objects without Comparison to any thing external;" while the latter he defined as "that which we perceive in Objects, commonly considered as *Imitations* or *Resemblances* of something else." (See Francis Hutcheson, *An Inquiry into the Original of our Ideas of Beauty and Virtue,* p. 15.) If Kant had attempted to map Hutcheson's distinction on the one here attributed to him (or *vice versa*), then something very much like the confusions and ambiguities I have indicated would have emerged. Nevertheless, I offer this merely as a speculative proposal for which I have no proof.

59. This may be taken as at least a partial response to Gadamer, who, echoing a widely shared sentiment, remarks that "It seems impossible to do justice to art if aesthetics is founded on the pure judgment of taste – unless the criterion of taste is made merely a precondition" (*Truth and Method,* p. 45). What is crucial is the inseparability of the formalism connected with the emphasis on purity contained in the Analytic of the Beautiful from the expression of aesthetic ideas that is characteristic of great art.

60. To my knowledge, the fullest discussion of this topic is by Otto Schlapp, *Kants Lehre vom Genie,* esp. pp. 33–34.

61. For example, Tonelli nicely documents Kant's wavering on the question of the relation between genius and rules in the *Reflexionen.* (See "Kant's Early Theory of Genius (1770–1779)," pp. 120–2, 210–11).

62. Two examples of contemporary discussions that clearly influenced Kant's views on the relation between genius and taste are Alexander Gerard's claim that a close connection between genius and taste is "so evident that it has almost passed into a maxim" (*An Essay on Taste,* p. 168); and Johann Georg Sulzer's statement that "The understanding and genius of the artist give to a work all the essential parts that belong to its inner perfection, but taste makes it into a work of fine art." ("Art," "*Geschmack,*" in *Allgemeine Theorie der schönen Künste,* in vol. #2, p. 372.

63. This is noted by Schlapp, *Kants Lehre vom Genie,* p. 334.

64. See, for example, KU 5: 316–17; 185.

65. Kant's "ironic intention" in his treatment of genius is emphasized by Zam-

mito, who also insists that there is no confusion at all in Kant's account, "just a variety of scores to settle" (particularly with the *Sturm und Drang*). See *The Genesis of Kant's Critique of Judgment*, pp. 142–3.

Chapter 13. The Sublime

1. See Samuel Monk, *The Sublime, A Study of Critical Theories in XVIII-Century England*, pp. 1–42, and Francis Ferguson, "The Sublime from Burke to the Present," vol. 4, pp. 326–31.
2. Monk, *The Sublime*, esp. pp. 26–42.
3. Ibid., pp. 84–100.
4. Edmund Burke, *A Philosophical Enquiry into the Origin of our Ideas of the Sublime and Beautiful*, p. 58.
5. Ibid., pp. 39–40.
6. Ibid., p. 36.
7. This is noted by Boulton in his "Editor's Introduction" to his edition of Burke's *Enquiry*, p. cxxv. In the same context, he also suggests that Kant's method in this early work is Burkean and that, although it is unlikely that he had firsthand knowledge of the *Enquiry* at that time, he was probably familiar with its essential themes and mode of analysis through the lengthy discussion of it by Moses Mendelssohn in his review summary.
8. See, for example, Anthro C 25: 175; Anthro P 25: 388–9; and R992–3 15: 436–7.
9. The basic scholarship on the dating of the inclusion of the sublime has been done by Michel Souriau, *Le jugement réfléchissant dans la philosophie critique de Kant*, and Giorgio Tonelli, "La formazione del testo della *Kritik der Urteilskraft*," pp. 423–48. These provide the bases for the more recent discussions of this topic by Donald Crawford, "The Place of the Sublime in Kant's Aesthetic Theory," pp. 161–83, and by John Zammito, *The Genesis of Kant's Critique of Judgment*, pp. 275–83.
10. They are not as sparse as Eva Schaper suggests, however, since she mysteriously claims that there are none at all. See "Taste, sublimity, and genius," p. 381.
11. In §25 of the published text, Kant also refers to a deduction of the sublime, but it is not clear whether he means a separate deduction or the one referred to in §30 as contained within the exposition.
12. In discussing these references, I am following the lead of Crawford, "The Place of the Sublime in Kant's Aesthetic Theory," pp. 178–9; he bases his analysis on the discussions of Souriau and Tonelli. Crawford, however, neglected the one at the end of §14 and therefore mistakenly denied that there are any references to the sublime in the Analytic of the Beautiful.
13. Actually, the situation is even worse, since Kant does not refer specifically to the moment of relation, though it seems reasonable to assume that this is the concern of §28, "On Nature as a Might." By contrast, at the beginning of the General Comment, Kant attempts to correlate each of the four likings discussed in the *Critique of Judgment* (for the agreeable, the beautiful, the sublime, and the morally good) with one of the moments, and he correlates that for the sublime with Relation (KU 5: 266–7; 126).

14. See KU 5: 272–5; 132–6. Kant begins the discussion by connecting these mental states with "nature within."

15. I here disagree with Crawford, who, in spite of following Tonelli in the late dating of the addition of the account of the sublime into the *Critique of Judgment,* insists that it is not a mere "afterthought" but instead reflects a shift of focus on Kant's part toward the ethical and the significance for it of aesthetic experience ("The Place of the Sublime in Kant's Aesthetic Theory," esp. pp. 176–83). Thus, though I agree with Crawford (and Zammito) that the belated inclusion of the sublime is probably due to Kant's shift of focus to the ethical, for the reasons given, I continue to insist on its merely parergonal status with respect to the very specific concerns of the third *Critique.*

16. Presumably this includes the modality of necessity, though Kant does not bring this into the story until §29.

17. As has been frequently pointed out, this characterization of the liking for the sublime as a "negative pleasure," marks Kant's major difference from Burke on the nature of the feeling of the sublime. For, as already noted, the latter denied the appropriateness of characterizing it as a pleasure at all because of its connection with displeasure, and termed it instead a "delight." (See note 6.) It should also be kept in mind, however, that in the same context Burke also speaks of "delight" as a "species of relative pleasure."

18. As we shall see in more detail later, Kant recognizes preconditions for the appreciation of the sublime that are not required for the beautiful.

19. Although Kant does not refer to heautonomy in connection with his account of teleological judgment, the conception is implicitly at work. For Kant makes clear in the Analytic of Teleological Judgment that the appeal to the idea of purpose is for the sake of judgment in its reflective capacity, since it is a condition of forming a determinate empirical concept (one capable of being used for classification and explanation) of objects that possess the peculiar properties of a *Naturzweck.* See especially KU 5: 376–7; 255–7, and the discussion of the concept of a *Naturzweck* in Chapter 12.

20. Even though two of the three definitions (or formulae) offered are in quantitative terms, I am distinguishing this discussion from the actual treatment of the "quantity" of the sublime. The latter is the topic of §26, which is concerned with the estimation of magnitude as it relates to the idea of the sublime. Admittedly, however, Kant does not make this clear, although he does explicitly connect §27 with the moment of quality. Another problem is that these nominal definitions are presented as of the sublime as such, not merely the mathematically sublime. All of this I regard as further evidence of the last-minute nature of the entire discussion of the sublime.

21. Unfortunately, at this point the Pluhar translation completely confuses matters by translating *"schlechtweg gross"* as "absolutely large" (p. 104), thereby leading the reader to assume that Kant is already talking about the sublime.

22. Herein lies the basis for the response to the criticism of Kant's account of the mathematically sublime by Paul Crowther (*The Kantian Sublime,* pp. 101–5). According to Crowther, it is possible to distinguish between a *"baroque"* and an *"austere"* version of the mathematically sublime. The former involves an explicit reference to infinity in connection with reason's demand on the imagination, whereas the latter takes reason's demand to be merely "the com-

prehension of the phenomenal *totality* of any given magnitude in a single whole of intuition – that is, irrespective of whether or not it is to be used as a measure in the estimation of magnitude" (p. 101). Given this distinction, Crowther dismisses the baroque version as "both phenomenologically counterintuitive and philosophically superfluous" (p. 104). If we take seriously the initial conception of the mathematically sublime as the absolutely great, however, the reference to infinity is clearly essential to the Kantian account, for reason's demand on the imagination follows directly from the latter's endeavor to provide an intuitive representation of something fitting that description. Moreover, Crowther's version of reason's demand suffers from a complete failure to distinguish between the totality required by the understanding, that is, "Allness" [*Allheit*], defined as "plurality considered as unity" (B111), which, like all the categories, expresses a condition of the unity of apperception (or the understanding), and the absolute totality or unconditioned required by reason. Consequently, "reason's demand" on Crowther's austere reading, which he claims to be all that is required by the Kantian mathematically sublime, is not even a demand of reason, and it is also one that the imagination can easily meet.

23. I am assuming that the phrase "by the eye" [*nach dem Augenmasse*] is to be taken metaphorically, since an aesthetic estimation of magnitude can be made by touch as well as by sight (and perhaps, in the case of intensive magnitudes, by the other senses as well).

24. This follows from the fact that mathematical estimation presupposes a unit of measure. Thus, whereas measurement in terms of yards is convertible to inches or centimeters, at some point appeal must be made to an aesthetic estimation, which is therefore the source of the basic unit of measure (KU 5: 251; 107).

25. The similarity between these "acts" and the first two parts of the threefold synthesis to which Kant refers in the A-Deduction (apprehension and reproduction) has been frequently noted in the literature. Indeed, Crowther simply identifies them (*The Kantian Sublime*, p. 96). Nevertheless, I do not think that such a direct identification can be maintained, at least in the case of reproduction and comprehension. For in the first *Critique* Kant connects the former with the representations of space and time, and there is no suggestion of any inherent limitations on the extent of the reproducibility of appearances. On the contrary, the introduction of any such limitation would run contrary to the intent of the analysis.

26. Kant characterizes this in terms of the Latin *"comprehensio aesthetica"* (KU 5: 251; 108) in order to differentiate it from comprehension in the usual sense of understanding, which presumably for Kant would be a *comprehensio intellectualis*.

27. The reference is to *Lettres sur l'Égypte* (1787) by Anne Jean Marie René Savary. See Pluhar's translation, p. 108–9, note 15.

28. This is suggested by Crowther, *The Kantian Sublime*, p. 103.

29. For Kant the unity of reason is essentially that of a system and features completeness, whereas the unity of the understanding is that of an aggregate brought together in one consciousness. See A326/B382–3; A 644/B672; A671/B699.

30. In view of Kant's claim in the discussion of the resolution of the First Antinomy that progress in the successive synthesis proceeds indefinitely rather
than infinitely, one might expect Kant to have said here that apprehension proceeds indefinitely rather than infinitely. But it is important to keep
in mind that he is here concerned with the apprehension of something that
is presumed to be already given in its entirety (an object that presents
itself as absolutely great) and, as Kant says in his resolution of the Second
Antinomy (concerning infinite divisibility) in this case the process may be
said to proceed *ad infinitum*. (See A523–4/B551–2.) For my discussion of
this distinction, see Allison, "The Antinomy of Pure Reason, Section 9,"
pp. 472–3.

31. For an analysis of Kant's conception of transcendental illusion, see Michelle
Grier, *Kant's Doctrine of Transcendental Illusion*.

32. Kant's conception of intellectual intuition, as sketched in §76 and §77 of the
Critique of Judgment, is discussed along lines similar to those taken here by
Sarah Gibbons, *Kant's Theory of Imagination*, pp. 136–9.

33. On the problematic yet noncontradictory status of the concept of an intuitive
intellect, see KU 5: 403; 286–7.

34. Perhaps the best example of this line of thinking is provided by Leibniz, who
was never far from Kant's thoughts on these matters. Of particular relevance
here is Leibniz's account of contingency in terms of an infinite analysis. The
difference between necessary and contingent truths on this account is that
the former can be reduced to identity by a process of conceptual analysis,
whereas contingent truths cannot because they require an infinite analysis.
Not even God can complete such an analysis, but he has no need to, since he
grasps the infinite in a single intuition. See, for example, "On Contingency,"
G. W. Leibniz, *Philosophical Essays*, p. 28; "On Freedom," loc. sit., p. 96; "The
Source of Contingent Truths," loc. sit., pp. 98–100. For an analysis of this
Leibnizian doctrine, see R. C. Sleigh, *Leibniz & Arnauld*, pp. 84–97.

35. The noumenon (in the positive sense) is defined by Kant as "the object of a
non-sensible intuition" (B307).

36. Admittedly, however, this is a very different kind of harmony than the one between the imagination and understanding brought about by aesthetic reflection on the beautiful. Kant later makes this difference clear by pointing
out that the imagination and reason are "harmonious by virtue of their contrast," and that they give rise to a purposiveness through their conflict [*Wider-
streit*] (KU 5: 258; 115–16).

37. The purely aesthetic nature of the feeling of the sublime, in contrast to the
practically grounded nature of moral feeling, is either downplayed or neglected by critics, who tend to deny the aesthetic nature of judgments of the
sublime. These include Crowther, *The Kantian Sublime*, esp. pp. 99, 165–6,
and Schaper, "Taste, sublimity, and genius," p. 382–4, who seems to have
closely followed Crowther. For a critique of these readings along the lines suggested here, see Patricia Matthews, "Kant's Sublime: A Form of Pure Aesthetic Reflective Judgment," esp. pp. 172–8.

38. Although she was not the first to make it, I am indebted to Patricia Matthews
for clarifying this important point. See her "Kant's Sublime," pp. 168–72.

39. Nevertheless, it must be kept in mind that Kant viewed the liking for the sub-

lime to be disinterested. (See KU 5: 244; 97, 5: 247; 100, 5: 249; 105, and 5: 267; 127.

40. As we shall see in the next section, Kant argues in §29 that a certain level of cultural development is necessary before one becomes capable of responding to the sublime. (See KU 5: 265; 104.)

41. This, in essence, is the response to the "everything may be sublime" objection that parallels the familiar and previously discussed objection to Kant's theory of beauty. This objection is raised by Crawford, "The Place of the Sublime in Kant's Aesthetic Theory," pp. 174–5.

42. In attempting to understand this account of the mathematically sublime, it is important to keep in mind Kant's claim that "every interest [of reason] is ultimately practical, even that of speculative reason being only conditional and reaching perfection only in practical use" (KpV 5: 121; 128).

43. See KpV 5: 72–81; 75–84. I analyze this conception of respect in *Kant's Theory of Freedom*, pp. 120–8.

44. In the General Comment on the Exposition of Aesthetic Reflective Judgments, Kant remarks: "It is in fact difficult to think of a feeling for the sublime in nature without connecting it with a mental attunement similar to that for moral feeling" (KU 5: 269–9; 128). He goes on to point out that it is merely similar, however, since in the case of the sublime (in contrast to "genuine morality"), the dominance of reason over sensibility is "exerted by the imagination itself as an instrument of reason" (KU 5: 269; 128).

45. The basic point is brought out nicely by Matthews against interpreters like Crowther and Schaper who tend to run together the sublime and moral feeling. See her "Kant's Sublime," p. 176.

46. In this regard, it is significant that Kant views the feeling of the sublime as an emotion [*Rührung*], which he describes as a weak type of affect [*Affekt*] (KU 5: 272; 133). And the latter is, in turn, defined as "an agitation of the mind that makes it unable to engage in free deliberation about principles with the aim of determining itself according to them" (KU 5: 272; 132). As already noted, Kant also holds that some affects, including anger and enthusiasm, are "aesthetically sublime," which hardly means that they have any moral worth. For Kant's account of affects, as distinguished from passions, see MS 6: 407–8; 208–9, and Anthro 7: 252–75; 120–42.

47. Burke, *Enquiry*, pp. 72–3.

48. Ibid., p. 64

49. Ibid., p. 65.

50. In order to avoid confusion, I am following all three English translators in rendering *"Macht"* by "might," but it should be kept in mind that the German term could be used to render Burke's "power."

51. Schiller seems to have had something like this distinction in mind, when in his own discussion of the sublime, which follows Kant's fairly closely, he distinguishes between two kinds of security: an external physical and inner or moral security. The basic idea is that the requisite lack of real danger concerns only the former, whereas the feeling of the sublime requires the latter as well. See Friedrich Schiller, "On the Sublime," pp. 30–1.

52. Burke, *Enquiry*, pp. 38–9.

53. For this reason Schiller insisted that the "practically-sublime," which is his

term for Kant's dynamically sublime, is much more important than the "the-oretically-sublime" (Kant's mathematically sublime). Thus, he claims that only through the former "do we really experience our true and complete independence from *nature*" ("On the Sublime," p. 26). Kant himself does not explicitly privilege the dynamically sublime in this way (perhaps because of his concern to relate even the mathematically sublime to our moral vocation), but it nonetheless seems to be implicit in his account.

54. The theological objection basically turns on the idea that the proper response to the sublimity of God, as He reveals his wrath in natural calamities such as tempests and earthquakes, is one of abject submission, rather than a feeling of the sublimity of one's own nature. Kant, of course, denies this in light of the conception of autonomy and equates such a view with superstition rather than genuine religion. (See KU 5: 263–4; 122–3.)

55. The point here is also virtually the same as the one Kant makes in the *Critique of Practical Reason*, concerning the example of someone threatened by a sovereign with sudden death unless he makes a false deposition against an honorable man. Such a person may not know what he *would in fact do* if confronted with such a situation because that is a matter of his level of autocracy, but he knows what he *ought to do*, since this is dictated by the autonomy of pure practical reason. See KpV 5: 30; 30 and the earlier discussion in Chapter 9, Part III.

56. See KU 5: 294; 160.

57. The point is noted by Crowther, *The Kantian Sublime*, p. 116.

58. A similar problem is posed by Kant's previously noted discussion in the General Comment of the sublimity of certain psychological states or affects, such as enthusiasm and anger (KU 5: 271–5; 132–5). Again, these are sublime insofar as they indicate a certain elevation of the self over the ordinary concerns of sensuous existence, and such "elevation" may, but need not, be morally based or praiseworthy.

59. See KU 5: 432–3; 319–21.

60. The contrary is argued by Crowther, *The Kantian Sublime*, p. 116.

61. For an interesting reading of this passage that turns on the sharp contrast between the standpoints of the actor and the spectator, see Arendt, *Lectures on Kant's Political Philosophy*, p. 53. Arendt does not, however, emphasize the purely aesthetic nature of the judgment of sublimity.

62. The point here is not that the presupposition of the universality of a predisposition to moral feeling does not require any justification, but rather that this does not form part of the project of a critique of judgment. Consequently, it is here simply presupposed. Presumably, this justification would be based on the "fact of reason" of the second *Critique*.

63. Kant's failure to mention artistic beauty here may simply be a reflection of his concern to maintain the parallelism with the sublime. But it may also indicate that he did not think that the claim holds in the case of the appreciation of artistic beauty, or at least not in the same way, since, as we have seen, that requires the consciousness of the object as art.

64. On this predisposition to moral feeling or, as it is there termed, the predisposition to personality, see Re 6: 26 and note; 74–5.

65. I have deliberately used Guyer's language of "opening up a gap in the argument" because the problem that arises for the sublime is somewhat analogous to that problem, which, according to Guyer and others, arises for the deduction of taste, if, in order to avoid the everything-is-beautiful objection, one distinguishes between the degree of attunement of the cognitive faculties required for cognition and that which is required for a judgment of beauty. See Chapter 8, Part VII.

66. This point has been insisted on most forcefully by Crowther, *The Kantian Sublime*, esp. pp. 152–65.

67. This point is completely missed by Crowther, perhaps because he fails to take seriously the aesthetic nature of the judgment of the sublime. Thus, he offers as genuine examples of the feeling of the sublime the sense of astonishment at the extent of human artifice and genius that one experiences in viewing the pyramids, buildings like St. Peter's, or, more generally, great works of art. (*The Kantian Sublime*, pp. 153–5). Kant would clearly acknowledge such a sense of astonishment, but for good reasons he would also deny that it is a pure feeling of the sublime.

68. It must be kept in mind here that this applies not *only* to art, which is why Kant emphasizes *crude* nature. In the General Comment he makes the same point in connection with the quintessentially sublime starry sky and ocean. The claim is that in order to appreciate their sublimity, we must base our judgment entirely on how we see them, setting aside completely any thoughts we might have in connection with them, such as that of distant worlds inhabited by other species of rational beings or of the ocean depths as containing a vast array of aquatic creatures (KU 5: 270; 130).

69. It should be noted in this context that Kant referred to both the pyramids and St. Peter's as examples of the sublime in *Observations on the Feeling of the Beautiful and Sublime*. The former is cited as an instance of the "the noble" [*das Edle*] sublime and the latter of "the splendid" [*das Prächtige*] sublime. (See Beob 2: 209–10; 49.)

70. A good example of an author with whom Kant was certainly familiar is Moses Mendelssohn. In his essay "On the sublime in the fine sciences," Mendelssohn defines the sublime essentially in terms of awe and admiration and distinguishes between two types of sublimity: an "objective" type, where the awe is generated by the nature of the object itself, and a "subjective" type, where it is directed to the way in which the object is depicted. The former pertains to objects of either nature or art, but the latter obviously concerns only artistic depiction. (See Moses Mendelssohn, *Philosophical Writings*, pp. 192–232.) The view that the sublime pertains primarily to art, or at least to art as much as to nature, seems to have been virtually universal during the eighteenth century. See, for example, the discussion of the sublime in painting by Monk, *The Sublime*, pp. 164–202.

71. This passage is cited by Crowther, who nevertheless complains that Kant attributes far too little significance to the place of the sublime in art (*The Kantian Sublime*, p. 152). Crowther's whole treatment of this question, however, is based on an uninformed and rather implausible "reconstruction" of Kant's position, which I cannot consider here except to note that he denies the

purely aesthetic nature of judgments of beauty and sublimity, with the result that the whole Kantian problematic is set aside. Moreover, Crowther completely neglects Kant's suggestive account in the *Anthropology*.

72. Kant also refers to this inscription in BDG 2: 151, and Ton 8: 399.

73. The "arts of speech" for Kant include oratory or rhetoric [*Beredsamkeit*] and poetry. See KU 5: 321; 190–1).

74. The distinction between the traditional rhetorical conception of the sublime, associated with a "high style," and the modern conception that is concerned with content and emotional effect is emphasized by Monk, *The Sublime*, esp. pp. 35–42.

75. This is also suggested by Kant's characterization in the General Comment of simplicity [*Einfalt*], defined as "artless purposiveness," as "as it were, nature's style in the sublime" (KU 5: 275; 136). Presumably, "nature's style" is here to be contrasted with that of the artist, which inevitably becomes anything but simple insofar as he attempts to incorporate sublimity into a work of art.

76. See also Anthro 7: 241; 109.

77. There is clearly an analogy here with the artistic depiction of the ugly, which, as we have seen, Kant allows within certain limits. The basic difference is that the ugly, in contrast to the sublime, is the *contrary* and not merely the *counterpoise* to the beautiful, which presumably puts further constraints on the conditions of its artistic representation.

78. I take it that this is Crowther's main point, though he does not present it in these terms. (See *The Kantian Sublime*, pp. 153–5).

79. These are suggested by Crowther, *The Kantian Sublime*, p. 155.

80. Although for the sake of simplicity the sublime is here and elsewhere treated as if it were itself an objective feature of things, it must be kept in mind that this is not the case for Kant.

81. See, for example, Crowther, *The Kantian Sublime*, pp. 155–61, and Gibbons, *Kant's Theory of Imagination*, pp. 139–43.

82. See also KU: 269; 129. In the secondary literature, the negative aspect of the sublime is emphasized by Lyotard, *Lessons on the Analytic of the Sublime*, pp. 150–3, and Makkreel, *Imagination and Interpretation in Kant*, p. 113.

83. It should also be noted, however, that in moral contexts, Kant often uses the term "sublime" and its cognates in a rhetorical rather than a technical sense, as, for example, in the famous paean to duty, "Thou sublime and mighty name" (KpV 86; 90).

84. Kant gives clear expression to the necessary interplay of love and respect as the two poles of the moral life in his account of friendship. (See MS 6: 469–74; 261–4.)

85. For the sake of simplicity, I am formulating the notion of a perfect duty in terms of the second formulation of the categorical imperative in the *Groundwork*, but this is also how Kant tends to characterize all duties in the *Metaphysics of Morals*.

86. This is not to deny that some imperfect duties are also entirely up to us, for example, one's moral perfection; but I am here interested only in the broad contours rather than the details of Kant's moral theory. Moreover, these contours do suggest at least a rough correlation between the perfect–imperfect

duty distinction and the distinction between duties that do and duties that do not require the cooperation of nature.

87. I am assuming here the controversial "nonrigorist" reading of Kant's conception of imperfect duties, according to which they allow for exceptions on the basis of inclination. For a discussion of this issue, see Mary Gregor, *Laws of Freedom*, pp. 95–112, and Thomas Hill, "Kant on Imperfect Duty and Supererogation," pp. 147–75.

88. This is not to deny that fulfilling imperfect duties often involves sacrificing some personal good; clearly it does. The point, however, is that precisely because such duties require a commitment to an end, rather than particular actions or omissions, these sacrifices are usually not as great as those that perfect duties may require.

BIBLIOGRAPHY

Allison, Henry E. *Kant's Transcendental Idealism*. New Haven: Yale University Press, 1983.

"The Concept of Freedom in Kant's 'Semi-Critical' Ethics," *Archiv für Geschichte der Philosophie*, 68 (1986), pp. 96–115.

Benedict de Spinoza: An Introduction. New Haven and London: Yale University Press, 1987.

Kant's Theory of Freedom. Cambridge: Cambridge University Press, 1990.

"Kant's Antinomy of Teleological Judgment," *System and Teleology in Kant's Critique of Judgment*, Hoke Robinson, ed., *Southern Journal of Philosophy* 30 (1992) (Spindel Conference 1991), supplemental volume, pp. 25–42.

"The Gulf between Nature and Freedom and Nature's Guarantee of Perpetual Peace," *Proceedings of the Eighth International Kant Congress Memphis 1995*, Hoke Robinson, ed. Milwaukee: Marquette University Press, 1996, vol. 1, pp. 37–49.

Idealism and Freedom. Cambridge: Cambridge University Press, 1996.

"We Can Act Only under the Idea of Freedom," *Proceedings and Addresses of the American Philosophical Association* 71 (1997), pp. 39–50.

"Pleasure and Harmony in Kant's Theory of Taste: A Critique of the Causal Reading," *Kants Ästhetik, Kant's Aesthetics, L'esthétique de Kant*, Herman Parret, ed. Berlin and New York: Walter de Gruyter, 1998, pp. 466–83.

"The Antinomy of Pure Reason, Section 9," *Immanuel Kant, Kritik der reinen Vernunft*, Georg Mohr and Marcs Willaschek, eds. Berlin: Akademie Verlag, 1998, pp. 465–90.

"Is the *Critique of Judgment* 'Post-Critical'?" *The Reception of Kant's Critical Philosophy: Fichte, Schelling, Hegel*, Sally Sedgwick, ed. Cambridge: Cambridge University Press, 2000, pp. 78–92.

Ameriks, Karl. Review of *Kant and the Claims of Taste* (by Paul Guyer), *New Scholasticism* 54 (1980), pp. 241–9.

"How to Save Kant's Deduction of Taste," *Journal of Value Inquiry* 16 (1982), pp. 295–302.

"Kant and the Objectivity of Taste," *British Journal of Aesthetics* 23 (1983), pp. 3–17.

"Kant on the Good Will," *Grundlegung zur Metaphysik der Sitten: Ein kooperativer Kommentar,* Otfried Höffe, ed. Frankfurt am Main: Vittorio Klostermann, 1989, pp. 45–65.

"New Views on Kant's Judgment of Taste," *Kants Ästhetik, Kant's Aesthetics, L'esthétique de Kant,* Herman Parret, ed. Berlin and New York: Walter de Gruyter, 1998, pp. 431–47.

Ameriks, Karl, and Dieter Sturma, eds. *The Modern Subject, Conceptions of the Self in Classical German Philosophy.* Albany: State University of New York Press, 1995.

Aquila, Richard. "A New Look at Kant's Aesthetic Judgments," *Essays in Kant's Aesthetics,* Ted Cohen and Paul Guyer, eds. Chicago and London: University of Chicago Press, 1982, pp. 87–114.

Arendt, Hannah. *Lectures on Kant's Political Philosophy,* Ronald Beiner, ed. Chicago: University of Chicago Press, 1982.

Baron, Marcia. "Freedom, frailty, and impurity," *Inquiry* 36 (1993), pp. 431–41.

Baum, Manfred. "Kants Prinzip der Zweckmässigkeit und Hegels Realisierung des Begriffs," *Hegel und die Kritik der Urteilskraft,* Hans-Friedrich Fulda and Rolf-Peter Horstmann, eds. Stuttgart: Klett-Cotta, 1990, pp. 158–73.

Beck, Jakob Sigismund. *Erläuternder Auszug aus den kritischen Schriften des Herrn Prof. Kant, auf Anrathen desselben.* Riga: Johann Friedrich Hartnoch, 1793–6, 3 vols.

Beck, Lewis White. *A Commentary on Kant's Critique of Practical Reason.* Chicago: The University of Chicago Press, 1980.

"Did the Sage of Königsberg Have No Dreams?" *Essays on Kant and Hume.* New Haven and London: Yale University Press, 1978, pp. 38–60.

"On the Putative Apriority of Judgments of Taste," *Essays on Kant and Hume.* New Haven and London: Yale University Press, 1978, pp. 167–70.

Brandt, Reinhard. "The Deductions in the *Critique of Judgment:* Comments on Hampshire and Horstmann," *Kant's Transcendental Deductions: The Three 'Critiques' and the 'Opus postumum,'* Eckart Förster, ed. Stanford, Calif.: Stanford University Press, 1989, pp. 177–90.

"Analytic/Dialectic," *Reading Kant,* Eva Schaper and W. Vossenkuhl, eds. Oxford: Blackwell, 1989, pp. 179–95.

"Die Schönheit der Kristalle und das Spiel der Erkenntniskräfte: Zum Gegenstand und zur Logik des ästhetischen Urteils bei Kant," *Autographen, Dokumente und Berichte, Kant-Forschungen* 5 (1994), pp. 19–57.

The Table of Judgments: Critique of Pure Reason A 67–76; B 92–101, Eric Watkins, trans. Atascadero, Calif.: Ridgeview Publishing Co., 1995. *North American Kant Society Studies in Philosophy,* Vol. 4.

"Zur Logik des ästhetischen Urteils," *Kants Ästhetik, Kant's Aesthetics, L'esthétique de Kant,* Herman Parret, ed. Berlin and New York: Walter de Gruyter, 1998, pp. 229–245.

Burke, Edmund. *A Philosophical Enquiry into the Origin of our Ideas of the Sublime and Beautiful,* J. T. Boulton, ed. (based on the text of the 2d ed.). London and New York: Routledge and Kegan Paul and Columbia University Press, 1958.

Cerf, Walter. Translator's Introduction and Comments to *Analytic of the Beautiful,* by Immanuel Kant. Indianapolis: The Bobbs-Merrill Company Inc., 1963, pp. vii–li, 81–141.

Cohen, Ted. "Why Beauty is the Symbol of Morality," *Essays in Kant's Aesthetics*, Ted Cohen and Paul Guyer, eds. Chicago and London: University of Chicago Press, 1982, pp. 221–36.

Cohen, Ted, and Guyer, Paul, eds. *Essays in Kant's Aesthetics*. Chicago and London: University of Chicago Press, 1982.

Crawford, Donald W. *Kant's Aesthetic Theory*. Madison: The University of Wisconsin Press, 1974.

"Kant's Theory of Creative Imagination," *Essays in Kant's Aesthetics*, Ted Cohen and Paul Guyer, eds. Chicago and London: University of Chicago Press (1982), pp. 151–78.

"The Place of the Sublime in Kant's Aesthetic Theory," *The Philosophy of Immanuel Kant*, Richard Kennington, ed. Washington, D.C.: The Catholic University of America Press, 1985, pp. 161–83.

Crowther, Paul. *The Kantian Sublime, From Morality to Art*. Oxford: Clarendon Press, 1989.

Danto, Arthur. *Beyond the Brillo Box: The Visual Arts in Post-Historical Perspective*. New York: Farrar, Straus and Giroux, 1992.

After the End of Art: Contemporary Art and the Pale of History. Princeton: Princeton University Press, 1997.

Derrida, Jacques. *The Truth in Painting*, Geoff Bennington and Ian McLeod, trans. Chicago and London: The University of Chicago Press, 1987.

Dickie, George. *The Century of Taste, The Philosophical Odyssey of Taste in the Eighteenth Century*. New York and Oxford: Oxford University Press, 1996.

Dunham, Barrows. "Kant's Theory of Aesthetic Form," *The Heritage of Kant*, George T. Whitney and David F. Bowers, eds. Princeton: Princeton University Press, 1939, pp. 359–75.

Düsing, Klaus. *Die Teleologie in Kants Weltbegriff*. Bonn: H. Bouvier u. Co. Verlag, 1968. *Kantstudien Ergängzungshefte*, vol. 96.

"Das Problem des höchsten Gutes in Kants praktischer Philosophie," *Kant-Studien* 62 (1971), pp. 5–42.

Ferguson, Francis. "The Sublime from Burke to the Present," *Encyclopedia of Aesthetics*, Michael Kelly, ed., vol. 4, pp. 326–31.

Floyd, Juliet. "Heautonomy: Kant on Reflective Judgment and Systematicity," *Kant's Ästhetik, Kant's Aesthetics, L'esthétique de Kant*, Herman Parret, ed. Berlin and New York: Walter de Gruyter, 1998, pp. 192–218.

Förster, Eckart, ed. *Kant's Transcendental Deductions: The Three 'Critiques' and the 'Opus Postumum.'* Stanford Calif.: Stanford University Press, 1989.

Fricke, Christel. *Kants Theorie des reinen Geschmacksurteils*. Berlin and New York: Walter de Gruyter, 1990.

"Explaining the Inexplicable. The Hypothesis of the Faculty of Reflective Judgment in Kant's Third Critique," *Noûs* 24 (1990), pp. 45–62.

"Kants Theorie der schönen Kunst," *Kants Ästhetik, Kant's Aesthetics, L'esthétique de Kant*, Herman Parret, ed. Berlin and New York: Walter de Gruyter, 1998, pp. 674–89.

Fulda Hans-Friedrich and Rolf-Peter Horstmann, eds. *Hegel und die Kritik der Urteilskraft*. Stuttgart: Klett-Cotta, 1990.

Funke, Gerhard, and Seebohm, Thomas M., eds. *Proceedings of the Sixth Interna-*

tional Kant Congress. Washington, D.C.: Center for Advanced Research in Phenomenology & University Press of America, 1989. 2 vols.

Gadamer, Hans-Georg. *Truth and Method*, 2d. revised ed., Joel Winsheimer and Donald G. Marshall, trans. New York: The Continuum Publishing Company, 1999.

Gammon, Martin. "Exemplary Originality: Kant on Genius and Imitation," *Journal of the History of Philosophy* 35 (1997), pp. 563–92.

"Kant: *parerga* and *pulchritudo adhaerens*", *Kant-Studien* 90 (1999), pp. 148–67.

Genova, A. C. "Aesthetic Justification and Systematic Unity in Kant's Third Critique," *Proceedings of the Sixth International Kant Congress*, Gerhard Funke and Thomas M. Seebohm eds. Washington, D.C.: Center for Advanced Research in Phenomenology & University Press of America, 1989, vol. 2, pt. 2, pp. 293–309.

Gerard, Alexander. *An Essay on Taste, the Second Edition, with corrections and additions*. Edinburgh, 1764. Reprinted New York: Garland, 1970.

Gibbons, Sarah. *Kant's Theory of Imagination, Bridging Gaps in Judgment and Experience*. Oxford: Clarendon Press, 1994.

Ginsborg, Hannah. *The Role of Taste in Kant's Theory of Cognition*. New York and London: Garland Publishing Company, 1990.

"Reflective Judgment and Taste," *Noûs* 24 (1990), pp. 63–78.

"On the Key to Kant's Critique of Taste," *Pacific Philosophical Quarterly* 72 (1991), pp. 290–313.

"Lawfulness without a Law: Kant on the Free Play of Imagination and Understanding," *Philosophical Topics* 25 (1997), pp. 37–81.

"Kant on the Subjectivity of Taste," *Kant's Ästhetik, Kant's Aesthetics, L'esthétique de Kant*, Herman Parret, ed. Berlin and New York: Walter de Gruyter, 1998, pp. 448–65.

Gotshalk, D. W. "Form and Expression in Kant's Aesthetics," *British Journal of Aesthetics* 7 (1967), pp. 250–60.

Gracyk, Theodore A. "Sublimity, Ugliness, and Formlessness in Kant's Aesthetic Theory," *Journal of Aesthetics and Art Criticism* 45 (1986), pp. 49–56.

Gregor, Mary J. *Laws of Freedom, A Study of Kant's Method of Applying the Categorical Imperative in the Metaphysik der Sitten*. Oxford: Basil Blackwell, 1963.

"Aesthetic Form and Sensory Content in the Critique of Judgment: Can Kant's 'Critique of Aesthetic Judgment' Provide a Philosophical Basis for Modern Formalism?" *The Philosophy of Immanuel Kant*, Richard Kennington, ed. Washington, D.C.: The Catholic University of America Press, 1985, pp. 185–99.

Grier, Michelle. *Kant's Doctrine of Transcendental Illusion*. Cambridge: Cambridge University Press, in press.

Guyer, Paul. "Formalism and the Theory of Expression in Kant's Aesthetics," *Kant-Studien* 68 (1977), pp. 46–70.

Kant and the Claims of Taste. Cambridge and London: Harvard University Press, 1979.

"Pleasure and Society in Kant's Theory of Taste," *Essays in Kant's Aesthetics*. Ted Cohen and Paul Guyer, eds. Chicago and London: University of Chicago Press, 1982, pp. 21–54.

"Reason and Reflective Judgment: Kant on the Significance of Systematicity," *Noûs* 24 (1990), pp. 17–43.

"Kant's Conception of Empirical Law," *Proceedings of the Aristotelian Society*, supp. vol. (1990), pp. 220–42.

Guyer, Paul, ed. *The Cambridge Companion to Kant*. Cambridge: Cambridge University Press, 1992.

Kant and the Experience of Freedom, Essays on Aesthetics and Morality. New York and Cambridge: Cambridge University Press, 1993.

Hegel, G. W. F. *Aesthetics, Lectures on Fine Art*, T. M. Knox, trans. Oxford: Clarendon Press, 1975. 2 vols.

Heimsoeth, Heinz. *Transzendentale Dialektik, Ein Kommentar zu Kants Kritik der reinen Vernunft*. Berlin: Walter de Gruyer & Co., 1966.

Henrich, Dieter. "Kant's Notion of a Deduction and the Methodological Background of the First *Critique*," *Kant's Transcendental Deductions, The Three 'Critiques' and the 'Opus Postumum,'* Eckart Förster, ed. Stanford, Calif.: Stanford University Press, 1989, pp. 29–46.

Aesthetic Judgment and the Moral Image of the World, Studies in Kant. Stanford, Calif.: Stanford University Press, 1992.

Hill, Thomas E., Jr. "Kant on Imperfect Duty and Supererogation," *Dignity and Practical Reason in Kant's Moral Theory*. Ithaca and London: Cornell University Press, 1992, pp. 147–75.

Höffe, Otfried, ed. *Grundlegung zur Metaphysik der Sitten: Ein kooperativer Kommentar*. Frankfurt am Main: Vittorio Klostermann, 1989.

Horstmann, Rolf-Peter. "Why Must There Be a Transcendental Deduction in Kant's *Critique of Judgment?*" *Kant's Transcendental Deductions, The Three 'Critiques' and the 'Opus postumum,'* Eckart Förster, ed. Stanford, Calif.: Stanford University Press, 1989, pp. 157–76.

Hudson, Hud. "The Significance of an Analytic of the Ugly in Kant's Deduction of Pure Judgments of Taste," *Kant's Aesthetics*, Ralf Meerbote, ed. Atascadero, Calif.: Ridgeview Publishing Company, 1991, pp. 87–103.

Hume, David. *A Treatise of Human Nature*, 2nd ed., revised by P. H. Nidditch. Oxford: Clarendon Press, 1978.

"The Sceptic," *Essays Moral, Political, and Literary*, revised ed. of the 1889, T. H. Green and T. H. Grose, eds., Eugene F. Miller, ed. Indianapolis: Liberty Fund, 1985, pp. 159–80.

Dialogues Concerning Natural Religion, Norman Kemp Smith, ed. Indianapolis and New York: The Bobbs-Merrill Co., 1947.

Hutcheson, Francis. *An Inquiry into the Original of Our Ideas of Beauty and Virtue*. 4th ed. London, 1738.

Iseminger, Gary. "Intentional Fallacy," *Encyclopedia of Aesthetics*, Michael Kelly, ed., vol. 2, pp. 515–17.

Juchem, Hans-Georg. *Die Entwicklung des Begriffs des schönen bei Kant*. Bonn: H. Bouvier u Co. Verlag, 1970.

Kelly, Michael, ed. *Encyclopedia of Aesthetics*. New York and Oxford: Oxford University Press, 1998, 4 volumes.

Kemal, Salim. "Aesthetic Necessity," *Kant-Studien* 74 (1983), pp. 176–205.

Kant and Fine Art, An Essay on Kant and the Philosophy of Fine Art and Culture. Oxford: Clarendon Press, 1986.

Kemp Smith, Norman. *A Commentary on Kant's Critique of Pure Reason*, reprint of 2d ed. New York: Humanities Press, 1962.

Kennington, Richard, ed. *The Philosophy of Immanuel Kant.* Washington, D.C.: The Catholic University of America Press, 1985. *Studies in Philosophy and the History of Philosophy,* vol. 12.

Kneller, Jane. "The Interests of Disinterest," *Proceedings of the Eighth International Kant Congress Memphis 1995,* Hoke Robinson, ed. Milwaukee: Marquette University Press, 1996, vol. 1, part 2, pp. 777–86.

Kulenkampff, Jens. *Kants Logik des ästhetischen Urteils.* Frankfurt am Main: Vittorio Klostermann, 1978.

"The Objectivity of Taste: Hume and Kant," *Noûs* 24 (1990), pp. 93–110.

Leibniz, G. W. *New Essays on Human Understanding,* Peter Remnant and Jonathan Bennett, trans. and eds. Cambridge: Cambridge University Press, 1981.

Philosophical Essays, Roger Ariew and Daniel Garber, eds. and trans. Indianapolis and Cambridge: Hackett Publishing Co., 1989.

Lewis, C. I. *Mind and the World Order.* New York: Dover Publications, 1956.

Locke, John. *Essay Concerning Human Understanding,* A. C. Fraser, ed. New York: Dover Publications, Inc., 1959.

Longuenesse, Béatrice. *Kant and the Capacity to Judge: Sensibility and Discursivity in the Transcendental Analytic of the Critique of Pure Reason,* Charles T. Wolfe, trans. Princeton: Princeton University Press, 1998.

"The Divisions of the Transcendental Logic and the Leading Thread," *Immanuel Kant, Kritik der reinen Vernunft,* Georg Mohr and Marcus Willaschek, eds. Berlin: Akademie Verlag, 1998, pp. 131–58.

Lories, Danielle. "Génie et goût: complicité ou conflit? Autour du Par. 50 de la Troisième Critique," *Kant's Ästhetik, Kant's Aesthetics, L'esthétique de Kant,* Herman Parret, ed. Berlin and New York: Walter de Gruyter, 1998, pp. 564–93.

Lüthe, Rudolf. "Kants Lehre von den ästhetischen Ideen," *Kant-Studien* 75 (1984), pp. 65–74.

Lyotard, Jean-François. *Lessons on the Analytic of the Sublime,* Elizabeth Rottenberg, trans. Stanford, Calif.: Stanford University Press, 1994.

MacMillan, Claude. "Kant's Deduction of Pure Aesthetic Judgments," *Kant-Studien* 76 (1985), pp. 43–54.

Makkreel, Rudolf A. *Imagination and Interpretation in Kant, The Hermeneutical Import of the Critique of Judgment.* Chicago and London: The University of Chicago Press, 1990.

Marc-Wogau, Konrad. *Vier Studien zu Kants Kritik der Urteilskraft.* Uppsala: A.-b. Lundequistka Bokhandeln, 1938.

Marx, Karl. *Early Writings,* T. B. Bottomore, trans. and ed. New York, Toronto, and London: McGraw Hill, 1964.

Matthews, Patricia. "Kant's Sublime: A Form of Pure Aesthetic Reflective Judgment," *Journal of Aesthetics and Art Criticism* 54 (1996), pp. 165–79.

McDowell, John. "Aesthetic value, objectivity, and the fabric of the world," *Pleasure, Preference & Value, Studies in Philosophical Aesthetics,* Eva Schaper, ed. Cambridge: Cambridge University Press, 1983, pp. 1–16.

McFarland, J. D. *Kant's Concept of Teleology.* Edinburgh: Edinburgh University Press, 1970.

"The Bogus Unity of the Kantian Philosophy," *Actes du Congrès d'Ottawa sur Kant dans les Traditions Anglo-Américaines et Continentales Tenu du 10 au 14 Octobre 1974, Proceedings of the Ottawa Congres on Kant in the Anglo-American and Con-*

tinental Traditions Held October 10–14, 1974, Pierre Laberge, François Duchesneau, and Bryan E. Morrisey, eds. Ottawa: The University of Ottawa Press, 1976, pp.180–96.

McLaughlin, Peter. *Kant's Critique of Teleology in Biological Explanation: Antinomy and Teleology.* Lewiston, N.Y.: The Edwin Mellon Press, 1990.

Meerbote, Ralf. "Reflection on Beauty," *Essays in Kant's Aesthetics,* Ted Cohen and Paul Guyer, eds. Chicago and London: University of Chicago Press, 1982, pp.55–86.

Meerbote, Ralf, ed. *Kant's Aesthetics.* Atascadero, Calif.: Ridgeview Publishing Company, 1991. *North American Kant Society Studies in Philosophy,* vol. 1.

Mendelssohn, Moses. *Philosophical Writings,* Daniel O. Dahlstrom, ed. Cambridge Texts in the History of Philosophy. Cambridge: Cambridge University Press, 1997.

Menzer, Paul. *Kants Ästhetik in ihrer Entwicklung.* Berlin: Akademie Verlag, 1952.

Mertens, Helga. *Kommentar zur Ersten Enleitung in Kants Kritik der Urteilskraft.* München: Johannes Berchmans Verlag, 1973.

Mohr, Georg, and Marcus Willaschek, eds. *Immanuel Kant, Kritik der reinen Vernunft.* Berlin: Akademie Verlag, 1998.

Monk, Samuel. *The Sublime, A Study of Critical Theories in XVIII-Century England.* Ann Arbor: University of Michigan Press, 1960.

Mothersill, Mary. "The Antinomy of Taste," *Kant's Aesthetics,* Ralf Meerbote, ed. Atascadero, Calif.: Ridgeview Publishing Company, 1991, pp. 75–86.

Munzel, G. Felicitas. "'The Beautiful Is the Symbol of the Morally-Good': Kant's Philosophical Basis of Proof for the Idea of the Morally-Good," *Journal of the History of Philosophy* 33 (1995), pp. 301–29.

"The Privileged Status of Interest in Nature's Beautiful Forms: A Response to Jane Kneller," *Proceedings of the Eighth International Kant Congress Memphis 1995,* Hoke Robinson, ed. Milwaukee: Marquette University Press, 1996, vol. 1, part 2, pp. 787–92.

O'Neill, Onora. *Constructions of Reason: Explorations of Kant's Practical Philosophy.* Cambridge: Cambridge University Press, 1989.

Parret, Herman ed. *Kants Ästhetik, Kant's Aesthetics, L'esthétique de Kant.* Berlin and New York: Walter de Gruyter, 1998.

Pippin, Robert B. *Kant's Theory of Form, An Essay on the Critique of Pure Reason.* New Haven and London: Yale University Press, 1982.

"The Significance of Taste: Kant, Aesthetic and Reflective Judgment," *Journal of the History of Philosophy* 34 (1996), pp. 549–69.

Posy, Carl J. "Imagination and Judgment in the Critical Philosophy," *Kant's Aesthetics,* Ralf Meerbote, ed. Atascadero, Calif.: Ridgeview Publishing Company, 1991, pp. 27–48.

Reich, Klaus. *The Completeness of Kant's Table of Judgments,* Jane Kneller and Michael Losonsky, trans. Stanford, Calif.: Stanford University Press, 1992.

Robinson, Hoke, ed. *System and Teleology in Kant's Critique of Judgment (Spindel Conference 1991), Southern Journal of Philosophy* 30 (1992), supp. vol.

Proceedings of the Eighth International Kant Congress Memphis *1995.* Milwaukee: Marquette University Press, 1996. 2 vol. in 5 parts.

Rogerson, Kenneth R. *Kant's Aesthetics: The Roles of Form and Expression.* Lanham, Md., New York, and London: University Press of America, 1986.

Rousseau, Jean Jacques. *The Social Contract, or Principles of Political Right,* Charles M. Sherover, ed. and trans. New York: Meridian, 1974.

Savile, Anthony. *Aesthetic Reconstructions: The Seminal Writings of Lessing, Kant and Schiller.* Oxford: Basil Blackwell, 1987.

Schaper, Eva. *Studies in Kant's Aesthetics.* Edinburgh: Edinburgh University Press, 1979.

"Taste, sublimity, and genius: the aesthetics of nature and art," The Cambridge Companion to Kant, Paul Guyer, ed. Cambridge: Cambridge University Press, 1992, pp. 367–93.

Schaper, Eva, ed. *Pleasure, Preference & Value, Studies in Philosophical Aesthetics.* Cambridge: Cambridge University Press, 1983.

Schaper, Eva, and W. Vossenkuhl, eds. *Reading Kant.* Oxford: Blackwell, 1989.

Schiller, Friedrich. "On the Sublime," *Essays,* Walter Hinderer and Daniel O. Dahlstrom, eds. New York: Continuum Publishing Company, 1993, pp. 22–44.

Schlapp, Otto. *Kants Lehre vom Genie und die Enstehung der 'Kritik der Urteilskraft.'* Göttingen: Vandenhoedt & Ruprecht, 1901.

Schulz, E. G. *Rehbergs Opposition gegen Kants Ethik.* Köln: Böhlau-Verlag, 1975.

Sedgwick, Sally, ed. *The Reception of Kant's Critical Philosophy: Fichte, Schelling, Hegel.* Cambridge, Cambridge University Press, 2000.

Shier, David. "Why Kant Finds Nothing Ugly," *British Journal of Aesthetics* 38 (1988), pp. 412–18.

Silber, John. "Kant's Conception of the Highest Good as Immanent and Transcendent," *Philosophical Review* 68 (1959), pp. 469–92.

Sleigh, R. C. *Leibniz & Arnauld, A Commentary on their Correspondence.* New Haven and London: Yale University Press, 1990.

Souriau, Michel. *Le jugement réfléchissant dans la philosophie critique de Kant.* Paris: Librairie Félix Alcan, 1926.

Stroud, Barry. *Hume.* London, Boston, and Henley: Routledge & Kegan Paul, 1977.

Strub, Christian. "Das Hässliche und die 'Kritik der ästhetischen Urteilskraft,' Überlegungen zu einer systematischen Lücke," *Kant-Studien* 80 (1989), pp. 416–46.

Sulzer, Johann Georg. *Allgemeine Theorie der schönen Künste.* Leipzig: Weidmanschen Buchhandlung, 1792. Reprint Hildscheim, Zurich, and New York: Georg Olms Verlag, 1994. 5 vols.

Thompson, Garrett. "Kant's Problems with Ugliness," *Journal of Aesthetics and Art Criticism* 50 (1992), pp. 107–15.

Tonelli, Giorgio. "La formazione del testo della *Kritik der Urteilskraft,*" *Revue Internationale de Philosophie* 8 (1954), pp. 423–48.

"Von den verschiedenen Bedeutungen des Wortes Zweckmässigkeit in der *Kritik der Urteilskraft,*" *Kant-Studien* 49 (1957–8), pp. 154–66.

"Kant's Early Theory of Genius," *Journal of the History of Philosophy.* 4 (1966), Part I pp. 109–31, Part II pp. 209–24.

Tuschling, Burkhard. "Intuitiver Verstand, absolute Identität, Idee. Thesen zu Hegels früher Rezeption der *Kritik der Urteilskraft,*" *Hegel und die Kritik der Urteilskraft,* Hans-Friedrich Fulda and Rolf-Peter Horstmann eds. Stuttgart: Klett-Cotta, 1990, pp. 174–88.

"The System of Transcendental Idealism: Questions Raised and Left Open in the Kritik der Urteilskraft," *System and Teleology in Kant's Critique of Judgment (Spindel Conference 1991)*, Hoke Robinson, ed. *Southern Journal of Philosophy* 30 (1992), supp. vol., pp. 109–27.

Uehling, Theodore E., Jr. *The Notion of Form in Kant's Critique of Aesthetic Judgment.* The Hague: Mouton, 1971.

Vleeschauwer, H. J. De. *La Déduction Transcendentale dans l'Oeuvre de Kant.* Original ed. Antwerp: De Sikkel, 1934–7. Reprint, New York and London: Garland Publishing, Inc., 1976. 3 vols.

Wenzel, Christian. *Das Problem der subjektiven Allgemeingültigkeit des Geschmacksurteils bei Kant* (Inaugural-Dissertation zur Erlangung des Grades eines Doktors der Philosophie des Fachbereichs Geschichte-Philosophie-Theologie der Universität-Gesamthochschule). Wuppertal, 1999.

Whitney, George T., and David F. Bowers, eds. *The Heritage of Kant.* Princeton: Princeton University Press, 1939.

Wolff, Michael. *Die Vollständigkeit der kantischen Urteilstafel.* Frankfurt am Main: Vittorio Klostermann, 1995.

Wood, Allen W., ed. *Self and Nature in Kant's Philosophy.* Ithaca and London: Cornell University Press, 1984.

"Kant's Compatibilism," *Self and Nature in Kant's Philosophy*, Allen Wood, ed. Ithaca and London: Cornell University Press, 1984, pp. 73–101.

"Unsociable Sociability: The Anthropological Basis of Kantian Ethics," *Philosophical Topics* 19 (1991), pp. 325–51.

Yovel, Yirmiahu. *Kant and the Philosophy of History.* Princeton: Princeton University Press, 1980.

Zammito, John H. *The Genesis of Kant's Critique of Judgment.* Chicago and London: The University of Chicago Press, 1992.

Zanetti, Véronique. "Teleology and the Freedom of the Self," *The Modern Subject, Conceptions of the Self in Classical German Philosophy*, Karl Ameriks and Dieter Sturma, eds. Albany: State University of New York Press, 1995, pp. 47–63.

Zumbach, Clark. *The Transcendent Science, Kant's Conception of Biological Methodology.* The Hague, Boston, and Lancaster: Martinus Nijhoff Publ., 1984.

INDEX